D0913014

EX LIBRIS

PACE
UNIVERSITY

THE HENRY BIRNBAUM
LIBRARY
PACE PLAZA, NEW YORK

NUREMBERG

A Renaissance City, 1500–1618

NUREMBERG

A RENAISSANCE CITY, 1500–1618 by Jeffrey Chipps Smith

Published for the Archer M. Huntington Art Gallery, The University of Texas at Austin

 University of Texas Press

Copyright © 1983 by the University of Texas Press
All rights reserved
Printed in the United States of America

First Edition, 1983

Requests for permission to reproduce material from this work should
be sent to Permissions, University of Texas Press, Box 7819, Austin,
Texas 78712.

Library of Congress Cataloging in Publication Data

Smith, Jeffrey Chipps, 1951–
    Nuremberg, a Renaissance city, 1500–1618.

    Catalog of an exhibition held at the Archer M.
Huntington Art Gallery at the University of Texas at
Austin.
    Bibliography: p.
    Includes index.
    1. Art, German—Germany (West)—Nuremberg—
Exhibitions.   2. Art, Renaissance—Germany (West)—Nurem-
berg—Exhibitions.   3. Reformation in art—Germany (West)
—Nuremberg—Exhibitions.   4. Nuremberg (Germany)—
Civilization—Exhibitions.   I. Archer M. Huntington Art
Gallery.   II. Title.

N6886.N9S64   1983   709'.43'32   83-10559
ISBN 0-292-75527-9

N
6886
.N9
S6483
1983

Contents

This exhibition is supported by an indemnity from
the Federal Council on the Arts and the Humanities.
Transportation from Germany was provided by the
Foreign Office of the Federal Republic of Germany.

Nuremberg

As the University of Texas at Austin celebrates its centennial, it is particularly appropriate that the Archer M. Huntington Art Gallery focus on one of the most visible of European nations, Germany. During the one hundred years of the University's existence, descendants of German settlers in Texas—one of the four major ethnic groups to immigrate to the Republic during the nineteenth century—have long supported and attended this state university. To recognize their ancestors' contribution to the visual arts is only fitting, and it is with great pleasure that the Huntington Art Gallery looks to the city of Nuremberg during the years 1500–1618.

When Jeffrey Chipps Smith, assistant professor of art and a specialist in northern European Renaissance and Baroque art, proposed a major international exhibition focusing upon approximately one hundred years in Nuremberg's history, enormous obstacles presented themselves. All were overcome: funding, borrowing objects from museums and collections in the United States, Canada, and Germany (some 21 in all), producing the catalogue—to name only the most formidable. To Professor Smith, who was part of the museum staff during the organization of the exhibition and the writing of the catalogue and who traveled diligently throughout the United States and Germany seeking the objects, the Huntington Art Gallery staff expresses its thanks for his dedication both to scholarship and to quality. Also, for his insightful essay on the historical background of the city of Nuremberg, we are grateful to Guy Fitch Lytle, assistant professor of history at the University of Texas at Austin.

During the one hundred years on which this exhibition focuses, painting, sculpture, printmaking, metalsmithing, and architecture were thriving, bringing Nuremberg to the forefront of artistic achievement in northern Europe. This creative thrust began with Dürer early in the sixteenth century and ended with Jamnitzer. Mercantilism and the Protestant Reformation combined to create an ambience in which the visual arts flourished.

Exhibitions at a university serve many purposes, all educational and all a part of our instructional mission as a visual arts resource. "Nuremberg: A Renaissance City, 1500–1618" was officially designated a University of Texas centennial exhibition by the Centennial Program Office under the direction of Vice-President Shirley Bird Perry. To her and her staff go the sincere appreciation of the gallery for her recognition of the important scholarly contribution this exhibition provides. Financial support from an Arts and Artifacts Indemnity Program (administered by the Museum Program of the National Endowment for the Arts), the Federal Republic of West Germany, and the Archer M. Huntington Museum Trust Fund made the exhibition possible. On behalf of the Huntington Art Gallery, I want to thank the Spencer Museum of Art at the University of Kansas and the University Art Museum at the University of California, Santa Barbara, for joining us in exhibiting these works. Having brought the objects so far geographically for the benefit of our students, we are delighted to share them with our university colleagues.

No exhibition of this magnitude can become a reality without the dedicated effort of an entire working-museum staff. Everyone at the Huntington Art Gallery who has been involved with the complexities of this exhibition deserves our sincere appreciation. On behalf of the Huntington Art Gallery, we invite you to enjoy this visually stimulating and scholarly accomplishment.

Eric McCready
Director

Preface

When discussing the Renaissance in Germany, art historians always cite Nuremberg and Augsburg as the two outstanding cultural centers of the sixteenth century, yet few critics have attempted to define either what qualities or what personalities made these two towns so important. Others have viewed art in Nuremberg as a one-man, one-act play starring Albrecht Dürer. While Dürer was unquestionably the most brilliant Nuremberg artist, the city's artistic vitality continued long after his death in 1528. When I originally proposed this exhibition to Eric McCready, director of the Archer M. Huntington Art Gallery at the University of Texas at Austin, I envisioned a small display of prints and drawings by Dürer, his pupils, and their immediate successors. The scope of the exhibition grew in direct relation to my fascination with the art of Peter Flötner, Wenzel Jamnitzer, and a host of others who were highly esteemed in their own lifetimes yet are comparatively unknown even to Renaissance art historians, who tend to focus upon Dürer's generation.

The purpose of the exhibition is to provide a general introduction to Nuremberg, its artists, and its cultural history between 1500 and 1618, the start of the Thirty Years War. This is a case study of the dynamics of one city from the advent of the Renaissance through the social and political upheavals of the Reformation to what one might call a conservative, comfortable old age in which its lead in artistic matters, bit by bit, passed to Augsburg, Munich, and Prague. I have referred to this entire period as the Renaissance because of the remarkable continuity of its artistic tradition. The term Mannerism is used here to define the style of one phase of the Renaissance rather than a distinctive era.

Many significant issues and avenues of research cannot be addressed adequately within the time and space constraints of the present catalogue. For example, Dürer's considerable influence on the other arts has been discussed only briefly. While I have not examined Nuremberg and its artists in a vacuum, I have not attempted to write an analytical study comparing Nuremberg with other towns, each of which had its own particular response to the cultural transformations of the period. Instead, my hope is that the information I have provided in the catalogue will be of service to others who are preparing more specialized research.

This exhibition catalogue is the first English-language study of the artistic patrimony of Nuremberg between 1500 and 1618. My research has been aided by the many excellent catalogues published by the Germanisches Nationalmuseum and the Stadtgeschichtliche Museen in Nuremberg; however, none has the same focus as the present exhibition.

The catalogue consists of two parts: a series of introductory essays and the catalogue proper, in which I have provided biographies and detailed commentaries on the art of forty-six masters. I have tried to address the central issues raised by each object rather than discuss the stylistic developments of the individual artists. The catalogue is arranged in a loose chronological fashion with special groupings for Dürer's followers, the medalists, the later printmakers, and the goldsmiths. On occasion, the chronological ordering within a single artist's oeuvre is altered for specific reasons. By contrast, the exhibition display follows a more thematic and stylistic grouping.

The objects included in the exhibition offer a representative sampling of the art of Renaissance Nuremberg drawn from North American collections supplemented by the loan of twenty-one works from the Germanisches Nationalmuseum and the Stadtgeschichtliche Museen in Nuremberg. The latter has been made possible through the assistance of Gerhard Bott, general director of the Germanisches Nationalmuseum, and his staff, notably Klaus Pechstein, who has handled the details of the loan. Since many of the finest paintings, sculptures, and goldsmith works by Nuremberg artists are still in situ or are scattered among European collections, the brilliance of certain artists, especially Wenzel Jamnitzer, can be judged adequately only in the comparative photographs in the catalogue. Other pieces in American museums are too fragile to withstand the rigors of a traveling exhibition.

In preparing this exhibition and the accompanying catalogue, I have benefited from the cooperation and knowledge of many individuals and institutions. My greatest debt is to Eric McCready and the staff of the Archer M. Huntington Art Gallery, who are listed at the end of the book, for their encouragement and good-humored patience as this project grew more ambitious. I have received research grants from the Archer M. Huntington Fund and the University Research Institute of the University of Texas at Austin. During the fall semester of 1981, I taught a graduate seminar on Nuremberg and its art. I wish to thank Martie Eickmann, Lisa Kelly, Sigrid Knudsen, Carolyn Nelson, Trudy Prescott, Teal Triggs, Ronnie Welch, and Eileen White for their many interesting observations. I have incorporated some of the research of Lisa Kelly (cat. nrs. 49–50, 163–170), Sigrid Knudsen (cat. nrs. 63, 115, 117, 160–161, 179–182, 194–195), and Ronnie Welch (cat. nrs. 61, 65, 69–70, 103, 105–108) into my entries. Knudsen, as my research assistant, provided invaluable help and editorial advice during our many months of frantic activity.

Of my colleagues at the University of Texas, I gratefully acknowledge the assistance I received from Thomas Boyd, John Clarke, Eleanor Greenhill, Brenda Preyer, and Richard Saunders of the Department of Art; Paul Willard, the Art History secretary; Robert Wills, dean of the College of Fine Arts; Hubert P. Heinem and Wolfgang F. Michael of the Department of Germanic Languages; David Armstrong of the Department of Classics; and Carole Cable and Chris Hanson of the General Libraries. My special thanks are due to Guy Fitch Lytle of the Department of History, who contributed the essay "The Renaissance and Reformation City of Nuremberg," and to Decherd Turner, director of the Humanities Research Center, for his support.

I wish to express my gratitude to the many individuals who contributed information or photographs to this project. Alison G. Stewart, NEA intern at the Philadelphia Museum of Art, graciously agreed to write the entry for Hans Sebald Beham's *Large Church Festival* (cat. nr. 84), which is the subject of part of her dissertation on peasant festivals. I benefited from the assistance of Christiane D. Andersson of Columbia University; Carl C. Christensen of the University of Colorado at Boulder; Hans Kammler of the Stadt Nürnberg Hochbauamt—Bildstelle; Thomas DaCosta Kaufmann and Robert A. Koch of Princeton University; Mrs. John A. Pope of the International Exhibitions Foundation, Washington; Alice Rössler of the Universitätsbibliothek Erlangen-Nürnberg; Martin Royalton-Kisch of the British Museum; Haide Russell, cultural counselor at the Embassy of the Federal Republic of Germany in Washington; I. A. Schmidt-Folkersamb of the Staatsarchiv in Nuremberg; Larry Silver of Northwestern University; Otto von Simson of the University of Berlin; Christian Theuerkauff of the Staatliche Museen in Berlin; and Kristin Zapalac, a graduate student in history at Johns Hopkins University in Baltimore.

Before acknowledging the help I received from individuals associated with the various museums and libraries lending to the exhibition, I wish to thank my wife, Sandy, and my son, Spencer, without whose encouragement and much needed distractions, this project would not have been completed. It is to Sandy and Spencer that this catalogue is dedicated.

The most logical manner of thanking the anonymous donor and the dozens of scholars and museum staff members at the lending institutions who have made this exhibition possible is to list them by museum or library. I hope that I shall be excused by those who so graciously gave their time and knowledge for this somewhat impersonal approach.

Ann Arbor, University of Michigan Museum of Art: Anne I. Lockhart, Curator of Western Art; Clifton Olds, former Acting Director (now at Bowdoin College)
Austin, The Humanities Research Center, The University of Texas: John Chalmers, Librarian; Cassandra James, Research Associate; Sally Leach, Assistant to the Director; Margarette Sharpe, Executive Assistant; Decherd Turner, Director
Baltimore, The Walters Art Gallery: Mrs. Thomas M. Baumann, Assistant Registrar; William R. Johnson, Chief Curator
Boston, The Museum of Fine Arts: Anne Poulet, Curator of European Decorative Arts and Sculpture; Sue W. Reed, Assistant Curator of Prints, Drawings, and Photographs; Eleanor A. Sayre, Curator of Prints, Drawings, and Photographs; Michelle Wilson, Assistant, Department of European Decorative Arts and Sculpture
Brunswick, Bowdoin College Museum of Art: Katharine J. Watson, Director

Cambridge, Fogg Art Museum, Harvard University: Suzannah Fabing, Deputy Director; Agnes Mongan, Former Director; Seymour Slive, Director; Miriam Stewart, Assistant, Drawing Department

Chicago, The Art Institute of Chicago: Harold Joachim, Curator of Prints and Drawings; Suzanne Folds McCullagh, Assistant Curator of Prints and Drawings

Chicago, The Newberry Library: Susan Dean, Assistant Curator of Special Collections

Cleveland, Cleveland Museum of Art: Sherman E. Lee, Director; Louise S. Richards, Chief Curator of Prints and Drawings; Patrick M. de Winter, Curator of Early Western Art

Dallas, Bridwell Library, Perkins School of Theology, Southern Methodist University: Jerry D. Campbell, Director

Detroit, The Detroit Institute of Arts: Ellen Sharp, Curator of Graphic Art

Fort Worth, The Kimbell Art Museum: William B. Jordan, Deputy Director; Edmund P. Pillsbury, Director; David M. Robb, Jr., Chief Curator

Hartford, The Wadsworth Atheneum: Jean K. Cadogan, Curator of European Paintings and Drawings; Gregory Hedberg, Chief Curator

Houston, The Museum of Fine Arts: Peter C. Marzio, Director; Edward B. Mayo, Registrar; David B. Warren, Associate Director

Indianapolis, Indianapolis Museum of Art: Allan W. Clowes; Anthony F. Janson, Senior Curator

Kansas City, Nelson-Atkins Museum of Art: Roger B. Ward, Assistant Curator in Charge of European Painting and Sculpture; Marc F. Wilson, Director

Lawrence, Spencer Museum of Art, University of Kansas: Elizabeth Broun, Acting Director

Los Angeles, Los Angeles County Museum of Art: Ebria Feinblatt, Curator of Prints and Drawings

Madison, Elvehjem Museum of Art, University of Wisconsin: Lisa Calden, Registrar; Katherine Mead, Director

Middleton, Davison Art Center, Wesleyan University: Ellen D'Oench, Curator

Minneapolis, The Minneapolis Institute of Arts: Marilyn Bjorklund, Registrar; Samuel Sachs II, Director

Minneapolis, James Ford Bell Library, University of Minnesota: Carol Urness, Assistant Curator

New York, Cooper-Hewitt Museum, The Smithsonian Institution's National Museum of Design: Elaine Dee, Curator of Prints

New York, The Metropolitan Museum of Art: Jacob Bean, Curator of Drawings; Suzanne Boorsch, Assistant Curator of Prints and Photographs; James David Draper, Associate Curator of European Sculpture and Decorative Arts; Colta Ives, Curator in Charge of Prints and Photographs; Helmut Nickel, Curator of Arms and Armor; Stuart W. Pyhrr, Associate Curator of Arms and Armor; George Szabo, Curator, Robert Lehman Collection

New York, The New York Public Library: Francis O. Mattson, Curator of Rare Books; Robert Rainwater, Keeper of Prints; Walter J. Zervas, Administrative Associate

New York, The Pierpont Morgan Library: Charles Ryskamp, Director; Felice Stampfle, Curator of Prints and Drawings

Nuremberg, Germanisches Nationalmuseum: Gerhard Bott, General Director; Günther Bräutigam, Curator of Sculpture; Kurt Löchner, Curator of Paintings; Klaus Pechstein, Curator of Goldsmith Work; Rainer Schoch, Curator of Prints and Drawings; Ludwig Veit, Curator of Coins and Medals; Leonie von Wilckens, Curator of Native Arts

Nuremberg, Stadtgeschichtliche Museen: Matthias Mende, Senior Curator

Oberlin, Allen Memorial Art Museum, Oberlin College: Richard E. Spear, Director

Ottawa, The National Gallery of Canada: Mimi Cazort, Curator of Drawings; Myron Laskin, Jr., Curator of European Art; Joseph Martin, Acting Director

Philadelphia, Pennsylvania Academy of the Fine Arts: Richard J. Boyle, Director

Philadelphia, Philadelphia Museum of Art: Ellen S. Jacobowitz, Acting Curator of Prints; Alison G. Stewart, N.E.A. Intern, Department of Prints, Drawings, and Photographs; Irene Taurins, Registrar

Princeton, The Art Museum, Princeton University: Barbara T. Ross, Custodian of Prints and Drawings

Sacramento, The Crocker Art Museum: Roger D. Clisby, Curator

St. Louis, St. Louis Art Museum: James D. Burke, Director; Helene Arnott Rundell, Registrar; Judith Weiss, Curator of Prints and Drawings

St. Louis, Special Collections, Washington University: Holly Hall, Head; Timothy D. Murray, Curator of Manuscripts

San Francisco, The Fine Arts Museums of San Francisco: Maxine Rosston, Assistant Curator, Achenbach Foundation for the Graphic Arts

Santa Barbara, University Art Museum, University of California: John David Farmer, Director; Phyllis Plous, Curator of Exhibitions; Alice Wong, Registrar

Seattle, Seattle Art Museum: Paula H. Wolf, Assistant to the Registrar

Urbana-Champaign, University of Illinois: N. Frederick Nash, Rare Book Room Librarian

Washington, Library of Congress: Jon D. Freshour, Registrar; Kathleen Hunt, Librarian of the Lessing J. Rosenwald Collection

Washington, National Gallery of Art: Lynn Gould, Assistant Curator of Graphic Arts; C. Douglas Lewis, Curator of Sculpture; Carlotta J. Owens, Curatorial Assistant; Andrew C. Robison, Curator of Graphic Arts; Jack C. Spinx, Chief of Exhibitions and Loans

Lenders
to the Exhibition

UNITED STATES

Ann Arbor	University of Michigan Museum of Art
Austin	Archer M. Huntington Art Gallery, The University of Texas
	Humanities Research Center, The University of Texas
Baltimore	The Walters Art Gallery
Boston	The Museum of Fine Arts
Brunswick	Bowdoin College Museum of Art
Cambridge	Fogg Art Museum, Harvard University
Chicago	The Art Institute of Chicago
	The Newberry Library
Cleveland	Cleveland Museum of Art
Dallas	Bridwell Library, Perkins School of Theology, Southern Methodist University
Detroit	The Detroit Institute of Arts
Fort Worth	The Kimbell Art Museum
Hartford	The Wadsworth Atheneum
Houston	The Museum of Fine Arts
Indianapolis	Indianapolis Museum of Arts
Kansas City	Nelson-Atkins Museum of Art
Lawrence	Spencer Museum of Art, University of Kansas
Los Angeles	Los Angeles County Museum of Art
Madison	Elvehjem Museum of Art, University of Wisconsin
Middleton	Davison Art Center, Wesleyan University
Minneapolis	The Minneapolis Institute of Arts
	James Ford Bell Library, University of Minnesota
New York	Cooper-Hewitt Museum, The Smithsonian Institution's National Museum of Design
	The Metropolitan Museum of Art
	The New York Public Library
	The Pierpont Morgan Library
Oberlin	Allen Memorial Art Museum, Oberlin College
Philadelphia	Pennsylvania Academy of the Fine Arts
	Philadelphia Museum of Arts
Princeton	The Art Museum, Princeton University
Sacramento	The Crocker Art Museum
St. Louis	St. Louis Art Museum
	Washington University, Special Collections
San Francisco	The Fine Arts Museums of San Francisco
Santa Barbara	University Art Museum, University of California
Seattle	Seattle Art Museum
Urbana-Champaign	University of Illinois
Washington	Library of Congress
	National Gallery of Art

CANADA

Ottawa	The National Gallery of Canada (Galerie nationale du Canada)

UNITED KINGDOM

London	Anonymous lender

WEST GERMANY

Nuremberg	Germanisches Nationalmuseum
	Stadtgeschichtliche Museen

Abbreviations

AGNM	*Anzeiger des Germanischen Nationalmuseum*
Andresen	A. A. Andresen, *Der Deutsche Peintre-Graveur*
Anzelewsky, *Dürer*	F. Anzelewsky, *Albrecht Dürer: Das malerische Werk*
B. or Bartsch	A. Bartsch, *Le Peintre-Graveur*
The Illustrated Bartsch	A. Bartsch, *The Illustrated Bartsch*
Boston: Dürer	*Albrecht Dürer: Master Printmaker*
Dodgson, I and II	C. Dodgson, *Catalogue of Early German and Flemish Woodcuts Preserved in the Department of Prints and Drawings in the British Museum*
Geisberg	M. Geisberg, *The German Single-Leaf Woodcut: 1500–1550*
H. or Hollstein	F. W. H. Hollstein, ed., *German Engravings, Etchings, and Woodcuts, ca. 1400–1700*
Habich	G. Habich, *Die Deutschen Schaumünzen des XVI. Jahrhunderts*
Hampe, *Nürnberger Ratsverlässe*	T. Hampe, *Nürnberger Ratsverlässe uber Kunst und Künstler im Zeitalter der Spätgotik und Renaissance (1449), 1474–1618 (1633)*
Hill and Pollard	G. F. Hill and G. Pollard, *Renaissance Medals from the Samuel H. Kress Collection at the National Gallery of Art*
JKSAK	*Jahrbuch der kunsthistorischen Sammlungen des allerhöchsten Kaiserhauses*
JKSW	*Jahrbuch der kunsthistorischen Sammlungen in Wien*
JPKS	*Jahrbuch der preussischen Kunstsammlungen*
M. or Meder	J. Meder, *Dürer-Katalog*
Morgenroth	U. Middeldorf and O. Goetz, *Medals and Plaquettes from the Sigmund Morgenroth Collection*
MJBK	*Münchner Jahrbuch der bildenden Kunst*
MVGN	*Mitteilungen des Vereins für Geschichte der Stadt Nürnberg*
Nuremberg: Dürer (1971)	*Albrecht Dürer, 1471–1971*
Nuremberg: Meister um Dürer	*Meister um Albrecht Dürer*
Nuremberg: Vorbild Dürer	*Vorbild Dürer: Kupferstiche und Holzschnitte Albrecht Dürers im Spiegel der europäischen Druckgraphik des 16. Jahrhunderts*
Reformation in Nürnberg	*Reformation in Nürnberg: Umbruch und Bewahrung*
Talbot, ed., *Dürer*	C. W. Talbot, ed., *Dürer in America: His Graphic Work*
Thieme-Becker	U. Thieme and F. Becker, eds., *Allgemeines Lexikon der bildenden Künstler von der Antike bis zur Gegenwart*
ZDVK	*Zeitschrift des deutschen Vereins für Kunstwissenschaft*
ZfK	*Zeitschrift für Kunstgeschichte*
ZfKW	*Zeitschrift für Kunstwissenschaft*

NUREMBERG

A Renaissance City, 1500–1618

Nuremberg's ascent from regional to international status occurred during the opening years of the sixteenth century as the influence of Dürer and his followers spread. Dürer introduced Renaissance ideas into Nuremberg and, through his prints, into other European cities. One reason for his success was his ability to combine Italian concepts of human form, spatial construction, and iconography with the underlying naturalism of German late Gothic art. Dürer translated the lessons of Italian art into a pictorial language that northern masters could comprehend, yet he never totally shed his late Gothic heritage. Indeed the tensions and awkward experiments of this transition from the late Gothic to the Renaissance will be significant characteristics of the art of the 1510s and 1520s.

In 1525 Nuremberg revolted against the Roman Catholic church and became the first free imperial city to adopt Lutheranism. This is a critical date in the history of Nuremberg and its art, for the Protestant Reformation brought new attitudes about the function and even the morality of religious art. Such traditional forms of religious art as altarpieces and devotional statues were openly challenged as idolatrous. Nuremberg's patricians had richly decorated local churches with paintings, sculptures, and liturgical objects during the first quarter of the century. Suddenly this source of artistic patronage ceased, and Nuremberg's artists were forced quickly to develop new secular themes and stylistic ideas. Dürer's teachings had prepared emerging artistic leaders Georg Pencz and Peter Flötner to appreciate the current innovations in northern Italian and Roman art. If Dürer introduced the Renaissance into Nuremberg, this next generation of masters naturalized it. Georg Pencz brought the latest innovations of Michelangelo and Giulio Romano into the pictorial programs of local patrician houses. Although the art of the second quarter of the century in some respects did not match the brilliance of the earlier period, it did not die with Dürer in 1528 as some critics have suggested. Instead it responded boldly to the dual challenges of the Reformation and the High Renaissance.

A third artistic period began approximately twenty-five years later. Pencz died in 1550; Flötner had died four years earlier. Their High Renaissance styles soon gave way to the inventive Mannerism of Wenzel Jamnitzer, Nuremberg's and Germany's greatest goldsmith, whose style and personality dominated the city for the next three and a half decades. Jamnitzer's deliberate distortion of Italian Renaissance and classical elements is first evident in the *Merkel Table Decoration* of 1549 (figs. 47 and 48). His technical innovations, notably his perfection of the art of casting after live models, and original compositional designs were widely emulated.

The complexities of Jamnitzer's Mannerism struck a sympathetic chord with his German colleagues. One reason for this is the inherent stylistic association between Mannerism and the intricate geometric patterns that characterize German late Gothic art. In Nuremberg, especially in its architecture, and elsewhere, Gothic forms persisted into the seventeenth century. In the designs of several of his tall standing cups, Jamnitzer intentionally revived certain Gothic features. This survival and revival of the late Gothic in all the arts were significant traits throughout the late sixteenth and early seventeenth centuries.

The year 1618 provides a fitting terminus for this study. In this year Christoph Jamnitzer, grandson of Wenzel and Nuremberg's last truly inventive artist, died. The flurry of artistic activity in the city during the 1590s and the opening two decades of the seventeenth century peaked around 1618 with the erection of Jakob Wolff the Younger's new west façade on the Rathaus, or city hall (fig. 8). With this Palladian-inspired building, Nuremberg had entered the Baroque period. Finally, 1618 marks the beginning of the Thirty Years War, a series of political and religious struggles that engulfed most of central Europe. The war soon sapped Nuremberg's financial and cultural resources to the point that the city never recovered its former prominence. From this time onward, despite the efforts of painter Joachim von Sandrart (1606–1688), Nuremberg's artists were of only regional note. Gradually the city and indeed much of Europe looked back upon the era of Dürer as an almost golden, mythical age. This cult of Renaissance Nuremberg subsequently inspired Wagner's *Die Meistersinger*, many nineteenth-century romantic paintings, and, in various ways, the politicians, writers, and artists of the twentieth century.[3]

The following essays and catalogue are intended as a general introduction to Nuremberg, its artists, and some of its specific contributions to the Renaissance in Germany. Dr. Guy Lytle's historical introduction, Section 2, provides a background for my detailed discussions about the city's art. A few words of explanation about the ordering of the essays are necessary: Section 3 is an examination of the religious function of art before and during the Reformation to demonstrate the magnitude of the cultural transformations that resulted from the adoption of Lutheranism in 1525. Simultaneously with the erection of great altarpieces and devotional monuments during the 1490s to the mid-1520s, Willibald Pirckheimer and other local intellectuals, with whom Dürer associated, introduced new humanistic ideas. Their early literary and artistic projects, treated in Section 4, opened up Nuremberg to the innovations of Italian and classical cultures, thereby setting the stage for the art of the late 1520s and 1530s that partially filled the void left by the loss of religious commissions. The central figure in the dissemination of Renaissance artistic concepts is, of course, Dürer. Therefore, in Section 5, his pedagogical ideas and the nature of his workshop are considered. Finally, the principal artists and stylistic trends during the sixteenth and early seventeenth centuries are surveyed in Sections 6 and 7.

Before turning to the historical and artistic essays, however, a brief description of Nuremberg is necessary to acquaint the reader with the principal churches, civic structures, residences, and other monuments that will be referred to repeatedly throughout the catalogue.

Visitors to Nuremberg have long admired its attractive skyline and the beautiful churches of St. Sebaldus and St. Lorenz. One such visitor, Aeneas Silvius Piccolomini, later Pope Pius II (1458–1464), came to Nuremberg while serving as secretary to Emperor Friedrich III (1440–1493). His long descriptions typify the remarks of contemporary travelers, chroniclers, and city eulogists. He writes:

. . . what a view this city offers! What splendor, what a pleasing location, what beauty, what culture, what an excellent government! Nothing is missing here to make it such a perfect civic community! Coming from lower Franconia and seeing the city in the distance, what grandeur, what magnificence it offers to the approaching viewer. And then within the city how neat the streets, how elegant the houses! What is there more glorious than the church of St. Sebaldus, what more splendid than the church of St. Laurentius, more majestic and mighty than the castle, and more praiseworthy than the moat and the city walls! How many homes of townsmen can one find here worthy of a king! The Scottish kings would have wished to live as elegantly as the average burgher of Nuremberg.[4]

Despite the obvious hyperbole, there is no doubt that Nuremberg was a well-fortified city filled with splendid houses and an abundance of richly endowed churches. The city's distinctive profile—with the towers of St. Sebaldus and St. Lorenz and the Burg, or imperial castle, dominating the northern rise—has been immortalized in Michael Wolgemut's famous woodcut view published in Hartmann Schedel's *Liber Chronicarum* (*Nuremberg Chronicle*) (cat. nr. 3) of 1493. Wolgemut depicted the city from the southeast. More complete views from the east and the west (cat. nrs. 163 and 164), etched by Hans Lautensack in 1552, provide a superb idea of Nuremberg's appearance in the sixteenth century.

As seen in Paulus Pfinzing's watercolor of Nuremberg and its surroundings (ca. 1596), the city is situated amid rolling forests and rather sparse farmland (fig. 1).[5] The Pegnitz River, flowing east to west, bisects the city into the parishes of St. Lorenz and, to the north, St. Sebaldus. A series of fortified walls, dating from the thirteenth, early fourteenth, and first half of the fifteenth centuries, ring the city. Some visitors, including humanist Conrad Celtis, claimed the walls had as many fortified towers as there were days in the year. Actually, the number never exceeded 150. There were six principal gates: Frauentor (*A*, southeast), Spittlertor (*B*, southwest), Neutor and Tiergärtnertor (*C* and *D*, northwest), Laufertor and Wöhrder Torlein (*E* and *F*, northeast). These are labeled in Pfinzing's portrait of the city.

The specific buildings within Nuremberg are better represented in a map by Wenzel Hollar (1607–1677), a wandering Bohemian artist famed for his cartographic

1. Paulus Pfinzing, *Plan of Nuremberg*, drawing from the *Pfinzing-Atlas*, ca. 1596, Nuremberg, Bayerisches Staatsarchiv, Karten & Pläne nr. 224.

talents (fig. 2). Letters that indicate the gates mentioned above and numbers that correspond to the list of buildings below have been added to Hollar's map.[6] As in Wolgemut's woodcut (cat. nr. 3), the visitor enters through the Frauentor to the southeast and then proceeds past St. Klara and St. Martha convents northward. The reader is advised to examine the list rather quickly but refer back to it as specific buildings and monuments are mentioned in the essays and the catalogue.

1. ST. KLARA (fig. 3). The Franciscan Convent of the Poor Clares was a major center of learning and, under Abbess Caritas Pirckheimer (1467–1532), one of the last bastions of Roman Catholicism.[7] The choir was completed in 1274, the nave was added in 1423–1427, and further building was continued until 1434. The church still stands, but the cloister and secondary buildings were demolished in 1897.

2. ST. MARTHA. Konrad Waldstromer founded this convent and pilgrims' hospital in 1363.[8] The building was completed by 1385, it was secularized in 1526, and from 1578 to 1620 it was used as the Meistersingers' school.

3. BAUMEISTERHAUS and PEUNT. The Peunt was the storage and work area for the city *baumeister* (building supervisor and architect).[9] Jakob Wolff the Younger erected the Baumeisterhaus in 1615.

4. KORNHAUS. Hans Beheim the Elder built this granary in 1498–1502 at the end of the Kornmarkt (Corn Market).[10] Around 1572 it became the local customs house. It was altered in the late nineteenth century to include ground-floor stores.

5. ZEUGHAUS. Hans Dietmair erected this city armory in 1588.[11]

6. KARTÄUSERKLOSTER. In 1380–1383 Marquard Mendel founded this Carthusian monastery on the south side of the Corn Market.[12] The chapel and cloister,

2. Wenzel Hollar, *Plan of Nuremberg*, engraving, mid-seventeenth century, Nuremberg, Germanisches Nationalmuseum, Sp. 6669.

3. Johann Ulrich Kraus (after Johann Andreas Graff), *The Church of St. Klara from the South*, engraving, 1688, Nuremberg, Germanisches Nationalmuseum, Sp. 6591.

now part of the Germanisches Nationalmuseum, were completed during the first half of the fifteenth century.

7. MENDEL ZWÖLFBRÜDERHAUS. In 1388 Konrad Mendel the Elder established a charitable home for twelve elderly craftsmen.[13] In exchange for an entrance fee and the transfer of their property, the craftsmen were provided food and lodging during their lifetimes.

8. ST. JAKOB. During the first half of the fifteenth century, a secondary parish church, St. Jakob, was incorporated into the city with the expansion of the walls.[14] The choir is fourteenth century and the nave was added around 1400.

9. ENCLAVE OF THE DEUTSCHE HERREN and ST. ELISABETH. The Teutonic Knights Hospitaler order was established in Nuremberg in 1212.[15] Their church of St. Elisabeth was built around 1220 and was replaced with a Rococo structure in the 1780s.

10. WEISSER TURM. The White Tower, a remnant of the thirteenth-century fortifications, was absorbed as the city expanded early in the fifteenth century.

11. UNSCHLITTHAUS. This large granary was built by Hans Beheim the Elder in 1491.

12. KARMELITERKLOSTER and SALVATORKIRCHE. The Carmelite monastery was established in 1287, and the church was built around 1340.[16]

13. NASSAUERHAUS. The oldest extant burgher house in the city was constructed around 1200.[17] The upper stories and the eastern *chörlein* (oriel or bay window) date to 1421–1423.

14. FOUNTAIN OF THE VIRTUES (fig. 46). Between 1584 and 1589, Benedikt Wurzelbauer cast the fountain after the wooden models of Johannes Schünnemann.[18]

15. ST. LORENZ (fig. 4). A shrine to St. Lawrence had existed on this site since 1235.[19] The nave of the parish church was started around 1270, and construction reached the crossing by about 1350. The elaborate west façade and the sculptural decoration were completed in 1355–1360 under the sponsorship of Emperor Charles IV (1346–1378). The great hall choir was built by Konrad Heinzelmann (1439–1477), Konrad Roritzer (1454–1464), and Jakob Grimm (1466–1477). The parish school was located just opposite the north transept.

16. FRANZISKANERKLOSTER (BARFÜSSERKLOSTER). The Franciscans are first recorded in Nuremberg in about 1224. This monastery was erected around 1256 and demolished partly in 1810 and partly in 1913.

17. VIATISHAUS (fig. 44). Viatis (1538–1624), one of the city's richest merchants, constructed this large house by the Pegnitz River.[20] In 1609 the city council criticized him for making his house too ostentatious. Paul Juvenel the Elder's 1615–1620 design for the painted façade survives.

18. BARFÜSSERBRÜCKE. The Franciscan bridge is now called the Museum bridge.

19. HEILIG-GEIST-SPITAL. The hospital and church of the Holy Spirit were founded in 1331 by patrician Konrad Gross (died 1356) and were erected between 1332 and 1339.[21] In 1424 the city council selected the church as the repository for the imperial relics and regalia that Emperor Sigismund (1410–1437) had entrusted to Nuremberg. Hans Beheim the Elder built the large addition over part of the river in 1506–1511.

20. ST. KATHARINENKLOSTER. This Dominican convent was founded by Konrad von Neumarkt (died 1296).[22]

21. FLEISCHBRÜCKE. The original bridge named for the adjacent meat market dated to 1335.[23] Jakob Wolff the Elder built this attractive stone bridge between 1596 and 1599.

22. FLEISCHHAUS. The meat market or butchers' house, built in 1570, was set along the Pegnitz River to permit the blood of the slaughtered beasts to be washed away.[24] In 1599 the butchers erected a large stone ox over the entrance to the house.

23. HAUPTMARKT (fig. 5). The High Market is the heart of the city.[25] As seen in Lorenz Strauch's view of the Hauptmarkt toward the north, patrician houses, including Willibald Pirckheimer's, lined the western and southern sides of the square. Number 15 (west side) is the Schopperhaus, site of the annual display

4. Johann Ulrich Kraus (after Johann Andreas Graff), *View of the Interior of St. Lorenz*, engraving, 1685, Nuremberg, Germanisches Nationalmuseum, Sp. 10449.

5. Anonymous artist (after Lorenz Strauch), *View of the Hauptmarkt to the North*, engraving, 1599, Nuremberg, Germanisches National-museum, Sp. 6580.

of the imperial relics. The Schöner Brunnen, Frauenkirche, and Rathaus are also visible to the north and east.

24. SCHÖNER BRUNNEN. The Beautiful Fountain was planned around 1370 and was erected by Heinrich Beheim between 1385 and 1396.[26] The fountain included figures of philosophy, the liberal arts, the church fathers, Moses and seven Old Testament prophets, the nine Worthies, and the seven electors. The remains of the fountain are in the Germanisches Nationalmuseum, as the original fountain was replaced with a replica at the end of the nineteenth century.

25. FRAUENKIRCHE (fig. 6). In 1349 the Jewish synagogue on this site was razed and between 1352 and 1358 this church, dedicated to the Virgin, was built.[27] The elaborate west porch, or Michaels-*chörlein*, was added in 1506–1509. Adam Kraft, Sebastian Lindenast, Jörg Heuss, and others produced the Männleinlaufen, the elaborate gable with a clock and automated statues of the seven electors and the emperor (Charles IV).

26. WAAGE. Hans Beheim the Elder built the city weighing house in 1497.[28] Adam Kraft's stone relief is now in the Germanisches Nationalmuseum. The building was destroyed in 1945.

27. AUGUSTINERKLOSTER. The Augustinian monastery was established in the thirteenth century.[29] The first church, dating to about 1275, was replaced with Hans Beer's hall church in 1479–1485. On 22 March 1525 the monks disbanded and transferred their property to the city. The church remained closed until 1615, when services were resumed. In 1816 the buildings were demolished.

28. ST. SEBALDUS (fig. 7). The northern parish church and shrine of Nuremberg's patron saint (who lived in the eighth or ninth century and was canonized in 1425) is on the site of a chapel dedicated to St. Peter.[30] The present church with its western choir, modeled after Bamberg Cathedral, was started in 1230. Most of the western sculpture was added between 1310 and 1350. The taller eastern hall choir was erected in 1361–1372. The two towers were begun in 1482 and 1483 and were completed before 1490 by Heinrich Kugler.

29. SEBALDER PFARRHOF. The house of the preacher of St. Sebaldus includes an attractively carved *chörlein* (now in the Germanisches Nationalmuseum) of about 1365.[31] The Sebaldus schoolhouse, the church of St. Moritz (1313), and a small cemetery once were located on the north and south sides.

30. RATHAUS (figs. 8 and 9). The core of the city hall, including the great hall, dates to 1332–1340.[32] Hans Beheim the Elder added the eastern wing, the expanded Ratsstube (city council meeting chamber), and new façades in 1514–1522. In 1520 and 1521 major painting and decorative programs were completed for the great hall and the building's exterior. New painting cycles and restoration were

Prospectiva Ædis, ad Divum B. MARIÆ Virginis, NORIBERGÆ. Prospect der MARIÆ-Kirche, zu ünser Lieben Frauen genannt in Nürnberg.

6. Johann Ulrich Kraus (after Johann Andreas
Graff), *View of the Interior of the Frauenkirche*, engraving, 1696, Nuremberg, Germanisches Nationalmuseum, St. Nbg. 3457.

7. Johann Ulrich Kraus (after Johann Andreas
Graff), *View of the Interior of St. Sebaldus*, engraving, 1693, Nuremberg, Germanisches Nationalmuseum, Sp. 9067.

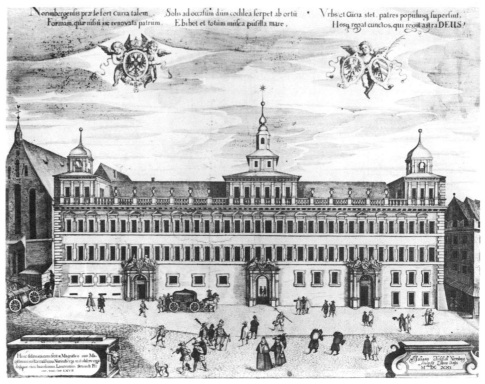

Norimbergenfis præ fe fert curia talem.   Solis ad occafium dum cochlea ferpet ab ortu   •   Vrbs et Curia ftet. patres populusq̃ fuperfint.
Formam,quæ nifi u fic renovata patrum.   E bibet et totiim mufca pufilla mare ,   Hosq̃ regat cunctos,qui regit aftra DEUS !

8. Johann Troschel (after Lorenz Strauch), *West Front of the Rathaus*, engraving, 1621, Nuremberg, Germanisches Nationalmuseum, Sp. 1528.

9. Anonymous artist, *View of the Painted West Façade of the Rathaus before the Rebuilding of the 1610s*, drawing, ca. 1530, Vienna, Graphische Sammlung Albertina, Mappe 75, Umschlag 8, Nr. 1 Architekturzeichnung 562.

undertaken in 1613. Between 1616 and 1622 Jakob Wolff the Younger built the great western façade and made other important changes. The city art collection and library were housed here from the fifteenth century until the nineteenth and late sixteenth centuries, respectively.

31. DOMINIKANERKLOSTER (PREDIGERKLOSTER). The Dominican monastery was founded in about 1270. After the order's disbanding, the building was used for various purposes, including housing the city library. The site was cleared in 1807.

32. BURGSTRASSE and FEMBOHAUS (fig. 10). Known in the sixteenth century as Bei den Predigern and Gasse unter der Veste, this major thoroughfare was lined with patricians' and craftsmen's houses.[33] Residents included Sebald Schreyer (nr. 9), superintendent of St. Sebaldus; Sebastian Kammermeister (nr. 15); Hartmann Schedel (nr. 19), author of the *Nuremberg Chronicle*; Michael Wolgemut (nr. 21); goldsmith Matthias Seidelmann (nr. 23); Albrecht Dürer the Elder (nr. 27) and his son from age four to thirty-eight; and, on the opposite side of the street, Johann Neudörfer and members of the Haller, Scheurl, and Harsdörfer families. Kammermeister's house was rebuilt in 1591–1600, probably by Jakob Wolff the Elder, for Netherlandish merchant Philipp van Oyrl. Since the nineteenth century it has been called the Fembohaus and is today the Stadtgeschichtliche Museen.

33. ALBRECHT DÜRERHAUS. In 1509 the artist moved from his family house to this large fifteenth-century residence by the Tiergärtnertor.[34]

34. PILATUSHAUS. This house, erected in 1489, was nicknamed Pilate's House after Adam Kraft's *Stations of the Cross* sculptural cycle, which extended from the Tiergärtnertor to the Johannisfriedhof (nr. 49).[35] Armorer Valentin Siebenbürger (cat. nr. 160) later resided here.

35. BURG (fig. 11 and cat. nr. 189). A fortress had occupied this site since the second quarter of the eleventh century.[36] The Romanesque double chapel dates to the late twelfth and early thirteenth centuries. The emperor's residence and that of the Burggraf, his representative, were destroyed by fire in 1420. The residence was rebuilt in the 1440s for Emperor Friedrich III. Extensive decorative work was executed in the early 1520s and early 1540s. Italian fortification engineer Antonio Fazuni rebuilt the walls around the castle in 1538–1545.

36. KAISERSTALLUNG. This is another granary built by Hans Beheim the Elder

10. Jakob Wolff the Elder (attributed), *Fembohaus*, 1591–1600; photo taken in 1942.

11. *Interior of the Burg toward the West*; the Heathens' Tower, the Double Chapel, and the Imperial Residence are seen on the left.

12. *Toplerhaus*, 1590–1597; photo taken in 1935.

(1494–1495). It was decorated with Adam Kraft's portal carving of Nuremberg's coats of arms.[37]

37. TOPLERHAUS (fig. 12). Located at Unter Söldnersgasse 17, this house, which dates from 1590–1597, was among the most elaborate of the late Renaissance residences in the city.[38] It was destroyed in 1945.

38. PELLERHAUS (figs. 13, 14, and 43). Jakob Wolff the Elder built this, the grandest of all patrician houses, for Martin Peller at Egidienplatz 23 in 1602–1607.[39] It was severely damaged in 1945 and now serves as the Stadtbibliothek and Stadtarchiv.

39. KOBERGERHAUS. Around 1470 Anton Koberger rented a large house on the west side of the Egidienplatz for his residence and printing establishment.[40] He purchased the building in 1489. At its peak his business employed twenty-four presses and about one hundred workers.

40. ST. EGIDIEN. The Benedictines, the first monastic order in Nuremberg, built this Romanesque basilica in 1140–1150.[41] A new choir was added in 1429–1433. After a fire in 1696 destroyed the church, Johann Gottlieb Trost erected the new structure in 1711–1718. The chapels of St. Martin (Wolfgangskapelle; rebuilt in 1437), Eucharius (ca. 1120–1130), and Tetzel (1345) were located on the south side. Only the Euchariuskapelle survived the 1696 fire.

41. EGIDIEN, OR MELANCHTHON, GYMNASIUM. In 1525 Philipp Melanchthon came to Nuremberg to design a new humanistic school, which opened the next year.[42]

42. HOUSE OF VEIT STOSS. The sculptor purchased the house at Wunderburggasse 7 in 1499, following the expulsion of the Jewish community.[43]

43. HERRENSCHIESSHAUS. Hans Dietmair built the shooting house of the archers company on Grübelstrasse in 1582–1583.[44] Peter Flötner's *Apollo Fountain* was originally located in the shooting yard behind the house (fig. 35).

44. LANDAUER ZWÖLFBRÜDERHAUS (fig. 15). In 1501 Mattheus Landauer and Erasmus Schiltkrot established this charitable home for twelve elderly craftsmen.[45] Hans Beheim the Elder erected the chapel in 1506–1508, and Dürer, together with his workshop, designed the chapel decorations (cat. nr. 35).

45. SIEBEN ZEILEN. In 1488 the city built these forty-one houses for fustian weavers who had moved from Augsburg.[46]

46. TUCHERHAUS (fig. 16). In 1533–1544 Lorenz II Tucher commissioned an architect, probably Paulus Beheim, to build a sumptuous new house and garden at

13. Jakob Wolff the Elder, *Pellerhaus* (main façade), 1602–1607; photo taken in 1935.

14. Interior courtyard of 13; photo taken in 1935.

15. Georg Christian Wilders, *Interior of the Chapel of the Zwölfbrüderhaus*, watercolor, 1836, Nuremberg, Germanisches Nationalmuseum, St. Nbg. 9556.

16. Paulus Beheim (attributed), *Tucherhaus*, 1533–1544; photo taken between 1934 and 1936.

Hirschelgasse 9–13.[47] Peter Flötner designed much of the furniture and interior decoration. The house was largely rebuilt after 1945.

47. HIRSCHVOGELHAUS (fig. 17). In 1534 Leonhard Hirschvogel commissioned a great room constructed on the garden side of his fifteenth-century house at Hirschelgasse 21.[48] Peter Flötner designed the decoration and, possibly, the architecture. Georg Pencz's *Fall of Phaeton* adorned the ceiling. In 1948 the remains of this room were moved to the Fembohaus.

48. PILGER-SPITAL HEILIG KREUZ. The Haller family founded the Holy Cross pilgrims' hospital and chapel before 1353.[49] The chapel was completed by 1362 and the choir of the church by 1402.

49. JOHANNISFRIEDHOF, JOHANNISKIRCHE, and HOLZSCHUHERKAPELLE. The St. John's Cemetery was the burial site for the parishioners of St. Sebaldus, especially after the city council decreed in 1518 that all nonecclesiastical burials must be outside the city walls.[50] Additional regulations of 1520 and 1522 required all tombs to be of simple stone. Decoration was limited to a bronze plate with the name, coat of arms, and profession of the deceased. A cemetery and church dedicated to St. John had occupied this site since the mid-thirteenth century. The Johanniskirche choir was built in 1377 and the nave in 1395. The Holzschuherkapelle was built in 1513 by Hans Beheim the Elder for Heinrich Marschalk von Rauheneck, the patron of Adam Kraft's *Stations of the Cross* and *Entombment*, located in the chapel. By 1515 the Imhoff family took over the chapel, and in 1523 it was transferred to the Holzschuhers.

50. ROCHUSFRIEDHOF and IMHOFFKAPELLE. The Cemetery of St. Roch was for the parishioners of St. Lorenz.[51] The heirs of Konrad Imhoff (1463–1519) had Hans Beheim the Elder design the chapel, and his son Paulus built it in 1520–1521. Veit Hirschvogel the Elder, Hans Burgkmair, and Wolf Traut provided the stained-glass windows and paintings.

17. Peter Flötner, *Chimneypiece for the Garden Room of the Hirschvogelhaus*, 1534, now in Nuremberg, Fembohaus (Stadtgeschichtliche Museen); photo taken between 1934 and 1936.

NOTES

1. G. Händler, *Fürstliche Mäzene und Sammler in Deutschland von 1500–1620*; G. Hartmann, *Reichserzkanzler, Kurfürst und Kardinal Albrecht II. von Brandenburg, der Führer deutscher Renaissancekunst*; J. Zimmer, *Hofkirche und Rathaus in Neuburg/Donau* (Neuburg an der Donau, 1971); R. Bruck, *Friedrich der Weise als Förderer der Kunst*; *Wittelsbach und Bayern, II.1/2 Um Glauben und Reich: Kurfürst Maximilian I.*, exh. cat. (Munich: Residenz, 1980); T. D. Kaufmann, *L'École de Prague, La Peinture à la Cour de Rodolphe II* (Paris, 1983).

2. N. Lieb, *Die Fugger und die Kunst*, esp. vol. 2; *Welt im Umbruch: Augsburg zwischen Renaissance und Barock.*

3. L. Grote, *Die Romantische Entdeckung Nürnbergs.*

4. *Enea Silvio Piccolomini, Deutschland*, ed. A. Schmidt (Cologne, 1962), pp. 102–103; the English translation is by S. Knudsen. Also see A. Buck, "Enea Silvio Piccolomini und Nürnberg," in *Albrecht Dürers Umwelt*, ed. G. Hirschmann and F. Schnelbögl, pp. 20–28.

5. Nuremberg, Bayerisches Staatsarchiv, Karten & Pläne nr. 224. On his career, see cat. nr. 208.

6. For the monuments discussed below, I have culled dates and factual information for various sources, including the following: W. Schwemmer and W. Kriegbaum, *Nürnberg, historische Entwicklung einer deutschen Stadt in Bildern*; G. Pfeiffer, ed., *Nürnberg, Geschichte einer europäischen Stadt*—this is the best general history; W. Schwemmer, *Das Bürgerhaus in Nürnberg*; A. von Reitzenstein and H. Brunner, *Bayern Baudenkmäler* (Reclams Kunstführer—Deutschland 1), (Stuttgart, 1974), pp. 664–694; G. Pfeiffer and W. Schwemmer, *Geschichte Nürnbergs in Bilddokumenten*. Please note that virtually all the buildings in Nuremberg were severely damaged in World War II, notably the 2 January 1945 bombardment. I have mentioned the destruction in only a few cases. See Pfeiffer, *Nürnberg*, pp. 548–549, and E. Mulzer, *Die Wiederaufbau der Altstadt von Nürnberg, 1945 bis 1970*, for specific literature on the destruction and rebuilding.

7. Pfeiffer and Schwemmer, *Bilddokumenten*, figs. 144, 146; L. Kurras and F. Machilek, *Caritas Pirckheimer, 1467–1532*, esp. pp. 69–70.

8. Schwemmer and Kriegbaum, *Nürnberg*, p. 45.

9. Ibid., p. 153.

10. Pfeiffer and Schwemmer, *Bilddokumenten*, fig. 253.

11. Ibid., fig. 34; D. von Dotzauer, "Das Zeughaus der Reichsstadt Nürnberg," *MVGN* 16 (1904): 151–178.

12. H. Maué, "Die Bauten der Kartause von ihrer Gründung 1380 bis zur Übernahme durch das Museum in Jahre 1857," in *Das Germanische Nationalmuseum Nürnberg, 1852–1977*, ed. B. Deneke and R. Kahsnitz (Munich, 1978), pp. 315–356.

13. On the history of the home and the beautiful manuscript with a stylized portrait of the members working at their crafts, see W. Treue et al., *Das Hausbuch der Mendelschen Zwölfbrüderstiftung zu Nürnberg. Deutsche Handwerkerbilder des 15. und 16. Jahrhunderts*, I: pp. 7–60.

14. *Reformation in Nürnberg*, nrs. 282–283.

15. Ibid.

16. K. Ulrich, "Das ehemalige Karmelitenkloster zu Nürnberg," *MVGN* 66 (1979): 1–110.

17. Pfeiffer and Schwemmer, *Bilddokumenten*, figs. 76–77.

18. See Section 7 below.

19. J. Viebig et al., *Die Lorenzkirche in Nürnberg*; H. Bauer, G. Hirschmann, G. Stolz, eds., *500 Jahre Hallenchor St. Lorenz zu Nürnberg, 1477–1977.*

20. Schwemmer, *Bürgerhaus*, pls. 70b, 99b; see Section 7 below.

21. Pfeiffer and Schwemmer, *Bilddokumenten*, figs. 161–162, 169.

22. Schwemmer and Kriegbaum, *Nürnberg*, p. 44.

23. Ibid., p. 154; K. Pechstein, "Allerlei Visierungen und Abriss Wegen der Fleischbrücken 1595," *AGNM* (1975): 72–89.

24. See note 23.

25. E. Mummenhoff, "Studien zur Geschichte und Topographie des Nürnberger Marktplatzes und seiner Umgebung," in *Aufsätze und Vorträge zur Nürnberger Ortsgeschichte*, pp. 194–279; Pfeiffer and Schwemmer, *Bilddokumenten*, figs. 249–252.

26. Pfeiffer and Schwemmer, *Bilddokumenten*, fig. 17; H. Herkommer, "Heilsgeschichtliches Programm und Tugenlehre—Ein Beitrag zur Kultur- und Geistesgeschichte der Stadt Nürnberg am Beispiel des Schönen Brunnens und des Tugendbrunnens," *MVGN* 63 (1976): 192–216; A. Legner et al., eds., *Die Parler und der schöne Stil, 1350–1400*, I: pp. 367–369, 371; K. Zapalac, "Through a Glass, Darkly: Reflections of Church, Empire, and City Government in Late Medieval Nürnberg" (unpublished paper); I wish to thank Ms. Zapalac for sharing her paper.

27. G. Bräutigam, "Die Nürnberger Frauenkirche und der Prager Parlerstil vor 1360," *Jahrbuch der Berliner Museen* 3 (1961): 38–75; Pfeiffer and Schwemmer, *Bilddokumenten*, figs. 22–24.

28. Schwemmer, *Bürgerhaus*, pls. 56a, 61.

29. J. Rosenthal-Metzger, "Das Augustinerkloster in Nürnberg," *MVGN* 30 (1931): 1–106; Pfeiffer and Schwemmer, *Bilddokumenten*, figs. 147, 153; *Reformation in Nürnberg*, nr. 91.

30. W. Schwemmer and M. Lagois, *Die Sebalduskirche zu Nürnberg.*

31. Pfeiffer and Schwemmer, *Bilddokumenten*, figs. 74, 114 (St. Moritz).

32. E. Mummenhoff, *Das Rathaus in Nürnberg*; M. Mende, *Das Alte Nürnberger Rathaus.*

33. Schwemmer, *Bürgerhaus*, pp. 71–72, figs. 66–73, pls. 92a–93 (Fembohaus), 57b (Wolgemuthaus); A. Wilson, *The Making of the Nuremberg Chronicle*, p. 16 lists the residents.

34. W. Schwemmer and H. Clauss, *Das Albrecht-Dürer-Haus in Nürnberg*.

35. Pfeiffer and Schwemmer, *Bilddokumenten*, fig. 79 (Dürer's house is in the center and Pilate's house is at the right side).

36. Ibid., figs. 4–10; E. Bachmann, *Imperial Castle Nuremberg: Official Guide*.

37. Schwemmer, *Adam Kraft*, fig. 31; Schwemmer and Kriegbaum, *Nürnberg*, p. 96 top.

38. K. Böllinger, *Das Toplerhaus in Nürnberg*; Schwemmer, *Bürgerhaus*, pl. 65.

39. R. Schaffer, *Das Pellerhaus in Nürnberg*; Schwemmer, *Bürgerhaus*, fig. 97, pls. 67, 92b, 100, 103, 106d, 107b, 113b, 128a, 129, 131.

40. Wilson, *Nuremberg Chronicle*, p. 14.

41. Pfeiffer and Schwemmer, *Bilddokumenten*, figs. 143, 145, 212–213.

42. Schwemmer and Kriegbaum, *Nürnberg*, p. 136.

43. K. Kohn, "Die Wohnhäuser zweier berühmter Nürnberger," *MVGN* 60 (1973): 296–299; Pfeiffer and Schwemmer, *Bilddokumenten*, figs. 75, 191.

44. Schwemmer, *Bürgerhaus*, pls. 51b, 96b.

45. Pfeiffer and Schwemmer, *Bilddokumenten*, fig. 148 (vault); and see Section 3.

46. Additional houses were added in 1524. Pfeiffer and Schwemmer, *Bilddokumenten*, fig. 284.

47. L. Grote, *Die Tucher: Bildnis einer Patrizierfamilie*, pp. 24ff., figs. 66–78; Schwemmer, *Bürgerhaus*, pls. 57a, 95, 120b; Pfeiffer and Schwemmer, *Bilddokumenten*, fig. 80.

48. Schwemmer, *Bürgerhaus*, pls. 23a, 105c. The garden room, before 1945, is illustrated in G. Glück, *Die Kunst der Renaissance in Deutschland, den Niederländen, Frankreich etc.*, p. 492.

49. H. Haller von Hallerstein and E. Eichhorn, *Das Pilgrimspital zum Heiligen Kreuz vor Nürnberg. Geschichte und Kunstdenkmäler*.

50. O. Glossner, *Der St. Johannisfriedhof zur Nürnberg* (Munich, 1968); Pfeiffer and Schwemmer, *Bilddokumenten*, p. 42, figs. 156, 157 (watercolor by Dürer), 165, 166 (Dürer's tomb).

51. Pfeiffer and Schwemmer, *Bilddokumenten*, fig. 164.

2. The Renaissance, the Reformation, and the City of Nuremberg

by Guy Fitch Lytle

The Renaissance was an urban phenomenon. Despite such relatively late developments as the French taste for rural châteaux or English admiration in poem and sermon alike of the virtuous, bucolic life, the Renaissance—economically, socially, politically, and culturally—was inseparable from the cities of southern and western Europe. Whether the beautiful, clean, and stable German towns celebrated by contemporary travelers; the fusions of princely courts and commercial communities in London, Dijon, or Paris; the intensely competitive yet elaborately chivalrous corporations of Flanders; or the brilliant, turbulent Italian metropolises that have intrigued both then and now virtually all who chanced to observe them, cities provided the arenas, and the populations furnished both players and audiences for the burgeoning dramas of Renaissance civilization.

During the sixteenth century, the Reformation was, to an almost equal extent, an urban matter. In many places, especially in the imperial free cities of the Holy Roman Empire in Germany, an increasingly literate, wealthy, and self-confident "middle-class"—pious, politically sophisticated, and frequently anticlerical—provided a highly receptive audience for the ideas of Luther and other reformers both on theological matters and on church organization. The practical minds of some urban merchants, lawyers, and artisans found in the new Reformation teachings both a welcome alternative to the overelaborate, expensive, and guilt-ridden nature of some aspects of late medieval Roman Catholic observance and an equally welcome chance to appropriate or somehow acquire much of the wealth and property of monasteries and other religious institutions. Others, for a variety of temporal and spiritual reasons, were much less ready to abandon the beliefs and practices of their predecessors and the social and political systems that had accompanied them. Thus, quite soon in the sixteenth century, the streets, pulpits, and council chambers of the cities, especially in German and Swiss areas, replaced the university lecture halls as the most important venues of religious conflict and change.

But these cities, in their own self-conceptions, were not the progeny of the novelties of Renaissance or Reformation. Their social structures and political organizations had long memories stretching back into medieval obscurity or classical fable. They each sought the ideal of the free, prosperous, self-sufficient Christian commonwealth, the definition of which was a central issue throughout the sixteenth century. Commercial, political, and religious rivalries sometimes led to unwanted, destructive wars, which marred their landscapes and depleted their treasuries; but this did not destroy the common experiences, ambitions, and values that produced a shared urban culture during the fifteenth and sixteenth centuries. Each city was different, yet each was also known to countless travelers from other cities who came to buy and sell, to study and teach, to negotiate or preach—travelers who also brought with them, and took away, ideas, impressions, and artifacts that would mold an international urban mentality amidst diversities of politics, religion, and language. Each city was unique, yet to study one carefully is to illuminate vital aspects of them all.[1]

Here our particular urban focus is the southern German city of Nuremberg. Because of its eminent standing as a Renaissance art center and its very important role in the events of the Lutheran Reformation, Nuremberg has attracted the attention of many excellent historians from the future Pope Pius II (Italian humanist Aeneas Silvius Piccolomini) and the "Nuremberg chronicler" (Hartmann Schedel) during the Renaissance itself to some of the leading American and German Reformation scholars of our own day. The serious student of this exhibition is, of course, commended post haste to this scholarly literature.[2] Also, in almost every respect, both the items on exhibit (and their descriptions) and the subsequent essays in this volume will add detail, complexity, and context to my overview; but it may still be useful for some viewers if I provide a brief glimpse at Nuremberg's general and changing situation during the sixteenth century.

With a population of some 40,000 to 45,000 souls within its walls (plus the 20,000 to 25,000 more that it controlled in the surrounding territory), Nuremberg was, if not one of the most populous cities of Renaissance Europe, certainly a very substantial force in the economic and political life of the Holy Roman Empire. It had been since 1219 an "imperial free city" (politically independent except for a general allegiance and some fiscal obligations owed to the emperor). In 1424, the emperor had entrusted to the city the imperial regalia (including the crown, Charlemagne's sword and ring, and such holy relics as the spear that had pierced Christ's side, a chip from his cross, items from the manger and the Last Supper, and thorns from his crown). Furthermore, a new emperor, although crowned elsewhere, usually held his first imperial diet in Nuremberg; and, between 1522 and 1524, it served as the tacit capital of the empire while the imperial court was in residence. (This imperial "tradition," along with fear and caution, partly explains the attempts of the city leaders to remain loyal to Charles V in temporal affairs during the troubles of the Reformation era.) By the early sixteenth century, Nuremberg was by all accounts one of the two or three most important German cities and had begun to expand into a small territorial state. All this brought both power and prestige to the city, as well as a continual stream of potential patrons for whatever the city had to offer.

If Renaissance Nuremberg wielded both a regional and an international political strength, this was paralleled in its economic life. The condition of a city's economy is always relevant to an understanding of its artistic attainments, since the availability of commissions, the type and wealth of patrons, the facilities for exporting finished craft products, and many similar concerns determine to a large extent the size and vigor of the artistic community. Further, a widespread, active international trade can provide cultural as well as business contacts and the chance to expose quality workmanship beyond its local market audience.

All these factors worked very much to Nuremberg's benefit during the fifteenth and early sixteenth centuries. After the dislocations caused by the Black Death in the fourteenth century, rapid urbanization, heightened productivity in manufacturing, specialization in certain technically more advanced crafts, and success in finding and supplying new markets had combined to produce a flourishing economy in most southern German cities. With the decline of the Hanseatic League of northern European and Baltic towns after 1400, burgher-merchants from Nuremberg, Strassburg, Augsburg, and Ulm began to control the international trade in such vital goods as textiles and skins, timber and metal ores, as well as spices and luxury items arriving from the East through Venice.

Enormous profits were realized by the leading patrician families of Nuremberg (who comprised perhaps 6%–8% of the population). Some of this wealth trickled far enough down to improve the living standards of many artisans, local merchants, and others in the middle ranks of society (probably some 60% of Nuremberg's people). And while it has never been pleasant to be one of any era's poor, even the conditions at the bottom of the social scale were seldom allowed to become dangerously wretched. The city council created the Common Chest and Great Almonry in 1522 to provide efficient relief for the needy. After 1525, this concern for social welfare intensified and precipitated a marked shift away from the patronage of religious art toward gifts of personal charity. This change, which occurred throughout Protestant Europe (and in some areas still loyal to Catholicism) during the sixteenth century, had major implications for social and political history, cultural developments, and the history of values and morals, which still require detailed comparative analysis.[3]

Nuremberg's leaders were ambitious and proud of their economic and political successes, but they were also concerned to achieve self-sufficiency, to maintain social order, to regulate the quality of workmanship among the city's renowned artisans (especially the goldsmiths, silversmiths, and others in the metal-working crafts), and to fulfill civic responsibilities to all citizens (and even to foreigners, who were welcome in the city as businessmen and property holders). A more aggressive Augsburg surpassed Nuremberg as the leading economic city in the area in the early sixteenth century, and perhaps Nuremberg's conservative policies were not always in its own best interests if our gauge is the maximization of profits. But Nuremberg, in the Renaissance, was—at least at first—prosperous enough; and it chose to cling to an older tradition of corporate unity and paternalistic restrictions that most citizens hoped would avoid the social conflicts erupting in many other parts of Europe, conflicts that produced suffering and disrupted business.

This social and economic conservatism was probably dictated in large part by the legally hierarchical nature of Nuremberg's social structure and political organization. Throughout the later Middle Ages and Renaissance, the city government was dominated by a small, stable class of urban aristocratic families, ranked socially in a fixed order. While there were some other administrative institutions, advisory groups, and professional civic bureaucrats, the final decision on all matters of policy rested with the council of forty-two, which was always controlled by these principal families. This is not to say that there were not divisions, factions, rivalry, and conflict within the elite. There were; and such competition can be a powerful motivation for, among other things, patronage of the arts and the Church. But, for the most part, the council tried to keep its disagreements sub rosa and present a united front to the town populace. The citizens at large were bound together by an annual oath and seem to have been contented to support this patrician constitution. Thus, actual political participation was not as widespread in Nuremberg as in many other Renaissance cities; but civic consciousness, with its sense of corporate responsibility in all matters affecting the daily lives of citizens, was a very important part of the Nuremberg leaders' conception of their roles. This most certainly included the issues of religion and the Church.

In the later Middle Ages, the city council had shown an ever increasing concern with such matters as public morals and the qualifications and behavior of the clergy, poor relief and education, ecclesiastical patronage, and the administration of monastic and other Church properties. Nuremberg, unlike many other important German cities, did not have a resident bishop (his see was at Bamberg), so the gradual development of an almost completely civic control over the institutional Church was not seriously challenged. While the absence of a large ecclesiastical power may have robbed Nuremberg's artists of an immediate source of patronage, this seems to have been made up in large part by numerous commissions from individual laymen and civic bodies who had been influenced both by the renewed spiritual and devotional movements, which developed even prior to the Reformation, and by that sense of civic and familial obligations that influenced patronage everywhere.

Nuremberg was not culturally isolated. Young members of important Nuremberg families had long traveled to Italy or elsewhere for their higher education, and the city (with its growing printing trade) had welcomed visiting scholars and teachers. If the ferment of Renaissance ideas was clearly an important factor in much of the artistic work just before and after 1500, the new ideas of the Reformation reached Nuremberg even more quickly. They were not, at first, either imposed from above by the council or demanded violently from below by the "rabble." Luther's views were brought first by Johann Staupitz during his frequent visits and were extensively discussed in certain monasteries and especially in the intellectual circle of the Christian humanist *sodalitas*. The members of this group (which later changed its name to the Martiniana) included Willibald Pirckheimer, Kaspar Nützel (who translated the Ninety-five Theses into German), Christoph Scheurl (a prominent lawyer), Lazarus Spengler (lawyer, council clerk, and one of the leading lay intellectuals of the early Reformation), and Albrecht Dürer, as well as other lay members of the patriciate and a number of reform-minded monks and priests. The Nuremberg printers were from the first very active in producing tracts that spread the opinions of Luther and his supporters (and sometimes those of his Protestant detractors as well). Indeed the importance of Nuremberg in the first stages of the Reformation was illustrated by the inclusion of two of its prominent citizens, Pirckheimer and Spengler (the first layman to write a defense of Luther), in the papal bulls of condemnation and excommunication aimed against Luther in 1520.[4]

The Reformation actually took hold in Nuremberg in the early 1520s, despite the presence in the city of the Imperial Council and three Imperial Diets. In many ways, the Nuremberg city council simply continued the control over the religious affairs of the city that it had asserted during the later Middle Ages, although it tried to appear as though it was simply going along with changes instituted by the clergy and thereby sought to assuage the anger (and military threats) of the emperor. Three councillors and several advisors had attended the Diet of Worms in 1521 and had returned very favorably impressed by Luther. The edict issued there proscribing Luther's views was posted by the ever-cautious town leaders, but only as a formality, and the Lutheran influence grew continuously. New clerics were appointed, most notably Andreas Osiander, an effective preacher and scholar. Changes were ordered (or allowed) that forbade many traditional religious customs and celebrations and banned the Good Friday passion play and the observance of most saints' feasts (although the council preserved some Marian observances). In turn, the council went along with the open reading of the Scriptures in German (although Latin services were continued), and the administration of communion in both kinds to the laity became common. In early March of 1525, Osiander debated and easily "defeated" his Roman Catholic opponent in a colloquy aimed at restoring uniformity and harmony in the town; and on the basis of this popular outcome, coupled with some previous administrative conflicts between the city and the bishop, the Reformation, under the control of the city council, was instituted. Throughout the 1520s and early 1530s, Nuremberg (led largely by Osiander's preaching and writing) developed coherent expressions of Lutheran beliefs (e.g., justification by faith alone; the sufficiency and authority of the Bible in all matters pertaining to religious life; the ethical implications of the concept of the priesthood of all believers), alternative forms of worship and church organization, and new schools to indoctrinate the young with Lutheran principles.

These accomplishments impressed other cities, which were themselves responding to the obvious appeals of many of Luther's reforms, and Nuremberg could have easily claimed a place of major leadership in the defense and spread of the Protestant cause. But throughout the process—and in the decades of conflict and danger that were to follow—the council always advocated caution, gradual change, moderate views, and protection of the city's independence at all costs.

On the one hand, the council maintained frequent negotiations both with Emperor Charles V and with other Protestant cities and princes; but the councillors either refused to join some of the Protestant military and political alliances (e.g., the League of Torgau-Gotha formed by Lutheran princes to oppose the Edict of Worms), which the patrician leaders felt might involve them in devastating wars, or, when they did join, they usually participated reluctantly and with restraint. (They did sign the important "Protestation" of Speyer in 1529.) By trying to remain on the sidelines during the conflict, Nuremberg forfeited its role as the leading spokesman for the imperial free cities and reaped the disdain of more committed Protestant politicians and preachers; but in these unsettled times, that was a price the city council seemed more than willing to pay.

On the other hand, the council avoided threats from the "left," or "below," to push the Reformation along more radical paths. It responded with concern and melioration to the complaints of the city's lower classes at the beginning of the Peasants' Revolt in 1525. It also pursued firm (though comparatively mild) policies against the spread of the teachings of some of the more extreme early reformers, such as Thomas Muntzer (who had one of his outspoken pamphlets against Luther's conservatism confiscated without any reimbursement to the Nuremberg printer), Andreas Bodenstein von Karlstadt (again the council destroyed a locally printed work that stressed the purely symbolic meaning of the Eucharist), Hans Denck, Anabaptist Wolfgang Vogel (the only radical actually put to death in Nuremberg during the intense repression of the sectaries by the Swabian League after the Peasants' Revolt), and others who favored radical views concerning the sacraments, church property (and iconoclasm), and the abolition of secular authority over "saved" Christians.[5] In at least one instance, even Osiander found himself in difficulties with the council when he attacked the merchants of Nuremberg for deceit and for making excessive profits by giving short weights, exploiting defenseless workers, and manipulating trade through monopolies. Was this anything "but concealed theft?" he asked. The Nurembergers were unaccustomed to such analysis and interference in their affairs, and similar sermons were discouraged.[6]

By rejecting both the return to Roman Catholicism and any accommodation with the radical reformers, Nuremberg played a significant role in the organization and consolidation of Lutheranism in the succeeding decades. As that Lutheranism was understood, with its emphases on the abolition of distinctions between laity and clergy and the submission of earthly Christians to properly constituted political authorities, it had as strong a practical appeal to the civic leaders of Nuremberg as it did a spiritual enticement to the citizenry as a whole in their search for a powerful, yet simple and understandable, creed that offered certainty of salvation and a form of worship and church organization stripped of many possibilities for abuse. (Among the most important immediate changes was the integration of the clergy more immediately into city affairs. They were now fully citizens with a voice in all matters, yet they were also even more closely tied to the council.) The rapid transformation in the behavior and beliefs of many people from eager participation in many aspects of late medieval Roman Catholic spirituality to an equally eager denunciation of those practices—often by the very same people—has considerable parallels with Luther's own emotional evolution and remains one of the most striking changes in European civilization. While the depth and lasting effects of these changes among the common people have recently become a matter of scholarly debate and research, the immediate effects in the 1520s and 1530s were both obvious and profound.[7]

For Nuremberg, the later sixteenth century lacked the heady excitement of its "golden age"; but, as much as this may be lamented by its modern historians, one suspects that it was not an altogether unwelcome respite for its leaders and many of its citizens. Survival had been the major goal of the city council in its arduous negotiations, compromises, and, when necessary, alliances for defense. Barring a major natural disaster or a devastating invasion, a city of substance such as Nuremberg could persevere for a long time as a vital social and cultural entity, even—in this case—in the midst of widespread warfare, a general economic decline, large-scale realignments of political forces and political attitudes (both in Germany and throughout western Europe), and continuing religious disunity. Although the adroit Nuremberg did manage to avoid the brunt of the Schmalkaldic League's religious and political civil wars, it was ironically humbled by the opportunistic adventurer Margrave Albrecht Alcibiades of Brandenburg-Kulmbach during two wars in the 1550s. Left with a very sizable debt and the need for substantial rebuilding both of its town defenses and in the villages of the surrounding countryside, Nuremberg faced severe financial problems. The shift of the center of economic activity from the Mediterranean to the Atlantic and the increased competition of Italian traders in Germany itself marked an end to the era of Nuremberg's commercial expansion and, thus, its ability to recover easily from the war damage after 1550. But the city still maintained its eminent reputation for quality workmanship and continued an active, if reduced, trade for another century at least. The increasing power, military might, and centralization of the "renaissance monarchies," and the international and civil wars of religion culminating in the Thirty Years War of the early seventeenth century, diminished the external role that any mere city-state such as Nuremberg could play (but it at least managed to maintain its political independence until 1806). In its religious life, Nuremberg continued to provide valuable support and organizational leadership for the consolidation of Lutheranism, despite the emergence of the dual challenges of an expansive Calvinism and a renewed, militant Roman Catholicism as the dynamic forces of the later Reformation. As late as 1609, Nuremberg helped form a "Union" of Lutheran powers (including the Elector of the Palatinate, several princes, and a number of southern German cities) to defend against any attacks on their rights to practice their religion; but the basic weaknesses of the old imperial cities in the new political and religious climate were clear to virtually everyone.[8]

Even in the area of religion itself, all was perhaps not well in the second half of the sixteenth century. In the visitation records of 1561, we find continuous complaints about the appalling ignorance among the people of even the most basic tenets of Christianity, despite years of Protestant pedagogy. Nuremberg adults set terrible examples for the young through "wanton prodigality in stuffing their guts and wearing extravagant clothing, also abominable cursing, lying, and deceiving." While one might perhaps argue that this is merely evidence that "Renaissance" Nuremberg was still alive, "Reformation" preachers despaired: "You cannot make them go to church, no matter what you say. To worldly affairs they turn with a passion, but for church they have no time and no interest." The countryside of the Nuremberg Territorium was apparently in even worse shape, according to these reports, despite thirty years of active "missionary" work. The city council was duly alarmed and demanded a simpler standard catechism, more indoctrination, harsher decrees and fines against the slothful, and more rigorous inspections.[9] Even if these complaints were somewhat hyperbolic, still it is clear that Nuremberg was hardly the Protestant paradise many had envisioned. Somehow I find it all the more human and interesting (and worthy of further research) because of this "failure."

While Nuremberg had quite obviously declined in both absolute and relative wealth, power, and prestige, it also resolutely endured as one of the more prominent cities in German lands. But decline does not of necessity entail artistic impoverishment or decadence. As the evidence of this current exhibition shows, Nuremberg's artists, craftsmen, and printers, who had earned such a very large reputation in the first decades of the sixteenth century, were still productive and still merited Europe's respect and patronage a hundred years later. The "Renaissance" city had, in one sense, been long overshadowed by the "Reformation" city. Yet, in many important respects, it too had endured all the change and remained vital, as many traditions do.

NOTES

1. The urban context of the Renaissance is a commonplace, dating back to the writings of the participants themselves. Similarly, the idea of a shared urban mentality (or value system) is generally accepted, yet it still requires extensive research and analysis. The bibliography already is massive, and I would refer readers to the writings of Hans Baron, Christian Bec, Gene Brucker, and Sylvia Thrupp as a beginning. My own approach to collective mentalities and the history of values will be somewhat different. On the Reformation, again the literature is very large, but basic perspectives can be found in B. Moeller, *Imperial Cities and the Reformation* (Philadelphia, 1972); B. Hall, "The Reformation City," *Bulletin of the John Rylands Library* 54 (1971): 103–148; S. E. Ozment, *The Reformation in the Cities* (New Haven, 1975); T. A. Brady, Jr., *Ruling Class, Regime, and Reformation at Strasbourg, 1520–1555* (Leiden, 1978).

2. The most important works on Nuremberg include G. Strauss, *Nuremberg in the Sixteenth Century*, rev. ed. (Bloomington, 1976), and *Luther's House of Learning* (Baltimore, 1978); G. Pfeiffer, ed., *Nürnberg, Geschichte einer europaischer Stadt*; H. J. Grimm, *Lazarus Spengler* (Columbus, 1978) and "The Role of Nuremberg in the Spread of the Reformation," in *Continuity and Discontinuity in Church History*, ed. F. F. Church and T. George (Leiden, 1979), pp. 182–197 (plus Grimm's other writings and the dissertations he directed at Ohio State); L. P. Buck and J. W. Zophy, eds., *The Social History of the Reformation* (Columbus, 1972); H.-D. Schmid, *Taufertum und Obrigkeit in Nürnberg* (Nuremberg, 1972); and the references to sources and older volumes contained in each of these works. There are countless studies on Dürer and his background, the best of which is still E. Panofsky, *The Life and Art of Albrecht Dürer*, 4th ed. (Princeton, 1955). (A facsimile ed. of the 1493 printing of Schedel's work has been produced recently by the Landmark Press of New York as *The Nuremberg Chronicle*.) For all the factual material that follows in this essay, unless otherwise documented, I am relying on information derived from these works. For the general political situation, see H. Holborn, *A History of Modern Germany: The Reformation* (New York, 1970).

3. I am currently at work on a book, tentatively entitled *Patronage, Piety, and Friendship: Toward a social history of values from feudalism to capitalism*, which tries to deal in part with these issues. See also G. F. Lytle and S. Orgel, eds., *Patronage in the Renaissance* (Princeton, 1981).

4. For the best introduction to Reformation issues, see S. E. Ozment, *The Age of Reform* (New Haven, 1980) and *The Reformation in the Cities* cited above. For Nuremberg per se and for much of what follows in the essay, Harold Grimm's book and article cited in note 2 are the most accessible guides and authorities. On the printers, see A. G. Dickens, *The German Nation and Martin Luther* (London, 1974); E. L. Eisenstein, *The Printing Press as an Agent of Change* (Cambridge, 1979), vol. 1; R. W. Scribner, *For the Sake of Simple Folk: Popular propaganda for the German Reformation* (Cambridge, 1982).

5. For the broader context here, see B. Scribner and G. Benecke, eds., *The German Peasant War of 1525—New Viewpoints* (London, 1979); G. H. Williams, *The Radical Reformation* (Philadelphia, 1962); S. E. Ozment, *Mysticism and Dissent* (New Haven, 1973).

6. Strauss, *Luther's House of Learning*, p. 243.

7. The reviews of Strauss's book, ibid., are too numerous to list here. See J. M. Kittelson, "The Confessional Age: The late Reformation in Germany," in *Reformation Europe: A Guide to Research*, ed. S. Ozment (St. Louis, 1982), pp. 361–383; my forthcoming article "Indoctrinating the Reformation" (tentatively in the *Journal of Interdisciplinary History*).

8. For different aspects of later Reformation urban history, see, in addition to Strauss, K. von Greyerz, *The Late City Reformation in Germany* (Wiesbaden, 1980); P. Benedict, *Rouen during the Wars of Religion* (Cambridge, 1980); the works discussed by Kittelson in his survey listed in note 7.

9. Strauss, *Luther's House of Learning*, pp. 296–297.

3. Religious Art and the Reformation

A. PRE-REFORMATION ART

"The piety at Nuremberg is remarkable, as well towards God as towards one's neighbor. The attendance at sermons is enormous, although preaching goes on in thirteen churches at the same time."[1] Johannes Cochlaeus's comments about Nuremberg's religious life, written in 1511, also pertain to the visual arts in Nuremberg prior to the city's adoption of Lutheranism in 1525, since these same worshippers were commissioning devotional images. Although the principal architectural projects of the fourteenth and fifteenth centuries, notably the choirs of St. Sebaldus and St. Lorenz, were completed, their adornment with paintings, statues, stained-glass windows, and liturgical objects continued until the eve of the Reformation. Johannes Andreas Graff's 1695 view of the interior of the Frauenkirche shows a monumental altarpiece behind the high altar of the choir (fig. 6). This is the *Welser Altar*, which painter Hans Springinklee and sculptor Hans Peisser(?) completed only in 1522 or 1523.[2] Graff's illustrations of the interiors of St. Sebaldus and St. Lorenz convey something of the wealth of art that once adorned Nuremberg's churches (figs. 4 and 7). Despite the removal of certain offending items during the Reformation, almost every available pillar and chapel is decorated with a statue or an altarpiece, all of which predate 1525.

Albrecht Dürer and his colleagues were fortunate to work during the period from 1490 to 1525 when Nuremberg's wealth peaked and individual spiritual piety was most fervent. The local patricians supported a large community of gifted painters and sculptors who benefited from the current practice of expressing personal religious devotion by means of pictorial images. Hans von Kulmbach, one of Dürer's first pupils, is a prime example of how a single highly talented, but not particularly innovative, artist thrived.[3] Prior to his death in 1522, Kulmbach designed the great *Bamberg*, *Kaiser (Emperor's)*, and *Markgraf (Margrave's) Windows* in St. Sebaldus. His painted masterpiece, the *Epitaph of Lorenz Tucher* (1513), hangs on the north ambulatory wall of this church. For St. Lorenz he planned the *Schmidtmair Window* and painted the wings of the *St. Anne Altarpiece* and the *St. Nicholas Altarpiece*. Additional stained-glass designs and paintings were created for the Frauenkirche, Rochuskapelle, Tetzelkapelle in St. Egidien, Sebalder Pfarrhof, and at least one of the Tucher family's house chapels.

To the modern observer living in a secular society, the ubiquity of the Church and the spiritual benefits of religious art are perhaps difficult to comprehend. One was baptized, educated, married, and buried under the aegis of the Church. The Roman calendar, with its movable feasts and saints' days, dictated holidays and periods of religious observance. Whether at mass or at home, one prayed to the Virgin and sought the assistance of the saints on all matters. One beseeched St. Apollonia to cure a toothache or petitioned St. Christopher to ensure a safe journey. On the streets of Nuremberg one could see pilgrims coming to venerate St. Sebaldus or, during the Easter season, to witness the display of the Holy Imperial relics in the Hauptmarkt. The city was home to the Augustinians, Benedictines, Carthusians, Dominicans, Franciscans, and the members of the Teutonic Order, among other monastic groups. Hans Sebald Beham's woodcuts published in *Das Babstum mit seynen gliedern gemalet vnd beschryben . . .* (Nuremberg, 1526; cat. nr. 78) capture something of the rich variety of religious costumes customarily seen in the city. In short, the Church's influence permeated all facets of daily life.

For the average Christian, art was the primary means for learning about the biblical narrative, the lives of the saints, and the spiritual mysteries of the Church. A Veit Stoss statue of the Virgin and Child is more physically accessible and easier to remember than a written or spoken description.[4] Strassburg preacher Johann Geiler von Kaisersberg (1445–1510) advised Christians to "take a picture of paper where Mary and Elizabeth are depicted as they meet each other, you buy it for a penny. Look at it and think how happy they had been and of good things . . . Thereafter show yourself to them in an outer reveration, kiss the image on the paper, bow in front of the image, kneel before it."[5] Although Johann Geiler von Kaisersberg's comments were directed primarily to an uneducated audience, his suggestion that art serves as an aid for personal meditation reflects contemporary devotional practices.

From the late fourteenth century on, the trend toward individual contemplation of the Christian mysteries had grown within the German church. The mystical writings of St. Birgitta and Thomas à Kempis's *De Imitatione Christi* enjoyed wide popularity.[6]

The devotional reliance upon art was certainly enhanced by the rise and proliferation of inexpensive prints that could be carried or tacked to a wall in the dwelling of even the poorest parishioner. The powerful visual impact of these prints is well illustrated by works in this exhibition. Hans Schäufelein's *Man of Sorrows* (cat. nr. 48), shaped like an altarpiece, focuses the viewer's thoughts upon Christ's sacrifice. Hans Sebald Beham's *Man of Sorrows* (cat. nr. 74), on the other hand, directs the worshipper to contemplate the redemptive mystery of the Eucharist as Christ's blood drips into the communion chalice. Dürer's *The Sudarium Held by One Angel* etching (cat. nr. 23) vividly recalls Christ's physical torture, while the same artist's *Virgin and Child Seated by the Wall* (cat. nr. 15) stresses the humanity and approachability of the holy pair as they sit before the western walls of Nuremberg.

The function of prints, such as Wolf Traut's *Man of Sorrows and Mater Dolorosa* (cat. nr. 59) of about 1515, is more specific. The large broadsheet, measuring 39.5 × 23.6 cm is made up of the image, the prayer, and the print's indulgence value. The half-length figures of Christ, displaying his wounds, and the Virgin, with the symbolic sword of her sorrows piercing her heart, are presented clearly with bold outlines and red highlights for Christ's wounds, lips, and other features. The passion instruments, including the lance of St. Longinus, which was then housed with the imperial relics in the Heilig-Geist-Spital, are neatly arranged behind. The bleeding Christ and sorrowful Virgin tug at the viewer's emotions, while the physical impact is heightened by Sebastian Brant's text, constructed as a dialogue between mother and son, explaining the need for his sacrifice. By reciting the printed prayer and contemplating the woodcut, the worshipper received an indulgence credit of three years. Thus this form of personal devotion using a print was rewarded with a specific spiritual credit each time the prayer was recited.

Erhard Schön's *Great Rosary* (cat. nr. 61) is another important example of the linking of image, prayer, and indulgence. At the bottom of the woodcut is a scene showing angels plucking souls from limbo. The obvious implication is that the more often the worshipper recites the Our Father (Pater Noster) and Hail Mary (Ave Maria) the sooner he or she can join the community of the Christian elect in the afterlife.

During these years Nuremberg was a major publishing center of spiritual texts. Aware of the popularity of religious prints, many authors provided their readers with richly illustrated books. Stephan Fridolin, the Franciscan preacher at the Convent of St. Klara, had Michael Wolgemut and Wilhelm Pleydenwurff design ninety-one woodcut illustrations for his *Schatzbehalter oder schrein der wahren reichtümer des heils . . .* (Nuremberg, 1491; cat. nr. 2). Ulrich Pinder engaged Hans Baldung Grien, Hans Schäufelein, Hans von Kulmbach, and Wolf Traut to decorate his *Der Beschlossen Gart des Rosencrantz Marie* (Nuremberg, 1505; cat. nr. 40) and *Speculum Passionis Domini Nostri Ihesu Christi* (Nuremberg, 1507; cat. nr. 43). The illustrated *Hortulus Animae* (cat. nr. 63) had eighteen editions either printed by or for Nuremberg publishers between 1516 and 1521.

The intense religious fervor of this pre-Reformation period, alluded to by Johannes Cochlaeus, prompted the erection of several sculptural cycles that stressed Christ's physical suffering and invited the viewer's empathy. In 1505 Bamberg knight Heinrich Marschalk von Rauheneck commissioned Adam Kraft, Nuremberg's finest stone sculptor, to carve seven reliefs illustrating the Stations of the Cross (fig. 18).[7] These sandstone carvings, each measuring about 122 × 165 cm, were mounted upon pillars and placed along the route between the Tiergärtnertor and Johannisfriedhof, which was the St. Sebaldus parish cemetery located west of town. The placement of each pillar was determined by the equivalent distances between the episodes of the Passion on the road from Pilate's house to Golgotha in Jerusalem, a route frequently walked by pilgrims to the Holy Lands. The inscription on the third pillar, for instance, reads:

Hir sprach Christus Ir Döchter von Jherusale[m] nit weynt über mich, sunder über euch un[d] eure kinder IIIc LXXX [380] schritt vo[n] pilat[us] haus.

18. Adam Kraft, *Third Station of the Cross*, ca. 1505, formerly in front of the house at Bürgschmietstrasse 18; the relief is now in Nuremberg, Germanisches Nationalmuseum; photo taken in about 1892.

Here Christ told the Daughters of Jerusalem not to weep over me, but over yourself and your children, 380 steps from Pilate's house. (Luke 23:28–29)

The large house on the Tiergärtenplatz, later owned by armorer Valentin Siebenbürger, immediately became known as Pilate's house.

The *Stations of the Cross* reliefs, now in the Germanisches Nationalmuseum and replaced with replicas along the route, culminated in a monumental *Crucifixion* and *Entombment* at the cemetery. Originally, the *Crucifixion* included life-size figures of Mary, John the Evangelist, Mary Magdalene, several Jews, and Roman soldiers. Today only the surviving statues of Christ and the two thieves, set in the courtyard of the Heilig-Geist-Spital, convey the powerful realism of the cycle. The *Entombment*, still at the cemetery in Marschalk's chapel (the Holzschuherkapelle), includes a painted topographical view of Jerusalem to heighten the veracity of the scene.

The purpose of the *Stations of the Cross* cycle, like the contemporary religious dramas that may have inspired it, was twofold: to reconstruct vividly the events of Christ's passion and to inspire the viewer to meditate upon the brutality of mankind and Christ's personal sacrifice for our salvation. This is one of the purest artistic portrayals of the pietistic *imitatio Christi*, or imitation of Christ, advocated by Thomas à Kempis and, earlier, the Franciscans. Kraft's sculptures also warned visitors to the Johannisfriedhof about their mortality and their need to prepare for their salvation.

In contrast to that in other German cities, the patronage of religious art in Nuremberg fell largely to the patricians. Ecclesiastical and craft guild sponsorship was negligible due primarily to civic control of the churches and the suppression of strong guilds. In a town where sumptuary laws were strictly enforced and showiness of any kind was discouraged, if not outlawed, such patrician families as the Tetzels, Holzschuhers, Imhoffs, Tuchers, Volckamers, Kresses, Pfinzings, Hallers, Mendels, Stromers, and Muffels used their wealth to embellish churches in the city and in surrounding villages.[8] Four of the most important artistic projects erected during this period are the Landauer Chapel, Adam Kraft's *Sacrament House* (St. Lorenz), the Vischer family's *Tomb of St. Sebaldus*, and Veit Stoss's *Angelic Salutation* (St. Lorenz) (figs. 19–23). These commissions demonstrate both the level of patrician patronage and something of the underlying spiritual and familial motivations that prompted each work.

In 1501, the year of his wife's death, Mattheus Landauer, a wealthy copper merchant, established the Zwölfbrüderhaus, or Twelve Brothers' House, a charitable home for twelve elderly craftsmen.[9] Landauer had Hans Beheim the Elder, the city's master mason, construct a small chapel (1506–1508) for the brothers' use. By this time Landauer himself was residing in the Zwölfbrüderhaus. In 1508 Landauer ordered Albrecht Dürer to paint the high altar and to design the rest of the interior decoration, which can best be seen in Georg Christian Wilder's 1836 watercolor (Germanisches Nationalmuseum; fig. 15). By 1511 Dürer had completed his *All Saints Altarpiece* (Vienna, Kunsthistorisches Museum; frame, Germanisches Nationalmuseum) for the main altar. Dürer's pupil Hans von Kulmbach planned several of the stained-glass windows, including the *Fall of the Rebel Angels* (cat. nr. 35).

Landauer erected the Zwölfbrüderhaus and chapel because of his concern for the spiritual well-being of its elderly inhabitants and himself. The inscription on the bottom of Dürer's altarpiece reads in translation: "Mattheus Landauer finally completed the chapel of the twelve brothers together with the charitable foundation and this altarpiece in the year 1511 after Christ's birth." He reminds the inhabitants and posterity of his generosity. Landauer, as did most of his contemporaries, subscribed to the fundamental Roman Catholic belief in the benefit of good works. By performing pious acts, including the erection of a chapel or the commissioning of religious art, an individual could enhance his or her chances at obtaining a shorter period of penance and ultimately salvation. Cardinal Albrecht von Brandenburg, archbishop of Mainz, calculated that his good deeds, his prayers, his religious establishments, and his huge collection of relics and art equaled an indulgence of 39,245,120 years of penance.[10] This strong incentive to influence one's future motivated many to commission paintings, sculptures, and stained-glass windows during this period.

Landauer's obsession with salvation is evident in the subject and the design of

Dürer's altarpiece. The wooden frame shows a traditional Last Judgment, with the Virgin and John the Baptist acting as intercessors for mankind. On the lintel, the souls are assigned to heaven or hell. The painting, like the chapel, was dedicated to the Trinity and the community of saints. Landauer is portrayed among the ranks of the Christians gathered to adore the Trinity; he is introduced by a cardinal, perhaps St. Jerome. The painting is a form of pictorial wish fulfillment since Landauer participates in the Augustinian City of God as if assured of his ultimate salvation.[11]

Although Landauer's level of artistic patronage exceeded that of the average Nuremberg merchant, his example and dual motives of salvation and a modicum of earthly fame were hardly unusual. For instance, the Imhoffs, one of Nuremberg's oldest and wealthiest families, had been major benefactors of St. Lorenz since the late fourteenth century. The most impressive of their donations was the towering *Sacrament House*, or eucharistic tabernacle, which Hans IV Imhoff contracted Adam Kraft to carve in 1493 (figs. 19 and 20).[12] The tabernacle, which rises up 18.7 meters before whimsically bending its spire at the springing of the vault, is one of the finest examples of German stone sculpture from any period. Hans Imhoff intended the tabernacle to benefit the entire parish community since, prior to the liturgical changes of Lutheranism, it was customary to house the host near the main altar until the celebration of the Eucharist.[13] The Imhoff *Sacrament House* replaced a much simpler, older niche. The relief carvings showing the institution of the sacrament at the Last Supper and other scenes of Christ's passion, culminating in the crucifixion, provide a didactic explanation of the meaning of the Eucharist. As did Landauer, Imhoff sought both public and celestial recognition of his largess by ordering Kraft to place his coats of arms on the balustrade socle.

For many patricians, the artistic beautification of local churches was a matter of civic and family obligation. The actions of Anton II Tucher (1458–1524) during the 1510s clearly demonstrate these points. Scion of the powerful Tucher family, Anton was the *vordester losunger*, or first treasurer, Nuremberg's most important public official, from 1507 to 1524.[14] Among his many duties was serving as the lay superintendent of St. Sebaldus and of St. Klara. Other family members, such as his brother Sixtus, the provost of St. Lorenz, were also involved in the affairs of local churches.

Prompted by his sense of civic and religious duty, Anton Tucher used his political office to ensure completion of the *Tomb of St. Sebaldus*, in the church of St. Sebaldus, the most complicated and expensive project of this time (figs. 21 and 22).[15] Peter Vischer the Elder had begun planning the tomb of Nuremberg's patron saint in 1488 on the order of Sebald Schreyer and Rupprecht I Haller. After several changes in design and repeated financial problems, Vischer and his sons modeled and cast the tomb between 1507 and 1519. In early 1519, when it became evident that the amassed funds were insufficient to pay for the monument, Tucher, a longtime overseer and financial sponsor of the tomb, assembled the town's wealthiest citizens in the Rathaus on 17, 18, and 19 March. By appealing to their civic pride and their veneration of St. Sebaldus, Tucher obtained the remaining balance of 800 gulden.[16] Among Tucher's arguments was his claim that the donors would receive rich material and spiritual rewards from God and St. Sebaldus for their generosity.[17] The successful campaign permitted the tomb to be placed into the church on 19 July.

Tucher was the sole donor of Veit Stoss's beautiful *Angelic Salutation* (1517–1518) in St. Lorenz (fig. 23).[18] The *Angelic Salutation* represents the Annunciation to the Virgin with life-size limewood statues of Mary and Gabriel surrounded by a huge rosary. It hangs at the entrance to the choir so that it is visible throughout the church. Tucher also commissioned Jacob Pulmann's accompanying *Marienleuchter*, a large candelabrum with a statue of the Virgin and Child, to illuminate Stoss's masterpiece.[19] Unlike Kraft's *Sacrament House*, which had a specific liturgical function, the *Angelic Salutation* is an elaborate devotional object. It is an expression of the intense veneration of the Virgin Mary during the early sixteenth century. By contemplating the joys of the Virgin, seen in the Annunciation and the surrounding roundels, and reciting ten Hail Marys for every Our Father, the worshipper obtained a papal indulgence. Just as in the case of the Traut broadsheet (cat. nr. 59) discussed above, art was a means for aiding the parishioners in their quest for salvation. The physical beauty of Stoss's carving and polychroming certainly encouraged veneration and

19. Adam Kraft, *Sacrament House*, 1493, St. Lorenz.

20. *Self-Portrait of Adam Kraft*, detail of fig. 19.

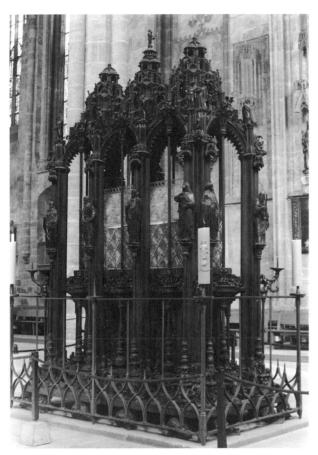

21. Peter Vischer the Elder and his sons, *The Tomb of St. Sebaldus*, completed in 1519, St. Sebaldus.

22. *Portrait of Peter Vischer the Elder*, detail of fig. 21.

contemplation of his statues. The rosary theme was especially appropriate for Tucher, the principal guardian of Nuremberg's well-being, since it symbolized the universal brotherhood of Christians joined together in faith. Faith indeed was the common bond of this community.

Nuremberg's patricians looked with pride upon the artistic commissions of family members. Tucher's heirs paid for the maintenance of the *Angelic Salutation* even though it does not bear the family coat of arms. When Kraft's *Sacrament House* required minor restorations in 1501, 1571, 1605, 1654, and 1670, the Imhoffs, not the church, paid the costs in spite of the fact that the tabernacle had been intended to benefit all the worshippers.[20] The significance of these works as symbols of family prestige is underscored by the futile attempt of Melchior Pfinzing, provost of St. Sebaldus, to replace the late fourteenth-century sacrament niche in the east ambulatory wall of his church with a more elaborate tabernacle. When the heirs of the original donors objected, the city council ruled that, in spite of its liturgical use, this was a family monument and only the heirs could make any alterations.[21]

Patrons like Landauer, Imhoff, and Tucher believed in the inherent value of their gifts.[22] Encouraged by the Church's promises of indulgences and the accumulated benefits of good works, as well as by personal, family, and civic pride, Nuremberg's patricians had lavish incentives to support the arts. Although the present exhibition consists primarily of prints and drawings, something of the artistic quality and range of themes in other media can be inferred.

The number of commissions between 1490 and 1525 was remarkably high and, one would think, certainly could not have been sustained much beyond the 1520s even if the Reformation had not brought a halt to most religious projects. The intense artistic production of these years had saturated local churches. Even the constant orders from such external patrons as Cardinal Albrecht von Brandenburg, Elector Friedrich the Wise, and King Sigismund I of Poland could not have slowed the inevitable decline in Nuremberg's religious art. Dürer and his colleagues benefited from the religious fervor that swept through Germany, but after 1525 Georg Pencz and other painters were forced to develop new artistic outlets.

B. THE IMPERIAL RELICS AND REGALIA

Nuremberg's religious life was greatly enriched by the presence of the imperial collection of holy relics and regalia within its walls. In 1423 Emperor Sigismund (1410–1437) decreed that these treasures should be permanently housed in Nuremberg rather than Aachen, Prague, or the various other cities where they had been stored at the whim of each new emperor. This decision, the result primarily of the city's constant political support of the emperor, was of tremendous spiritual, economic, and artistic significance to Nuremberg since these were among the most sacred of relics—they embodied the divine right and continuity of the empire. Nuremberg's status as a free imperial city was greatly enhanced by the presence of the Holy Lance of St. Longinus, a fragment of the True Cross, a splinter from the manger, a piece of the tablecloth used at the Last Supper, part of the apron worn by Christ while wiping the Apostles' feet, the tooth of John the Baptist, the arm bone of St. Anne, a portion of John the Evangelist's garment, and the chains that once bound Sts. Peter, Paul, and John the Evangelist.[23] The collection also contained the symbols of the imperial office, including the crown of Otto I (dated 962), the reputed sword of St. Maurice, the scepter and orb; the coronation cloak, stockings, gloves, alba, and dalmatica; and Friedrich II's sword and scabbard.

23. Veit Stoss, *Angelic Salutation*, 1517–1518, St. Lorenz.

Shortly after obtaining these venerable relics, the city council and local religious leaders established an annual celebration, the feast of the Holy Lance on the second Friday after Easter. This quickly became the city's most important church feast as crowds of pilgrims joined local citizens in the Hauptmarkt to view the relics. The patrician government also scheduled a large two-week trade fair to coincide with the display to ensure maximum financial profits. On the Thursday following Easter and eight days before the feast of the Holy Lance, the city *baumeister* (building superintendent and architect) supervised the transfer of the Heiltumsstuhl, a three-story wooden display tower, from its storage at the Peunt, behind St. Martha, to the Schopperhaus (nr. 15) on the west side of the Hauptmarkt.[24] The city-owned Schopperhaus was used for storing the relics before and after the ceremony. During the rest of the year the relics were housed in the church of the Heilig-Geist-Spital, neutral ground between the parishes of St. Sebaldus and St. Lorenz.

The best representation of the Heiltumsstuhl and the ceremony is in a woodcut published in 1487 (fig. 24).[25] Below, heavily armed soldiers are stationed to control the press of the crowd seen in the foreground. In the open upper story of the platform are the *ältere herren*, the elders of the city council, holding candles. A cleric, reading from a sheet of parchment, describes each of the relics to the faithful. The preachers of St. Sebaldus and St. Lorenz and other dignitaries, including occasionally the emperor and the bishop of Bamberg, hold the individual reliquaries. From left to right are the splinter from the manger, the arm bone of St. Anne, the tooth of John the Baptist, the piece of John the Evangelist's garment, and the three sets of chains. Painted banners showing the Cross, the Crown of Thorns, the Holy Lance, and the imperial eagle flutter at the top of the tower. Each of the onlookers gathered in the square who had completed the appropriate prayers was granted an indulgence of 34 years and 34 quadregenes (1 quadregene equals 40 days), or a total of 37 years and 275 days.[26] Other sources placed the indulgence at 230,660 days, or approximately 632 years.

24. *Heiltumsstuhl* (*The Display Tower of the Holy Relics*), woodcut published by Peter Vischer in 1487, Nuremberg, Bayerisches Staatsarchiv, Reichsstadt Nürnberg Handschriften, nr. 399a.

The Hauptmarkt was an appropriate place for the annual ceremony since its setting symbolized Nuremberg's identity as a free imperial city.[27] As seen in Lorenz Strauch's view of the Hauptmarkt, the city's largest square is lined with patrician houses (fig. 5). The Rathaus looms to the north. On the east side is the Frauenkirche, which Emperor Charles IV (1346–1378) had founded. An elaborate new façade was added between 1506 and 1509 that included a tall gable with statues of Charles IV and the seven imperial electors. The electors were automated to move around the emperor at certain hours of the day. The cycle refers to Charles IV's 1356 Golden Bull that formalized the election of each new emperor and required that their initial diets (Reichstag) be held in Nuremberg. In the northwest corner of the marketplace stood

25. Albrecht Dürer, *Emperors Charlemagne and Sigismund*, ca. 1510–1513, Nuremberg, Germanisches Nationalmuseum, Gm. 167–168.

the Schöner Brunnen, the richly carved fountain dating to the 1380s whose iconographic program again refers to the emperor and the seven electors.

The presence of the imperial treasures in Nuremberg prompted several artistic projects. In about 1438 the city council commissioned Hans Schesslitzer, Peter Ratzko, Hans Nürnberger, and a painter named Lucas to make the large silver shrine (today in the Germanisches Nationalmuseum) to house all the relics during the rest of the year.[28] New leather cases were produced for the coronation cloak and a ceremonial cross in 1495 and for the True Cross in 1517.[29] The following year Anton II Tucher, Hieronymus Ebner, and Martin Geuder paid Hans Krug the Younger to fashion two nearly identical reliquaries for the pieces from the apron of Christ and from the tablecloth of the Last Supper.[30] The scenes of the Last Supper engraved on the backsides of the silver reliquaries are based upon Hans Schäufelein's woodcut illustration in Pinder's *Speculum Passionis Domini Nostri Ihesu Christi* (cat. nr. 43).

By far the most significant art work commissioned in connection with the imperial relics is Albrecht Dürer's painting, *Emperors Charlemagne and Sigismund* (Germanisches Nationalmuseum), ordered by the city council in 1510 (fig. 25).[31] Surprisingly, this was Dürer's first major civic project. He made careful studies of Charlemagne's crown, sword, and orb, based upon direct examination of the relics either during one of the annual displays or at the Heilig-Geist-Spital.[32] Like an antiquarian, Dürer desired to provide accurate pictorial records of the imperial collection.

While his portrayal of Charlemagne is necessarily imaginary, the figure of Sigismund is modeled after known likenesses. These two rulers were singled out, according to the inscriptions on the painting, because Charlemagne had founded the German Empire and had collected, it was believed, many of the relics, which Sigismund had placed in the city's custody in 1423.

The actual function of Dürer's large (190 × 90 cm) painting is not totally clear. Dürer's preliminary drawing (London, Courtauld Institute Gallery, Count Seilern Collection) shows the panels as hinged pendants, presumably to be set against the wall of the large room in the Schopperhaus where the imperial relics and regalia were temporarily stored during the feast of the Holy Lance.[33] However, since the painting, as completed in 1512 or 1513, contains inscriptions on the reverse side, the panels may have served as doors for a tall cabinet in which the relics were arranged until their display. Dürer's paintings may also simply have replaced a 1430s panel documented in this storage chamber.[34]

With Nuremberg's adoption of Lutheranism, the feast of the Holy Lance and the display of the imperial relics ceased. The last appearance occurred in 1523. Dürer's panels remained in the Schopperhaus until the city council ordered them transferred to the Rathaus in October 1526.[35] The relics and the regalia were kept in their silver shrine in the Heilig-Geist-Spital until the end of the eighteenth century. The shrine was proudly suspended from the vault at the top of the nave.[36] Although these objects were no longer subject to pious veneration, they continued to be esteemed as artifacts of Germany's imperial heritage.[37] Charles V and later emperors did not attempt to transfer the relics and regalia to a Roman Catholic city.

C. ART AND THE REFORMATION

The Nuremberg city council voted to adopt Lutheranism on 17 March 1525, following twelve days of debate between local Roman Catholic and Protestant theologians.[38] Although popular, the decision was difficult since there was still strong support for the Roman Catholic church within the city. Furthermore, Nuremberg was now in direct opposition to their Roman Catholic Emperor Charles V. The imperial relics, reduced to objects of historical, but not spiritual, significance, were no longer shown. Consequently, Nuremberg's special association with the imperial house was irreparably weakened.

The city moved quickly in its transition to Lutheranism. Iconoclasm was minimal. However, the artistic blossoming of the first quarter of the century soon faded. Since religious commissions had been the major source of revenue for most artists, the economic dislocation was acute. To silence some artisans who blamed their plight on Luther, Hans Sachs wrote *Ein neuwer Spruch wie die Geystlichkeit vnd etlich Handwercker vber den Luther clagen* (Nuremberg: H. Höltzel, 1525[?]), for which Hans Sebald Beham provided the woodcut illustrations.[39] Sachs reminded them that Luther was not to be faulted for writing the words of God, and he accused the artisans of being motivated only by their selfish personal greed.

Nuremberg's leaders had long been receptive to Luther's complaints against the distant Roman papacy and his concept of grace. In 1516 Anton II Tucher, Hieronymus Ebner, Hieronymus Holzschuher, Christoph Scheurl, Lazarus Spengler, Georg Behaim (the prior of St. Lorenz), and Albrecht Dürer, among others, had gathered in the Augustinian church to listen to the sermons and thoughts of Johann Staupitz, general vicar of the Augustinian order and Luther's mentor.[40] In the following year, Staupitz sent Wenzel Linck from Wittenberg to Nuremberg to head the Augustinian church and meet with this group, which was known as the Sodalitas Staupitziana.

Dürer's response to Luther was intense and provides a good barometer of the changes in religious attitudes that occurred in Nuremberg between 1516 and 1525. Dürer had always been fervently pious, as is evident in the emotionalism of the *Large Passion* (cat. nr. 12), the orthodoxy of the *Mass of St. Gregory* (cat. nr. 13), and even the 1500 *Self-Portrait* (Munich, Alte Pinakothek) with its implicit *imitatio Christi* intent.[41] The artist was open-minded however. His participation in the Sodalitas Staupitziana proves his willingness to debate, on an intellectual level, traditional religious beliefs. Dürer soon embraced many of Luther's ideas. When Jan van Scorel visited Dürer in Nuremberg in 1519, he found the master preoccupied with the religious debate.[42] An inventory of Dürer's books made in 1520 before he departed on his trip to the Low Countries shows that he possessed at least sixteen of Luther's writings.[43] According to his travel diary, he purchased several more of Luther's books while in Cologne and later in Antwerp he exchanged his three books (*Apocalypse*, *Life of the Virgin*, and *Large Passion*) for the theologian's *Babylonian Captivity*.[44]

Dürer and Luther never met, yet each was impressed by the other's talents. In a 1520 letter to Georg Spalatin, chaplain and personal secretary to Friedrich the Wise, Dürer wrote: "God helping me, if ever I meet Dr. Martin Luther, I intend to draw a careful portrait of him from the life and to engrave it on copper, for a lasting remembrance of a Christian man who helped me out of great distress. And I beg your worthiness to send me for my money anything new that Dr. Martin may write."[45] When news that Luther had been arrested and possibly killed reached Dürer in Antwerp on 17 May 1521, the artist penned the most moving passage in his travel account.[46] He speaks of Luther as a modern prophet and "knight of Christ." He goes on to condemn bitterly the corruption of the Roman papacy.

For his part, when Luther learned of Dürer's death in 1528, he wrote the following to Eobanus Hessus in Nuremberg: "As to Dürer it is natural and right to weep for so excellent a man; still you should rather think him blessed, as one whom Christ has taken in the fullness of his wisdom and by a happy death from these most troublous times, and perhaps from times even more troublous which are to come, lest one, who was worthy to look upon nothing but excellence, should be forced to behold things most vile. May he rest in peace. Amen."[47]

Dürer's art and writings convey the image of a highly devout individual who intellectually assessed the merits and flaws of both Roman Catholicism and Lutheranism. Although evidence suggests that Dürer was a Lutheran when he died, the artist and his best friend, Willibald Pirckheimer, disliked the extremism of some of the radical Protestants. Pirckheimer broke with Luther and remained in the Roman Catholic fold. He wrote that "I was a good Lutheran, and so was my friend Albrecht (Dürer) of blessed memory, for we hoped that the roguery of Rome and the knavery of monks and priests would be bettered. But instead of that, things have so gone from bad to worse that the Protestants make the Popish look pious by contrast."[48]

Dürer's last great painting, the so-called *Four Apostles* (Munich, Alte Pinakothek), best expresses his position within the religious struggle (fig. 26).[49] In the early fall of 1526, Dürer presented two life-size panel paintings to the city council of Nuremberg with the explanation that he had long wished to give one of his works "to show my respect for your wisdoms." It was also a personal remembrance. On the left panel are painted Sts. John the Evangelist and Peter and, opposite on the right panel, Sts. Paul and Mark. The arrangement is highly unusual since John and Paul dominate the two panels and overshadow the figures of Peter and Mark. The Roman Catholics based their claims to religious primacy upon Peter, but in this case he is obscured by John, who was Luther's favorite apostle. Peter leans over to read John's gospel, which Luther had praised as the "one fine, true, and chief Gospel." Dürer emphasizes the significance of the written word of the gospel rather than the institution of the church established by Peter. St. Paul, whom Luther considered the best teacher after Christ, was referred to as the "apostle of the Reformation." Early Protestants even called themselves Paulines.[50]

The inscriptions at the bottom of the panels provide the key to deciphering Dürer's intended meaning. Mixing biblical passages, all taken from Luther's 1522 German translation of the New Testament, with his own comments, Dürer warns of false prophets and the peril of the moment. The inscriptions begin: "All worldly rulers in these dangerous times should give good heed that they receive not human misguidance for the Word of God, for God will have nothing added to His Word nor taken away from it. Hear therefore these four excellent men, Peter, John, Paul, and Mark, their warning."[51] Critics have correctly interpreted the ensuing biblical texts as Dürer's plea to the city council to shun radical preachers and vainglorious men seeking power, not truth. Dürer was also praising the city council for their moderate course through the turmoil. The city fathers had expelled the Anabaptists and such radicals as Hans Denck. Likewise, Andreas Osiander and other Protestant preachers were warned to modify their behavior.

Dürer shared the conservative, cautious approach of the patrician government. Where Pirckheimer lamented the Protestant excesses, Dürer still clung to the teachings of Luther. Luther and Dürer both bitterly condemned the 1525 Peasants' Revolt and opposed the splintering of the evangelical movement. Given the Protestant theme of the paintings, it was not surprising that when in 1627 Elector Maximilian I, Duke of Bavaria and a staunch Roman Catholic, acquired the panels he ordered the offending inscriptions sawed off. Fortunately, these were preserved.

The radicalism about which Dürer warned had already touched some of

Nuremberg's artists. Georg Pencz, Barthel Beham, and his brother Hans Sebald Beham had moved dangerously close to atheism. On 16 January 1525, the three were interrogated at the Rathaus by a committee consisting of Christoph Scheurl, two other city lawyers, and five local preachers.[52] The transcript of this hearing, today in the Staatsarchiv, reads in part:

Georg Pen[c]z replies to the questionnaire as follows: Does he believe in God? Yes, he feels there is a God, but what he should take to be this God he cannot say. What does he think of Christ? He thinks nothing of Christ. Does he believe in Holy Scripture as the word of God? He does not believe in Scripture. What is his opinion of the Sacrament of the Altar? He has no use for it. Of baptism? He has no use for baptism. Does he believe in worldly authority and does he recognize the Council of Nuremberg as lord over his body, his goods, and all that is material? He recognizes no lord but God alone.[53]

On 26 January the trio was exiled from Nuremberg. By 16 November they were permitted to return. Whether their statements were prompted by youthful intemperance or by strong personal convictions cannot be determined. The episode had no ill effects on Pencz's career in Nuremberg, since in 1532 he was appointed the official city painter. The Behams, on the other hand, returned briefly to Nuremberg but within a few years had permanently moved away. Barthel became the portraitist at the Roman Catholic court of the Duke of Bavaria in Munich.

27. Erhard Schön, *Complaint of the Poor Perse-
cuted Gods and Church Images*, woodcut, ca. 1530,
Nuremberg, Germanisches Nationalmuseum,
H. 7404.

The events of 1525 did result in important changes in the function of art in
Nuremberg. The adornment of local churches ceased immediately, and many Protestant theologians demanded the destruction of religious art as idolatrous. Andreas
Bodenstein von Karlstadt published his pamphlet *Von abtuhung der Bylder Vnd das
Keyn Betdler vnther den Christen seyn sollen* (About the Abolishing of Pictures and How
Christians Should Not Be Begging; Wittenberg, 27 January 1522) advocating icono-
clasm of religious images. He wrote: "My heart since childhood has been brought
up in the veneration of images and a harmful fear has entered me which I gladly
would rid myself of and cannot . . ."[54] Many of the reformers recognized that the
thin dividing line between image and idol was frequently crossed. Johann Geiler von
Kaisersberg's advice on how to meditate upon a print or a painting invited abuse.
This sort of idolatry is illustrated in Michael Ostendorfer's 1520 woodcut *Pilgrimage to
the Shrine of the Beautiful Virgin at Regensburg*, in which worshippers, seeking miraculous cures, crowd around the famous Byzantine icon and the Virgin and Child
statue outside the church.[55]

Luther bitterly opposed the abuses at Regensburg, but he never abandoned his
appreciation for the pedagogical function of religious art. He wrote:

Of this I am certain, that God desires to have his works heard and read, especially the
passion of our Lord. But it is impossible for me to hear and bear it in mind without
forming mental images of it in my heart. For whether I will or not, when I hear of
Christ, an image of a man hanging on a cross takes form in my heart, just as the reflec-
tion of my face naturally appears in the water when I look into it. If it is not a sin but
good to have the image of Christ in my heart, why should it be a sin to have it in my
eyes? This is especially true since the heart is more important than the eyes.[56]

Whereas Luther accepted biblical representations and the stories of the Apostles, he
rejected nonbiblical devotional images of Christ and Mary and the spurious legends
of saints.

Dürer's feelings about idolatry parallel those of Luther. He wrote in the introduction of his *Art of Measurement* (cat. nr. 31) of 1525:

And they ["all eager students of Art"] will not be misled by those now amongst us
who, in our own day, revile the Art of Painting and say that it is the servant to Idolatry.
For a Christian would no more be led to superstition by a picture or effigy than an
honest man to commit murder because he carries a weapon by his side. He must indeed
be an unthinking man who would worship picture, wood, or stone. A picture therefore
brings more good than harm, when it is honourably, artistically, and well made.[57]

The radical iconoclasm advocated by Karlstadt, Zwingli, and others was
parodied by poet Hans Sachs and artist Erhard Schön in their broadsheet entitled
Klagrede der armen verfolgten Götzen vnd Tempelbilder of ca. 1530 (fig. 27).[58] The poem is
a lament by the statues about their sorry state and how it was not their fault they had
been carved into religious images. In the woodcut, a church is being stripped of its
art. One man holds a statue of the Virgin and Child, a second threatens St. Peter, a
third has a Crucifixion on his shoulder, while two others carefully burn the offending statues. At the upper right is a rich man pointing out the splinter in another
man's eye while ignoring the beam in his own. The biblical reference (Luke 6:42) is

used here to criticize the blindness of such reformers as Karlstadt to see where the true problem lies.

The city council's firm stand against all iconoclastic acts resulted in minimal artistic damage. Following the lead of the Augustinians, many of the local monasteries had sold their property and art objects to the city by the end of 1525. Chalices, plate, and other liturgical items no longer needed in the Lutheran service were either sold to patrons, such as Cardinal Albrecht von Brandenburg, or were melted down to finance other projects.[59] Many religious objects reverted to the ownership of their original donors or the donors' families. For example, in 1523 sculptor Veit Stoss had presented a monumental *Altar of the Virgin Mary* to the Carmelite church in Nuremberg where his son Andreas was the prior.[60] The altarpiece remained in the monastery until the order's suppression in 1543. The city council ordered the altarpiece returned to Stoss's heirs, who soon sold it to the bishop of Bamberg.

The patrician government valued personal property and the familial associations of much of the art in local churches. Except for the removal of some offending works from St. Sebaldus, St. Lorenz, the Frauenkirche, and the Heilig-Geist-Spital, the artistic decorations of these churches remained essentially intact.[61] A few of the works mentioned earlier were specifically affected by the change in religious observances. Veit Stoss's *Angelic Salutation* had fallen into disfavor well before 1525 as reformers attacked the cult of the Virgin. In 1519 Anton Tucher had installed a permanent cover over the sculptural group, as is illustrated in the 1685 engraved view of the interior of St. Lorenz (fig. 4). The *Angelic Salutation* was, however, never removed from the church. Luther's demystification of the Eucharist meant that there was no longer any purpose for Kraft's *Sacrament House* (fig. 19). Although some criticized the tabernacle as idolatrous, it was never damaged. Likewise, the continuing popular veneration for the saint spared the *Tomb of St. Sebaldus*. The city council did however remove his feast day (19 August) from the liturgical calendar in order to defuse any potential problems.

Not surprisingly, Nuremberg's artists used their talents to ridicule the Roman Catholic church. Around 1524, Hans Greiffenberger, a little-known painter, was censured for his caricatures of the papacy.[62] Of greater importance was the publication of the tiny book *Eyn wunderliche Weyssagung von dem Babstum* (cat. nr. 65), printed by Hans Guldenmund in 1527. Andreas Osiander, the intense preacher of St. Lorenz, had found a collection of fourteenth- and fifteenth-century prophecies about the papacy in the library of the Carthusian monastery. His edition of this text, which was intended to show that the decadence of the papacy was recognized centuries earlier, included thirty crude woodcuts by Erhard Schön with accompanying rhymes by Hans Sachs.

The opening image shows the pope as a worldly soldier, while in the second the pope, with French assistance, battles the German emperor. Others stress his worldliness, vanity, and contempt for mankind. Number twenty, illustrated in the catalogue, is a flattering allusion to Luther. The Nuremberg city council, anxious not to draw imperial attention to its politically awkward position, seized all the copies on 27 March 1527. Osiander, Sachs, and Guldenmund, but interestingly not Schön, were sharply rebuked. Osiander had to promise that the pamphlet would not be reissued without city council permission.

While this antipapal polemic was temporarily suppressed, it was just one of the many instances in which Hans Sachs and other Lutheran supporters enlisted Nuremberg's artists to disseminate their message. Just as the reformers acknowledged the deeply rooted influence of religious art on devotional attitudes of the populace, they recognized the propaganda potential of the graphic arts in support of their ideas.

Most of this propaganda was polemical directed against the Roman Catholic church. Hans Sachs and Erhard Schön had also collaborated earlier for this purpose. In the *Hunting of Monks and Clerics* (cat. nr. 64) of about 1525, a hunting party of devils track down the Catholic clergy and drive them toward a pig-snouted hell mouth. The pope, holding court in the hell mouth, is clearly the anti-Christ in league with the devil to trick Christian souls. In *God's Lament for the Fate of His Vineyard* of 1532, Schön contrasts the leafless trees filled with relics, rosary beads, and indulgences tended by the Catholics with the fertile vines of the true garden of Christ tended by angels.[63] A Protestant preacher, at the left, explains the differences to his parishioners. Still other prints portray the theologically weak foundation of the Roman Catholic church, the clergy sowing a field with indulgences, and the devil playing a bagpipe shaped like a fat monk.[64]

At the same time that Peter Flötner was designing elaborate Italianate decorative programs for Nuremberg's patricians, he was devising stinging woodcuts like the *Procession of the Clergy* (cat. nr. 123) of 1535. Flötner mocks the gluttonous habits of the monks and nuns, who carry food, wine, and even a backgammon board in their decidedly unsolemn procession. In the contemporary *New Passion of Christ*, it is the Roman Catholic church, not the Jews, that condemns, flagellates, humiliates, and crucifies Christ.[65] In the final scene Christ rises from the tomb guarded by sleeping monks; that is, the message of Christ will triumph over all obstacles posed by the Catholics. Among Flötner's most satirical prints is the *Triumphal Arch of Johann Eck* (ca. 1530), which parodies Eck's reported victory over Luther at the 1519 Leipzig disputation.[66] The pillars of Eck's church are not John the Baptist and John the Evangelist but luxury, drunkenness, and lust. Eck's coat of arms is changed to a fool's cap.

The majority of the anti-Catholic representations, which continued to appear well into the second half of the sixteenth century, are artistically crude since the prints were directed at a mass audience rather than the discerning collector. Even the attractive polemical prints of Hans Holbein the Younger or the Cranachs are stylistically simple.[67] The sheer number of local prints and the range of their themes demonstrate that Nuremberg remained one of the principal centers for the creation of Lutheran propaganda. For instance, in 1559 an anonymous Cranach follower published the *Allegory of the Reformation in Nuremberg* (fig. 28).[68] The skyline of Nuremberg, viewed from the southeast, provides the backdrop for the baptism of Christ. God blesses John the Baptist's anointment of Christ with the water of the Pegnitz River. On the northern shore kneel a group of church reformers, including Johann Huss (died 1415), Luther, Melanchthon, Nuremberg-born Georg Maier (or Major; 1502–1574), and Erasmus. Opposite are the major Protestant princes, such as Friedrich the Wise, Johann the Steadfast, Johann Friedrich the Magnanimous, other Saxon nobles, and the margraves of Brandenburg. The woodcut stresses the importance Luther placed upon baptism and the holy sacraments. More significantly, the image is a memorial to Nuremberg's unwavering support of Lutheranism during the uneasy decades leading up to the 1555 Treaty of Augsburg that formally approved the religious status quo in Germany.

Some religious art continued to be produced in Nuremberg after 1525, but the themes were primarily restricted to Old Testament stories, scenes from Christ's ministry and passion, the Acts of the Apostles, and the Apocalypse.[69] Most of the books, prints, small paintings, and sculptural pieces were intended for personal domestic use or export rather than for church ornamentation. As noted earlier, the decoration of Nuremberg's churches dates primarily to the pre-Reformation period. In the Heilig-Geist-Spital, a few Baroque altars were erected in the seventeenth century.[70]

28. Anonymous (Cranach school), *Allegory of the Reformation in Nuremberg*, woodcut, 1559, Nuremberg, Germanisches Nationalmuseum, Sp. 2416.

The principal additions in St. Sebaldus were Johannes Kreutzfelder's painted *Beheim Epitaph* (1603), Johann Wurzelbauer's bronze *Crucifix* (1628), the *Holzschuher Lamentation* (1650), and the *Muffel Altar* (1663).[71] These compare modestly to the profusion of works donated to the church between 1490 and 1525. No Protestant churches were built in Nuremberg in the sixteenth century. Thus the opportunity to include Protestant altarpieces as part of an integrated ecclesiastical program never materialized in Nuremberg as it had in Torgau at the chapel of the Schloss Hartenfels, which Luther consecrated in 1544.[72]

While Lucas Cranach and his shop created new Protestant iconographic images, Nuremberg's artists were content to repeat well-worn themes. Even the presence of the elder Cranach in Nuremberg for six months in 1539 had no discernible influence on the local school.[73]

Matthias Zündt's *Das Apostelschiff*, or *The Apostle Ship*, etching of 1570 (cat. nr. 185) is a rare exception. Zündt shows the Christian church as a ship steady on its course in spite of the attacks of such enemies as Nero, Pilate, Mohammed, Attila the Hun, Herod, the Turks and Tartars, and even the whore of Babylon. Christ is the mast. The four evangelists, John the Baptist, and James the Major are the true navigators. The sacraments of baptism and communion are celebrated on the deck. Zündt's allegory is not anti-Catholic. Rather it reiterates the Lutheran emphasis on scripture and the sacraments. Luther and Melanchthon, who are included among the oarsmen, are shown to be the most recent of the great church fathers who endeavor to support the church's ministry.

The Reformation in Nuremberg prompted significant artistic changes. Deprived of their traditional religious commissions, except for the occasional orders from Roman Catholic princes and clergy outside the city, most artists turned to portraiture or representative themes drawn from classical literature or daily life. If Albrecht Dürer and the early humanists had paved the way for artists to understand the lessons of Italian art and culture, the Reformation pushed local artists fully into the Renaissance. Faced with the alternatives of either developing new artistic ideas or abandoning their crafts for want of traditional patronage, most Nuremberg artists were forced to adopt new, secularized ideas expressed in Renaissance, rather than Gothic, forms.

NOTES

1. J. Janssen, *History of the German People at the Close of the Middle Ages*, 1: p. 39. On the general subject of religious life in Germany and Nuremberg during the opening years of the sixteenth century, see I. Höss, "Das religiösgeistige Leben in Nürnberg am Ende des 15. und am Ausgang des 16. Jahrhunderts," *Miscellanea Historiae Ecclesiasticae*, pp. 17–36; idem, "Das religiöse Leben vor der Reformation," in *Nürnberg*, ed. Pfeiffer, pp. 137–146; B. Moeller, "Piety in Germany around 1500," in *The Reformation in Medieval Perspective*, ed. S. Ozment, pp. 50–75; K. Schlemmer, *Gottesdienst und Frömmigkeit in der Reichsstadt Nürnberg am Vorabend der Reformation*.

2. K. Pechstein, "Zu den Altarskulpturen und Kunstkammerstücken von Hans Peisser," *AGNM* (1974): 38–74; J. Dettenthaler, "Hans Springinklee als Maler," *MVGN* 63 (1976): 178–180. The altar was dismantled in 1815–1816.

3. On Kulmbach, see his biography in the catalogue.

4. E. Lutze, *Veit Stoss*, figs. 46–47.

5. S. Ringbom, *Icon to Narrative*, p. 29. Also see E. J. D. Douglass, *Justification in Late Medieval Preaching: A Study of John Geiler of Kaisersberg*, pp. 189–200 (attitudes on meditation).

6. Moeller, "Piety in Germany around 1500," pp. 56–57; Birgitta, *Revelationes* (Nuremberg: A. Koberger, 1500), with woodcuts designed by Dürer's workshop; see *Nuremberg: Dürer (1971)*, nr. 365.

7. Schwemmer, *Adam Kraft*, pp. 34–47, figs. 56–65.

8. K. R. Greenfield, "Sumptuary Law in Nürnberg: A Study in Paternal Government," *Johns Hopkins University—Studies in Historical and Political Science* 36 (1918): 7–139.

9. J. Ahlborn, *Die Familie Landauer, vom Maler zum Montanherrn*; Anzewelsky, *Dürer*, nr. 118, figs. 141–148; F. Klauner, "Gedenken zu Dürers Allerheiligenbildern," *JKSW* 75 (1979): 57–92.

10. Moeller, "Piety in Germany around 1500," p. 55.

11. Schwemmer, *Adam Kraft*, pp. 31–32, figs. 52–53, for the Landauer family epitaph erected by Kraft in 1503 in the cloister of St. Egidien. The iconography of this work anticipates Dürer's *All Saints Altarpiece*.

12. Ibid., pp. 19–24, figs. 6–27; Johann Neudörfer, *Des Johann Neudörfer Nachrichten von Künstlern und Werkleuten daselbst aus dem Jahre 1547*, p. 10. For a translation of the contract, see

W. Stechow, *Northern Renaissance Art, 1400–1600—Sources and Documents*, pp. 81–82. And see C. Frhr. von Imhoff, "Die Imhoff- Handelsherren und Kunstliebhaber," *MVGN* 62 (1975): 1–42, esp. figs. 10, 12–13, 15.

13. E. Maffei, *La Réservation eucharistique jusqu'à la renaissance* (Brussels, 1942); A. A. King, *Eucharistic Reservation in the Western Church* (London, 1965).

14. W. Schwemmer, "Das Mäzenatentum der Nürnberger Patrizierfamilie Tucher vom 14.–18. Jahrhundert," *MVGN* 51 (1962): 24–29. For Tucher's activities at St. Klara, see Kurras and Machilek, *Caritas Pirckheimer*, nrs. 53, 92, 102, 106, 113, 126.

15. For a more complete discussion of the tomb, see K. Pilz, *Das Sebaldusgrabmal im Ostchor der St.-Sebaldus-Kirche in Nürnberg—Ein Messinggus aus der Giesshütte der Vischer*; cat. nr. 117 below.

16. Schwemmer, "Mäzenatentum . . . Tucher," pp. 28–29.

17. C. Christensen, *Art and the Reformation in Germany*, pp. 16–17.

18. Schwemmer, "Mäzenatentum . . . Tucher," pp. 25–27; Lutze, *Veit Stoss*, pp. 52–55, figs. 66–72; M. Baxandall, *The Limewood Sculptors of Renaissance Germany*, p. 271.

19. J. Viebig et al., *Die Lorenzkirche in Nürnberg*, p. 23.

20. Schwemmer, *Adam Kraft*, p. 23. See Schwemmer, "Mäzenatentum . . . Tucher," p. 27, for repairs to the *Angelic Salutation*.

21. Christensen, *Art and the Reformation in Germany*, pp. 71–72; Schwemmer and Lagois, *Die Sebalduskirche zu Nürnberg*, pp. 10, 32.

22. The primary source for the following section is J. Schnelbögl, "Die Reichskleinodien in Nürnberg. 1424–1523," *MVGN* 51 (1962): 78–159. Emperor Sigismund's decree is illustrated in Pfeiffer and Schwemmer, *Bilddokumenten*, fig. 18. The relics were carried into Nuremberg amid great celebration on 22 March 1424.

23. In 1796 the relics were transferred to Vienna and are now in the Schatzkammer of the Kunsthistorisches Museum. On these pieces, see H. Fillitz, *Die Insignien und Kleinodien des Heiligen Römischen Reiches*, esp. pp. 12ff., 29–31, figs. 1–51.

24. Schnelbögl, "Die Reichskleinodien in Nürnberg," pp. 107–110.

25. *Wie das hochwirdigist auch kaiserlich heiligthum und die grossen römischen gnad darzu gegen alle jaer au(ss)gerufft und geweist wirdt in der löblichen statt Nuremberg* (Nuremberg: Peter Vischer, 1487). This publisher is not to be confused with Peter Vischer the Elder, the creator of the *Tomb of St. Sebaldus*. A second edition was published in 1493. Schnelbögl, "Die Reichskleinodien in Nürnberg," pp. 124–125; and *Reformation in Nürnberg*, nr. 48.

26. Schnelbögl, "Die Reichskleinodien in Nürnberg," p. 125; *Reformation in Nürnberg*, nr. 48.

27. G. Bräutigam, "Nürnberg als Kaiserstadt," in *Kaiser Karl IV.—Staatsmann und Mäzen*, ed. F. Seibt, pp. 339–343.

28. H. Kohlhaussen, *Nürnberger Goldschmiedekunst des Mittelalters und der Dürerzeit, 1240 bis 1540*, nr. 169.

29. Fillitz, *Die Insignien und Kleinodien*, fig. 13; Schnelbögl, "Die Reichskleinodien in Nürnberg," p. 101.

30. Fillitz, *Die Insignien und Kleinodien*, figs. 47–50; Schnelbögl, "Die Reichskleinodien in Nürnberg," p. 101; Kohlhaussen, *Nürnberger Goldschmiedekunst*, nrs. 404–405 (as Krug workshop).

31. A. Strange, "Zwei neu endeckte Kaiserbilder Albrecht Dürers," *ZfK* 30 (1957): 1–21; Schnelbögl, "Die Reichskleinodien in Nürnberg," p. 102; Anzelewsky, *Dürer*, nrs. 123–124; P. Strieder, "Noch einmal zu Albrecht Dürers Kaiserbildern," *AGNM* (1979): 111–115; and K. Löcher, "Dürers Kaiserbilder—Nürnberg als Hüterin der Reichsinsignien," in *Das Schatzhaus der Deutschen Geschichte*, ed. R. Pörtner, pp. 305–330.

32. F. Winkler, *Die Zeichnungen Albrecht Dürers*, II: nrs. 505–507; F. Zink, *Die Deutschen Handzeichnungen*, I: nrs. 53–55; cf. Fillitz, *Die Insignien und Kleinodien*, figs. 1–6, 17–22.

33. Winkler, *Zeichnungen Dürers*, II: nr. 503.

34. Löcher, "Dürers Kaiserbilder," p. 314.

35. Anzelewsky, *Dürer*, pp. 233–234.

36. It is seen in the 1696 engraving by Jeremius Wolff after Johann Andreas Graff; illustrated in *Reformation in Nürnberg*, nr. 143.

37. Georg Pencz was paid by the city on 18 July 1532 for copying Dürer's panels. The panels served as a record of the imperial relics and as such were sent to a Saxon prince, likely Johann Friedrich the Magnanimous, the recently named Elector of Saxony. Hampe, *Nürnberger Ratsverlässe*, I: nr. 1937; also cited by Anzelewsky, *Dürer*, p. 235.

38. G. Strauss, *Nuremberg in the Sixteenth Century*, pp. 175–176. On the Reformation, see Strauss, pp. 154–186; G. Pfeiffer's four short articles in Pfeiffer, ed., *Nürnberg*, pp. 146–170; *Reformation in Nürnberg*. During the summer of 1983 there will be a major exhibition, *Martin Luther und die Reformation in Deutschland*, held at the Germanisches Nationalmuseum in Nuremberg.

39. *A New Judgment Concerning the Complaints about Luther by the Clergy and Some Artisans*; Geisberg, nr. 222; H. Zschelletzschky, *Die 'Drei gottlosen Maler' von Nürnberg: Sebald Beham, Barthel Beham, und Georg Pencz* (Leipzig, 1975), pp. 230–234; *Reformation in Nürnberg*, nr. 116; R. W. Scribner, *For the Sake of Simple Folk: Popular Propaganda for the German Reformation*, p. 30.

40. I. Höss, "Das religiose Leben vor der Reformation," pp. 145–146; *Reformation in Nürnberg*, nrs. 91–92 (Staupitz's published Nuremberg sermons).

41. The literature on Dürer and his religious convictions is extensive. A good summary is provided in G. Seebass, "Dürers Stellung in der reformatorischen Bewegung," in *Albrecht Dürers Umwelt*, ed. Hirschmann and Schnelbögl, pp. 101–131; see the list in M. Mende, *Dürer-Bibliographie*, pp. 405–413; G. Wiederanders, *Albrecht Dürers theologische Anschauungen*.

42. C. van de Wall, intro. and tr., *Carel van Mander, Dutch and Flemish Painters* (New York, 1936), p. 161; also cited by Christensen, *Art and the Reformation in Germany*, p. 177.

43. W. M. Conway, ed. and tr., *The Writings of Albrecht Dürer*, pp. 156–157; H. Rupprich, ed., *Dürer schriftlicher Nachlass*, I: p. 221.

44. Conway, *Writings of Dürer*, pp. 107 and 123; Rupprich, *Dürer schriftlicher Nachlass*, I: p. 160 (lines 8off.), 175 (lines 101ff.); Meder, nrs. 113–123, 163–178, 188–207.

45. Conway, *Writings of Dürer*, p. 89; Rupprich, *Dürer schriftlicher Nachlass*, I: pp. 85–87 (letter nr. 32).

46. Conway, *Writings of Dürer*, pp. 158–159; Rupprich, *Dürer schriftlicher Nachlass*, I: pp. 170–172.

47. Conway, *Writings of Dürer*, p. 136; Rupprich, *Dürer schriftlicher Nachlass*, I: p. 281 (nr. 125—12 or 13 May 1528?).

48. Strauss, *Nuremberg in the Sixteenth Century*, p. 172; Rupprich, *Dürer schriftlicher Nachlass*, I: pp. 283–288, specifically 285 (lines 115ff.—letter to Johann Tschertte November 1530).

49. Rupprich, *Dürer schriftlicher Nachlass*, I: p. 243 (nr. 23 [6 October]); Anzelewsky, *Dürer*, nrs. 183–184; *Reformation in Nürnberg*, nr. 105; P. Strieder, "Albrecht Dürers 'Vier Apostel' im Nürnberger Rathaus," in *Festschrift Klaus Lankheit zum 20. mai 1973* (Cologne, 1973), pp. 151–157; Christensen, *Art and the Reformation in Germany*, pp. 181–206. The city provided Dürer with a gift of 100 gulden plus 12 for his wife and 2 for his servant.

50. Christensen, *Art and the Reformation in Germany*, p. 182.

51. Ibid., p. 183.

52. Zschelletzschky, *Die 'Drei gottlosen Maler' von Nürnberg*, pp. 31–55; *Reformation in Nürnberg*, nrs. 182–183.

53. Strauss, *Nuremberg in the Sixteenth Century*, p. 180.

54. Christensen, *Art and the Reformation in Germany*, p. 25 (Karlstadt, p. 19), and generally pp. 23–25; *Reformation in Nürnberg*, nr. 135. Karlstadt corresponded with Dürer on 1 November 1521; see Rupprich, *Dürer schriftlicher Nachlass*, I: pp. 92–93 (letter nr. 37).

55. Geisberg, nr. 967; *Reformation in Nürnberg*, nr. 130 with literature.

56. Christensen, *Art and the Reformation in Germany*, pp. 51–52. On Luther's attitude toward art, see Christensen, pp. 42–65; M. Stirm, *Die Bilderfrage in der Reformation*, pp. 17–68.

57. Conway, *Writings of Dürer*, p. 212.

58. *Complaint of the Poor Persecuted Gods and Church Images*; Geisberg, nr. 1145 (with reproduction of the lengthy text); *Reformation in Nürnberg*, nr. 137.

59. Christensen, *Art and the Reformation in Germany*, p. 78. On this subject, see C. Christensen, "Iconoclasm and Preservation of Ecclesiastical Art in Reformation Nürnberg," *Archive für Reformationsgeschichte* 61 (1970): 205–221, portions of which appear in chapters 1 and 3 of his book.

60. Lutze, *Veit Stoss*, pp. 57–62, figs. 74–81, 84–91; now in Bamberg Cathedral.

61. Christensen, *Art and the Reformation in Germany*, pp. 66–78, esp. 73 (Caritas Pirckheimer's lament over local rowdiness and the destruction of some stained-glass windows by vandals), 75–77.

62. Ibid., p. 70.

63. Geisberg, nr. 1140.

64. Ibid., nrs. 1139, 1141, 1144. Schön, Pencz, Hans Sebald Beham, and other artists created a sizable corpus of polemic prints. For a few of these, see *Die Welt des Hans Sachs*, nrs. 9, 18, 33, 60, 73. Also see K. Hoffmann, "Typologie Exemplarik und reformatorische Bildsatire" in *Kontinuität und Umbruch*, ed. J. Nolte, pp. 189–210; Scribner, *For the Sake of Simple Folk*.

65. Geisberg, nrs. 823–824.

66. Ibid., nr. 814; Scribner, *For the Sake of Simple Folk*, pp. 65–67.

67. F. Saxl, "Holbein and the Reformation," *Lectures—I* (London, 1957), pp. 277–285; D. Koepplin and T. Falk, *Lukas Cranach*, 1: pp. 360ff., 2: pp. 498ff.

68. *Reformation in Nürnberg*, nr. 89. For a discussion of the iconography and participants, see Scribner, *For the Sake of Simple Folk*, pp. 224–227.

69. See cat. nrs. 125–127. Also see *Bibel und Gesangbuch in Zeitalter der Reformation, 1517–1967*.

70. Some of these altars are visible in Jeremias Wolff's engraving after Johann Andreas Graff's view of the interior of the church in 1696; *Reformation in Nürnberg*, nr. 143.

71. The print after Graff (fig. 7) shows an elaborate Baroque high altar added later in the seventeenth century. Schwemmer and Lagois, *Die Sebalduskirche zu Nürnberg*, illustrates only the Wurzelbauer *Crucifix* on p. 18. Also see the general comments in *Barock in Nürnberg, 1600–1750*.

72. H. C. von Haebler, *Das Bild in der evangelischen Kirche*; Stirm, *Die Bilderfrage in der Reformation*, pp. 69–119; Koepplin and Falk, *Lukas Cranach*, 2: pp. 498–522; Christensen, *Art and the Reformation in Germany*, pp. 110–163; C. Andersson, "Religiöse Bilder Cranachs im Dienste der Reformation," in *Humanismus und Reformation als kulturelle Kräfte in der deutschen Geschichte*, ed. L. Spitz, pp. 43–79. I wish to thank Professor Andersson for sharing her text with me prior to its publication. After this section was completed, I received from C. Christensen a copy of his essay "Reformation and Art" in *Reformation Europe: A Guide to Research*, ed. S. Ozment (St. Louis: Center for Reformation Research, 1982), pp. 249–270, which the reader should consult for additional literature.

73. Hampe, *Nürnberger Ratsverlässe*, I: nr. 2443. Several portraits of the electors and dukes of Saxony later found in the Rathaus may have been painted by Cranach during this period.

4. Art and the Rise of Humanism

"I have chosen Nuremberg as a permanent dwelling place, because I can easily procure here all necessary instruments, particularly those which are indispensable for the study of astronomy, and also because I can easily keep up a connection with scholars of all countries from here, for this city, on account of its concourse of merchants, may be considered the central point of Europe."[1] When Johannes Regiomontanus (1436–1476), Germany's most famous early astronomer and mathematician, penned these comments to his colleague Christian Roger at Erfurt in about 1471, Nuremberg was quickly becoming a major intellectual center blessed with a growing community of highly trained artists and active publishers. Through its international trade Nuremberg had access to the latest ideas and innovations throughout the continent. Martin Behaim's *Erdapfel* (*Earth Apple*) of 1491–1492 is the oldest extant world globe and predates Christopher Columbus's voyage to the New World.[2] Increasingly, the young patricians studied medicine and law at the universities of Padua, Bologna, or Heidelberg. One direct result was Nuremberg's adoption of Roman law in 1484 when Anton Koberger published, at the request of the city council, the *Newe Reformacion der Stat Nureberg* (cf. cat. nr. 24), the first printed municipal law code in Germany.[3]

The intellectual advances, found at first in the sciences and law, gradually extended to the arts during the last years of the fifteenth century and the opening decades of the sixteenth. The rise of humanism in Nuremberg was one significant reason for this expansion.[4] Humanism was an intellectual movement that, through its study of Greek and Roman cultures rather than just the theological concerns of the Middle Ages, stressed the importance of man, his institutions, and his creative endeavors, notably in the arts and letters. A contemporary author could draw upon the language structures and thematic ideas of Cicero or Virgil. Dürer could refer to Vitruvius's canon of proportions or Euclid's thoughts on geometry in order to perfect his figural forms.

Nuremberg's early humanists and in particular four of Dürer's friends and neighbors, namely Hartmann Schedel (1440–1514), Sebald Schreyer (1446–1520), Conrad Celtis (1459–1508), and Willibald Pirckheimer (1470–1530), were instrumental in interesting local artists in the ancient world and in ideas then being generated in Italy. Beyond introducing specific classical themes and Italian artistic models, the humanists inspired artists to experiment and to innovate. Pirckheimer taught Dürer a scholarly method for his theoretical research. In fact, Dürer was so thoroughly involved in the activities of Pirckheimer's scholarly circle that he can legitimately be considered the first artist-humanist in northern Europe.

Hartmann Schedel settled in Nuremberg in the early 1480s following his training as a medical doctor at Padua, where he also studied Greek and law.[5] While in Italy, Schedel copied dozens of manuscripts and collected the writings of Cicero, Horace, Livy, and Virgil, as well as those of Jerome and Augustine, and contemporary literature on medicine, geography, and mathematics. His real passion was his library. Celtis dubbed him a "bibliophage," or devourer of books. His library grew rapidly, especially with the inclusion of part of his elder cousin Hermann Schedel's collection of Italian authors. At his death, Hartmann's library numbered well over 370 manuscripts and 600 printed books, making it one of the largest personal holdings in Germany. His collection ultimately formed the nucleus of the Bayerisches Staatsbibliothek in Munich. Schedel's library, like those of Schreyer and Pirckheimer, made available classical literature and the latest scientific treatises to his friends and colleagues in Nuremberg.

Schedel's own writings include his *Liber Antiquitatum*, a catalogue of antique inscriptions, and the *Nuremberg Chronicle* (cat. nr. 3), which Anton Koberger published in 1493 in Latin and German editions.[6] While the *Liber Antiquitatum* is of only minor importance, Schedel's *Nuremberg Chronicle*, published in at least 1,500 Latin and 1,000 German copies, is truly the first mass-produced illustrated history text intended for both learned and general audiences. The structure of the *Nuremberg Chronicle* follows the medieval or Augustinian format of different ages of human history beginning with the creation of man. However, Schedel's generally critical approach to his sources and his frequent rejection of implausible explanations link him with the historiographic method of Florentine Leonardo Bruni and other humanistic authors. Artistically, the *Nuremberg Chronicle* was a new type of history text. Schedel and publisher Koberger engaged artists Michael Wolgemut, Wilhelm Pleydenwurff, and, indirectly, Wolgemut's pupil Albrecht Dürer to design the approximately two thousand woodcut illustrations used in the volume. The reader is provided with accurate maps and many city views, as well as hundreds of stylized portraits of important historical figures, to supplement the text. This was the start of the intimate collaboration between Nuremberg's humanists and artists that continued throughout Dürer's lifetime.

Schedel's principal sponsor was his neighbor Sebald Schreyer. As the *kirchenmeister*, or superintendent, of St. Sebaldus, Schreyer is well known for ordering Adam Kraft to carve the *Schreyer-Landauer Funerary Monument* in 1490–1492 on the outside of the choir, initiating the *Tomb of St. Sebaldus* in about 1488, and prompting the construction of the two spires of the church.[7] In addition to church-related activities, Schreyer was the principal benefactor of several important humanistic projects of the 1490s and 1500s.[8] While the *Nuremberg Chronicle* was in press in 1493, Schreyer requested Peter Danhauser, a Nuremberg lawyer and astrologer, to write the *Archetypus Triumphantis Romae*, a compendium of texts by classical authors.[9] He engaged Michael Wolgemut to design the accompanying woodcut illustrations. This was one of the few occasions when Wolgemut turned to Italian models for several of his woodcuts. For instance, he copied Ferrarese *Tarocchi* (tarot) engravings of about 1465–1470 for his nine Muses.[10] This ambitious undertaking was left incomplete when Danhauser followed Conrad Celtis to the University of Vienna in about 1497. Some of Wolgemut's illustrations and blocks are today in Berlin (Kupferstichkabinett).

Schreyer's library functioned as an important gathering place for local humanists. To provide an appropriate setting for his friends, Schreyer paid an unnamed artist, likely Wolgemut or a member of his workshop, in 1495 to paint the walls of this chamber.[11] The classical scheme was probably the first of its type in Nuremberg and perhaps in Germany. On one side Apollo was portrayed surrounded by the nine Muses (Clio, Euterpe, Melpomene, Talia, Polimnia, Erato, Terpsicore, Urania, and Caliope) and seven ancient wisemen (Thales, Solon, Chilo, Pittacus, Bias, Cleobolus, and Periander). On the adjacent wall were half-length portraits of Schreyer and his friends Conrad Celtis, Peter Danhauser, and Master Petrus Schoberlein. Celtis composed the epigrams written beneath each of the figures and he may have helped Schreyer design the overall program. Schreyer was inspired by accounts of classical and contemporary Italian humanist libraries, such as that at Urbino.[12] The decorative program of his library expresses Schreyer's and his colleagues' conviction that under their aegis Apollo, his Muses, and the collective knowledge of the ancients had triumphantly emerged in Nuremberg.

The appearance of Apollo and his Muses in Nuremberg echoes Conrad Celtis's lifelong campaign to transform Germany into the principal cultural center of Europe.[13] Celtis's concept of intellectual nationalism evolved about the time that Emperor Friedrich III crowned him the first German poet laureate on 18 April 1487 in a ceremony performed in the Burg in Nuremberg. Four years later Celtis wrote to Sixtus Tucher, Anton II's brother: "When you read my writings, you will be convinced that I did not send them to you to display my poetic genius . . . , but you will understand that I spared no trouble to accomplish a certain end. For if these efforts do not match those of the Italians, I wish to stimulate and awaken those men among the Germans who excel in learnedness and genius . . . then the Italians, most effusive in self-praise, will be forced to confess that not only the Roman imperium and arms, but also the splendor of letters has migrated to the Germans."[14] Many of Celtis's Nuremberg friends shared the poet's desire to rally humanistic learning and the arts in Germany. Albrecht Dürer, stung by Venetian criticism of his painting style, lavished attention upon his *Feast of the Rose Garland*, executed in 1505–1506 for the Fondaco dei Tedeschi, to prove his painterly abilities.[15] When the picture was finished he proudly signed it "Albertus Dürerus Germanus" as if to remind the viewer that a German artist, not a Venetian, painted this altarpiece.

Celtis, though born in Wipfeld bei Schweinfurt, considered Nuremberg his spiritual home. It was here that the poet's laurel had been placed upon his head and that he maintained a close cadre of friends. His important writings were published in Nuremberg. Sebald Schreyer was an important patron for Celtis. Besides the library epigrams, Schreyer had Celtis compose the *Ode to St. Sebaldus* (*In vitam divi Sebaldi carmen*), which first appeared in a Basel edition of ca. 1494 with a woodcut attributed to Wolgemut and later in a Nuremberg edition of ca. 1501 with a woodcut depiction of the saint by Dürer.[16] More significantly, it was Schreyer who subsidized Celtis's *Norimberga*, written in 1496 and published locally by Hieronymus Höltzel in 1502.[17] *Norimberga* is an elaborate eulogy to the city's government, citizens, buildings, and history. While this work is now considered one of the finest Renaissance examples of this genre, the Nuremberg city council, to whom Celtis dedicated his book, sadly did not fully appreciate his efforts and only rewarded him with a miserly twenty gulden.

Celtis did have a core of admirers who under the title Sodalitas Celtica, or the Celtis Society, published his two principal humanistic writings, his edition of Hroswitha von Gandersheim's *Opera* (1501), and his poetic masterpiece *Quatuor Libri Amorum* (cat. nr. 10) of 1502.[18] Shortly after 1490 Celtis had discovered the manuscript of Hroswitha, a tenth-century German nun, in the monastery of St. Emmeram at Regensburg. Although this was a medieval text, the form of Hroswitha's six comedies was classical in style. Celtis heralded her writings as proof of early German cultural prominence. Dürer designed the dedication pages to Emperor Otto I (962–973) and Friedrich the Wise; his pupil Hans von Kulmbach added the six title pages. Celtis's *Quatuor Libri Amorum* consists of four allegorical love poems, written in part in Pirckheimer's home, which Celtis dubbed "a poet's refuge." Dürer's woodcut *Allegory of Philosophy* (folio A 12v) carries Celtis's cultural chauvinism one step further by defining the four great human cultures as Egyptian, Greek, Roman, and German.

Dürer and Celtis maintained a warm personal relationship, and both appreciated the other's contributions to the Renaissance in Germany. Celtis composed a flattering ode to Dürer in about 1500. The Latin text reads:

> *Ad Pictorem Albertum Durer Nurnbergensem*
> Alberte, Almanis pictor clarissime terris,
>   Norica ubi vrbs celsum tollit in astra caput,
> Alter ades nobis Phidias et alter Apelles
>   Et quos miratur Grecia docta manu.
> Italia haud talem nec lubrica Gallia uidit
>   Et neque in Hispanis quisque uidebit agris.
> Pannonios superas et quos modo Teutonus ora
>   Continet et si quos Sarmatis ora colit.
> Des operam, nostram depinges Philosophiam,
>   Cognita que faciet cuncta sub orbe tibi.[19]

In this ode, Celtis praised Dürer, the brilliant German painter, as the Phidias and the Apelles of the present and as an artist without rivals in Italy, Gaul (France and the Low Countries), or Spain. Celtis observed that the fame of Dürer's art, including the image of Philosophy (see cat. nr. 10), had extended throughout the German lands, as far as Sarmatia, and, indeed, everywhere under the heavens. Dürer, for his part, included a portrait of Celtis standing beside him in the *Martyrdom of 10,000* (Vienna, Kunsthistorisches Museum), which was painted in 1508 for their mutual patron Friedrich the Wise.[20] Dürer added Celtis as an afterthought to honor the recently deceased poet.

Willibald Pirckheimer, Dürer's best friend and true mentor, was Nuremberg's foremost humanist.[21] Pirckheimer was able to read Greek and he possessed a rich understanding of the ancient world. He was a gifted editor and translator of classical texts, his works including editions of Plutarch, Xenophon, Theophrastus, Lucian, Gregory of Nazianzus, and John of Damascus, as well as Ptolemy's *Geography*, based on Regiomontanus's notes. For Emperor Maximilian, Pirckheimer translated into Latin Horopollo's *Hieroglyphica*, an important emblematic text to which Dürer supplied drawings in 1512–1513.[22] His personal library, the hub of local and visiting scholars, included the writings of both classical and contemporary authors. Pirckheimer also amassed a major collection of ancient coins that later served as the primary source for his study of antique inscriptions, the *Priscorum Numismaticum*, published posthumously in 1533 by one of his followers.[23]

Pirckheimer's influence on Dürer was threefold: he introduced Dürer to the classical world, he taught Dürer a humanist's critical methodology, and he was Dürer's frequent iconographic collaborator. Dürer's friendship with Pirckheimer really began shortly after the artist had returned from his first Venetian trip in late spring 1495. Pirckheimer had also just returned to Nuremberg after spending the years 1488–1495 studying in Padua and Pavia. Perhaps it was their common association with Italy that initially drew the men together. Their approach to Italian culture was different yet complementary. When Dürer viewed the prints of Mantegna or Pollaiuolo, he was captivated by the heroic figures wholly independent of their classical origins. Pirckheimer, on the other hand, was able to explain to Dürer the antique sources and allusions behind Mantegna's *Death of Orpheus* (now lost) or *Bacchanal with Silenus*.[24] Dürer's few early mythological works, notably his painted *Hercules and the Stymphalides* (Nuremberg, Germanisches Nationalmuseum) of 1500, were made under Pirckheimer's direction.[25] Pirckheimer imposed a critical methodology into Dürer's native curiosity and scientific inclination. Dürer spent much of his career grappling with the theoretical problems of human proportion and perspective. Like a scholar, he turned to the writings of Euclid and Vitruvius for answers. He queried his mathematician friends. He returned to Venice, thanks to a loan from Pirckheimer, to study Italian solutions and to learn from a specialist in Bologna. Dozens of drawings demonstrate his intellectual pursuit of logical answers as he created the human body from geometrical forms or from strict mathematical ratios. He then sought to codify his knowledge, much as Pirckheimer systematized his classical coin inscriptions, in a series of incomplete artist's manuals and in his *Art of Measurement* (1525; cat. nr. 31), *Treatise on Fortifications* (1527), and *Treatise on Human Proportion* (1528; cat. nr. 89). His rational, intellectual methodology derives, to a large degree, from his association with Pirckheimer and his circle of scholarly friends.

The intricate iconographies of such works as Dürer's *Adam and Eve* (cat. nr. 11), *Melencolia I* (cat. nr. 19), or the *Portrait of Johannes Kleberger* (Vienna, Kunsthistorisches Museum), painted in 1526 in emulation of classical portrait busts, are most likely due to Pirckheimer's creative participation.[26] Pirckheimer is documented as the overseer of various imperial projects, notably the *Triumphal Arch of Maximilian I* (cat. nr. 20), the *Great Triumphal Chariot* (cat. nr. 26), and the 1521 *Portrait of Emperor Charles V* (cat. nr. 138). The Nuremberg city council ordered Pirckheimer and Dürer to devise the new decorations for the great hall of the Rathaus and, apparently, the exterior mural cycles as well. These imperial and civic commissions were issued to both men, as their contemporaries recognized that they frequently collaborated. What a brilliant union it was, since Dürer's creative genius was combined with Pirckheimer's probing scholarly mind.

The humanist pursuits of Schedel, Schreyer, Celtis, and Pirckheimer prove that Nuremberg was a dynamic cultural center during the last years of the fifteenth century and the opening decades of the sixteenth. These individuals were later replaced by mathematician Joachim Camerarius; Eobanus Hessus, who was a professor of rhetoric and poetry; and famed astronomer and geographer Johann Schöner—all faculty members of the Egidien, or Melanchthon, Gymnasium, the humanist school founded by Philipp Melanchthon in 1525.[27] While Anton Koberger's printing firm declined quickly following his death in 1513, other local publishers, notably Hieronymus Höltzel, Johann Petreius, Friedrich Peypus, Johann Stüchs, and Johann Weissenburger, produced an impressive number of scientific and humanistic texts throughout the first half of the century.[28] The city library, housed in the Rathaus, continued its rapid expansion, including the acquisition of the library and scientific tools of Regiomontanus.[29] Although the intense intellectual ferment of the first third of the century waned following the deaths of Dürer and Pirckheimer, important scholarly contributions continued to be made until the outbreak of the Thirty Years War in 1618.

For Nuremberg's artists this scientific and intellectual movement had lasting effects. Dürer and, to a lesser degree, Peter Vischer the Younger revealed to them the profound lessons of the Italian Renaissance. New generations of artists absorbed Dürer's discoveries and went on to create their own dialogue with Italian and German Renaissance cultures.

NOTES

1. Janssen, *History of the German People*, I: p. 141. Also see E. Zinner, *Leben und Wirken des Johannes Müller von Konigsberg, genannt Regiomontanus* (Munich, 1938; reprinted Osnabrück, 1968); *500 Jahre Regiomontan—500 Jahre Astronomie*, exh. cat. (Nuremberg: Germanisches Nationalmuseum, 1976).

2. *Martin Behaim und die Nürnberger Kosmographen*, exh. cat. (Nuremberg: Germanisches Nationalmuseum, 1957); R. Pörtner, "Der 'Erdapfel,' der Wie ein Augapfel gehüet wird," in *Das Schatzhaus der deutschen Geschichte*, ed. Pörtner, pp. 277–304.

3. Strauss, *Nuremberg in the Sixteenth Century*, pp. 219ff.

4. Ibid., pp. 241–250; J. Pfanner, "Geistewissenschaftlicher Humanismus," and J. Hofmann, "Naturwissenschaftlicher Humanismus," in *Nürnberg*, ed. Pfeiffer, pp. 127–133, 134–137; L. Spitz, "The Course of German Humanism," in *Itinerarium Italicum*, ed. H. Oberman and T. Brady, Jr., pp. 371–436; F. Machilek, "Klosterhumanismus in Nürnberg um 1500," *MVGN* 64 (1977): 10–45.

5. Wilson, *Nuremberg Chronicle*, pp. 25–26. See cat. nr. 3 for additional information. On his library and its history, see R. Stauber, *Die Schedelsche Bibliothek* (Freiburg, 1908).

6. G. B. De Rossi, "Dell' opus de antiquitatibus di Hartmann Schedel Norimberghese," *Nuove Memorie dell' Istitutio de Corrispondenza Archeologica* (Lipsia, 1865), pp. 500–514.

7. Schreyer's artistic commissions have been mentioned in Section 3. See also E. Caesar, "Sebald Schreyer, ein Lebensbild aus dem vorreformatorischen Nürnberg," *MVGN* 56 (1969): 1–213, esp. 79–103, 146–149, 152–156, for these artistic projects.

8. Ibid., pp. 104–135; and see comments immediately below.

9. L. Grote, "Die 'Vorderstube' des Sebald Schreyer—Ein Beitrag zur Rezeption der Renaissance in Nürnberg," *AGMN* (1954–1959): 43–67, esp. 52ff.; *Nuremberg: Dürer (1971)*, nr. 177; Wilson, *The Making of the Nuremberg Chronicle*, pp. 243–244 (he publishes the contract).

10. On these models, see J. Levenson, K. Oberhuber, and J. Sheehan, *Early Italian Engravings from the National Gallery of Art*, pp. 81–113. The same models were used by Dürer and the Vischer family; see J. Seznec, "Apollo and the Swans on the Tomb of St. Sebald," *Journal of the Warburg and Courtauld Institutes* 2 (1938–1939): 75.

11. Grote, "Die 'Vorderstube' des Sebald Schreyer," provides a thorough discussion of the program, its sources, and its documentation.

12. R. von Busch, *Studien zu deutschen Antikensammlungen des 16. Jahrhunderts*, pp. 70–72.

13. L. Spitz, *Conrad Celtis: The German Arch-Humanist*, esp. pp. 66–67, 93–106, pertaining to Celtis's edition of and lectures about Tacitus's *Germania*. Incidentally, Friedrich Creussner of Nuremberg published the first Latin edition of the *Germania* in 1473; see *Nuremberg: Dürer (1971)*, nrs. 283–284.

14. Spitz, "The Course of German Humanism," p. 372.

15. Prague, Nationalgalerie; Anzelewsky, *Dürer*, nr. 93.

16. C. Dodgson, "Die illustrierten Ausgaben der sapphischen Ode des Konrad Celtis an St. Sebald," *JKSAK* 23 (1902): 45–52; Spitz, *Conrad Celtis*, p. 41; Meder, nr. 234; *Nuremberg: Dürer (1971)*, nr. 359.

17. Spitz, *Conrad Celtis*, pp. 35–40; Strauss, *Nuremberg in the Sixteenth Century*, pp. 9–14; *Nuremberg: Dürer (1971)*, nr. 237.

18. On Hroswitha and her writings, see Spitz, *Conrad Celtis*, p. 42; *Nuremberg: Meister um Dürer*, nr. 225; *Nuremberg: Dürer (1971)*, nr. 288.

19. Kassel, Landesbibliothek, ms. poet. fol. 7, folio 69v–70; D. Wuttke, "Unbekannte Celtis-Epigramme zum Lobe Dürers," *ZfK* 30 (1967): 321–325; Rupprich, *Dürer schriftlicher Nachlass*, III: p. 460, which gives the texts of three additional odes to Dürer.

20. E. Panofsky, "Conrad Celtes and Kunz von der Rosen: Two Problems in Portrait Identification," *Art Bulletin* 24 (1942): esp. 39–43; Anzelewsky, *Dürer*, nr. 105.

21. On Dürer's artistic work for Pirckheimer, see cat. nr. 30, Dürer's 1524 engraving of Pirckheimer. Pirckheimer was also an important member of the Nuremberg city council. F. X. Pröll, *Willibald Pirckheimer, 1470–1970—eine Dokumentation in der Stadtbibliothek Nürnberg*; H. Rupprich, "Dürer und Pirckheimer, Geschichte einer Freundschaft," in *Albrecht Dürer Umwelt*, ed. Hirschmann and Schnelbögl, pp. 78–100; N. Holsberg, "Willibald Pirckheimer als Wegbereiter der griechischen Studien in Deutschland," *MVGN* 67 (1980): 60–78.

22. Pröll, *Pirckheimer*, nr. 74; the manuscript is now Vienna, Österreichischen Nationalbibliothek, ms. Cod. Vind. 3255; some of the drawings are in the Germanisches Nationalmuseum, see *Nuremberg: Dürer (1971)*, nr. 297.

23. Pröll, *Pirckheimer*, nr. 73, which is London, British Museum, ms. Egerton 1926. R. von Busch, *Studien zu deutschen Antikensammlungen*, pp. 99–102, 231, mentions the coin collections of Stephan Fridolin, Hans Tucher, and artist Peter Vischer the Elder of Nuremberg. Pirckheimer's collection later passed to Willibald Imhoff in Nuremberg and, still later, parts to Thomas Howard, Earl of Arundel.

24. Levenson, Oberhuber, and Sheehan, *Early Italian Engravings*, nrs. 73–74, 75; Winkler, *Zeichnungen Dürers*, I: nrs. 54–56.

25. Anzelewsky, *Dürer*, nr. 67.

26. Ibid., nr. 182. In 1528 Kleberger married Pirckheimer's daughter Felicitas.

27. On Melanchthon, Camerarius, and Hessus, see cat. nrs. 32–34. On Schöner, see F. Schnelbögl, *Dokumentie zur Nürnberger Kartographie—mit Katalog*, pp. 7, 52–53.

28. J. Beuzing, "Humanismus in Nürnberg, 1500–1540. Eine Liste der Druckschriften," in *Albrecht Dürers Umwelt*, ed. Hirschmann and Schnelbögl, pp. 255–299.

29. K. Goldmann, *Geschichte der Stadtbibliothek Nürnberg*.

5. Dürer as Teacher

Art in Nuremberg changed drastically during the first third of the sixteenth century. The crowded passion scenes of Adam Kraft's *Schreyer-Landauer Epitaph* (1490–1492) outside St. Sebaldus gave way to the new spirit embodied in Peter Vischer the Younger's *Epitaph of Dr. Anton Kress* (1513) in St. Lorenz (fig. 29).[1] Whereas Kraft incorporated himself and Sebald Schreyer into a Lamentation sequence, Vischer's sole subject was Anton Kress, the deceased prior of St. Lorenz. Kress kneels before the altar, alone in prayer. The balanced orderly composition strongly anticipates Dürer's *Erasmus* engraving of 1526.[2] The decorative vocabulary of the shell niche, coffered vault, grotesque ornament, and putti is closer in spirit to Renaissance Padua than Nuremberg of the early 1490s. A similar transformation is evident when comparing Michael Wolgemut's modest imitations of the Ferrarese *Tarocchi* with Georg Pencz's *Fall of Phaeton* painted in 1534 for the ceiling of the garden wing of the Hirschvogel house (fig. 33).[3] Pencz's illusionistic ceiling drew upon the models of Andrea Mantegna and Giulio Romano but it is a highly original product.

Vischer and Pencz belong to a new generation of artists trained to understand and to appreciate the innovations of Italian Renaissance art. The transition from the late Gothic to the Renaissance was inevitable given sufficient time; however, in Nuremberg it was achieved within a few decades due largely to Albrecht Dürer. While Panofsky's famous claim that Dürer brought the Renaissance to northern Europe oversimplifies the complexity of the issue, it is basically correct.[4] Dürer was the catalyst and the bridge between an older generation of artists trained in the Flemish-influenced styles of Martin Schongauer and Michael Wolgemut and younger artists, such as Pencz, who delighted in copying Raphael and Michelangelo. Dürer was an ideal intermediary since through his prints he could communicate his discoveries about human form, Vitruvian proportion, and mathematical perspective in terms comprehensible to his contemporaries. Dürer presents the art of Mantegna, Pollaiuolo, Giovanni Bellini, and Jacopo de' Barbari in a northern European vocabulary. Dürer prepares his audience to appreciate classical sculpture, which he knew through Italian prints, by casting the *Apollo Belvedere* and the, perhaps, *Medici Venus* as Adam and Eve in his 1504 engraving (cat. nr. 11).

In the following section I shall concentrate upon Dürer the teacher by examining his workshop, pupils, and pedagogical ideas.[5] It was the transmission of Dürer's technical and theoretical knowledge to his apprentices and other masters that prompted the changes from Gothic to Renaissance artistic visions.

About the time of Albrecht Dürer's death in 1528, Hans Baldung Grien wrote from Strassburg requesting a lock of the artist's hair.[6] Dürer's hair was still in Baldung's possession when his goods were inventoried following his own death in 1545. Baldung's unusual demand illustrates his lifelong admiration for Dürer, who was his teacher from 1503 to 1506 or early 1507. During the subsequent years, the two masters remained in touch. Dürer mentioned in his Netherlandish travel diary that during his stay in Antwerp in June and July 1521 he presented some of Baldung's prints to famed landscape painter Joachim Patinir.[7] Long after Baldung himself had become one of Germany's great artists, he still revered Dürer as his master.

This incident, however minor, typifies Dürer's critical role as teacher to a generation of German artists. His crusade to educate German artists has direct parallels to Conrad Celtis's campaign to rally northern humanists to surpass the scholars of Italy. Dürer spent his career trying to convey his discoveries and thoughts on nature and artistic theory to other artists. Inspired by Pirckheimer and his other humanist friends, Dürer was the first northern artist to publish treatises on measurement and human proportion (cat. nrs. 31 and 34).

In 1512 or 1513, Dürer began drafting a painter's manual entitled *Speis der Malerknaben*, or *Food for Young Painters*, which he humbly offered to the reader as a substitute for the recorded but lost treatises of Phidias, Praxiteles, Apelles, and other ancient artists. Dürer wrote, "Often do I sorrow because I must be robbed of the aforesaid masters' books of art."[8] He willingly shares his knowledge so that his readers will become "artistic painters"; that is, they will become well versed in the technical and scientific bases of art. His text begins: "Now I know that in our German nation at the present time are many painters who stand in need of instruction, for they lack real art, yet they nevertheless have many great works to make. Forasmuch, then, as they are so numerous, it is very needful for them to learn to better their work. . . . Whosoever will, therefore, let him hear and see what I say, do, and teach, for I hope it may be of service and not for a hindrance to the better arts, nor lead you to neglect better things."[9] Somewhat earlier Dürer had made an outline for a detailed treatise on painting that was to include chapters on "how the lad should be taught," the freedom of painting, how to make the proportions of men and buildings correctly, how to represent things in one view, and such practical matters as where to dwell and how much to charge for one's work.[10]

Dürer's strengths as a teacher can best be gauged by his remarkable influence on the artists in Nuremberg. Almost every major painter and printmaker active in Nuremberg between 1500 and 1528 either trained with Dürer or worked in his atelier. Grote has ordered his pupils into three groups.[11] The initial batch included his brother Hans (1502–1509), Hans Baldung Grien (1503–1506/07), Hans Süss von Kulmbach (ca. 1500/03–1511), and Hans Schäufelein (1503/04–1506/07). Excepting his brother Hans, the artists had all received their preliminary training with other masters before coming to Dürer to complete their education. Kulmbach, for instance, had worked with Jacopo de' Barbari, Dürer's Venetian friend who briefly settled in Nuremberg in 1500. Baldung was educated in Strassburg and Schäufelein possibly in Nördlingen before seeking Dürer's knowledge, just as Dürer had traveled to Colmar in 1490 hoping to complete his own training with Martin Schongauer. Around 1510 Zurich artist Hans Leu the Younger (ca. 1490–1531) and in 1519 Utrecht painter Jan van Scorel (1495–1562) both journeyed long distances to study with Dürer.[12] The second group of pupils consisted of Wolf Traut (by 1505–before 1512), Hans Springinklee (by 1507–1510), who is the only artist Neudörfer specifically mentions living in Dürer's household, and possibly Erhard Schön (1510s[?]).[13] The third set of pupils included Georg Pencz (before 1521–1523), Hans Sebald Beham (late 1510s), and his younger brother, Barthel Beham (late 1510s). This group is more problematic since none of the members is firmly documented in Dürer's shop. Pencz collaborated with Dürer on the Rathaus paintings of 1521. The Behams closely copied Dürer's compositions and his techniques, so that if they were not actually in his shop they were, at the very least, totally immersed in his art. Grote has also linked Nikolaus Glockendon, a member of the famous family of manuscript illuminators, and a host of anonymous artists, notably the Master of the *Ansbach Mystical Wine Press*, with Dürer.[14]
Ansbach Mystical Wine Press, with Dürer.[14]

The lack of firm information about the precise number of pupils and journeymen in Dürer's workshop and the organization of his shop is partially due to the unusual history of the painting trade in Nuremberg. There was no painters' guild.[15] In most German cities, the painters established trade guilds that regulated such matters as the number of apprentices per master, the nature and length of training, the specifications of the required masterpiece, the qualities of materials and craftsmanship, and, occasionally, price structures. Guilds provided painters and other artisans with a group identity and political clout.

In Nuremberg the guilds were suppressed following an unsuccessful craftsmen's revolt in the mid-fourteenth century. The city council assumed the task of regulating every facet of these trades. In the fifteenth century, the city council divided the crafts into two categories: the *geschworne Handewerke* and the *freien Kunste*. The *geschworne Handewerke*, or "sworn artisans," were so called because each artist was required annually to pledge his allegiance to Nuremberg and to promise not to leave the city without obtaining the permission of the council. This group included the goldsmiths, silversmiths, metalworkers, and other craftsworkers considered vital to the city's economic strength. The city council did permit these crafts to organize very weak guilds that did little more than set loose requirements for training and for an applicant's masterpiece.

Painting, manuscript illuminating, and printmaking were included among the *freien Kunste*, or "free arts." Since these trades were not economically as significant as the *geschworne Handewerke*, the council sought to encourage talented new masters to settle in Nuremberg and to ensure the free exchange of ideas by removing all barri-

29. Peter Vischer the Younger, *Epitaph of Dr. Anton Kress*, 1513, St. Lorenz.

ers beyond the council's requirements concerning length and rules of apprenticeship. The council repeatedly rejected attempts by painters (1509 and 1534) and manuscript illuminators (1477, 1482, 1527, 1531, and 1548) to organize as groups. Not until 1571 and 1596 were the illuminators and painters allowed to establish even minimal rules and ordinances. Even then these two groups were barred from demanding either a masterpiece or an entrance fee for new artists.

The city council, rather than a craft organization, kept records of its artists and of new masters entering the city; however, no roster of pupils working for Dürer and other contemporary artists survives. The list of Dürer's pupils is based upon other documentary evidence or upon stylistic associations.

The city council did require that all heads of independent workshops be Nuremberg citizens. Locally born artists were automatically citizens. Outsiders were charged between four and ten gulden, depending on the value of their property, to acquire citizenship. This requirement had one interesting result for Dürer's workshop. Such artists as Baldung and Schäufelein, who came to Nuremberg to train with Dürer and then settle elsewhere, never acquired Nuremberg citizenship. Technically, they were ineligible to receive their own commissions since they were not independent masters. In fact, however, they were working on their own important projects, as for example Baldung's stained-glass designs for the Loeffelholz window in St. Lorenz.[16] I suspect that the actual contract and payment documents, which do not survive, listed Dürer as the artist of record even though all parties knew that Baldung would produce the window design. Several fully trained artists apparently continued working in Dürer's shop rather than acquire citizenship and open their own shops.

The city council also required that all independent artists marry. Dürer married Agnes Frey immediately upon his return to Nuremberg in 1494. Young apprentices occasionally married the widows of their masters in order to lower their citizenship and trade fees. Michael Wolgemut was working as a journeyman in Munich when his teacher, Hans Pleydenwurff, died on 9 January 1472. Wolgemut soon returned to Nuremberg, married Pleydenwurff's widow, Barbara, and took over the deceased artist's workshop.[17] A century later Balthasar Jenichen married the wife of his master Virgil Solis shortly after the master's death in 1562. It was so unusual for an artist to remain a bachelor that Neudörfer considered Wolf Traut's unmarried status noteworthy enough to mention in his biography of the painter.[18] Difficulties arose, however, when an artist married before becoming an independent master. Hans Vischer, one of Peter the Elder's sons, was severely censured by Nuremberg's metalworkers because of his early marriage.[19] Only action by the city council in 1514 prevented punitive sanctions from being leveled against Hans.

Dürer's pupils received the standard education in the basics of drawing and design and the technical requirements of painting and printmaking. In many respects, Dürer's teaching was highly traditional, varying little from his own experiences in Wolgemut's shop. What does distinguish Dürer's atelier is his emphasis upon understanding the human form and the mathematics of art. The lessons of his trips to Italy and his theoretical musings were given practical applications in his shop. Dürer's stylistic imprint, learned by patiently copying his work and participating with him in many commissions, is stamped upon each of his followers. Some, like Kulmbach, never really freed themselves from Dürer's style.

During his initial trip to Venice and northern Italy in 1494 and 1495, Dürer was greatly impressed by the emphasis placed upon the human form, especially in the classicizing nudes of Pollaiuolo and Mantegna. The influence upon his art is readily apparent if his beautiful 1498 *Nude Woman with a Herald's Wand* (cat. nr. 8) is compared with the 1493 *Nude Girl* (Bayonne, Musée Bonnet).[20] The latter is highly stylized with an accentuated abdomen. The 1498 drawing shows the woman placed in raking light. The imperfect musculature of her shoulders, the shifting contour lines, and the quiet spontaneity prove that during the interim years Dürer had adopted the practice of using live nude models. By having his wife, pupils, other models, and even himself pose, or by sketching at one of the local bathhouses (cf. cat. nr. 5), Dürer sought to comprehend the mechanics of the human body.[21] There is also evidence to suggest that Dürer used wooden model puppets, such as the example now in Berlin (Staatliche Museen), to study various poses.[22] In all his work Dürer returned to nature and absorbed its lessons before developing his theoretical expositions, as for instance his ideas on human proportions expounded in the ca. 1501–1502 *Nemesis* (cat. nr. 9) and the 1504 *Adam and Eve* (cat. nr. 11) engravings.

Dürer certainly lectured on the correct ways to represent the human body in different positions. He seems to have arranged for models in his studio, and a few of his pupils' nude studies survive. Among Kulmbach's earliest drawings are the sketches of a standing nude man and an older nude man seated on a floor, both at Coburg (Veste).[23] Kulmbach's youthful *Nude Mother and Child* (Erlangen, Universitätsbibliothek) is a study sheet examining the pair in three different postures.[24] Even after leaving Dürer's shop in 1511, Kulmbach continued with his figural studies, as seen in *Nude Male Figure Study* (cat. nr. 38). The wavering contour lines and the stress upon duplicating the shading patterns on the torso, legs, and arms suggest that Kulmbach was working from a live model. Hans Schäufelein's *Nude Man with a Dragon* (Paris, Louvre) of about 1506 or 1507 is not drawn from life, yet the muscular male figure shows that the artist was accustomed to sketching from a model.[25] Baldung's extant nudes date from 1513, well after he left Nuremberg; however, I suspect that his lifelong fascination with the sensuality of the human body dates back to his years with Dürer. Of the later artists, Barthel Beham, in his earliest prints, such as the *Battle for the Banner* (cat. nr. 97), revealed his fascination with the twisting human body. Beham's or Pencz's interest in the human form depended more upon their study of the prints of Agostino Veneziano or Giulio Romano than upon direct observation of nature.[26] This shift parallels Dürer's own gradual move toward the theoretical as he worked on his *Treatise on Human Proportions* (cat. nr. 34).

As Dürer experimented to determine the proper ratios for each body type, he transmitted his ideas to his apprentices. For example, Kulmbach's early *Proportional Study* (Berlin, Kupferstichkabinett) depicts the left side of a nude male with outstretched arm.[27] Eight equally spaced concentric circles and a radius line are inscribed over the figure to define the proportional ratios of the different parts of the body. Dürer's figural and facial experiments later inspired two didactic manuals by his followers: Hans Sebald Beham's 1546 *Kunst und Lehr Büchlin* (cat. nr. 95) and Erhard Schön's 1538 *Vnnderweissung der Proportzion vnnd Stellung der Possen* (cat. nr. 71). Schön was especially interested in presenting different solutions for arranging figures correctly within perspectival boxes.

Dürer expected his pupils to copy his prints, drawings, and paintings as a primary means of learning his style. The extant oeuvre of each pupil includes groups of figures or entire compositions borrowed from Dürer. For example, among Kulmbach's drawings, his *Landsknecht* (Vienna, Albertina) and *Loving Pair* (Munich, Staatliche Graphische Sammlung) derive from Dürer's *Joys of the World* drawing (Oxford, Ashmolean Museum).[28] Kulmbach copied *Sts. Joachim and Simeon* (London, British Museum) from Dürer's *Jabach Altarpiece* (Munich, Alte Pinakothek) and the *Arrest of Christ* and *Flagellation* (Milan, Biblioteca Ambrosiana) from his teacher's *Green Passion* (Vienna, Albertina).[29]

Schäufelein was especially successful in copying Dürer's art. In 1675 Sandrart wrote that Schäufelein "was able to imitate drawings by Albrecht Dürer so exactly that often the greatest experts have been uncertain whether they were done by Dürer or by Schäufelein, just as connoisseurs mistake Schäufelein's woodcut illustrations in many books for Dürer's work."[30] Schäufelein's early *Adoration of the Magi* drawing (Berlin, Kupferstichkabinett) replicates the composition of Dürer's *Paumgartner Altarpiece* (Munich, Alte Pinakothek) with only minor alterations.[31] Schäufelein also borrowed from his fellow pupils, as is evident in his Baldung-style *St. Sebastian* sketch (Berlin, Kupferstichkabinett).[32] Baldung's *Dead Christ* (New York, Metropolitan Museum of Art, Lehman Collection) derives from Dürer's 1500 *Deposition of Christ* painting in Munich (Alte Pinakothek).[33] Springinklee's *Adam and Eve* (cat. nr. 53) depends on Dürer's 1504 engraving.

Like other contemporary artists, Dürer involved his pupils in many of his painting commissions. It was commonplace for apprentices and journeymen to prepare the panels and canvases and to paint the less important features, such as the

30. Hans Frey, *Design for a Table Fountain with a Mountain Scene and Morris Dancers*, drawing, ca. 1490s, Erlangen, Universitätsbibliothek, B 147.

background or the secondary figures. This was both sound economic practice and an integral part of an artist's training. When Dürer wrote to Frankfurt merchant Jakob Heller on 24 August 1508, "and no one shall paint a stroke on it [the Heller Altarpiece] except myself, wherefore I shall spend much time on it,"[34] he implied that it was highly unusual for him to paint a panel all on his own. In fact Dürer used this excuse to obtain a higher payment from Heller. And while the central panel of the now-lost altarpiece may well have been autograph, the wings were painted by his shop.

As Dürer obtained an ever larger number of orders, he utilized the talents of his workshop. His actual participation varied. His hand is more evident in the *Deposition of Christ* panel (ca. 1500) in Munich (Alte Pinakothek) than in the painting of the same subject now in Nuremberg (Germanisches Nationalmuseum).[35] In the case of the *St. Sebaldus Altarpiece*, which Sebald Schreyer commissioned for the Heilig-Kreuz-Kirche in Schwäbisch-Gmund, Dürer turned most of the project over to his assistants, a fact tacitly acknowledged in the text of Schreyer's payment.[36] In still other instances, Dürer supplied the drawing and the pupils did all of the actual painting, as, for example, when he left for his second Italian trip in 1505 he prepared the design drawings and assigned Hans Schäufelein to make the *Ober-Sankt-Veit Altarpiece* (Vienna, Erzbischöfliches Dom- und Diozäsanmuseum), which Friedrich the Wise had commissioned for the Schlosskirche at Wittenberg.[37] This practice occasionally continued after the pupil had left the workshop, the prime instance occurring in 1511 when the heirs of Lorenz Tucher (died 1503) commissioned a monumental epitaph painting for the church of St. Sebaldus.[38] Dürer created the design for this powerful, Italianate *sacra conversazione*, while Kulmbach executed the painting, his greatest work, with only minor additions and changes to Dürer's drawing.

One of the most significant lessons that Dürer taught his pupils was how to think graphically. Dürer appears to have seen forms in terms of swelling and tapering lines; chiaroscuro effects, in his printed works, were reduced to varying patterns of black on white. Even in his paintings, Dürer's strokes and shading patterns are arranged as if he were working with a burin. Dürer's revolutionary graphic style was transmitted to his followers. This black-and-white mentality of the workshop is evident when Springinklee's *Adam and Eve* (cat. nr. 53) is contrasted with Ludwig Krug's woodcut of the same subject (cat. nr. 114). While Krug was strongly influenced by and occasionally worked with Dürer, he never understood Dürer's use of line to define forms and create chiaroscuro values. Springinklee's figures are highly plastic or sculpturesque. He models his bodies with a myriad of different types of straight and curving lines, of varying lengths and intensities, juxtaposed with carefully placed patches of light. Adam and Eve are fully rounded, with light dancing across their bodies and defining their volume. By contrast, Krug's couple is extremely flat. Adam's torso is a confusion of misplaced shading lines that barely distinguish the figure from his background. The tremendous success of Nuremberg's printmakers during this period is due largely to Dürer's ability to teach his students how to create forms, textures, space, and certain tonal values in black and white. Because of their concern for high quality and inventiveness, the Dürer school prints were eagerly collected by artists and connoisseurs.[39]

Dürer also taught his pupils how to create designs, both drawings and prints, useful to artists in other crafts. Doubtlessly, Dürer's own interest in the needs of other artists resulted from his initial training as a goldsmith and his close association with his father-in-law, Hans Frey, a table-fountain maker. Among Dürer's most interesting early drawings is his design for a *Great Table Fountain with Soldiers* (London, British Museum) of 1495, which is similar to Frey's *Table Fountain with a Mountain Scene and Morris Dancers* drawing at Erlangen (Universitätsbibliothek; fig. 30).[40] Dürer's design for the *Apple Cup* inspired an artist working in the Krug workshop to fashion the wonderful covered cup in the shape of an apple (cat. nr. 116) now in Nuremberg (Germanisches Nationalmuseum). In 1522 Anton II Tucher commissioned Dürer to devise the *Chandelier* in the shape of a dragon (Nuremberg, Germanisches Nationalmuseum), which Veit Stoss then carved from lindenwood and antler for the Regimentsstube at the Rathaus (fig. 31).[41] Dürer also provided designs for the reliefs in the Fugger Chapel in St. Anne in Augsburg, the tomb statues of

31. Veit Stoss (after Albrecht Dürer), *Chandelier*, formerly in the Rathaus, 1522, Nuremberg, Germanisches Nationalmuseum, HG. 68.

Maximilian I that Peter Vischer the Elder cast for the emperor's mausoleum in the Hofkirche at Innsbruck, and numerous other projects.[42]

The majority of Dürer's pupils supplemented their income by providing designs for other artists. There are extant drawings by Wolf Traut for a silver *Crucifixion* (Nuremberg, Germanisches Nationalmuseum) and by Kulmbach for an elaborate *Monstrance* (Schwerin, Landesmuseum).[43] Steingräber has identified a gold enamel medallion of the *Adoration of the Magi* (London, Victoria and Albert Museum) as part of the *Pax Reliquary*, once owned by Cardinal Albrecht von Brandenburg, that is illustrated in the *Halle Heiltumscodex*.[44] Kulmbach's design for this piece was formerly in Dresden (ex. Coll. Johann Friedrich Lahmann). At least one other reliquary in Albrecht von Brandenburg's famous collection is attributed to Kulmbach.[45] Hans Sebald Beham's prints provided a rich repository of designs and motifs for goldsmiths, sculptors, and artists in other trades. Beham's extremely beautiful drawing for a *Fountain with Satyrs and Nude Woman* (Erlangen, Universitätsbibliothek) could be constructed either as a table decoration or as the centerpiece for a courtyard.[46]

If Dürer's fame as a teacher can be gauged by the subsequent contributions of his pupils, he had no pedagogical peer in Germany or, perhaps, in northern Europe. Dürer sought to create "artistic painters," his term for an artist educated in the fundamentals of both technique and mathematics. He exposed his pupils to lessons in Vitruvian proportional schemes, human anatomy, Euclidian geometry, and the intricacies of humanistic imagery. He prepared them to comprehend both the northern and the Italian traditions of art. In this, he really was the artistic bridge into the Renaissance.

Dürer sought to fire the imaginations of his pupils. In the rough draft for his *Speis der Malerknaben*, he defined a good painter as one who "is inwardly full of figures, and were it possible for him to live forever he would always have from his inward 'ideas,' whereof Plato writes, something new to pour forth by the work of his hand."[47] Dürer's compositional and iconographic experiments were continued by his pupils as is evident by the sampling of works included in this exhibition.

What little that can be reconstructed about Dürer's personal relationships with his pupils suggests that he was a warm, encouraging teacher. The story about Baldung's quest for a lock of his hair tells a great deal about the pupils' affection for their master. Years after some of the pupils had completed their training, they continued to be involved in Dürer's major artistic projects for Emperor Maximilian I (cat. nrs. 20 and 26) and the city (cf. cat. nrs. 26 and 213). This association demonstrates his lasting friendship with his pupils and his respect for their skills. Indeed, the Dürer school paintings and prints played a significant role in transmitting Renaissance ideas throughout all of central Europe.

NOTES

1. Schwemmer, *Adam Kraft*, figs. 1–5; H. Stafski, *Der Jüngere Peter Vischer*, pp. 40–41, figs. 78–79.

2. Meder, nr. 105.

3. On the Wolgemut prints, see Section 4, notes 9–10. On Pencz's ceiling, see Section 6, notes 35, 37.

4. E. Panofsky, "Albrecht Dürer and Classical Antiquity," in *Meaning in the Visual Arts*, pp. 236–294, esp. p. 281.

5. The two best essays on the Dürer shop are L. Grote, "Dürer-Werkstatt und Dürer-Schule," and P. Strieder, "Meister um Albrecht Dürer," in *Nuremberg: Meister um Dürer*, pp. 11–16, 17–33. Also see Mende, *Dürer-Bibliographie*, pp. 498–518. For specific works by the members of Dürer's workshop, see the catalogue biographies and entries.

6. A. Shestack, "An Introduction to Hans Baldung Grien" in *Hans Baldung Grien*, ed. J. Marrow and A. Shestack, p. 6.

7. Conway, *Writings of Dürer*, p. 123; and Rupprich, *Dürer schriftlicher Nachlass*, I: p. 167 (lines 266–267).

8. Stechow, *Northern Renaissance Art*, pp. 111–112; Rupprich, *Dürer schriftlicher Nachlass*, II: p. 135 (lines 38ff.). Rupprich, II: pp. 83–394, has reassembled Dürer's scattered notes for a manual for young painters of which the *Speis der Malerknaben* is but a small section. See II: pp. 131ff.

9. Stechow, *Northern Renaissance Art*, p. 111; Rupprich, *Dürer schriftlicher Nachlass*, II: p. 132 (lines 56–57).

10. Stechow, *Northern Renaissance Art*, pp. 110–111; Rupprich, *Dürer schriftlicher Nachlass*, II: pp. 92–93.

11. Grote, "Dürer-Werkstatt und Dürer-Schule," in *Nuremberg: Meister um Dürer*, pp. 12–15.

12. On Leu, see *Nuremberg: Meister um Dürer*, pp. 130–142. On Scorel, see Section 3, note 42.

13. Neudörfer, *Nachrichten von Künstlern*, p. 144.

14. *Nuremberg: Meister um Dürer*, pp. 15, 94–97, 142–150, 166.

15. My comments on the Nuremberg painters' organization are based upon the following sources: G. Betz, "Der Nürnberger Maler Michael Wolgemut und seine Werkstatt," pp. 167–186; C. C. Christensen, "The Nuernberg City Council as a Patron of the Fine Arts, 1500–1550," pp. 34–65; Strauss, *Nuremberg in the Sixteenth Century*, pp. 97–98; W. Schultheiss, "Albrecht Dürers Beziehungen zum Recht," in *Albrecht Dürers Umwelt*, ed. Hirschmann and Schnelbögl, esp. pp. 229–233. The principal study for all these is E. Mummenhoff, "Freie Kunst und Handwerk in Nürnberg," *Korrespondenzblatt des Gesamtvereins der deutschen Geschichts- und Alterstumsvereine* (1906), cols. 105–120, and an earlier essay, both of which I have been unable to obtain. The best general study on the structure of artists' workshops during this period is H. Huth, *Künstler und Werkstatt der Spätgotik*.

16. K.-A. Knappe, "Das Löffelholz-Fenster in St. Lorenz in Nürnberg und Hans Baldung," *ZfKW* 12 (1958): 163–178.

17. Betz, "Wolgemut," pp. 93, 97. For the next example, see Schnelbögl, *Dokumentie zur Nürnberger Kartographie*, pp. 18–19.

18. Neudörfer, *Nachrichten von Künstlern*, p. 136.

19. Christensen, "The Nuernberg City Council," p. 49; and Hampe, *Nürnberger Ratsverlässe*, I: nr. 983.

20. Winkler, *Zeichnungen Dürers*, IV: nr. 947, I: nr. 28. See Talbot, ed., *Dürer*, nr. V, for a good discussion of the 1498 drawing.

21. Winkler, *Zeichnungen Dürers*, I: nr. 267, is Dürer's *Nude Self-Portrait* (Weimar, Schlossmuseum). His painted nude portrait of his wife, dated 1519, was in Paulus Praun's collection around 1600; C. T. de Murr, *Description du Cabinet de Monsieur Paul de Praun à Nuremberg*, nr. 156.

22. The female model puppet is inv. nr. 2167. See J. von Schlosser, "Aus der Bildnerwerkstatt der Renaissance," *JKSAK* 31 (1913–1914): 67–136, esp. 111–118, figs. 40–41; esp. C. Theuerkauff's comments in *Berlin: Der Mensch um 1500, Werke aus Kirchen und Kunstkammern*, ed. H. Gagel, exh. cat. (Berlin: Staatliche Museen, 1977), nr. 30. On the general subject, also see L. Fusco, "The Use of Sculptural Models by Painters in Fifteenth-Century Italy," *Art Bulletin* 64 (1982): 175–194.

23. F. Winkler, *Die Zeichnungen Hans Süss von Kulmbachs und Hans Leonhard Schäufeleins*, Kulmbach nrs. 14–15.

24. Ibid., Kulmbach nr. 26.

25. Ibid., Schäufelein nr. 8.

26. This is not to suggest that they did not continue using live models. For instance, see Hans Sebald Beham's *Nude Man with a Club* (Berlin, Kupferstichkabinett); *Nuremberg: Meister um Dürer*, nr. 76, pl. 12.

27. Winkler, *Zeichnungen Kulmbachs und Schäufeleins*, Kulmbach nr. 13.

28. Ibid., nrs. 3–4.

29. Winkler, *Zeichnungen Kulmbachs und Schäufeleins*, Kulmbach nrs. 57–58, 143–144; cf. Anzelewsky, *Dürer*, nrs. 74–75, and Winkler, *Zeichnungen Dürers*, II: nrs. 300, 307.

30. R. A. Peltzer, ed., *Joachim von Sandrarts Academie der Bau-, Bild- und Mahlery- Künste von 1675*, p. 263; translation given in W. Strauss, *Albrecht Dürer: Woodcuts and Woodblocks*, p. 651. Dürer encouraged them to learn the mechanics of his style by emulating his works. The artist was less pleased with the outright theft of his ideas by Marcantonio Raimondi and other artists. Hans Sebald Beham stole part of Dürer's theoretical exposition on the proportions of horses and pub-

lished it as his own work; see cat. nr. 95. On the issue of copyright, see Christensen, "The Nuernberg City Council," pp. 52–65; Schultheiss, "Albrecht Dürers Beziehungen zum Recht," pp. 247–253.

31. Many of Schäufelein's youthful works derive from Dürer's. Winkler, *Zeichnungen Kulmbachs und Schäufeleins*, Schäufelein nr. 10; cf. Anzelewsky, *Dürer*, nrs. 50–52.

32. Winkler, *Zeichnungen Kulmbachs und Schäufeleins*, Schäufelein nr. 13; cf. Baldung's *Martyrdom of St. Sebastian* painting (Nuremberg, Germanisches Nationalmuseum) of 1507; Marrow and Shestack, eds., *Hans Baldung Grien—Prints & Drawings*, fig. 4.

33. Marrow and Shestack, eds., *Hans Baldung Grien*, nr. 14, fig. 14a; Anzelewsky, *Dürer*, nr. 70.

34. Stechow, *Northern Renaissance Art*, p. 92; and Rupprich, *Dürer schriftlicher Nachlass*, I: pp. 66–67 (letter 14, lines 16ff.).

35. Anzelewsky, *Dürer*, nrs. 70, 55.

36. Ibid., pp. 26, 44, 221; *Nuremberg: Meister um Dürer*, p. 12; Mende, *Dürer-Bibliographie*, nrs. 8164–8171.

37. Anzelewsky, *Dürer*, pp. 26, 38–39; Winkler, *Zeichnungen Dürers*, II: nrs. 319–323.

38. *Nuremberg: Meister um Dürer*, nrs. 162, 403. Dürer's drawings are in Berlin (Kupferstichkabinett); see Winkler, *Zeichnungen Dürers*, II: nr. 508.

39. Three major Nuremberg collectors of prints were Melchior Ayrer (1520–1570), Paul III Behaim (1592–1637), and Paulus Praun (1548–1616). See W. W. Robinson, "'This Passion for Prints': Collecting and Connoisseurship in Northern Europe during the Seventeenth Century," in *Printmaking in the Age of Rembrandt*, by C. S. Ackley, p. xxxiv; de Murr, *Description du Cabinet de Monsieur Paul de Praun à Nuremberg*, pp. 197–213, which lists 276 engravings and 4 woodcuts by Hans Sebald Beham.

40. See Section 7, notes 90, 91. On Dürer's designs for goldsmith work, sculpture, and stained glass, see *Nuremberg: Dürer (1971)*, pp. 364–393. And for the general influence of his art on sculptors of his and later periods, see H. Beck and B. Decker, eds., *Dürers Verwandlung in der Skulptur zwischen Renaissance und Barock*.

41. Winkler, *Zeichnungen Dürers*, III: nr. 708 (Constance, Städtische Wessenberg-Gemäldegalerie), and cf. nr. 709 (Vienna, Kunsthistorisches Museum), a 1513 drawing of a mermaid chandelier made for Pirckheimer. On the project, see D. Heikamp, "Dürers Entwürfe für Geweihleuchter," *ZfK* 23 (1960): 42–55; *Nuremberg: Dürer (1971)*, nrs. 708–709.

42. *Nuremberg: Dürer (1971)*, nrs. 699–702 (Fugger), 707 (Maximilian); E. Egg, *Die Hofkirche in Innsbruck*.

43. On Traut, see Zink, *Die Handzeichnungen*, nr. 101 (attributed to an artist in Traut's circle); Kohlhaussen, *Nürnberger Goldschmiedekunst*, fig. 388 (attributed to Traut). On the Kulmbach drawing, see Winkler, *Zeichnungen Kulmbachs und Schäufeleins*, Kulmbach nr. 86.

44. E. Steingräber, "Süddeutsche Goldemailplastik der Frührenaissance," in *Studien zur Geschichte für europäischen Plastick—Festschrift für Theodor Müller*, ed. K. Martin, pp. 223–233, esp. 223–224, figs. 1, 3, 4, which is Aschaffenburg, Schlossbibliothek, ms. Man. 14, fol. 156v.

45. Ibid., fig. 5, fol. 106v.

46. See Beham's drawings for a medal or a seal of *Status Pacis and Constantia Triumphans* (cat. nrs. 89–90) and his *Ornament with Two Genii* woodcut (cat. nr. 94). E. Bock, *Die Zeichnungen in der Universitätsbibliothek Erlangen*, nr. 310, which measures 84.2 × 32.5 cm.

47. Stechow, *Northern Renaissance Art*, p. 112; Rupprich, *Dürer schriftlicher Nachlass*, II: p. 109 (lines 62–63).

6. Artistic Developments of the First Half of the Sixteenth Century

Nuremberg was a vibrant artistic center throughout the first half of the sixteenth century. Slowly its artists shed the last vestiges of the late Gothic and adopted the forms of Italian classicism and the High Renaissance. Religious themes yielded to secular subjects, especially after 1525. While no single German city or princely court can claim primacy in bringing about this transition, such Nuremberg artists as Dürer, the Vischers, Peter Flötner, Melchior Baier, and Georg Pencz made vital contributions. The close collaboration among these Nuremberg masters ensured that Renaissance ideas reached all artistic fields. Overall, however, the city's artistic progress was uneven. The brilliance of the paintings and prints produced by Dürer and his followers could not be matched by their successors, with the single exception of Pencz. Nuremberg's architecture remained old-fashioned if judged against the innovations of Regensburg or Cracow or even the architectural forms employed by some of Nuremberg's sculptors. Only in the fields of goldsmith work and, to a lesser degree, sculpture was the city consistently innovative.

This section provides an examination of a few of the principal accomplishments in individual media and describes cross-media influences in the first half of the sixteenth century. Secondary categories of portrait medals, plaquettes, and small bronzes will be discussed in the exhibition catalogue.[1] Brief biographies of artists not included in the exhibition can be found in the Appendix.

A. PAINTING

Painting in Nuremberg can be almost evenly divided into two distinctive periods. During the first quarter-century, Dürer, briefly Hans Baldung Grien, Hans Schäufelein, Hans von Kulmbach, Hans Springinklee, and Wolf Traut filled local churches with altarpieces and produced a significant corpus of patrician portraits. By the early 1530s all of these masters were either dead, had moved away (Baldung and Schäufelein), or were largely inactive (Springinklee). Of Dürer's last group of followers, Hans Sebald Beham, living in Frankfurt, restricted himself to prints, and his brother Barthel had departed for the court of Duke Wilhelm IV of Bavaria in Munich. Only Georg Pencz remained, serving as the official city painter from 1532. Among other artists, the talented Augustin Hirschvogel, who was a glass painter, cartographer, and print maker, achieved prominence only after leaving Nuremberg in 1536.[2] Hans Lautensack's paintings from this period do not survive or, at least, cannot be identified, and his landscape and portrait etchings date to the 1550s. Even the six-month visit of Lucas Cranach the Elder in 1539 and the presence of Jacopo da Strada (1507–1588), the painter, goldsmith, and antiquarian who lived in Nuremberg between 1546 and 1552, had minimal influence on local painters.[3] Nevertheless, some major advances were made during the second quarter of the century.

Dürer transformed the course of early Nuremberg painting. Michael Wolgemut's mature works, such as the *Peringsdörffer Altar* and *Straubinger Altar*, both dating between 1485 and 1490 and originally located in the Augustinian Church, are spatially cramped, with a prevailing agitated linearism similar to that of the statues of Stoss and Kraft.[4] Wolgemut's influence on his star pupil is evident in Dürer's youthful *Miraculous Rescue of a Drowning Child* (Bregenz, Private Collection) and the problematic *Seven Sorrows of the Virgin Altarpiece* (Dresden, Staatliche Kunstsammlungen, and Munich, Alte Pinakothek), which was painted in 1496 for Friedrich the Wise.[5] The anatomically more sound and powerfully sculptural figures exhibited in his *Paumgartner Altarpiece* (Munich, Alte Pinakothek) of 1503–1504 reflect how deeply his first trip to Italy and subsequent figural studies altered his former style.[6] The central scene of the *Nativity* displays a carefully calculated one-point perspective scheme that converges toward the approaching shepherds at the rear of the composition. Dürer's *Self-Portrait* of 1500 (Munich, Alte Pinakothek) was based upon rigorous geometric calculations to ensure rational order and balance, traits wholly absent in Wolgemut's art.[7]

Dürer's predilection for a mathematically logical structure is more classically stated in the Landauer *All Saints Altarpiece* (Vienna, Kunsthistorisches Museum) of 1511 and in the quiet dignity of the 1519 *Virgin and Child with St. Anne* (New York, Metropolitan Museum of Art).[8] His success in teaching this lesson to his students can be judged by Kulmbach's *Epitaph of Lorenz Tucher* in St. Sebaldus and in Wolf Traut's *St. John the Baptist Altarpiece* (Nuremberg, Germanisches Nationalmuseum) of 1517, which was formerly in the Heilsbronn Kloster outside Nuremberg.[9]

If Dürer influenced the figural conceptions and compositional structures of Nuremberg painting, he was unable to transform the traditional altar-with-wings format that continued to be created until 1525. Traut's beautiful *High Altar* (1511) in the Johanniskirche and the *St. Rochus Altar* (1521–1522) in the Rochuskapelle both display carved statues of saints in the center and paintings on the wings.[10] The elaborate Gothic tracery that remained so popular throughout Germany is found as late as Kulmbach's 1521 *St. Anne Altarpiece*, which Haintz Mayer and his wife gave to St. Lorenz.[11] Dürer's design for the frame of the *All Saints Altarpiece* (frame in Nuremberg, Germanisches Nationalmuseum) with its rounded arch and Italian decorative features is the exception.[12] Only gradually are these latter motifs adopted by other masters, for instance the Veit Stoss follower who in 1521 carved the marvelous *Johannes-Altar* in St. Lorenz with its Renaissance-style pilasters, Corinthian capitals, and niches (see fig. 4 with the *Johannes-Altar* in the center of the crossing).[13] Cycles with numerous small narrative scenes, a feature common in early German painting, doggedly persisted, for instance, Georg Pencz's passion program on the exterior wings of the *Silver Altar* (Cracow, Wawel Cathedral), made for King Sigismund I of Poland, dates to 1531.[14]

Given the paucity of large paintings from the second quarter of the century, the artistic changes between 1500 and 1550 can best be demonstrated by contrasting two of the pictures in the exhibition: Schäufelein's *Portrait of a Man* (cat. nr. 42), dated 1504, and Pencz's *Portrait of a Girl* (cat. nr. 111), dating to about 1545. Schäufelein presents his sitter in half-length with a three-quarters view of the face, an arrangement frequently used by earlier Nuremberg painters, such as Hans Pleydenwurff and Wolgemut. By setting the dark figure against a lighter background, Schäufelein creates the optical suggestion of space surrounding the sitter. Dürer had used the same effect in his 1497 *Portrait of Albrecht Dürer the Elder* (replica: London, National Gallery), which may derive from the more common practice of including a window at the rear of the composition to define the architectural space.[15] Schäufelein's strong attention to the facial likeness and expression again has its roots in such Dürer portraits as the 1499 *Oswolt Krel* (Munich, Alte Pinakothek) or the 1500 *Young Man* (Munich, Alte Pinakothek).[16] The gesture of the man with flowers in his hand has precedents in Wolgemut's *Portrait of a Young Man* (Detroit, Institute of Arts) of 1486 and Dürer's 1493 *Self-Portrait* (Paris, Louvre).[17] Schäufelein's painting thus nicely sums up Nuremberg portraiture of the previous two decades.[18]

Pencz's *Portrait of a Girl*, painted about forty years later, conveys a totally different spirit. Where Schäufelein's man has a raw immediacy as he leans forward slightly and rests his hands on the bottom of the frame, Pencz's sitter, with her body turned parallel to the picture plane, is more distant, more aloof. Pencz's portrait has a cool reserve, or an absence of emotion. The emphasis is upon the clarity of the materials with their strong outlines and meticulous textural detail. This smooth, polished style focuses as much upon the social station of the young woman as it does on the individual. Little competes with the face for the viewer's attention in the Schäufelein painting. Pencz created a complicated, if faulty, interior setting. The light, entering through the window at the upper left and reflected in the glass vase, casts shadows on the sitter's face and on the back wall.

Pencz's portrait is strongly influenced by the brilliant, cool naturalism of Dürer's late portraits, notably *Jacob Muffel* and *Hieronymus Holzschuher*, both in Berlin (Staatliche Museen); however, it owes even more to Barthel Beham's innovative pictures of the late 1520s and early 1530s.[19] In Beham's *Portrait of a Man* (Munich, Alte Pinakothek), *Portrait of an Umpire* (Vienna, Kunsthistorisches Museum), and, to a lesser degree, *Portrait of a Nobleman* (cat. nr. 102), the artist presents his figures in hip-length views within atmospheric settings.[20] Beham stresses the personal dignity of his sitters while creating a clear physical and psychological distance between them and the viewer. This cool detachment is reminiscent of the portraits of Jacopo da Pontormo and Jacopo Palma (Il Vecchio) or, closer at hand, the courtly southern German portrait style of Hans Holbein the Younger and, later, Christoph Amberger and

Jakob Seisenegger.[21] Pencz's late paintings, including the *Portrait of a Girl* and espe-cially *Portrait of a Young Sculptor* (Dublin, National Gallery of Ireland) of 1549, carry this trend still further, recalling the enamellike colors and figural isolation of Agnolo Bronzino.[22] The intense power of the *Portrait of Sebald Schirmer* (Nuremberg, Germa-nisches Nationalmuseum) and *Portrait of Jörg Herz* (Karlsruhe, Staatliche Kunsthalle), both dated 1545, clearly establish Pencz as one of the premier portraitists active in central Europe.[23]

Nuremberg's artists excelled in producing large scale decorative ensembles that, unfortunately, are little known today since few traces remain. In preparation for the anticipated visit of Emperor Charles V, the Nuremberg city council in 1520 or-dered Hans Springinklee to paint the ceiling of the reception room at the Burg with Charles's coats of arms and emblems.[24] Springinklee covered the paneled walls of the adjacent living room with classical grotesques and added frescoes of the *Annuncia-tion*, *Adoration of the Magi*, *Flight into Egypt*, and *Crucifixion* in the imperial oratorium.

Also in 1520 the city council decided that the paintings in the great hall and on the exterior of the Rathaus had so badly deteriorated that two new pictorial pro-grams were needed.[25] The original decorations in the great hall dated back to around 1340, but, unfortunately, nothing is known about their appearance. Pirckheimer and Dürer were charged with devising the iconographic programs and stylistic designs for the great hall and, it seems likely, for the illusionistic architecture and didactic scenes on the exterior. Both cycles were completed by 1522.

The original appearance of the great hall before the 1619 transformations sur-vives only in the small painting attributed to Paul Juvenel the Elder included in the exhibition (cat. nr. 213). On the north wall (right side) are the *Great Triumphal Chariot*, based upon Dürer's woodcut series (cat. nr. 26); a group of musicians performing on a balcony; and the *Calumny of Apelles*. Dürer's original drawing for the latter is now in Vienna (Albertina).[26] Scenes illustrating Roman civic virtue (e.g., Justice of Trajan) and the power of women (e.g., Bathsheba at her bath, Samson and Delilah, and Phyllis and Aristotle after Dürer's drawing in New York [Morgan Library]) cover the south wall. Juvenel also depicts Wolgemut's *Last Judgment* on the west wall and the great bronze grille, completed by the Vischer workshop in 1540, and its stone sup-ports carved by Sebald Beck. Not shown in the painting is the east wall with the new imperial throne and stained-glass windows with the city's coats of arms, designed by Kulmbach and executed by Veit Hirschvogel the Elder in 1521.

The varied program reflects the multiple functions of the great hall. It was the site of the imperial Reichstag, which explains the throne and the references to Nuremberg's happy association with Charles V's predecessor, Maximilian I. The western end of the hall served as a court, so the looming Wolgemut *Last Judgment*, the *Calumny of Apelles*, and the various scenes of virtue on the south wall were espe-cially appropriate. The elaborate patrician dances held in the hall prompted the painted musicians and the playful allusions to man's basic weakness in the represen-tations of the power of women.

Dürer created the designs, based upon his earlier discussions with Pirck-heimer, while he was in the Netherlands in 1520 and 1521. He received 100 gulden as payment at the beginning of 1522. The actual execution of the paintings was left to others. Sandrart (1675) and later critics have attributed the majority of the painting to Georg Pencz.[27] Springinklee may also have contributed certain decorative motifs. Subsequent restorations and the complete destruction of the pictures in 1945 prevent any stylistic investigations.[28]

In 1521 the paintings on the exterior walls of the Rathaus were completed. Nuremberg, like most southern German towns, was famous for its painted houses and public buildings. When Dürer devised his plans for the 1520–1521 campaign, the exterior was still covered with pictures, of unknown subjects, dating either to 1340 or to Master Berthold's work in 1423.[29] However, these older paintings had badly deteriorated and had to be replaced with a new cycle. Part of Dürer's program was still visible in the nineteenth century, while other portions were destroyed dur-ing the building campaign of the 1610s.[30] A set of Nuremberg school drawings of ca. 1530, now in Vienna (Albertina), provides the best idea of the appearance of Dürer's cycle that covered the south, east, and west sides of the building.[31] The illusionistic architecture skillfully incorporated the extant windows. On the west façade were painted tall figures of Sts. George, Peter, Sebaldus, and Lawrence between the windows and, below, such justice scenes as the Judgment of Solomon, the Justice of Cambyses, the Shooting of the Dead Father, and Christ and the Adulterous Woman (fig. 9). The architecture of the south façade with the elaborate fake doorways and gallery is the most impressive. The biblical moralizations included Bathsheba at her Bath, the Death of Absalom, and Esther and Ahasuerus. The cycle is prominently dated 1521 at the southeast corner.

Georg Pencz is traditionally credited with the execution of the exterior paintings. Considering that Pencz was probably at work on the paintings inside the great hall at this time, however, it is difficult to imagine his producing the exterior cycle as well, unless it was completed before the interior. Michael Graf, later Pencz's father-in-law, and Hans Graf are documented working on the exterior paintings in 1520 although their precise roles are not specified.[32] Mende has suggested that Kulmbach may have designed or painted the four saints on the west façade. In any event, the Rathaus paintings of 1520–1521 are valuable evidence of the creative collaboration among Nuremberg's artists.

As city painter from 1532, Georg Pencz was continually involved in civic artistic projects. Among the most politically significant, if impermanent, of these was the *Triumphal Arch of Emperor Charles V*, a great wood and painted canvas structure placed across the Burgstrasse between the Rathaus and the castle on the occasion of the emperor's first visit to Nuremberg on 16 February 1541. According to Hans Sachs, who penned a poetic account of the visit, the arch was "sixty work shoes high." Charles and his party passed through the large central arch as they progressed up to the imperial apartments.

Pencz's final plan for the arch is preserved in a colored drawing still in Nuremberg (Staatsarchiv; fig. 32).[33] Anxious not to remind Charles of the serious religious rift that separated the city and its ruler, Pencz devised a program that stressed their imperial bonds. As the plaque held by two putti informs the viewer, the Senatus Populusque Norembergensis (S.P.Q.N.) welcomed the "Imperators Caesari Avgvsto Carlo V." Above the musicians performing in the loggia are Charles's symbols: the double-headed imperial eagle, the twin pillars of Hercules, and his coats of arms. As he passed through the arch, winged victories in the spandrels reached out to crown Charles with wreaths of laurel. Statues of Justitia and Prudentia adorned the front of the arch and Fortitudo and Modestia appeared on the back side.

32. Georg Pencz, *Design for the Triumphal Arch Erected in Nuremberg for Emperor Charles V*, drawing, 1540–1541, Nuremberg, Bayerisches Staatsarchiv, Reichsstadt Nürnberg SI L134, nr. 19.

33. Georg Pencz, *The Fall of Phaeton*, drawing for the 1534 ceiling painting formerly in the garden room of the Hirschvogelhaus, Nuremberg, Germanisches Nationalmuseum, Hz. 5212.

Pencz's arch was part classical and part fantastic in design. The upper portions of the large central arch were largely his own invention. The lower part, however, was a composite of the Arch of Constantine (A.D. 315), what little was then visible of the Arch of Titus (A.D. 81), and the Arch of Septimius Severus (A.D. 203), all of which he studied during his trip to Rome around 1540. The winged victories, the coffered vault of the arch, the projecting fluted columns and lintel, and other features are carefully rendered. The two flanking arches with the imitation ashlar may reflect his examination of more contemporary structures.

Pencz's drawing is corroborated by Peter Flötner's woodcut (Geisberg 822) commemorating the occasion. The only substantive differences are the decorations of the lintels, jambs, and bases with classical grotesques and foliate patterns. Because these features are the trademark of Flötner's style, it seems likely that he participated in the final execution of the arch (cf. fig. 17). These minor changes from Pencz's original design are still evident in Jost Amman's etching *The Triumphal Entry of Emperor Maximilian II into Nuremberg on 7 June 1570*.[34] The arch was sufficiently expensive that the business-minded city council ordered it stored at the Peunt and then later reused it for Maximilian II's entry with only minor changes to the coats of arms and personal emblems.

Besides these large civic projects, other major decorative programs were commissioned by local patricians for their townhouses. In 1534 Pencz and sculptor Peter Flötner decorated the large garden wing that Leonhard Hirschvogel had added to his house on the Hirschelgasse. Flötner planned the wall designs and carved the elaborate chimneypiece (fig. 17).[35] Pencz painted on canvas the *Fall of Phaeton* that was placed on the ceiling. Following the severe damage to the Hirschvogel house in 1945, what remained of this room was transferred to the Fembohaus.

During his travels through northern Italy in 1529 or 1530, Pencz must have stopped in Mantua, where he carefully studied Andrea Mantegna's frescoes in the Camera degli Sposi of the Palazzo Ducale, which were completed in 1474, and Giulio Romano's 1527–1528 ceiling in the Sala di Psiche at the Palazzo del Tè.[36] Pencz's involvement with Dürer the theorist and with the Rathaus paintings made him receptive to these seemingly infinite, mathematically rendered architectural fantasies. The Hirschvogel ceiling provided Pencz with the initial opportunity to translate the lessons of his journey into an actual program.

Pencz's *Fall of Phaeton*, a theme drawn from Ovid's *Metamorphoses* (Book Two), survives both in the original drawing and in the heavily restored painting (fig. 33).[37] The artist has seized the most dramatic moment when Jupiter strikes down Phaeton, Apollo's son, with a thunderbolt. Jupiter killed the inexperienced youth because he had lost control of the chariot of the sun and had scorched the earth. The fire-breathing horses, no longer held by the reins, tumble in all directions, while the falling Phaeton threatens to land upon the viewer entering the garden room. Hercules, Neptune, Bacchus, and other deities flank Jupiter. At the lower right, Apollo grieves for his lost son.

Pencz created a strongly unified composition that is carefully balanced yet conveys the explosive action of the event. The three-dimensional projections of his figures are quite believable. Ovid's account specifies that Jupiter was unable to gather clouds about him when he cast the thunderbolt; Pencz, however, retains the clouds as an expressive space-suggesting device much in the way Correggio used layers of clouds in his 1520–1524 dome in S. Giovanni Evangelista in Parma.[38]

Probably during the early 1540s, Pencz painted a scene of working carpenters on the ceiling of the garden house of the Volckamer family. According to Sandrart, it had "the appearance of a room without a roof, so that looking upwards the eye travelled to the sky beyond and caught sight of carpenters at work among the rafters. This being all so deceptively rendered that the spectator mistook it for real."[39] Drawings in Oxford (Christ Church Library) and London (University College) have been linked with the Volckamer ceiling. In the Oxford sketch, the viewer stares up at naked putto carpenters erecting cross beams on the unfinished building. They straddle the supports and pass timbers to each other. The London drawing shows a rectangular architectural frame with putti hoisting building materials. A bearded man (the artist?) peers down at the viewer. The London drawing is the finer of the two; however, it is impossible to determine which, if either, Pencz used here.

By far the most extraordinary of Pencz's illusionistic drawings meant as a design for a ceiling or a floor is the *Last Judgment* (Leningrad, Hermitage), dating to the early 1540s.[40] Pencz totally inverts the traditional view by showing the event from the vantage point of the throne of heaven. The viewer looks down through an opening in the clouds, around which angels stand and welcome the saved, toward the earth below, where the dead rise up from their tombs. Pencz borrowed a few figures from Michelangelo's *Last Judgment* in the Sistine Chapel, which he had seen during a second Italian trip to Rome in 1539–1540.

With these and other ceiling decorations, Pencz strongly influenced patrician taste for Renaissance art. The process of educating the patricians about the wealth of Renaissance forms and themes, begun by Dürer and the Vischer family, bore fruit in Nuremberg art of the 1530s. Perhaps Pencz's personal contribution would not seem quite so outstanding if we knew more about the many painting cycles by other artists that once adorned Nuremberg's houses and public buildings.[41]

B. PRINTS

In 1617 Antwerp master Frans II Francken painted *The View of a Collector's Cabinet* (Brentfort, The Duke of Northumberland Collection).[42] It shows an elaborate painted and lacquered wooden chest filled with precious objects, such as exotic shells, ancient coins, jewelry, a richly illuminated manuscript, small paintings, and statues of marble and bronze. Classical sculptures decorate the gallery behind. In the center of Francken's collector's chest, pinned carefully to the door, is Dürer's 1524 engraved *Portrait of Friedrich the Wise* (cat. nr. 29). Lucas van Leyden's ca. 1520 engraving *Vanitas: A Young Man with a Skull* (B. 174) is propped up on the table nearby.

The prints of Dürer and Lucas van Leyden were eagerly sought as artistic treasures for the collections of the most discriminating of connoisseurs. Archduke Ferdinand II's *kunstkammer* (art collection) in the Schloss Ambras outside Innsbruck included 224 prints and 8 drawings by Dürer alone.[43] The 1580 inventory of Nuremberg patrician Willibald Imhoff's collection lists twenty-nine books filled with Dürer's prints plus the copper plate of the artist's *Portrait of Willibald Pirckheimer* (cat. nr. 30).[44] The inventory of Nuremberg collector Paulus Praun (1548–1616) boasted all Dürer's prints in their first editions, apparently originally assembled by Wenzel Jamnitzer.[45]

Dürer and his generation of artists are largely responsible for the public acceptance of prints as significant artistic products. Dürer, Albrecht Altdorfer, Baldung, Hans Burgkmair, Lucas Cranach the Elder, and Hans Holbein the Younger all considered the print media as vital and lucrative outlets for their creative expression. Of the major painters only Grünewald (Matthaus Gotthart Neithart) apparently shunned printmaking. Augsburg, Basel, Strassburg, and Erfurt were active printmaking centers, but primacy during the lifetime of Dürer goes again to Nuremberg. Dürer and his followers were remarkably active, as the selection of works in the exhibition demonstrates. Their compositional ideas quickly spread throughout Europe and, in the case of at least one Pencz engraving, to India, where it was copied in the *Album of Jahangir* (Washington, Freer Gallery of Art) of 1590–1600.[46] Dürer, for instance, recognized that his fame in Italy and in the Netherlands was due to knowledge of his prints. In each of their master prints, Dürer and his colleagues strived to develop new artistic solutions and technical perfection.

The master print, that is, one of high artistic merit, can be contrasted with a second category of print: the popular image, most often a woodcut, which was intended to appeal to a mass audience. These works were inexpensive and drew their themes from important contemporary events (Erhard Schön's *Siege of Münster* [cat. nr. 69] or the *Turkish Atrocities* series of the late 1520s); religious beliefs (Traut's *Man of Sorrows and Mater Dolorosa* [cat. nr. 59] or Springinklee's *St. Sebaldus in a Niche* [cat. nr. 55]); miraculous abnormalities (Dürer's *Great Sow of Landser*); celebrated personages (Schön's *Portrait of Albrecht Dürer* [cat. nr. 66] or Virgil Solis's *Albrecht, Margrave of Brandenburg on Horseback* [cat. nr. 174]); and didactic moralizations (Pencz's *Rabbits Catching the Hunter* [cat. nr. 106] or Hans Sebald Beham's *Large Church Festival* [cat. nr. 84]).[47] Often these prints were the tabloids of the day, providing rich insight into contemporary attitudes. Hans Sachs, Nuremberg's famous shoemaker, poet, and playwright, used the broadsheets of Schön, Pencz, Flötner, and others to pass his commentary on life and man's foibles.[48] A strong case can be made that Nuremberg popular prints greatly influenced the ideas and imagery of Flemish master Pieter Bruegel the Elder.[49]

The publishing of most woodcuts was a collaborative effort. Early in his career, Dürer cut his own blocks, but from 1498 he employed a *formschneider*, or special woodblock cutter, such as Hieronymus Andreae, his usual collaborator from 1515 on. The *formschneider* received the drawing either on paper or already on the block. He cut the block and then together with the *briefmaler*, who colored prints by hand or by stencil, oversaw the printing and distribution.[50] The prints frequently are marked with the names of the *formschneider* or the *briefmaler*. For instance, Hans Guldenmund, a *briefmaler* working "in Sanct Gilgengassen," that is by "St. Egidien," published Schäufelein's *Princes' Dance* (cat. nr. 51) and *Wild Man and His Family* (cat. nr. 50). Albrecht Glockendon, an *illuminist*, or manuscript illuminator, who worked as a *briefmaler*, published Hans Sebald Beham's *Feast of Herodias* (cat. nr. 82), *Large Church Festival* (cat. nr. 84), and *Fountain of Youth* (cat. nr. 85), as well as Pencz's *Venus* (cat. nr. 103) and Schön's *Twelve Clean and Twelve Unclean Birds* (cat. nr. 70). Book publisher Hieronymus Höltzel occasionally printed woodcuts, such as Traut's *Man of Sorrows and Mater Dolorosa* (cat. nr. 59). The major individuals who published prints in Nuremberg include Hans Glaser, Georg Glockendon, Stephan Hamer, Georg Lang, Niclas Meldemann, Wolfgang Resch, Simon Tunckel, Hans Wandereisen, and Christoph Zell, plus those already mentioned.

The quality of Nuremberg prints remained high until the end of the 1540s, when a sharp decline occurred in the work of both the printmakers and the publishers. Hans Lautensack, Virgil Solis and his pupil Jost Amman, and a few others were often outstanding printmakers; however, they lacked the broad supporting cast found in the first half of the sixteenth century.

C. ARCHITECTURE

Nuremberg's architectural history during this period is essentially the story of Hans Beheim the Elder (ca. 1455–1538).[51] Beheim is recorded working for the city as early as 1491. By 1503 he was appointed *stadtwerkmeister* (*anschicher auf der Peunt*), the master mason of city works. In actuality, Beheim was an architect, too, a fact tacitly acknowledged by the city when in 1520 the council ordered the *stadtbaumeister*, the city building master or architect, not to interfere with any of Beheim's projects.

His fame is primarily local since he specialized in utilitarian civic structures. He designed and erected the Waage (1497), or city weighing house, and three massive granaries: the Unschlitthaus (1491), the Kaiserstallung (1494–1495), which he ingeniously blended with the adjacent Burg to suggest a unified complex, and the Kornhaus or Maut (1498–1502). The huge scale of the latter, with its tall pitched roof, is relieved only by the delicate late Gothic tracery on the eastern and western gables.

Somewhat more creative were his additions to the Heilig-Geist-Spital (1506–1511) and the Rathaus (1514–1522). When new construction at the hospital was condemned by Beheim as unsafe, he devised the two-story wing built over part of the Pegnitz River. The city council commissioned Beheim to expand the Ratsstube, or council meeting chamber, build a new façade for this room, and add the large east wing, or gallery, on the great courtyard.[52] The Ratsstube façade and east gallery are again ornamented only with bands of flamboyant carved tracery, which was a characteristic feature of many of his buildings.

Beheim's chapels are all modest in scale and design. The Landauer Zwölfbrüderkapelle (1506–1508) is merely a simple hall relieved only by the large windows and the delicate ribbing with pendant keystone over the main altar (fig. 15). Beheim was responsible for the Holzschuher Chapel (1513) in Johannisfriedhof and the design of the Rochus or Imhoff Chapel in Rochusfriedhof, which his son Paulus (ca. 1496–1561) erected in 1520–1521.

Beheim also built several houses, the most significant of which was the Welserhaus (Theresienstrasse 7) of 1510, where he devised a large central courtyard with open galleries on three stories.[53] Perhaps he was influenced by the recently completed Fondaco dei Tedeschi, the German merchants' establishment in Venice.[54] The rounded arches here do little to offset Beheim's dogged adherence to Gothic decorative elements.

Beheim was a sound builder, but like his friend and frequent collaborator Adam Kraft, he was essentially a late Gothic artist. Little is known about his later career. In 1519 Beheim was one of several architects who submitted wooden scale models of the new pilgrimage church Zur schönen Maria (The Beautiful Mary) to the Regensburg city council.[55] Hans Hieber was selected as the architect, however, and his model is today in the Stadtmuseum in Regensburg. Hieber's design, like Albrecht Altdorfer's painted architecture, combines Gothic and Renaissance features well beyond the creative capabilities visible in Beheim's known oeuvre.

Paulus Beheim, Hans's son, is credited with the house of Lorenz II Tucher (Hirschelgasse 9–13), erected in 1533–1544 (fig. 16). This is one of Nuremberg's first Renaissance-style houses that includes a garden as an integral part of the design. I suspect that the probable French Renaissance sources for the Tucher house were suggested not by Beheim but by sculptor Peter Flötner, who was charged with the interior decoration.

One of the most important themes in German Renaissance art and architecture, as in the other arts, is the introduction and ever more frequent and idiomatic use of classical elements. While Nuremberg's architects lagged well behind their colleagues in Regensburg, Cracow, or, to a lesser degree, Augsburg in applying the forms of the classical revival, such artists as Dürer, Peter Vischer the Younger, his brother Hermann II, and Flötner often included the architectural vocabulary of the Italian Renaissance in their work.[56] In 1515 Hermann Vischer traveled to Mantua, Siena, and Rome. His sketches (Paris, Louvre) include careful architectural renderings of the interior of the Pantheon and the Colosseum, the buildings of Raphael and Bramante, and other known monuments.[57] His two drawings for a totally renovated *Tomb of St. Sebaldus* are classic High Renaissance designs reminiscent of Michelangelo's early plans for the *Tomb of Pope Julius II*.[58] Hermann died in 1517 before ever implementing his new vision, but he was responsible for the altered architectural details of the top of the *Tomb of St. Sebaldus* (fig. 21). His sketchbook includes four drawings for totally transforming the choir of Bamberg Cathedral into a modern structure. Whether these are simple idle doodles or the beginning of a serious architectural project is unclear.

Although Peter Flötner was a brilliant designer rather than an aspiring architect, he nevertheless played an important role in introducing many classical motifs into all branches of the visual arts. His woodcuts of elaborate doorways (Geisberg 835–837), columns (Geisberg 845–846), and capitals (Geisberg 847–855) brought a mature Renaissance vision to his broad audience. While Dürer and the Vischers were trailblazers in bringing the Renaissance to Germany, Flötner has been called the Praeceptor Germaniae, or teacher of Germany.[59] His ideas were quickly transferred by others into virtually all media, as will be seen later. One critic compared Flötner's role with that later performed in the Low Countries by Cornelis Floris. Flötner also provided several of the woodcut illustrations for the *Vitruvius teutsch* (Nuremberg: J. Petreius, 1548, cat. nr. 136), the first German edition of Vitruvius's architectural treatise.

Flötner can be credited with the design of the garden room of the Hirschvogelhaus of 1534.[60] The classical architectural moldings and the garland frieze of the exterior have no local precedents. Neither does the carved doorway to the garden. His style is best seen in the large chimneypiece with its classical cornice, metopes, and triglyphs (fig. 17). An eagle, the family symbol, and two putti are placed within the rounded arch over the lintel. Garlands encircle their armorial shields. The lintel with its rinceaux and putti riding mermen, the framing pilasters with grotesques, and the base frieze with its musical putti form an extremely attractive if overly energetic ensemble. Flötner's lintel decoration, columns, and pilasters are then repeated in wood around the rest of the room. The marriage of Flötner's architectural forms with Pencz's *Fall of Phaeton* in the garden room of the Hirschvogelhaus demonstrates that a new era has indeed begun in Nuremberg art.

D. SCULPTURE

An abundance of talented sculptors and bronze casters lived in Nuremberg during the first half of the century.[61] Rich varieties of styles existed simultaneously and no single artist dominated to the degree that Dürer overshadowed his fellow painters and printmakers. Veit Stoss, Adam Kraft, and Peter Vischer the Elder were contemporaries, yet very different artistic personalities. The sweet, ethereal poetry of Stoss's *Angelic Salutation* in St. Lorenz, like the limewood carvings of Tilmann Riemenschneider of Würzburg, represents the final blossoming of German late Gothic art (fig. 23).

The beauty of his oeuvre notwithstanding, Stoss did not blaze new artistic paths. The same is basically true for Adam Kraft. The powerful figures and energetic naturalism of his *Stations of the Cross, Schreyer-Landauer Epitaph,* and *Sacrament House* in St. Lorenz (figs. 18–20) are rooted in the Netherlandish-influenced art of Nikolaus Gerhaert (active 1462–1473).[62] Like Michael Wolgemut, his counterpart among painters, Kraft absorbed the lessons of Rogier van der Weyden and Dirk Bouts and then created his own inventive variations, yet he never aspired to build new artistic solutions from this base. When comparing the Madonna and Child house statues of Stoss and Kraft with the so-called *Nuremberg Madonna* (Nuremberg, Germanisches Nationalmuseum), a limewood sculpture of ca. 1515 modeled after Dürer's realistic, bourgeois Virgin type, they appear strikingly old-fashioned.[63] They are busy and overly decorative, while the Düreresque Madonna conveys quiet, inner grief. The statues of Stoss and Kraft do not offer any precedents for Dürer's classical balance and psychological insight.

Peter Vischer the Elder, head of Nuremberg's most important bronze foundry, on the other hand, was a transitional figure. He was trained in the Gothic tradition of the late fifteenth century, yet he was open to the innovations occurring in northern Italy. The tone of his workshop was first established in 1490 when he designed and cast the free-standing *Branch Breaker* (Munich, Bayerisches Nationalmuseum). Von der Osten has demonstrated that Vischer employed an Etruscan Silenus or similar classical figure as his model.[64] Although Vischer adopted the posture, he transformed his source into an oafish German peasant. The artist may have even owned the model since he possessed a collection of 300 to 400 "*alt frenkischen pild,*" or old Frankish images, usually interpreted to mean classical and early medieval coins and small statues.[65]

The Vischer workshop continued to evolve due to Peter the Elder's active collaboration with his sons, Peter the Younger, Hermann II, and Hans. Often the attribution of specific works, such as the *Tomb of Elisabeth and Hermann VIII of Henneberg* (ca. 1507; Römhild, Stadtkirche), which is given to Peter the Elder by some critics and to Hermann by others, is difficult to establish.[66] Peter the Elder encouraged his sons to travel and was willing to incorporate their new ideas in such family projects as the *Tomb of St. Sebaldus* (figs. 21 and 22). Peter the Younger's careful study of the figure style and lost wax technique of Andrea Riccio (1470–1532) in Padua resulted in the inclusion of the numerous putti, nude deities, and other Italianate forms ornamenting the tomb. Hermann's fascination with the architecture of ancient Rome and of Bramante influenced the elaborate spires of the tomb.

The career of Hermann was tragically cut short when he died in 1517, barely two years after returning from Italy. The only work from this brief period that bears his creative imprint is the grille once in the great hall of the Rathaus.[67] It is just visible at the rear, or western end, of Juvenel's painting (cat. nr. 213). The Fugger family originally commissioned the Vischer shop to make the grille for their funerary chapel in St. Anne in Augsburg in 1512. After many delays and alterations, the grille was instead erected in the Nuremberg Rathaus in 1540. Between 1515 and 1517 Hermann designed the frame for the grille, whose classical architectural forms and rhythmic alternation recall those of contemporary Roman palaces. The grotesques and the mythological sculptural friezes were added later by Peter the Younger and Hans.[68]

34. Peter Vischer the Younger, *Orpheus and Eurydice*, bronze plaquette, after 1515, Washington, National Gallery of Art.

Peter the Younger's absorption of Italian artistic ideas was already evident in 1513, when he created the *Epitaph of Dr. Anton Kress* (St. Lorenz), which is arguably the first true Renaissance funerary monument in Germany (fig. 29).[69] The simple clarity of this humanistic portrait would influence Dürer's late portrait engravings, notably that of *Erasmus*. In 1525 and 1527 Cardinal Albrecht of Brandenburg and Elector Friedrich the Wise, two of the empire's most discerning patrons, ordered Peter the Younger to erect their tomb monuments.[70] The artist has placed Friedrich the Wise beneath a classical triumphal arch ornamented with dancing putti and grotesques. While the motif of the ruler holding the sword of authority is commonplace, Vischer's figure, isolated beneath the spacious arch, has an elegant majesty rarely matched in northern funerary monuments. Peter the Younger can also be credited with introducing small bronzes and plaquettes into Nuremberg art. His mythological plaquettes, such as the *Orpheus and Eurydice* (Washington, National Gallery; fig. 34) were avidly collected by connoisseurs and artists alike.[71] The multiplicity of artistic styles in Nuremberg sculpture is especially evident when one realizes that Vischer's nude figures predate Veit Stoss's *Angelic Salutation* (fig. 23) by a year or two.

The third brother, Hans, ran the workshop during the 1530s. He completed and placed the Rathaus grille. Hans's tomb sculpture, such as the bronze plaques for Seweryn Boner and his wife of 1535–1538 in Cracow (Church of Our Lady), tend to be crowded variants of Peter the Younger's conceptions.[72] Several small bronze statues, including the *Striding Youth* (Munich, Bayerisches Nationalmuseum), are based on Roman prototypes.[73] However, the exaggerated broad stance and swaying upper torso of the *Striding Youth* are more mannerist than classical in feeling.

Hans probably also cast Peter Flötner's famous *Apollo Fountain* in 1532 (fig. 35).[74] The subject of the fountain was dictated by its original placement in the shooting yard of the Schiesshauses am Sand, the gentlemen's archery clubhouse. Flötner based his statue of Apollo on Jacopo de' Barbari's 1503 or 1504 engraving of *Apollo and Diana*,[75] although Flötner's Apollo is trimmer, especially in the upper torso. The artist has likewise corrected the shooting position for his patrons. At the corners of the fountain base four putti ride sea monsters.

35. Peter Flötner, *The Apollo Fountain*, 1532, now in the courtyard of the Pellerhaus (Stadtbibliothek).

Flötner's creative genius is recorded not only in the myriad of prints but also in plaquettes, small bronzes, and such sculptural works as the chimneypiece for the Hirschvogelhaus (fig. 17).[76] His art was a conduit for disseminating Renaissance motifs and forms. Frequently, he provided designs and wooden models for Nuremberg goldsmiths. His collaboration with Melchior Baier will be discussed shortly.

Several of Nuremberg's renowned medalists were active sculptors as well. Between 1518 and 1520 Hans Schwarz carved the wooden *Allegory of Misjustice*, which was placed over the door to the Ratsstube in the Rathaus.[77] The presiding judge is seated between a rich merchant and a poor man. The scales of justice tip in favor of the rich merchant, who is seen reaching into his bulging purse to influence the decision. The carvings served to remind the city council to act fairly. Matthes Gebel created, in addition to numerous medals, several life-size portrait busts, including *Philipp von Pfalz*(?) and *Friedrich II von Pfalz*(?) in Munich (Bayerisches National-

36. Pancraz Labenwolf (after the design of Hans Peisser), *The Putto Fountain*, in the courtyard of the Rathaus, ca. 1555; photo taken in about 1938.

museum).[78] The *Portrait of an Unknown Man* (1527) by goldsmith Melchior Baier is now in Basel (Historisches Museum).[79]

The period ends fittingly with the *Putto Fountain* (ca. 1555; fig. 36) and the *Goose-Bearer Fountain* (ca. 1550), designed by wood sculptor Hans Peisser and cast in bronze by Pankraz Labenwolf.[80] The fountains embody the two prevailing thematic trends in Nuremberg art of the first half of the century. The putto, perched on a tall classical column that rises from an oversized scalloped basin, is Italianate while the goose-bearer, seemingly extracted from the prints of Dürer and Hans Sebald Beham (cat. nr. 84), typifies the continuing fascination with rustic peasant subjects.[81] Each is appropriate to its site: the *Putto Fountain* stands in the Great Courtyard of the Rathaus and the *Goose-Bearer Fountain* was originally in the Obstmarkt, or fruit market, where poultry was sold behind the Frauenkirche. The distinction between patrician and popular tastes in art is obvious. The artists may have understood the latter better than the former since the *Goose-Bearer Fountain* is more successful ultimately than the *Putto Fountain*. The putto, only fifty-three centimeters tall, is overwhelmed by the size of the column and base of the fountain and it is much too small to compete with the surrounding architecture. The goose-bearer is a considerably larger figure and the fountain is set lower to the ground. Its scale and relation to its setting are more appropriate than those of the *Putto Fountain*.[82]

E. GOLDSMITH WORK

Nuremberg's goldsmiths, praised by Regiomontanus in the early 1470s, dominated their trade within central Europe throughout the sixteenth century.[83] Such cities as Augsburg, Lüneburg, and Dresden enjoyed periods of brilliance, yet none could match the consistent quality and output of Nuremberg.[84] One hundred twenty-nine gold- and silversmiths are recorded working in Nuremberg in 1514.[85] The Krugs, Melchior Baier, Wenzel Jamnitzer and his family, Jonas Silber, Friedrich Hillebrandt, Hans Petzoldt, and Christoph Jamnitzer form an unbroken succession of masters whose fame spread throughout the continent.

Nuremberg's goldsmiths had achieved full guild status by 1449.[86] All regulations and activities were, however, tightly controlled by the city council. As members of a *geschworne Handwerke*, the goldsmiths annually swore their allegiance to the city. Since they were highly trained craftsmen, goldsmiths were forbidden to leave Nuremberg, even for short periods, without city council approval. This did prevent individual masters from being easily lured to another city or court where they could share any technical innovations.

A goldsmith's training was rigorous. One apprenticed for at least three years with a master before serving elsewhere as a journeyman for three or four years. To become a master goldsmith, the applicant had three months to design and to make three items: a columbine cup, a gold ring set with a precious stone, and a steel seal-die. Passing this hurdle demonstrated general technical proficiency. From 1535 on the applicant was permitted to use someone else's designs, and in 1572 a columbine cup by Wenzel Jamnitzer served as the standard model for all aspirants to follow.[87] In 1572 the guild restricted the size of each shop to the master, four journeymen, and two apprentices in order to prevent an artist like Wenzel Jamnitzer from accepting a large number of commissions to the detriment of his fellow goldsmiths.

Particularly during the first half of the century, goldsmiths maintained a close business relationship with other Nuremberg artists since it was generally a wood sculptor, a specialized patternmaker, or, occasionally, a printmaker who supplied the wooden, lead, and plaster models. This creative collaboration is nicely illustrated in the execution of the *Silver Altar*, which King Sigismund I of Poland commissioned in 1531 for the Sigismund Chapel in Wawel Cathedral in Cracow.[88] Hans Dürer, Albrecht's younger brother who was Sigismund's court painter in Cracow, made the drawings for the scenes from the life of the Virgin. Peter Flötner transformed these into wooden models, which Pankraz Labenwolf then cast in bronze. Next, Melchior Baier made silver reliefs and assembled the altar, which bears his signature. Finally, Georg Pencz painted the *Passion of Christ* on the exterior of the wings. Guild regulations were designed to prevent the goldsmith from making his own models; however, in many instances Baier, the Jamnitzers, and others skirted the rule.[89]

The *Silver Altar* demonstrates how difficult it is to refer to some goldsmith pieces as the work of a single master. Hans Frey, Albrecht Dürer's father-in-law, was famed for his elaborate automated table fountains, such as the one illustrated in the *Table Fountain with a Mountain Scene and Morris Dancers* drawing at Erlangen (Universitätsbibliothek; fig. 30).[90] Frey created the designs and wooden models, then teamed with a goldsmith, usually Ludwig Krug, who cast the fountains in silver and applied the enamel decorations.[91] Veit Stoss carved the model for a 1477 monstrance, made in Nuremberg, now in the Obere Pfarre at Bamberg.[92] Paulus Müllner specialized in silver statues of saints. He often designed the original drawing, such as the *St. Jerome* in Weimar (Staatsarchiv), and engaged a sculptor to make the wooden model.[93] Tilmann Riemenschneider produced the model for Müllner's *Bust of St. Kilian*, commissioned by the cathedral chapter in Würzburg.[94] Ludwig Krug, whose range of talents is well illustrated in the exhibition, used both the models of other masters and his own, such as the wooden *Naked Warrior* (Berlin, Kunstgewerbemuseum).[95]

37. Anonymous goldsmith, *The Schlüsselfelder Ship*, 1503, Nuremberg, Germanisches Nationalmuseum, HG. 2146.

At the outset of the sixteenth century, Nuremberg's goldsmiths supplied religious statues (such as those by Müllner and Sebastian Lindenast the Elder), monstrances, reliquaries, and other ecclesiastical objects to churches throughout the empire.[96] More utilitarian cups, dishes, and plates also accounted for a sizable percentage of their oeuvre. Purely decorative pieces were occasionally commissioned by a patrician for his house or by the city council as a gift for a visiting dignitary. The most outstanding early example of this latter category is the *Schlüsselfelder Ship* (Nuremberg, Germanisches Nationalmuseum) completed in 1503 (fig. 37).[97] The ship, made of cast silver that has been chased, partially gilt, and engraved, was intended as an automated wine dispenser. It is a highly accurate replica of a contemporary galley, or carrack. Seventy-four tiny cast figures scramble to their battle positions; a few tightly secure the main sail. The ship is supported by a siren set on a lobated base. The artist of the ship is unknown. Kohlhaussen and others have suggested that Albrecht Dürer the Elder was the master, but the attribution is doubtful since no known works can be linked with the artist. The identity of the initial patron is also a mystery. Mattheus Landauer may have commissioned the ship, which subsequently passed into the collection of his nephew Wilhelm Schlüsselfelder (1483–1549).

If the *Schlüsselfelder Ship* demonstrates the technical proficiency of local goldsmiths, the artistic differences that separate the first and second quarters of the century are evident in the Krug and Baier workshops. Hans Krug the Elder (died 1519) and his sons, Hans the Younger (died 1529) and Ludwig (ca. 1488/90–1532), specialized in religious vessels, such as the 1518 *Reliquary of the Apron of Christ* and *Reliquary of the Table Cloth from the Last Supper* (Vienna, Kunsthistorisches Museum, Schatzkammer) mentioned in the discussion of the imperial relics.[98] In spite of the constraints imposed by traditional reliquary shapes, the family created strikingly original designs. The *Pelican-Ostensorium*, made before 1519 for Maximilian I and owned, during the 1520s, by Cardinal Albrecht of Brandenburg, is such a bizarre combination of Renaissance architectural motifs, hybrid foliate forms, angels, pearls, and precious gems that the underlying core, which is still typically late medieval, is obscured.[99] In the contemporary *Nautilus Shell Reliquary*, also owned by Cardinal Albrecht von Brandenburg, the Krug workshop placed the saintly relic within the mouth of the shell and then totally enveloped the shell in the branches of a tree whose stem forms the shrine's base.[100] These twisting organic forms are a particular characteristic of the Krugs' work. In the *Apple Cup* (cat. nr. 114) they adhered to the simplicity of Dürer's drawing and produced a highly naturalistic stem. In other works these stems are radically off axis, and the intricate leaf patterns threaten to run wild. Frequently, coins, ivory plaques, and narrative carvings were inserted along the bodies or lids of cups. The Krug workshop, and Ludwig in particular, stood with one foot in the waning style of late Gothic and the other at the threshold of Mannerist fascination with technical virtuosity and the bizarre.

38. Melchior Baier and Peter Flötner, *Pfinzing Dish*, 1534–1536, Nuremberg, Germanisches Nationalmuseum, HG. 8397.

Nuremberg's goldsmiths might have leaped directly into Mannerism had it not been for the High Renaissance style of Melchior Baier and his frequent collaborator, Peter Flötner.[101] Baier (master 1525; died 1577) continued producing religious objects for his Roman Catholic patrons, especially King Sigismund I of Poland, though he is most famous for his elaborate covered cups and dishes.[102] Between 1534 and 1536

39. Melchior Baier and Peter Flötner, *Holz-schuher Covered Cup*, before 1540, Nuremberg, Germanisches Nationalmuseum, HG. 8601.

Baier and Flötner created the *Pfinzing Dish* (Nuremberg, Germanisches National-museum), ordered to commemorate the fraternal ties of Martin, Melchior, and Sigmund Pfinzing, who are portrayed in Matthes Gebel's three medals on the lid (fig. 38).[103] Where the Krug *Pelican-Ostensorium* is intentionally complex, the *Pfinzing Dish* is simple and clear. The three medals are balanced with attractive enamel rinceaux patterns. The bowl is ornamented with minute chisel marks arranged in neat concentric rings. The architectural forms of the base and stem are elegant, with the enamel and chiseled decorations instantly legible. Even in the masters' *Agate Dish* (Munich, Residenz, Schatzkammer) of 1536, the opulence of the decoration does not obscure the clarity of structural forms.[104]

The diversity of the Baier-Flötner style is seen in the *Holzschuher Covered Cup* (Nuremberg, Germanisches Nationalmuseum), completed before 1540 (fig. 39).[105] Once again Flötner was responsible for the overall design. He carved into the coconut wood bacchanal scenes that recall his contemporary plaquettes (cf. cat. nr. 134). On top of the finial a satyr pours wine into a man's mouth. Below, cast figures of amorous couples and copulating goats, set beneath the twisting vines that form the stem, suggest the properties of wine. The arcadian subjects are part of what Kris has defined as the rustic style in German art of the period.[106] The circular motion of the base figures, the stem, the triumphal procession of Bacchus, and the finial figures is consistent and highly regular in its design. The creative and technical talents of Baier and Flötner, as seen in these two works, set the stage for Wenzel Jamnitzer, Nuremberg's greatest artist of the second half of the sixteenth century.

NOTES

1. See cat. nrs. 137–157 (medals), 125–135 (plaquettes), and 117–121, 158, 209 (small bronzes).

2. K. Schwarz, *Augustin Hirschvogel: Ein deutscher Meister der Renaissance*; J. S. Peters, "Early Drawings by Augustin Hirschvogel, 1503–1553," *Master Drawings* 17 (1979): 359–392, and "Frühe Glasgemälde von Augustin Hirschvogel," *AGNM* (1980): 79–92.

3. On Cranach, see Hampe, *Nürnberger Ratsverlässe*, I: nr. 2443. On Strada's stay, see J. F. Hayward, *Virtuoso Goldsmiths*, pp. 46–48.

4. Betz, "Wolgemut," pp. 288–311; the paintings are in the Heilig-Kreuz-Kapelle and in Straubing (Stadtpfarrkirche).

5. Anzelewsky, *Dürer*, nrs. 5, 20–38, pp. 27–28.

6. Ibid., nrs. 50–54K.

7. Ibid., nr. 66.

8. Ibid., nrs. 118–147.

9. *Nuremberg: Meister um Dürer*, nrs. 162, 365.

10. Ibid., nr. 360; Pfeiffer and Schwemmer, *Bilddokumenten*, figs. 156, 164.

11. *Nuremberg: Meister um Dürer*, nr. 154. Also see H. Schindler, *Der Schnitzaltar* (Regensburg, 1978), pp. 54–79, for a discussion of the type.

12. Anzelewsky, *Dürer*, nr. 118, fig. 148.

13. Viebig et al., *Die Lorenzkirche in Nürnberg*, p. 43.

14. H. G. Gmelin, "Georg Pencz als Maler," *MJBK* 17 (1966): 76–79 (nr. 6), figs. 18–31.

15. Anzelewsky, *Dürer*, nr. 48.

16. Ibid., nrs. 56–58; *Nuremberg Durer (1971)*, nr. 87.

17. Betz, "Wolgemut," pp. 282–283; Anzelewsky, *Dürer*, nr. 10. Also see W. Wenke, "Das Bildnis bei Michael Wolgemut," *AGNM* (1932–1933): 61–73.

18. For a specific study of local portraiture, see P. Strieder, "Zur Nürnberger Bildniskunst des 16. Jahrhunderts," *MJBK* 7 (1956): 120–137.

19. Anzelewsky, *Dürer*, nrs. 178–179.

20. L. von Baldass, "Zur Bildniskunst der Dürerschule, II. Die Bildniskunst des Jörg Pencz und Bartel Beham," *Pantheon* 26 (1940): 258, where he credits Beham with the introduction of the hip-length portrait into German art. *Nuremberg: Meister um Dürer*, nr. 34; G. von der Osten and H. Vey, *Painting and Sculpture in Germany and the Netherlands, 1500 to 1600*, pp. 231–234, fig. 214, for comments on the painting styles of Beham and Pencz. The Beham portrait in the exhibition lacks the atmospheric background.

21. Pencz copied the portraits of Holbein and Amberger; see Gmelin, "Georg Pencz als Maler," nr. 39, fig. 62. His contact with Amberger's work is, I think, critically important. On their association and on Amberger, see K. Löcher, "Studien zur oberdeutschen Bildnismalerei des 16. Jahrhunderts," *Jahrbuch der Staatlichen Kunstsammlungen in Baden-Württemberg* 4 (1967): 31–84, esp. 43–49, and "Die Malerei in Augsburg, 1530–1550," in *Welt im Umbruch: Augsburg zwischen Renaissance und Barock*, II: pp. 23–30, nrs. 444–460. See generally J. Pope-Hennessy, *The Portrait in the Renaissance*, ch. IV, figs. 117, 243; O. Benesch, *La Peinture Allemande: De Dürer à Holbein* (Geneva,

1966), pp. 151–175; von der Osten and Vey, *Painting and Sculpture in Germany*, pp. 214, 216, 227–230, 234.

22. Gmelin, "Georg Pencz als Maler," nrs. 37, 38 (*Portrait of a Seated Youth*; Florence, Uffizi); Pope-Hennessy, *The Portrait*, esp. fig. 261 (*Ugolino Martelli*; Berlin, Staatliche Museen).

23. Gmelin, "Georg Pencz als Maler," nrs. 47, 42; cf. nrs. 36, 44, 46.

24. Dettenthaler, "Hans Springinklee als Maler," p. 177, nrs. 9–11; Bachmann, *Imperial Castle Nuremberg*, pp. 23–24, 31, figs. 1, 11, 21.

25. Christensen, "The Nuernberg City Council," pp. 82–89; especially Mende, *Rathaus*, I: pp. 38–88, 192–409 (interior decorations), 410–440 (exterior decorations), with extensive commentary and literature on all facets of the program.

26. Winkler, *Zeichnungen Dürers*, IV: nrs. 922, 921 (Pierpont Morgan Library drawing). On the *Last Judgment* and grille, see Mende, *Rathaus*, II: nrs. 604, 615–658; also see notes 67–68 below.

27. Peltzer, ed., *Sandrarts Academie*, p. 78; Mende, *Rathaus*, I: pp. 80–81.

28. Mende, *Rathaus*, I: pp. 383–409, for the 1613 and later restorations.

29. Ibid., p. 410. It has been suggested that this artist was a member of the Landauer family.

30. Ibid., nrs. 578–579, for two ca. 1829 views by Georg Christoph Wilder.

31. Ibid., nrs. 575–577.

32. Ibid., p. 413. On page 80, Mende states that Pencz married Graf's daughter in 1530.

33. Reichsstadt Nürnberg, Losungsamt Akten, SI L134, nr. 19, folio 52. A brief discussion of the arch, including Sachs's comments on its size, is in *Reformation in Nürnberg*, nr. 275.

34. Andresen 71 and Hollstein, II: p. 17. On Maximilian II's entry, see cat. nr. 192.

35. For illustrations of the Hirschvogelhaus before 1945, see Schwemmer, *Bürgerhaus*, pls. 23a, 105c; G. Glück, *Die Kunst der Renaissance in Deutschland*, p. 492, for a whole view of the garden room. On the subject of this and other ceiling painting by Pencz, see E. Kris, "Georg Pencz als Deckenmaler," *Mitteilungen der Gesellschaft für vervielfält Kunst* 46 (1923): 45–53; W. Pfeiffer, "Zwei Zeichnungen von Georg Pencz," *Pantheon* 22 (1964): 81–90; Gmelin, "Georg Pencz als Maler," esp. pp. 64, 86, nr. 22; Zink, *Die Handzeichnungen*, nr. 103. K. Lange, *Peter Flötner, ein Bahnbrecher der deutschen Renaissance auf Grund neuer Entdeckungen*, pp. 64–74.

36. F. Hartt, *History of Italian Renaissance Art* (Englewood Cliffs, N.J., 1969), figs. 426, 636, and *Giulio Romano*, pp. 126–140, figs. 226, 258. Romano's influence on Pencz has been cited by many writers, including Kris ("Georg Pencz als Deckenmaler," p. 49) and Zink (*Die Handzeichnungen*, nr. 103). For Pencz's copy of a Romano drawing, see cat. nr. 107.

37. Gmelin, "Georg Pencz als Maler," fig. 17.

38. Hartt, *History of Italian Renaissance Art*, fig. 621, and cf. 638, Romano's frescoes of 1530–1532 in the Sala dei Giganti in the Palazzo del Tè.

39. Peltzer, ed., *Sandrarts Academie*, p. 78. I have given the English paraphrase in H. and E. Tietze, "Georg Pencz: Design for a Ceiling-Painting, Oxford, Christ-Church-Library," *Old Master Drawing* 14 (1939–1940): 18. On the London drawing, see H. Geissler, ed., *Zeichnung in Deutschland: Deutsche Zeichner, 1540–1640*, I: nr. A 34.

40. W. Pfeiffer, "Zwei Zeichnungen von Georg Pencz," pp. 82–83, fig. 7. Pencz executed other ceiling paintings and drawings. Sandrart mentioned a ceiling in the *Chamber of Diana* in the Residenz at Landshut; see Peltzer, ed., *Sandrarts Academie*, p. 78.

41. Between 1533 and 1544, Lorenz II Tucher had Paulus Beheim(?) erect his new residence. Flötner was in charge of the decorations and, possibly, the original architectural plan. Either Veit the Younger or Augustin Hirschvogel executed the stained-glass windows illustrating the exploits of Jupiter, Hercules, Mars, Venus, and Ceres. On the house and its decoration, see Grote, *Die Tucher*, pp. 24ff., figs. 66–78. See also fig. 16.

42. F. Anzelewsky, M. Mende, and P. Eeckhout, *Albert Dürer aux Pays-Bas: Son voyage (1520–1521), son influence*, nr. 426. Dürer prints appear in other Francken *cabinets d'amateurs* paintings.

43. Robinson, "'This Passion for Prints,'" p. xxxiii. Ferdinand II lived from 1529 to 1595.

44. A. Springer, "Invertare der Imhoff'schen Kunstkammer zu Nürnberg," *Mitteilungen der kaiserl. königl. Central Commission* (Wien) 5 (1860): 356.

45. De Murr, *Description du Cabinet de Monsieur Paul de Praun à Nuremberg*, pp. 67, 107–108, for his drawings.

46. Pencz's *Geometria* (B. 46 and cat. nr. 109) is accurately copied, including the artist's monogram, among the marginal scenes. The other prints have yet to be attributed. See M. C. Beach, *The Imperial Image: Paintings from the Mughal Court*, Freer Gallery of Art (Washington, 1981), pp. 162–163, cat. nr. 16C (Freer 56.12B); and cat. nr. 109.

47. On Schön's *Turkish Atrocities*, see Geisberg, nrs. 1239–1244. Dürer's *Great Sow of Landser* is Meder 82. On the popularity of images of miraculous celestial events, see A. Janeck, *Zeichen am Himmel: Flugblätter des 16. Jahrhunderts*.

48. For Amman's *Portrait of Hans Sachs*, see cat. nr. 193, where additional information is provided. Also see H. Röttinger, *Die Bilderbogen des Hans Sachs*; R. Freitag-Stadler et al., eds., *Die Welt des Hans Sachs*, exh. cat. (Nuremberg, 1976); J. K. W. Willers, ed., *Hans Sachs und die Meistersinger in ihrer Zeit*.

49. F. Würtenberger, *Pieter Bruegel d. Ä. und die deutsche Kunst* (Wiesbaden, 1957); the subject still needs more research.

50. See Amman's illustrations of the *formschneider* and *briefmaler* (cat. nr. 190). For a good, brief introduction to printing, see W. L. Strauss, *The German Single-Leaf Woodcut, 1550–1600*, I: pp. 1–9.

51. His name is spelled either Beheim or Behaim. E. Lutze, "Hans Behaim der Ältere," *ZDVK* 5 (1938): 181–203; W. Schultheiss, "Der Nürnberger Architekt Hans Behaim d. Ä., seine Herkunft und Bautätigkeit bis 1491," *MVGN* 47 (1956): 426–443; C. Schaper, "Studien zur Geschichte der Baumeisterfamilie Behaim," *MVGN* 48 (1958): 125–182, esp. 125–142 for Hans the Elder, and 161–179 for his son Paulus; Christensen, "The Nuernberg City Council," pp. 72–73. For illustrations of these buildings, see the specific references given in the description in Section 1.

52. Mende, *Rathaus*, I: figs. 9, 20, 24, 33–34, 36–37.

53. Schwemmer, *Bürgerhaus*, pls. 82, 111a. Beheim worked with Kraft on Winklerstrasse 5, dated 1496–1497; see ibid., pls. 112a, 121b; Schwemmer, *Adam Kraft*, figs. 38–39.

54. H.-R. Hitchcock, *German Renaissance Architecture*, pl. 1.

55. Ibid., pp. 25–26, pl. 25. Beheim served as an advisor for Ottheinrich, Count Palatine; see p. 132.

56. Ibid., chs. 1, 2, for these three cities. Also see J. Bialostocki, *The Art of the Renaissance in Eastern Europe*, esp. pp. 18–25, 35–44, for the Wawel Castle and the Sigismund Chapel in Wawel Cathedral in Cracow. H. Stierhof, "Augsburger Architektur, 1518–1650," in *Welt im Umbruch: Augsburg zwischen Renaissance und Barock*, I: pp. 100–112.

57. L. Demonts, *Musée du Louvre—Inventaires général des Dessins des Écoles du Nord—Écoles Allemande et Suisse*, II: pp. 70–74, nrs. 333–352. Very general comments about Hans are given in von der Osten and Vey, *Painting and Sculpture in Germany*, pp. 22–23; Hitchcock, *German Renaissance Architecture*, pp. 5, 34–35, pls. 2, 34.

58. Demonts, *Musée du Louvre—Dessins*, nrs. 347–348. For Hermann's work on the tomb, see Pilz, *Das Sebaldusgrabmal im Ostchor der St.-Sebaldus-Kirche in Nürnberg*, pp. 58, 60, 72, 75.

59. Von der Osten and Vey, *Painting and Sculpture in Germany*, p. 268. The role of Flötner in bringing Renaissance motifs to the north was first discussed in Lange, *Peter Flötner*; also see *Peter Flötner und die Renaissance in Deutschland*.

60. See note 35 above.

61. A thorough history of Nuremberg sculpture has yet to be written. See H. Höhn, *Nürnberger Renaissanceplastik*; selected comments in E. F. Bange, *Die Kleinplastik der deutschen Renaissance in Holz und Stein*, and *Die Deutschen Bronzestatuetten des 16. Jahrhunderts*; H. R. Weihrauch, *Europäische Bronzestatuetten*; and von der Osten and Vey, *Painting and Sculpture in Germany*, chs. 2, 30.

62. Baxandall, *The Limewood Sculptors of Renaissance Germany*, pp. 248–251.

63. *Nuremberg: Dürer (1971)*, nr. 703 with literature; Pfeiffer and Schwemmer, *Bilddokumenten*, fig. 192.

64. G. von der Osten, "Uber Peter Vischers Törichten Bauern und den Beginn der 'Renaissance' in Nürnberg," *AGNM* (1963): 71–83, esp. 71–78.

65. Ibid., pp. 80–81.

66. E. Panofsky, *Tomb Sculpture* (New York, n.d.), fig. 274 (Peter the Elder); von der Osten and Vey, *Painting and Sculpture in Germany*, fig. 5 (Hermann).

67. Mummenhoff, *Das Rathaus in Nürnberg*, pp. 97–105, 251–253 (documents), figs. pp. 99, 103, the sixth plate at the end of the book; Christensen, "The Nuernberg City Council," pp. 99–108; forthcoming comments in Mende, *Rathaus*, II: nrs. 615–658. Hans Vischer was helped in the installation of the grille by sculptor Sebald Beck, who carved the stone frames at either side. Little is known about his career. He arrived in Nuremberg in 1538. On 7 May, the city council ruled that the cabinet makers guild, which included wood sculptors, must stop trying to prevent Beck from working in the city since he was "more talented and famous than them all." Christensen, "The Nuernberg City Council," p. 50; Hampe, *Nürnberger Ratsverlässe*, I: nrs. 2325, 2336. For a good illustration of Beck's carved frames, see Mende, *Rathaus*, I: fig. 64.

68. Stafski, *Der Jüngere Peter Vischer*, pp. 47–48, figs. 86–87. The grille was removed from the great hall in 1806 and sold. Some of the figures are today in the Château Montrottier in Annecy.

69. Ibid., pp. 40–41, figs. 78–79; also see comments in Section 5.

70. Ibid., pp. 41–44, figs. 80–81.

71. Ibid., pp. 38–39, figs. 76–77, for the Washington plaquette and a second, different *Orpheus and Eurydice* in Berlin (Staatliche Museen). On his small bronzes, see ibid., pp. 45–47, figs. 82–85; also see cat. nr. 118.

72. Bialostocki, *The Art of the Renaissance in Eastern Europe*, figs. 161–162.

73. Höhn, *Nürnberger Renaissanceplastik*, fig. 83.

74. Weihrauch, *Europäische Bronzestatuetten*, p. 318, suggests that Pankraz Labenwolf not Hans Vischer cast the *Apollo Fountain*.

75. Levenson, Oberhuber, and Sheehan, *Early Italian Engravings*, nr. 141.

76. Flötner created small bronzes, architectural motif wood paneling for rooms, and a variety of other items. See the catalogue biography.

77. Pfeiffer and Schwemmer, *Bilddokumenten*, fig. 52; Mende, *Rathaus*, I: fig. 67. Mende (I: p. 7) suggests that Dürer may have provided the design. A thorough discussion is promised in Mende, *Rathaus*, II: nr. 606–607. These statues have also been attributed to Hans Leinberger of Landshut.

78. Inv. K 919–920. J. Jahn, *Deutsche Renaissance*, pl. 141a. See the catalogue biography for additional comments.

79. Kohlhaussen, *Nürnberger Goldschmiedekunst*, fig. 634.

80. The wooden models for both of these statues survive. The *Putto* is in the Germanisches Nationalmuseum and the *Goose-Bearer* is now on display in the Fembohaus. On these and the

career of Peisser, see K. Pechstein, "Der Bildschnitzer Hans Peisser," *AGNM* (1973): 84–106, esp. 84–92, figs. 1–2, 7–8. On Labenwolf, see Weihrauch, *Europäische Bronzestatuetten*, pp. 318–319, fig. 388.

81. For Dürer's peasants, see Meder 84–89; also see Winkler, *Zeichnungen Dürers*, IV: nr. 946 (Oxford, Ashmolean Museum) for a design for a table fountain with a man carrying a goose.

82. On Labenwolf, also see cat. nr. 158.

83. The definitive study is Kohlhaussen's *Nürnberger Goldschmiedekunst*, especially the first half of the book, which treats the fourteenth and fifteenth centuries. Excerpts of Regiomontanus's comments are quoted at the beginning of Section 4.

84. H. Selig, *Die Kunst der Augsberger Goldschmiede, 1529–1868*, esp. vol. I. On Lüneburg, see the comments in K. Pechstein, *Goldschmiedewerke der Renaissance—Kataloge des Kunstgewerbemuseums Berlin V*, nrs. 1–27. On Dresden's goldsmiths, see W. Holzhausen, *Prachtgefässe—Geschmeide—Kabinettstücke—Goldschmiedekunst in Dresden*, esp. pp. XIV–XXII.

85. Kohlhaussen, *Nürnberger Goldschmiedekunst*, p. 305.

86. The following two paragraphs are taken from Hayward, *Virtuoso Goldsmiths*, pp. 35–47, esp. 38.

87. Ibid., pl. 425 (Nuremberg, Germanisches Nationalmuseum), for a similar columbine cup made for the Tucher family around 1564. Also see K. Pechstein, "The 'Welcome' Cup—Renaissance Drinking Vessels by Nuremberg Goldsmiths," *Connoisseur* 199 (November 1978): 180–187, fig. 2.

88. Kohlhaussen, *Nürnberger Goldschmiedekunst*, nr. 458; see note 14 above.

89. Hayward, *Virtuoso Goldsmiths*, pp. 64–65.

90. The drawing, attributed to Frey (1450–1523), is full scale (75.1 × 34.4 cm); see Bock, *Zeichnungen*, nr. 147. On the subject of table fountains and Frey, see Kohlhaussen, *Nürnberger Goldschmiedekunst*, pp. 255–265.

91. Kohlhaussen, *Nürnberger Goldschmiedekunst*, p. 262, cites Neudörfer for the association between Frey and Krug. See Neudörfer, *Nachrichten von Künstlern*, p. 124.

92. Kohlhaussen, *Nürnberger Goldschmiedekunst*, nr. 313.

93. Ibid., nr. 423.

94. Ibid., nr. 283.

95. Ibid., nr. 423; Pechstein, *Goldschmiedewerke der Renaissance*, nr. 151.

96. On Lindenast, see Kohlhaussen, *Nürnberger Goldschmiedekunst*, pp. 280–281, nr. 347. For Müllner's art, see ibid., nrs. 341–343.

97. Ibid., pp. 272–273, nr. 338; also see nr. 339, which is another Nuremberg ship now in Padua (San Antonio). On the general subject of table nefs, see C. Oman, *Medieval Silver Nefs* (London, 1963), which both mentions the Nuremberg examples and cites an engraving by the Master W with the Key (active in Bruges 1465–1485) as the source for the design of the *Schlüsselfelder Ship*; see pp. 21, 24, fig. 15. Also see M. Lehrs, *Late Gothic Engravings of Germany & the Netherlands*, nr. 459.

98. See Section 3 and note 30. Also see Kohlhaussen, *Nürnberger Goldschmiedekunst*, nrs. 404–405. On the Krug workshop, see ibid., pp. 351ff., nrs. 390–425.

99. Ibid., nr. 395. The cardinal owned at least five Krug works.

100. Ibid., nr. 393.

101. Ibid., pp. 437ff., for a discussion of the collaboration.

102. Ibid., nrs. 460–463.

103. Ibid., nr. 465; on the medals, see the comments on Gebel in the catalogue.

104. Ibid., nr. 467.

105. Ibid., nr. 469.

106. Ibid., p. 479; E. Kris, "Der Stil 'Ristique,' die Verwendung des Naturabgusses bei Wenzel Jamnitzer und Bernard Palissy," *JKSW* 1 (1926): 137ff., esp. 165–166.

7. Art Prior to the Thirty Years War

During the first half of the sixteenth century, German art was enriched by numerous strong local schools. A work from this period can usually be associated with Nuremberg, Regensburg, Strassburg, or another center. However, during the second half of the century, the artistic situation in Nuremberg and most other German cities was rather muddled.[1] Local peculiarities had been swept aside by the influx of Netherlandish and Italian Mannerism. While not totally homogeneous, the artistic currents of this period were international rather than local or regional. Even the principal artists working in Nuremberg, Augsburg, or Munich were often not Germans. In the second half of the sixteenth century, the most outstanding portrait painter in Nuremberg was Nicolas Neufchâtel from Mons (Hainaut); sculptor Johann Gregor van der Schardt was from Nijmegen (Gelderland), printmaker Jost Amman was from Zurich, and even Wenzel Jamnitzer, Germany's most brilliant goldsmith, was born and trained in Vienna.

The general artistic pre-eminence of Nuremberg was not sustained during the latter half of the sixteenth century. While major contributions were made in all fields, notably in printmaking and goldsmith work, Nuremberg's artistic influence gradually waned. Augsburg, Munich, and Prague were often more innovative, more receptive to new ideas from the 1580s onward. Nevertheless, Nuremberg remained an active center until 1618, when war broke out in central Europe.

A. PAINTING

The history of painting in the city during the second half of the sixteenth century can be summarized by examining three basic trends: the continued demand for portrait paintings, especially those by Nicolas Neufchâtel and his followers; Hans Hoffmann's revival of Albrecht Dürer's art; and patrician interest in mythological cycles to decorate homes.

Following the death of Georg Pencz in 1550, Nuremberg was without a first-rate portraitist. Therefore, when Nicolas Neufchâtel arrived in 1561, he enjoyed immediate success.[2] Neufchâtel was born around 1527 in Mons, where he worked following his training in the workshop of Pieter Coecke van Aelst in Antwerp in 1539. None of his paintings from the 1540s or 1550s have been identified. Because he was a Calvinist his departure from Mons may be linked with the political and religious upheavals caused by Charles V's heir, Philip II, king of Spain (1556–1598). Neufchâtel may initially have been drawn to the growing artistic community of Netherlandish exiles near Frankfurt before moving to Nuremberg, but between 1561 and 1573 he lived in Nuremberg and his entire oeuvre of about forty paintings dates to these years. It is unclear when (1573 or 1590) and where he died.

The reasons for Neufchâtel's rapid success are visible in his best known painting, the *Portrait of Johann Neudörfer and His Son* (Munich, Alte Pinakothek, on loan to the Germanisches Nationalmuseum) dated 1561 (fig. 40).[3] The famous mathematician, calligrapher, and biographer of artists is shown explaining the structure of a dodecahedron to his son. Neufchâtel captured the intimacy of the occasion as he depicted the intense concentration of Neudörfer and the strict attentiveness of his son. The warm gray-brown tones unify the composition, and the strong facial lighting draws the figures out of the shadows of the room. The harmonious composition has a soft, atmospheric quality that is much closer to the style of earlier sixteenth-century Antwerp portraitists, such as Quentin Massys and his sons, than the chilly clarity and rigidly defined forms of Georg Pencz's portraits.[4] Neufchâtel's chiaroscuro is also evidence of the spread of Titian's influence in southern Germany.[5] Neufchâtel's ability to blend the styles of Antwerp and Germany is all the more evident when his oeuvre is contrasted with the drier, nonatmospheric qualities seen in the paintings of the Master of the 1540s or Willem Key, two of his Antwerp contemporaries. Neufchâtel's style, however, never equaled the elegant courtliness of Antonio Moro, the finest of the Netherlandish portraitists.[6]

Neufchâtel's *Portrait of Wenzel Jamnitzer* (Geneva, Musée d'Art et d'Histoire), dating to about 1565, conveys something of the goldsmith's creative energy (fig. 41).[7] Although the figure is rather stiffly posed, there is the anticipation of motion as if momentarily Jamnitzer will address the viewer about the design of the Neptune finial statue. Neufchâtel achieves this effect by lowering Jamnitzer's left shoulder and

GRAPHICES·MVLTITVDINE·CELEBRIS·INCŌPARABILIS·INDVSTRIÆ·EXĒPLAR

MAGNV·ORNAMETV·PATR·REIP·NORIB·CVI·DESIDERATISS·CIVIS·EFFIGIE·V·ÆTAT·LXIII

IOANNES·NEVDORF·PER·EVROPA·VNIVERSA·IFINITA·DISCIPVLOR·ARITHMETICES

AVTOR·NICOLAVS·DE·NOVO·CASTELLO·HOSPES·GR·ER·DD·AN·M·D·LXI·

40. Nicolas Neufchâtel, *Portrait of Johann Neudörfer and His Son*, 1561, Munich, Alte Pinakothek (on loan to the Germanisches Nationalmuseum).

twisting the body toward his right side. The implied movement and the dignity of his sitter link Neufchâtel's art with the more famous portraits of Antonio Moro. Neufchâtel's paintings also influenced the attractive portrait sculptures of his friend Johann Gregor van der Schardt.

Neufchâtel trained or inspired most of the next group of Nuremberg portraitists, including Nicolas Juvenel, who moved to Nuremberg from Dunkirk; Andreas Herneisen, who painted the *Portrait of Hans Sachs*, later etched by Jost Amman (cat. nr. 193); Hans Strauch; and Hans Hoffmann. Although Hoffman is better known for his copies after Dürer, he was a talented portraitist, as seen in his drawing *Paulus Pfinzing* (cat. nr. 208). This sketch was made in 1591 while Hoffmann was one of Emperor Rudolf II's court painters at Prague. Since it was probably Hoffmann's last portrait before he died in 1591 or 1592, it reveals less of Neufchâtel's specific influence than the continuous inroads of Netherlandish art in both Nuremberg and Prague.

The artistic changes of the last decades of the century are evident when Neufchâtel's *Wenzel Jamnitzer* is compared with Lorenz Strauch's *Christoph Jamnitzer* (Nuremberg, Germanisches Nationalmuseum) dated 1597 (fig. 42).[8] Lorenz (1554–1632), son of Hans, was less successful in conveying the power and intellect of the younger Jamnitzer, who was Wenzel's grandson and one of Nuremberg's most innovative later artists. The face is broad and strangely masklike when contrasted with the careful modeling in Wenzel's face. Where Neufchâtel lavished attention upon the structure and detailing of Wenzel's robe and the table covering, Strauch's depiction of his sitter's costume was shapeless, although it did show the local adoption of the Span-

41. Nicolas Neufchâtel, *Portrait of Wenzel Jamnitzer*, ca. 1565, Geneva, Musée d'Art et d'Histoire.

42. Lorenz Strauch, *Portrait of Christoph Jamnitzer*, 1597, Nuremberg, Germanisches Nationalmuseum, Gm. 1453.

ish black robe with ruffled lace collar then popular throughout much of Europe.[9] The overly flat wall and the window with its view of the Heathen's Tower next to the Imperial Chapel at the Burg do little to unify Strauch's composition.

Strauch's talents are more evident in his architectural views.[10] He specialized in creating faithful reproductions of buildings in Nuremberg and other cities. His designs were then transformed into engravings by various local artists. His *Hauptmarkt* of 1599 is the finest extant record of the arrangement of the main square and its buildings (fig. 5). Earlier Nuremberg masters Michael Wolgemut (cat. nr. 3) and Hans Lautensack (cat. nrs. 163 and 164) had created careful reproductions of the city's skyline. While Strauch developed from this tradition, his work more correctly belongs to the *veduta*, or topographical view, painting that became popular in Germany and, especially, in the Low Countries during the second half of the sixteenth century. These artists specialized in portraying major buildings and other architectural scenes within a city for commercial purposes. For instance, Strauch's 1621 *Rathaus* engraving celebrates the completion of the new western façade, an event of sufficient local and regional interest to guarantee sales of the print (fig. 8).

It is perhaps symptomatic of the general malaise in Nuremberg and German painting of the last quarter of the sixteenth century and in the early seventeenth century that there was a strong revival of interest in Dürer's art.[11] His paintings, drawings, and prints were avidly collected and duplicated. Much of Hans Hoffmann's reputation, then and now, rests upon his abilities to reproduce Dürer's paintings and drawings or to create new works in Dürer's manner. Andreas Gulden, who, around 1663, continued Neudörfer's biography of artists, claimed that Hoffmann was so successful in emulating Dürer's style that many of his own works passed for original Dürers.[12] Hoffmann may be responsible for several of the drawings of plants and insects that Winkler and other critics have long ascribed to Dürer.[13]

Hoffmann's talents are evident when his *Dead Blue Jay* drawing (Cleveland,

Museum of Art), which is signed and dated 1583, is compared with Dürer's 1512 watercolor, now in Vienna (Albertina), or when his *Hieronymus Holzschuher* painting (Nuremberg, Germanisches Nationalmuseum) of 1578 is contrasted with Dürer's 1526 panel, now in Berlin (Staatliche Museen).[14] The precise accuracy of his copies is very impressive.

Hoffmann's patrons were often local patricians who already possessed original paintings and drawings by Dürer. The prime example is Paulus Praun, who owned at least ten Dürer paintings and literally dozens of Hoffmann's paintings and drawings, including the *Hieronymus Holzschuher* and the *Ecce Homo* painting, which can likely be identified as the picture now in Nieborow in Poland.[15] In 1585 Emperor Rudolf II, perhaps the most avid Dürer collector, engaged Hoffmann as a court painter at Prague specifically because of his abilities to reproduce Dürer's style.[16]

After Hoffmann's death in 1591 or 1592, other Nuremberg masters continued to duplicate Dürer's work. In 1607 Archduke Maximilian I commissioned Frederick van Valckenborch (ca. 1570–1623), who was a member of a famous family of Flemish landscapists, and Paul Juvenel the Elder (1579–1643) to reproduce the middle panel of Dürer's *Heller Altarpiece*, now lost but then in the Dominikanerkirche in Frankfurt.[17] Although their version does not survive either, another copy, by their colleague Jobst Harrich (ca. 1580–1617), is today in Frankfurt (Historisches Museum).[18] After Hoffmann, Georg Gärtner the Younger (ca. 1575/80–1654) was the best of the Dürer copyists. Certain of Gärtner's paintings, such as his *Man of Sorrows* (Göttingen, Kunstsammlung der Universität), are valuable records of lost works by Dürer.[19] Gärtner also painted the version of Dürer's *Four Apostles* that is now in Nuremberg (Germanisches Nationalmuseum; see fig. 26).[20]

Of this latter group of artists, only Paul Juvenel the Elder achieved real prominence in Nuremberg. His true talents lay not in reproducing Dürer's pictures but in painting large decorative cycles on the ceilings and façades of patrician houses or in the Rathaus. In 1607 Martin Peller commissioned Juvenel to paint the ceiling of the Schöne Zimmer (beautiful chamber) in his just-completed townhouse (see figs. 13 and 14).[21] This ceiling, now in the Fembohaus, consists of twenty-one pictures set amid a richly carved wooden frame (fig. 43). The central scene shows the *Fall of Phaeton*, the same subject Georg Pencz painted for the ceiling of the Hirschvogelhaus in 1534 (fig. 33). Whereas Pencz's depiction of this mythological tale filled the entire ceiling, Juvenel placed it at the center of a more elaborate cosmological program that includes the four elements, Venus (left), Luna (right), and, in the corners, Mercury, Mars, Jupiter, and Saturn. Juvenel's solution lacks the dramatic composition and the carefully foreshortened figures found in Pencz's painting, but this commission occurred early in Juvenel's career, while Pencz's work reflects the style of a mature master.

Between about 1612 and 1615, Juvenel traveled to Italy to complete his training. He sought to improve his skill in foreshortened figures by examining decorative cycles in both Rome and Mantua. His subsequent fame as a perspective painter is one clear result of this trip.[22] Juvenel also studied the landscapes of German expatriate Adam Elsheimer (1578–1610) while in Rome.

His production after returning to Nuremberg was more successful. He was immediately involved in the restoration and repainting of parts of the great hall of the Rathaus. His painted view of the great hall (cat. nr. 213) is the only record of the room's decoration before the major changes begun in 1619. In 1622 he received 400 florins for painting the ceiling of the Schönen Saal (beautiful chamber) of the Rathaus with scenes from Roman history glorifying personal sacrifices for the good of the country.[23]

Juvenel was the finest of the many artists who painted elaborate mythological and historical cycles on the façades of patrician houses. Nuremberg's long-standing fame in this form of decoration, already seen in the 1520 program at the Rathaus (fig. 9), was commented upon by many visitors. For instance, after a trip to Nuremberg, French jurist Jacques Esprinchard (1573–1604) wrote, "The houses of the city are almost all painted on the exteriors, and that is to say nothing of their magnificence."[24] Some local citizens, such as Wolf Jakob Stromer, who was the city *baumeister* from

43. Paul Juvenel the Elder, *The Fall of Phaeton*, ceiling painting formerly in the Pellerhaus, ca. 1607, Nuremberg, Fembohaus (Stadtgeschichtliches Museen); photo taken between 1934 and 1936.

1597 until 1614, criticized many of the new patrician houses and their painted façades as too ostentatious.[25]

Although Juvenel's actual paintings have long since disappeared, his drawings for the Meierhaus (Hauptmarkt 26) and the Viatishaus (Königstrasse 2) are still extant (fig. 44).[26] Bartholomaus Viatis, one of Nuremberg's wealthiest merchants, erected a large new house by the banks of the Pegnitz River between 1615 and 1620. Juvenel's program reveals both the artist's strengths and weaknesses. The doorway is transformed into a triumphal arch with winged victories. The story of Judith and Holophernes, with the Battle of Betulia, extends across the entire façade. The Fall of Phaeton and Neptune driving his chariot fill the large registers above, while below are scenes of Diana and Acteon and the Justice of Trajan. The Labors of Hercules, the exploits of Samson, various depictions of birds and animals, and series of decorative patterns complete the cycle. Juvenel was able to create powerful figures and dramatic scenes that individually must have been extremely attractive. Yet, either because of his patron's wishes or due to his own volition, the overall program is not linked by a readily apparent theme or by design. The façade lacks a coherent unity; Juvenel concentrated instead on the individual compositions.

The importance of Juvenel, Gärtner, and the other Nuremberg painters at this time was strictly local. The innovative late Mannerist styles of Bartholomäus Spranger (1546–1611), Hans von Aachen (1552–1615), or Johann Rottenhammer (1564–1625), artists working in Prague, Munich, and Augsburg, had comparatively little influence on the mainstream of Nuremberg painting.[27] By the 1620s Nuremberg was becoming increasingly conservative and provincial in its artistic tastes. Even the pedagogical activities of Joachim von Sandrart (1606–1688), who had studied with Rembrandt and spent many years working in Italy, did little to slow the city's decline.

B. PRINTS

When, in 1967, Konrad Oberhuber selected German printmakers for an exhibition in Vienna of European graphics between 1540 and 1600, half of the twenty

44. Paul Juvenel the Elder, *Design for the Painted Façade of the Viatishaus*, drawing, between 1615 and 1620, Nuremberg, Fembohaus (Stadtgeschichtliches Museen).

masters were from Nuremberg.[28] Two observations can be drawn from the choice of the artists and the prints for this exhibition: first, Nuremberg remained by far the most active print center in Germany; and second, the quality of German graphics slipped dramatically after the passing of Dürer, Hans Burgkmair, and *kleinmeisters* Pencz and the two Behams. There were, of course, three outstanding exceptions: Tobias Stimmer (1539–1584) of Strassburg and Nuremberg artists Hans Lautensack and Jost Amman.[29]

Other capable, though lesser, graphic artists also lived in Nuremberg. Erasmus Hornick, Bernhard Zan, Matthias Zündt, and Paul Flindt the Younger devoted most of their energies to designing models and decorative patterns for local goldsmiths. Representative examples of their prints and drawings are included in this exhibition. Zündt's *Apostle Ship* (cat. nr. 185) is one of the artist's finest nondecorative prints. Virgil Solis, long considered one of Germany's greatest printmakers, is ultimately less significant than either Lautensack or Amman.[30] During his career, Solis created over two thousand prints, including a vast number of book illustrations for Frankfurt publisher Sigmund Feyerabend. Not surprisingly, the quality of his prints is extremely uneven, especially since he made active use of Balthasar Jenichen and other shop assistants. Solis squandered his obvious technical and creative talents by succumbing to trade demand for his prints. He has no great or master prints, for only rarely did he devote the time to produce a first-rate design.

Lautensack and Amman concerned themselves much more with artistic problems than did Solis. Lautensack, active mainly in the 1550s, is best known for his landscape and portrait etchings. He is Germany's last significant landscape artist until Adam Elsheimer's brief career. In *Landscape with Workers in a Vineyard* (cat. nr. 169) or *Landscape with a Town on a River* (cat. nr. 165), Lautensack displays the mossy wind-swept trees and pantheistic sense inherent in the Danube school of landscapists that included Altdorfer, the Elder Cranach, Jörg Breu, and Wolf Huber.[31] Like his colleague Augustin Hirschvogel, a Nuremberg expatriate, Lautensack stands at the end of this earlier German landscape style and at the beginning of a new trend then being developed in Antwerp and other Flemish towns.[32] The atmospheric feeling and quick, deft strokes defining the trees and countryside in his *Landscape with a*

Town recall Pieter Bruegel the Elder's early landscape prints and drawings made during the 1550s.[33] Lautensack, however, could never match Bruegel's mood and animation of natural forms.

While the majority of Lautensack's landscapes represent imaginary settings, he was also a skilled view painter as demonstrated in his magnificent 1552 etched prospects of Nuremberg from the east (cat. nr. 163) and the west (cat. nr. 164). Like Wolgemut, Erhard Etzlaub, or Hans Wurm before him, Lautensack offered a detailed portrait of the city.[34] Each of the principal churches and buildings was accurately reproduced and located. Not only are Lautensack's views more panoramic than those of his predecessors, but he also included local citizens working in the fields, strolling in the countryside, or stopping to watch the artist sketching. By including himself and a group of onlookers on a knoll just west of Nuremberg, Lautensack successfully pulls the viewer into the composition. This is also an unusually early example of an artist showing himself working directly from nature. The motif of the artist sketching can be found in Bruegel's *Alpine Landscape* drawing (London, Courtauld Institute Galleries, Count A. Seilern Collection) of about 1555; otherwise, it is relatively rare until the end of the sixteenth century.[35] The significance of these Lautensack views is twofold: these are the finest city portraits made in Germany during the sixteenth century and the artist has created two vivid encomia to Nuremberg's prosperity, telling more about the city than most of the lengthy written eulogies.

Lautensack's talents as a portraitist are evident in his etchings *Georg Roggenbach* (cat. nr. 167) or *Hieronymus Schürstab* (cat. nr. 166). If these prints lack the penetrating impact of some of Dürer's portrait engravings, they still admirably convey both the likeness and stature of each sitter. Lautensack's frequent use of a landscape view behind the sitter often has a specific purpose. For instance, Schürstab was the major benefactor of the church of St. Leonhard located just outside Nuremberg, which can be seen in the background of his portrait. In other cases, the artist sets his sitters within elaborate scrolled frames. His portrait of his father, *Paul Lautensack*, of 1552 is a direct forerunner to vivid, framed portrait engravings, such as *Dirk Volkertsz. Coornhert* of 1590, by Hendrik Goltzius (1558–1617), working in Haarlem.[36]

Although Jost Amman lacked Lautensack's skills as a landscapist and portraitist, he was a much more versatile printmaker.[37] Born and trained in Zurich, in 1561 Amman arrived in Nuremberg, where he worked briefly with Virgil Solis until the latter's death in 1562. Amman assumed many of Solis's activities, especially his book illustration work for Feyerabend (cat. nr. 194). Amman was as prolific as Solis, yet he managed to produce a corpus of significant prints that establishes him as Germany's finest graphic artist of the second half of the sixteenth century.

As did Lautensack, Amman created several attractive portraits with the sitter placed within elaborate scrolled frames. His 1573 *Gaspar de Coligny* shows the French admiral and Huguenot martyr proudly posed.[38] The surrounding allegorical figures, such as Caritas, refer to his character. Below, Amman represents the slaughter of the Huguenots and Coligny's death during the St. Bartholomew's Eve Massacre (24 August 1572). The print thus provides considerable information about Coligny and his support for the Protestant cause in France, a topic of great interest in Protestant areas of Germany. In *Wenzel Jamnitzer in His Studio* (cat. nr. 191), Amman portrays his friend and frequent collaborator engaged in a geometric calculation. Amman successfully conveys the serious, scholarly nature of the Nuremberg goldsmith. This print also reveals the influence of the portraits of Nicolas Neufchâtel, discussed earlier (cf. figs. 40 and 41).

Amman and Jamnitzer worked together on several occasions. Using Jamnitzer's drawings, Amman produced the title page and elaborate geometric forms in Jamnitzer's *Perspectiva Corporum Regularium* (Nuremberg, 1568; cat. nr. 197). Jamnitzer's sketches were also the source for Amman's *Apotheosis of Emperor Maximilian II* and its pendant, the *Triumph of the Christian Church*, both dated 1571, which are among his greatest prints.[39]

Lautensack's views of Nuremberg may have inspired Amman's *Display of Fireworks on the Castle of Nuremberg* (cat. nr. 192). Amman communicates the excitement of the spectators as they watch the exploding rockets. The rearing horses and barking dogs add to the commotion. By using a low horizon line, Amman draws the viewer into the field north of Nuremberg. Even more than in Lautensack's views, Amman develops a strong sense of immediacy.

Amman's ability to organize diverse scenes coherently is evident in his most complex print, the *Allegory of Commerce* (cat. nr. 195), dating about 1585. This woodcut is extremely large, measuring 87.5 × 60.3 cm. Mercury, the god of trade, oversees this elaborate exposition of the various aspects of commerce. Dozens of small scenes show the mining for metals, the transportation of goods, and the inherent risks of business. By using strong horizontal divisions, such as that separating the landscape scenes from the large trading establishment outlined below, and the vertical thrusts of Fortune's fountain, Amman develops a balanced, organized composition that in a lesser artist's hands would have quickly become chaotic.

Whether working on a large scale, such as in the *Allegory of Commerce*, or in the more modest sized *Daughter of Jephthah* drawing (cat. nr. 196), Amman maintains high quality and technical perfection. Even his mass-produced book illustrations never sink to the substandard level of Solis's. Yet, for all his artistic success, Amman died a poor man in 1591. Perhaps his economic plight discouraged other talented Nuremberg artists, because, with his death, Nuremberg's great era of prominence in the graphic arts ended.

C. ARCHITECTURE

Nuremberg's architecture continued to be extremely old-fashioned up until the 1590s. Hans Dietmair's Herrenschiesshaus, the shooting house for the local archers' organization, built in 1582–1583 with a tall balanced façade and modest scroll gable, is an exception.[40] More typical are such houses as the 1612 Hertelshof (Paniersplatz 9) or the 1590 Toplerhaus (Unter Söldnersgasse 17), which continue using Gothic decorative forms.[41] The Toplerhaus is particularly bizarre (fig. 12). The rhythmic regularities of the two façades are overlaid with repeated Gothic *chörleins* (oriel or bay window) and the high, multicolumned gable. This tall finial gable can be found on the eastern façade of the great hall of the Rathaus, built in 1332–1340, and in numerous other intermediary structures, including the garden façade of the Tucherhaus, built between 1533 and 1544.[42]

A vestige of this local taste for tall gables linked by columns is still apparent in the first really modern private house in Nuremberg: the Fembohaus, which today serves as the Stadtmuseum (fig. 10).[43] Netherlandish merchant Philipp van Oyrl commissioned a local architect, generally believed to have been Jakob Wolff the Elder, to design and erect a new residence in 1591. Construction was completed in 1600. The later-added stone *chörlein* (1680–1685) and the doorway (1735), seen in the photograph, disturb the harmony of Wolff's façade, yet the proportional balance is still evident. The decoration of the lower stories is limited to the large window frames. This simplicity contrasts with repeating horizontal stringcourses, the columns that link the upper stories, and the elaborate gable with its convex C-scroll and rusticated obelisk finials and urns. The triangular thrust of the roof culminates in the statue of Fortune. Here the Gothic holdovers found on the Toplerhaus have been banished.

Wolff's conservative use of these modern decorative motifs, as seen in the Fembohaus, disappeared when he designed the opulent Pellerhaus, which is Nuremberg's most important private residence (figs. 13, 14, and 43).[44] At Martin Peller's order, Wolff erected the house between 1602 and 1607. Wolff's original plan was even more Italianate than the completed building, but Peller's neighbors objected to it since it did not match the Gothic or early Renaissance styles of their houses.[45] The three lower stories are covered with a heavy rustication that is broken only by the projecting fluted pilasters of the *chörlein* and the balustrade above. The complex gable is far more imposing, if less legible, than that of the Fembohaus. The three orders (Ionic, Corinthian, and Tuscan), the tall obelisks, the caryatids, and the scalloped pediment and scroll work bring to mind the architectural designs of Cornelis Floris of Antwerp. Floris's forms, seen in the Antwerp City Hall, were widely disseminated in his *Weeldeley Niewe Inventien van Antycksche* (Antwerp, 1557) and in Hans Vredeman de Vries's *Architectura* (Antwerp, 1563).[46] Floris's influence can be observed in the later sixteenth-century city halls of Bremen and other northern German towns.[47] In Nuremberg, Floris's motifs were occasionally used by goldsmith Wenzel Jamnitzer, among others.

The interior courtyard of the Pellerhaus, added in 1607–1608, is just as elaborate as the façade. The three stories of galleries and the lavishly carved gable have more in common with contemporary palaces than with the other houses in Nuremberg. However, in spite of Wolff's obvious advances, the courtyard is overly busy, and modest Gothic tracery work has reappeared in the balustrades.

This trend in Nuremberg architecture toward even greater decoration was thoroughly rejected by Wolff's son, Jakob the Younger, who between 1616 and 1622 built the western wing and façade of the Rathaus.[48] Unlike the city halls of most German towns, the one in Nuremberg is not set on a large square. It is thus difficult to see and certainly less imposing than it would have been given a better site. Lorenz Strauch's 1621 engraving of the Rathaus provides the best view (fig. 8).

The Nuremberg Rathaus follows the new, more classicizing trend in northern European architecture. This is one of the earliest Palladian or academic-style structures north of the Alps. Before Palladio's architecture appeared in Inigo Jones's Queen's House at Greenwich (1616–1635) or the 1619–1622 Banqueting House at Whitehall in London, Augsburg architect Elias Holl had constructed several buildings based upon Palladio's own structures and his ideas as expressed in his *Quattro libri dell' architettura* (Venice, 1570).[49] Holl's Stadtmetzg (1609), Gymnasium St. Anne (1613–1615), Neuer Bau (1614), and the new Augsburg Rathaus (1615–1620) provided Jakob Wolff the Younger with a new architectural vocabulary of classical forms and balanced designs.[50] Wolff may have had a first-hand knowledge of some of Palladio's buildings since the city council sent him to Italy prior to 1616 to study current architectural styles.

The Nuremberg Rathaus façade is characterized by its clean lines and strong symmetrical harmony. The façade is long and low, as opposed to Holl's much taller Augsburg Rathaus. The three towers and three portals create a five-part rhythm that unifies the façade. The horizontal thrust of the building is emphasized by the strong stringcourses and the cornice and balustrade of the roof. The massive ground floor is ornamented only by the three portals and small square windows. The upper two floors share the regular fenestration set at very close intervals though the third floor has alternating rounded and pointed pediments. Wolff abandoned the intricate decorative style used by most previous Nuremberg architects.

Wolff's Rathaus façade is an important contribution to the nascent German Baroque. Wolff and Holl helped to end what one might term the tyranny of the Gothic style in German architecture. Architectural forms of the Renaissance can be found in the work of Nuremberg painters, sculptors, and printmakers, notably the Vischer family, Flötner, Pencz, and Wenzel Jamnitzer. However, Nuremberg's architects were remarkably slow in following their initiative or that of several other German cities. While the attractive late-sixteenth and early-seventeenth century townhouses, especially those built by Jakob Wolff the Elder, can be considered Renaissance structures, Nuremberg's architecture largely went directly from the Gothic to the Baroque.

D. SCULPTURE

Just as Nuremberg had very little civic and no religious architecture during the second half of the sixteenth and the opening years of the seventeenth centuries, the city sponsored little large-scale sculpture. Nuremberg has nothing similar to Hans Steinmüller's statues *Christ and the Apostles* (1585–1586) in Sts. Ulrich and Afra in Augsburg, Hans Reichle's *St. Michael Vanquishing Lucifer* (1603–1606) on the Augsburg Arsenal, or Hubert Gerhard's sculptures for St. Michael's in Munich of the late 1580s.[51] Rather, Nuremberg's patrician patrons continued to favor small bronzes and cabinet pieces, such as those made by Hans Jamnitzer (cat. nrs. 200–203), Benedikt Wurzelbauer (cat. nr. 209), or Johann Gregor van der Schardt.

Van der Schardt (1530–after 1581) was one of Germany's finest sculptors during the 1570s.[52] He was born in Nijmegen (Gelderland) and studied during the 1560s in Rome and, probably, Florence. Although little is known about his early career, both Guicciardini (1566) and Vasari (1568) praise his talents. By 1568 Van der Schardt was in Venice, where in the following year he began working for Emperor Maximilian II.

By 1570 van der Schardt had settled in Nuremberg. In that year Willibald Imhoff paid him for producing a life-size terra-cotta portrait bust, which is now in Berlin (Staatliche Museen; fig. 45).[53] Van der Schardt's portrait of Imhoff is the best extant example of his work. Imhoff (1519–1580), Willibald Pirckheimer's nephew, was an avid art and jewelry collector, a point the sculptor stressed in his portrait as Van der Schardt sought to capture the essential character of his patron. Shown staring intently at a large ring in his left hand, Imhoff is the consummate connoisseur evaluating the merits and beauty of the ring.

Most sixteenth-century portrait busts lack the relaxed, introspective quality that characterizes van der Schardt's work. More typical is the impassive stare of Conrad Meit's terra-cotta bust *Charles V* (Bruges, Gruuthuse Museum) of 1520, which van der Schardt might have known since he was trained in the Netherlands.[54] In the 1530s Matthes Gebel of Nuremberg and Christoph Weiditz of Augsburg created portrait busts that again show the sitters looking out toward or beyond the viewer.[55] Twenty years later either Dietrich Schro of Mainz or Nuremberg medalist Joachim Deschler produced the exquisite, if tiny (about 16 cm tall), half-length bust *Ottheinrich, Count Palatine* (Paris, Louvre).[56] Although the German portrait busts are far less idealized than the classically inspired bust *Ottavio Grimani* (Berlin, Staatliche Museen), which Venetian master Alessandro Vittoria carved in about 1576, none matches the realism of van der Schardt's *Willibald Imhoff* with its raised arm and lifelike painted surfaces.[57]

Van der Schardt's art is instead closer in spirit to the better paintings of fellow Netherlandish expatriate Nicolas Neufchâtel (figs. 40 and 41).[58] The quiet intimacy of the geometry lesson in Neufchâtel's *Johann Neudörfer and His Son* and the creative energy reflected in *Wenzel Jamnitzer* are matched by the intense concentration of *Willibald Imhoff*. Both masters impart the essential characters of their sitters in a dignified yet unpretentious manner. The artists have conformed the essential features of their Netherlandish training to the bourgeois tastes of Nuremberg's patrons. That the pair knew each other is confirmed by a Neufchâtel portrait of the sculptor once in the local collection of Paulus Praun (1548–1616).[59]

If Imhoff was van der Schardt's first Nuremberg patron, Praun was his most important one, for Praun possessed the largest art collection in Nuremberg. Besides the 1580 portrait medallion of Praun now in Stuttgart (Landesmuseum), van der Schardt created most of the 171 clay statues after classical sculptures in Rome and Florence recorded in the inventory of Praun's holdings.[60] Whether Praun sent van der Schardt back to Italy or whether the artist simply relied on his own earlier sketches and whatever contemporary models he could obtain is not clear. Praun owned many of Giovanni Bologna's small bronzes, which may have inspired van der Schardt's two *Mercury* statues in Stockholm (National Museum) and Vienna (Kunsthistorisches Museum) or his *Pallas Athena* in London (private collection).[61] Van der Schardt's bronzes share the elegant elongation and twisting rhythms of Giovanni Bologna's powerful form of Mannerism. Interestingly, van der Schardt's bronzes are wholly different in style from his more subdued portrait busts and medallions. Giovanni Bologna (1529–1608), the Netherlandish artist who became Florence's leading sculptor, seems to be the common thread linking van der Schardt's bronzes with those of Adrian de Vries (ca. 1560–1626), the last great Mannerist sculptor who was trained in The Hague and in Bologna's workshop in Florence before working for Rudolf II in Prague.[62]

Many of van der Schardt's bronzes were cast by Georg Labenwolf (active 1559–1585) and his pupil Benedikt Wurzelbauer (1548–1620).[63] Labenwolf and Wurzelbauer were the latest in the long succession of talented bronze founders, from the Vischers onward, active in Nuremberg. While most of their production involves casting after other artists' models, Wurzelbauer, in particular, created some of his own designs.

Wurzelbauer was also responsible for the erection of the *Fountain of the Virtues* (1583–1589), the only significant civic sculptural commission of the entire second

45. Johann Gregor van der Schardt, *Portrait Bust of Willibald Imhoff*, terra cotta, 1570, Berlin (West), Skulpturengalerie, Staatliche Museen Preussischer Kulturbesitz.

46. Benedikt Wurzelbauer (after the wooden models of Johannes Schünnemann), *The Fountain of the Virtues*, 1583–1589, adjacent to St. Lorenz.

half of the sixteenth century (fig. 46).[64] The fountain is set just to the north of the west façade of St. Lorenz. Although little-known Dutch(?) sculptor Johannes Schünnemann is credited with carving the wooden figure models, Wurzelbauer probably produced the initial design.[65] His signature is proudly inscribed on the completed bronze fountain.

The three-tiered fountain's compact, intricate design is strikingly similar to then-current Nuremberg goldsmith work, notably that by Wenzel Jamnitzer and his followers.[66] Crowning the fountain is the figure of Justice. Immediately below are trumpet-playing putti, who hold the city's coats of arms. Beneath the putti are the female personifications of Faith, Hope, Charity, Fortitude, Patience, and Temperance. A comparison of these statues with the finial, or base, figures on Jamnitzer's *Kaiserpokal*, or *Emperor's Cup* (Berlin, Kunstgewerbemuseum), dating before 1572, reveals that Wurzelbauer has adopted the general arrangement, specific strapwork decorative motifs, and something of the figure types from his goldsmith colleague (fig. 50). Wurzelbauer's women are, however, shorter, less curvaceous, and cruder in appearance than Jamnitzer's female figures, such as Mother Earth from the *Merkel Table Decoration* or the frontispiece of his *Perspectiva Corporum Regularium* (Nuremberg, 1568; cat. nr. 197; fig. 48).

Conceivably, Wurzelbauer was so accustomed to working on a small scale that he was totally unable to conceive a powerful, monumental design. His fountain, while very attractive, is extremely old-fashioned when compared with Hubert Gerhard's contemporary *Augustus Fountain* (1589–1594), formerly in Augsburg, in which the large statue of Augustus dominated and projected outward in all directions.[67] Gerhard is responding to Giovanni Bologna's *Neptune Fountain* (1563–1567) in Bologna or Bartolommeo Ammanati's *Neptune Fountain* (1560–1575) in Florence.[68] While Wurzelbauer demonstrably borrowed models (see cat. nr. 209) from Giovanni Bologna, he never understood this artist's intentions. In this respect Wurzelbauer's *Fountain of the Virtues* can be equated with the Toplerhaus and other contemporary patrician residences in Nuremberg that occasionally utilize Renaissance and Mannerist forms without fully comprehending the underlying artistic concepts (fig. 12).

Wurzelbauer's fountain would provide a fitting end to this study of the principal trends in Nuremberg sculpture since it is so closely associated with the table fountains designed by Dürer and his contemporaries early in the century. However, just as architect Jakob Wolff the Younger rejected the overly decorative style of his father in favor of the academic Palladian style, the portal statues on Wolff's west façade of the Rathaus reject the art of Wurzelbauer (fig. 8). In 1616–1617 Christoph Jamnitzer designed the portal decoration, and the actual carving was executed by Joachim Toppmann and Leonhard Kern.[69] Each portal is dominated by two principal figures. From north to south are the statues of Ninus and Cyrus, Prudence and Justice, and Alexander the Great and Caesar. The figures recline on the portal pediments, an arrangement used by Michelangelo for the *Medici Tombs* in S. Lorenzo in Florence and in dozens of other works during the sixteenth century. The powerful, muscular figures, if somewhat overladen with symbolic attributes, recall the more dynamic works by Giovanni Bologna, Hubert Gerhard, and Adrian de Vries, notably the last's *Hercules Fountain* (completed in 1602) in Augsburg.

That Nuremberg's sculptors were capable of creating important large-scale ensembles is demonstrated by the few monumental statues of the seventeenth century, such as Johann Wurzelbauer's bronze *Crucifix* (1625), now on the exterior of St. Sebaldus, or Georg Schweigger's *Neptune Fountain* (1660–1668).[70] However, the opportunity came all too rarely.

E. GOLDSMITH WORK

Although the quality of the various artistic trades in Nuremberg fluctuated from generation to generation, the city's goldsmiths exhibited a steady rise in prominence. The fame of the Krugs and Melchior Baier was soon eclipsed by Germany's greatest goldsmith, Wenzel Jamnitzer, and his host of talented followers.[71] From the late 1540s until the death of Christoph Jamnitzer in 1618, the artistic ideas generated in Nuremberg were widely emulated throughout central Europe. Just as Albrecht Dürer's paintings and prints encouraged artists in other cities to experiment, Wenzel

Jamnitzer was the catalyst behind the blossoming innovations produced in Augsburg and, later, in Dresden and Leipzig.

The analogy between Jamnitzer's and Dürer's careers is rather striking. Both understood the mechanics and the inherent potentials of their respective crafts as they strove for new solutions. Jamnitzer and Dürer based their art on the direct observation of nature mixed with a thorough grounding in the laws of mathematics. Dürer wrote his various treatises to educate his fellow artists in the theoretical bases of art. Jamnitzer was renowned as a mathematician and a geometrician. His principal treatise was the *Perspectiva Corporum Regularium* (Nuremberg, 1568; cat. nr. 197), a collection of his designs, etched by Jost Amman, showing elaborate perspectival projections of geometric forms. His title page, illustrated in the catalogue, pronounces that the successful artist must understand "Arithmetica, Geometria, Architectura, and Perspectiva"—sentiments exactly paralleling Dürer's. Indeed, Amman's *Wenzel Jamnitzer in His Studio* (cat. nr. 191) recalls Dürer's woodcuts at the end of his *Art of Measurement* (cat. nr. 31) representing artists using various scientific tools for aiding their perspective calculations. Jamnitzer not only was a student of Dürer's writings but was also an avid collector of his prints, possessing all of Dürer's prints in their first editions.

Comparatively little is known about Jamnitzer's production before his first great work, the *Merkel Table Decoration* (Amsterdam, Rijksmuseum), which the Nuremberg city council acquired in 1549 (figs. 47 and 48).[72] When he received his Nuremberg citizenship in 1534, he was already a trained master. He is likely to have learned his craft in Vienna, where he was born in 1508. He moved to Nuremberg with his brother Albrecht, an accomplished goldsmith who worked with Wenzel during much of his career.

The *Merkel Table Decoration* is shaped somewhat like a table fountain.[73] It consists of the caryatid figure of Mother Earth standing amid an abundance of grasses and tiny animals. She supports an elaborate bowl totally covered with foliate, scroll, strapwork decorations, and pendant putti. Inside the bowl are intricate patterns of

47. Wenzel Jamnitzer, *Merkel Table Decoration*, by 1549, Amsterdam, Rijksmuseum, RBK 17040.

48. Detail of fig. 47.

49. Wenzel Jamnitzer, *Design for the Merkel Table Decoration*, drawing, before 1549, Nuremberg, Germanisches Nationalmuseum, Hz. 5360.

Moresque designs, partially based upon Dürer woodcuts, and numerous miniature creatures. The finial is composed of a base with the busts of three nude women, an enamel urn, and more flowers and grasses cast from life.

Although the inscriptions on the bottom of *Merkel Table Decoration* state that the fruits of the earth can be placed in the bowl, it is highly unlikely that Jamnitzer ever intended his work to be functional.[74] Rather, it is purely decorative and a significant early German Renaissance example of art for art's sake; it was to be appreciated solely for its beauty. Although the city council probably commissioned the *Merkel Table Decoration* with the intention of presenting it as a gift to Emperor Charles V or perhaps his son, Philip II, as suggested by the blank shield to be filled in with the appropriate coat of arms at a later date, the council members retained it for their own enjoyment.[75] The *Table Decoration* remained in the Rathaus until 1806, when it was acquired by Paul Merkel of Nuremberg.[76]

The salient characteristics of Jamnitzer's style are already evident in this early masterpiece. The elegantly swaying figure of Mother Earth is among the first Mannerist sculptures produced in Germany (fig. 48). The strong contrapposto, elegant elongated lines, and clinging drapery are as advanced as those of Benvenuto Cellini. As seen in Jamnitzer's drawing for the *Merkel Table Decoration* (Nuremberg, Germanisches Nationalmuseum), Mother Earth was originally equally elaborate, but instead of being a caryatid figure she held a large cornucopia that supported the dish above (fig. 49).[77] The caryatid design is at once more classical and more exotic since it offers a wonderful contrast to the surrounding natural forms. The Mannerist delight in unusual juxtapositions and technical virtuosity has rarely been better expressed than here.

Although most Nuremberg goldsmiths relied on such sculptors as Peter Flötner or Johann Gregor van der Schardt to carve their wooden models, Jamnitzer is believed to have produced his own.[78] One of the wooden models for Mother Earth, though not the final one, is today in Berlin (Kunstgewerbemuseum). In Neufchâtel's *Portrait of Wenzel Jamnitzer*, the goldsmith is shown with a drawing of Neptune and the completed Neptune finial figure on the table before him as if to emphasize the artist's role in the creation of the work from beginning to end (fig. 41). This point is even more explicitly stated in Strauch's *Portrait of Christoph Jamnitzer*, in which Wenzel's grandson is represented carving the wax model (fig. 42). Furthermore, Wenzel's characteristic figure types reappear with little variation throughout his career, as for instance on the title page to his *Perspectiva Corporum Regularium* (cat. nr. 197) or in Spring, one of four caryatid figures (Vienna, Kunsthistorisches Museum) made before 1578 as the legs to a huge silver table fountain owned by Emperor Maximilian II.[79]

The figure of Mother Earth is surrounded by terrestrial abundance in the form of minute leaves, grasses, and tiny creatures. This design is both a brilliant iconographic solution and one of Jamnitzer's trademarks. While Flötner, not Jamnitzer, was the first Nuremberg artist to adopt the Paduan practice of casting directly from real grains or insects, Jamnitzer perfected the technique. The Cleveland *Mortar* (cat. nr. 198), by his workshop, provides a humble idea of his skill. Johann Neudörfer wrote admiringly about his good friends' talent: "Their [Wenzel's and his brother Albrecht's] skill in making castings of little animals, worms, grasses and snails in silver and decorating silver vessels therewith has never been heard of before and they have presented me with a whole silver snail, cast with all kinds of flowers and grasses around it; and the said flowers and grasses are so delicate and thin that they move when one blows on them."[80] Tiny silver lizards and grasses by Jamnitzer can be seen in Nuremberg (Germanisches Nationalmuseum) and Berlin (Kunstgewerbemuseum).[81] The silver vase in the niche at the rear of Neufchâtel's *Portrait of Wenzel Jamnitzer* is also filled with the artist's cast plants (fig. 41). This practice was soon emulated by goldsmiths throughout southern Germany.

Jamnitzer's superb technical abilities are evident in his fired and cold polychromed enameling and, especially, in his decorative forms.[82] Jamnitzer invented the goldsmith's roller stamp, a device that permitted a specific decorative motif to be reproduced repeatedly with no variation. A roller stamp was used for the geometric pattern on the inside lip of the dish of the *Merkel Table Decoration*. The triglyph and metope design that he adopted from Flötner and used so often in his goldsmith pieces can be seen on the outer lip of the dish in his drawing for the *Merkel Table Decoration* (fig. 49). Jamnitzer likewise popularized the use of scroll and strapwork decorative patterns, seen here, as well as a type of etched borders previously used only by contemporary armor makers (cf. cat. nr. 161).

Nuremberg goldsmiths had long specialized in creating sumptuous covered cups, such as the *Holzschuher Cup* by Baier and Flötner (fig. 39). Most of Jamnitzer's cups have disappeared; however, the *Kaiserpokal*, or *Emperor's Cup*, now in Berlin (Kunstgewerbemuseum), was certainly among his finest (fig. 50).[83] The *Kaiserpokal* was produced around 1565, at the order of the city council, to be presented to Maximilian II on some future occasion. The specific moment was likely the emperor's initial entry into Nuremberg on 7 June 1570.

The cup is decorated with finial figures of the emperor and, below, Albrecht V, Duke of Bavaria (1550–1579), the archbishop of Salzburg, and the bishops of Bamberg and Würzburg. The four virtues of Prudence, Faith, Hope, and Charity, adorning the base, recall the contrapposto and form of Mother Earth.

Jamnitzer's combination of cast statues in the round, relief casting, rollwork, and engraved decoration reveal the characteristic complexity of his style. In fact, as Hayward has observed, Jamnitzer's figures are highly Manneristic, his rollwork is purely classical, and the lobed foot of the cup is typically Gothic.[84] This delight in intentionally mixing styles typifies contemporary tastes for ambiguity.

Among Jamnitzer's most Manneristic works is the ewer in Munich (Residenz, Schatzkammer).[85] Jamnitzer has set a trochus shell in a richly enameled silver-gilt mount. The base depicts an eagle devouring a snail that rests on a bed of wiggling snakes. The spout and handle form a voluptuous harpy. Like the *Merkel Table Decoration*, the ewer was never intended to be functional. Rather, it is the sort of precious rarity, a blending of the natural and the man-made, eagerly collected for contemporary princely *kunstkammern* (art collections).

Jamnitzer also created collector's chests to house these wonder artifices and natural curiosities. Among his finest chests and jewelry caskets are the examples now in Munich (Residenz, Schatzkammer; ca. 1560), two in Dresden (Grünes Gewölbe; 1562 and a second completed before 1589 by his colleague Nikolaus Schmidt), Madrid (Convent of Descalzas Reales; made in 1570 for Emperor Maximilian II), and Berlin (Kunstgewerbemuseum; 1570s).[86] Closely related to the Berlin chest is the signed ebony chest now in Chicago (Martin D'Arcy Gallery, Loyola University of Chicago), the best example of Jamnitzer's art in the United States (fig. 51).[87] The exotic character of the design suggests that it was used to store jewelry and precious curios. The chest rests on four sphinxes and is decorated with silver-gilt figural reliefs, decorative plaques, footed pilasters and hermae, and semiprecious stones (lapis lazuli, feldspar, bloodstone, and amethyst quartz). Identical hermae, pilasters, and reliefs also appear on the Munich chest.

Since Jamnitzer's better works were destined for the major merchant and princely collections, his artistic and technical innovations were quickly disseminated throughout most of central Europe. Locally, he inspired the chests and writing cabinets produced by his son Hans, Hans Straub (active 1568–1610), and Hans (died 1585) and Elias Lencker (died 1591).[88] The Nuremberg city council valued Wenzel as one of the city's greatest citizens and bestowed him with many commissions and civic honors. In 1600 the city council paid 50 gulden to Hans Jamnitzer for a painted portrait of Wenzel, which was prominently hung alongside the portraits of German emperors and several of Dürer's civic paintings in the Regimentsstuben of the Rathaus.[89]

Hans Jamnitzer and Jonas Silber are among the most noteworthy of Wenzel's immediate followers. Hans made the attractive mother-of-pearl casket now in Stuttgart (Landesmuseum) and many small bronze plaques, including several in the present exhibition (cat. nrs. 200–203). Silber created similar plaques and numerous goldsmith designs. However, Silber is most famous for his last dated work, the 1589 *Weltallschale (World Dish) of Emperor Rudolf II* (Berlin, Kunstgewerbemuseum; fig. 52).[90]

Silber's *Weltallschale* is a good example of the intricate iconographic programs

50. Wenzel Jamnitzer, *Kaiserpokal* (*Emperor's Cup*), ca. 1565, Berlin (West), Kunstgewerbemuseum, Staatliche Museen Preussischer Kulturbesitz.

51. Wenzel Jamnitzer, *Collector's Chest*, 1570s,
Chicago, The Martin D'Arcy Gallery, Loyola
University of Chicago.

52. Jonas Silber, *Weltallschale* (*World Dish*) *of Emperor Rudolf II*, 1589, Berlin (West), Kunstgewerbemuseum, Staatliche Museen Preussischer Kulturbesitz.

occasionally found in Nuremberg goldsmith work. It is thought that Rudolf II devised the dish's symbolic content to express both the extent of the imperial realm and his specific importance. The base of this dish shows Adam and Eve beside the Tree of Life. The design loosely recalls the table fountains of Hans Frey or Baier's *Holzschuher Cup* (figs. 30 and 39). The trilobe base has reliefs representing the continents of Africa (an elephant), Asia (a camel), and America (a chimera). The allegorical figure of Europe, contorted to conform to the cartographic shape of the continent, is found on the interior of the dish. The underside of the dish is ornamented with stylized portraits of the emperor and the seven electors as well as the principal coats of arms of the empire. The twelve ancient kings and princes of Germany figure on the inside of the cover, the top of which is a map of the heavens. Finally, the figure of Christ as judge is perched on top of the arch of the firmament. Only one of the four pendant angels is still attached to this arch. Rudolf is presented as Christ's vicar on earth, elected by his subjects, and responsible for the empire's well-being.

At the end of the sixteenth century and the beginning of the seventeenth, Hans Petzoldt, Hans Kellner, Jörg Ruel, Melchior Königsmüller, Hans Beutmüller, Friedrich Hillebrandt, and Christoph Jamnitzer numbered among the many extraordinarily talented goldsmiths active in Nuremberg.[91] Works by several of these artists are included in the exhibition.

Petzoldt was the most prolific of these masters. Over forty works by him survive, and between 1595 and 1616 the Nuremberg city council commissioned at least eighty-four silver cups from him.[92] The *Ostrich Egg Cup* (dated 1594), now in Minneapolis (Institute of Arts), is a prime example of his style (fig. 53). The female term mounts, the scrollwork of the stem, and the warrior finial strongly recall Wen-

53. Hans Petzoldt, *Ostrich Egg Cup*, 1594, Minneapolis Institute of Arts, Christina N. & Swan J. Turnblad Fund.

54. Hans Petzoldt, *Dianapokal* (*Diana Cup*), ca. 1610, Berlin (West), Kunstgewerbemuseum, Staatliche Museen Preussischer Kulturbesitz.

zel Jamnitzer's art. The delicately painted ribbons and foliage together with the elegant terms mimic Roman decorative patterns.

A multiplicity of styles flourished during this period. Whereas the painters of Nuremberg resurrected the art of Albrecht Dürer, local goldsmiths developed a neo-Gothic style. Actually, Gothic elements persisted in such forms as the columbine cups that the goldsmiths required applicants to make for their masterpieces. The structural shape and lobated patterns of late Gothic cups are still evident in Petzoldt's famous *Dianapokal* (ca. 1610) in Berlin (Kunstgewerbemuseum; fig. 54).[93] While such trappings as the female masks, grotesques, and sirens recall contemporary goldsmith works, Petzoldt's *Dianapokal* has less in common with Wenzel Jamnitzer's *Kaiserpokal* than with the late fifteenth-century Nuremberg covered cups, such as those now in Budapest (Kunstgewerbemuseum) and Vienna (Kunsthistorisches Museum).[94]

The last of the important masters from this period is Christoph Jamnitzer, whose art also ranges from the neo-Gothic to the threshold of the Baroque. The intricate ewers in Dresden (Grünes Gewölbe) and Vienna (Kunsthistorisches Museum) or the bizarre hybrid forms of his *Neuw Grottessken Buch* (Nuremberg, 1610; cat. nr. 212) rank among the most unusual of all Mannerist creations.[95] The precious and esoteric tastes of the princely connoisseurs of the period are fully evident in Christoph's *Elephant Ewer* of about 1600, now in Berlin (Kunstgewerbemuseum; fig. 55).[96] This is Hannibal's war elephant at the Battle of Zama. Other scenes of Hannibal's fight

55. Christoph Jamnitzer, *Elephant Ewer*, ca. 1600, Berlin (West), Kunstgewerbemuseum, Staatliche Museen Preussischer Kulturbesitz.

against Scipio once figured on the now lost accompanying basin. The technical virtuosity, the sense of momentary action, and the lack of a single intended vantage point of the *Elephant Ewer* typify Christoph Jamnitzer's Mannerist sensibilities. However, at almost the same time, Jamnitzer was capable of creating the models for the monumental portal statues of the Nuremberg Rathaus and the coherent structure of his beautiful *Shell Dish with Milo of Crotona* (Nuremberg, Germanisches National-museum) of 1616.[97] The seeds of Nuremberg's Baroque period are fully evident in these works.

NOTES

1. There exists no thorough study of this later period of art beyond the general comments in some of the survey books listed below and a few exhibition catalogues, including *Aufgang der Neu-*

zeit: Deutsche Kunst und Kultur von Dürers Tod bis zum Dreissig; ährigen Krieg, 1530–1650, which has no text; *Barock in Nürnberg, 1600–1750;* Geissler, ed., *Zeichnung in Deutschland.*

2. R. A. Peltzer, "Nicholas Neufchâtel und seine Nürnberger Bildniss," *MJBK* N.F. 3 (1926): 187–231; K. Pilz, "Nürnberg und die Niederlande," *MVGN* 43 (1952): 72–76; Strieder, "Zur Nürnberger Bildniskunst des 16. Jahrhunderts," pp. 132–133; von der Osten and Vey, *Painting and Sculpture in Germany*, p. 310.

3. Peltzer, "Neufchâtel," nr. 21. On Neudörfer, see cat. nr. 164.

4. M. J. Friedländer, *Early Netherlandish Painting, VII. Quentin Massys*, ed. H. Pauwels (Leiden, 1971), nrs. 36–50.

5. Titian was in Augsburg from January to October 1548 and again in late 1550 until the summer of 1551. See *Welt im Umbruch: Augsburg zwischen Renaissance und Barock*, II: pp. 29–30, 139–148. Neufchâtel's portraits are particularly close to those of Giovanni Battista Moroni (died 1578). Compare Moroni's *Bernardo Spini* (Bergamo, Accademia Carrara) of about 1570 with Neufchâtel's full-length *Wolfgang Müntzer von Babenberg* (Nuremberg, Germanisches Nationalmuseum) of about 1565; see F. Boucher, *20,000 Years of Fashion: The History of Costume and Personal Adornment* (New York, n.d.), fig. 462; Peltzer, "Neufchâtel," nr. 25.

6. M. J. Friedländer, *Early Netherlandish Painting, XIII. Antonis Mor and His Contemporaries*, ed. H. Pauwels and G. Lemmens (Leiden, 1975).

7. Hayward, *Virtuoso Goldsmiths*, p. 64, pl. 5; Peltzer, "Neufchâtel," did not know of this painting, which was formerly attributed to Georg Pencz. Compare Neufchâtel's double portrait of Nuremberg goldsmith *Hans Lencker and His Son* (Copenhagen, Statens Museum), dated 1567; Peltzer, "Neufchâtel," nr. 17.

8. Hayward, *Virtuoso Goldsmiths*, p. 65, pl. 6; also see H. H. Mahn, *Lorenz und Georg Strauch*; *Barock in Nürnberg*, nr. A10.

9. Bucher, *20,000 Years of Fashion*, pp. 226–229.

10. Andresen, I: pp. 47–61; Mahn, *Lorenz und Georg Strauch*. For Strauch's 1614 view of the interior of the Hofkirche and Emperor Maximilian I's tomb, see Egg, *Die Hofkirche in Innsbruck*, p. 67. On the development of view painting, see the brief comments by Volkmar Schauz in Geissler, ed., *Zeichnung in Deutschland*, II: pp. 204–206; *The Dutch Cityscape in the 17th Century and Its Sources*, exh. cat. (Amsterdam: Historisch Museum, 1977).

11. H. Kauffmann, "Dürer in der Kunst und im Kunsturteil um 1600," and A. Ernstberger, "Kurfürst Maximilian I. und Albrecht Dürer," *AGNM* (1940–1953): 18–60, 143–196; Anzelewsky, *Dürer*, pp. 100ff.; G. Goldberg, "Zur Ausprägung der Dürer-Renaissance in München," *MJBK* 31 (1980): 129–175.

12. Neudörfer, *Nachrichten von Künstlern*, p. 198.

13. Talbot, ed., *Dürer in America*, p. 108.

14. On Hoffman, see K. Pilz, "Hans Hoffmann—Ein Nürnberger Dürer-Nachahmer aus der 2. Hälfte des 16. Jahrhunderts," *MVGN* 51 (1962): 236–272. For these comparisons, see H. S. Francis, "Drawing of a Dead Blue Jay by Hans Hoffmann," *Bulletin of the Cleveland Museum of Art* 34 (1947): 13–14, with Winkler, *Zeichnungen Dürers*, III: nr. 615; and Pilz, "Hoffmann," nr. 2, fig. 2, with Anzelewsky, *Dürer*, nr. 179.

15. De Murr, *Description du Cabinet de Monsieur Paul de Praun à Nuremberg*, for Dürer's work, see nrs. 81, 87–91, 119–120, 150, 156, plus prints and drawings; for Hoffmann, see nrs. 38, 128–148, 157, 226, 236–237, among other works.

16. Pilz, "Hoffmann," pp. 239–242; E. Fučikov, "Umělci na dvoře Rudolfa II a jejich vztah k tvorbe Albrechta Dürera," *Umeni* 20 (1972): 149–166, with summary in French.

17. Peltzer, ed., *Sandrarts Academie*, p. 136. On Valckenborch, see Geissler, ed., *Zeichnung in Deutschland*, I: pp. 203–206.

18. Anzelewsky, *Dürer*, text fig. 82.

19. Ibid., text figs. 95–96; Geissler, ed., *Zeichnung in Deutschland*, I: pp. 218–219.

20. Anzelewsky, *Dürer*, text figs. 118–119.

21. For comments on the architecture, see below. Also see Schaffer, *Das Pellerhaus in Nürnberg*.

22. Neudörfer, *Nachrichten von Künstlern*, p. 199, by Neudörfer's continuator Andreas Gulden.

23. Mummenhoff, *Das Rathaus in Nürnberg*, pp. 144–145, 292.

24. My translation after Mende, *Rathaus*, I: p. 410; for literature on façade painting in Nuremberg and southern Germany see ibid., p. 108.

25. Schwemmer, *Bürgerhaus*, p. 76.

26. *Barock in Nürnberg*, nrs. A 53–54.

27. Von der Osten and Vey, *Painting and Sculpture in Germany*, pp. 343–345; Geissler, ed., *Zeichnung in Deutschland* I: nrs. B9–12 (Spranger), B14–19 (Aachen), F9–12 (Rottenhammer).

28. K. Oberhuber, ed., *Die Kunst der Graphik IV: Zwischen Renaissance und Barock—Das Zeitalter von Bruegel und Bellange*, pp. 126–166.

29. Ibid., pp. 151ff. In this section, I have omitted any reference to the many lesser printmakers, *formschneiders*, and *briefmalers*. See the catalogue comments on Hans Glaser (cat. nr. 171) and see the general comments in Strauss, *The German Single-Leaf Woodcut, 1550–1600*, I–III.

30. Oberhuber, ed., *Zwischen Renaissance und Barock*, pp. 139ff.; I. O'Dell-Franke, *Kupferstiche und Radierungen aus der Werkstatt des Virgil Solis*; see the catalogue comments (cat. nrs. 172–178).

31. C. W. Talbot and A. Shestack, eds., *Prints and Drawings of the Danube School*; A. Strange, *Malerei der Donauschule*.

32. Ibid., pp. 88–93, and see Section 6, note 2, for literature on Hirschvogel. On the Netherlandish landscapes, see H. G. Franz, *Niederländische Landschaftsmalerei im Zeitalter des Manierismus*; M. Winner, ed., *Pieter Bruegel d. Ä. als Zeichner: Herkunft und Nachfolge*.

33. L. Münz, *Bruegel Drawings: A Complete Edition* (London, 1961), nrs. 1–22.

34. See cat. nr. 3; fig. 1; Zink, *Die Handzeichnungen*, nr. 107.

35. Münz, *Bruegel Drawings*, nr. 14. For general comments on artists sketching landscapes, see W. Stechow, *Dutch Landscape Painting of the Seventeenth Century* (London, 1966); J. C. Smith, ed., *Seventeenth-Century Dutch Landscape Drawings*, exh. cat. (Austin, Archer M. Huntington Art Gallery, 1982), pp. 3–4.

36. Oberhuber, ed., *Zwischen Renaissance und Barock*, nrs. 175, 313; also H. Mielke, *Manierismus in Holland um 1600*, nr. 41.

37. For information on Amman, see the catalogue comments (cat. nrs. 188–195).

38. Andresen, I: Amman nr. 2; Hollstein, II: p. 9.

39. Andresen, I: Amman nrs. 30–31; Hollstein, II: p. 14.

40. Schwemmer, *Bürgerhaus*, pls. 51, 96b.

41. Ibid., pls. 84 (Hertelshof), 65 (Topler), and see 86–87 for other examples. Also see Böllinger, *Das Toplerhaus in Nürnberg*.

42. Schwemmer, *Bürgerhaus*, pls. 54 a–b (Rathaus); Pfeiffer and Schwemmer, *Bilddokumenten*, fig. 80 (Tucherhaus).

43. Schwemmer, *Bürgerhaus*, pp. 71ff., figs. 66–73, pls. 92a–93; also see Hitchcock, *German Renaissance Architecture*, p. 250.

44. Schaffer, *Das Pellerhaus in Nürnberg*; Schwemmer, *Bürgerhaus*, pls. 67, 91c, 92b, 100, 103, 106d, 107b, 113b, 128a, 129, 131; Hitchcock, *German Renaissance Architecture*, pp. 304–306.

45. Christensen, "The Nuernberg City Council," p. 69.

46. Hitchcock, *Netherlandish Scrolled Gables of the Sixteenth and Early Seventeenth Centuries* (New York, 1978), pp. 50–52, figs. 45 (Antwerp, City Hall), 47–48.

47. Hitchcock, *German Renaissance Architecture*, pls. 376–378, and cf. 379–385.

48. Mummenhoff, *Das Rathaus in Nürnberg*, pp. 123–158, with general plans and plates at the end of the text; Hitchcock, *German Renaissance Architecture*, pp. 325–326, pl. 421.

49. Hitchcock, *German Renaissance Architecture*, pp. 309–327. On Jones, see J. Summerson, *Architecture in Britain, 1530–1830*, 6th rev. ed. (Harmondsworth, 1977), pp. 111–112, figs. 77–80, 88–90. On Palladio, see J. S. Ackerman, *The Architect and Society: Palladio*, 2d ed. (Harmondsworth, 1977).

50. Hitchcock, *German Renaissance Architecture*, pp. 314ff., pls. 404–405, 409, 413–416, 418.

51. Von der Osten and Vey, *Painting and Sculpture in Germany*, figs. 289–290; Hitchcock, *German Renaissance Architecture*, pls. 254, 256.

52. R. A. Peltzer, "Johann Gregor van der Schardt (Jan de Zar) aus Nymwegen, ein Bildhauer der Spätrenaissance," *MJBK* 10 (1916–1918): 198–216. Peltzer provides some additional biographical information, such as the artist's work for King Frederick II of Denmark.

53. *Berlin: Der Mensch um 1500*, nr. 5, and also see nr. 6, the 1580 portrait of Imhoff's wife, Anna Harsdörffer. I wish to thank Dr. Christian Theuerkauff for providing me with information about the Berlin statues. On Imhoff's art collection, which has been mentioned earlier in the text, see Springer, "Invertare der Imhoff'schen Kunstkammer zu Nürnberg," pp. 352–357.

54. *Charles-Quint et son Temps*, nr. 374, fig. 119.

55. Jahn, *Deutsche Renaissance*, pls. 141a, 142.

56. G. Kauffmann, *Die Kunst des 16. Jahrhunderts*, nr. 173 (Schro); *Berlin: Der Mensch um 1500*, fig. 21 (Deschler).

57. Kauffmann, *Die Kunst des 16. Jahrhunderts*, nr. 225. Peltzer, "van der Schardt," p. 211, also mentions the differences between these two artists. Peltzer also makes the interesting observation that van der Schardt's busts strongly anticipate those of Hendrik de Keyser (1565–1621), Amsterdam sculptor and architect. See J. Leeuwenberg and W. Halsema-Kubes, *Beeldhouwkunst in het Rijksmuseum* (Amsterdam, 1973), nrs. 223–233.

58. This observation is also made by Vey in von der Osten and Vey, *Painting and Sculpture in Germany*, p. 286.

59. De Murr, *Description du Cabinet de Monsieur Paul de Praun à Nuremberg*, nr. 72, and also see 39 (Hans Hoffmann's 1581 painted *Portrait of Johann Gregor van der Schardt*); Peltzer, "van der Schardt," p. 201.

60. E. F. Bange, "Ein Tonrelief des Johann Gregor van der Schardt," *MJBK* N.F. 1 (1924): 169–171, fig. 2; *Der Mensch um 1500*, fig. 23. De Murr, *Description du Cabinet de Monsieur Paul de Praun à Nuremberg*, pp. 230ff., 240; Peltzer, "van der Schardt," p. 201.

61. Peltzer, "van der Schardt," pp. 210–211, figs. 5–5A, 6. On Giovanni Bologna, see C. Avery and A. Radcliffe, *Giambologna, 1529–1608: Sculptor to the Medici*.

62. Von der Osten and Vey, *Painting and Sculpture in Germany*, pp. 326–327, figs. 287–288; Kauffmann, *Die Kunst des 16. Jahrhunderts*, pls. 257a–b.

63. H. Weihrauch, *Europäische Bronzestatuetten*, p. 324. On Georg Labenwolf, see E. W. Braun, "Nürnberger Bronzestatuetten aus der Werkstätte von Georg Labenwolf," *Kunst und Kunsthandwerk* 23 (1920): 129ff.; on Wurzelbauer, see cat. nr. 211.

64. Herkommer, "Heilsgeschichtliches Programm," esp. pp. 212–216.

65. Weihrauch, *Europäische Bronzestatuetten*, p. 329; Herkommer, "Heilsgeschichtliches Programm," p. 212.

66. Vey also noticed the strong association between the fountain's design and Nuremberg's

goldsmiths, especially Jamnitzer; von der Osten and Vey, *Painting and Sculpture in Germany*, pp. 323–324. He did not give any specific comparisons.

67. Ibid., pp. 324–325, fig. 286.

68. J. Pope-Hennessy, *Il Cinquecento e il Barocco* (Milan, 1966), I: figs. 94, 98.

69. Mummenhoff, *Das Rathaus in Nürnberg*, esp. pp. 134–135.

70. Schwemmer and Lagois, *Die Sebalduskirche zu Nürnberg*, p. 18; H. R. Weihrauch, "Georg Schweigger (1613–1690) und sein Neptunbrunnen für Nürnberg," *AGNM* (1940–1953): 87–142.

71. Superb research on German goldsmiths has been published by John Hayward and Klaus Pechstein in recent years. I have relied heavily on Hayward, *Virtuoso Goldsmiths*, and on numerous articles and catalogues by Pechstein, which are cited in the following notes and in the bibliography. I wish to thank Dr. Pechstein for discussing several issues with me.

72. Hayward, *Virtuoso Goldsmiths*, comments to pls. 416–420; Pechstein, "Der Merkelsche Tafelaufsatz von Wenzel Jamnitzer," *MVGN* 61 (1974): 90–121.

73. Compare Wenzel's *Drawing for a Table Fountain* (Coburg, Veste); Hayward, *Virtuoso Goldsmiths*, pl. 127.

74. Pechstein, "Der Merkelsche Tafelaufsatz," pp. 95–96.

75. Ibid., p. 99.

76. K. Pechstein, ed., *Paul Wolfgang Merkel und die Merkelsche Familienstiftung*, p. 33.

77. Pechstein, "Der Merkelsche Tafelaufsatz," pp. 94–95, with color plate. The drawing is inv. Hz. 5360.

78. Hayward, *Virtuoso Goldsmiths*, pp. 60, 64–65, which cites various reasons for Jamnitzer's activities as a model maker. Sandrart also praised Wenzel's ability to make wax models; see Peltzer, ed., *Sandrarts Academie*, p. 266. On the Berlin model, see Pechstein, *Goldschmiedewerke der Renaissance*, nr. 155.

79. Bange, *Die Deutschen Bronzestatuetten des 16. Jahrhunderts*, pl. 184, and see pls. 185–187 for the remaining seasons; von der Osten and Vey, *Painting and Sculpture in Germany*, fig. 254; for a good description, see Hayward, *Virtuoso Goldsmiths*, pp. 129–130.

80. Hayward, *Virtuoso Goldsmiths*, p. 208 (with the translations used in my text), and also see p. 12 on casting; Neudörfer, *Nachrichten von Künstlern*, p. 126. The best discussion of casting from live models is Pechstein, "Wenzel Jamnitzers Silberglocken mit Naturabgüssen," *AGNM* (1967): 36–43.

81. Pechstein, "Silberglocken," and *Bronzen und Plaketten von ausgehenden 15. Jahrhundert bis zur Mitte des 17. Jahrhunderts*, nrs. 134–138.

82. The material in this paragraph is based upon Hayward, *Virtuoso Goldsmiths*, pp. 53–54.

83. Pechstein, *Goldschmiedewerke der Renaissance*, nr. 100; Hayward, *Virtuoso Goldsmiths*, pls. 424, 426.

84. Hayward, *Virtuoso Goldsmiths*, pls. 424–426.

85. Ibid., p. 334, and color pl. XIII.

86. Ibid., pls. 427 (Munich), 428 (Dresden); *The Splendors of Dresden: Five Centuries of Art Collecting*, nr. 25 (1562 Dresden casket); K. Pechstein, "Jamnitzer-Studien," *Jahrbuch der Berliner Museen* 8 (1966): 263–283 (Madrid), and *Goldschmiedewerke der Renaissance*, nr. 89.

87. I wish to thank Fathers Donald F. Rowe and Leo J. Martin of the Martin D'Arcy Gallery for supplying me with photographs and information. See D. F. Rowe, *The First 10 Years: Notable Acquisitions of Medieval, Renaissance, and Baroque Art, the Martin D'Arcy Gallery of Art, the Loyola University Museum of Medieval and Renaissance Art* (Chicago, 1979), nr. 54.

88. Pechstein, *Goldschmiedewerke der Renaissance*, nr. 88 (Straub); Hayward, *Virtuoso Goldsmiths*, pls. 210–211 (Hans Jamnitzer), 491 (Lencker).

89. For specific information about his public honors, see the catalogue biography. The painting of Wenzel is mentioned in Mummenhoff, *Das Rathaus in Nürnberg*, p. 72.

90. A. Schönberger, "Die 'Weltallschale' Kaiser Rudolfs II," in *Studien zur Geschichte der Europäischen Plastik: Festschrift für Theodor Müller*, ed. K. Martin, pp. 253–262; Pechstein, *Goldschmiedewerke der Renaissance*, nr. 101; Hayward, *Virtuoso Goldsmiths*, pp. 216–217, pls. 474–475.

91. A general discussion of these later masters is given in Hayward, *Virtuoso Goldsmiths*, pp. 215–225; see Ruel's *Agate Cup* (Minneapolis Institute of Arts) and Beutmüller's *Standing Covered Cup* (Toledo Museum of Art), ibid., pls. 492, 487, for good examples of their work in the United States. Hillebrandt's most beautiful piece is the Neptune Nautilus-Shell Cup, dated 1595, in Nuremberg (Germanisches Nationalmuseum); see *Germanisches Nationalmuseum Nürnberg: Führer durch die Sammlungen*, nr. 380.

92. On Petzoldt (Petzolt), see appendix biography; Hayward, *Virtuoso Goldsmiths*, pp. 218–219, pl. 481.

93. Pechstein, *Goldschmiedewerke der Renaissance*, nr. 105, and cf. nr. 106, the *Grape Cluster Cup*. On the neo-Gothic style, see O. von Falke, "Die Neugotik im deutschen Kunstgewerbe der Spätrenaissance," *JPKS* 40 (1919): 75–92; Hayward, *Virtuoso Goldsmiths*, p. 219.

94. Kohlhaussen, *Nürnberger Goldschmiedekunst*, nrs. 352, 381.

95. Hayward, *Virtuoso Goldsmiths*, pls. 511–514; *The Splendors of Dresden*, nr. 265.

96. Pechstein, *Goldschmiedewerke der Renaissance*, nr. 102; Hayward, *Virtuoso Goldsmiths*, pl. 517; J. Hildebrand and C. Theuerkauff, *Die Brandenburgisch-Preussische Kunstkammer: Eine Auswahl aus den alten Beständen*, nr. 43.

97. K. Pechstein, "Eine unbekannte Entwurfsskizze für eine Goldschmiedeplastik von Christoph Jamnitzer," *ZfK* 31 (1968): 321, fig. 7.

Catalogue of Artists

Etzlaub was a compass maker, surveyor, cartographer, astronomer, designer of almanacs and horoscopes, and an amateur physician.[1] He was born in the house *zum Schachzagel* in Erfurt between 1455 and 1460. He matriculated at the University of Erfurt on 2 May 1468 and four years later entered the Collegium maius in Erfurt. First recorded in Nuremberg in 1484, when he was granted citizenship, Etzlaub is frequently mentioned in local records and contemporary correspondence. His wife's name was Ursula; they had no children. In 1507 he was referred to as the official city land surveyor. In this capacity, he created several parchment maps, including the *Imperial Forest around Nuremberg* of 1516 and the *Territory of the Imperial City of Nuremberg* of 1519.[2] In 1511 he was the captain, or civil defense coordinator, for the Haymarket quarter of the city. A self-taught physician, Etzlaub worked part-time as a practicing doctor from 1513 until his death in late January or early February 1532.

Etzlaub was a friend of Pirckheimer and other Nuremberg humanists. Johann Neudörfer offered the following description of Etzlaub:

My intention is not to write of clever or eloquent men or of those versed in medicine, but only of those cunning in the work of their hands, as this Etzlaub showed himself skilful and industrious in making compasses of many kinds. He was also an experienced astronomer, and depicted the country many miles round Nuremberg in a land-map printed by Georg Glockendon. What was held by my lords the Council in and around the city, in flowing waters, roads, tracks, towns, markets, villages, hamlets, woods, rights of jurisdiction, and other excellences, he showed forth for them in the district office in fair maps and pictures; he was the first who instructed me in "Coss" [Algebra]. He was lastly a physician and was held by common people in affection and esteem, and he had good fortune from his practice of medicine. He died without heirs.[3]

Etzlaub was Germany's finest compass maker and cartographer. His folding compasses, such as the 1511 example in Nuremberg (Germanisches Nationalmuseum), were used throughout the empire and as far away as Lisbon.[4] A compass similar to his is illustrated in Gualtherus Rivius's *Vitruvius teutsch* of 1548 (cat. nr. 136) with the inscription that the example shown was the "form and true counterfeit of the compass used in all navigation at this time."[5]

Etzlaub continued the succession of Nuremberg astronomers and cartographers.[6] Regiomontanus had worked in Nuremberg during the early 1470s. Martin Beheim designed and Georg Glockendon painted the *Erdapfel*, or *Earth Apple*, of 1492, the oldest extant terrestrial globe. Etzlaub certainly was familiar with the work of Hieronymus Münzer, who supplied the maps for the *Nuremberg Chronicle* (cat. nr. 3), and Johann Schöner. Etzlaub is credited with at least six printed or parchment maps, the most important of which is included in the exhibition.[7]

1. The following biographic information is drawn primarily from F. Schnelbögl, "Life and Work of the Nuremberg Cartographer Erhard Etzlaub (+1532)," *Imago Mundi—A Review of Early Cartography* 20 (1966): 11–26, esp. 11–14. The original German text of this article appeared in *MVGN* 57 (1970): 216–231.

2. Ibid., p. 20, nrs. 5, and 4. Both are in the Germanisches Nationalmuseum (S.P. 10419 and La. 1217); see Schnelbögl, *Dokumentie zur Nürnberger Kartographie*, pp. 56–59, with illustrations. The 1516 map was likely painted by his frequent collaborator printer Georg Glockendon. The 1519 map was painted by Nuremberg artist Michel Graf.

3. Schnelbögl, "Life and Work," p. 18. I have corrected the translation in places. Also see Neudörfer, *Nachrichten von Künstlern*, p. 172.

4. Schnelbögl, "Life and Work," p. 25.

5. Folio LII. Cited in ibid.

6. For a general survey, see Schnelbögl, *Dokumentie zur Nürnberger Kartographie*, esp. pp. 4–8, 50–53. He mentions that of the twenty-three incunabula maps, six were published in Nuremberg. The globes by Beheim and Schöner, mentioned below, are today in the Germanisches Nationalmuseum.

7. Schnelbögl, "Life and Work," pp. 18, 20.

1. ROAD MAP FOR CENTRAL EUROPE

ca. 1500
Printed by Georg Glockendon the Elder in
Nuremberg
Woodcut
40.2 × 28.5 cm
Lent by the National Gallery of Art, Washington, Rosenwald Collection, 1943

The correct title is *Das is der Rom weg von meylen zu meylen mit puncten verzeychnet von eyner stat zu der andern durch deutzsche lant* (or *This is the way to Rome mile by mile with points from one city to another through the German lands*).[1] Etzlaub created this map to assist travelers from northern Europe journeying to Rome for the Jubilee Year in 1500.[2] This map, like all of Etzlaub's printed maps and the fifteenth-century Cusanus-type maps, is oriented from south to north. The oldest published map of Germany,[3] it shows the principal cities, topographic features, and trade routes from Viborg in Denmark to Naples and from Cracow to Ypres and Narbonne. Nuremberg is situated at the center. The map encompasses latitudes 58° to 41° north. The scale is 1:5,300,000. Etzlaub has carefully calculated the distances between cities. Each dot on the designated routes stands for the distance of one common German mile (7,400 meters). Most towns are designated by simple circles, but a few important cities and pilgrimage sites are marked with small buildings or churches. The German names for the cities and topographic features are given.

Etzlaub designed the *Road Map for Central Europe* to be used with a compass.[4] At the bottom of the print is a small illustration of a compass and a detailed text telling the traveler how best to use the map. Ideally, the traveler would carry one of Etzlaub's finely crafted compasses, which were sold with instructions for the novice.[5]

Etzlaub's map was immediately successful. On 11 August 1500, Sebald Schreyer, humanist and superintendent of St. Sebaldus, sent Conrad Celtis a copy of this map. Schreyer's accompanying letter included the following comments: "You also receive in the present packet a representation of Upper Germany with parts of the adjacent provinces, prepared by a certain craftsman in this art, namely the one who made those sundials or hand-horoscopes. Though professing none of the liberal arts, he is not wanting in letters and has great natural talent in other ways. Some years ago he was granted citizenship of Nuremberg. He regularly practices those arts here and he is called in our tongue Erhard Etzlauben."[6] Etzlaub's map would influence the design of one of Hans von Kulmbach's woodcuts in Celtis's *Quatuor Libri Amorum* of 1502 (cat. nr. 10).[7]

The large demand for this map prompted Etzlaub to publish the *Roadmap through the Roman Empire* in 1501.[8] Although the general design is the same, the 1501 map covered more territory by extending to Salerno in the south and as far as Paris and Canterbury in the west. This map was printed by Georg Glockendon and reprinted in 1533 by his son Albrecht.

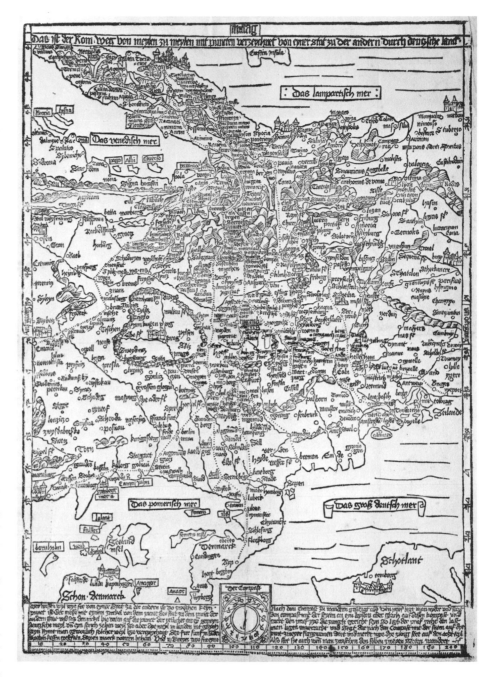

1. H. Krüger, "Das Heilige Jahr 1500 und Erhardt Etzlaubs Romwegkarte," *Erdkunde* 4 (1950): 137–141; *The World Encompassed*, exh. cat. (Baltimore: Baltimore Museum of Art, 1952), nr. 45; R. Field, *Fifteenth Century Woodcuts and Metalcuts from the National Gallery of Art*, nr. 281; Schnelbögl, *Dokumentie zur Nürnberger Kartographie*, pp. 5–7, and "Life and Work," pp. 18, 20 (nr. 2); *Reformation in Nürnberg*, nr. 16.

2. Although some critics have dated this map as early as 1492, circumstantial evidence suggests the later date of 1500. For a thorough discussion of the dating, see Krüger, "Das Heilige Jahr 1500," pp. 138–140.

3. Etzlaub's earliest printed map showing the environs of Nuremberg and the cities within a 118.4-km radius of Nuremberg was published in 1492 by Georg Glockendon. Glockendon published most of Etzlaub's works and is credited with the 1500 map. Schnelbögl, "Life and Work," p. 20.

4. Ibid., p. 25, for comments on his designing of compasses.

5. Ibid. Schnelbögl mentions that a printed explanation sheet on how to use one of Etzlaub's folding compasses was once in the Staatsbibliothek in Munich.

6. Ibid., p. 12.

7. Ibid., p. 23.

8. Ibid., p. 20, fig. 3.

Wolgemut is best known today as Albrecht Dürer's teacher from 1486 to 1489. Wolgemut was also Nuremberg's principal painter and printmaker during the last third of the fifteenth century.[1] Dürer's *Portrait of Michael Wolgemut at Age 82* (Nuremberg, Germanisches Nationalmuseum), dated 1516, is the only definite likeness of the artist; the painting also informs us that he was born in about 1434.[2] He is thought to be the son of painter Valentin Wolgemut, who appears in the city's tax records between 1461 and 1469. Michael likely trained with his father. A trip to the Netherlands during the 1450s or early 1460s is possible and would explain the strong Flemish influence on his style.[3] By 1470 he was a journeyman under a Munich painter named Gabriel. By late 1471 or early 1472, Wolgemut had returned to Nuremberg.[4] Since he did not become an independent master until 1473, he may have worked in the shop of Hans Pleydenwurff. Pleydenwurff died in 1472 and Wolgemut soon after married his widow, Barbara.[5] Wolgemut took over the Pleydenwurff workshop and subsequently trained his stepson and future partner, Wilhelm Pleydenwurff. Wolgemut lived and worked in a large house at Burgstrasse 21 (then called Gasse unter der Veste). In 1493 he purchased the adjacent house and expanded his residence.

Wolgemut's long and prolific career can be divided into four periods.[6] Little is known about the early years before 1473, and no paintings from this period have been identified; however, he may have helped Hans Pleydenwurff paint the 1465 *Hofer Altarpiece* (Munich, Alte Pinakothek). Between 1473 and 1485, Wolgemut established his reputation as a painter, printmaker, and stained-glass designer. His major picture is the 1479 *Altar* in Zwickau (Marienkirche), for which he was paid the remarkably high sum of 1,400 gulden. He provided the woodcut for the title page of *Reformation der Stadt Nürnberg* (Nuremberg: Anton Koberger, 1484).[7] He also designed several stained-glass windows, including those ordered by Emperor Friedrich III (1476–1477) and the Kunhofer and Schlüsselfelder families in the choir of St. Lorenz.[8]

The works associated with his third, or mature, period from 1486 to about 1500 involve the active participation of his large workshop. His stepson was now his collaborator on many projects, while Dürer's precise role within the workshop is still actively debated.[9] A large workshop was necessary to provide the woodcuts for Wolgemut's three great publication projects: the *Schatzbehalter* (1491; cat. nr. 2), the *Nuremberg Chronicle* (1493; cat. nr. 3), and *Archetypus Triumphatis Romae*, which was never completed.[10] Around 1486 he created the *Peringsdörffer Altar* for the Augustinerkloster, a painting justifiably praised by Neudörfer and Sandrart.[11] His altar in Straubing (St. Jakob) probably dates to about 1488.

Wolgemut continued painting until shortly before his death on 30 November 1519. Among his late altarpieces are those in Schwabach (Stadtpfarrkirche) of 1506–1508 and Windelsbach (Pfarrkirche) of 1510. Wolgemut's style changed little after the mid-1480s, but due to the ever increasing participation of his assistants, the quality of the late works is uneven.

1. The literature on Wolgemut is extensive; see Mende, *Dürer-Bibliographie*, nrs. 5808–5830. My comments are specifically taken from the following: F. Stadler, *Michel Wolgemut und der nürnberger Holzschnitt im letzten Drittel des fünfzehnten Jahrhunderts*; Wenke, "Das Bildnis bei Michael Wolgemut"; Betz, "Wolgemut"; and the various other sources listed below and in the notes for cat. nrs. 2 and 3.

2. Anzelewsky, *Dürer*, nr. 132.

3. Betz, "Wolgemut," p. 238, largely accepts the claim by C. Willnau ("Rogier van der Weyden und Michael Wolgemut," *Die Weltkunst* 24 [1954]: 7–8) that Wolgemut was in van der Weyden's workshop in 1451. This seems very doubtful.

4. Betz, "Wolgemut," p. 97.

5. Ibid., pp. 120, 125, 140. Barbara died in 1500. Wolgemut soon thereafter married a woman named Christina, who died in 1550.

6. For the paintings listed below and the general classification, see ibid., pp. 261–329.

7. Stadler, *Wolgemut*, p. 67; Field, *Fifteenth Century Woodcuts and Metalcuts*, nr. 243; *Nuremberg: Dürer (1971)*, nr. 231.

8. U. Frenzel, "Michael Wolgemuts Tätigkeit für die Nürnberger Glasmalerei. Dargestellt an der Bildnisscheibe des Dr. Lorenz Tucher von 1485," *AGNM* (1970): 27–46.

9. For instance, see L. Sladeczek, *Albrecht Dürer und die Illustrationen zur Schedelchronik* (Strassburg, 1965).

10. Betz, "Wolgemut," pp. 156–162; Grote, "Die 'Vorder-Stube' des Sebald Schreyer," pp. 52ff.; see also the comments on Schreyer in Section 4.

11. Neudörfer, *Nachrichten von Künstlern*, p. 128; Peltzer, ed., *Sandrarts Academie*, p. 58. Both the *Peringsdörffer* and *Straubing* altars were formerly in the Augustinerkloster. Today the *Peringsdörffer Altar* is located in the Heilig-Kreuz-Kirche, just outside Nuremberg. The best discussion of these paintings is E. Pfeiffer, "Der 'Augustiner-Hochaltar' und vier weitere Altäre des ausgehenden 15. Jahrhunderts," *MVGN* 52 (1963–1964): 305–398, esp. 363–396.

Wilhelm was the son of painter Hans Pleydenwurff, who had settled in Nuremberg by 1457.[1] Wilhelm was born between 1458 and 1460. After Hans's death in 1472, Wilhelm continued his training with Michael Wolgemut, who had married Hans's widow, Barbara, in 1472 or early 1473 and taken over the family workshop. He collaborated with Wolgemut on several altarpieces, including that commissioned in the mid-1480s by Levinus Memminger for St. Lorenz. A wing from *St. Martin Altar* (Nuremberg, Germanisches Nationalmuseum) of about 1490 has been attributed to him.[2] In 1490 Wilhelm and Wolgemut were paid to repaint the Schöner Brunnen in the Hauptmarkt.[3] Wilhelm's major contributions were the woodcuts he designed for the *Schatzbehalter* (cat. nr. 2) and the *Nuremberg Chronicle* (cat. nr. 3). He was buried on 31 January 1494.

1. Most of the literature on Wilhelm deals with his role in producing the *Schatzbehalter* and the *Nuremberg Chronicle*. For very general comments, see K. Oettinger, "Zu Dürers Beginn," *ZDVK* 8 (1954): 153–168, esp. 164–165, where he discusses Wilhelm's possible influence on Dürer; Betz, "Wolgemut," pp. 146, 342–353.

2. Betz, "Wolgemut," pp. 312–313. This painting was originally in St. Jakob.

3. Hampe, *Nürnberger Ratsverlässe*, I: nrs. 416–417 (12–14 August 1490); also cited in Betz, "Wolgemut," p. 105.

2. STEPHAN FRIDOLIN, SCHATZBEHALTER ODER SCHREIN DER WAREN REICHTÜMER DES HEILS VNND EWYGER SELIGKEIT GENANNT

Nuremberg: Anton Koberger, 8 November 1491
352 leaves (lacks first and final blanks)
96 woodcuts
(woodcuts) 17.5 × 25–25.2 cm
Contemporary stamped pigskin binding with clasps
The University of Texas at Austin, The Humanities Research Center [ex.: the Jesuit College in Munich (1606) and the Kupferstichkabinett in Berlin (1881)]

The *Schatzbehalter* (or treasury of the richness of the saints and of eternal salvation) was the first of the two great picture books that these two artists produced for publisher Anton Koberger.[1] It is a collection of devotional and edifying texts compiled by Stephan Fridolin (1430–1498), a local Franciscan friar and preacher at the Convent of St. Klara.[2] The ninety-one full-page woodcuts, five of which are repeated for a total of ninety-six, represent biblical and allegorical subjects, such as the Coronation of Christ (page F 5 recto) illustrated here.[3] These images are not, however, specifically linked to the accompanying text.

The artists' names do not appear in the *Schatzbehalter*. Therefore, the attribution of the illustrations to Wolgemut and Pleydenwurff is based on the stylistic similarities with the *Nuremberg Chronicle* (cat. nr. 3), which is firmly documented to these artists. The woodcut of the Coronation of Christ is a trinitarian devotional image representing God offering his martyred son the crown of heaven. The figure of the bearded and crowned God reappears in several of the *Nuremberg Chronicle* Genesis scenes, including the opening woodcut of God creating the universe (folio I verso). The style of the throne and the techniques of shading are shared by these two woodcuts.

While the attribution to Wolgemut, Pleydenwurff, and their workshop is secure, the task of sorting out the individual hands is more difficult. Bellm, following the scheme of Stadler, attributes thirty-three woodcuts, including the first twelve, to Wolgemut, twenty-five to Pleydenwurff, and the remaining thirty-three to shop assistants.[4] Since work on the *Schatzbehalter* may have begun as early as 1486 or so, it is possible that Dürer may have been involved in a minor way in the execution of the woodcuts.

Many of Wolgemut's and Pleydenwurff's preparatory drawings for the *Schatzbehalter* are in a sketchbook in Berlin (Kupferstichkabinett).[5] Among Wolgemut's thirty pen-and-ink drawings, which Bellm has dated between 1480 and 1488, is the design for the Coronation of Christ (fol. 4). When creating these drawings, Wolgemut borrowed figural and compositional motifs from contemporary sources; for instance, the Coronation of Christ is patterned in part after Martin Schongauer's *Coronation of the Virgin* engraving.[6] Wolgemut's Baptism of Christ (page N 5 verso) derives from Schongauer's engraving of the same subject. Bellm has identified the source

of other drawings as the *Speculum Humanae Salvationis* (Basel: B. Richel, 1476), which publisher Anton Koberger may have shown to Wolgemut.

1. Dodgson, I: pp. 241–245; Betz, "Wolgemut," pp. 96–101, 330ff.; R. Bellm, *Der Schatzbehalter—Ein Andachts- und Erbauungsbuch aus dem Jahre 1491*; F. Geldner, *Die Deutschen Inkunabeldrucker*, I: p. 163; *Reformation in Nürnberg*, nr. 50. Anton Koberger (ca. 1440–1513) was Nuremberg's most important publisher from 1470 until his death. Neudörfer claimed that his establishment on Egidienplatz contained twenty-four presses and one hundred workmen. For Koberger and his career, see Neudörfer, *Nachrichten von Künstlern*, p. 173; O. Hase, *Die Koberger*; and Wilson, *Nuremberg Chronicle*, pp. 175–180.

2. Fridolin's name does not appear in the text. The attribution of the text to him is based largely upon a copy of this book (Munich, Bayerisches Staatsbibliothek, Inc. c.a. 2606/19), which gives Fridolin's death date and the information that he was the author. On Fridolin's life, see U. Schmidt, *P. Stephan Fridolin. Ein Franziskanerprediger des ausgehenden Mittelalters*. On his collection of antiquities, see von Busch, *Studien zu deutschen Antikensammlungen*, p. 231.

3. The woodcuts numbered 25, 39, 46, 68, and 71 are repeated. The only detailed study of any of the woodcuts is W. Brücker, "Hand und Heil im 'Schatzbehalter' und auf volkstümlicher Graphik," *AGNM* (1965): 60–109, esp. 60–66, which examines the four opening and closing woodcuts of hands covered with numbers and with depictions of saints.

4. Bellm, *Schatzbehalter*, pp. 5–8.

5. Ibid., pp. 8–10; idem, *Wolgemuts Skizzenbuch—im Berliner Kupferstichkabinett*, pl. 1, the *Coronation of Christ*. The manuscript is inv. nr. 78b 3a.

6. Bellm, *Schatzbehalter*, pp. 9–10, for the following. Also see A. Shestack, *The Complete Engravings of Martin Schongauer*, nrs. 101 (B. 72), 97 (B. 34).

3. HARTMANN SCHEDEL, LIBER CHRONICARUM (NUREMBERG CHRONICLE)

Nuremberg: Anton Koberger, 12 July 1493
326 leaves; 47 × 32.5 cm
1809 woodcuts using 645 different woodblocks
The University of Texas at Austin, The Humanities Research Center [ex.: Hanley Collection]

After Johann Gutenberg's forty-two-line Bible (Mainz, 1453–1456), Hartmann Schedel's *Nuremberg Chronicle* is the most famous fifteenth-century publication.[1] It is a lavishly illustrated history of the world from creation until 1493, following the format of many late medieval chronicles.[2] It is distinguished from its predecessors both by Schedel's careful scholarship and by the unprecedented number of illustrations. Publisher Anton Koberger's advertisement promised the prospective buyer that "nothing like this has hitherto appeared to increase and heighten the delight of men of learning and of everyone who has any education at all. . . . Indeed, I venture to promise you, reader, so great delight in reading it that you will think you are not reading a series of stories, but looking at them with your own eyes. For you will see there not only portraits of emperors, popes, philosophers, poets, and other famous men each shown in the proper dress of his time, but also views of the most famous cities and places throughout Europe. . . . Farewell, and do not let this book slip through your hands."[3] Although the portraits are not as accurate as Koberger suggested, the thirty-two accurate views of such cities as Jerusalem, Constantinople, Rome, Venice, Nuremberg (illustrated here), and other German towns, as well as the many more fanciful city representations, do successfully transport the armchair traveler across the continent.[4]

The creation of the *Nuremberg Chronicle* is well documented.[5] In either late 1487 or early 1488, Nuremberg patricians Sebald Schreyer, the superintendent of St. Sebaldus, and his brother-in-law Sebastian Kammermeister contracted Wolgemut and Pleydenwurff to illustrate Schedel's text, which was still being written, and Anton Koberger to publish the work.[6] This contract was restated on 29 December 1491. The artists were paid 1,000 gulden and they were to equally divide any subsequent profits with the two investors.

Work was well under way by 1490, the date on Wolgemut's magnificent drawing *God the Creator* (London, British Museum) that is the design for the opening woodcut (page I verso).[7] These two masters created exemplars, or layout models, for both the Latin and German editions of the *Nuremberg Chronicle*.[8] The earlier, Latin exemplar ranges from extremely sketchy outlines to fairly complete drawings. The Wolgemut-Pleydenwurff workshop produced 645 woodblocks, many of which were used repeatedly to illustrate different historical figures or distant cities.[9]

The contract specified that during the printing either Wolgemut or Pleydenwurff would be present in Koberger's publishing house to correct any defects. One such mistake occurs in the copy exhibited: accidentally, the woodblock for Moses receiving the Ten Commandments was

Berta etas mūdi

NVREMB

set above that showing Moses leading the Israelites across the Red Sea on page XXX verso. This mistake appeared in a few early impressions but was soon corrected. Another reason for requiring the artists' presence at the publisher's was to guard against theft or the possible loss of a block, and, indeed, the contract required Koberger to set aside a locked room for storing the woodblocks. However, these precautions did not prevent Augsburg publisher Hans Schönsperger from printing a pirated edition of the chronicle in 1496.[10]

As mentioned above, the *Nuremberg Chronicle* was published in Latin and German editions. The more carefully laid out and printed Latin edition appeared first, on 12 July 1493. The Latin text is also longer, with additional woodcuts. The German edition, *Das Buch der Cronicken*, was printed on 23 December 1493. Scholars have estimated that approximately 1,500 Latin and 1,000 German copies were published.[11] The cost of an unbound and uncolored copy was slightly under 2 gulden (Rhine guilder).[12] This price can be compared with the average annual salaries of

a printer (32 gulden), a legal court scribe (40 gulden), or a physician (100 gulden) or the rough equivalent of buying 120 pounds of beef at prices for the year 1500. Thus the price, while not exorbitant, was relatively high. By contemporary standards, the *Nuremberg Chronicle* sold fairly well. When the final settlement of the artists and investors was made on 22 June 1509, 509 Latin and 49 German copies remained unsold.[13] Interestingly, the records of 1509 provide a glimpse into Koberger's marketing and distribution system, for copies were held by booksellers throughout central Europe, France, and Italy.

1. The literature on the *Nuremberg Chronicle* is vast. Most of the comments below are based upon E. Rucker, *Die Schedelsche Weltchronik—Das grösste Buchunternehmen der Dürer-Zeit*; Wilson, *Nuremberg Chronicle*. On Schedel, see Wilson, pp. 25ff., and the comments in Section 4 above.

2. It is divided according to the six ages of mankind: (1) Creation to the sons of Noah; (2) Noah's Ark to the destruction of Sodom and Gomorrah; (3) Abraham to Saul; (4) David to the destruction of Jerusalem; (5) the Babylonian captivity to the death of John the Baptist; and (6) the birth of Christ to the present. The illustrations are linked to the text.

3. A copy of this rare book advertisement is in Schedel's own Latin edition of the chronicle (Munich, Staatliches Bibliothek, Cim. 187, folio 2 of the pages added before the text). Also attached is Etzlaub's *Road Map of Central Europe* (cat. nr. 1). See Wilson, *Nuremberg Chronicle*, pp. 208–209 (gives the full text), 217.

4. Wolgemut's depiction of Nuremberg will be discussed in cat. nrs. 163–164. On the views of cities and some of the sources, see Rucker, *Weltchronik*, pp. 72–77, 85–135.

5. The documents are published in Wilson, *Nuremberg Chronicle*, pp. 45–54.

6. The 1487–1488 document no longer survives. Schedel, Schreyer, Kammermeister, Wolgemut, and, presumably, Pleydenwurff were all neighbors. On their relationships and careers, see above Section 4 (Schreyer); Rucker, *Weltchronik*, pp. 14, 17–18; Wilson, *Nuremberg Chronicle*, pp. 16–17, 22–23 (comments by P. Zahn).

7. Dept. of Prints and Drawings, 1885.5.9.43. See Rucker, *Weltchronik*, fig. 43, and cf. 8; A. Wilson, "The Early Drawings for the Nürnberg Chronicle," *Master Drawings* 13 (1975): 115–130.

8. Nuremberg, Stadtbibliothek, Cent. II-98 (Latin) and II-99 (German). See Rucker, *Weltchronik*, pp. 20–42; Wilson, *Nuremberg Chronicle*, pp. 42, 63–174. Four additional but separate layout drawings are also in the Stadtbibliothek; see Rucker, *Weltchronik*, pp. 49–60.

9. An adequate analysis of the specific roles of Wolgemut, Pleydenwurff, and the individual shop members has yet to be done. See Wilson, *Nuremberg Chronicle*, pp. 193–206. Equally unclear is the contribution of the young Dürer; see L. Sladeczek, *Albrecht Dürer und die Illustrationen zur Schedelchronik* (Strassburg, 1965); and E. Panofsky, *The Life and Art of Albrecht Dürer*, pp. 19–20.

10. Schönsperger commissioned Augsburg artists to make reduced-size copies of all the prints in the *Nuremberg Chronicle*. His edition is much smaller (20.5 × 29 cm vs. 47 × 32.5 cm) and cheaper. His edition undercut the market and prevented the Nuremberg group from continuing with their stated plan to publish a new edition. See Rucker, *Weltchronik*, p. 82, figs. 1, 62.

11. Wilson, *Nuremberg Chronicle*, p. 43. The large editions explain why so many copies of this book survive. For instance, the University of Texas at Austin possesses five Latin (one hand colored) and two German copies.

12. Ibid., pp. 237–241, for the following.

13. Ibid., pp. 229–236.

Albrecht Dürer, Germany's greatest Renaissance painter, printmaker, and art theorist, was born in Nuremberg on 21 May 1471, the son of goldsmith Albrecht the Elder (died 1502) and Barbara Holper (died 1514).[1] After beginning his training as a goldsmith in his father's workshop in 1485–1486, Albrecht changed his artistic direction. On 30 November 1486 he started his four-year apprenticeship with Michael Wolgemut, who taught him painting and printmaking. In 1490 Dürer left Nuremberg to work as a journeyman in Basel (1491–1493), Colmar (1492), and Strassburg (1493–1494). Through the assistance of his godfather, Anton Koberger, a Nuremberg publisher, the young Dürer supported himself by preparing book illustrations for publishers in these cities. This early period ended when he returned to Nuremberg in 1494 and married Agnes Frey, daughter of artist Hans Frey, on 7 July.

Soon after this event, Dürer departed for Venice, where he remained from fall 1494 to late spring 1495. This introduction to Italian art and theory and classical culture profoundly altered the course of his career as he became increasingly interested in theories of perspective and human proportions. His friendships with Willibald Pirckheimer (cat. nr. 30) and his longtime patron Friedrich the Wise (cat. nr. 29) began shortly after his return to Nuremberg. The inspiration of the Italian journey and his association with Pirckheimer, among others, prompted a period of dramatic graphic activity that would establish his fame throughout Europe. *The Apocalypse* (cat. nr. 6), *Nemesis* (cat. nr. 9), and *Adam and Eve* (cat. nr. 11) were published during the years between the two Italian trips, that is, between 1495 and 1505.

In the summer of 1505, Dürer went back to Venice. His letters from there to Pirckheimer provide insight into his thoughts on Italians, their art, and himself. In 1505–1506 Dürer painted the *Feast of the Rose Garlands* for the German merchants in Venice; Dürer labored on this picture in order to silence Italian criticisms of his painting and colors. The success of this work prompted the Venetian senate to offer Dürer a post as civic painter with an annual stipend of 200 ducats.[2]

Upon returning to Nuremberg in January 1507, Dürer received numerous painting commissions, the most important of which were the *Heller Altar* (1508–1509), now lost, and *All Saints Altarpiece* (1508–1511), formerly in the Zwölfbrüderhaus chapel (fig. 15).[3] On 14 June 1509, Dürer acquired the large house by the Tiergärtnertor, and in the same year he was appointed to the larger city council, the highest honor accorded to someone who was not a member of the patrician class. In 1511 Dürer published the *Large Passion* (cat. nr. 12), the *Small Passion*, the *Life of the Virgin*, and the second edition of *The Apocalypse*.

Dürer's association with Emperor Maximilian I began in 1512 when the ruler resided in Nuremberg between 4 February and 21 April. The artist's many projects for Maximilian included the *Triumphal Arch* (cat. nr. 20) and the *Great Triumphal Chariot* (cat. nr. 26). On 6 September 1515, Maximilian rewarded Dürer with an annual salary of 100 gulden.

Dürer participated in the meetings of the Sodalitas Staupitziana in 1516 and 1517.[4] This group of Nuremberg patricians and intellectuals gathered to discuss the dissident ideas of Martin Luther. In later years Dürer would become a staunch supporter of Luther and moderate Protestantism. Dürer's religious thoughts were expressed in his writings and in his art, most notably in his *Last Supper* woodcut (cat. nr. 28) and his *Four Apostles* painting of 1526 (fig. 26).

Dürer made a series of brief trips to Bamberg in 1517, to Augsburg in 1518, and to Switzerland in 1519. On 12 July 1520, Dürer, his wife, Agnes, and their maid started their journey to the Netherlands that would last until the summer of 1521. Dürer's travel diary is a careful record of his expenditures, his artistic activities, his reception in Antwerp, Bruges, Brussels, and other towns, and his thoughts on contemporary events, including the reported death of Luther.[5] While searching for a beached whale in Zeeland, Dürer contracted malaria, which broke his health.

Dürer's last years were devoted primarily to his theoretical writings. His *Art of Measurement* (cat. nr. 31) appeared in 1525, the *Treatise on Fortification* was published two years later, and the *Treatise on Human Proportions* (cat. nr. 34) was printed, posthumously, in 1528. He also prepared painted and graphic portraits of many of his friends (cat. nrs. 25, 29, 30, and 32).

Dürer died on 6 April 1528 and was buried near his father-in-law in the Johannisfriedhof. His current tomb was erected in the mid-seventeenth century by Joachim von Sandrart.[6]

1. The following biographical comments are based mainly upon Panofsky, *Dürer; Nuremberg: Dürer (1971)*. Many of the biographical facts, the art objects, and the artist's friendships are discussed at length in Sections 3 through 6 above. The exhaustive literature on Dürer is summarized in Mende, *Dürer-Bibliography*. On Dürer's writings and contemporary literary references to the artist, see Rupprich, *Dürer schriftlicher Nachlass*. On his paintings, see Anzelewsky, *Dürer*. On his drawings, see Winkler, *Zeichnungen Dürers*. On his prints, see Meder, *Dürer-Katalog*; and the excellent discussion in *Boston: Dürer*. Also see Talbot, ed., *Dürer*, for a superb summary of the scholarship on Dürer's prints and drawings; G. Hirschmann and F. Schnelbögl, eds., *Albrecht Dürers Umwelt*, with fourteen essays on specific facets of his career; more recently, F. Anzelewsky, *Dürer: His Art and Life*, and P. Strieder, *Albrecht Dürer: Paintings, Prints, Drawings*, both excellent general surveys.

2. Conway, *Writings of Dürer*, p. 59. He was later offered a similar post in Antwerp; see ibid., p. 126.

3. A. Pfaff, *Studien zu Albrecht Dürers Heller-Altar* (Nuremberg, 1971).

4. See Section 3 C.

5. For a good English translation, see J.-A. Goris and G. Marlier, *Albrecht Dürer: Diary of His Journey to the Netherlands, 1520–1521* (Greenwich, Conn., 1971). Also see Anzelewsky, Mende, and Eeckhout, *Albert Dürer aux Pays-Bas*.

6. Illustrated in Anzelewsky, *Dürer: His Art and Life*, fig. 240.

4. THE HOLY FAMILY BENEATH A TREE

ca. 1490–1494; false monogram
Drawing: pen and brown ink
22.8 × 14.6 cm
Private Collection, London

Winkler has correctly identified this drawing as one of Dürer's earliest works.[1] Since it does not show any influence of his trip to Italy in 1494–1495, Winkler dated the drawing to Dürer's *wanderjahre*. In support of Winkler's thesis, I would add that the drawing, especially the style of the Virgin, recalls the engravings of Martin Schongauer, with whom Dürer sought to study when he left Nuremberg for Colmar in 1490.[2] During the four-year period before his return to Nuremberg, Dürer made several drawings of either the Virgin and Child or the Holy Family in which he experimented with different poses for Mary and Christ. The exhibited example is very sketchy as the central tree, the landscape, and even the figures are rendered with a few quick strokes of the pen. Greater attention is given to the patterns of the Virgin's robe. The *Mary and Child* (London, Private Collection) is very similar in style.[3] Both of these drawings probably predate the more complete Holy Family sketches at Erlangen (Universitätsbibliothek) and Berlin (Kupferstichkabinett).[4] All the drawings were preparatory for the *Holy Family with the Butterfly* of 1495–1496, Dürer's first important engraving.[5]

1. Winkler, *Zeichnungen Dürers*, I: nr. 24. The drawing was first firmly attributed to Dürer by C. Dodgson in "Albrecht Dürer: The Holy Family," *Vasari Society for the Reproduction of Drawings by Old Masters*, 1 (Oxford, 1905–1906), nr. 30. Also see the comments in *Nuremberg: Dürer (1971)*, nr. 140.
2. This association is also made in *Nuremberg: Dürer (1971)*, nr. 140. See Schongauer's *The Madonna and Child on a Grassy Bench* (B. 30), with the landscape behind, and *The Madonna and Child in the Courtyard* (B. 32); Shestack, *The Complete Engravings of Martin Schongauer*, nrs. 21, 23.
3. Winkler, *Zeichnungen Dürers*, I: nr. 22.
4. Ibid., nrs. 25, 30. The authors of *Nuremberg: Dürer (1971)*, nrs. 140, 142, suggest that the motif of Joseph behind the bench derives from the Master of the Housebook's *Holy Family in a Landscape* drypoint (nr. 138).
5. Meder 42. Also see the comments in Talbot, ed., *Dürer*, nr. 2. None of the drawings cited above is specifically the model for this print; rather these drawings are reworkings of the same theme from which the artist borrowed certain motifs for the engraving.

5. THE BATHHOUSE

ca. 1496–1497; monogram
Woodcut
38.7 × 28 cm
B. 128; M. 266; H. 266
Lent by the Philadelphia Museum of Art, The
SmithKline Corporation Fund

Upon his return from Venice in 1495, Dürer began a period of tremendous graphic activity that culminated with the publication of *The Apocalypse* (cat. nr. 6) and *Large Passion* (cat. nr. 12). The woodcuts from the years 1496–1499, including *The Bathhouse*, are extremely large in scale.[1] There exists a clarity of design and monumentality of form not evident in his earlier prints. In this woodcut, Dürer's contour and shading lines define the figures more thoroughly. The whiteness of the paper is used in conjunction with strong outlines to provide the impression of substance.

Dürer represents six men standing and sitting in a public bath. Local bathhouses were social meeting places for both men and women. The open-air setting seen here is highly unusual. More typical is the closed wooden room with a large ceramic stove represented in Dürer's *Women's Bath* drawing of 1496,[2] which was originally planned for use as a pendant to *The Bathhouse*. Dürer took advantage of his trips to the bathhouses of Nuremberg to study human anat-

omy. The figures in *The Bathhouse* are muscular and more correctly formed than those in the *Lamentation* woodcut made a year or two earlier.[3]

The figure standing by the waterspout may be a self-portrait.[4] Dürer's earthy humor is evident both in the placement of the spout and in the little cock (*hahn*), which conveys the same range of meanings in English and German. Attempts to identify the fat man as Pirckheimer are not as convincing as the association of the two foreground figures with Stephan and Lucas Paumgartner because he does not look like the known portraits of Pirckheimer. These four figures have also been associated with the four humors.[5]

1. Talbot, ed., *Dürer*, nr. 84; *Boston: Dürer*, nr. 18. Compare Meder 107, 212, 236, among other prints.
2. Winkler, *Zeichnungen Dürers*, I: nr. 152; formerly in Bremen, Kunsthalle. Dürer's pupil Hans Springinklee used this drawing as the source for his woodcut (Geisberg, nr. 1347) of about 1518. Also see Hans Sebald Beham's *Women's Bathhouse* (cat. nr. 81). Dürer represented another outdoor bath in his drawing *Joys of the World* (Oxford, Ashmolean Museum); Winkler, *Zeichnungen Dürers*, I: nr. 163.
3. Meder 186.
4. On the various iconographic interpretations of this print, see E. Wind, "Dürer's 'Männerbad': A Dionysian Mystery," *Journal of the Warburg and Courtauld Institutes* 2 (1938–1939): 269–271; Panofsky, *Dürer*, pp. 49–50; Talbot, ed., *Dürer*, nr. 84.
5. See note 4. Dürer(?) is the melancholic; the fat man is phlegmatic; the choleric man holds a scraping knife; and the sanguine man holds a flower.

6. THE APOCALYPSE

1496–1498; published by Dürer in 1498 and re-issued with a new frontispiece in 1511
15 woodcuts
B. 60–75; M. 163–178; H. 163–178

A. SEVEN ANGELS WITH THE TRUMPETS

Revelation 8:1–13 and 9:1–6 (seventh in the sequence of fifteen)
ca. 1496; monogram
39.2 × 27.9 cm
B. 68; M. 170; H. 170
The University of Texas at Austin, Archer M. Huntington Art Gallery

B. THE BABYLONIAN WHORE

Revelation 17:1–5, 18:21, and 19:11–15 (fourteenth in the sequence of fifteen)
ca. 1496–1497; monogram
39.2 × 28.1 cm
B. 73; M. 177; H. 177
Private Collection, London

While Dürer was completing work on *The Bathhouse* (cat. nr. 5), he began designing *The Apocalypse*, his greatest series.[1] Each of the fifteen woodcuts is printed on a recto page with the accompanying text on the verso, or facing, page. The 1498 edition was published with texts in Latin and, separately, in German.[2] A second Latin edition with a new frontispiece was issued in 1511.

The Apocalypse immediately established Dürer's fame throughout Europe. In spite of certain minor borrowings from the Quentell Bible (Cologne, 1480), Dürer reinterpreted each episode. He successfully conveyed the awe and cataclysmic horror of St. John's words with an immediacy rarely, if ever, equaled. In the *Seven Angels with the Trumpets*, a great mountain of burning fire and a fiery star rain down upon the earth destroying one-third of mankind. The violence of the text is matched or even heightened by Dürer's depiction. Equally brilliant is the union of fire, clouds, and the earth in the *Babylonian Whore*, where the fire consuming Babylon pours directly out of the sky and the water at the left miraculously vaporizes to form the cloud enveloping the righteous army above. To portray the wanton, luxury-loving whore, Dürer reused a drawing of a wealthy Venetian woman he had made in 1495 and added a sumptuous lobed columbine cup of the sort made in Nuremberg.[3]

A major factor for the success of the series was Dürer's technical virtuosity. Each line expresses a different nuance as it tapers or swells. Strongly outlined forms are enriched with dramatic chiaroscuro contrasts. Although the compositions are densely packed, this crowding is coherently organized and contributes to the impact of the individual scenes. Critics believe that Dürer himself carved the woodblocks for this series since the variety of lines is rarely matched in later woodblocks that were cut by professional *formschneiders*.[4]

Dürer encouraged the dissemination of his prints, especially to other artists. For instance, when he traveled to the Netherlands in 1520 and

1521, he recorded in his diary that he either sold or gave away over one hundred copies of the *Apocalypse*.[5] Not surprisingly, his series influenced most subsequent representations of this theme. Hieronymus Greff (ca. 1460–after 1507) of Strassburg produced an identical version and simply replaced Dürer's monogram with his own,[6] but Dürer had few legal means for preventing other artists from making exact copies of his work.[7] Later *Apocalypse* cycles by Anton Woensam (before 1500–1541) of Worms and Matthias Gerung (ca. 1500–ca. 1568/1570) of Lauingen are merely variations on Dürer's work.[8]

1. On the two exhibited prints, see Talbot, ed., *Dürer*, nrs. 98, 105; *Boston: Dürer*, nrs. 36, 45.

2. The German text is based on the 1483 Bible published by Anton Koberger. Koberger, Dürer's godfather, probably permitted the artist to use his presses and type for this series.

3. Winkler, *Zeichnungen Dürers*, I: nr. 69 (Vienna, Albertina); generally on goldsmith cups, see Kohlhaussen, *Nürnberger Goldschmiedekunst*, pp. 296ff.

4. See W. Ivins, Jr., "Notes on Three Dürer Woodblocks," *Metropolitan Museum Studies* 2 (1929): 102–111; A. G. Stewart, "Early Woodcut Workshops," *Art Journal* 39 (1980): 189–194.

5. Rupprich, *Dürer schriftlicher Nachlass*, I: pp. 146–202. For instance, Dürer distributed ninety-three copies of the three books (*Apocalypse*, *Life of the Virgin*, *Large Passion*). To artists Lucas van Leyden, Jean Mone, Adriaen Horenbouts, and others he gave copies of all his prints.

6. *Nuremberg: Vorbild Dürer*, nrs. 59, 61, 64, 68.

7. On Dürer's legal position and rights, see Schultheiss, "Albrecht Dürers Beziehungen zum Recht," in Hirschmann and Schnelbögl, eds., *Albrecht Dürers Umwelt*, esp. pp. 235–244. On 3 January 1512, the Nuremberg city council ordered an unnamed individual to stop selling copies of Dürer's work bearing his monogram in the Hauptmarkt. Rupprich, *Dürer schriftlicher Nachlass*, I: p. 241. On the subject of copies after Dürer, see J. Held, ed., *Dürer through Other Eyes: His Graphic Work Mirrored in Copies and Forgeries of Three Centuries*; *Nuremberg: Vorbild Dürer*.

8. *Nuremberg: Vorbild Dürer*, nrs. 62, 65–66.

7. THE SEA MONSTER (DAS MEERWUNDER)

ca. 1498; monogram
Engraving
25.2 × 19 cm (plate); 24.8 × 18.7 cm (sheet)
B. 71; M. 66; H. 66
Private Collection, London

In 1498 at about the time he had completed the *Apocalypse* (cat. nr. 6) and the *Large Passion* (cat. nr. 12), Dürer began working on a group of independent engravings, including the *Sea Monster*, the *Virgin and Child with the Monkey*, and *Hercules*.[1] These prints show a steady progress in the artist's ability to define shapes using varied hatching strokes.[2]

The subject of this print remains a mystery. Dürer called it *Das Meerwunder*, or the wonder or monster of the sea.[3] The reclining nude woman is very classical in appearance. She reappears in the *Hercules*, which has prompted scholars to search for possible ancient literary sources.[4] Most recently, it has been suggested that the print represents the abduction of Syme by Glaukos, a tale recounted in Philostratus's *Eikones*, written in the third century A.D.[5] Other critics, especially Lange, plausibly posit that Dürer was inspired instead by a contemporary event, a mysterious occurrence that became ever more fanciful as the story crossed Europe.[6] Prints of miraculous deformed births, portentous celestial happenings, and other wondrous incidents enjoyed great popularity at the time. Dürer's *Great Sow of Landser* belongs to this category.[7]

1. *Nuremberg: Dürer (1971)*, nr. 516; Talbot, ed., *Dürer*, nr. 15; P. Strieder, "Antike Vorbilder für Dürers Kupferstich 'Das Meerwunder,'" *AGNM* (1971–1972): 42–47. For the other two prints, see Meder 30 and 62.

2. Dürer's hatching is more tentative in the *Sea Monster* than in the *Hercules*, so it is usually placed slightly earlier. There is also a certain awkwardness in his figural constructions and their placement in space. It has been suggested that the castle by the shore is loosely modeled on the Burg in Nuremberg.

3. Rupprich, *Dürer schriftlicher Nachlass*, I: p. 162 (lines 28–29), a reference made on 24 November 1520 while in Antwerp.

4. Talbot, ed., *Dürer*, nr. 15, gives a summary of older suggestions.

5. Strieder, "Antiker Vorbilder," pp. 42–47.

6. Talbot, ed., *Dürer*, nr. 15, gives a summary of older suggestions. For a study of the celestial events that were recorded in broadsheets, see Janeck, *Zeichen am Himmel*.

7. Meder 82. The *Sea Monster* was frequently copied; see *Nuremberg: Vorbild Dürer*, nrs. 37–41.

8. NUDE WOMAN WITH A HERALD'S WAND

1498; monogram
Drawing: pen and brown ink on paper
31 × 20.9 cm
Lent by the Crocker Art Museum, Sacramento

During the period between his two Italian trips, Dürer repeatedly returned to the subject of the female nude. Before journeying to Venice in 1494, Dürer's concept of the female nude was based primarily on the existing conventions, in which the woman is represented with a large, pear-shaped abdomen, stylized contour, and an axial symmetry, as seen, for instance, in his 1493 sketch in Bayonne (Musée Bonnat).[1] Upon returning to Nuremberg in 1495, Dürer, in his drawings, reveals something new: he had begun the practice of sketching from live models. In his *Women's Bath* (Bremen, Kunsthalle) of 1496, a man (Dürer?) can be seen peering through a window at the bathing women.[2] Many of Dürer's models may have been bathhouse attendants and customers.

These early nude drawings are not without their flaws. As Talbot has noticed in the Sacramento sketch, Dürer had considerable difficulty in foreshortening the woman's right shoulder, and a certain indecision about where to place the contour lines of the left shoulder and arm resulted in the wavy outlines.[3] Nevertheless, this drawing is extremely attractive especially in its use of light and dark contrasts to enliven the surface of the figure. His technique of crosshatching is the same that he employed in his prints.

While retaining his interest in using live models, Dürer subsequently tried to adapt the human form to a Vitruvian proportion, as in the case of *Nemesis* (cat. nr. 9), to a more classicizing ideal of beauty, as in *Adam and Eve* (cat. nr. 11), or, still later, into a flexible system of figural ratios, as seen in his *Treatise on Human Proportions* (cat. nr. 34). Dürer never abandoned the use of the live model. In 1519 he painted a nude portrait of his wife, *Agnes Frey*, that passed later into the collection of Paulus Praun of Nuremberg but is now lost.[4]

1. Winkler, *Zeichnungen Dürers*, I: nr. 28; also see Talbot, ed., *Dürer*, fig. V a.

2. Winkler, *Zeichnungen Dürers*, I: nr. 152; also see nrs. 85, 89 (both Paris, Louvre), 154 (New York, Metropolitan Museum of Art, Lehman Collection).

3. Ibid., IV: nr. 947; Talbot, ed., *Dürer*, nr. V, which supplies the best discussion of this drawing; *Master Drawings from Sacramento* (Sacramento: E. B. Crocker Art Gallery, 1971), nr. 7. The drawing has been trimmed along the bottom margin.

4. De Murr, *Description du Cabinet de Monsieur Paul de Praun à Nuremberg*, nr. 156.

9. NEMESIS

ca. 1501–1502; monogram
Engraving
33.3 × 22.9 cm
B. 77; M. 72; H. 72
St. Louis Art Museum, 32: 1926

Nemesis, a goddess of fortune, floats above the world rewarding some, as symbolized by the covered cup, and, in the guise of the goddess of retribution, punishing others, as symbolized by the bridle.[1] The mountain village below is the Tyrolean town of Klausen im Eisacktal (Chiuso), doubtlessly based upon a watercolor made during Dürer's first trip to Venice. The artist's specific literary source is a passage in Politian's *Manto* (Milan, 1499), owned by Pirckheimer.[2]

The figure of Nemesis, worked out in preliminary drawings, is not based upon his study of a live model.[3] Rather, she is a pear-shaped late-Gothic-style nude that Dürer has drawn according to a set of proportional ratios developed by Roman theorist Vitruvius.[4] Ideally, the head is one-eighth the length of the body, the face is one-tenth, and the foot is one-seventh. Although Dürer's calculations vary slightly, the artist was employing a similar scheme to formulate the structure of his female form. During this period of his career, Dürer experimented with Vitruvian proportions in an attempt to create the ideal human figure. After his second trip to Venice in 1505–1507, when he studied the theoretical ideas of Leonardo da Vinci, among others, Dürer shifted his attention to the codification of the infinite variations of the human body rather than one specific set of proportions. His work culminated in the *Art of Measurement* (cat. nr. 31).

During the period from about 1500 to 1504, Dürer actively experimented with his engraving technique in such prints as *St. Eustace*, *Nemesis*, and *Adam and Eve* (cat. nr. 11).[4] A comparison with *The Sea Monster* (cat. nr. 7) of about 1498 reveals that Dürer's skill at rendering chiaroscuro values through his net of hatchings has advanced dramatically. He is now fully capable of rendering subtle gradations of tone and surface textures. In the upper portion of the *Nemesis* he has wiped the plate clean to accentuate the contrast between the ink and the white paper.

1. Panofsky, *Dürer*, pp. 81–82; *Nuremberg: Dürer (1971)*, nr. 481; Talbot, ed., *Dürer*, nr. 25; *Boston: Dürer*, nr. 60. The term Nemesis is Dürer's own; see Rupprich, *Dürer schriftlicher Nachlass*, I: p. 154 (line 250), 160 (line 146). For other iconographic sources, see E. Panofsky, "'Virgo et Victrix,' a Note on Dürer's *Nemesis*," in *Prints: Thirteen Illustrated Essays*, ed. C. Zigrosser (New York, 1962), pp. 13–38.
2. *Nuremberg: Dürer (1971)*, nr. 481.
3. Winkler, *Zeichnungen Dürers*, I: 266 (London, British Museum) illustrating a study for her wing and a second profile sketch of Nemesis, minus the goldsmith cup. Compare his drawing *Nude Woman with a Herald's Wand* (cat. nr. 8).
4. Panofsky, *Dürer*, pp. 81–82; Talbot, ed., *Dürer*, nr. 25.
5. Meder 1 (*Adam and Eve*), 60 (*St. Eustace*).

10. CONRAD CELTIS, QUATUOR LIBRI AMORUM (Nuremberg: Sodalitas Celtica, 5 April 1502)

11 woodcuts
21.9 × 14.8 cm (woodcut *Philosophy*)
M. 244–245; H. 244–245
Lent by the Library of Congress, Washington, Lessing J. Rosenwald Collection

In 1501 the Sodalitas Celtica, a group of Conrad Celtis's Nuremberg friends, published Hroswitha von Gandersheim's *Opera*, edited by Celtis and containing woodcuts by Dürer and his pupil Hans von Kulmbach.[1] The following year Dürer and Kulmbach again collaborated with this group and provided the eleven woodcuts for Celtis's *Quatuor Libri Amorum*, or *Four Books of Love*, an allegorical description of Celtis's loves and the union of the German lands.[2] Celtis envisioned this book to be the prologue of a greater corpus, the *Germania illustrata*. However, as with most of Celtis's grandiose projects, the remaining volumes were never written.

Dürer's participation in this project was limited to designing two woodcuts: the unsigned scene of Celtis presenting the book to Maximilian I (fol. a i verso) and the monogrammed image of Philosophy (fol. a vi verso). Dürer followed drawings made by Celtis. Philosophy, the queen of the Muses and the basis of knowledge, is based upon the description in Boethius's *Consolatione Philosophiae* (Book 1). She is enthroned and holds a scepter and a book. The Greek letters, arranged in the form of a ladder, refer to the ascent from practice to theory. In the roundels are Ptolemy (Egypt), Plato (Greece), Cicero (Virgil is also listed; Rome), and Albertus Magnus (Germany), the philosophers of the four great cultures as defined by Celtis. Champion of German culture, Celtis intentionally excluded any association with modern Italy. In the corners are the four winds, each linked with the elements, humors, and plants. For instance, Boreas, at the lower right, is the freezing northern wind and is associated with the earth, melancholy, and the oak leaf. The explanation lies in the inscription below:

Whatever heaven contains, what earth, the air, and the water,

Whatever can exist among all things that are human,

Whatever the fire-god makes in the whole circle of earth,

All that I, Philosophy, carry within my own breast.[3]

That is, all human knowledge is based on philosophy.

1. *Nuremberg: Dürer (1971)*, nr. 289; Talbot, ed., *Dürer*, nr. 211; the comments in Section 4.
2. *Nuremberg: Dürer (1971)*, nr. 289; Talbot, ed., *Dürer*, nr. 212; Strauss, *Albrecht Dürer Woodcuts and Woodblocks*, pp. 230–236, 612–613. On Kulmbach's participation, see *Nuremberg: Meister um Dürer*, nr. 226.
3. Talbot, ed., *Dürer*, nr. 212, citing L. Spitz, *The Religious Renaissance of the German Humanists*, p. 87.

11. ADAM AND EVE

1504; inscribed "ALBERTVS DVRER NORICVS
FACIEBAT [monogram] 1504"
Engraving
24.9 × 19 cm
B. 1; M. 1; H. 1
Lent by the Los Angeles County Museum of
Art: Purchased with Funds Provided by the Art
Museum Council

If the *Apocalypse* series (cat. nr. 6) established Dürer's fame, the *Adam and Eve*, his most accomplished engraving to date, firmly secured his position as Europe's foremost printmaker.[1] *Adam and Eve* is the culmination of a large sequence of preparatory drawings and an elaborate iconographic program.

From the time of Jacopo de' Barbari's arrival in Nuremberg in 1500, Dürer had become increasingly engrossed in the pursuit of an ideal beauty based upon correct proportions and classical forms. While the figure of *Nemesis* (cat. nr. 9) had been based upon the Vitruvian canon, she was still a German *hausfrau*. Adam and Eve, on the other hand, bring to mind the *Apollo Belvedere*, the *Medici Venus*, or related Roman statues that Dürer knew of second hand by way of Italian prints and drawings.[2] The figure of Adam first emerged in the ca. 1501–1503 drawing of Apollo in New York (Metropolitan Museum of Art) and in the contemporary *Apollo and Diana* in London (British Museum) in which the artist experimented with the classical weight shift and the emphasis upon the carefully muscled torso.[3] His *Apollo* in Zurich (Kunsthaus) offers a slightly different positioning of the body and another facial type.[4] Eve's pose gradually evolved out of a set of six quick sketches done to address the relationships of the different planes and parts of the body.[5] The *Nude Woman with a Staff* in Ottawa (National Gallery of Canada) seems to be the summation of these other studies.[6] Nevertheless, the definitive designs for both Adam and Eve are stated only in the 1504 drawing in New York (Pierpont Morgan Library).[7] The dark, brushed backgrounds in these last two drawings silhouette the figures just as the woods did in the final engraving.

None of Dürer's earlier engravings matches the technique of *Adam and Eve*. Dürer developed the surfaces of his figures with subtle modulations of light. There is a quick transition from the whiteness of the paper, visible in their bodies, to the velvety blacks of the woods behind. There is an extraordinary variety of textures even in single objects, such as the tree between Adam and Eve. Two trial impressions of this print exist.[8] They reveal that he blocked out the figures and largely completed the background details before finishing Adam and Eve.

As Panofsky has shown, the print's iconography is equally complex.[9] Since the twelfth century it was held that, before the fall, Adam and Eve lived in a sinless state of perfect physical equilibrium and, as a result, were immortal. This balance of the bodily humors, or temperaments, was irrevocably altered following the fall; the couple was subject to the dominance of any of these humors and they became mortal. The original harmonies are still evident in Dürer's engraving; however, the animals on the ground

each refer to a different temperament that will be unleashed with the first couple's fall from grace. The cat stands for choleric cruelty, the rabbit for sanguine sensuality, the elk for melancholic gloom, and the ox for phlegmatic sluggishness. The cat will soon pounce upon the mouse, much as the serpent will prey on mankind. The parrot at the upper left offers the viewer hope since the parrot symbolized the virgin birth of Christ.

This engraving was immediately popular. Agostino Veneziano, Johann Ladenspelder, and Johann Wierix, among others, produced exact copies.[10] Hans Springinklee's *Adam and Eve* (cat. nr. 53) was directly inspired by Dürer's engraving. The nucleus of Dürer's design can be found in wood sculptures and works in other media.[11]

1. Panofsky, *Dürer*, pp. 84–87; *Nuremberg: Dürer (1971)*, nr. 484; Talbot, ed., *Dürer*, nr. 30; *Boston: Dürer*, nrs. 84–85. I have relied primarily on these sources for this entry.

2. Panofsky, *Dürer*, pp. 85ff.; Talbot, ed., *Dürer*, p. 39, note 7.

3. Winkler, *Zeichnungen Dürers*, I: nrs. 262, 261; Talbot, ed., *Dürer*, nr. VII.

4. Winkler, *Zeichnungen Dürers*, I: nr. 264.

5. Ibid., II: nrs. 411–416.

6. Ibid., I: nr. 265; Talbot, ed., *Dürer*, nr. VIII. The date of 1508 was added by someone else at a later date.

7. Winkler, *Zeichnungen Dürers*, II: nr. 333; Talbot, ed., *Dürer*, nr. XII.

8. All the different states are illustrated in C. Dodgson, *Albrecht Dürer Engravings and Etchings* (1926; reprint: London, 1967), pp. 51–55.

9. Panofsky, *Dürer*, pp. 84–87.

10. *Nuremberg: Vorbild Dürer*, nrs. 98, 102–103.

11. For instance, the wooden Adam and Eve by Master H. L. that dates to about 1520. The carving is in Freiburg (Augustinermuseum); see Beck and Decker, *Dürers Verwandlung in der Skulptur zwischen Renaissance und Barock*, nr. 177.

12. CHRIST IN LIMBO (from the LARGE PASSION)

1510; monogram
Woodcut
39.6 × 28.4 cm
B. 14; M. 121; H. 121
Lent by the Art Institute of Chicago. The John
H. Wrenn Memorial Collection. 1934.462

The *Large Passion* was designed in two stages.
Dürer made seven of the Passion scenes between 1497 and 1499. He then set the project
aside until 1510, when he added four more
woodcuts, including *Christ in Limbo*, and a frontispiece.[1] These woodcuts were published with
the title *Passio domini nostri Jesu* by Hieronymus
Höltzel of Nuremberg in 1511. Benedictus Chelidonius, a Benedictine monk in St. Egidien, supplied the accompanying Latin text.[2] The exhibited print is a strong, clear impression made
before this text was added.

Christ in Limbo is among Dürer's most technically advanced woodcuts. The artist has developed what Panofsky aptly termed the "graphic
middle tone."[3] This can best be seen in the figures of Adam and Eve on the left-hand side. In
his earlier woodcut the *Bathhouse* (cat. nr. 5), the
light and dark contrasts are achieved by using
strong contour lines and varying hatchings and
crosshatchings to suggest shade. Dürer still
used this system in *Christ in Limbo*; however, to
show that Eve is standing largely in shadow,
Dürer introduced a series of parallel, horizontal
strokes that extend unbroken from contour to
contour, that is, from one side of the leg or arm
to the other. These lines are not as densely
placed as the intricate web of crosshatchings
used for Eve's back and side and therefore convey a middle tone between the contour lines and
the dark shading strokes.

1. Also see *Nuremberg: Dürer (1971)*, nrs. 375, 597;
Talbot, ed., *Dürer*, nr. 130; *Boston: Dürer*, nr. 157. The
theme is based upon the apocryphal Gospel of Nico-
demus; see E. Hennecke, *New Testament Apocrypha*,
2 vols. (Philadelphia, 1963), I: pp. 470–484. Dürer returned to this theme in the 1511 *Small Woodcut Passion*
(M. 150) and the 1512 *Engraved Passion* (M. 16).
2. Chelidonius supplied the texts for Dürer's *Small
Woodcut Passion* and *Life of the Virgin*, both published
by Höltzel in 1511. See *Nuremberg: Dürer (1971)*, nrs.
374, 376.
3. Panofsky, *Dürer*, pp. 134–135; Talbot, ed., *Dürer*,
p. 175.

13. MASS OF ST. GREGORY

1511; monogram
Woodcut
30 × 20.5 cm
B. 123; M. 226; H. 226
Lent by the St. Louis Art Museum: Bequest of
Horace M. Swope, 264: 1940

1511 was one of the most important years of
Dürer's career. He published *The Apocalypse*, the
Large Passion, and the *Life of the Virgin* plus two
of his finest woodcuts, the *Mass of St. Gregory*
and the *Trinity*.[1] In the *Mass of St. Gregory*, Dürer
experimented further with the use of varied
graphic tones. The middle tone lines now are
rendered as concentric strokes that define both
shadow and structure. These lines are more
skillfully integrated with his crosshatchings.
Rarely will his later woodcuts match the wealth
of tonal variations and descriptive employment
of line. None of Dürer's contemporaries, including talented Hans Burgkmair, could match Dürer's technique. By this period, Dürer was also
employing a trained woodblock cutter.[2]

The theme of the mass of St. Gregory the
Great, who was pope from 590 to 604, enjoyed
great popularity during the fifteenth and early
sixteenth centuries.[3] According to a twelfth-
century biographer, the pope was performing
mass in the church of S. Croce in Gerusalemme
in Rome. While preparing to bless the eucharistic wine and host, he experienced a vision of
Christ as the man of sorrows standing on the
altar. In this vision of the physical transubstan-
tiation of Christ, the savior is seen in his
sepulchre surrounded by the instruments of the
Passion, the cock of St. Peter, and the hanging
figure of Judas. The other ecclesiastics, who do
not share in this revelation, are isolated by action and position from Gregory. Dürer heightened the visionary mood by dissolving the architecture of the church behind the clouds.

1. Also see *Nuremberg: Dürer (1971)*, nr. 339; Talbot,
ed., *Dürer*, nr. 194; *Boston: Dürer*, nrs. 167–168. See
Meder 187 (*Trinity*), 188–207 (*Life of the Virgin*).
2. The identity of his *formschneider*(s) during this
period is unknown. By 1515 Hieronymus Andreae
(died 1556) was his usual collaborator. See cat. nr. 6;
note 4.
3. J. A. Endres, "Die Darstellung der Gregorius-
messe im Mittelalter," *Zeitschrift für Christlichen Kunst*
30 (1917): 146–156; G. Schiller, *Iconography of Christian
Art*, II: pp. 199, 226–228. With the advent of Lutheranism, such visionary themes, of questionable validity,
were challenged by Luther and his followers. These
themes rapidly disappeared in Nuremberg's art. See
Schiller, *Iconography of Christian Art*, fig. 807, for an illustration of a painting of the mass of St. Gregory by a
Nuremberg follower of the Master of the Augustinian
Altar that dates to about 1490.

14. VIRGIN AND CHILD WITH THE PEAR

1511; monogram
Engraving
15.7 × 10.7 cm
B. 41; M. 33; H. 33
The University of Texas at Austin, Archer M.
Huntington Art Gallery

15. VIRGIN AND CHILD SEATED BY THE WALL

1514; monogram
Engraving
14.7 × 10 cm
B. 40; M. 36; H. 36
Lent by the Museum of Fine Arts, Houston:
Gift Marjorie G. and Evan C. Horning

Throughout his career, Dürer repeatedly returned to the theme of the Virgin and Child. While he varied the background and the trappings, Dürer's concern with the maternal relationship remained constant. In these two prints, Mary's face is tinged with resigned sadness as she contemplates her son's fate.[1] Christ often holds an apple or a pear that symbolically alludes to his role as the second Adam or to his incarnation. The Virgin and Child are shown without halos to accent their humanity. In related prints dating to 1519 and 1520, Dürer's figures radiate tremendous energy as he emphasizes their divine natures.[2]

Certain stylistic changes are evident when comparing these two engravings. In the 1511 print, Dürer is interested in sharp chiaroscuro contrasts as the whiteness of the paper is juxtaposed with the deep shadows, as in Mary's robe. Three years later, Dürer avoided these tonal polarities in favor of a greater range of medium tones that lend a warm, intimate mood to the scene.

The 1511 engraving is based upon a preparatory drawing of the same year now in Berlin (Kupferstichkabinett).[3] The setting is vaguely Italianate, perhaps a recollection from his second journey to Italy in 1505–1507. The scene in the background of the *Virgin and Child Seated by the Wall* is the Burg in Nuremberg. Although one critic identified it as the view from the northern gable window of Dürer's house by the Tiergärtnertor, I would suggest that Dürer stood outside the western wall of the city.[4] Although Dürer was not particularly concerned with providing a meticulously accurate city view, his representation gives a general idea of the appearance of the western fortifications before the major rebuilding by Antonio Fazuni between 1538 and 1545.

1. Also see Talbot, ed., *Dürer*, nrs. 37, 63; *Boston: Dürer*, nrs. 109, 185. My stylistic comments are largely based upon these two catalogues.
2. Meder 39–41.
3. Winkler, *Zeichnungen Dürers*, III: nr. 516.
4. W. Funk, "Die Landschaft auf Albrecht Dürers Kupferstich 'Die Madonna an der Stadtmauer,'" in *Albrecht-Dürer-Festschrift*, ed. G. Biermann (Leipzig, 1928), pp. 107–111. Early in his career, Dürer executed several watercolor views in and around Nuremberg; see Winkler, *Zeichnungen Dürers*, I: nrs. 61 (*Wire Mill*), 62 (*Johanniskirche*), 116 (*Nuremberg from the West*), among others. Cf. cat. nrs. 163–164, 192.

16. FOUR HEADS IN PROFILE

1513 (partially cut off); monogram
Drawing: pen and brown ink
21 × 20 cm
Lent by the Nelson-Atkins Museum of Art,
Kansas City, Missouri (Nelson Fund)

Shortly after returning from his second trip to
Venice in 1507, Dürer began investigating the
range of human facial types. In this drawing, the
artist first sketched an average male head.[1] In
each of the successive faces, the proportions of
the different parts of the face are altered. The
nose may be elongated or shortened or flattened. Chins can be varied to recede or to jut
out. By defining the face not simply as an ideal
type but as a series of parts that can be arranged in almost infinite combinations, Dürer
sought to establish a flexible system of human
proportions.[2]

During this Venetian trip, Dürer apparently
saw some of the caricatures by Leonardo da
Vinci or a follower in which faces were gro-
tesquely distorted.[3] These abnormal physiog-
nomies may have inspired Dürer's experiments.
Dürer used one of his grotesque designs for the
painting *Christ among the Doctors* of 1506.[4]

1. Winkler, *Zeichnungen Dürers*, III: nr. 657; Talbot,
ed., *Dürer*, nr. XX. This drawing is listed in the inventory of Willibald Imhoff as "Vier Mannsköpf hinter
einander." The drawing was probably in the possession of Imhoff's uncle Willibald Pirckheimer until 1530.
See cat. nr. 30 for comments on these two collections.
2. Dürer made other drawings of this type. A study
of ten heads in profile is in Berlin (Kupferstichkabinett). See Winkler, *Zeichnungen Dürers*, III: nr. 656; Talbot, ed., *Dürer*, fig. XXb. Either Baldung or Hans Leu,
another of Dürer's pupils, made two drawings of seventeen heads and nine heads that are based upon
Dürer's ideas; see *Hans Baldung Grien im Kunstmuseum
Basel*, exh. cat. (Basel: Kunstmuseum, 1978), nrs.
29–30, figs. 38–39.
3. Panofsky, *Dürer*, p. 269. For examples of
Leonardo's grotesques, see K. Clark and C. Pedretti,
*The Drawings of Leonardo da Vinci in the Collection of Her
Majesty the Queen at Windsor Castle*, rev. ed., 3 vols.
(London, 1968), I and II: nrs. 12449 recto to 12493.
4. Castagnola (Thyssen-Bornemisza Collection);
Anzelewsky, *Dürer*, nr. 98. Grotesque faces had
already been used in German and Netherlandish art to
represent Christ's tormentors in Passion scenes. See
J. Marrow, *Passion Iconography in Northern European Art
of the Late Middle Ages and Early Renaissance* (Kortrijk,
1979).

17. KNIGHT, DEATH, AND THE DEVIL

1513; monogram
Engraving
24.6 × 18.9 cm
B. 98; M. 74; H. 74
Lent by the Spencer Museum of Art, University of Kansas, Lawrence (Gift of the Max Kade Foundation)

In 1513 and 1514 Dürer created his so-called three master engravings: *Knight, Death, and the Devil*, *St. Jerome in His Study* (cat. nr. 18), and *Melencolia I* (cat. nr. 19). These three prints are linked by their large size, their technical virtuosity, and their thematic associations.

Knight, Death, and the Devil shows a knight mounted on a powerful horse riding resolutely through the rough terrain.[1] He ignores the horrific specter of a devil and the corpse-like figure of death who seeks to deter the knight by reminding him of his own mortality. As Panofsky has shown, the knight is the embodiment of the Church militant and the *vita activa*, or the active life of the Christian in the real, as opposed to cloistered, world.[2] Dürer was inspired by Erasmus's *Enchiridion militis Christiani* (*Handbook of the Christian Soldier*), which was published in 1504. Erasmus viewed the life of a Christian as a form of pilgrim's progress, in which one's beliefs are constantly challenged by self-doubts and the devil.

The design for this print is an assemblage of drawings Dürer had made over a fifteen-year period. The position of the knight and the style of his armor are based upon a sketch of a German soldier that Dürer penned in 1498;[3] this knight's horse, however, was shown at rest. In 1503 Dürer produced two further studies of horses in motion that were incorporated in his final print.[4] In a double drawing of about 1513, Dürer combined these earlier sketches and added the running dog.[5] The figure of death is an elaboration upon the 1505 *Memento Mori* charcoal drawing in London (British Museum).[6] The devil generally recalls the tormentors in Martin Schongauer's *The Temptation of St. Anthony*.[7]

1. Panofsky, *Dürer*, pp. 151–154; *Nuremberg: Dürer (1971)*, nr. 503; Talbot, ed., *Dürer*, nr. 58; *Boston: Dürer*, nrs. 179–182. See these sources for more thorough discussions of the iconography of this print.
2. Panofsky, *Dürer*, pp. 151–154.
3. Vienna (Albertina); Winkler, *Zeichnungen Dürers*, I: nr. 176.
4. Venice (Accademia) and Cologne (Wallraf Richartz Museum); ibid., II: nrs. 360–361. Dürer may have been inspired by Leonardo's designs.
5. The drawings are on the recto and verso of one sheet. Milan (Biblioteca Ambrosiana); ibid., III: nrs. 617–618; *Nuremberg: Dürer (1971)*, nr. 502.
6. Winkler, *Zeichnungen Dürers*, II: nr. 377.
7. Shestack, *Martin Schongauer*, nr. 4 (B. 47).

18. ST. JEROME IN HIS STUDY

1514; monogram
Engraving
24.7 × 19 cm (plate); 26.2 × 20 cm (sheet)
B. 60; M. 59; H. 59
Lent by the Kimbell Art Museum, Fort Worth

For many critics *St. Jerome in His Study* is Dürer's finest engraving, his technical masterpiece.[1] Dürer created a warm, sun-drenched chamber through the deft juxtaposition of tones, ranging from the pure whites of the paper, as seen in Jerome's halo, to the mottled surfaces of the window frame to the intense near-blacks of the lower wall. The artist has incorporated a seemingly limitless variety of lines and stipples to form objects and to suggest their textures.

Although the print is in black and white, the subtle tonal shifts have a colorific effect. Erasmus's admiration for Dürer's talent for implying color through his lines was expressed in his 1528 eulogy to the artist. In comparing Dürer with ancient Greek painter Apelles, he wrote:

> . . . Apelles was assisted by colors. . . . But Dürer, though admirable also in other respects, what does he not express in monochromes, that is, in black lines? Light, shade, splendor, eminences, depressions; and, though derived from the position of one single thing, more than one aspect offers itself to the eye of the beholder. He observes accurately proportions and harmonies. Nay, he even depicts that which cannot be depicted: fire, rays of light, thunder, sheet lightning, lightning, or, as they say, the "clouds on a wall"; all the sensations and emotions; in fine, the whole mind of man as it reflects itself in the behavior of the body, and almost the voice itself. These things he places before the eye in the most pertinent lines—black ones, yet so that if you should spread on pigments you would injure the work. And is it not more wonderful to accomplish without the blandishment of colors what Apelles accomplished with their aid?[2]

St. Jerome appears frequently in Dürer's art.[3] He can be the scholar, the penitent, or the elderly man contemplating death. In this engraving, Dürer shows Jerome within his quiet study as the thinker, wholly absorbed in the religious treatise, perhaps his translation of the Bible into Latin, on the writing desk. Like the evangelists portrayed in medieval manuscripts, Jerome is the spiritually inspired intellect. Just as the Christian knight in the 1513 engraving (cat. nr. 17) is the embodiment of the *vita activa*, or active life, Jerome represents the *vita contemplativa*, or the contemplative life of the theologian.[4] These two prints thus form pendants illustrating the dual character of the Christian church.

St. Jerome in His Study was frequently copied by other artists. Lucas Cranach used the composition as the framework for two of his portraits of Cardinal Albrecht von Brandenburg.[5] Nuremberg printmaker Wolfgang Stuber, who was active between 1580 and 1588, transformed Jerome into a portrait of Martin Luther.[6]

1. Jerome lived from about 340 to 420. On the print, also see Panofsky, *Dürer*, pp. 154–155; *Nuremberg: Dürer (1971)*, nr. 273; Talbot, ed., *Dürer*, nr. 60; *Boston: Dürer*, nrs. 186–187; P. W. Parshall, "Albrecht Dürer's St. Jerome in His Study: A Philological Reference," *Art Bulletin* 53 (1971): 303–305.
2. Panofsky, *Dürer*, p. 44; Rupprich, *Dürer schriftlicher Nachlass*, I: pp. 296–297, with the full text.
3. Meder 57–58, 227–229; Anzelewsky, *Dürer*, nrs. 14, 162.
4. Panofsky, *Dürer*, p. 156, for a more complete discussion.
5. *Nuremberg: Dürer (1971)*, nr. 274; Koepplin and Falk, *Lukas Cranach*, I: nr. 45, with color plate of Cranach's painting in Darmstadt (Hessisches Landesmuseum). Another version is in the Ringling Museum of Art in Sarasota, Florida.
6. *Nuremberg: Dürer (1971)*, nr. 275; esp. *Nuremberg: Vorbild Dürer*, nr. 186, also see 185 (by Hieronymus Hopfer), 187 (by Mario Cartaro), 188 (by Hieronymus Wierix).

19. MELENCOLIA I

1514; monogram
Engraving
23.9 × 18.9 cm (the right side has been cut with
a loss of .5–.7 cm)
B. 74; M. 75; H. 75
Lent by the Bridwell Library, Perkins School of
Theology, Southern Methodist University,
Dallas, Gift of the Everett Lee DeGolyer, Jr.,
family

Melencolia I was the most enigmatic of the three
master engravings until Panofsky demonstrated
that the figure of melancholy must be understood as a spiritual self-portrait of Dürer.[1] Dürer
fused the iconographic traditions of geometry,
one of the seven liberal arts, with melancholy,
the most severe of the four humors that control
man's temperament. Geometry was for Dürer
one form of the scientific basis of art, that is, the
knowledge all artists must be equipped with. The
attributes of geometry, including the sphere,
truncated rhombo-hedron, saw, wood plane,
scales, hourglass, bell, and magic square, are
haphazardly arranged around Melancholy.

Melancholy is identifiable both by the inert,
brooding pose and by her wreath of watercress
and water ranunculus, plants traditionally pre-
scribed because of their watery characteristics as
a curative to counterbalance the dryness of
melancholy. During the late fifteenth and early
sixteenth centuries, the melancholic humor was
increasingly viewed as a trait shared by all men
of genius. It was associated with the planet Saturn, which controlled the mind. Neoplatonic
writer Marsilio Ficino observed that all artists
suffer from varying degrees of melancholy.[2]
While subject to fits of depression, the melancholic was "known to walk a narrow ridge of
creativity, high above other mortals."[3] Cornelius
Agrippa of Nettesheim carried this analogy further by defining three types of melancholy. Artists and others of the first type were restricted
only by the heights of their imagination. Scien-
tists and physicians were dominated by reason.
And the third type, composed mainly of theologians, excelled in intuitive thought. Thus,
artists suffer from the first type of melancholy,
hence the print's title, *Melencolia I*.

Dürer's figure of Melancholy has mastered
geometry, yet she is rendered immobile by the
realization that there are boundaries beyond
which her creative knowledge can never transcend. During this period, Dürer was immersed
in his theoretical writings. Increasingly, he came
to understand that his scientific formulas did not
offer answers to all artistic problems. His frus-
trations are elegantly expressed in this engraving and in his comment that "the lie is in our
understanding, and darkness is so firmly entrenched in our mind that even our groping will
fail."[5] Whereas St. Jerome is busily engaged in
his spiritually inspired work and his chamber is
most orderly, the secular Melancholy, thwarted
by the limitations of human knowledge, sits inactive and surrounded by disorder. These two
prints represent opposite ideals of human
action.[6]

1. Panofsky, *Dürer*, pp. 156–171. This summarizes
much of his earlier research that is contained in Panofsky and F. Saxl, *Dürers 'Melencolia I.' Eine quellen- und
typengeschichtliche Untersuchung* (Leipzig, 1923). Also
see R. Klibansky, E. Panofsky, and F. Saxl, *Saturn and
Melancholy* (London, 1964). On this print, see *Nuremberg: Dürer (1971)*, nr. 270; Talbot, ed., *Dürer*, nr. 59,
which provides an excellent summary of Panofsky's
ideas; *Boston: Dürer*, nrs. 188–189; S. Rösch,
"Gedanken eines Naturforschers zu Dürers 'Melan-
cholie,'" *MVGN* 58 (1971): 161–167, which recon-
structs the engraving's perspective structure; H. von
Einem, "Notes on Dürer's Melencolia I," *Print Review* 5
(1976): 35–39.
2. Panofsky, *Dürer*, pp. 165ff.
3. Talbot, ed., *Dürer*, nr. 59.
4. Panofsky, *Dürer*, p. 169; *Nuremberg: Dürer (1971)*,
nr. 276.
5. Panofsky, *Dürer*, p. 171.
6. Ibid., p. 156.

20. TRIUMPHAL ARCH OF EMPEROR MAXIMILIAN I (DIE EHRENPFORTE)

1515 (dated); 1512–1517/18
Woodcut: 192 blocks cut by Hieronymus
Andreae
340.9 × 292.2 cm
B. 138; Dodgson, I: pp. 311–328; M. 251; H. 251

A. *Ehrenpforte des Kaisers Maximilian I. Des aller
   durch leuchtigisten gross mechtigsten fürsten
   schlachten vnd thaten* (Vienna: Raphael
   Hofhalter, 1559)
   Fourth edition of the twenty-four historical
   scenes
   Lent by the John M. Wing Foundation of
   The Newberry Library, Chicago

B. Photograph of the 1799 edition of the entire
   arch on display at the New York Public
   Library

Emperor Maximilian I was the first Renaissance prince to recognize the propaganda potential of the graphic arts. Flattering allegorical conceits could be reproduced in multiple copies and disseminated throughout the empire. Indeed, much

of Maximilian's subsequent fame is due to such artistic projects as the *Triumphal Arch*, the *Great Triumphal Chariot* (cat. nr. 26), *Theuerdank* (cat. nr. 47), *Weisskunig* (cat. nr. 54), and the incomplete *Freydal*.[1] Maximilian reportedly said that "whoever prepares no memorial for himself during his lifetime has none after his death and is forgotten along with the sound of the bell that tolls his passing. Thus the money I spend for the perpetuation of my memory is not lost; in fact, in such a matter to be sparing of money is to suppress my future memory."[2]

The *Triumphal Arch* was the greatest of these projects.[3] Court astronomer Johannes Stabius (died 1522) devised the iconographic program in conjunction with Jörg Kölderer, a painter and architect who worked for Maximilian in Innsbruck.[4] It consists of seven basic parts: the three gates of honor, praise, and nobility; the central tower; twenty-four historical scenes from Maximilian's life (exhibited here); busts of emperors and kings (left); busts of Maximilian's ancestors from Clovis to Friedrich III to his six grandchildren (right); the two round towers with eleven scenes from Maximilian's private life; and various decorative and symbolic ornaments.

Originally, the *Triumphal Arch* was to be displayed in conjunction with the fifty-four–meter-long *Great Triumphal Chariot* and the *Arch of Devotion* (*Die Andachtspforte*), the religious counterpart of the secular arch, which was never designed.

Dürer's participation in this project likely began between 4 February and 21 April 1512, when Maximilian and Stabius were in Nuremberg. Since Kölderer's watercolor drawings for the arch are lost, it is uncertain how specific the preliminary designs were. Dürer was assisted by his former pupils Hans Springinklee and Wolf Traut, as well as Regensburg artist Albrecht Altdorfer. Springinklee created seven of the historical scenes and much of the family tree while Traut is credited with making twelve historical woodcuts. Altdorfer added the two flanking towers with the scenes from Maximilian's private life.

The arch is dated 1515. Although the artistic designs were completed by this date, Nuremberg *formschneider* Hieronymus Andreae did not finish the monumental task of cutting the 192 woodblocks until 1517.[5] A proof edition of the arch was printed in 1517 and in January and Feb-

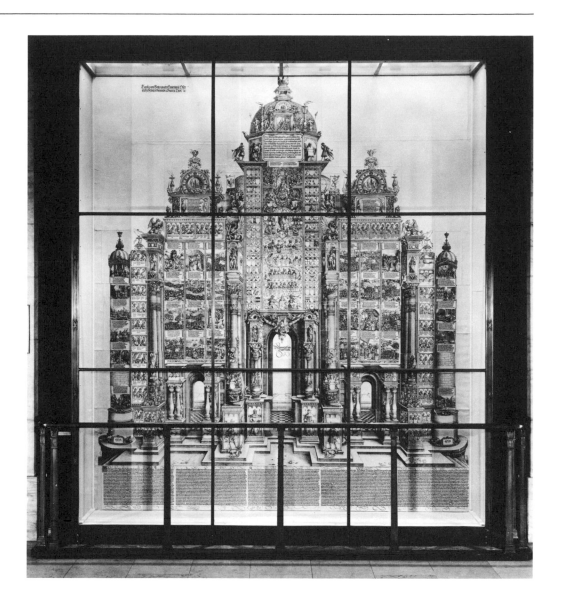

ruary 1518 the first edition of two hundred copies was delivered to Maximilian. Shortly afterward the annual pensions of Stabius and Dürer were doubled by the emperor.

The *Triumphal Arch* was published both in its entirety and in a book format containing only the twenty-four historical woodcuts after Maximilian's death in 1519. In 1526 Archduke Ferdinand I of Austria obtained the original woodblocks, which had remained in the possession of Hieronymus Andreae. He had a second complete edition printed in Vienna between 1526 and 1528. Ferdinand received 300 copies. The woodblocks, which today are in Vienna, were reused in 1559 by Raphael Hofhalter, in 1799 by Adam Bartsch, and in 1885–1886 as a facsimile in the periodical *Jahrbuch der kunsthistorisch Sammlungen des allehöchsten Kaiserhauses*. Hofhalter also issued the fourth book edition of the historical scenes.[6] The first three printings by Hieronymus Andreae are incomplete.

Illustrated here are Traut's woodcut (number one) of Maximilian as the perfect prince, surrounded by the symbols of warfare, chivalry, venery, construction, and literature, and Dürer's scene (number two) of Maximilian's marriage to Mary, Duchess of Burgundy, on 19 August 1477.[7] Dürer's woodcut was replaced by another on the same subject by Springinklee in the 1799 and 1885–1886 editions, as can be seen in the photograph of the 1799 version on display at the New York Public Library.

1. *Vienna: Maximilian I. 1459–1519*, pp. 21–39, 68–115, nrs. 66–69 on the *Freydal*.

2. Cited without a source in S. Appelbaum, ed., *The Triumph of Maximilian I: 137 Woodcuts by Hans Burgkmair and Others*, p. v.

3. My comments are taken from the following sources: E. Chmelarz, "Die Ehrenpforte des Kaisers Maximilian I.," *JKSAK* 4 (1886): 289–319; Dodgson, I: pp. 311–328; P. Strieder, "Zur Entstehungsgeschichte von Dürers Ehrenpforte für Kaiser Maximilian," *AGNM* (1954–1959): 128–142; *Vienna: Maximilian I. 1459–1519*, pp. 69–78, nrs. 350–377; *Nuremberg: Meister um Dürer*, nr. 341; *Nuremberg: Dürer (1971)*, nr. 261; *Boston: Dürer*, nr. 204; *Maximilian's Triumphal Arch: Woodcuts by Albrecht Dürer and Others* (New York: Dover Publications, 1972), which is a copy of the 1885–1886 edition; Strauss, *Albrecht Dürer Woodcuts and Woodblocks*, pp. 500–507, 639, 726–731.

4. Strauss, *Albrecht Dürer Woodcuts and Woodblocks*, pp. 726–731, provides an English translation of the Stabius text at the bottom of the arch. On Stabius, also see the comments for cat. nr. 21. Kölderer also produced the elaborate drawings that Burgkmair and others used for the *Triumphal Procession*; see *Vienna:*

Maximilian I. 1459–1519, nrs. 216–274. His role in the planning of the *Triumphal Arch* must have been considerable since his coat of arms was added along with those of Stabius and Dürer at the lower right of the arch.

5. The Museum of Fine Arts in Boston possesses the copy owned by Niclas Meldemann, Nuremberg painter, publisher, and woodblock cutter. Since it bears his notations on the backside, H. R. Rossiter suggested that Meldemann must have assisted Andreae in the cutting of the blocks. See Rossiter, "Maximilian's Triumphal Arch," *Bulletin of the Museum of Fine Arts, Boston* 49 (1951): 95–98; *Boston: Dürer*, nr. 204.

6. Dodgson, I: pp. 321–328, fully describes the four book editions.

7. Traut's dog is copied from Dürer's *St. Eustace* (Meder 60).

21. NORTHERN HEMISPHERE

1515
Woodcut
42.7 × 42.7 cm
B. 151; M. 260; H. 260
Lent by the Metropolitan Museum of Art, New York, Harris Brisbane Dick Fund, 1951

In 1515, at the request of Johannes Stabius, Maximilian I's court astronomer, Dürer completed woodcut maps of the northern and southern celestial hemispheres and of the earth.[1] Stabius dedicated these three maps to Cardinal Matthäus Lang of Wellenburg, the emperor's former secretary. The two celestial maps, the first ever printed, were designed as a pair. The *Southern Hemisphere* displays the coats of arms of Stabius, Dürer, and Conrad Heinfogel, a Nuremberg astronomer who suggested certain corrections to the heavenly maps.

Dürer's specific source was a pair of hand-drawn maps (Nuremberg, Germanisches Nationalmuseum) that were made in Nuremberg in 1503.[2] Dürer's two woodcuts are almost exact copies of these drawings. The artist altered the individual constellations only slightly and added the four astronomers Aratos, Ptolemy, Azophi (Alsufi), and Manilius in the corners of the *Northern Hemisphere*. According to the research of Voss and others, the 1503 map is based upon an Arabic prototype that was once in the possession of Johannes Regiomontanus in Nuremberg.[3] A local astronomer, probably Heinfogel, updated the map so that it would be correct for the years 1499–1500. The numbers marked on the constellations and surrounding zodiacal signs correspond to the arrangement of stars listed in books eight and nine of Ptolemy's *Algamest*.[4]

1. On the *Northern Hemisphere*, also see *Nuremberg: Dürer (1971)*, nr. 309; Talbot, ed., *Dürer*, nr. 199. On the *Southern Hemisphere* and the terrestrial map, see Meder 259 and 261; *Nuremberg: Dürer (1971)*, nrs. 308, 315; Talbot, ed., *Dürer*, nr. 198 (*Southern Hemisphere*). For detailed discussions of these three woodcuts, see E. Weiss, "Albrecht Dürer's geographische, astronomische und astrologische Tafeln," *JKSAK* 7 (1888): 207–220; F. Saxl, *Verzeichnis astrologischer und mythologischer illustrierter Handschriften des lateinischen Mittelalters* (Heidelberg, 1927), II: pp. 19–40; W. Voss, "Eine Himmelskarte vom Jahre 1503 mit den Wahrzeichen des Wiener Poetenkollegiums als Vorlage Albrecht Dürers," *JPKS* 64 (1943): 89–150; G. Hamann, "Albrecht Dürers Erd- und Himmelskarten," in Hirschmann and Schnelbögl, eds., *Albrecht Dürers Umwelt*, pp. 152–177. The woodblocks for the two celestial prints are today in Berlin (Kupferstichkabinett); see Strauss, *Albrecht Dürer Woodcuts and Woodblocks*, pp. 635–636.
2. Voss, "Eine Himmelskarte vom Jahre 1503"; Zink, *Die Handzeichnungen*, nrs. 99–100; *Nuremberg: Dürer (1971)*, nrs. 307–308.
3. The map owned by Regiomontanus was probably in the possession of his follower and heir Bernhard Walther.
4. Talbot, ed., *Dürer*, nr. 199. For the influence of Dürer's celestial maps on later art, notably Giovanni Antonio Vanosino's Sala Bolognese (1570s) in the Vatican, see J. Hess, "On Some Celestial Maps and Globes of the Sixteenth Century," *Journal of the Warburg and Courtauld Institutes* 30 (1967): 406–409, esp. 406–407.

22. CHRIST ON THE MOUNT OF OLIVES

1515; monogram
Etching on iron
22.1 × 15.3 cm
B. 19; M. 19; H. 19
Private Collection, London

Dürer was one of the first German artists to experiment with the etching technique, which
prior to the first decade of the sixteenth century
had been employed primarily by armor makers
and goldsmiths.[1] Between 1514 and 1518, Dürer
made six etchings and then abandoned the technique.[2] As Talbot has noted, Dürer never fully
exploited or, perhaps, understood the spontaneity of line that is possible in etching.[3] Instead, he carefully placed his strokes and developed his shading contrasts much in the same
way he did in his engravings. Dürer faithfully
followed the pen-and-ink preliminary sketch
that is now in Vienna (Albertina).[4]

Following the Last Supper, Christ and his disciples went to the garden of Gethsemane on the
Mount of Olives.[5] Taking Peter, John, and James
with him, Christ entered into the garden. Apart
from the others, Christ knelt in prayer and beseeched God to take away the cup, an Old Testament symbol of divine judgment and, here, an
allusion to Christ's pending martyrdom. Dürer's
Christ is resigned to his fate, comforted only by
the angel. By placing Christ in the foreground
and contrasting his divine light with the darkness of night, Dürer isolated Christ. The drama
of the event is strengthened by the approach of
Judas and the soldiers toward the garden gate.

1. On the etching technique, see A. M. Hind, *A
History of Engraving & Etching from the 15th Century to
the Year 1914*, 3d rev. ed. (New York, 1963), ch. III; esp.
Boston: Dürer, p. XVIII.
2. *Desperate Man* of about 1514–1515 (Meder 95);
Christ on the Mount of Olives; the *Man of Sorrows Seated*
of 1515 (Meder 22); *Abduction of the Unicorn* (Meder 67)
and *Sudarium Held by One Angel* (cat. nr. 23), both
dated 1516; and *Landscape with a Cannon*, dated 1518
(Meder 96). See Talbot, ed., *Dürer*, nrs. 65–69.
3. Talbot, ed., *Dürer*, nr. 66. On this etching, also
see *Nuremberg: Dürer (1971)*, nr. 612; *Boston: Dürer*, nrs.
191–192. The plate is in Bamberg (Staatsbibliothek).
The exhibited print is from the first edition.
4. Winkler, *Zeichnungen Dürers*, III: nr. 585, and see
nr. 584 (Paris, Louvre), which shows another version
of the same theme that Dürer made in 1515.
5. Schiller, *Iconography of Christian Art*, II: pp. 48–51,
provides a discussion of the subject.

23. THE SUDARIUM HELD BY ONE ANGEL

1516; monogram
Etching on iron
18.3 × 13.4 cm
B. 26; M. 27; H. 27
Lent by the Spencer Museum of Art, University of Kansas, Lawrence

In 1513 Dürer designed an engraving of two angels holding the sudarium, or veil, of St. Veronica.[1] Although the faces of the angels mirror their grief over the death of Christ, the emotionalism of this print cannot match the supreme drama of Dürer's 1516 etching.[2] The sudarium is now held by just one angel, but rather than simply displaying the veil to the viewer, the angel, overcome with anguish, races madly through the heavens. Unlike the group of angels below who transport the instruments of the Passion, this angel has broken away and intently stares at the wind-whipped veil. Dürer has placed the veil upside down and in an uncustomary, asymmetrical spot at the top of the composition. These features, coupled with the remarkable interplay of lines and wide range of chiaroscuro contrasts, most notably in the angel's robe, heighten the theatrical animation of the scene.

The veil, or sudarium, of St. Veronica was a popular subject in German art.[3] The saint frequently appears at the edge of the road in scenes of Christ carrying the cross. According to legend, Veronica took pity on the struggling Christ and used her veil to wipe his brow. Christ's sweat and blood left an indelible portrait of the Lord on the cloth. Numerous miracles were attributed to the sudarium. Today the cloth is in St. Peter's in Rome.

This particular impression of the etching was pulled during the artist's lifetime or shortly thereafter before the plate began to rust.

1. Meder 26.
2. *Nuremberg: Dürer (1971)*, nr. 340; Talbot, ed., *Dürer*, nr. 68; *Boston: Dürer*, nr. 193. Dürer's drawing for this etching is now in London (British Museum); see R. Pickvance, "Sixty Years of Patronage," *Connoisseur* 160 (1965): 103, fig. 7.
3. L. Réau, *Iconographie de l'Art Chrétien*, III.3, pp. 1314–1317.

116

24. REFORMACION DER STAT NÜREMBERG . . . (Nuremberg: Friedrich Peypus, 21 January 1521)

1 woodcut (on the verso of the title page—folio aa i verso)
24.5 × 16.6 cm (woodcut only); original binding
B. 162; M. 285; H. 285
Lent by the Library of Congress, Washington, Lessing J. Rosenwald Collection

The *Reformacion der Stat Nüremberg*, when initially printed by Anton Koberger in Nuremberg in 1484, was Germany's first printed civil legal code.[1] Michael Wolgemut supplied the woodcut with Nuremberg's coats of arms. In 1519 or early 1520, the city council ordered a new, revised edition. Since Dürer left for the Netherlands on 12 July 1520 and was away for a full year, he must have designed the woodcut before his departure.[2] Peypus probably added the date 1521 to signify the year of publication.

The woodcut is entitled *Sancta Ivsticia*, or Holy Justice. At the top are the virtues Justice and Liberality, who refer to the inherent character of both the law code and the city council.[3] Below, two angels support the city's three coats of arms.[4] In the center is the emperor's crown and double-headed eagle, signifying Nuremberg's status as a free imperial city. At the lower left is the crowned, human-headed female eagle and, opposite, is a split shield with half of an eagle and five diagonal bars.

Although Dürer did not add his monogram, which he probably felt would be out of place among the city's coats of arms, the attribution is secure based upon the figure style and the artist's shading scheme. The original woodblock is in the Derschau Collection in East Berlin.[5]

1. *Nuremberg: Dürer (1971)*, nr. 231; *Reformation in Nürnberg*, nr. 67. The title of the 1484 edition was *Newe Reformacion der Stat Nureberg*.

2. On this woodcut, see *Nuremberg: Dürer (1971)*, nr. 232; Talbot, ed., *Dürer*, nr. 214; Schultheiss, "Albrecht Dürers Beziehungen zum Recht," in *Albrecht Dürers Umwelt*, ed. Hirschmann and Schnelbögl, pp. 248–249. The woodcut appeared in a second edition in 1522 and in several unrelated publications; see Hollstein, nr. 285.

3. The role of the city council in dispensing justice, alluded to in this code, is explicitly portrayed in an anonymous watercolor of the second half of the sixteenth century. It shows a model of the city placed on the shoulder of a seated patrician. Hanging above are the sword and scales of justice. See *Reformation in Nürnberg*, nr. 6.

4. On the city's coats of arms, see R. Schaffer, "Die Siegel und Wappen der Reichsstadt Nürnberg," *Zeitschrift für bayerische Landesgeschichte* 10 (1937): 157–203.

5. Strauss, *Albrecht Dürer Woodcuts and Woodblocks*, ill. on p. 644.

25. PORTRAIT OF ULRICH VARNBÜLER

A. 1522; signed in text
Woodcut
48.7 × 32.6 cm
B. 150; M. 256; H. 256
Lent by the New York Public Library, Prints
Division, Astor, Lenox and Tilden
Foundations

B. Early seventeenth century; signed in text
Chiaroscuro woodcut in black, brown,
yellow, and white
48.7 × 32.6 cm
B. 150; M. 256; H. 256
Lent by the New York Public Library, Prints
Division, Astor, Lenox and Tilden
Foundations

In 1522 Ulrich Varnbüler (1474–ca. 1544), the prothonotary of the Imperial Supreme Court, attended the imperial diet held in Nuremberg. Dürer used the occasion to make the charcoal-and-chalk profile drawing of his friend that is now in Vienna (Albertina).[1] This drawing served as the design for the printed portrait that is the largest of Dürer's woodcuts and only the second portrait that Dürer had made in this technique.[2] It is inscribed

VLRICHVS VARNBVLER ETC M.DXXII
Albrecht Dürer of Nuremberg wishes to make

known to posterity and to preserve by this likeness his singular friend, Ulrich surnamed Varnbüler, Chancellor of the Supreme Court of the Roman Empire and at the same time privately a distinguished scholar of language.[3]

The flourishing script may have been written by calligrapher Johann Neudörfer, who penned the explanatory text at the bottom of Dürer's *Four Apostles* (fig. 26) in 1526.

The subsequent fate of the woodblock used to print this portrait is only partially known.[4] By the beginning of the seventeenth century, the woodblock was in the possession of Hendrick Hondius in The Hague, who continued to issue impressions. Around 1620 the woodblock was owned by Willem Jansen in Amsterdam. According to Meder, the woodblocks were in rather poor condition so Jansen added two tone blocks to improve the appearance of the print. The exhibited example was printed with yellow and brown tone blocks; green versions are also recorded.

1. Winkler, *Zeichnungen Dürers*, IV: nr. 908.
2. *Nuremberg: Dürer (1971)*, nr. 545; Talbot, ed., *Dürer*, nrs. 203–204; *Boston: Dürer*, nr. 207. Dürer's first woodcut portrait was of Emperor Maximilian; see Meder, nr. 255. The only other woodcut portrait is of Eobanus Hessus (cat. nr. 33), which is after Dürer's drawing rather than designed entirely by the artist.
3. The translation is from Talbot, ed., *Dürer*, nr. 203. The last part of the inscription alludes to Varnbüler's

translation of Erasmus's essay *Dulce bellum inesperto*. Panofsky suggested that the letters covered by the strip that runs through the inscription form an anagram, "Varennulere," for Varnbüler's name; see E. Panofsky, *Albrecht Dürer*, 2 vols. (Princeton, 1943), II: p. 45, nr. 369.
4. See Meder, nr. 256. Also see W. Strauss, *Chiaroscuro: The Clair-Obscur Woodcuts by the German and Netherlandish Masters of the XVIth and XVIIth Centuries*, nr. 1.

26. THE GREAT TRIUMPHAL CHARIOT (*See p. 120*)

27. CRUCIFIXION IN OUTLINE (GREAT CRUCIFIXION)

1523
Engraving
32 × 22.5 cm
M. 25; H. 25
Lent by the St. Louis Art Museum, 138: 1916

Dürer never finished this engraving, a fact that has long puzzled art historians.[1] He made at least thirteen elaborate preparatory drawings on green or blue prepared paper that are dated 1521 or 1523.[2] The figures of the Virgin and John the Evangelist are sketched in reverse so that they would be oriented correctly in the print.

Panofsky suggested that Dürer found the print overly crowded and abandoned the project.[3] Winkler thought that the plate, set aside temporarily by Dürer, was accidentally scratched, forcing Dürer to scrap any plans to complete the engraving.[4] Recently, Rasmussen has argued that Dürer's changing religious attitudes caused him not to finish the print.[5] Rasmussen developed Panofsky's earlier identification of St. John as an idealized portrait of Luther. He goes on to claim that while it had been acceptable to portray Luther as a saint, as Baldung did in a 1521 woodcut, it was no longer permissible in 1523, given the ever more stringent Protestant condemnations of Catholic veneration of saints.[6] Therefore, in 1523 or 1524 it would have been blasphemous to represent Luther in the guise of St. John.

Whatever the actual reason, the incomplete engraving provides a superb idea of Dürer's technical practices. First, Dürer worked out the composition in a series of preparatory drawings. It is unclear whether he used these individual drawings or created a definitive sketch of the entire composition that has not survived. The drawing or drawings could be placed on the copper plate and lightly incised to transfer the image, or the artist could work directly on the plate with the drawing(s) before him. With his burin he outlined the figures on the copper plate, but he never finished this stage. The figure of St. Longinus, whose lance tip is seen in the center, was not added. The *Sultan*, another unfinished engraving, shows that Dürer next strengthened the contour lines and added details and shading lines in select sections of the print, here the robe.[7] The unique impression of the *Sultan*, now in Amsterdam, was printed with hand pressure as a trial proof so that the artist could study the progress of his work. Trial proofs exist for Dürer's *Adam and Eve* (cat. nr. 11) and *Hercules*.[8] In the case of *Adam and Eve*, Dürer finished all the background and the figure of Eve before completing the legs of Adam.

Dürer never published the *Crucifixion in Outline*. The impression exhibited here is one of the rare engravings made using the original plate. The watermark places the date between 1558 and 1588. Dürer's plate was copied, with only minor variations, by another artist and impressions from this second plate are more common.

1. *Nuremberg: Dürer (1971)*, nr. 223; Talbot, ed., *Dürer*, nr. 74, which provides a good summary of earlier literature.
2. Winkler, *Zeichnungen Dürers*, IV: pp. 56–61, nrs. 762, 766, 768, 858 (*Mary and Two Holy Women*), 859 (*John the Evangelist*), 860–865, 867–869.
3. Panofsky, *Dürer*, pp. 223–235, esp. 224.
4. Winkler, *Zeichnungen Dürers*, IV: p. 57; Talbot, ed., *Dürer*, nr. 74.
5. J. Rasmussen, "Zu Dürers unvollendetem Kupferstich 'Die Grosse Kreuzigung,'" *AGNM* (1981): 56–79.
6. Marrow and Shestack, eds., *Hans Baldung Grien*, fig. 41.
7. Meder 91.
8. Meder 1, 63.

26. THE GREAT TRIUMPHAL CHARIOT

1522 (1523 Latin edition); signed
Woodcut: 8 blocks
45 × 228.1 cm
B. 139; M. 252; H. 252
Lent by the Spencer Museum of Art, University of Kansas, Lawrence

In 1512 Emperor Maximilian I conceived of one of his greatest artistic projects: a series of prints depicting a vast triumphal procession glorifying himself and his family. It was to be displayed in conjunction with the *Triumphal Arch* (cat. nr. 20) that Dürer and his workshop finished in 1515.[1] Court artist Jörg Kölderer created the preliminary miniatures that were to serve as the designs for the woodcuts by Hans Burgkmair, Leonhard Beck, Albrecht Altdorfer, Wolf Huber, Hans Schäufelein, and, perhaps, Hans Springinklee. The design for the central chariot with Maximilian and his first wife, Mary of Burgundy, was made by Dürer in about 1516.[2] This series, which was incomplete when Maximilian died in 1519, measures fifty-four meters long.

In 1518 Dürer and Willibald Pirckheimer began working on a new chariot design for the emperor. The program became increasingly elaborate. Dürer's drawing of 1518, now in Vienna (Albertina), shows that the chariot has been expanded to include Maximilian, his two wives, his two children (Philip the Fair and Margaret of Austria), and Philip's children (Charles V, Ferdinand, and his four daughters).[3] Surrounding Maximilian are various allegorical figures. The chariot is pulled by six teams of horses led by virtues. Correspondence between Maximilian and Pirckheimer proves that the emperor examined and approved either this drawing or, less likely, the final print.[4]

With Maximilian's death in January 1519, Dürer altered the design. He retained Maximilian and the virtues surrounding him, but removed all the other family members. The cycle became an allegory of Maximilian as the ideal emperor rather than a glorification of his genealogy. Dürer first published the *Great Triumphal Chariot* in 1522.[5] Detailed texts were added to explain all the different symbolic features. Exhibited here is the first Latin edition, which was issued in 1523. Since Maximilian had died before the series was completed, Dürer resorted to his independent

publication of the *Great Triumphal Chariot* in order to obtain some remuneration for years of work on the cycle.[6] For reasons that are somewhat unclear, the *Great Triumphal Chariot* was replaced by Dürer's *Small Triumphal Chariot* in the 1526 publication of the *Triumphal Procession of Maximilian I*.

Each of the eight blocks is lettered; from left to right are the following images:

A and B   Maximilian is seated in the center of the triumphal chariot. The canopy is adorned with a sun and the imperial coat of arms. The inscription reads, "That which the sun is in the heavens, the Emperor is on earth." Victory crowns Maximilian. Standing on pedestals are Justice, Temperance, Fortitude, and Prudence, the four cardinal virtues. Running beside the chariot are Security, Confidence, Gravity, and Perseverance. Reason drives the chariot, whose wheels are inscribed Honor, Glory, Magnificence, and Dignity. The reins are marked Nobility and Power.

C   Providence and Moderation lead the first pair of horses. They are preceded by

D   Eagerness and Fitness
E   Firmness and Quickness
F   Virility and Keenness
G   Magnanimity and Courage
H   Experience and Cleverness.

Dürer's final design was finished by 1521, at the latest, since in this year Georg Pencz and other artists connected with Dürer's atelier used the print as the model for the mural they painted on the north wall of the great hall of the Nuremberg Rathaus.[7] In 1520 the city council had requested Dürer and Pirckheimer to plan the program for the interior decorations of this room. Since the Golden Bull (1356) required that the first diet (Reichstag) held by a new emperor must be in Nuremberg, specifically in the great

hall of the Rathaus, Dürer and Pirckheimer determined that this allegory of imperial virtues and glorification of Maximilian would be an appropriate subject for this chamber. Except for minor decorative changes and the addition of cartouches, with the explanatory texts, suspended for garlands above the horses, the painting closely replicates Dürer's woodcut cycle. The earliest view of this chamber showing the various decorative programs is the painting by Paul Juvenel the Elder (cat. nr. 213).

1. The literature on this cycle is extensive. See especially F. Schestag, "Kaiser Maximilian I. Triumph," *JKSAK* 1 (1883): 154–181, and plate volume (1884); *Vienna: Maximilian I. 1459–1519*, pp. 69–104, nrs. 216–340; Appelbaum, ed., *The Triumph of Maximilian I*; H. Appuhn and C. von Heusinger, *Riesenholzschnitte und Papiertapeten der Renaissance*, pp. 55–61.

2. Dürer's *Small Triumphal Chariot* is Meder 253. It was cut by Hieronymus Andreae.

3. Winkler, *Zeichnungen Dürers*, III: nr. 685. Cf. nr. 671 (Vienna, Albertina), which is Dürer's first drawing; it is based largely upon Jörg Kölderer's initial design. See *Vienna: Maximilian I. 1459–1519*, nr. 258. Dürer also made drawings of trophy bearers to be used in the triumphal procession; see Winkler, III: nrs. 690–699; *Vienna: Maximilian I. 1459–1519*, nrs. 344–349.

4. Rupprich, *Dürer schriftlicher Nachlass*, I: p. 261, nrs. 40 (Pirckheimer's letter to Maximilian, which was written at the beginning of the year), 41 (Maximilian's response, dated 29 March 1518). English translations of these two letters are provided in Strauss, *Albrecht Dürer Woodcuts and Woodblocks*, p. 536.

5. On the *Great Triumphal Chariot*, also see *Vienna: Maximilian I. 1459–1519*, nr. 343; *Nuremberg: Dürer (1971)*, nr. 264; Talbot, ed., *Dürer*, nr. 202; *Boston: Dürer*, nr. 205. Hieronymus Andreae also cut this series.

6. According to Meder, nr. 252, and Hollstein, nr. 252, seven editions using Dürer's woodblocks were issued before 1600. Hans Guldenmund of Nuremberg printed a copy of this series that initially appeared in 1529 and was reissued in 1545 and 1609. One additional sixteenth-century copy and an eighteenth-century copy were also published.

7. See Mende, *Rathaus*, I: pp. 224–245, nrs. 221–272, for a thorough discussion of the mural picture. Also see the comments in Section 6 and cat. nr. 213.

28. LAST SUPPER

1523; monogram
Woodcut
21.3 × 30 cm
B. 53; M. 184; H. 184
Lent by the Cleveland Museum of Art, Norman
O. Stone and Ella A. Stone Memorial Fund

The *Last Supper* is Dürer's last major woodcut.[1] Christ is placed in the center at the focal point of the perspective scheme. Dürer has selected the moment when Christ commands his followers to love each other. Christ's gesture is calm but forceful. The resigned expression on his face recalls his sad appearance in the *Christ on the Mount of Olives* etching (cat. nr. 22). Judas has already departed. Peter, to Christ's left, is visibly shaken by the knowledge that he will deny his master three times before the coming dawn. By stripping the room of all unessential features, Dürer concentrated the viewer's attention upon the individual emotional responses of the disciples.[2]

The only portable objects in the room are the chalice on the table and the charger, basket of bread, and wine pitcher on the floor. As Lenz, Panofsky, and others have observed, the *Last Supper* is Dürer's commentary on the contemporary chalice controversy.[3] In his "Sermon on the New Testament, that is, on Holy Mass" of 1520, Luther argued that Christ instituted the Eucharist as a testament and sacrament, not as a sacrifice.[4] The laity should therefore be permitted to partake of both the host and the wine rather than just the host as was then customary in Germany. The next year Luther's follower Andreas Bodenstein von Karlstadt dedicated his "On the Adoration and Reverence for the Miracles of the New Testament," a treatise on the chalice controversy, to Albrecht Dürer.[5] On Easter Sunday in 1523, the Nuremberg city council permitted the Holy Communion service at the Augustinerkloster to follow Luther's changes in the eucharistic liturgy.[6] St. Sebaldus, St. Lorenz, and the other churches in Nuremberg were required to follow the traditional Roman Catholic rite. According to the later account of Caspar Peucer, Dürer and Pirckheimer hotly debated the issue while Melanchthon resided at Pirckheimer's house in late 1525 and early 1526.[7] Dürer strongly supported Luther's stand, while his friend adhered to the Roman Catholic form of the service.

In Dürer's woodcut, the chalice alone is set on the table to indicate that Christ shared this sacrament with his disciples. The sacrificial paschal lamb is not represented, as the charger on the floor is empty.[8] Finally, equal stress is placed upon the basket of bread and the wine pitcher on the floor.

1. *Nuremberg: Dürer (1971)*, nr. 396; Talbot, ed., *Dürer*, nr. 206; *Boston: Dürer*, nrs. 208–209.

2. Although it is occasionally suggested that Dürer used either Leonardo da Vinci's *Last Supper* in Milan (S. Maria delle Grazie) or Raimondi's print (B. 26) of the subject after a drawing attributed to Raphael as his model, his woodcut owes little to either work beyond a general placement of figures around three sides of a table and a concentration upon individual gestures. See I. H. Shoemaker and E. Broun, *The Engravings of Marcantonio Raimondi*, nr. 30.

3. O. Lenz, "Der Dürersche Holzschnitt 'Des Abendmahl' von 1523," *Die christliche Kunst* 21 (1924–1925): 232–236; Panofsky, *Dürer*, pp. 221–223; see note 1 above.

4. Panofsky, *Dürer*, p. 222. Also see Luther's *Von beyder gestalt des Sacraments tzu nemen vnd anter newrung* (Wittenberg, 1522); *Reformation in Nürnberg*, nr. 206, and also see nrs. 173–177.

5. *Von anbetung vnd eer erbietung der zaychen des newen Testaments* (Augsburg, 1521); *Nuremberg: Dürer (1971)*, nr. 392. Karlstadt's dedication to Dürer is published by Rupprich, *Dürer schriftlicher Nachlass*, I: pp. 92–93 (nr. 37), and, in English translation, by Strauss, *Albrecht Dürer Woodcuts and Woodblocks*, p. 568.

6. This ruling is discussed in *Reformation in Nürnberg*, nr. 207.

7. Rupprich, *Dürer schriftlicher Nachlass*, I: pp. 306–307 (nr. 21). This account includes quotations attributed to Dürer and Pirckheimer. In 1526 and 1527, Pirckheimer wrote two treatises about the Last Supper and the sacrament. See G. Krodel, "Nürnberger Humanisten am Anfang des Abendmahlsstreites," *Zeitschrift für bayerische Kirchengeschichte* 25 (1956): 40–50; *Nuremberg: Dürer (1971)*, nr. 407.

8. The lamb was placed in the center of the table in Dürer's other two Last Supper woodcuts in the *Large Passion* (1510) and *Small Woodcut Passion* (1511); see Meder 114 and 133. The chalice and the bread are both on the table before Christ in Dürer's drawing (Vienna, Albertina) of 1523; see Winkler, *Zeichnungen Dürers*, IV: nr. 889.

123

29. PORTRAIT OF FRIEDRICH THE WISE, ELECTOR OF SAXONY

1524; signature and monogram
Engraving
19.3 × 12.7 cm
B. 104; M. 102; H. 102
Lent by the New York Public Library, Prints Division, Astor, Lenox and Tilden Foundations

Friedrich the Wise (1463–1525), Dürer's first and most steadfast princely patron, was an enlightened supporter of the arts and of learning.[1] For instance, he founded the university at Wittenberg in 1502. For Friedrich, Dürer painted his portrait in 1496, the *Adoration of the Magi* in 1504, and the *Martyrdom of 10,000* in 1508.[2] Before he departed for Venice in 1505, Dürer instructed his pupil to paint the *Ober-Sankt-Veit Altar*, using his drawings, for the elector.[3]

Friedrich was one of the most devout German princes. By 1509 his collection of relics housed in Wittenberg numbered about five thousand items, including thirty-three pieces of the True Cross. Part of his collection is recorded in Lucas Cranach the Elder's woodcuts for *Das Wittenberger Heiligtumsbuch* (Wittenberg, 1509).[4] Although Friedrich remained Catholic, he was the staunch protector of Luther, especially after Luther had been condemned at the Diet of Worms in 1521. Friedrich's men kidnapped Luther and took him to Wartburg to shield him from imperial troops. As a result, Friedrich frequently appears in Protestant art, as for instance the Cranach school *Allegory of the Reformation in Nuremberg* of 1559 (fig. 28).

Dürer probably already entertained the notion of making a printed portrait of Friedrich as early as 1522.[5] Friedrich resided in Nuremberg between November 1522 and the beginning of February 1523 while attending the imperial Reichstag. During this occasion Dürer created the silverpoint-over-chalk drawing of the prince, now in Paris (École des Beaux-Arts), which subsequently served as the design for the engraving.[6] Dürer represented Friedrich in a full-face view. His coats of arms ornament the upper corners of the print. The inscription below alludes to Friedrich's religious nature and his protection of Luther. The text reads: "He was dedicated to Christ and loved the word of God with great piety, worthy to be revered by posterity. Albrecht Dürer from Nuremberg drew Friedrich, Duke of Saxony, Archmarshal and Elector of the Holy Roman Empire. He drew the picture for the man of great merit, as a living man for the living man. 1524."[7]

There is no evidence that Friedrich commissioned Dürer to make this portrait; rather, Dürer seems to have conceived of the portrait as an appropriate way of honoring the prince. The precise number of impressions of the engraving that Dürer printed is unknown. In 1519 Dürer produced two hundred copies of the small portrait of Cardinal Albrecht von Brandenburg.[8] His second portrait of the cardinal, dated 1523, had an initial run of five hundred impressions.[9] These engraved portraits had a variety of purposes, including use as bookplates.

1. Pieter Vischer the Younger made the prince's grave monument in 1527; see Stafski, *Der Jüngere Peter Vischer*, pp. 41–42, fig. 81. For a general study of his patronage, see Bruck, *Friedrich der Weise*.
2. Anzelewsky, *Dürer*, nrs. 19, 20–38 (the *Wittenberg Mary Altar* of 1496 may have been made by Dürer for Friedrich), 82, 105.
3. Ibid., pp. 26, 38–39; Winkler, *Zeichnungen Dürers*, II: nrs. 319–323.
4. J. Jahn, *Lucas Cranach d. Ä., 1472–1553: Das gesamte graphische Werk*, pp. 456–544.
5. On the engraving, also see *Nuremberg: Dürer (1971)*, nr. 547; Talbot, ed., *Dürer*, nr. 76.
6. Winkler, *Zeichnungen Dürers*, IV: nr. 897.
7. The translation is from Anzelewsky, *Dürer* (1980), p. 227. The Latin text reads:

CHRISTO SACRVM / ILLE DEI VERBO MAGNA PIETATE FAVEBAT / PERPETVA DIGNVS POSTERITATE COLI / D[omino] FRID[e]R[ico] DVCI SAXON[iae] S[acri] R[omani] IMP[erii] / ARCHIM[areschallus] ELECTORI / ALBERTVS DVRER NVR[imbergensis] FACIEBAT / B[ene] M[erenti] F[ecit] V[ivus] V[ico] / M.D. XXIIII.

8. Meder 100. For two hundred impressions plus the copper plate, Dürer received 200 florins in gold and 20 ells of damask for a coat. For Dürer's letter to the cardinal, see Rupprich, *Dürer schriftlicher Nachlass*, I: pp. 85–87 (letter nr. 32).
9. Meder 101. Dürer also sent Albrecht the copper plate. For Dürer's letter to the cardinal, see Rupprich, *Dürer schriftlicher Nachlass*, I: p. 95 (letter nr. 41).

30. PORTRAIT OF WILLIBALD PIRCKHEIMER

1524; monogram
Engraving
18.2 × 11.5 cm
B. 106; M. 103; H. 103
Lent by the Cleveland Museum of Art, Gift of
Edward B. Greene

Willibald Pirckheimer (1470–1530) was Dürer's closest friend and intellectual mentor.[1] Dürer's portrait engraving is a testament to their relationship.[2] Unlike his portraits of Erasmus or Melanchthon (cat. nr. 32), which are somewhat idealized, the unflinching depiction of Pirckheimer does not attempt to down play the humanist's massive bulk and fleshy face. Rather, these features are exploited to convey his physical and mental energy. Dürer's portrait is also a searching study of how age had transformed the face of his friend. In 1524 Pirckheimer, who suffered from gout, was certainly thinking about death and about his memory. These concerns are suggested in the inscription:

Portrait of Willibald Pirckheimer at the age of 53. We live by the spirit; the rest belongs to death.[3]

The engraving is therefore a record of Pirckheimer's likeness and, more intangibly, of his spirit. Four years later, Pirckheimer had the words "Whatever was mortal of Albrecht Dürer is covered by this tomb" inscribed on the artist's tomb in the Johannisfriedhof. Both texts reflect the pair's awareness of their respective contributions to their time.

Although Dürer and Pirckheimer collaborated on such important artistic projects as the planning of the *Triumphal Arch of Emperor Maximilian I* (cat. nr. 20), the *Great Triumphal Chariot* (cat. nr. 26), or the decorations for the Nuremberg Rathaus, Dürer never made a painting of Pirckheimer.[4] The humanist commissioned a bookplate (ca. 1501), miniatures in a few Italian editions of classical texts in his library, and the title page for his translation of Plutarch's *De vitanda usura* (Nuremberg: Friedrich Peypus, 1515).[5] Dürer also produced the pen illustrations for Pirckheimer's Latin translation of Horopollo's *Hieroglyphica* that was presented to Maximilian in 1514.[6]

Pirckheimer was, however, an active collector of Dürer's watercolors, drawings, prints, and, in a few cases, paintings. Most of these were probably gifts from the artist. For instance, the drawing *Four Heads in Profile* (cat. nr. 16) is listed in the inventory of Willibald Imhoff's possessions. Imhoff was Pirckheimer's nephew and heir to most of his art collection. Imhoff also owned the copper plate for the Pirckheimer engraving,[7] paintings of Dürer's parents (possibly by the artist's shop), a watercolor self-portrait of Dürer done in 1497, paintings of the Crucifixion and the Descent from the Cross, twenty-nine books of prints by Dürer, and many other items.[8]

1. Pirckheimer's influence on Dürer is discussed briefly in Section 4. For literature on Pirckheimer, see Section 4, note 21; also see W. P. Eckert and C. von Imhoff, *Willibald Pirckheimer Dürers Freund im Spiegel seines Lebens, seiner Werke und seiner Umwelt.*
2. *Nuremberg: Dürer (1971)*, nr. 293; Talbot, ed., *Dürer*, nr. 77. Dürer's drawing for this engraving has not survived. His silverpoint and charcoal portrait

sketches of Pirckheimer, both dating around 1503, are in Berlin (Kupferstichkabinett), see Winkler, *Zeichnungen Dürers*, II: nrs. 268, 270; *Nuremberg: Dürer (1971)*, nr. 529. Yet another drawing may have been employed as the model for the Nuremberg portrait medal of Pirckheimer of 1517 (cat. nr. 137).
3. Panofsky, *Dürer*, p. 239; Talbot, ed., *Dürer*, nr. 77.
4. Such a picture may have existed, but I have not found any supporting documentation.
5. Pirckheimer's face was used for the *Caput Physicum* that appeared in Ludovicus de Prussia, *Triligium animae* (Nuremberg: Anton Koberger, 1498). On these various works, see *Nüremberg: Dürer (1971)*, nrs. 292, 295, 296, 298.
6. Ibid., nr. 297.
7. Springer, "Inventare der Imhoff'schen Kunstkammer zu Nürnberg," p. 356. "Mein An herr Wilbaldtt pirkamer Inn Kupfer gestochen von Albrecht Dürer, welches Kupfher noch wol drucktt. Ist Sonst seiner Kupfer keins hir schlag Ich an auf 40 fl." (1580 inventory).
8. Ibid., pp. 353–356.

31. THE ART OF MEASUREMENT

*Albertvs Dvrervs Nvrembergensis pictor hvivs
aetatis celeberrimus, versus a Germanica lingua in
Latinam . . .* (Paris: Christian Wechel, 1534)
M., pp. 284–286; H., p. 258
The University of Texas at Austin, The Humanities Research Center

*A Course in the Art of Measurement with Compass
and Ruler*, as the original German title is translated, was the first of Dürer's three published treatises.[1] It was issued by Dürer in 1525. The second Latin edition, translated by Joachim Camerarius (1500–1574), a professor at the Egidien Gymnasium, is exhibited.[2] Dürer dedicated the book to his friend Pirckheimer.

Dürer wrote this treatise to overcome an omission that he perceived in the training of young artists in Germany. Dürer writes that they have "never learned the art of measurement, without which no one can become a true artisan. It is the fault of their masters who themselves were ignorant of this skill. . . . It is this skill which is the foundation of all painting."[3] The text is intended as a practical manual for artists in all media.

The book is divided into four chapters, beginning with a discussion of the problems of linear geometry.[4] Chapter 2 is concerned with the construction of two-dimensional figures. This is followed by a chapter on the application of geometrical principles to the practical tasks of architecture, engineering, and decoration, including the just shaping of letters. The fourth chapter is about the geometry of solid bodies and the treatment of linear perspective. Included in this final chapter are Dürer's depictions of two devices to aid the artist in making portraits and in determining perspective.[5] Two further woodcuts of the draftsmen sketching a jug and of a reclining woman were designed by the artist but first appeared in the 1538 edition of the treatise.[6]

In the third chapter Dürer provides instructions about how to design different types of monuments. Figures 16 and 17, illustrated here, represent a monument to commemorate a victory over the rebellious peasants and a memorial to a drunkard.[7] The former is one of Dürer's most strident social commentaries as he shows a defeated peasant with a sword in his back perched on top of a tall column composed of farm tools, a chicken basket, milk jug, and other commonplace farm objects. A lengthy text accompanying the image explains each feature.

Dürer describes the monument to a drunkard as follows:

First, make the drunkard's casket, inscribed with an epitaph that mockingly praises his easy living. Place a beer barrel on top of it, covered by a board game, topped in turn by two bowls which would hold a glutton's portion and are joined at their rims. On the bottom of the upper bowl put a low beer mug with two handles and cover it with a plate which serves as the base of a high beer glass turned upside down. The entire structure is to be surmounted by a basket filled with bread, butter, and cheese. In this manner, but with other paraphernalia, one can decorate memorials according to the way of life of the person being commemorated. For the sake of adventure, I wanted to explain this, and I have drawn it below as part of this section on columns.[8]

The date inscribed on both monuments originally read 1525 but was changed in this edition to 1530.

1. The *Treatise on Fortification* was published in 1527 and the *Treatise on Human Proportions* (cat. nr. 34) first appeared in 1528. On the *Art of Measurement*, see Panofsky, *Dürer*, pp. 253–260; Rupprich, *Dürer schriftlicher Nachlass*, III: pp. 307–367; *Nuremberg: Dürer* (1971), nr. 640, pp. 341–354; Talbot, ed., *Dürer*, nr. 215; *Boston: Dürer*, nrs. 218–219; W. Strauss, ed., *The Painter's Manual*, which includes an English translation of the treatise.
2. On the different editions of the treatise, see Meder, *Dürer-Bibliographie*, pp. 451–456.
3. Strauss, ed., *The Painter's Manual*, p. 37 (part of the dedication to Pirckheimer).
4. Panofsky, *Dürer*, pp. 254–260, provides the clearest introduction to and description of the four chapters. For discussions of the mathematics of the treatise, see J. E. Hofmann, "Dürers Verhältnis zur Mathematik," in Hirschmann and Schnelbögl, eds., *Albrecht Dürers Umwelt*, pp. 132–151; E. Pfeiffer, "Dürers Masseinheiten und Werkzahlen in der Unterweisung der Messung," *MVGN* 64 (1977): 111–164.
5. Meder, nrs. 268–269; Strauss, ed., *The Painter's Manual*, pp. 390, 392.
6. Meder, nrs. 270–271; Strauss, ed., *The Painter's Manual*, p. 434.
7. Pages 102 and 103 in the Latin edition. The number 17 is left off the page in the Latin edition. In the German edition, there are six lines of text about the construction of a tower under figure 17.
8. Strauss, ed., *The Painter's Manual*, p. 233.

ALBERTI DVRERI

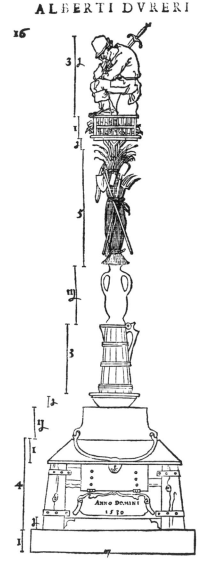

GEOMETRIAE LIB· III.

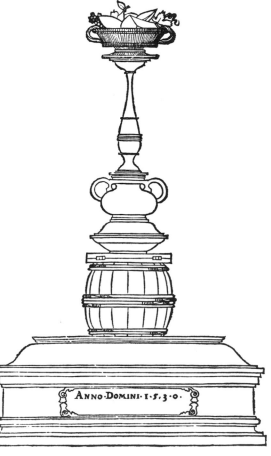

32. PORTRAIT OF PHILIPP MELANCHTHON

1526; monogram
Engraving
17.5 × 12.8 cm
B. 105; M. 104; H. 104
Lent by the Museum of Fine Arts, Houston,
Gift of Marjorie and Evan C. Horning

Melanchthon (1497–1560) was a renowned teacher and one of the most eloquent spokesmen for the Lutheran cause.[1] He studied at Heidelberg (1509) and Tübingen (1512) before being named professor of Greek at the new university at Wittenberg in 1518. Melanchthon established education programs for high schools and Latin schools throughout Germany, thereby earning the sobriquet *praeceptor Germaniae*, or teacher of Germany. Between November 1525 and May 1526, Melanchthon resided at Pirckheimer's house in Nuremberg while organizing the new Egidien Gymnasium.[2] Melanchthon composed most of the Augsburg Confession, a clear statement of the Protestant beliefs that were debated at the Reichstag in 1530. Melanchthon is often prominently displayed by Luther's side in Protestant prints and paintings.[3]

Dürer made this portrait engraving while Melanchthon was living in Nuremberg,[4] although the two men had been friends since 1518. Melanchthon is known to have answered Dürer's questions about the nature of the Last Supper, and he certainly advised the artist on other theological matters. Dürer's drawing for this print, today in Florence (Casa Horne), is the oldest known portrait of Melanchthon.[5] It lacks the vivacity of Dürer's contemporary silverpoint of Eobanus Hessus (see cat. nr. 33) and may be the artist's reworking of another sketch made from life. The resulting engraving represents Melanchthon in near profile set against a sky or wall sketchily defined with horizontal hatchings. Dürer emphasizes Melanchthon's intense gaze and prominent forehead to convey his intellectuality.

The inscription beneath reads in translation: "Dürer was able to depict Philipp's features as if living, but the practical hand could not portray his soul."[6] Rupprich credits Eobanus Hessus, one of the professors at the Egidien Gymnasium, with composing the inscription.[7]

1526
VIVENTIS·POTVIT·DVRERIVS·ORA·PHILIPPI
MENTEM·NON·POTVIT·PINGERE·DOCTA
MANVS

2. His remarks at the opening of the school are given in Pröll, *Pirckheimer*, nr. 82. The school is also called the Melanchthon-Gymnasium.

3. For instance, see fig. 28 and cat. nr. 187. G. Pfeiffer has suggested that St. Paul in Dürer's *Four Apostles* (fig. 26) is a portrait of Melanchthon; see his "Die Vorbilder zu Albrecht Dürers 'Vier Aposteln,'" *Wissenschaft Beilage zum Jahresbericht über das Melanchthon-Gymnasium in Nürnberg für der Schuljahr 1959/60* (Nuremberg, 1960), pp. 12–16, 20–21.

4. The plate is in Gotha and a counterproof is in Berlin (Kupferstichkabinett). Also see *Nuremberg: Dürer (1971)*, nr. 409; Talbot, ed., *Dürer*, nr. 78; *Boston: Dürer*, nr. 217. Additional literature is provided in Mende, *Dürer-Bibliographie*, nrs. 7457–7461.

5. Winkler, *Zeichnungen Dürers*, IV: nr. 901.

6. The translation is from Talbot, ed., *Dürer*, nr. 78.

7. Rupprich, *Dürer schriftlicher Nachlass*, I: p. 275 (nr. 98).

33. PORTRAIT OF HELIUS EOBANUS HESSUS

1526 (1540)
Woodcut
12.7 × 9.5 cm (woodcut); 29.5 × 16.1 cm (sheet with texts)
M. 257; H. 257
The University of Texas at Austin, The Humanities Research Center, Iconography Collection

In 1526 Dürer created a silverpoint sketch of his friend Eobanus Hessus (1488–1540) that ranks among his finest drawings because of the extreme beauty and delicacy of the lines and because of his success in conveying Hessus's sharp intellect.[1] In this year Hessus became professor of Latin, rhetoric, dialectic, and poetry at the Egidien Gymnasium, which Melanchthon had founded. Hessus was an accomplished poet and author. His *Urbs Noriberga Illustrata Carmine Heroico* of 1532 includes descriptions of the Vischer family's *Tomb of St. Sebaldus* (figs. 21 and 22) and other local artistic programs.[2] Following Dürer's death in 1528, Hessus and Thomas Venatorius composed an eight-page eulogy to the artist.[3]

Hessus may have commissioned Dürer to draw his portrait with the intention of using the sketch as the design for a woodcut frontispiece for his book *Ad illustrissimim Principem Joannen Fridericum Ducem Saxoniae Elegia*, which Friedrich Peypus of Nuremberg published in August of 1526. The resulting woodcut is considerably inferior to Dürer's woodcuts, especially in the uninspired cutting; therefore, it would seem that another artist produced the woodcut after Dürer's drawing rather than from a block planned by Dürer. The lack of the artist's monogram supports his distance from the final woodcut.

The woodcut was also published separately.[4] The example exhibited here was issued in 1540 on the occasion of Hessus's death. The top inscription reads:

H. EOBANO HESSO POE=
tae Clarissimo qui obiit Anno domini
XXXX. ETATIS SVE LI.S.R. IOANNES GIGAS

Following the portrait are fifty-two lines of verse, arranged in two columns, praising Hessus. At the bottom of the lefthand column is the name Volffgangum Meyerpeck, the author of the verse. It was likely printed in Zwickau. Meder lists four subsequent copies after this woodcut.[5]

---

1. Winkler, *Zeichnungen Dürers*, IV: nr. 905 (London, British Museum).
2. Stechow, *Northern Renaissance Art*, pp. 125–126, provides an English translation of the description of the tomb. Also see Helius Eobanus Hessus, *Noriberga Illustrata und andere Städtegedichte*, ed. J. Neff, in *Lateinische Litteraturdenkmäler des XV. und XVI. Jahrhunderts*, ed. M. Herrmann, 12 (Berlin, 1896).
3. Rupprich, *Dürer schriftlicher Nachlass*, I: pp. 298–301.
4. *Nuremberg: Dürer (1971)*, nr. 300. The print is praised by Hessus's friend Euricius Cordus, physician and poet; see Rupprich, *Dürer schriftlicher Nachlass*, I: p. 296.
5. Meder 257 provides a full list of editions and copies.

34. TREATISE ON HUMAN PROPORTIONS

Alberti Dureri clarissimi pictoris et Geometrae de Symetria partium in rectis formis humanorum corporum, Libri in latinum conversi (Nuremberg: Hieronymus Andreae, 1532 and 1534)
M., pp. 288–289; H., p. 259
The University of Texas at Austin, The Humanities Research Center

Although Dürer's ideas about human proportions were largely formulated by 1512 and written by 1523, this book was first published on 31 October 1528, over six months after the artist's death.[1] The publication was due to the efforts of Dürer's wife, Agnes, who helped fund the printing, and his friends. Pirckheimer wrote an elegy to Dürer and Hieronymus Andreae, Dürer's longtime *formschneider*, published the text. The first edition was in German.[2] Joachim Camerarius translated the work into Latin in 1528. Exhibited here is the second edition, which appeared in 1532 (books one and two) and 1534 (books three and four).

The *Treatise on Human Proportions* is the culmination of three decades of theoretical musings about the design of the human body and how to codify the wide variety of different body types. The treatise is divided into four books.[3] The first book is a discussion of the measurements of male and female heads, hands, and feet. Eight additional types (tall, short, fat, and thin males and females) are presented in book two. This is followed by mathematical variations of basic proportions. Several of the grotesques are related to the physiognomic experiments seen in *Four Heads in Profile* (cat. nr. 16). The final book tries to explain human movement in terms of perspective and geometry.

The profile view of a woman, illustrated here, lists the different body parts and the relative proportion of each part to the whole body. Dürer based his proportional scheme upon the *exempeda* method of Leonbattista Alberti, the fifteenth-century Italian architect and theorist, in which the body is divided into six equal parts.[4] Each part, called a *messtsab*, or stick, is equivalent to one-sixth of the total height. This basic unit, denoted by the symbol $\mathcal{L}$, is further subdivided into ten *zalls*, or numbers ($\mathcal{E}$), each of which is one-sixtieth of the total body length. Each *zall* is broken down into ten *teills*, or parts ($\perp$), and each *teill* is comprised of three *trümles*, or bits (%). In the case of the length of the foot, Dürer has indicated that it should be nine *zalls*, that is, nine-sixtieths or fifteen percent of the total body height. The distance from the sole of the foot to the kneecap is marked as one stick (one-sixth), five *zalls* (five-sixtieths), and six *teills* (six-six hundredths), or a total of 26 percent of the total height. From the lower part of the ankle to the knee is just over 22 percent of the body height. The same simple calculations can be applied to any part of the body. Dürer has also marked with triangles the joints of the knee, hip, and arm, as well as the vertebras of the spine.

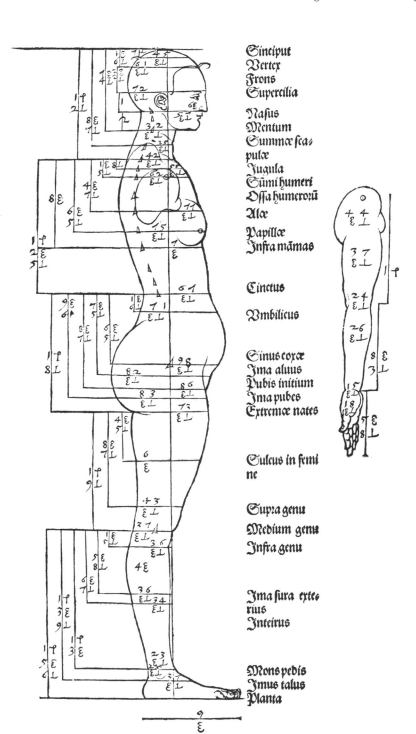

1. On the treatise, see Panofsky, *Dürer*, pp. 260–270; Rupprich, *Dürer schriftlicher Nachlass*, III: pp. 17–305; *Nuremberg: Dürer (1971)*, nrs. 494–495; Talbot, ed., *Dürer*, nr. 217; *Boston: Dürer*, nr. 221. A facsimile of the 1528 German edition was published by Verlag Walter Uhl of Unterschneidheim in 1969.

2. Meder, *Dürer-Bibliographie*, pp. 458–465, lists the different editions and translations.

3. Panofsky, *Dürer*, pp. 260–270, and *Boston: Dürer*, nr. 221, provide brief descriptions of the contents of the four books.

4. The illustration is from Book Two, page N ii verso (Latin edition), and L ii verso (German edition). The page is followed by two further representations of this woman and a table listing some of the proportions. Cf. Dürer's preparatory drawing for this type of figure, now in London (British Museum, Sloane 5228/9 lv); see W. L. Strauss, *The Complete Drawings of Albrecht Dürer*, V: pp. 2539–2540, and his comments on this proportional scheme on pp. 2530–2531.

Also see cat. nrs.

Born around 1480 in the town of Kulmbach north of Bayreuth,[1] Kulmbach was in Nuremberg by 1500; however, it is unclear whether he went immediately into Dürer's workshop or served as an assistant to Venetian painter and printmaker Jacopo de' Barbari, who is recorded working for Maximilian I in Nuremberg from April onward.[2] By 1501 Kulmbach collaborated with Dürer on the woodcut illustrations for Conrad Celtis's edition of Hroswitha von Gandersheim's *Opera* and, in 1502, Celtis's *Quatuor Libri Amorum* (cat. nr. 10).[3] Kulmbach remained in Dürer's workshop until March 1511, when he acquired Nuremberg citizenship. During this long apprenticeship, Kulmbach participated in many of the workshop projects, including the illustrations for the writings of Ulrich Pinder in 1505 and 1507 (cat. nrs. 40 and 43) and the stained-glass designs for the Landauer Zwölfbrüder-kapelle (cat. nr. 35). In actuality, Kulmbach was an independent master working with Dürer. He produced several important paintings, including the wings for the *St. Nicholas Altar* and, in 1510, the *St. Anne Altar*, both in St. Lorenz.[4]

Kulmbach traveled to Cracow in 1510 and returned to Nuremberg by March 1511.[5] The purpose of this trip may have been to deliver his *Sts. Peter and Paul Altar* (Florence, Uffizi).[6] While in Cracow he painted the *Adoration of the Magi Altar*, dated 1511, perhaps for the monastery na Scalce.[7] On his return trip, Kulmbach made the *Portrait of Margrave Kasimir von Brandenburg-Kulmbach* (Munich, Alte Pinakothek).[8]

Once back in Nuremberg, Kulmbach began painting the *Epitaph of Lorenz Tucher* (St. Sebaldus), his greatest picture.[9] Anton II Tucher and other family members commissioned Dürer to design the composition and Kulmbach to execute the painting. Dürer's drawing, dated 1511, was followed with minor alterations, and Kulmbach finished the epitaph in 1513.

Kulmbach returned to Cracow in 1514 for a two-year period. During this stay he created two of his finest paintings, the *St. Catherine Altar* (Cracow, Church of Our Lady), dated 1515, and the *St. John Altar* (Cracow, St. Florian), dated 1516.[10]

Kulmbach achieved renown for his designs for goldsmith works, sculptures, and, especially, stained-glass cycles.[11] Among his major glass designs during the 1510s are the *Kaiser (Emperor's) Window* (1514–1515), *Markgraf (Margrave's) Window* (1515), and *Haller Window* (ca. 1520) in St. Sebaldus, the *Welser-Thurmer Window* in the Frauenkirche (ca. 1516), and the *Imhoffkapelle Windows* (1520).[12] In a few instances, Kulmbach must have made his designs either before his departure for Cracow or while living in this Polish capital.

Kulmbach was the finest painter in Nuremberg after Dürer. His rather sudden death sometime between 29 November and 3 December 1522 was an unfortunate loss for the city.[13]

1. His birthplace is mentioned first by Sandrart; see Peltzer, ed., *Sandrarts Academie*, pp. 76–77. The biographical information is largely taken from F. Stadler, *Hans von Kulmbach*; F. Winkler, *Hans von Kulmbach*; *Nuremberg: Meister um Dürer*, pp. 97–139, nrs. 149–233.

2. Neudörfer is the source for Kulmbach's association with Barbari; see Neudörfer, *Nachrichten von Künstlern*, p. 134. On 8 April 1500, Maximilian I appointed Barbari as his portraitist and miniature painter for a period of one year, during which time he resided in Nuremberg. He came to Nuremberg because of his association with Nuremberg merchant Anton Kolb, who had initiated and financed Barbari's monumental *View of Venice* woodcut in 1500. The artist probably remained here until 1503, when he left to work for Friedrich the Wise. Stylistic associations between the two painters are occasionally suggested by Stadler and others.

3. Spitz, *Conrad Celtis*, p. 42; Winkler, *Hans von Kulmbach*, pp. 33–37; *Nuremberg: Meister um Dürer*, nr. 225; *Nuremberg: Dürer (1971)*, nr. 288.

4. Stadler, *Kulmbach*, nrs. 11–12, 79; Winkler, *Hans von Kulmbach*, pp. 47, 51–52; *Nuremberg: Meister um Dürer*, nrs. 149, 154. The *St. Nicholas Altar* is usually dated between 1500 and 1505.

5. Stadler, *Kulmbach*, p. 18, gives this return date.

6. The painting dates 1509–1510. Stadler, *Kulmbach*, nr. 29; Winkler, *Hans von Kulmbach*, pp. 48–49; *Nuremberg: Meister um Dürer*, nr. 152.

7. Stadler, *Kulmbach*, nr. 33; Winkler, *Hans von Kulmbach*, pp. 59ff.; *Nuremberg: Meister um Dürer*, nr. 158.

8. Stadler, *Kulmbach*, nr. 47; Winkler, *Hans von Kulmbach*, p. 71; *Nuremberg: Meister um Dürer*, nr. 159.

9. See the comments for cat. nr. 38.

10. The *St. John Altar* was largely destroyed in World War II; the predella is in Warsaw (Muzeum Narodowe). Stadler, *Kulmbach*, nrs. 109–110; Winkler, *Hans von Kulmbach*, pp. 55–56, 66; *Nuremberg: Meister um Dürer*, nrs. 164, 168.

11. On his work for goldsmiths, see Winkler, *Zeichnungen Kulmbachs und Schäufeleins*, pp. 31–32, nrs. 82–93; and especially Steingraber, "Süddeutsche Goldemailplastik der Frührenaissance," pp. 223–233. Also see the comments in Section 5. A. Schädler, in "Zum Meister der 'Nürnberger Madonna,'" *AGNM* (1976): 63–71, has suggested, I think incorrectly, that Kulmbach designed this famous wooden statue (now in the Germanisches Nationalmuseum) and may also have carved it.

12. Winkler, *Zeichnungen Kulmbachs und Schäufeleins*, pp. 28–31, nrs. 61–81. Specifically on these windows, see *Nuremberg: Meister um Dürer*, nrs. 187–191. The best discussion of Nuremberg stained glass and Kulmbach's role is K.-A. Knappe, *Albrecht Dürer und das Bamberger Fenster in St. Sebald in Nürnberg*.

13. Barbara Butts, a graduate student at Harvard University, is currently writing her dissertation on Kulmbach. She is focusing on Kulmbach's paintings, notably the problems of attribution and original arrangement.

56. Veit Hirschvogel the Younger (after Hans von Kulmbach), *The Fall of Rebel Angels*, stained-glass windows formerly in the Zwölfbrüder-haus Chapel, 1508–1510, located in Berlin, Schlossmuseum (Kunstgewerbemuseum) until their destruction in World War II (H. Schmitz, *Die Glasgemälde des königlichen Kunstgewerbemuseums in Berlin* [Berlin, 1913], II: pl. 39).

35. FALL OF THE REBEL ANGELS (ST. MICHAEL WITH THE DRAGON)

1508 or early 1509
Drawing: brush with gray-and-black wash
31.8 × 41.9 cm
Lent by the Museum of Fine Arts, Boston,
Harvey D. Parker Collection

This drawing is approximately one-third of the original cartoon for the *Fall of the Rebel Angels* stained-glass window that the workshop of Veit Hirschvogel the Younger made for the chapel of the Zwölfbrüderhaus (fig. 56).[1] This tiny chapel was founded in 1506 by Mattheus Landauer and erected by architect Hans Beheim the Elder.[2] When the building was completed in 1508, Landauer commissioned Dürer to paint the *All Saints Altarpiece* (Vienna, Kunsthistorisches Museum) for the eastern altar.[3] Dürer and his workshop were also charged with preparing the designs for the chapel's stained-glass windows. The interior of the chapel is best illustrated in Georg Christian Wilder's 1836 watercolor (fig. 15), which, unfortunately, does not reproduce the stained-glass windows since these had been purchased by the Duke of Sagan in the 1810s. These windows were in the Schlossmuseum in Berlin until their destruction in World War II.[4]

The three eastern windows were filled with stained glass. The *Fall of the Rebel Angels* was paired with the *Sacrifice of Isaac* and set in the right-hand, or southernmost, double-lancet window. These windows admonish the worshippers not to be prideful and to place their trust in God. The central, triple-lancet window contained an image of the Trinity, while Landauer and his family, along with the wise and foolish virgins, were represented in the left-hand window.[5] The windows on the north and south walls were decorated with images of the evangelists, prophets, and the Virgin.[6]

The attribution of the Boston drawing to Kulmbach is fairly secure based upon comparison with the artist's prints and drawings; however, the drawing's relationship to the original plans by Dürer is less clear.[7] In 1509 Dürer produced an attractive drawing of the *Fall of the Rebel Angels* for the Schilling family of Nuremberg.[8] Kulmbach's two angels and the demons are seemingly free adaptations of the Dürer drawing. The latter cannot be intended for the Landauer chapel since its shape does not conform to the building's double lancets and because the Schilling family was not connected with the Zwölfbrüderhaus. Consequently, either Dürer made another earlier drawing of this subject that served as the model for both his 1509 sketch and the Boston drawing or Kulmbach made his own design for the chapel window that was loosely based upon Dürer's 1509 sketch.

Kulmbach's contribution to the creation of the other windows has never been adequately addressed. The Boston drawing is, unfortunately, the only one of the glass cartoons to survive.

1. The drawing was first published as a Dürer school piece by C. Dodgson in "School of Dürer, The Fall of the Rebel Angels: Fragment of a Cartoon for Stained Glass," *Old Master Drawings* 5 (1930): 42–43, who linked it with the Landauer Chapel. Also see Winkler, *Hans von Kulmbach*, pp. 23–24; K. A. Knappe's review of Winkler's book in *ZfK* 23 (1960): 186, and G. Frenzel, "Veit Hirsvogel: Eine Nürnberger Glas-

malerwerkstatt der Dürerzeit," p. 206, fig. 10; *Nuremberg: Meister um Dürer*, nr. 210. This stained-glass window was formerly in the Schlossmuseum in Berlin; see H. Schmitz, *Die Glasgemälde des königlichen Kunstgewerbemuseums in Berlin*, I: pp. 142–146, esp. 143, II: pl. 39 (which is the source for the photograph). Schmitz (p. 142) attributed this and the other windows to Veit Hirschvogel the Elder. Frenzel ("Veit Hirsvogel," pp. 193–210) credits Veit the Younger. Frenzel also gives a general discussion about the collaboration between Dürer, his pupils, and the Hirschvogel family.

2. The chapel measures 8.35 × 8.93 meters. See Section 3 for comments about the chapel and its foundation.

3. Anzelewsky, *Dürer*, nr. 118.

4. The windows entered the museum in 1891. See Schmitz, *Die Glasgemälde*, I: pp. 142–143.

5. Ibid., I: p. 143, II: pls. 37–38.

6. Ibid., I: p. 143, fig. 233.

7. Winkler, *Hans von Kulmbach*, pp. 23–24. Winkler based his argument for the attribution upon a comparison with Kulmbach's prints. I would add that such features as the faces, especially the construction of the mouths, and the draperies can be related to the slightly later Kulmbach drawings of *St. Leonhard* (Erlangen, Universitätsbibliothek) and *St. Veronica* (Dresden, Kupferstichkabinett), both designs for windows. See Winkler, *Zeichnungen Kulmbachs und Schäufeleins*, Kulmbach nrs. 62, 64.

8. Winkler, *Zeichnungen Dürers*, II: nr. 468 (London, British Museum).

36. ST. JOHN THE BAPTIST IN THE WILDERNESS

ca. 1510
Drawing: pen and brown ink with touches of
black chalk
27.2 cm diameter
Lent by the Metropolitan Museum of Art, New
York, Harris Brisbane Dick Fund, 1953

Between 1509 and 1511, Kulmbach produced at
least a dozen drawings of saints that were designs for stained-glass roundels.[1] These circular
drawings, averaging between 27 and 27.5 cm
in diameter, belong to several different series
rather than one large program. For example, the
three sketches of the *Church Fathers* (Dresden,
Kupferstichkabinett) are part of one group,
while the three drawings of martyred saints in
Bremen (Kunsthalle) constitute the remnants of
a second set.[2]

St. John the Baptist in the Wilderness is stylistically related to these other roundel drawings,
but it can be specifically linked only with the *St.
Wenzel* (Dresden, Kupferstichkabinett).[3] Both
works share such features as the short, hooked
shading strokes used in the draperies, the undu-
lating, parallel pen marks to define the ground
lines, and the tight crosshatchings to form
stands of trees. The *St. Wenzel*, with its gray
wash, is somewhat more finished. Kulmbach's
landscapes are still somewhat tentative in these
two drawings and in his *Sts. Peter and Paul Altar*
(Florence, Uffizi) of 1509–1510.[4] Over the ensuing five or six years, Kulmbach would learn how
to create more complex and more mysterious
landscapes, as, for instance, in his *St. Catherine
Altar* (Cracow, Church of Our Lady) and *St. John
Altar* (Cracow, St. Florian).[5]

1. Stadler, *Kulmbach*, nr. 57; Winkler, *Zeichnungen
Kulmbachs und Schäufeleins*, Kulmbach nr. 110; and see
the following note.

2. Winkler, *Zeichnungen Kulmbachs und Schäufeleins*,
nrs. 103–105 (Church Fathers), 106, 108–109, 111–113
(martyrdoms), among others.

3. Ibid., nr. 109, which also associated the two
drawings. These sketches were made shortly before
the *St. Nicholas* (cat. nr. 37). The more rigid and carefully defined drapery of *St. Wenzel* is very similar to
that of *St. Nicholas*.

4. See Kulmbach biography, note 6.

5. See ibid., note 10.

37. ST. NICHOLAS

ca. 1511
Drawing: pen and ink with blue, pink, and gray washes; cut out and glued to a second sheet of paper
34 × 16 cm
Lent by the Fogg Art Museum, Harvard University, Cambridge, Bequest of Meta and Paul J. Sachs

St. Nicholas (ca. 270–342), bishop of Myra, is dressed in his episcopal robe and mitre.[1] He holds a crozier and, in his left hand, a book with three purses, a reference to the dowries he provided for three poor girls. The drawing illustrates Kulmbach's definitive bishop type: the single figure stands erect; the face is rectangular and ringed with curling hair; and the mouth is formed with a wavy, down-turned line. This type or formula was well established by about 1508 and would be repeated throughout his career. In Kulmbach's earliest paintings, such as the *St. Nicholas Altar* in St. Lorenz, the smile of the bishop can be rather awkwardly formed.[2] The mature bishop type can be seen in the drawing of *St. Othmar* (Dresden, Kupferstichkabinett) and in the figures of Sts. Willibald and Dionysius from the *St. Anne Altar*, formerly in St. Lorenz.[3] A less forceful St. Nicholas of this basic design appears in the late *Tabernacle Altar* (Schwabach, Stadtpfarrkirche).[4]

Kulmbach made the *St. Nicholas* as a preparatory sketch for a painting or a stained-glass cycle. Winkler credited Kulmbach with the windows of eight standing and three seated saints in the Pfarrkirche at Inglostadt.[5] While the Harvard drawing is considerably different in expression and costume details from the Inglostadt window of St. Nicholas, both are images of a standing saint set beneath a frame of branch tracery. Similar arrangements are evident in Kulmbach's *St. Nicholas Altar* in St. Lorenz and the *Sts. Peter and Paul Altar*.[6]

1. Stadler, *Kulmbach*, nr. 38; Winkler, *Zeichnungen Kulmbachs und Schäufeleins*, Kulmbach nr. 141; A. Mongan and P. J. Sachs, *Drawings in the Fogg Museum of Art*, nr. 388. Stylistically, the drawing is most closely related to the figures in the *Sts. Peter and Paul Altar* (Florence, Uffizi) of 1509–1510 and especially the *St. Anne Altar*, parts of which date to 1510. Kulmbach likely executed the drawing shortly before his departure for Cracow in 1511. On the paintings, see Kulmbach biography, notes 4, 6. On the saint's iconography, see Réau, *Iconographie de l'Art Chrétien*, III. 2, pp. 976–988.
2. See Kulmbach biography, note 4. The painting is usually dated between 1500 and 1505.
3. Ibid., note 4, for the *St. Anne Altar*. The drawing is usually dated between 1510 and 1515; see Winkler, *Zeichnungen Kulmbachs und Schäufeleins*, Kulmbach nr. 135.
4. The altar is dated 1520; see Stadler, *Kulmbach*, nr. 142; Winkler, *Hans von Kulmbach*, pp. 91–92, pl. 67.
5. Winkler, *Hans von Kulmbach*, p. 27, pl. 15. These windows may date as early as 1505. The window of St. Nicholas is not as monumental in design as the Harvard drawing.
6. For references to these two altars, see notes 1 and 2 above. This branch tracery frame is a common feature of Kulmbach's windows and drawings. See, for instance, the *Kaiser (Emperor's) Window* in St. Sebaldus and the preparatory drawings in Berlin (Kupferstichkabinett); Stadler, *Kulmbach*, nr. 99; Winkler, *Zeichnungen Kulmbachs und Schäufeleins*, Kulmbach nrs. 77–80. On this topic, see M. Braun-Reichenbacher, *Das Ast- und Laubwerk: Entwicklung, Merkmale und Bedeutung einer spätgotischen Ornamentform* (Nuremberg, 1966).

38. NUDE MALE FIGURE STUDY and on the reverse TWO STUDIES OF THE VIRGIN AND CHILD

ca. 1511–1513
Drawing: pen and brown ink
17.9 × 9.1 cm
Lent by the Germanisches Nationalmuseum, Nuremberg, Hz. 82

Kulmbach used this sheet of paper on two occasions, perhaps a year or two apart.[1] The *Two Studies of the Virgin and Child* date to 1511 or early 1512 because, as Winkler and others have observed, these are preliminary drawings for Kulmbach's greatest painting, the *Epitaph of Lorenz Tucher* in St. Sebaldus.[2] The Tucher family commissioned Dürer to make the overall design; Dürer's 1511 drawing is in Berlin (Kupferstichkabinett).[3] Kulmbach began working on this project shortly after his return from Cracow in 1511. Although he adopted most of Dürer's design, he changed the positions of several of the figures, including the Virgin and Child. This sheet contains two quick alternative positions. Kulmbach's final solution is very similar to the central, larger drawing. Since Kulmbach completed the painting in 1513, these two sketches belong to the early stages of the project.

The principal drawing on the other side of this sheet represents a study of a nude male who holds a water bucket. He is often referred to as St. Florian, a third-century Roman soldier in Austria who was credited with dousing a roaring fire with a single bucket of water. More likely, Kulmbach was posing an assistant or someone in one of the local bathhouses. Like his teacher Dürer, Kulmbach employed live models as is evident in such drawings as the *Man with a Stool* (Coburg, Veste).[4] During the years after leaving Dürer's workshop, Kulmbach became increasingly confident in his ability to represent the human body. This drawing stands midway between his earlier nude sketches, notably the *Lady with a Mirror* (*Vanitas*) (Florence, Uffizi) and *St. Christopher* (Oxford, Christ Church Library), both made before 1510, and the more sculpturesque St. John in the *St. John Altarpiece* (Cracow, St. Florian), which is dated 1516.[5] The *Nude Male Figure Study* should be dated 1512 or 1513.

1. Stadler, *Kulmbach*, nrs. 126a–b; Winkler, *Zeichnungen Kulmbachs und Schäufeleins*, Kulmbach nrs. 33 (*Nude Male Figure Study*), 90 (*Two Studies of the Virgin and Child*); Winkler, *Hans von Kulmbach*, p. 64; *Nuremberg: Meister um Dürer*, nr. 206; Zink, *Die Handzeichnungen*, nr. 82. Most of these authors supply illustrations of both sides of this sheet.

2. Stadler, *Kulmbach*, nr. 78; Winkler, *Hans von Kulmbach*, pp. 63ff.; *Nuremberg: Meister um Dürer*, nr. 162.

3. Winkler, *Zeichnungen Dürers*, II: nr. 508.

4. See Section 5 for a discussion of the use of models in Dürer's workshop. On this drawing, see Winkler, *Zeichnungen Kulmbachs und Schäufeleins*, Kulmbach, nr. 15.

5. Ibid., nrs. 25, 35, with a discussion of the dating. On the painting, which was largely destroyed in World War II, see Stadler, *Kulmbach*, nr. 110b; Winkler, *Hans von Kulmbach*, p. 66; *Nuremberg: Meister um Dürer*, nr. 168.

39. HOLY FAMILY

ca. 1511–1513
Drawing: pen and brown ink. Retouchings with brush and white lead and pencil by Peter Paul Rubens.
29 × 20 cm
Lent by the Pierpont Morgan Library, New York

This drawing of the Holy Family, midwives Zebel and Salome, a shepherd, and angels is among Kulmbach's most problematic works.[1] Winkler dated it to 1507–1510, claiming that it was the first great religious drawing by the artist; however, he also observed that it was the only early drawing to represent a complex spatial stage.[2] Stadler, on the other hand, believed that it was one of Kulmbach's last drawings. A comparison with the most important late painting, the *Tabernacle Altar* (Schwabach, Stadtpfarrkirche) of 1520, reveals very few stylistic similarities.[3]

A dating between 1511 and 1513 for the *Holy Family* seems more plausible. I suspect that Winkler's early placement of this drawing was largely due to its obvious association with Dürer's *Paumgartner Altar* (Munich, Alte Pinakothek) of about 1500.[4] Dürer developed a complex architectural stage consisting of a thatched lean-to, side and rear stone arches, and an abbreviated landscape behind. Kulmbach's angels and other figures loosely recall Dürer's figures. Kulmbach, however, did not apply Dürer's more complicated spatial ideas until around 1510 or so, as, for instance, in the 1511 *Adoration of the Magi* (Berlin, Staatliche Museen).[5] Upon his return from Cracow in March 1511, Kulmbach began working on the *Epitaph of Lorenz Tucher* (St. Sebaldus). Besides simply using Dürer's design for this painting, Kulmbach re-examined Dürer's figural and compositional ideas.[6] The *Holy Family* shares the greater monumentality of the *Epitaph of Lorenz Tucher*. In both works the figures are more sculpturesque and better integrated into the composition than in any of his earlier paintings or drawings.

The *Holy Family* may also be related to other works from this period between the two trips to Cracow. The shepherd climbing through the window recalls both the facial type and the linear hatching of the *Nude Male Figure Study* (cat. nr. 38). The face and the headdress of the standing midwife reappear in the *Mary Salome and Family* (St. Louis Art Museum) of about 1511 and in the *Holy Kinship Altar* of 1513.[7] In these and other paintings and drawings of this period, Kulmbach has yet to exhibit the overly theatrical gestures and settings of the *St. Catherine Altar* (1515) and *St. John Altar* (1516) made upon his return to Cracow.[8]

This drawing has the unusual distinction, or misfortune, of having been owned by Peter Paul Rubens (1577–1640) or one of his friends, presumably in Antwerp.[9] Rubens eagerly collected the drawings of Italian and Northern Renaissance masters, but he had few qualms about "correcting" these drawings. Using a brush and white lead and pencil, Rubens altered the face and shoulders of Kulmbach's Virgin. According to Held and Jaffé, Rubens retouched this drawing and ones by Bernard van Orley, Hans Holbein, and Jan Vermeyen, among others, in order to bring out the beauties of these works or to stimulate his own imagination.[10] Rubens often used images by older artists as inspiration for his own production. In this specific instance, Rubens marred and muddied Kulmbach's clearly defined forms.

1. A. E. Popham, "An Orley Drawing Retouched by Rubens," *Old Master Drawings* 1 (1926–1927): 45–47, esp. 47; E. Schilling, *Nürnberger Handzeichnungen des XV. und XVI. Jahrhunderts*, nr. 31; Stadler, *Kulmbach*, nr. 145; Winkler, *Zeichnungen Kulmbachs und Schäufeleins*, Kulmbach, pp. 18, 22, nr. 21; Winkler, *Hans von Kulmbach*, p. 17; also see additional references in note 9 below.

2. Winkler, *Zeichnungen Kulmbachs und Schäufeleins*, p. 22.

3. Stadler, *Kulmbach*, nr. 142; Winkler, *Hans von Kulmbach*, pl. 67.

4. Anzelewsky, *Dürer*, nr. 50.

5. See Kulmbach biography, note 7.

6. See Kulmbach biography, note 9.

7. Stadler, *Kulmbach*, nrs. 71–72; Winkler, *Hans von Kulmbach*, p. 69. For a general discussion of the St. Louis painting, see L. Silver, "Early Northern European Paintings," *Saint Louis Art Museum Bulletin* (Summer 1982): 10–11.

8. See Kulmbach biography, note 10.

9. F. Lugt, "Rubens and Stimmer," *Art Quarterly* 6 (1943): 99–115, esp. 114; J. Held, *Rubens—Selected Drawings* (London, 1959), esp. p. 59; M. Jaffé, "Rubens as Collector of Drawings," *Master Drawings* 2 (1964): 383–397, and 3 (1965): 21–35, esp. 26; see note 1 above. Note that there exists no documentary evidence that Rubens actually possessed this Kulmbach drawing. He frequently touched up older drawings for friends.

10. Held, *Rubens*, pp. 58–61; Jaffé, "Rubens as Collector of Drawings," 1964, p. 384, and 1965, p. 26; see esp. E. Mitsch, ed., *Rubenszeichnungen*, exh. cat. (Vienna: Albertina, 1977), nrs. 60–66.

Also see cat. nrs.

10 Celtis, *Quatuor Libri Amorum* (Nuremberg, 1502)

40 Pinder, *Der Beschlossen Gart des Rosenkrantz Marie* (Nuremberg, 1505)

Hans Baldung, nicknamed Grien or Green, was the most gifted of all Dürer's pupils and achieved renown as a painter, a printmaker, and a designer of stained-glass windows.[1] Whereas most artists came from artisan families, Baldung's father was an attorney for the bishop of Strassburg and his brother and cousins were lawyers and doctors. He was born in 1484 or early 1485 in Schwäbisch-Gmund.[2] By 1499 he was apprenticed to an artist in Strassburg. Around 1503 Baldung moved to Nuremberg and entered Dürer's workshop to complete his training. He remained in Nuremberg until late 1506 or early 1507.

While in Dürer's workshop, Baldung frequently used the master's pictorial ideas. He also learned Dürer's graphic style, though Baldung never sought the same level of technical perfection. As did Dürer, he developed a strong interest in the human form, but his tastes tended to the erotic rather than the scientific.

A sizable corpus of paintings, drawings, and prints has been assigned to this period, from 1503 to 1506/07.[3] Dürer permitted his pupils to work on their own projects. With Hans von Kulmbach and Hans Schäufelein, his fellow apprentices, Baldung lavishly illustrated two devotional texts compiled by Ulrich Pinder (cat. nrs. 40 and 43). He painted two wings for an altar now in Schwabach (Kirchengemeinde) and the *Knight with Death and a Maiden* in Paris (Louvre).[4] He designed the *Löffelholz Window* (1506) in St. Lorenz and, with Kulmbach, a New Testament cycle for a window in the Karmeliterkloster.[5] Baldung also created a series of twelve devotional woodcuts (cat. nr. 41) that combined his ideas with the designs of Dürer.

By 1507 he had left Nuremberg and moved to Halle to paint the *Altar of St. Sebastian* (Nuremberg, Germanisches Nationalmuseum) and the *Adoration of the Magi Altar* (Berlin, Staatliche Museen).[6] These two paintings and most of his art up until 1512 continued to show Dürer's strong influence.

Baldung purchased his citizenship in Strassburg during the Easter season of 1509. The following year he married Margarethe Herlin and joined the painters' guild. Baldung would remain in Strassburg for the rest of his life with the exception of the years 1512–1516, when he was in Freiburg. With the help of his brother, Caspar, a professor of law at the University of Freiburg, Baldung obtained the commission to paint the *Coronation of the Virgin* for the high altar of the Münster.[7] During this period he made his attractive portrait *Margrave Christoph I von Baden* (1515; Munich, Alte Pinakothek).[8] Most of his religious paintings predate the iconoclastic riots in Strassburg of the late 1520s. Such prints as his 1521 portrait *Luther with a Nimbus and Dove* reveal his support for the Protestant reformation.[9] He continued to paint portraits and make paintings and prints of nonreligious themes, notably those dealing with death and witchcraft imagery, including the 1544 *Bewitched Groom* woodcut.[10] When he died in September 1545 he was an esteemed citizen of Strassburg.

1. It is often suggested that the nickname was given to Baldung while he was in Dürer's workshop to distinguish him from Hans Dürer, Hans von Kulmbach, and Hans Schäufelein. His self-portrait in the 1507 *Altar of St. Sebastian* (Nuremberg, Germanisches Nationalmuseum) shows him dressed in green. On Baldung, see C. Koch et al., *Hans Baldung Grien*; P. Halm, "Die Hans-Baldung-Grien-Ausstellung in Karlsruhe," *Kunstchronik* 13 (1960): 123–140; Marrow and Shestack, eds., *Hans Baldung Grien*, especially A. Shestack, "An Introduction to Hans Baldung Grien," pp. 3–18; see also the literature in the following notes.
2. T. A. Brady, Jr., "The Social Place of a German Renaissance Artist: Hans Baldung Grien (1484/85–1545) at Strasbourg," *Central European History* 8 (1975): 295–315.
3. H. Beenken, "Zeichnungen aus der Nürnberger Frühzeit Hans Baldungs," *Jahrbuch für Kunstwissenschaft* 5 (1928): 169–175; *Nuremberg: Meister um Dürer*, pp. 47–63, nrs. 1–29; K. Oettinger and K.-A. Knappe, *Hans Baldung Grien und Albrecht Dürer in Nürnberg*, pp. 1–46; L. Hults-Boudreau, "Hans Baldung Grien and Albrecht Dürer: A Problem in Northern Mannerism," dissertation (University of North Carolina, 1978), ch. II; Marrow and Shestack, eds., *Hans Baldung Grien*, nrs. 1–17; the comments in Section 5.
4. C. Koch, "Zwei Altarflügel mit Gemälden Baldungs aus seiner frühen Epoche," *ZfKW* 12 (1958): 157–162; *Nuremberg: Meister um Dürer*, nrs. 1, 2.
5. The window from the Karmeliterkloster is now divided between Grossgrundlache (Pfarrkirche) and Nuremberg-Wöhrd (St. Bartholomaus). See Knappe, "Das Löffelholz-Fenster in St. Lorenz," pp. 163–178; *Nuremberg: Meister um Dürer*, nrs. 4, 5.
6. *Nuremberg: Meister um Dürer*, nr. 3.
7. Marrow and Shestack, eds., *Hans Baldung Grien*, figs. 9, 60a.
8. Ibid., fig. 79a.
9. Ibid., fig. 41. On this subject, see L. Hults, "Baldung and the Reformation," in ibid., pp. 38–59.
10. Ibid., nr. 87. On his style after 1520, especially his developing Mannerism, and his choice of themes, see G. Bussmann, *Manierismus im Spätwerk Hans Baldung Grien: Die Gemälde der zweiten Strassburger Zeit*; Hults-Boudreau, "Hans Baldung Grien," chs. III (style), IV (iconography); C. Talbot, "Baldung and the Female Nude," in Marrow and Shestack, eds., *Hans Baldung Grien*, pp. 19–37.

40. ULRICH PINDER, DER BESCHLOSSEN GART DES ROSENKRANTZ MARIE

2 volumes; Nuremberg: Friedrich Peypus, 9 October 1505
Volume I: 306 leaves (Books 1–5); volume II: 302 leaves (Books 6–11)
Lent by the Library of Congress, Washington

Ulrich Pinder (died 1519), a Nuremberg physician, compiled the *Closed Garden of the Rosary of Mary* for the local confraternity of the rosary.[1] It is a collection of older devotional tracts about the Virgin and Christ. Two years later Pinder would publish another text, *Speculum Passionis Domini Nostri Ihesu Christi* (cat. nr. 43), focusing specifically on Christ's passion. The cult of the Virgin and the devotion of the rosary were extremely popular during the last years of the fifteenth century and the opening years of the sixteenth. In 1495 Pope Alexander VI (1492–1503) sought to encourage the formation of brotherhoods dedicated to the rosary by granting an indulgence value of seven years for the recitation of the prayers Our Father and Hail Mary.[2] Kulmbach, Schön, and Traut, among others, created paintings and prints of rosary themes. Veit Stoss's *Angelic Salutation* was the most elaborate of the rosary images produced in Nuremberg (fig. 23).

Pinder's book is more important than other contemporary rosary texts since it contains over one thousand woodcuts illustrating biblical and allegorical themes. The folio size of the two volumes and the integration of text and illustration were inspired by the earlier picture books the *Schatzbehalter* and the *Nuremberg Chronicle* (cat. nrs. 2 and 3). The illustrations are by Baldung, Kulmbach, Schäufelein, Traut, and an unidentified artist, all apprentices and journeymen in Dürer's workshop. Although Pinder must have contracted an agreement with Dürer as the head of the workshop, Dürer does not seem to have participated. Dürer's faith in the talents of his pupils and his current involvement in other projects explain why such a major undertaking was left to the workshop.

Not surprisingly, many of these woodcuts were influenced by Dürer's drawings and prints. For instance, Baldung's Crucifixion (I: cci verso) derives in part from Dürer's 1505 drawings of Christ and the two thieves.[3] Yet Baldung skillfully blended these figures into a highly personalized composition that emphasized the event's emotional drama. The backturned soldier on the left nicely draws the viewer into the scene.

More original is Baldung's woodcut of the origin of the Eucharist (II: ccxxix verso), in which the crucified Christ divides the fall of Adam and Eve from the celebration of the communion service. In this highly compact image, Baldung clearly explained that Christ's sacrifice was nec-

essary to remove the original sin caused by the transgressions of Adam and Eve. Through the mystery of the Eucharist, symbol of Christ's sacrifice, the worshipper partakes of Christ's redemption of mankind.

Critics disagree about the precise division of labor. Strieder attributed 125 woodcuts to Baldung, 159 to Schäufelein, 51 to Kulmbach, and 13 to Traut, excluding the many replicas.[4] Hollstein gave only 35 woodcuts to Baldung, while Oettinger and Knappe suggested that he made 199 woodcuts, but not necessarily all those listed by Strieder.[5] Oldenbourg credited Schäufelein with 166 woodcuts. It is also unclear which pupil oversaw this project.[6] Wolgemut provided the title woodcut but was less involved in the production than Baldung or Schäufelein. Given the artistic maturity of Baldung and Schäufelein during the years 1503–1505, they probably shared this responsibility.

1. Peypus, Pinder's son-in-law, used presses owned by Pinder. On this book, see H. Vollmer, "Die Illustratoren des 'Beschlossen gart des rosenkranz mariae.' Ein Beiträge zur Kenntnis des Holzschnittes der Dürerschule," *Repertorium für Kunstwissenschaft* 31 (1908): 18–36, 144–158; Koch et al., *Hans Baldung Grien*, nr. II B II; *Nuremberg: Meister um Dürer*, nr. 25; Oettinger and Knappe, *Baldung*, nr. 70, pp. 132–137; M. C. Oldenbourg, *Die Buchholzschnitte des Hans Schäufelein*, I: pp. 15–26.

2. Erzbischöfliches Diözesan-Museum Köln, *500 Jahre Rosenkranz 1475 Köln 1975*, exh. cat. (Cologne, 1975), provides a thorough discussion of the institution of the rosary; see nr. A 55 for the Pinder volume. For comments on the rosary in Nuremberg, see Schön's *The Great Rosary* (cat. nr. 61) below.

3. Winkler, *Zeichnungen Dürers*, II: nrs. 324–326 (Vienna, Albertina).

4. Strieder's comments are in *Nuremberg: Meister um Dürer*, pp. 58–60.

5. Hollstein, II: p. 84, nrs. 15–49; Oettinger and Knappe, *Baldung*, nr. 70. The first systematic separation of hands was attempted by Vollmer, "Die Illustratoren," pp. 23–25, 33–36, 148–151, 157–158.

6. Oldenbourg, *Buchholzschnitte des Schäufelein*, I: pp. 15–26.

41. CRUCIFIXION

ca. 1505
Woodcut
23.8 × 16.2 cm
Geisberg 63; Hollstein, II: nr. 12
Lent by the St. Louis Art Museum; Bequest of
Horace M. Swope, 79: 1940

Shortly after completing the illustrations for
Pinder's *Der Beschlossen Gart des Rosenkrantz
Marie* in 1505, Baldung began work on a series of
twelve devotional woodcuts.[1] One of the most
moving is the *Crucifixion*.[2] Certain features, such
as the figure of Christ, are adopted directly from
Baldung's earlier woodcut in the Pinder volume.
However, important differences exist that require this unsigned and undated single woodcut
to be later than the text illustration. For instance,
Baldung's hatching style more successfully de-
fines the figural forms and the shading patterns
here than in the Pinder Crucifixion scene. Baldung has stripped the subject of its unessential
details. Christ, alone, is dramatically silhouetted
against the darkened sky. The onlookers have
been reduced to the Virgin, John the Evangelist,
and, clutching the cross, the grieving Mary
Magdalene. They are compositionally balanced
by Stephaton holding the sponge on a lance.

Baldung relied on designs by Dürer for the
Crucifixion and many of the other woodcuts in
this series.[3] The four figures below the cross derive from Dürer's *Crucifixion* drawing in the
Green Passion series (Vienna, Albertina) of
1504–1505. The posture of Mary Magdalene
holding the cross is identical to the representation in Dürer's *Calvary* woodcut of 1500–1502.
Precedents for the inclusion of the sun and the
moon and the obliquely angled cross can also be
found in Dürer's oeuvre. These borrowings do
not, however, lessen the impact of Baldung's
composition.

Critics have suggested that Baldung intended
the *Crucifixion* to be displayed with the woodcuts the *Descent from the Cross* and the *Lamentation* to form a triptych.[4] Baldung used this arrangement formula for the woodcuts *St.
Catherine*, the *Virgin and Child*, and *St. Barbara*,
which are part of this series of twelve.[5] Although triptychs are common in painting and
sculpture, there are no precedents in prints. Because of the sequential problems of placing the
Descent from the Cross in the center between the
Crucifixion and the *Lamentation*, critics are less
certain that Baldung conceived these three
prints as an independent triptych.

Also see cat. nr.

43 Pinder, *Speculum Passionis Domini Nostri
Ihesu Christi* (Nuremberg, 1519 [1507])

1. Marrow and Shestack, eds., *Hans Baldung Grien*,
nrs. 4–10, with a discussion of this series.
2. This print was later published with a six-line text
in Latin and German; see Geisberg, nr. 63. Dürer's
monogram was also erroneously added to the print at
a later date. On this print, see Koch et al., *Hans Baldung Grien*, nr. II H 8; Oettinger and Knappe, *Baldung*,
nr. 56; Marrow and Shestack, eds., *Hans Baldung
Grien*, nr. 7 (written by Lorraine Karafel). I have relied
on the latter for much of this entry.
3. Marrow and Shestack, eds., *Hans Baldung Grien*,
nr. 7, esp. figs. 7b and 7c for the following.
4. Oettinger and Knappe, *Baldung*, p. 15, nrs.
57–58; Marrow and Shestack, eds., *Hans Baldung
Grien*, nrs. 7–8.
5. Marrow and Shestack, eds., *Hans Baldung Grien*,
nrs. 4–6, with additional literature.

Hans Leonhard Schäufelein

The artist was born probably in Nuremberg between 1480 and 1485.[1] His father, Franz, a successful merchant, moved there from Nördlingen in 1476; however, since Franz continued to reside off and on in both towns, it is unclear where Hans was raised and received his initial training. He entered Dürer's workshop in about 1503.[2] He was already a highly skilled artist, as evidenced by his portraits dated 1503 and 1504 (cat. nr. 42). During Dürer's second trip to Venice, from fall 1505 to January 1507, Schäufelein painted the *Ober-Sankt-Veit Altarpiece*, after Dürer's drawings, which Friedrich the Wise had ordered for the Schlosskirche at Wittenberg.[3] Schäufelein was responsible for the majority of the woodcuts illustrating Ulrich Pinder's *Speculum Passionis Domini Nostri Ihesu Christi* of 1507 (cat. nr. 43). By this time he began to sign his works with his monogram and a small shovel (*schäufel*), a punning reference to his name. Hans left Dürer's workshop in late 1506 or, more likely, in early 1507. He may have stopped briefly in Augsburg before journeying through the Tyrol in 1509 and 1510. The period 1510–1515 witnessed a dramatic increase in his graphic production, especially for Augsburg publisher Hans Schönsperger. He contributed to several of Emperor Maximilian I's woodcut projects, including the *Theuerdank* (cat. nr. 47) and the *Weisskunig* (cat. nr. 54).

In 1515 he moved to Nördlingen, his father's hometown, where he was appointed city painter. His most important picture was the *Battle of Betulia* of 1515, which he painted on the walls of the chamber of the Bavarian league in the town hall.[4] In 1521 he made the *Ziegler Altar* in Nördlingen.[5] Until his death, shortly before St. Martin's day (11 November) 1540, Schäufelein remained extremely active as a portraitist and printmaker. The portraits *Lorenz II Tucher* and, one of his wife, *Katharina Straub*, signed and dated 1534, and the fact that most of his later prints were published by Hans Guldenmund prove that Schäufelein remained in extremely close touch with Nuremberg.[6] It is likely that he returned occasionally to meet with Guldenmund or poet Hans Sachs, with whom he often collaborated. Dürer's influence on Schäufelein's late woodcuts and paintings was still quite strong, and Schäufelein's art contributed to the spreading of Dürer's style and ideas to Augsburg and Nördlingen.

Guldenmund, see cat. nr. 50, note 4. When Dürer journeyed to Antwerp, he took some of Schäufelein's work with him. His diary entry for 12 February 1521 reads: "I sold 2 sketches and 4 books of Schäufelein's prints for 3 fl[orins]." This supports my contention about Schäufelein's continued ties to Nuremberg. See Conway, *Writings of Dürer*, p. 114; Rupprich, *Dürer schriftlicher Nachlass*, I: p. 165 (lines 158–160).

1. A thorough monograph on Schäufelein is needed. The information below is largely taken from the following: Peltzer, ed., *Sandrarts Academie*, pp. 263, 308, 333, 412; E. Buchner, "Der junge Schäufelein als Maler und Zeichner," in *Festschrift für Max J. Friedländer zum 60. Geburtstage*, pp. 46–76, and "Schäufelein," in Thieme-Becker, 29: pp. 557–561; Winkler, *Zeichnungen Kulmbachs und Schäufeleins*; *Nuremberg: Meister um Dürer*, pp. 167–186, nrs. 289–328; Oldenbourg, *Buchholzschnitte des Schäufelein*; P. Strieder, "Schäufelein, Hans," *Kindlers Malerei Lexikon* (Zurich, 1968), V; pp. 222–227.

2. Buchner, "Der junge Schäufelein," and *Nuremberg: Meister um Dürer*, pp. 167ff., are the only detailed studies of his early period.

3. Vienna, Erzbischöfliches Dom- und Diozäsanmuseum. See Anzelewsky, *Dürer*, pp. 26, 38–39; Winkler, *Zeichnungen Dürers*, II: nrs. 319–323.

4. See cat. nr. 49.

5. Buchner in Thieme-Becker, 29: p. 558.

6. Ibid.; L. Grote, *Die Tucher*, figs. 64–65. Lorenz II built the Tucher house (fig. 16). On his work for

42. PORTRAIT OF A MAN

Inscribed: 1504 ALT 23; and on the shirt: A
Painting: oil on panel
44.5 × 30.5 cm
Lent by The Clowes Fund Collection, Indianapolis Museum of Art

Schäufelein's picture is an engagement or marriage portrait of a twenty-three-year-old man.[1] He holds some eryngo, a plant symbolizing luck in love. This feature can also be seen in Michael Wolgemut's 1486 *Portrait of a Man* (Detroit Institute of Arts) and in Dürer's 1493 *Self-Portrait* (Paris, Louvre).[2] The identity of the sitter is unknown. The "A" on his shirt likely refers not to his name but to either that of his bride or the first letter of a personal motto.

The painting has previously been attributed to Dürer and to Baldung, which is not surprising given Schäufelein's specific borrowings from Dürer's portraits of the 1490s.[3] Many of these stylistic associations have been commented upon in Section 6. Since Schäufelein and Baldung were both in Dürer's workshop at the same time and did collaborate with each other, their art, even as late as the mid-1510s, reveals strong similarities. For instance, Baldung's self-portrait painted in the *Altar of St. Sebastian* (Nuremberg, Germanisches Nationalmuseum) of 1507 exhibits the same abstraction of the face, with the emphasis on a strong contour rather than subtle modeling, that is evident in the Schäufelein portrait.[4]

The Indianapolis painting is closely related to Schäufelein's 1503 *Portrait of Sixtus Oelhafen* in Würzburg (Martin-von-Wagner-Museum der Universität) and, especially, to the *Portrait of a Man* in Warsaw (Muzeum Narodowe), which is undated but contemporary.[5] The use of an extremely wavy contour line to define the right side of the sitters' faces or strong circular strokes that form the left eyebrow and then continue downward to provide form and shading to the nose are identical in the Indianapolis and Warsaw pictures. These features can also be found in Schäufelein's signed and dated portrait drawings of the 1510s.[6]

1. References to older literature can be found in A. F. Janson, *100 Masterpieces of Painting: Indianapolis Museum of Art* (Indianapolis, 1980), pp. 54–55. The best discussion of Schäufelein's early paintings is Buchner, "Der junge Schäufelein."

2. *Nuremberg: Dürer (1971)*, nr. 100; Anzelewsky, *Dürer*, nr. 10. Anzelewsky has questioned the traditional interpretation of the eryngo since in other instances it can symbolize Christ's passion. The German name for this thistle-like plant is Männertreu, or man's devotion. I suspect the plant could convey either idea. In Dürer's painting, he is dressed very much as the young dandy, not the attire appropriate to a reference to the Passion.

3. H. Tietze, *Meisterwerke Europäischer Malerei in Amerika* (Vienna, 1936), pp. 338–339, nr. 202; G. Glück, "Ein Neu gefundenes Werk Albrecht Dürers," *Belvedere* 7–8 (1934–1936): 117–118, attributed it to Dürer. E. Panofsky, *Albrecht Dürer* (1943 ed.), II: p. 19, nr. 92, suggested that Baldung or someone in his circle painted this picture.

4. *Nuremberg: Meister um Dürer*, nr. 3.

5. Janson, *100 Masterpieces*, p. 54, states that Dr. Kurt Löcher, now curator of painting at the Germanisches Nationalmuseum, first attributed the picture to Schäufelein during a visit to Indianapolis. Löcher suggested the comparison with the Würzburg portrait. I think that the Warsaw portrait is even closer in style

and feeling. On these pictures, see *Nuremberg: Meister um Dürer*, nrs. 294, 298. The Warsaw painting is discussed in Buchner, "Der junge Schäufelein," pp. 72, 74, fig. 18. All three pictures are illustrated in P. Vaisse and A. Ottino della Chiesa, *Tout l'Oeuvre Peint de Dürer* (Paris, 1968), nrs. 108, 200, 202.

6. Winkler, *Zeichnungen Kulmbachs und Schäufeleins*, Schäufelein nrs. 69–70.

43. ULRICH PINDER, SPECULUM PASSIONIS DOMINI NOSTRI IHESU CHRISTI

Nuremberg: Friedrich Peypus, 30 August 1507; exhibited: second edition Peypus, 19 October 1519
76 woodcuts
Lent by the George N. Meissner Collection, Special Collections, Washington University Libraries, St. Louis

Two years after completing the illustrations for Pinder's *Der Beschlossen Gart des Rosenkrantz Marie* (cat. nr. 40), Schäufelein and Baldung collaborated on the decoration of the *Mirror of the Passion of Our Lord Jesus Christ*, a collection of New Testament passages and texts by the Church Fathers compiled by Pinder.[1] This folio volume is considerably less ambitious than its predecessor. Of the seventy-six woodcuts, forty-four had already appeared in the 1505 book. Schäufelein contributed twenty-nine new woodcuts and Baldung just three.[2]

Many of Schäufelein's woodcuts reveal both his continued dependence upon Dürer and his rapidly developing originality. For example, in the woodcut *Christ's Descent into Limbo*, illustrated here, the woman (Eve?) on the left is copied directly after Dürer's *Adam and Eve* drawing (Paris, École des Beaux-Arts) of the 1490s.[3] Yet Schäufelein then places her in a dramatic composition seemingly of his own design. Although Dürer, who had returned from his second trip to Venice at the beginning of 1507, may have offered specific design suggestions, there is no firm evidence that Dürer was the source for Schäufelein's woodcuts.[4] In fact, Winkler may have been correct when he observed that Dürer studied Schäufelein's woodcuts while preparing his *Small Woodcut Passion* of 1509–1511.[5] Dürer certainly appreciated the emerging inventiveness of his pupil.

1. Wolf Traut or Hans von Kulmbach have occasionally, if inconclusively, been linked with this cycle. See Dodgson, II: pp. 5–6, 17; F. Winkler, "Dürers kleine Holzschnittpassion und Schäufeleins Speculum-Holzschnitte," *ZDVK* 8 (1941): 197–208; Koch et al., *Hans Baldung Grien*, nr. II B IV; *Nuremberg: Meister um Dürer*, nr. 27; Oettinger and Knappe, *Baldung*, pp. 137–138; Oldenbourg, *Buchholzschnitte des Schäufelein*, nrs. 167–195; *Nuremberg: Dürer (1971)*, nr. 373.
2. For the attribution of specific woodcuts to the two artists, see *Nuremberg: Meister um Dürer*, nr. 27.
3. Winkler, "Dürers kleine Holzschnittpassion," p. 201; Winkler, *Zeichnungen Dürers*, I: nr. 148. *The Descent into Limbo* is on folio 67 verso of the 1507 edition and 58 of the 1519 edition.
4. Talbot, ed., *Dürer*, p. 184.
5. Winkler, "Dürers kleine Holzschnittpassion," passim, cf. figs. 3 and 4.

44. CRUCIFIXION

ca. 1507; monogram and shovel
Woodcut
34.1 × 26.6 cm (sheet that has been trimmed)
B. 30; Geisberg, nr. 1042; Dodgson, II: nr. 33
Lent by the Metropolitan Museum of Art, New
York, Joseph Pulitzer Bequest, 1917

Schäufelein produced this woodcut shortly after
leaving Dürer's workshop,[1] and Dürer's influence
is evident in the figures, the Christ type, and in
the overall composition. Schäufelein's mourners
recall the costumes, gestures, and styles of Dürer's grieving figures in such works as his *Lamentation* painting of 1500.[2] Dürer had developed a
new heroic, muscular Christ, as seen, for instance, in his 1505 *Christ on the Cross* drawing,
that soon transformed most contemporary depictions of Christ made in Nuremberg.[3] The
similarities between Schäufelein's Christ and,
for example, the monumental *Calvary* that Adam
Kraft carved between 1506 and 1508 for the Johannisfriedhof result from their common dependence on Dürer.[4] The handling of the composition and landscape in Schäufelein's woodcut
recalls such Dürer prints as *Samson and the Lion*
(ca. 1496) or *Joachim and the Angel* from *The Life of
the Virgin* (ca. 1504).[5]

The early dating of this print is supported by
its similarities in style and design to the *Crucifixion* that Schäufelein made in 1504 or 1505 for Ulrich Pinder's *Der Beschlossen Gart des Rosenkrantz
Marie* (cat. nr. 40).[6] In the intervening two or
three years, Schäufelein had gained more confidence in his ability to arrange a large number of
figures in space. His later mourners are more
sculptural and more expressive. The *Calvary* was
made at the same time as the smaller, undated
Bearing of the Cross and the large *Martyrdom of St.
Sebastian*.[7]

1. This woodcut is sometimes referred to as the
Great Calvary because of its size. *Nuremberg: Meister um
Dürer*, nr. 312.
2. Anzelewsky, *Dürer*, nr. 70.
3. Winkler, *Zeichnungen Dürers*, II: nr. 325 (Vienna,
Albertina). Schäufelein painted the *Crucifixion* in the
Ober-Sankt-Veit Altar (Vienna, Erzbischöfliches Dom-
und Diozäsanmuseum) of 1505–1506 after Dürer's
drawings. See Winkler, *Zeichnungen Dürers*, II: nrs.
319–323; *Nuremberg: Meister um Dürer*, nr. 293, fig. 57.
This painted version is more crowded, less heroic than
the print.
4. Schwemmer, *Adam Kraft*, fig. 66. Kraft's Christ is
more linear, less muscular than Schäufelein's.
5. Meder, nrs. 107, 190.
6. Oldenbourg, *Buchholzschnitte des Schäufelein*, nr.
153, pl. 12.
7. Geisberg, nrs. 1041, 1056.

142

45. ADORATION OF THE MAGI

ca. 1507–1510
Drawing: pen and black and brown ink over charcoal on white paper
23.8 × 22.3 cm
Lent by the Fogg Art Museum, Harvard University, Cambridge, Bequest of Meta and Paul J. Sachs

This drawing shows Schäufelein's continued reliance upon the work of Dürer and the stylistic changes that occurred in the years immediately after he left Dürer's workshop.[1] His composition derives from Dürer's *Adoration of the Magi* painting of 1504 (Florence, Uffizi), as evidenced by the general arrangement of the figures, the placement of the hat on the kneeling magus, and the shape of the apple cup with serpent finial.[2]

Schäufelein's early drawings tend to be freely sketched with little stress upon the structures of the figures. Shortly after leaving Dürer's workshop around 1507, Schäufelein developed a tighter hatching style and greater confidence in his ability to arrange figures. These traits are evident here and in the closely related, but somewhat later, drawings of *Apostles* in Leipzig (Museum).[3] The faces of the two elder magi are especially close to *St. Andrew* and *St. Simon*.

The artist reused portions of this composition in two woodcuts published in *Evangelienbuch* (Augsburg, 1512) and *Plenarium* (Basel, 1514).[4]

Schäufelein added abbreviated inscriptions indicating colors, as seen next to the Virgin's veil, by her right sleeve, by her right leg, and just below the knee of the kneeling magus. Conceivably, the drawing was intended as a design either for a stained-glass window or, more likely given the amount of detail in the composition, for another artist.

1. Mongan and Sachs, *Drawings in the Fogg Museum of Art*, nr. 393; A. Mongan, ed., *Memorial Exhibition: Works of Art from the Collection of Paul J. Sachs (1878–1965) Given and Bequeathed to the Fogg Art Museum, Harvard University* (Cambridge, Mass., 1965), nr. 10. On Schäufelein's copying of Dürer's work, see the comments in Section 5.

2. Anzelewsky, *Dürer*, nr. 82. Compare also Dürer's *Adoration of the Magi* drawing in Bayonne (Musée Bonnat); Winkler, *Zeichnungen Dürers*, II: nr. 294. Also compare the famous *Apple Cup* (*Apfelpokal*) (cat. nr. 116). Schäufelein's *Adoration of the Magi* painting (Innsbruck, Ferdinandeum), probably made around 1504–1505, also derives from Dürer's painting; see Buchner, "Der junge Schäufelein," pp. 50–52, fig. 3.

3. Winkler, *Zeichnungen Kulmbachs und Schäufeleins*, Schäufelein nrs. 26–38, esp. 26, 33.

4. Oldenbourg, *Buchholzschnitte des Schäufelein*, nrs. 220 (pl. 39), esp. 495 (pl. 77); also cited by Mongan, *Memorial Exhibition*, nr. 10. The artist also executed several paintings of this theme.

46. ST. BIRGITTA GIVING THE RULE TO HER ORDER

Dated 1513 (lower right)
Woodcut
24.1 × 22.4 cm
Geisberg, nr. 1058; Dodgson, II: p. 29
Lent by the New York Public Library, Prints Division, Astor, Lenox and Tilden Foundations

In 1900 Dodgson was the first scholar to attribute this woodcut to Schäufelein. Although Dodgson did not give his reasons, the attribution is correct. St. Birgitta's (St. Bridget) figure type and pose are identical to St. Anne's in Schäufelein's signed and dated (1511) drawing in Bremen (Kunsthalle).[1] The figures and the style of hatching reappear in other woodcuts of the early 1510s, notably *St. Sebastian and St. Roch*.[2] The heads of the nuns and monks are cut on separate blocks, which Dodgson believes were designed by Leonhard Beck of Augsburg.

St. Birgitta of Sweden (1302–1373; canonized in 1391) enjoyed immense popularity in Germany and Italy because of her writings on the cult of the Virgin and the passion of Christ.[3] Nuremberg publisher Anton Koberger printed her *Revelationes* in Latin in 1500 and in German in 1502.[4] St. Birgitta's comments on the nativity of Christ and especially on his crucifixion influenced the compositions of Grünewald and many other artists.

In this woodcut, St. Birgitta is shown seated and presenting her writings to the nuns and monks of the Birgittine Order (Order of the Holy Savior), which she had founded in 1346.[5] Her three principal symbols are the crown on the ground, the pilgrim's staff, and the angel. She was erroneously believed to have been a princess ("principessa di Nericia") who exchanged her crown for her habit. The pilgrim's staff and the angel derive from a vision of Dom Gerekin, a Cistercian monk at Alvastra in Spain, where St. Birgitta resided for four years following the death of her husband in 1344.

The format of the lower half of the woodcut plus the figures of Christ and the Virgin Mary directly above are based upon earlier prototypes. Nordenfalk has published a German manuscript of the second half of the fifteenth century that displays an almost identical composition.[6] While it is doubtful that Schäufelein saw this specific manuscript while he was in the Tyrol in 1509–1510, he must have seen a related image.

The upper half of the woodcut is a genealogical tree. On the right, between St. Birgitta and the Swedish coat of arms, is a man who must be identified as her husband, Ulf Gudmarsson. This pious man died while on a pilgrimage with his wife to Compostela, but not before they had produced eight children, including St. Catherine of Sweden (1332–1381), who is depicted holding a lamp and lilies immediately above.[7] The other seven children are represented in the branches of the tree.

The monk is most likely Augustinian canon Alfonso de Vadaterra, a Spanish bishop and refugee, whom St. Birgitta met in Italy in 1369 or 1370.[8] He was St. Birgitta's literary editor, who, between 1375 and early 1377, when her canonization petition was initiated, completed the *Re-velationes*. In manuscript representations Alfonso de Vadaterra is shown in both monastic and episcopal attire.

1. Winkler, *Zeichnungen Kulmbachs und Schäufeleins*, Schäufelein nr. 50, cf. 41.
2. Geisberg nr. 1057.
3. C. Nordenfalk, "Saint Bridget of Sweden as Represented in Illuminated Manuscripts," in *De Artibus Opuscula XL: Essays in Honor of Erwin Panofsky*, ed. M. Meiss (New York, 1961), pp. 371–393; U. Montag, *Das Werk der heiligen Birgitta von Schweden in oberdeutscher Überlieferung* (Munich, 1968).
4. *Nuremberg: Meister um Dürer*, nr. 397; *Nuremberg: Dürer (1971)*, nr. 365. Schäufelein was not influenced by the woodcuts in this edition. See A. Schramm, *Die Bilderschmuck der Frühdrucke*, 17: nrs. 600–617.
5. On the iconography of the saint, see Nordenfalk, "Saint Bridget," pp. 374, 377–378, 383.
6. Ibid., p. 383, fig. 31 (Vienna, Nationalbibliothek, cod. 1316, fol. 7v).
7. Dodgson correctly identified St. Catherine, but he erroneously claimed that the woman with the book on the opposite side of the genealogical tree was St. Birgitta once again.
8. Nordenfalk, "Saint Bridget," pp. 373, 379, discusses Alfonso de Vadaterra and his representations.

47. [MELCHIOR PFINZING], DIE GEUERLICHEITEN VND EINSTEILS DER GESCHICHTEN DES LOBLICHEN STREYTPAREN VND HOCHBERÜMBTEN HELDS VND RITTERS HERR TEWRDANNCKHS (THEUERDANK) (Nuremberg: Hans Schönsperger the Elder, 1 March 1517)

290 vellum leaves
118 handcolored woodcuts (each numbered)
15.8 × 13.8 cm (woodcut)
Lent by the New York Public Library, Rare Book Manuscripts Division, Astor, Lenox and Tilden Foundations

On 19 August 1477, Maximilian, then Duke of Austria, married Mary, Duchess of Burgundy, at Ghent. Although their union proved to be brief, since Mary was killed in a riding accident in 1482, two children, Philip the Fair and Margaret of Austria, were born. Throughout his life, Maximilian looked back on this period as a time of personal happiness and idealism. In 1505 Maximilian conceived of writing a long allegorical poem about his personal trials and his courtship of Mary. The result was the *Theuerdank*, a largely fictitious story of a hero's battles, hunts, and character-building escapades.[1] Courtiers Sigismund von Dietrichstein and Marx Treitzsauerwein helped to compose the text and its versification. By 1514 Melchior Pfinzing, provost of St. Sebaldus, had edited the text and prepared it for publication. Early textual editions and a proof edition with woodcuts are still in Vienna.[2]

The first edition was published in Nuremberg by Augsburg printer Hans Schönsperger the Elder.[3] The example of the *Theuerdank* in the exhibition is one of the very rare copies printed on parchment and with hand-colored woodcuts. Most of these were distributed to nobles and courtiers only after Maximilian's death in 1519. This particular copy was at least briefly in Nuremberg, since on the end page is the printed and hand-colored bookplate of Muffel von Eschenau (1509–1569) of Nuremberg created by Virgil Solis.[4] Schönsperger published a second edition two years later in Augsburg. A total of seven editions were printed in the sixteenth century.[5]

Schäufelein contributed 20 of the 118 woodcuts.[6] His work was finished before he moved to Nördlingen in 1515. The principal artist of the series was Leonhard Beck of Augsburg, who made as many as 77 woodcuts.[7] He was helped by Hans Burgkmair, Augsburg's finest painter and printmaker, who produced 13 images. Other woodcuts have been attributed to Wolf Traut, Erhard Schön, and other unidentified artists. *Formschneider* Jost de Negker carved some of the woodblocks.[8]

While Schäufelein's woodcuts are comparatively simple in design and add little to our broader understanding of his artistic development, these serve to document his collaborative relationship with Beck. Illustrated here is figure 58, representing Theuerdank threatened by a sack of gunpowder. He stands on a ship between Ehrenhold (favorable honor) and, on the shore, Unfallo (misfortune). During the course of production, but probably after Schäufelein had moved to Nördlingen or started work on another project, Beck altered the image. The head

of Unfallo, the upper body of Theuerdank, and the area from Theuerdank's legs to the bottom of the sack were removed and replaced with new designs by Beck. The additions are quite obvious upon close examination of the composition. Beck apparently sought to standardize the heads of the principal characters. In all, he changed seventeen of Schäufelein's twenty woodcuts.[9]

1. Simon Laschitzer, "Der Theuerdank. Facsimile-Reproduction nach der ersten Auflage vom Jahre 1517," *JKSAK* 8 (1888), is still the most thorough study; also see *Maximilian I. 1459–1959*, nrs. 70–75; *Nuremberg: Meister um Dürer*, nr. 327; Oldenbourg, *Buchholzschnitte des Schäufelein*, pp. 75–77, nrs. 591–611 (L 119); *Hans Burgkmair: 1473–1973. Das graphische Werk*, exh. cat. (Augsburg: Städtische Kunstsammlungen, 1973), nrs. 167–177.

2. Laschitzer, "Der Theuerdank," pp. 14–69, esp. 61–64, for Vienna, Nationalbibliothek, Cod. Vindob. 2833 (proof edition); *Maximilian I. 1459–1959*, nrs. 70–72. Woodcut number 58 illustrated here is folio 94 verso in this Vienna proof edition.

3. Schönsperger was responsible for the pirated edition of Schedel's *Nuremberg Chronicle*; see cat. nr. 3, note 10.

4. Solis died in 1562, so the book was likely in Muffel von Eschenau's possession before this time. See Morgenroth, nr. 162, for Matthes Gebel's 1532 portrait medal of Jacob Muffel.

5. For information about the different editions, see Laschitzer, "Der Theuerdank," pp. 108–116, esp. 108–110, on the first edition. He mentioned that Maximilian kept the first edition and that in 1526 Arch-

duke Ferdinand ordered the copies distributed. Also see *Nuremberg: Meister um Dürer*, p. 185.

6. Laschitzer, "Der Theuerdank," pp. 71–75; *Nuremberg: Meister um Dürer*, p. 185. He designed numbers 10, 13 (signed), 16, 21, 26, 30 (signed), 32, 39, 42, 45 (signed), 46, 48 (signed), 50, 57, 58 (signed), 69 (signed), 70 (signed), 72, 87, and 105.

7. Laschitzer, "Der Theuerdank," pp. 75–81 (Burgkmair), 81–90 (Beck); *Nuremberg: Meister um Dürer*, p. 185, mentions that numbers 40 and 79 have been attributed to Traut and that Dodgson had linked others with Schön; *Hans Burgkmair: 1473–1973*, introductory remarks before nr. 167.

8. Laschitzer, "Der Theuerdank," pp. 91–94. For instance, Schäufelein's woodcut number 70 contains his monogram and that of Negker.

9. On Beck's changes, see ibid., pp. 94–103. Beck is credited with the addition of the faces of the monks and nuns in Schäufelein's *St. Birgitta Giving the Rule to Her Order* (cat. nr. 46). Another prominent example is Springinklee's *Emperor Maximilian I and Archduke Charles Receiving Three Portuguese Ambassadors* (cat. nr. 54).

48. MAN OF SORROWS

ca. 1520; monogram and shovel
Woodcut
24.3 × 17.1 cm
B. 41; Dodgson, II: pp. 30–31
Lent by the New York Public Library, Prints Division, Astor, Lenox and Tilden Foundations

"I bear these cruel wounds for thee, O man! And I hear thy frailty with my blood. I heal thy wounds with my wounds, with my death I expiate thy death. I am God and have become man for thee. But thou dost not thank me. With thy sins thou often tearest open my wounds. I am still lashed for thy misdeeds. Have done now. I once suffered great torment from the Jews. Now, friend, let peace be between us."[1] This text, written by Benedictus Chelidonius beneath the *Man of Sorrows* woodcut on the title page of Dürer's *Large Passion*, creates a dialogue between Christ and the viewer. The worshipper is asked to ponder both the reasons for Christ's sacrifice and his or her own continuing transgressions. Chelidonius's text typifies how Man of Sorrows paintings and prints were understood during this period. The immediacy and impact of Schäufelein's woodcut and related representations are intended to encourage the worshipper to meditate and to offer prayers for forgiveness.[2]

The design of Schäufelein's woodcut is highly unusual since it is conceived as an altarpiece. He has placed the Man of Sorrows, like a painting, within a heavy, carved wooden frame. It is decorated with a shell niche and a grieving putto above and, below, two putti holding a garland from which hangs a mirror. While later fifteenth-century prints occasionally have narrow printed frames, this imitation of an altarpiece design seems to have occurred first in the 1510s, perhaps in Augsburg.[3] Schäufelein's woodcuts in Wolfgang von Maen's *Das leiden Jesu Christi vnnsers erlösers . . .* (Augsburg: Hans Schönsperger the Younger, 1515) are set within imitation carved frames that approximate this basic design.[4] Much closer in style and purpose to Schäufelein's *Man of Sorrows* are Hans Burgkmair's *King Solomon Praying to Idols* and Albrecht Altdörfer's *Beautiful Virgin of Regensburg*, both dating around 1519 or 1520.[5] Other artists adopted this printed altarpiece concept in the 1520s.[6]

1. Schiller, *Iconography of Christian Art*, II: p. 197; on the theme and related bibliography, see pp. 197, 224. On the development of half-length devotional images, see Ringbom, *Icon to Narrative*, esp. ch. I.
2. See cat. nr. 59.
3. For instance, Master E. S.'s *Man of Sorrows* (1467); A. Shestack, *Master E. S.—Five Hundredth Anniversary Exhibition*, nrs. 78–79.
4. Oldenbourg, *Buchholzschnitte des Schäufelein*, p. 42 (L. 25), pls. 50–54. The borders were likely added by another artist.
5. *Hans Burgkmair: 1473–1973*, nr. 115, fig. 85; the frame was added by Jost de Negker. On Altdörfer's woodcut, see Geisberg, nr. 31.
6. For instance, Hans Sebald Beham's *Altarpiece with the Life of the Virgin*; Geisberg, nr. 192.

49. BATTLE OF BETULIA

ca. 1530; monogram and shovel on central tree
Woodcut (four blocks)
39.5 × 116.8 cm
Geisberg, nrs. 1021–1024
Lent by the Philadelphia Museum of Art:
Charles M. Lea Collection

The story of the battle of Betulia comes from the Book of Judith in the Old Testament Apocrypha.[1] According to this account, the Israelites were being routed by the stronger Assyrian army, led by Holofernes, when Judith, a Jewish widow, decided to help her people by using her feminine charms. Dressed in her finest clothing and jewelry, Judith and a servant went to the Assyrian camp. On the pretext that she had information about the Israelite army, she was led before Holofernes. Captivated by her beauty and her wisdom, Holofernes permitted Judith to wait upon him. On the fourth night, Holofernes was seized by his desire for her and had her admitted into his tent; however, Holofernes passed out on his bed, having drunk too much. At this moment, Judith seized Holofernes's sword, severed his head from his body, and placed the head in the sack held by the servant. They quickly returned to Betulia, where, in the print, they are being welcomed by King Ozias. Holofernes's head was displayed about the city walls. The leaderless Assyrians withdrew and the war ended. For her heroic exploits, Judith is included in medieval and Renaissance cycles of the nine female worthies, as well as in programs representing the power of women over men.

Schäufelein illustrated this theme repeatedly during his career. A drawing (Bamberg, Staatsbibliothek), made while Schäufelein was still in Dürer's workshop, is a design for a wall painting set around a door or a window.[2] In 1515 he painted the battle in the chamber of the Bavarian league in the Rathaus at Nördlingen, where he was the city painter.[3] This mural cycle shows the two scenes of Judith meeting Holofernes and the decapitation, with the attacking troops depicted behind. This painting was widely acclaimed by his contemporaries and such later critics as Sandrart in 1675.[4]

Perhaps the success of this painting and the popularity of his other battle compositions, notably the *Battle of Pavia* of about 1526, inspired Schäufelein to design this extremely large woodcut representation of Judith's exploits.[5] The coherently organized composition, which reads from right to left, combines features from the earlier Nördlingen painting with the artist's other military scenes, such as the battle of Cividale in the *Weisskunig* (cat. nr. 54) and his many prints of soldiers.[6] A roughly contemporary drawing of the *Death of Holofernes* (London, University College Library) may have been executed as a preliminary study for the print; however, Schäufelein rejected the design.[7] This woodcut, like many of Schäufelein's large-format prints, was intended to be mounted or displayed on a wall much like a painting.

1. Réau, *Iconographie de l'Art Chrétien, II.1*, pp. 329–335.
2. Buchner, "Der junge Schäufelein," pp. 55–56, fig. 6; Winkler, *Zeichnungen Kulmbachs und Schäufeleins*, Schäufelein nr. 14. Buchner dated the drawing about 1505 and Winkler placed it about five years later.
3. Although this painting is considered his finest work and is usually mentioned in the literature on the artist, it has not, to my knowledge, been thoroughly studied. Very brief comments are given in Buchner, "Der junge Schäufelein," p. 56. For a pre-1914 photograph, see the Marburger Index: Nördlingen 5 2514, 124 594.
4. Peltzer, ed., *Sandrarts Academie*, pp. 263, 412.
5. Geisberg, nrs. 1089–1095. Also see the *Battle with the Turks*; Geisberg, nrs. 1096, 1097, which dates around 1532.
6. Oldenbourg, *Buchholzschnitte des Schäufelein*, nr. 854, pl. 159; it is dated between 1514 and 1516. On the soldiers, see Geisberg, nrs. 1099–1105, and cf. the figures in Schäufelein's *Triumphal Procession of Emperor Charles V* (cat. nr. 52).
7. Winkler, *Zeichnungen Kulmbachs und Schäufeleins*, Schäufelein nr. 80.

50. WILD MAN AND HIS FAMILY

1530 (1545)
Woodcut on two blocks
25.1 × 26.4 cm (image); 26.1 × 27.7 cm (sheet)
Geisberg, nr. 1106; Dodgson, II: p. 53
Lent by the Metropolitan Museum of Art, New York, Gift of Harry G. Friedman, 1957

The concept of the wild man enjoyed tremendous popularity in Germany during the later fifteenth century and the first half of the sixteenth. The wild man, a forerunner of the werewolf or the modern Big Foot, resembled man except that most of his body was covered with thick hair. Occasionally, leaves and branches would ring his head and genitals. The wild man was a primitive creature who lived simply in the dense German forests. He avoided man except when he occasionally left the forest to steal a child for his dinner.[2] Schäufelein shows him with an uprooted tree for a walking staff, a reference to his wild, physical power.

During the early sixteenth century, the image of the wild man began to change.[3] He was no longer devoid of intelligence. He had become a noble creature cleansed by the purity of nature who criticizes mankind and his social structures. The woodcut exhibited here lacks its original eighty-five lines of verse by Hans Sachs, which were used for the 1530 and 1545 editions of this print as published by Hans Guldenmund of Nuremberg.[4] The correct title is *Klag der wilden Holtzleüt vber die vngetrewen Welt* or *Lament of the Wild Forest Folk over the Perfidious World*. Using the wild man as his spokesman, Sachs offers a blistering commentary upon man's corrupt behavior. The wild man, not the civilized urban burgher, is the superior creature.

Portions of Sachs's text read as follows:

Alas! Society corrupts
And rampant perfidy erupts
As justice suffers out of sight
Injustice prospers in the light
The loan shark sits in Honor's seat
While honest workers cannot eat

. . . .

The world's in such a sorry state
With lies, and knavery, and hate
And so to sum it up in short
We find the things of evil sort
Embraced by all society

. . . .

A man who would be well employed
And finds the world in such a mess
Must forsake this faithlessness
And so we left our worldly goods
To make our home in these deep woods
With our little one protected
From that falsehood we rejected
We feed ourselves on native fruits
And from the earth dig tender roots

. . . .

And thus removed from civilization's
Shams we've lived for generations
United in our simple life

. . . .

When all the world will see the light
And everyman live true, upright,
In equal, unconniving good
It's then we'll gladly leave the wood
And rejoin mankind in tears
Of joy; We've waited for years and years.
This turn to virtue Man now mocks,
Will soon occur, hopes friend Hans Sachs.[5]

The transformations in the wild man's image belong to a broader trend that glorified the beauty and simplicity of the natural world in contrast to the complex and often immoral, man-made cities. In art, Albrecht Altdörfer and other Danube School painters and printmakers created wild, evocative scenes of forests and mountains.[6] Some are arcadian, others powerfully pantheistic. Whether the hero is the wild man or Altdörfer's satyr, he embodies a simpler, more primeval stage in man's evolution.

---

1. T. Husband and G. Gilmore-House, *The Wild Man: Medieval Myth and Symbolism*, provides an excellent introduction to this subject and its transformations; see their nrs. 52 (a pair of ewers) and 58 (Dürer's *Coat of Arms of Death*) for other Nuremberg examples of this theme. Carnival actors dressed as wild men and wild women were frequently part of the annual Schembart festival in Nuremberg; see S. L. Sumberg, *The Nuremberg Schembart Carnival*, pp. 98–103, figs. 16, 17, 56.
2. See Lucas Cranach the Elder's woodcut (ca. 1510–1515; Geisberg 619); Husband and Gilmore-House, *The Wild Man*, nr. 25.
3. Ibid., pp. 15–17.
4. On this print, also see Röttinger, *Die Bilderbogen des Hans Sachs*, nr. 405; *Die Welt des Hans Sachs*, nr. 71; Husband and Gilmore-House, *The Wild Man*, nr. 33. Guldenmund probably published the first edition of the print that appeared on 2 June 1530. Husband and Gilmore-House, *The Wild Man*, fig. 85, illustrates the ca. 1530 version (Berlin, Kupferstichkabinett), which has a more complete landscape background. Guldenmund's name appears at the bottom of the text of the more numerous 1545 edition. Nuremberg *formschneider* and publisher Wolfgang Strauch produced a third edition in 1569. Strauch's print is not mentioned in Strauss, *The German Single-Leaf Woodcut, 1550–1600*, III: p. 1063, where he discusses Strauch's career; however, see Röttinger, *Die Bilderbogen des Hans Sachs*, nr. 405.
5. The translation is by F. Childs and is published in Husband and Gilmore-House, *The Wild Man*, pp. 202–204.
6. Talbot and Shestack, eds., *Prints and Drawings of the Danube School*, esp. pp. 10–14. Also see L. Silver, "Forest Primeval: Wilderness Images by Albrecht Altdörfer (1506–1516)," which will appear in *Simiolus* in 1983.

51. PRINCES' WEDDING DANCE: DANCING COUPLE

1531–1535 or 1570
Woodcut
24.7 × 17.8 cm (block); 25.3 × 19.3 cm (sheet)
Geisberg, nr. 1078; Dodgson, II: p. 52 (nr. 231)
Lent by the Art Museum, Princeton University
(Junius S. Morgan Collection)

The *Dancing Couple* is one of the series of nineteen woodcuts that comprise the *Princes' Wedding Dance*. The actual composition of this series, the artists involved, and the date have puzzled many critics, including Geisberg and Dodgson. Röttinger's solution is now accepted.[1] He claimed that this series consisted of nineteen woodcuts, sixteen by Schäufelein, one by Pencz, and two by Schön.[2] A second, unrelated series of different dimensions was made by Pencz and Hans Sebald Beham.[3] *Briefmaler* Hans Guldenmund of Nuremberg published the series sometime between 1531 and 1535. The original edition contained Guldenmund's signature and texts penned by Hans Sachs above each figure.[4] Although the *Dancing Couple* may be from this first edition with the accompanying inscriptions cut off, the lack of Guldenmund's signature beneath the feet of this couple and the imperfect impression suggest that it belongs instead to the incomplete 1570 edition published in Nuremberg by Wolfgang Strauch.[5] Nuremberg *form-schneider* Peter Steinbach produced a later, third edition.[6]

The series has been variously titled. The *Princes' Wedding Dance* appears to be correct since the seventeen couples are richly attired and several of the men wear the collars of the Order of the Golden Fleece.[7] One of Schön's two woodcuts depicts the bride and groom. Schäufelein provided representations of the dance leader, the torch bearer, musicians, and even an audience.

While the cycle is not intended to commemorate any specific occasion, it does recall the elaborate patrician dances held in the great hall of the Nuremberg Rathaus.[8] Schäufelein was certainly familiar with the mural paintings of musicians and onlookers executed in this chamber by Pencz and others after Dürer's designs.[9]

---

1. Röttinger, *Die Bilderbogen des Hans Sachs*, pp. 39–46, nr. 198a; also see *Die Welt des Hans Sachs*, nrs. 94–112.

2. Geisberg, nrs. 1001 (Pencz), 1064–1079 (Schäufelein), 1169–1170 (Schön). The total length of the series would be about 3.60 meters. For an incomplete view of the ensemble, see Horst and von Heusinger, *Riesenholzschnitte*, fig. 55.

3. Röttinger, *Die Bilderbogen des Hans Sachs*, nr. 5305; Geisberg, nrs. 246–248 (Beham), 1002–1003 (Pencz).

4. Röttinger, *Die Bilderbogen des Hans Sachs*, pp. 42–46, provides the entire text; the text for the *Dancing Couple* is given in lines 73–80. See Geisberg, nr. 1078, for an illustration of this print with its text and Guldenmund's signature.

5. Röttinger, *Die Bilderbogen des Hans Sachs*, p. 40, provides information about the different editions. Strauch was active between 1554 and 1572; see Strauss, *The German Single-Leaf Woodcut, 1550–1600*, III: p. 1063, nr. 32.

6. Steinbach was active between 1577 and 1636. He also republished Schäufelein's *Triumphal Procession of Emperor Charles V* (cat. nr. 52).

7. On the costumes and general figure types, cf. the revelers in Hans Sebald Beham's contemporary *Feast of Heriodias* (cat. nr. 82).

8. A mid-sixteenth-century watercolor illustrating a patrician dance in the great hall is reproduced in *Reformation in Nürnberg*, nr. 79. Also see the later watercolor of a dance held sometime between 1620 and 1625; Pfeiffer and Schwemmer, *Bilddokumenten*, fig. 60.

9. Mende, *Rathaus*, I: nr. 191; see cat. nr. 213 for a discussion of these paintings.

52. TRIUMPHAL PROCESSION OF EMPEROR CHARLES V

ca. 1600 (after original 1537 edition)
Published by Peter Steinbach ("Gedruckt zu
Nurnberg durch Peter Steinbach
Formschneider")
Woodcut: 9 blocks
42 × 274.3 cm
B. 1; P. iii 247, 1; Geisberg, nrs. 1080–1088;
Dodgson, II: pp. 49–50
Lent by the Germanisches Nationalmuseum,
Nuremberg, HB 26536 (Rolle)

This series, one of Schäufelein's last important
works, was designed in 1536 and published by
Hans Guldenmund of Nuremberg in January
1537. On 29 January 1537, Guldenmund presented a copy of the German-text edition to the
Nuremberg city council, thereby providing a terminus.[1] A second entry in the city council records, dated between 5 and 9 April, states that
the council decided to postpone its discussion
about how much to reward Guldenmund until
they had seen the Latin-text edition the printer
was preparing.[2] Guldenmund also published an
edition without the accompanying long inscriptions that laud the emperor.[3] There exist at least
two later editions: one published by Johann
Kramer, a minor Nuremberg *formschneider* who
was active between 1551 and 1556, and that exhibited here, by Peter Steinbach.[4]

Schäufelein's design is extremely clear and orderly.[5] The procession begins on the left with
two groups of trumpeters and a drummer, followed by two sets of mounted nobles, some
wearing the collar of the Order of the Golden
Fleece of which Charles V was the current sov-
ereign, and foot soldiers. Their clothes and the
textiles covering the horses are decorated with
Charles V's emblems, the pillars of Hercules; the
imperial eagle; the flints and firestones, cross of
St. Andrew, and pendant ram of the Order of
the Golden Fleece; the sun; and the emperor's
various coats of arms. Four teams of horses pull
the chariot. Charles V is shown being crowned.
Four other princes, whom Dodgson identified as
Maximilian I, Philip the Fair, Charles the Bold,

and Ferdinand of Aragon, flank the emperor.[6]
More puzzling is the identity of the sleeping
prince represented on the textile covering the
rear wheel of the chariot. Dodgson thought he
was Charles V's ancestor Rudolf of Hapsburg;
however, the identity is by no means definite.

This triumphal procession celebrates the imperial dignity of Charles V rather than an entry
into any specific town.[7] He is the "TRIVMPHVS
CAROLI IMPERATORIS EIVS NOMINIS
QVINTI," or "The Triumphant Emperor Charles
fifth of his name."[8] He is the embodiment of the
thirty-six virtues (moderation, justice, might,
perseverance, etc.) inscribed on the leaves of
the laurel wreath that hovers in front of his
chariot. Earlier, Dürer had used the same virtues, in the form of young maidens leading
horses, in his *Great Triumphal Chariot* (cat. nr.
26).

While preparing his program, Schäufelein
studied the more elaborate *Triumphal Procession
of Emperor Maximilian I* made by Hans Burgkmair
and a host of other artists during the 1510s.[9]
Schäufelein had contributed at least two woodcuts. The artist adopted many of the costume
designs, facial types, and horse postures from
the woodcuts traditionally attributed to Hans
Springinklee.[10] However, Schäufelein rejected
the ponderous chariots, with their implausible
modes of propulsion, and complicated arrangements in favor of a more conventional, horse-
drawn procession. He used the movement of
the figures and their informal conversations to
enliven the series.

takes. For instance, in the sixth woodcut with the
laurel wreath, the principal horse has its right rear
hoof closer to the viewer than the left hoof. The flowing tail masks or at least obscures part of this flaw.
  6. Dodgson, II: p. 49.
  7. Cf. Jörg Breu the Elder's *Entry of Emperor Charles V
into Augsburg in 1530* (Geisberg, nrs. 357–366), which
nicely captures the confusion and haphazardness of
an actual rather than idealized entry. Also see the elaborate cityscape in Hans Sebald Beham's *Entry of Emperor Charles V into Munich in 1530* (Geisberg, nrs. 292–
296), which was published by Niclas Meldemann in
Nuremberg.
  8. In the 1537 edition, this text read "SOLA TVO
CAPITI DIGNA EST HAEC LAVREA CAESAR."
  9. Applebaum, ed., *The Triumph of Maximilian I*;
Schäufelein is attributed nrs. 127–128. See the comments for cat. nr. 26.
  10. Ibid., nrs. 91–95, 103–110. I wonder whether
Schäufelein might have made these woodcuts as well,
given the stylistic similarities to such contemporary
drawings as his *Landsknecht* (Vienna, Collection Fürst
Liechtenstein), the 1518 *Child on a Horse* (Frankfurt,
Städelsches Kunstinstitut), and his borrowings twenty
years later. On the drawings, see Winkler, *Zeichnungen
Kulmbachs und Schäufeleins*, Schäufelein nrs. 53, 60.

Also see cat. nrs.

  1. Hampe, *Nürnberger Ratsverlässe*, I: nr. 2225.
  2. Ibid., nr. 2237; also cited by Dodgson, II: p. 50. It
is likely that this series would have been publicly displayed on such ceremonial occasions as Charles V's
entry into Nuremberg in 1541. The Latin edition is illustrated in Geisberg, nrs. 1080–1088. The inscriptions, other than those on the laurel wreath by the
chariot, were printed with separate blocks from the
woodcuts.
  3. Illustrated in *Reformation in Nürnberg*, nr. 276.
  4. On the career of Kramer, see Strauss, *The German
Single-Leaf Woodcut, 1550–1600*, II: p. 537, which does
not mention this print. Steinbach was active between
1577 and 1636. He also reissued Schäufelein's *Princes'
Wedding Dance* (cat. nr. 51).
  5. Schäufelein did make a few compositional mis-

Springinklee was a painter, woodcut designer, and manuscript illuminator.[1] Critics have suggested that he was born probably in Nuremberg between 1490 and 1495. This dating is based upon the facts that his earliest work appears in 1510 and that a 7 September 1520 document refers to the artist as "den jungen Springenclee."[2] Springinklee was a pupil in Dürer's workshop by 1507. Neudörfer, writing in 1547, stated that Springinklee lived in Dürer's house.[3] Springinklee was in Constance in 1510 and 1511, when he illuminated the *Missal of Bishop Hugo von Hohenlandenberg*, among other manuscripts.[4]

Throughout the 1510s, Springinklee worked closely with Dürer. *Adam and Eve* (cat. nr. 53) is based upon Dürer's oeuvre. Springinklee made woodcuts after Dürer's *Women's Bath* drawing and the Dürer workshop drawing of *St. Anne with the Virgin and Child*.[5] Through Dürer, Springinklee became involved in several of the graphic projects of Emperor Maximilian and his astronomer, Johannes Stabius. In 1512 he provided the woodcut for Stabius's *Horoscope of Maximilian*.[6] Soon afterward he contributed woodcuts to the *Small Triumphal Procession*, the *Weisskunig* (cat. nr. 54), and the *Triumphal Arch of Emperor Maximilian I* (cat. nr. 20) and added drawings to Pirckheimer's Latin edition of Horopollo's *Hieroglyphica*.[7] When Maximilian died in 1519, Springinklee designed two commemorative prints (cat. nrs. 56 and 57).

During the 1510s, Springinklee produced an important corpus of woodcuts and book illustrations, including those for the immensely popular *Hortulus Animae* (cat. nr. 63). Dettenthaler has attributed to Springinklee seven paintings, done primarily for churches in and around Nuremberg during this decade.[8] The city council employed Springinklee in 1520 and 1521 to redecorate the emperor's private chambers in the Burg.[9] Springinklee painted Charles V's twenty-four coats of arms on the ceiling of the reception room. Classical grotesques were added to the paneling of the emperor's living room. He also painted frescoes of the Annunciation, Adoration of the Magi, Flight into Egypt, and Crucifixion on the walls of the emperor's oratory in the upper chapel of the Burg. Springinklee may have been involved in a minor way in the decorative cycles of the great hall of the Rathaus.

Virtually nothing is known about Springinklee's subsequent career. Dettenthaler claimed that Springinklee produced the paintings for the monumental *Welser Altar*, formerly in the Frauenkirche (fig. 6), and several lesser pictures made before 1525.[10] On 7 December 1533, Springinklee married Barbara Wagnerin according to the records of St. Sebaldus.[11] Johann Gabriel Doppelmayr, writing in 1730, said that Springinklee died in 1540; however, there exists no corroborative evidence.[12] In all likelihood, Springinklee left Nuremberg sometime after 1525 and died abroad.

1. New research on Springinklee is desperately needed. On his oeuvre and life, see Dodgson, I: pp. 369–417; F. T. Schulz, "Springinklee, Hans," in Thieme-Becker (1937), 31: pp. 412–416; *Nuremberg: Meister um Dürer*, pp. 15, 187–203, nrs. 329–357; Dettenthaler, "Hans Springinklee als Maler," pp. 145–182.

2. Schulz, "Springinklee," p. 412; Dettenthaler, "Hans Springinklee als Maler," p. 146.

3. Neudörfer, *Nachrichten von Künstlern*, p. 144.

4. Schulz, "Springinklee," p. 412; *Nuremberg: Meister um Dürer*, nr. 330.

5. Geisberg, nrs. 1338, 1347; Winkler, *Zeichnungen Dürers*, I: nrs. 152, 220. The drawing *St. Anne with the Virgin and Child* (Nuremberg, Germanisches National-museum) is now attributed to Dürer's workshop rather than to the master; see Zink, *Die Handzeichnungen*, nr. 70.

6. *Vienna: Maximilian I. 1459–1519*, nr. 448; *Nuremberg: Dürer (1971)*, nr. 311. Springinklee made woodcuts for four horoscopes.

7. Dodgson, I: pp. 398–404; *Vienna: Maximilian I. 1459–1519*, nrs. 305–317, for the *Small Triumphal Procession*, nrs. 200, 435, on the Horopollo illustrations.

8. Dettenthaler, "Hans Springinklee als Maler," pp. 173–176, nrs. 1–7. Dettenthaler credits Springinklee with sixteen paintings or painted programs.

9. Ibid., p. 177, nrs. 9–11, for the following cycles.

10. Ibid., pp. 178–182, nrs. 12 (*Welser Altar*)–16. On Springinklee's woodcuts for books published after 1524, see Dodgson, I: pp. 373–374, 377–378. Most of these seem to have been made before 1524 and simply reused.

11. Dettenthaler, "Hans Springinklee als Maler," p. 147.

12. Ibid. This comment was in J. G. Doppelmayr, *Historische Nachricht von den Nürnbergischen Mathematics und Künstlern.*

53. ADAM AND EVE

ca. 1512
Woodcut
22.8 × 14.6 cm
Geisberg, nr. 1337
Lent by the Metropolitan Museum of Art, New
York, Gift of Paul J. Sachs, 1922

Springinklee's *Adam and Eve* is generally believed to be his earliest print, predating his signed and dated *Miracle of St. Wilgefortis* (Geisberg, nr. 1342) by about a year.[1] His woodcut is directly based upon Dürer's 1504 engraving *Adam and Eve* (cat. nr. 11) and the 1507 painting of this theme now in Madrid (Prado).[2] The basic compositional design of two large figures set in the extreme foreground and backed by a stand of dense foliage is adopted from Dürer's print, as are the essential features of Springinklee's two figures. Springinklee used the body of Dürer's Adam for his Adam. However, his Adam's face, with its long, angular lines and baggy cheeks, as well as the wind-swept hair, is taken from Dürer's Eve. The position of the shoulder and the reaching right arm recall Dürer's painted Adam. Springinklee's Eve is a combination of the body of the engraved Eve, the shoulders of the painted Adam, and the head and hair of the painted Eve by Dürer. Yet, in spite of all these borrowings, Springinklee's figures are highly attractive and much warmer in their human interaction than are those in Dürer's engraving.

Various secondary features in the woodcut also derive from Dürer's oeuvre. For instance, the serpent with the apple in the tree is quite similar to that in Dürer's 1507 painting. Although Springinklee did not include the emblematic creatures found in Dürer's engraving of 1504, the small owl in the tree comes from the *Marriage of the Virgin* woodcut in Dürer's *Life of the Virgin* series.[3] Springinklee carefully studied Dürer's use of hatchings and crosshatchings in this series and used dark, ink-filled shadows to form the contour on the left half of Eve.[4]

1. *Nuremberg: Meister um Dürer*, nr. 338; P. Strieder, "Copies et interprétations du cuivre d'Albrecht Dürer Adam et Eve," *Revue de l'Art* 21 (1973): 44–47; *Nuremberg: Vorbild Dürer*, nr. 100.
2. Anzelewsky, *Dürer*, nrs. 103–104.
3. Meder 194.
4. Compare the Adam and Eve prints by Ludwig Krug (cat. nr. 114) and Hans Sebald Beham (cat. nr. 93).

54. MARX TREITZSAUERWEIN, WEISSKUNIG (Vienna: Joseph Kurzböck, 1775)

251 woodcuts; exhibited: Springinklee, *Emperor Maximilian I and Archduke Charles Receiving Three Portuguese Ambassadors* (woodcut number 156a)
ca. 1514–1516
23.7 × 21.2 cm
Dodgson, I: p. 374
Lent by the Art Institute of Chicago. 1977. 233

The *Weisskunig*, or story of the white king, is one of the most ambitious of Emperor Maximilian I's literary and artistic projects.[1] In about 1505, the emperor decided to write a biography of his father, Emperor Friedrich III (1440–1493), and himself. He dictated large portions of the text, especially the sections on his own life, to his court secretary, Marx Treitzsauerwein, who did the actual writing of the narrative. The book is divided chronologically into three sections. The first describes the life of Friedrich III; the second covers the period from Maximilian's birth in 1459 to his marriage to Mary of Burgundy in 1477; and the third treats Maximilian's life and deeds up to 1513. In 1526 King Ferdinand of Hungary requested Treitzsauerwein to write the fourth section, which would extend the narrative up to Maximilian's death in 1519; however, the secretary died in 1527 and the project was never finished. In fact, the completed three sections and their illustrations were only first published in 1775.

The 251 woodcuts were made in Augsburg between 1514 and 1516. The principal artists were Hans Burgkmair and Leonhard Beck who, respectively, created 118 and 127 of the woodcuts.[2] Hans Schäufelein designed the *Throne of the Blue King* (nr. 123) and the *Battle of Cividale* (nr. 200) woodcuts.[3] The remaining four illustrations were added by Hans Springinklee.[4]

The basic composition of Springinklee's *Emperor Maximilian I and Archduke Charles Receiving Three Portuguese Ambassadors*, illustrated here, was used for three separate woodcuts. An examination of the print quickly reveals that it is composed using two woodblocks. The three ambassadors and the herald holding the Portuguese coat of arms are printed from a smaller, irregularly shaped woodblock that has been added to the principal block. Since Springinklee was instructed, probably by Beck, to represent three different groups of foreign envoys seeking marriages with the three daughters of Philip of Castile, he simply repeated the principal woodblock and inserted three slightly different secondary blocks depicting the kneeling ambassadors. This use of interchangeable woodblocks is unusual but hardly unique.

Springinklee's scene is a carefully constructed one-point perspective scheme. The young artist is applying his teacher's lessons on spatial design. In particular, he seems to have studied carefully the spatial expositions in Dürer's *Life of the Virgin* series published in 1511.[5]

proof edition with annotations by Maximilian that is in the Department of Prints, Drawings & Photographs of the Museum of Fine Arts in Boston; *Nuremberg: Meister um Dürer,* nr. 328.

2. On Burgkmair and Beck, see Schultz, "Der Weisskunig," pp. xxv–xxvi; Augsburg, *Hans Burgkmair: 1473–1973,* nrs. 178–203, with a discussion of the project and its artists.

3. Oldenbourg, *Buchholzschnitte des Schäufelein,* p. 118 (L246–247).

4. Schultz, "Der Weisskunig," pp. xxv, 67, 383–385; Dodgson, I: p. 374. Besides the three woodcuts discussed below, Springinklee made woodcut nr. 199 representing Maximilian dictating the feats of his forebears to a painter and a group of writers.

5. Meder 188–207.

1. A. Schultz, "Der Weisskunig," *JKSAK* 6 (1888), is a facsimile edition with a short critical introduction; T. H. Musper, ed., *Kaiser Maximilians Weisskunig,* 2 vols. (Stuttgart, 1955–1956); *Maximilian I. 1459–1959,* nrs. 76–89, 387–389, with a discussion of the textual editions, which, however, neglects to include the

55. ST. SEBALDUS IN A NICHE

1518
Woodcut
30.1 × 20.9 cm
Dodgson, I: pp. 395–396; M., p. 18; H.: Dürer
School, nr. 18
Lent by the Cooper-Hewitt Museum, The
Smithsonian Institution's National Museum of
Design, New York (1950-5-25)

St. Sebaldus was Nuremberg's principal patron
saint.[1] Little is known about his life other than
that he lived during the eighth or ninth century.
An Augsburg chronicle of 1070 or 1072 mentioned Nuremberg's veneration of Sebaldus. Although he was not canonized until 26 March
1425, the parish church for the northern half of
Nuremberg had already been named in his
honor (fig. 7). Sebaldus was frequently represented in local art. For example, the Vischer family constructed his shrine, which contains scenes
of his life, between 1507 and 1519 for the church
of St. Sebaldus (figs. 21 and 22). In about 1494
and 1501, Wolgemut and Dürer designed woodcuts of the saint for two editions of Conrad Celtis's ode to Sebaldus, commissioned by Sebald
Schreyer.[2] In 1514 Springinklee planned the
woodcut for the title page of *Die hystori des lebes
. . . des . . . Sant Sebalds* (Nuremberg: Hieronymus Höltzel).[3]

Springinklee is also credited with the design
of *St. Sebaldus in a Niche*, dated 1518.[4] Sebaldus is
dressed as a pilgrim with a walking stick and
with pilgrimage badges on his hat. In his right
hand is a model of the west façade of the Nuremberg church. One legend claimed that Sebaldus belonged to the Danish royal family and
married a French princess; therefore, the coats
of arms of Denmark and France are placed at the
upper left. Opposite are two of Nuremberg's
three coats of arms. The 1518 figure of Sebaldus
is more monumental than his 1514 counterpart.
Springinklee is now using Dürer's "graphic middle ground" shading technique to achieve a
greater range of tonal values and to create more
sculpturesque forms. Springinklee will make
even better use of this technique in a woodcut of
1519 (cat. nr. 57). The artist is less successful in
his rendering of the architecture, especially the
awkward juncture of the ceiling and the top of
the niche. Similarly, the source of his lighting is
puzzling as it seems to shine through the solid
wall by Sebaldus's right foot.

1. S. Sprusansky, ed., *Der heilige Sebald, seine Kirche
und seine Stadt*, provides the best introduction to the
saint's history and his representation in art. Also see
H. Martin von Erffa, "Der Nürnberger Stadtpatron auf
Italienischen Gemälden," *MVGN* 64 (1977): 1–9.

2. Sprusansky, ed., *Der heilige Sebald*, nr. 7
(Wolgemut); Meder, nr. 234 (Dürer); C. Dodgson, "Die
illustrierten Ausgaben der sapphischen Ode des
Konrad Celtis an St. Sebald," *JKSAK* 23 (1902): 45–52;
Spitz, *Conrad Celtis*, p. 41; *Nuremberg: Dürer (1971)*, nr.
359; see the comments in Section 4.

3. Dodgson, I: p. 381; *Nuremberg: Meister um Dürer*,
nr. 350; *Reformation in Nürnberg*, nr. 47; Sprusansky,
ed., *Der heilige Sebald*, nr. 3.

4. Passavant attributed the woodcut to Dürer; however, most critics agree with Dodgson (I: pp. 395–396),
who credits Springinklee.

56. RICHARDUS SBROLIUS, RICHARDI SBRVLII FOROIVLIANI POETAE CAESAREU IN DIVI MAXIMILIANI CAESARIS P. F. AUG. OBITUM NENIA (Augsburg, 17 February 1519)

One woodcut: *The Imperial Family Mourning the Death of Maximilian I* with monogram
15.6 × 13.8 cm (woodcut only)
Geisberg, nrs. 1344–1345; Dodgson, I: p. 409
Lent by the John M. Wing Foundation of the Newberry Library, Chicago

RICHARDI SBRVLII FOROIVLIANI
Poetæ Cæfarei in diui MAXIMI
LIANI Cæfaris P. F. Aug.
obitum Nenia.

Emperor Maximilian I died on 12 January 1519, inspiring Richardus Sbrolius, a court writer active in Augsburg during the 1510s, to compose a long poem extolling the emperor's character.[1] Shorter poems laud Maximilian's daughter Margaret of Austria (1480–1530), and his grandsons and heirs, Charles V (1500–1558) and Ferdinand I (1503–1564). These poems and the accompanying woodcut by Springinklee were published in a small four-page pamphlet, exhibited here, and in a larger broadsheet.[2]

Springinklee's woodcut represents Maximilian's family gathered around his coffin, on which are placed the imperial regalia. The artist adopted his image from contemporary funerary miniatures illustrating the office of the dead in books of hours.[3] Springinklee simply replaced the customary monks praying beside a bier with Maximilian's daughter and six grandchildren. On the left are Charles, Ferdinand, and Margaret. Opposite are the four daughters of Maximilian's deceased son Philip the Fair (1478–1506), King of Castile: Eleanor (1498–1558), Isabella (1501–1526), Mary (1505–1558), and Catherine (1507–1578).[4] Since Maximilian's family was scattered across the continent, Springinklee's is an ideal not historical gathering.

This woodcut is simple in design. Springinklee likely made the woodcut rather quickly during the second half of January. This scene of mourning forms an appropriate, though unintended, pendant to Springinklee's contemporary woodcut *Emperor Maximilian I Presented by His Patron Saints to the Almighty* (cat. nr. 57).

1. *Vienna: Maximilian I. 1459–1519*, nr. 208. Sbrolius, or Sbrulius, also worked on one of the textual editions of *Theuerdank*; see ibid., nr. 75. The pamphlet is dated "quarto. Id. Februa," which I read as the fourth day after the ides (13th), or the seventeenth of February.
2. The broadsheet, published by Geisberg (nrs. 1344–1345), contains the same text. It measures 49 × 34 cm.
3. Generally, on this subject, see A. Erlande-Brandenburg, *Le Roi est Mort* (Geneva, 1975).
4. The three interchangeable woodcuts that Springinklee made for the *Weisskunig* (cat. nr. 54) represent the marriage negotiations for the first three of Philip the Fair's daughters.

57. EMPEROR MAXIMILIAN I PRESENTED BY HIS PATRON SAINTS TO THE ALMIGHTY

1519
Woodcut
37.4 × 37.7 cm (woodcut only)
Geisberg, nr. 1343; Dodgson, I: pp. 407–409
Lent by the University of Michigan Museum of Art, Ann Arbor

Shortly after Maximilian's death on 12 January 1519, his court historian and astronomer, Johannes Stabius, formulated the program for this apotheosis image.[1] Springinklee represented Maximilian in heaven being introduced by his patron saints to God. Maximilian is dressed in a sumptuous pearl-and-jewel-trimmed robe decorated with the imperial eagle. He wears the imperial crown and his regalia are set on the pillow at his feet. His profile view and crown design recall Dürer's 1518 drawing for the *Great Triumphal Procession* (cf. cat. nr. 26).[2] Maximilian addresses God with the words:

Tu autem Domine Susceptor meus es:
gloria mea: & exaltans Caput meum.

Moreover, you O Lord are my supporter
You are my glory and you glorify my reign.[3]

Surrounding the emperor are the Virgin and Child and his saints: George, patron of the Order of St. George; Andrew, patron of the Order of the Golden Fleece; Maximilian, his name saint; Sebastian and Barbara, who were the patrons of archers and artillery soldiers, respectively; and Leopold, a former Austrian noble. They intercede on Maximilian's behalf by reminding God of the emperor's virtuous character and many good works for the Church. The banderole above their heads reads:

Domine saluum fac Regem, & exaudi
Nos in Die qua inuocauerimus te.

Lord save the King & listen
To us this day in which we invoke you.

God stands within the triumphal arch above the suppliants. He is dressed in a rich robe similar in design to that of Maximilian. He blesses the emperor and says:

Preueni eum in Benedictionibus dulcedinis posui in
Capite eius Coronam de Lapide precioso & letificabo
eum in gaudio cum vultu meo: —.

I came before him with sweet blessings
On his head I placed a crown of precious stones & I caused
Him to rejoice at the sight of my countenance.

This woodcut is one of Springinklee's greatest works. Although certain features—notably, God's face, St. Leopold, and the little winged angels—derive from Dürer's prints, these borrowings do not diminish the attractive architectural design and balanced composition by Springinklee. The young artist's ability to render different materials and to achieve very subtle tonal variations has never been more evident than in this woodcut.

Below the woodcut, Stabius supplied a long text listing the emperor's various titles, his death date, the length of his reign, and, at the bottom,

an enumeration of his princely virtues. Springinklee added Stabius's coat of arms at the lower left corner of the woodcut.

---

1. On Stabius (died 1522), see cat. nrs. 20–21. The best discussion about this print is Dodgson, I: pp. 407–409; also see H. S. Francis, "A Woodcut by Hans Springinklee," *Bulletin of the Cleveland Museum of Art* 40 (1953): 17–18; *Vienna: Maximilian I. 1459–1519*, nr. 436; *Nuremberg: Meister um Dürer*, nr. 347; C. Olds, E. Verheyen, and W. Tresidder, *Dürer's Cities: Nuremberg and Venice*, nr. 95.
2. Vienna, Albertina. Winkler, *Zeichnungen Dürers*, III: nr. 685.
3. I wish to thank John Clarke for his assistance with the translation of this and the following Latin quotations.

Also see cat. nrs.
20 *Triumphal Arch of Emperor Maximilian I*
63 *Hortulus Animae* (Lyon: Johannes Clein for Johann Koberger, 9 November 1517)

Wolf Traut

A painter and printmaker, Wolf Traut was born about 1480 in Nuremberg, the son of Hans Traut.[1] Although critics have ascribed woodcuts dating as early as 1503 to Wolf, his first firmly attributed woodcuts appeared in Pinder's *Der Beschlossen Gart des Rosenkrantz Marie* of 1505 (cat. nr. 40).[2] Therefore, Traut was a pupil in Dürer's workshop by 1504 or 1505 at the latest. During 1506 and 1507, Traut designed illustrations for three devotional treatises published in Nuremberg by Hieronymus Höltzel.[3] Critics suggested that he collaborated with Hans von Kulmbach during the period from 1505 to 1507 when Dürer was in Venice.[4]

In spite of Dodgson's statement that "Traut is an artist of mediocre taste and accomplishment," it is clear that he created an attractive group of important paintings and prints during the 1510s.[5] Wolf painted the *High Altar* (1511) and the wings for a second altar in the Johanniskirche.[6] In 1511 and 1512 he produced fifty-one woodcuts for St. Bonaventura's *Die Legend des heyligen vatters Francisci*.[7] Between 1512 and 1515 Traut collaborated with Dürer and other artists in the production of the *Triumphal Arch of Emperor Maximilian I* (cat. nr. 20). The signed and dated *Artelshofener Altar*, formerly in the Tuchmacherkapelle at St. Lorenz, was finished in 1514.[8]

Traut's principal patron between 1513 and 1518 was Abbot Sebald Bamberger of the Kloster Heilsbronn, west of Nuremberg.[9] Traut painted the *St. Vincent and St. Maurice Altar* (1516–1518); the *St. John the Baptist Altar* (1517), which is one of his finest works; the *St. Peter and St. Paul Altar* (1517–1518); and a portrait of the abbot (ca. 1516–1518).

Since Traut continued to be involved in other projects at this time, he seems to have remained in Nuremberg. His woodcuts for the *Hallesche Heiltumsbuch* appeared in 1520.[10] Traut died during the summer of this year according to an entry in the St. Sebaldus death register.[11]

Recht," in Hirschmann and Schultheiss, eds., *Albrecht Dürers Umwelt*, p. 231. Neudörfer stated that Traut remained unmarried. He was also a good friend of Hermann Vischer. See Neudörfer, *Nachrichten von Künstlern*, p. 136.

1. Hans Traut was a painter and goldsmith. On the family, see C. Rauch, *Die Trauts*. On Wolf, see Dodgson, I: pp. 500–524; F. T. Schulz, "Traut, Wolf," in Thieme-Becker (1939), 33: pp. 351–354; L. von Baldass, "Zur Bildniskunst der Dürerschule. I. Zur Bildniskunst des Wolf Traut und H. L. Schäufelein," *Pantheon* 26 (1940): 225–229; *Nuremberg: Meister um Dürer*, pp. 204–220, nrs. 358–394; P. Strieder, "Traut, Wolf," *Kindlers Malerei Lexikon* (Zurich, 1968), 5: pp. 554–558.
2. Andreas Stiborius, *Libellus Linconiensis De Phisicis Lineis* (Nuremberg: J. Weissenburger, 1503); see *Nuremberg: Meister um Dürer*, nr. 383, for comments on the attribution of this early work to Traut.
3. Ibid., 384, 386–387; see cat. nr. 59.
4. Strieder, "Traut," p. 554.
5. Dodgson, I: p. 500. He then proceeds to talk rather positively about Traut's specific works.
6. *Nuremberg: Meister um Dürer*, nrs. 359–360, both still in situ.
7. Ibid., nr. 390.
8. Ibid., nr. 362 (Munich, Bayerisches Nationalmuseum). Pfeiffer and Schwemmer, *Bilddokumenten*, fig. 183.
9. *Nuremberg: Meister um Dürer*, nrs. 364–367 (Heilsbronn, Münster, except the *St. John the Baptist Altar*, the center panel of which is in Nuremberg, Germanisches Nationalmuseum).
10. Ibid., nr. 393, made for Cardinal Albrecht von Brandenburg. See P. M. Halm and R. Berliner, *Das Hallesche Heiltum: Man. Aschaffenb.* 14.
11. Schulz, "Traut," p. 351. Relatively little is known about his personal life. Local records mention that he got into a fight with fellow painter Hans Rab in 1512; see Schultheiss, "Albrecht Dürers Beziehungen zum

58. NATIVITY, PASSION OF CHRIST, AND THE CHRISTIAN ESTATE

1511
Woodcut
43.5 × 59.2 cm
Dodgson, I: p. 515; Geisberg, nr. 1404
Lent by the Cleveland Museum of Art, Delia E. Holden Fund

This highly attractive broadsheet is one of Traut's finest prints. It also exhibits how dependent the artist was on the designs of his contemporaries. The broadsheet consists of fifteen woodblocks plus a long German prayer. The Nativity in the center is copied in reverse from a woodcut by Hans von Kulmbach, with whom Traut had worked while in Dürer's atelier.[1] Traut added a few minor details to the figures and the setting. At the right is the date 1511 with the 5 cut backward. The hand of God directs the viewer to the eleven Passion scenes at the top of the broadsheet. Traut loosely based his designs upon Dürer's *Small Passion*, which was published in 1511 but largely completed by 1510.[2] Below are groups of ecclesiastics and secular figures who comprise the Christian estate. Directly

behind the German emperor is a portrait of Friedrich the Wise. Traut had made an independent woodcut of Friedrich in 1510 that he reused in this broadsheet.[3] His source for both images was Lucas Cranach the Elder's 1509 woodcut of the Elector of Saxony.[4] Traut reissued his portrait of Friedrich the Wise and the Nativity after Kulmbach in a second broadsheet made in 1511 or shortly thereafter.[5]

The viewer, as a member of the Christian estate, shares in the veneration of Christ. The accompanying German text begins: "O Lord Jesus Christ a son of the Living God . . ." The prayer recalls that Christ was sent to earth and born of Mary in order to redeem mankind through his ultimate sacrifice.

1. Geisberg, nrs. 891–892. Also see comments by Dodgson, I: p. 515.
2. Meder, 135, 137–138, 140–143, 146, 149, 152, 154.
3. Dodgson, I: p. 514; Koepplin and Falk, *Lukas Cranach*, I: nr. 105.
4. Koepplin and Falk, *Lukas Cranach*, I: nr. 104. For an illustration, see Jahn, *Lucas Cranach*, p. 203.
5. Geisberg, nr. 1405. Since the Nativity was reused, it is not necessary that the print date to 1511. Because this broadsheet includes seven Passion scenes not by Traut, I am assuming that the exhibited broadsheet, which is entirely by Traut, predates it.

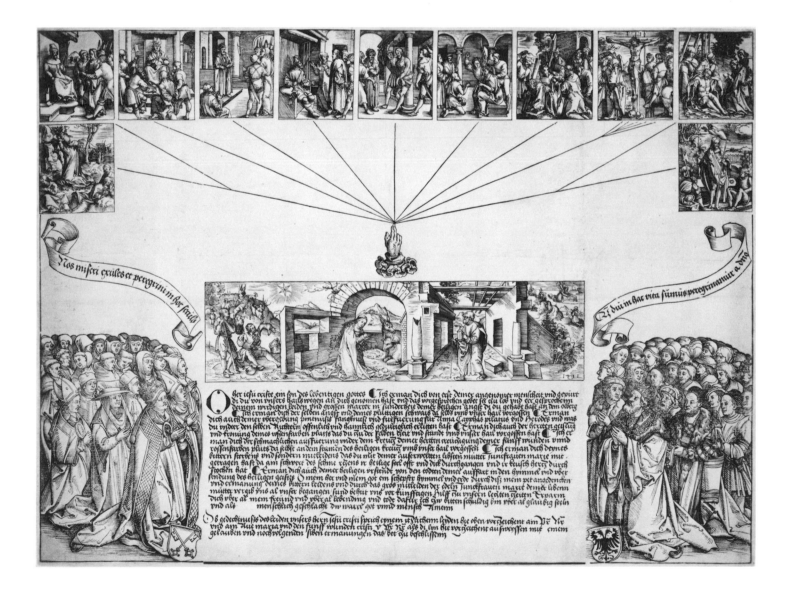

59. MAN OF SORROWS AND MATER DOLOROSA

1512
Woodcut highlighted with red ink
42.5 × 26 cm
Dodgson, I: pp. 519–520; Geisberg, nr. 1408
Lent by the National Gallery of Art, Washington, Rosenwald Collection, 1952

This indulgence broadsheet was published by Hieronymus Höltzel of Nuremberg in Latin in 1512, as exhibited here, and in a slightly smaller German edition shortly afterward.[1] Image and text are joined to help the worshipper contemplate the sacrifice of Christ and the Virgin. Traut's half-length figures are simply defined yet powerful in impact. Christ displays his wounds, which are colored in red. Mary is the Virgin of Sorrows with a sword piercing her heart. Behind the two figures are the instruments and symbols of the Passion. The raw immediacy of the image is enhanced by the eye contact of Christ and the Virgin. The frame is inscribed:

ASPICE QVI TRANSIS QVIA TV MIHI CAVSA DOLORIS

Behold [you] who pass by because you [are] the cause of my sorrow

The eucharistic nature of Christ's sacrifice is reiterated in the second woodcut of a gardener who holds a grape vine in a pot.[2]

Printed on both sides of the gardener woodcut is Sebastian Brant's *Querulosa Christi consolatio ad dolorosam virginis Marie compassionem*, a sixty-eight–line poetic dialogue between the Virgin and Christ about the cosuffering of the Virgin. Beneath this is an eight-line prayer composed by Benedictus Chelidonius, the Nuremberg Benedictine who collaborated with Dürer and Höltzel on several projects; a dedication to city council member Hieronymus Ebner (1477–1533); and Höltzel's colophon with the date [15]12.[3] The two lines of text at the bottom of the sheet list the indulgence assigned to the recitation of prayers to Christ and the Virgin.[4] Pope Leo IX (1049–1054), not Leo X (1513–1521) as Dodgson stated, established an indulgence value of three years, which was augmented by almost another full year by Pope Innocent IV (1243–1254) and the Council of Lyon in 1251.[5]

Traut may have modeled his composition and text after a woodcut printed in Basel(?) around 1500.[6] However, his monumental figures owe more to the art of his teacher, Albrecht Dürer.

1. On the devotional function of this print, see the comments in Section 3. The print was briefly described by E. Schilling, "An Indulgence Printed at Nuremberg in 1512," in *Essays in Honor of Georg Swarzenski* (Chicago, 1951), pp. 125–128. The German edition of the print is not dated and it lacks the prayer by Benedictus Chelidonius (see below); it is reproduced in Geisberg, nr. 1408. Traut and Höltzel collaborated on the 1509 *Legend of Sts. Henry and Kunigunde* broadsheet (Geisberg, nr. 1412) and at least four religious texts; see *Nuremberg: Meister um Dürer*, nrs. 384, 386, 387, 390.

2. *The Gardener* is often incorrectly attributed to Dürer. See Meder 263. It is either by Traut or by another member of Dürer's circle.

3. Chelidonius provided the prayers accompanying Dürer's *Large Passion* and *Life of the Virgin* series, which Höltzel published in 1511.

4. For another indulgence print, see Erhard Schön's *The Great Rosary* (cat. nr. 61).

5. Dodgson was unaware of the dated Latin edition that was made before the coronation of Leo X in 1513.

6. Dodgson, I: p. 520. I have not seen this earlier print. His suggestion that the Virgin derives from Martin Schongauer's *The Crucifixion* engraving (B. 25) seems unlikely.

60. STS. PAUL AND IDA VON TOGGENBURG

ca. 1515
Drawing: pen with black and red ink
30.4 cm diameter
Lent by the Germanisches Nationalmuseum,
Nuremberg, Hz.4097

Small stained-glass roundels with scenes of the patron's saints and coat of arms adorned many houses in Nuremberg and other German towns. Hans von Kulmbach produced numerous stained-glass designs and may have encouraged his colleague Wolf Traut to make the drawings of *Sts. Paul and Ida von Toggenburg* or the 1509 *Two Putti* (formerly Rotterdam, Koenig Collection).[1] None of Traut's windows have survived or, at least, been identified.

While Traut's drawing style is somewhat more refined than that of his prints, he employed the same shading technique. His hatchings tend to flatten rather than heighten the plasticity of the forms. The artist applied short, parallel lines to the faces of the two saints that mask the contour lines and confuse the facial structure. A similar misuse of hatchings can be seen in the face of the Virgin in cat. nr. 59.[2]

1. *Nuremberg: Meister um Dürer*, nr. 375; Zink, *Die Handzeichnungen*, nr. 90 (Hz.4097). Ida, Countess of Toggenburg (died 1226), is a minor saint venerated primarily in southern Germany and Switzerland. She is buried at Fischingen (Thurgau), where a new tomb was erected in 1496. See Réau, *Iconographie de l'Art Chrétien*, III.2: p. 670. On the 1509 drawing for a glass roundel, see F. Winkler, "Wolf Traut," *Old Master Drawings* 11 (1936–1937): 37–38, pl. 31. On Kulmbach's roundels, see cat. nr. 36.

2. Also compare the style of the drawing with Traut's *St. John the Baptist Altar* (Nuremberg, Germanisches Nationalmuseum) of 1517; *Nuremberg: Meister um Dürer*, nr. 365; cited by Zink, *Die Handzeichnungen*, nr. 90.

Also see cat. nr.
20   *Triumphal Arch of Emperor Maximilian I*

Erhard Schön, a prolific woodcut designer and a minor painter, was born in Nuremberg about 1491.[1] His teacher is unknown, though Grote has suggested that Schön may have been loosely associated with Dürer and Springinklee.[2] Schön is best known for his prints. Röttinger estimated that he created over 1,200 book illustrations, beginning with those in *De spirituali vinea* (Nuremberg: Johann Stüchs, 1513).[3] In 1516 and 1517 Schön and Hans Springinklee designed the woodcuts for *Hortulus Animae* (cat. nr. 63), an anthology of prayers that enjoyed tremendous popularity.

During Schön's early period, which lasted until about 1524, he concentrated primarily upon religious themes, such as *The Great Rosary* (cat. nr. 61). With Nuremberg's adoption of Lutheranism in 1525, Schön became one of the principal anti-Catholic propagandists, often in collaboration with poet Hans Sachs. The *Hunting of Monks and Clerics* (cat. nr. 64), the *Wondrous Prophecy of the Papacy* (cat. nr. 65), or his satire on the iconoclasts (fig. 27) typify his barbed wit and the simpler, more expressive style that emerged during these years. Because Schön designed his broadsheets for the general public not the connoisseur, the technical and aesthetic issues that concerned Dürer and most of his pupils were not of great interest to him.

Schön and Hans Sachs commonly poked fun at human nature.[4] Many of their broadsheets analyze man's folly by portraying such themes as the wicked wife, the properties of wine, the lament of the housewife, the distribution of fools' hats, the land of Cockaigne, and other popular subjects drawn from contemporary literature, theater, and folklore.

Schön also illustrated scenes of battles and soldiers. His portrait woodcuts include *Albrecht Dürer* (cat. nrs. 66 and 67), *Johann Huss, Sultan Suleiman II*, the sultan's wife, and other central European dignitaries.[5]

During the mid-1530s Schön became interested in representing classical themes, such as *Diane, Acteon, and Nymphs* (cat. nr. 72), and perspective experiments. Schön created striking anamorphic prints (cat. nr. 68), in which the true subject is hidden by a distorted perspective. In 1538 Schön published his *Unnderweissung der proportzion vnnd stellung der possen* (cat. nr. 71), a short treatise on the designing and placement of figures in space.

Comparatively little is known about his personal life. His wife Helena died in 1540 and he remarried in the following year. He was living in a house on the Weinmarkt, just west of St. Sebaldus, when he died sometime between 14 September and 13 December 1542.[6]

1. As with most of the artists in this exhibition, a thorough, critical study of Schön's work and his stylistic associations with other Nuremberg artists remains to be done. The best study to date is H. Röttinger, *Erhard Schön und Niklas Stör, der Pseudo-Schön.* Also see Dodgson, I: pp. 418–438; Geisberg, nrs. 1119–1315; H. Röttinger, "Schön, Erhard," in Thieme-Becker (1936), 30: pp. 218–220. On his few paintings, see H. Stegmann, "Erhard Schön als Maler," *Mitteilungen aus dem Germanisches Nationalmuseum* (1908): 49–61. Schön occasionally made designs for sculpture. Around 1533 he made a drawing for a fountain that was made in Nuremberg by sculptors Peter Flötner and Heinrich Zeckhorn and cast by Pankraz Labenwolf. The fountain was ordered by Cardinal Bernhard von Cles, bishop of Trient. See Weihrauch, *Europäische Bronzestatuetten*, p. 289.

2. Grote in *Nuremberg: Meister um Dürer*, p. 15. Among the reasons given for linking Schön with Dürer's workshop are his questionable involvement in the *Triumphal Arch of Emperor Maximilian I* (cat. nr. 20) and the *Theuerdank* (cat. nr. 47), his portrait of Dürer (cat. nr. 66), and his later interest in perspective and the theory of figural positioning (cat. nr. 71). Dürer's influence can be demonstrated by examining Schön's prints; however, Schön's knowledge of Dürer was obtained secondhand.

3. Röttinger, "Schön," p. 218.

4. Schön and Sachs collaborated on at least sixty books and broadsheets. See ibid., p. 219, and the literature in note 1.

5. See Geisberg, nrs. 1296, 1289–1290, and generally 1276–1298.

6. Röttinger, "Schön," p. 218.

61. THE GREAT ROSARY

1515; monogram
Woodcut: hand colored with green-brown, purple, red, and blue washes
44.7 × 29.9 cm
Dodgson, I: pp. 427–429; Röttinger, *Schön*, nr. 133; Geisberg, nr. 1133
Lent by the Metropolitan Museum of Art, New York, Rogers Fund, 1920

The Great Rosary is one of Schön's earliest and finest woodcuts.[1] Unlike the majority of his prints, which are finished in a quick, expressive style, *The Great Rosary* is extremely detailed and carefully composed. The handcoloring of this copy of the print heightens its strong pictorial qualities.

The woodcut represents the celestial hierarchy and Christendom's veneration of the rosary. It is inscribed at the top: "Jesus this is the praiseworthy brotherhood of the heavenly rosary." The rosary is a form of religious devotion instituted by St. Dominic in 1213.[2] It consists of prayers and meditations on the events of the life of the Virgin from the annunciation to the crucifixion and resurrection of Christ. Aided by a string of beads in the form of either a single strand or a circular chaplet, the worshipper recites one Pater Noster (Our Father), symbolized by the large bead usually red in color, for every 10 Ave Marias (Hail Mary), symbolized by the small white beads. In the print the beads are represented as roses. The large, red beads (or roses) signify the passion of Christ while the small, white beads (or roses) signify the purity of the Virgin, who is considered the second Eve and the rose without thorns, free from original sin. The complete rosary consists of 150 Ave Marias and 15 Pater Nosters. The ordinary, or short, form of the devotion is in the same ten-to-one ratio and consists of 50 Ave Marias and 5 Pater Nosters. Either the complete or ordinary form is said in three parts and in each part the Pater Nosters are recited and counted in meditation of the joys, sorrows, and glories of the Virgin and Child.

The brotherhood of the rosary was founded by Jacob Sprenger of Cologne in 1475.[3] It was based upon the idea of a universal Christian brotherhood of the laity and clergy that were united by their common veneration of Christ and the Virgin Mary. The local chapters of the brotherhood, which quickly emerged in Nuremberg and other German towns, commissioned numerous art objects bearing rosary themes. For instance, Ulrich Pinder's *Der Beschlossen Gart des Rosenkrantz Marie* (1505; cat. nr. 40) was created for the Nuremberg chapter. One of Albrecht

Dürer's greatest paintings, *The Feast of the Rose Garlands*, was executed for the brotherhood formed by the German merchants in Venice.[4] In this picture, the Virgin, the Christ Child, and the angels are depicted placing garlands of roses on the heads of the celebrants.

In Schön's print, the crucified Christ is set in the center of the garland. God the Father and the Holy Spirit, above, complete the Trinity. The garland is divided into three zones. From left to right and top to bottom are the prophets and patriarchs, apostles and evangelists, holy martyrs, doctors and confessors, virgins, widows, and holy women. Surrounding them are the nine orders of angels. Beginning with those encircling God and moving clockwise are the Seraphs, Thrones, Virtues, Principalities, Angels (Angeli), Archangels, Powers, Dominations, and Cherubs. Outside the garland are scenes of the Mass of St. Gregory, St. Francis receiving the stigmata, and groups of ecclesiastical and secular worshippers. Finally, at the bottom is a depiction of purgatory with angels retrieving those souls who had served their time.

This last scene is of special significance since this woodcut is an indulgence sheet. The specific indulgence value accorded the recitation of the rosary changed slightly in the different editions of this print. In this case, it is listed as 107 years, 100 quadragenes (each equals 40 days), and 1,780 days which, when totaled, would equal 122 years and 305 days. By repeating the rosary prayers, the worshipper could shorten the time that he or she would spend in the flaming purgatory illustrated at the bottom of the print. The indulgence values were assigned by Popes Alexander VI (1492–1503) and Leo X (1513–1521), Cardinals Raymund, Innocent, and Albrecht von Brandenburg, and Veit von Pommersfelden, bishop of Bamberg (1501–1503).

There were two principal categories of rosary images: the great rosary and the rosary of the Virgin. The first type is seen in Schön's print and the closely related 1515 woodcut by Hans von Kulmbach, which emphasize the crucified Christ and the universal brotherhood of Christianity.[5] The rosary of the Virgin, on the other hand, stresses the role of the Virgin Mary. Such images as Veit Stoss's *Angelic Salutation* (fig. 23) or Wolf Traut's woodcut of about 1510 illustrate the joys and sorrows of Mary.[6]

Luther and his followers subsequently would criticize the rosary devotion. In 1531 Melanchthon wrote: "Then there is the worship of saints which is guilty of a double fault: it arrogates Christ's place to the saints, and it worships them wickedly. Thus the Dominicans made up the rosary of the blessed Virgin, which is mere babbling, as stupid as it is wicked, nourishing a false confidence. This wickedness, too, is used only for the sake of profit. . . . But they spend their time either on philosophical discussions or on ceremonial traditions that obscure Christ."[7]

1. *Nuremberg: Dürer* (1971), nr. 347; *Cologne: 500 Jahre Rosenkranz 1475 Köln 1975*, nr. A 60; *Reformation in Nürnberg*, nr. 118.

2. On the history of the rosary, see E. Wilkins, *The Rose Garden Game* (New York, 1969); esp. K. J. Klinkhammer, "Die Entstehung des Rosenkranzes und sein ursprüngliche Geistigkeit," and G. Ritz, "Der Rosenkranz," in *Cologne: 500 Jahre Rosenkranz 1475 Köln 1975*, pp. 30–50, 51–101.

3. *Cologne: 500 Jahre Rosenkranz 1475 Köln 1975*, pp. 118–120. Sprenger was the Dominican prior in Cologne.

4. Prague (Nationalgalerie). Anzelewsky, *Dürer*, nr. 93, with additional comments about the iconography of the rosary.

5. Geisberg, nrs. 891–897. This woodcut may predate Schön's by a few months, but the chronological relationship of these two prints is not clear. The compositions are largely the same. Schön's print contains much more detail and includes the kneeling figures below. Although I suspect that Schön patterned his design after Kulmbach's, the opposite relationship cannot be excluded. Kulmbach produced a painted version (Munich, Alte Pinakothek) between 1516 and 1518; see *Nuremberg: Meister um Dürer*, nr. 170. Master MTR of Nuremberg incorporated Kulmbach's woodcut into his large confessional broadsheet of 1519; see Geisberg, nr. 953.

6. On Stoss's carving, see Section 3. On Traut's woodcut, see Geisberg, nr. 1415.

7. T. G. Tappert, ed., *The Book of Concord: The Confessions of the Evangelical Lutheran Church* (Philadelphia, 1959), p. 278 (section 53).

62. LEONHARD REYNMANN, NATIUITET KALENNDER (Nuremberg: Friedrich Peypus, 7 December 1515)

1 woodcut on p. 1 verso
17.4 × 12.7 cm (woodcut)
Dodgson, I: p. 423; Röttinger, *Schön*, nr. 6
Lent by the Library of Congress, Washington, Lessing J. Rosenwald Collection

Leonhard Reynmann (Reinmann) was an astronomer-astrologer in Nuremberg who specialized in designing horoscopes, such as the *Natiuitet Kalennder* (*Birth Calendar*). By using a series of tables and dials at the end of this booklet, readers could determine their zodiacal sign and the positions of the sun and the moon at the time of their births in order to plot a personal horoscope.[1]

The single woodcut on the verso of the title page is by Schön.[2] It represents God the father in the heavens. Below is a large disk surrounded by the four winds. The disk consists of four concentric bands. At the center is the earth, which is cosmographically surrounded by the seven planets, the twelve signs of the zodiac, and the twelve celestial houses.[3] These are the forces that affect one's nature and life. Schön presents a schematized view of the universe as it was then understood.

Reynmann and Schön collaborated on at least one other project.[4] In 1523 they produced a forecast of the calamitous events that would occur in the following year due to the unusual conjunction of the planets. Interestingly, some contemporaries cited the movement of the planets as the reason for the peasant uprisings in 1524 and 1525.[5]

1. Occasionally, dials were added to zodiacal scenes in order to determine the phases of the moon in relation to the planets. One very attractive example was made by Albrecht Glockendon the Younger, Nuremberg illuminator and publisher, in the *Geomantie Ottheinrichs von der Pfalz* (Heidelberg, Universitätsbibliothek, ms. 833) of 1537. See A. W. Biermann, "Die Miniaturenhandschriften des Kardinals Albrecht von Brandenburg (1514–1545)," *Aachener Kunstblätter* 46 (1975): 146, fig. 184. For contemporary horoscopes, see those made by Hans Springinklee; *Nuremberg: Dürer (1971)*, nrs. 311–312. On planetary influences, see cat. nr. 103.

2. The only thorough description of this woodcut is A. Hagelstange, "Erhard Schöns Titelholzschnitt zum Nativität-Kalender des Leonhard Reynmann," *Zeitschrift für Bücherfreunde* 9 (1905–1906): 403–408.

3. Ibid., p. 407, identifies the twelve houses as follows: 1. life (Vita), 2. gain (Lucrum), 3. brother (Fratres; here shown as a monk and a nun), 4. father (Genitor), 5. birth (Nati), 6. health (Valetudo), 7. spouse (Uxor), 8. death (Mors), 9. piety (Pietus), 10. authority (Regnum), 11. good deeds (Benefacta; here shown as a wheel of fortune), and 12. confinement (Carcer). This list is also given in the book opposite the woodcut.

4. Reynmann, *Practica vber die grossen vnd manigfeltigen Coniunction der Planeten, die imm jar M.D. XXiiij. erscheinen, vnd vngezweiffelt vil wunderparlicher ding geperen werden* (Nuremberg: Hieronymus Höltzel, 1523); *Nuremberg: Dürer (1971)*, nr. 435; esp. *Reformation in Nürnberg*, nr. 57.

5. *Nuremberg: Dürer (1971)*, nr. 435, citing H. Buszello. *Der deutsche Bauernkrieg von 1525 als politische Bewegung* (Berlin, 1969), pp. 54–55.

63. HORTULUS ANIMAE (Lyon: Johannes Clein for Johann Koberger, 9 November 1517)

83 woodcuts
8.8 × 6.8 cm (for the large woodcuts)
Dodgson, I: pp. 382–393, 429–430, 562–563;
Röttinger, *Schön*, nr. 7
Lent by the Library of Congress, Washington

The *Hortulus Animae*, or *Garden of the Spirit*, was the most popular anthology of prayers published during the years immediately prior to the Reformation. Oldenbourg has documented 103 editions printed between 1498 and 1523.[1] Of these, 36 exist in unique copies; therefore, the original number of editions was probably somewhat higher. At least twenty German and Latin editions were published by or for Johann or Anton II Koberger of Nuremberg between 1516 and 1522.[2]

Humanist Sebastian Brant (1457–1521) of Strassburg is credited with conceiving this prayer book,[3] but it is unclear whether he edited the first Strassburg edition of 1498. He is occasionally listed as translator or editor from 1501 on.

Oldenbourg has defined four basic groups of the *Hortulus Animae*. The exhibited example belongs to the fourth, or Nuremberg, group, done for the Koberger publishing house. Johann Koberger had printed several early editions (1511, 1513) using woodcut illustrations from another group. In 1515 he ordered Hans Springinklee and Erhard Schön to design two new series of woodcuts, which were used in various combinations between 1516 and 1523. The 15 March 1516 edition and the 9 November 1517 edition are essentially the same and are the only versions containing all fifty-one of Springinklee's woodcuts.[4] Schön contributed four large woodcuts, including that of St. Birgitta illustrated here, one small print, and two diagrams. The framing borders used for all the woodcuts are by Springinklee.[5] The remaining illustrations are re-used from a 1511 Lyon edition.[6]

1. M. C. Oldenbourg, *Hortulus Animae (1494)–1523: Bibliographie und Illustration*, p. 5. This is the principal source for what follows.
2. Ibid., p. 117. Dodgson, I: pp. 562–563, listed eighteen.
3. Oldenbourg, *Hortulus Animae*, p. 17. The author suggests that the idea and a lost textual edition probably date to 1494.
4. Ibid., L 62 (1516), L 69 (1517); on Springinklee's work, see pp. 121–125, and on a second set of woodcuts made in 1518, see pp. 125–128. Neudörfer, writing in 1547, praised Springinklee's woodcuts and borders; Neudörfer, *Nachrichten von Künstlern*, p. 144.
5. Oldenbourg, *Hortulus Animae*, pp. 117–121.
6. Ibid., L 38.

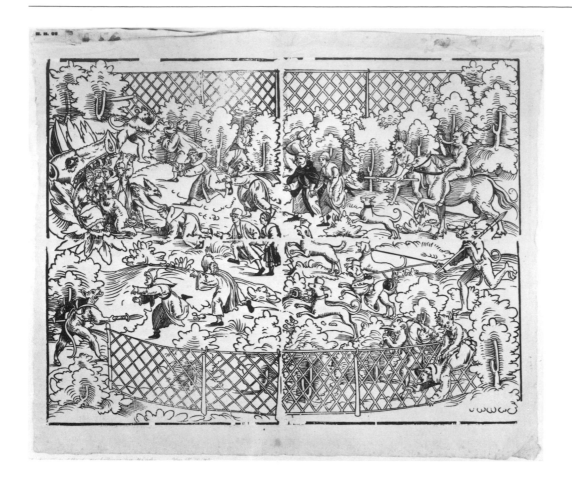

64. THE HUNTING OF MONKS AND CLERICS

ca. 1525
Woodcut
37.6 × 49.2 cm
Röttinger, *Schön*, nr. 143; Geisberg, nr. 1143
Lent by the Germanisches Nationalmuseum,
Nuremberg, HB 22

During the years immediately following Nuremberg's adoption of Lutheranism in 1525, local printmakers created numerous anti-Catholic broadsheets, often with satirical texts supplied by Hans Sachs. To protect themselves from the civic authorities, these artists did not sign their works.

Schön's woodcut illustrates Hans Sachs's poem *Das münich- und pfaffenjaid*, the text of which is lacking in this particular copy.[1] Sachs describes a dream in which he saw demons and their dogs hunting down an unusual quarry: monks, clerics, and their concubines. Just as in contemporary images of princely hunts where stags are penned in by nets and herded toward the slaughter, ropes frame this clearing and prevent the clergy from escaping.[2] The poet and artist may have been inspired by, or may have inspired, a 1525 carnival pageant in nearby Zwickau in which students dressed as devils chased others clad as monks through the streets.[3]

At the left is a gaping, pig-snouted hell mouth toward which the quarry is being driven. The pope holds court as he blesses both monk and demon. The message of the print is that obedience to the pope and the Roman Catholic church will result in damnation rather than salvation since the pope is in league with the devil. Similar hell mouths were common in contemporary carnivals, such as the Schembart festival in Nuremberg.[4]

1. Röttinger, *Die Bilderbogen des Hans Sachs*, nr. 1143; *Nuremberg: Die Welt des Hans Sachs*, nr. 17. Geisberg illustrates the Coburg (Veste) copy with the full text. Also see Geisberg, nrs. 1139–1141, 1144, for related woodcuts.

2. Cf. cat. nr. 106.

3. Scribner, *For the Sake of Simple Folk*, p. 63, also see 62, 166, 168, fig. 45. Scribner cites a contemporary drawing by the workshop of Lucas Cranach the Elder showing women hunting monks. See Zink, *Die Handzeichnungen*, nr. 117.

4. Sumberg, *The Nuremberg Schembart Carnival*, p. 134, fig. 47. In Nuremberg, a dragon was more common for a hell mouth. On the subject, see D. C. Stuart, "The Stage Setting of Hell and the Iconography of the Middle Ages," *Romanic Review* 4 (1913): 330–342.

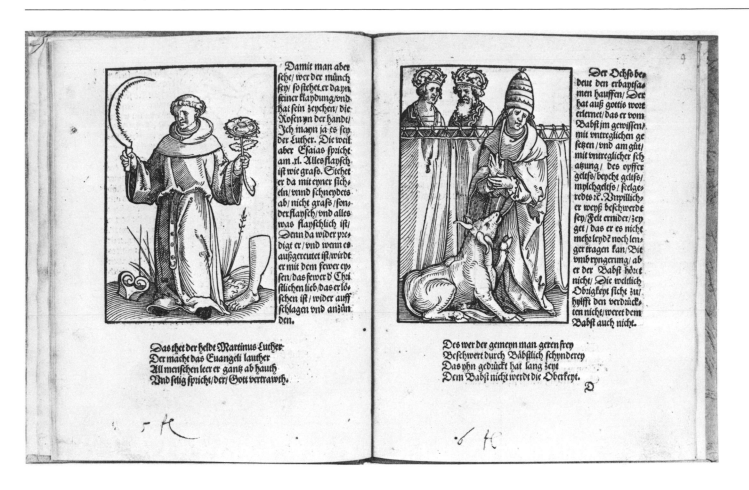

65. ANDREAS OSIANDER AND HANS SACHS, EYN WUNDERLICHE WEYSSAGUNG VON DEM BABSTUM (Nuremberg: Hans Guldenmund, 1527)

30 woodcuts
11 × 7.5 cm (average size of the woodcuts)
Röttinger, *Schön*, nr. 48
The University of Texas at Austin, The Humanities Research Center

A Wondrous Prophecy of the Papacy was an opening salvo in the antipapal and anti-Catholic propaganda campaign waged by Nuremberg's Lutherans.[1] In 1526 or early 1527 Andreas Osiander, the preacher of St. Lorenz, discovered in the library of the Kartäuserkloster a collection of prophecies about the future of the Church at the end of the age of Christ. Some of the writings were attributed to Joachim of Fiore (ca. 1145–ca. 1202), a Calabrian monk and sectarian advocate, and others to a mysterious "Anselmus." Although the texts probably date to the fourteenth and fifteenth centuries, Osiander proclaimed the work as proof that others had foreseen the impending corruption of the papacy. Osiander determined that since this book had been published in Bologna in 1515 the text had been edited to delete the original authors' true meaning.[2] Therefore, he decided to dispense entirely with the actual text and simply use the illustrations. Osiander wrote a new foreword and had Hans Sachs compose couplets for each of the thirty woodcuts, which were copied, with certain changes, by Schön. The Lutheran preacher thereby totally transformed the booklet into a strident condemnation of the papacy.

The woodcuts represent the pope turning away from the Holy Spirit and deceiving mankind.[3] He takes his orders from Satan, not God. The pope becomes a temporal rather than spiritual leader who surrounds himself with soldiers. God removes his spiritual powers and the pope is identified as a beast of the Apocalypse. Luther and the patient flock challenge the pope's rule. The Diet of Worms is characterized as a meeting under human and not divine law. Only at the later Reichstags at Nuremberg does God's word prevail. The pope's supporters are derisively characterized as cunning foxes. The final five woodcuts foretell future events. The pope's power is stripped away and he sits alone and naked mocked by the world. A confessor gives the papal crown to the Christian flock. God selects another man as head of the Church who returns the spiritual authority of the church to God at the end of the world.

Illustrated here are scenes twenty and twenty-one. In the first, Schön has converted the image into a stylized portrait of Luther, wearing his Augustinian robes.[4] He is equated with the *homo spiritualis* of the prophecy. Like Saturn or Cronus, the god of time, the monk holds a jagged sickle with which he cuts a rose just as he will also cut down the unworthy pontiff. The leg is described by Osiander as a reference to Isaiah (40:6): "All flesh is as grass." The branding iron, considerably altered from the B used in the 1515 edition, signifies the fire of Christian love. In a letter written to Osiander on 19 May 1527, Luther expressed his approval of the image and the text.[5]

The second scene is less obscure. The patient Christians, symbolized by the ox, have long shouldered the pope's financial demands. Having learned from the Holy Spirit that these requests are unjust, they refuse to pay any longer. In the subsequent image the ox is transformed into an angry bear.

This little booklet immediately angered the Nuremberg city council, which was trying to mend its relationship with Emperor Charles V following its decision to break away from the Roman Catholic church.[6] On 27 March 1527 the city council ordered the confiscation of all copies of the book, and Osiander was forbidden to publish any further works without the council's permission. The reprimand extended to Sachs and the publisher, Guldenmund, but interestingly no mention is made of Schön. This is but one of several incidents of civic censorship during this politically sensitive period.

1. R. H. Bainton, "Eyn wunderliche Weyssagung: Osiander-Sachs-Luther," *Germanic Review* 21 (1946): 161–164; *Nuremberg: Die Welt des Hans Sachs*, nr. 25; *Reformation in Nürnberg*, nr. 156; Scribner, *For the Sake of Simple Folk*, pp. 142–147.
2. *Joachimi Abbatis Vaticinia circa Apostolicos viros et Ecclesiam Romanam* (Bologna, 1515).
3. The clearest description of the illustrations is in Scribner, *For the Sake of Simple Folk*, pp. 143–146.
4. Bainton, "Weyssagung," pp. 163–164, figs. 1–3, for the following.
5. Ibid., p. 162.
6. *Reformation in Nürnberg*, nr. 281: Nuremberg, Staatsarchiv, Reichsstadt Nürnberg Ratsbuch 13, fols. 256–257. On the subject of civic censorship, see A. Müller, "Zensurpolitik der Reichsstadt Nürnberg. Von der Einführung der Buchdruckkunst bis zum Ende der Reichsstadtzeit," *MVGN* 49 (1959): 66–169, esp. 82–84, on this incident.

66. PORTRAIT OF ALBRECHT DÜRER AT AGE FIFTY-SIX

ca. 1528
Woodcut
31.8 × 25.2 cm
Dodgson, I: pp. 360–361; Röttinger, *Schön*,
nr. 280; Geisberg, nr. 1295; M., pp. 240–242;
H. (Dürer School), nr. 32; *Nuremberg: Dürer
(1971)*, nr. 46
Lent by the Art Museum, Princeton University
(Laura P. Hall Memorial Collection)

In a letter to Willibald Pirckheimer written in Venice on 13(?) October 1506, Albrecht Dürer lamented, "Oh, how I shall long for the sun! Here I am a gentleman, at home only a parasite."[1] Dürer was referring to the fact that artists were more esteemed in Venice than in the patrician-dominated city of Nuremberg. However, Dürer's status did indeed change shortly after his return to Nuremberg. In 1509 he was elected a *genannter* of the greater city council, the highest honor accorded to a person of nonpatrician birth. In the same year he acquired his large house by the Tiergärtentor, and three years later he began working for Maximilian. Dürer was regularly included at Pirckheimer's gathering of scholars and he was the only artist to participate in the meetings of the Sodalitas Staupitziana in 1516. His 1520–1521 journey to the Netherlands was a triumph. Thus, at home and abroad Dürer had become a celebrity. Hans Schwarz produced a

portrait medal of Dürer in 1520 (cat. nr. 143). Previously, portrait medals were generally made only for the nobility and wealthy merchants, not for artists.

Albrecht Dürer was famous throughout Europe when he died on 6 April 1528 at the age of fifty-six. His death inspired Erhard Schön to design this woodcut portrait, which was accompanied by a short text by Hans Sachs. The image is based upon Matthes Gebel's 1527 portrait medal of the artist.[2] Dürer is shown in profile with short hair rather than the long locks seen in Hans Schwarz's earlier medal (cat. nr. 143). At the upper left is his coat of arms, an open door, a play on his surname. While most printed portraits were published in only one or at most two editions, Schön's woodcut was reissued at least three times during the 1540s by Nuremberg *formschneider* Hans Wolff Glaser and five times by Wolfgang Drechsel of Nuremberg during the

67. PORTRAIT OF ALBRECHT DÜRER AT AGE FIFTY-SIX

ca. 1528
Woodblock
30 × 25.4 × 2 cm
Lent by the Art Museum, Princeton University
(Gift of Alexander P. Morgan)

last quarter of the sixteenth century.[3] The text of each version differs slightly.

The exhibited print lacks the signature of the publisher and Hans Sachs's text. It is an edition not recorded by Dodgson, Meder, or Hollstein.[4] Based upon the quality of the impression, notably the clarity of the lines and the fine inking, it would seem to be an early example. The text reads:

Albrecht Dürer Conderfeyt in seinem alter
Des L V I. Jars.
(Albrecht Dürer represented in his
fifty-sixth year.)

Princeton also possesses what may be the original woodblock for this print. The date of 1527 and Dürer's monogram added to Dürer's coat of arms are features not found in the early impressions of this print; however, an examination by Barbara Ross of Princeton reveals that these features have been carefully inlaid rather than plugged into the Princeton woodblock.[5] Therefore, the Princeton woodblock, when first cut, conformed to the appearance of the original impressions of the print. A hand-rubbed impression pulled from the Princeton woodblock shows that the contour and shading lines are identical with those of the exhibited print.

Dürer's monogram and the date 1527 were added perhaps by Glaser or, more likely, by Drechsel. The date was taken either from Gebel's medal of 1527 or by adding fifty-six to Dürer's birth date of 1471. Dürer was, however, still fifty-six when he died in 1528. Therefore, it should not be assumed that the original print dated to 1527. By the 1580s the woodblock had split slightly. Most of the subsequent impressions were printed from a new woodblock now in Vienna (Albertina).[6]

1. Stechow, *Northern Renaissance Art*, p. 91, whose translation is given here; and Rupprich, *Dürer schriftlicher Nachlass*, I: p. 59 (lines 90–91).
2. *Nuremberg: Dürer* (1971), nr. 77.
3. Dodgson, I: pp. 360–361; Meder, pp. 240–242; Hollstein (Dürer School) nr. 32, list the different editions. The different versions of this print are also examined in H. Meier, "The Aged Dürer: A Question of Editions," *New York Public Library Bulletin* 32 (1928), pp. 490–492.
4. Ibid. The peculiar spelling of the word "conderfeyt" rather than "conterfeyt" is not mentioned in any of these lists. Furthermore, the text form "alter // Des L V I. Jars" is unique. I wish to thank Professor Robert Koch of Princeton University for supplying me with additional information about this print and woodblock. See B. Ross, "Prints Depicting Albrecht Dürer," *Record of The Art Museum, Princeton University* 31, no. 2 (1971): 72–75.
5. Ross, "Prints Depicting Albrecht Dürer," p. 74.
6. On the Vienna woodblock, see Meder, p. 242, cf. figs. 167, 168.

68. PICTURE PUZZLE WITH LOVING COUPLE

ca. 1535
Woodcut: hand colored with red, yellow, green, black, purple, and brown washes
21.4 × 57.1 cm
Röttinger, *Schön*, nr. 204; Geisberg, nr. 1197-1
Lent by the Germanisches Nationalmuseum, Nuremberg, HB 26686

Schön was among the first German artists to make anamorphic images, perspective distortions that can be clearly viewed only from one side or with the assistance of a mirror. The *Picture Puzzle with Loving Couple* appears highly confused at first glance.[1] A stag hunting sequence and a boat with a woman and four men are placed at the top and the bottom of the print. The central scene cannot be read unless the viewer stands to the left-hand side and looks back or, preferably, places a mirror along the left-hand margin and looks at the reflected image. This will reveal three naked figures standing in a room. In the middle is a woman. With her right arm she pushes the rejected elderly suitor toward the door. With her other hand she fondles the younger man who in turn caresses her breast. "Out, you old fool!" (AVS DV ALTER TOR) reads the accompanying inscription. The woman, like the hunter above or the alluring, single woman in the boat below, has captured her quarry. Just as the central image is not immediately clear, love distorts man's judgment.[2]

An expanded version of the print includes a bedroom scene, in regular perspective, at the left. An old man caresses a young woman, who occupies herself with removing the coins from the man's purse and passing them on to her young male accomplice. A fool peers around the other side of the bed. It is a variation on the unequal-couple theme that enjoyed tremendous popularity in contemporary prints.[3]

An anamorphic design can be produced rather easily. Once a drawing is made, a grid of horizontal and vertical lines is placed over it so that an object, such as a body, is covered with a series of squares. In the case of Schön's print, the grid is then distorted or pulled incrementally toward the right; each square has now become a trapezoid. The artist next transfers the pictorial information in each original square to the trape-

zoid. The relationships of the horizontal and vertical lines are thus altered and highly exaggerated. This process, at its simplest level, can be seen in the diagram.

During the 1530s, Schön produced three anamorphic prints. The most elaborate is the *Landscapes with the Portraits of Charles V, Ferdinand I, Francis I, and Clement VII*, in which the four portraits are ingeniously woven into the fabric of a landscape just as the four rulers' actions affect the lives of all the citizens within their realms.[4] A moral is thus hidden along with the portraits. The third print represents *Jonah and the Whale* and was published in Nuremberg by Stefan Hamer in 1538.[5]

1. J. Baltrusaitis, *Anamorphic Art*, pp. 11–16, fig. 9. This is the best study on the subject.
2. In a similar fashion, death confronts man when he least expects it in the form of the skull added in the center of Hans Holbein the Younger's *French Ambassadors* painting, dated 1533, now in London (National Gallery). See P. Ganz, *The Paintings of Hans Holbein*, nr. 74, fig. 113.
3. On the subject, see A. G. Stewart, *Unequal Lovers*, pp. 68ff.
4. Röttinger, *Schön*, nr. 205; Geisberg, nr. 1197.
5. Röttinger, *Schön*, nr. 203; Geisberg, nr. 1197-2. Compare his perspective experiment in his artistic treatise of 1538 (cat. nr. 71).

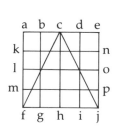

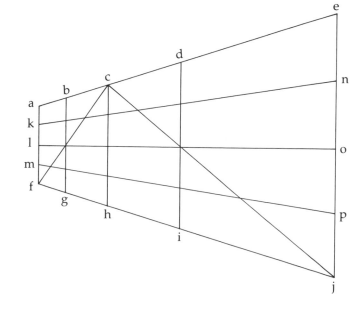

69. SIEGE OF MÜNSTER

ca. 1535
Woodcut (2 blocks)
29.8 × 55.6 cm
Röttinger, *Schön*, nr. 248; Geisberg, nrs.
1256–1257
Lent by the University of Michigan Museum of
Art, Ann Arbor

The siege of Münster was among the Reformation's bloodiest episodes.[1] Through the efforts of Bernard Rothmann, this northwestern German city had adopted Lutheranism in 1532. Soon, however, the Melchorite Anabaptists led by Jan Mathijs expelled the city's Roman Catholics and conservative Lutherans and established an Old Testament–style theocracy. The Lutherans joined forces with the Catholic Prince-Bishop Franz von Waldeck and troops from Hesse, Cologne, Cleves, and Frisia. After a yearlong siege, the city fell on 25 June 1535 and most of Münster's inhabitants were slaughtered.

Hoping to capitalize upon public fascination with the radicalism and subsequent fall of the Anabaptists, Schön created this and a second print showing the Lutheran and Catholic forces encircling the city.[2] The emphasis is not upon historical accuracy but upon lively scenes of skirmishes, the movements of troops, incidents in the camps, and, generally, the mood of the occasion. In this print Schön adopted a broad aerial view. Narrative considerations outweigh scale and perspective inconsistencies. Schön's second woodcut series of the siege focuses upon a single cannon emplacement overlooking the city, whose skyline bears no resemblance to that of his first print.

Prints of famous battles by Schön, Schäufelein, Hans Sebald Beham, and others enjoyed considerable popularity as the public's only illustrated source of information.[3] Schön represented the Turkish siege of Vienna in 1529 and of Budapest in 1541.[4] When Emperor Charles V conquered Tunis in 1535, Schön published a topographical view of the city and the surrounding coastline.[5] The woodcut is titled *VENI VIDI VICI* (*I Came, I Saw, I Conquered*) and the accompanying text describes the exploits of Charles V, the "new Julius Caesar."

---

1. On the siege and its history, see G. H. Williams, *The Radical Reformation* (Philadelphia, 1962), ch. 13.
2. Röttinger, *Schön*, nr. 249; Geisberg 1258–1264, printed on seven blocks and measuring 29 × 270.9 cm. The exhibited print lacks the title and four lines of descriptive text below; see illustration in Geisberg.
3. Geisberg, nrs. 283–288 (*Siege of Vienna*, 1529), 289 (*Siege of Rhodes*, 1522), 290 (*Siege of Greek Weissenburg*, 1522), 291 (*Siege of Landstuhl*, 1523), 291-1 (*Siege of Ebernburg Castle*) by Beham. On Schäufelein's *Battle of Pavia* of ca. 1526, see Geisberg 1089–1094.
4. Röttinger, *Schön*, nrs. 241, 253; Geisberg 1246–1247, 1269–1273.
5. Röttinger, *Schön*, nr. 250; Geisberg 1265.

70. THE TWELVE CLEAN AND TWELVE UNCLEAN BIRDS

1537(?); published by Albrecht Glockendon
Woodcut: hand colored
55.4 × 38.2 cm
Röttinger, *Schön*, nr. 200; Geisberg, nr. 1194
The University of Texas at Austin, The Humanities Research Center, Iconography Collection

Schön and poet Hans Sachs once again collaborated to make this large broadsheet.[1] The didactic intention of the print is clearly stated at the top. It reads in part as follows:

. . . all creatures of God, however insignificant they may be, can serve to the benefit of the select company of humankind. As Christ admonishes us through the parables of the birds to pay heed to that which is transitory . . . Regard the birds of the sky; they do not sow, nor do they reap . . . Christ teaches us to be gentle as Doves and . . . Christ compares Himself to a mother hen. . . . Therefore, I have undertaken to illustrate briefly the life and actions of true Christians who live according to the spirit . . . with twelve clean birds and their nature, to the right below the Dove and on the other hand the life of the godless humans who live according to the flesh . . . with the nature of twelve unclean birds to the left under the Raven . . .[2]

The compositional arrangement is based on medieval Last Judgment scenes. In the center is the pelican, a traditional symbol of Christ since it willingly sacrifices itself to save its children. On its right, the viewer's left, are the good birds arranged under the dove. These birds correspond to the saved in a Last Judgment. Opposite, under the raven, are the unclean birds, or the symbols of the damned. Each bird is described briefly. For instance,

The Parakeet 3

The Parakeet greets its master
Thus a Christian in this wilderness
Cries out to Christ his master alone
Who can indeed help him in his distress.

The Sparrowhawk 10

The Sparrowhawk is a bird of prey
Thus the Godless man always
Only seeks his own self-interest,
Deceives, oppresses, forces, robs people of their goods.

Or

The Bee 9

The bee makes honey and harms no one
Thus a pious Christian in his country
Is harmless to everyone
And employs no deceitful cunning.[3]

The Bat 8

The bat flies at night
Just as he is deemed godless
Who does his works secretly, slyly
Since they are false and not good.

Although the program is ultimately modeled upon medieval bestiaries, it is devoid of any references to the pope, the Roman Catholic church, the Virgin, or the hierarchy of saints.[4] Instead, it stresses the moral conduct advocated by Luther.

1. Röttinger, *Die Bilderbogen des Hans Sachs*, nr. 87, which states that it was first published sometime between 1534 and 1538; *Nuremberg: Die Welt des Hans Sachs*, nr. 169.

2. Professor Hubert Heinem of the University of Texas at Austin prepared the translations used in this entry.

3. The bee, although an insect, is included among the clean birds.

4. On the subject, see F. McCulloch, *Mediaeval Latin and French Bestiaries* (Chapel Hill, 1962).

Die dryt figur.

Hie hab ich Neun angesicht mit Jrer virung das du sicht wie vnnd wa sy hin treffenn mit irenn habstrychen vbersich neben sich vnnd fursich wie du sy dan sichts.

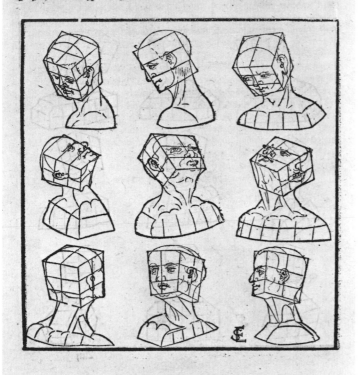

Die zehennd figur.

Die zehennd Figur zaygt an von Fünf possen / in eittem Gehaus von dreyen ligenden / vnd zweyen knieenden / mit Jren dreyen beweglichen gelidere wie sie in der virung begriffen sind so wayst du dich darnach zu richten

71. ERHARD SCHÖN, UNNDERWEISSUNG DER PROPORTZION VNND STELLUNG DER POSSEN (Nuremberg: Christoph Zell, 1538)

31 woodcuts
18.5 × 15.5 cm (page)
B. 34; Röttinger, *Schön*, nr. 76.
Lent by the Library of Congress, Washington, Lessing J. Rosenwald Collection

The title page reads: "Manual of Proportion and the Positioning of Jointed Mannequins: lying or standing, drawn as they appear before our eyes in this little book by Erhard Schön from Nuremberg for the instruction of apprentices and the young who are enamored of art, printed 1540."[1] Next are the artist's monogram and symbol, two quick pen strokes intersecting to form an acute angle. This is followed by a long foreword on page A ii. Since this nicely describes the purpose of the book, it is quoted in full.

Hail and good fortune, I, Erhard Schun [sic] wish all those who favor art. Because many of my apprentices have many times begged me to make it easier for them to understand the art of proportion and measurement, based on Dürer, Vitruvius, and other books, I have ventured to write this little book for my apprentices in the simplest and easiest manner. It is not intended for those who already know art, but for those who may gain from it better understanding. Let no one think that what he finds in this book is the only information, but let him proceed and discover (invent) more. For instance, a mason who wishes to draw a structure in the proper manner or how to construct a perfect square; or a goldsmith's requirements for his artistry. If I have not included every subject, I have made a start with one skill, and if anyone tries it, let him not be dissuaded by another, even if he does not understand everything immediately. Things which are easy cannot be skillful, but skillfully made things require diligence and work until one has acquired and learned the skill. I shall restrict myself in this manual to contour lines and squares.

I dedicate this little book to my friends and to my dear apprentices with special affection and the sincere desire that they will learn, God willing, what is written therein within a brief span of time.[2]

The manual consists primarily of simple woodcuts with very brief annotations. Schön illustrates the proper technique for constructing heads and faces, for establishing the relative proportions and poses of figures in a group, for rendering gestures and figures in action, for shaping heraldic shields, and for portraying horses. Reproduced here are figures 3 and 10. Figure 3 depicts nine heads, placed within cubes, set in varying positions. In figure 10, three lying and two kneeling mannequins are placed within a chamber that is designed in one-point perspective. While devising his figure studies, Schön used a jointed wooden mannequin, probably something like the female puppet now in Berlin (Staatliche Museen).[3] Earlier Dürer had employed mannequins while working on the illustrations to his studies of human anatomy.[4]

The significance of Schön's treatise lies not in the brilliant insight, or lack of it, in any of the individual illustrations. Rather it is important as a milestone in the cultural emergence of the artist as a theoretician. Like Dürer (cat. nrs. 31 and 34) or Hans Sebald Beham (cat. nr. 95), Schön sought to aid other artists by publishing his own knowledge on selected subjects.

---

1. The translation of W. L. Strauss is given in *The Illustrated Bartsch*, 13: p. 139; on pp. 139–176 the entire 1542 edition of the treatise is reproduced. Also see L. Baer, ed., *Erhard Schön, Unterweisung der Proportion und Stellung der Possen*, Nürnberg, 1542 (Frankfurt a. M., 1920). The treatise was published in 1538 (exhibited here), 1540, 1542, 1543, and 1561.
2. *The Illustrated Bartsch*, 13: p. 140.
3. *Berlin: Der Mensch um 1500*, nr. 30, pp. 166–171, with additional literature.
4. Rupprich, *Dürer schriftlicher Nachlass*, III: pls. 35–37; W. L. Strauss, ed., *The Human Figure by Albrecht Dürer: The Complete Dresden Sketchbook*, nrs. 96–105.

72. DIANA, ACTEON, AND NYMPHS

1540
Drawing: pen and black ink
12.2 × 20.6 cm
Lent by the Seattle Art Museum, LeRoy M.
Backus Collection

This drawing illustrates an episode described in Ovid's *Metamorphoses* (Book III) in which Acteon accidentally encounters Diana, the goddess of the hunt, and her nymphs bathing.[1] Diana, enraged, splashes water at Acteon, thereby transforming him into a stag. He is killed by his own hunting dogs at the left.

Although this sketch is not signed, the attribution to Schön is secure. The calligraphy of the date and the general style are very similar to the many drawings that Schön made between 1535 and 1540. The crudely formed faces, general figure types, and characteristic shading using simple hatchings on only one side of the body seen in the Seattle sketch can be found in his signed *Mercury and the Hermaphrodite* (1540) and *Laocoon* (1540) at Erlangen and *Judgment of Paris* (1536) and *Temptation of Adam and Eve* (1540) at Berlin.[2] Schön's five mythological drawings at Erlangen may be designs for book illustrations or projected print series. The horizontal format and more thoroughly developed landscape in the Seattle drawing suggest it was intended as a separate project.[3]

1. E. Mandowsky, *Old Master Drawings: Seattle Art Museum Collection Guide* (Seattle, 1980), nr. 5.
2. Bock, *Zeichnungen*, nrs. 257–258, cf. also 256, 259–261; idem, *Staatliche Museen zu Berlin: Die Zeichnungen alter Meister im Kupferstichkabinett, Die deutschen Meister* I: p. 77, nrs. 188, 919, II: pls. 108–109.
3. Cf. the landscape design in the *Judgment of Paris* drawing in Berlin.

73. BEHEADING OF JOHN THE BAPTIST

ca. 1530(?)
Drawing: pen and black ink
22.7 × 22.6 cm
Lent by the Art Institute of Chicago. 1922.2070.
Gurley Collection

The *Beheading of John the Baptist* is a drawing for a stained-glass roundel. The artist is the same one who made the *Christ and the Adulterous Woman* sketch in Erlangen (Universitätsbibliothek) that Bock linked with the workshop of Schön.[1] Both roundels are identical in size and style and doubtlessly belong to a larger biblical cycle. The subjects would have been appropriate for either a Protestant or Catholic church.

The artist of this drawing based his composition almost entirely upon Albrecht Altdorfer's 1512 woodcut of the same subject.[2] The foreground figures (except the man on the extreme left-hand side), the pointed and broken arches, and the architecture at the right are copied with only minor changes. He has added the background with the banquet of Herod.

1. Bock, *Zeichnungen*, nr. 263; cited in the museum's curatorial files.
2. *The Illustrated Bartsch*, 14: nr. 152.

Hans Sebald Beham

Hans Sebald, elder brother of Barthel Beham, was a prolific printmaker and book illustrator.[1] He was born in Nuremberg in 1500, a date verified by Matthes Gebel's portrait medal of Hans Sebald at age forty made in 1540.[2] Hans Sebald may have trained with Dürer during the late 1510s; however, this association is based upon stylistic influences rather than any documentation.[3] His earliest drawings and prints date to 1518.[4]

Hans Sebald's career in Nuremberg was fraught with crises. On 16 January 1525 Hans Sebald, his brother Barthel, and Georg Pencz were interrogated by three city lawyers and five preachers.[5] The artists' atheistic and somewhat anarchistic views were too radical for the city officials, and on 26 January the trio was banished from Nuremberg. Only in late November were they permitted to return. Three years later, Hans Sebald was again censored by the city council when he was charged with appropriating information contained in Dürer's unpublished study on horses and then having it printed under his own name.[6] These events help to explain why Sandrart, writing in 1675, stated that Hans Sebald had a very bad reputation.[7]

The artist fled to Ingolstadt, returned briefly to Nuremberg in 1529, spent 1530 in Munich, and in the following year entered the service of Cardinal Albrecht von Brandenburg, the archbishop of Mainz. His principal work during this period is the *Prayer Book* of the cardinal (Aschaffenburg, Hofbibliothek, ms. 8).[8]

By 1532 the artist had settled in Frankfurt-am-Main, where he remained until his death on 22 November 1550. Beham collaborated extensively with Frankfurt publisher Christian Egenolff on such books as the *Biblische Historien* of 1533 (cat. nr. 80) and Beham's *Kunst und Lehrbuchlein* (cat. nr. 95).[9] While maintaining close ties with Nuremberg print publishers, notably Albrecht Glockendon, throughout his career, Beham renounced his Nuremberg citizenship on 24 July 1535 and five years later obtained Frankfurt citizenship.

Beham's prints cover a remarkable range of themes, both religious and secular. He was noted for his large-scale woodcuts, such as the *Large Church Festival* (cat. nr. 84), the *Fountain of Youth* (cat. nr. 85), and, arguably his most beautiful print, the *Siege of Vienna*.[10] His engravings and etchings are much finer in detail and smaller in size, hence the appellation *kleinmeister*, or small master, given to Hans Sebald.[11] The artist frequently copied Barthel's work after his death in 1540, as may be seen in the *Adam and Eve* (cat. nr. 93) and *Death and Three Nude Women* (cat. nr. 91). Hans Sebald's drawings and prints served as designs for artists in other media; for instance, the *Entombment* (cat. nr. 76) is a drawing for a stained-glass roundel, and catalogue numbers 79, 89, and 90 are patterns for seals or medals.

1. A new monograph on Beham is needed. My comments are based upon Neudörfer, *Nachrichten von Künstlern*, p. 138; Peltzer, ed., *Sandrarts Academie*, p. 77; G. Pauli, *Hans Sebald Beham, ein kritisches Verzeichnis seiner Kupferstiche, Radierung, und Holzschnitte*; H. Röttinger, *Ergänzungen und Berichtigungen des Sebald Beham-Kataloges Gustav Paulis* (Strassburg, 1927)—Pauli and Röttinger's books were reprinted in a single volume in 1974 (Baden-Baden); *Nuremberg: Meister um*

Dürer, pp. 73–91, nrs. 69–141; Zschelletzschky, *Die 'Drei gottlosen Maler' von Nürnberg*.

2. A. Suhle, *Die Deutsche Renaissance-Medaille*, pl. 23, fig. 1; Zschelletzschky, *Die 'Drei gottlosen Maler' von Nürnberg*, fig. 3.

3. See cat. nrs. 74, 76; Strieder's comments in *Nuremberg: Meister um Dürer*, pp. 29–30.

4. For example, his *Sketch with Eight Heads* and his *Head of a Young Maiden* (B. 204); *Nuremberg: Meister um Dürer*, nrs. 72, 94. Beham used the monogram ⊩SP or HSP throughout the 1520s and occasionally during the early 1530s before he transformed the P into a B. Since his signed works always include the triple initials, I have used the forename Hans Sebald rather than the shorter Sebald that is often given by other scholars.

5. See Section 3 C; Zschelletzschky, *Die 'Drei gottlosen Maler' von Nürnberg*, pp. 31–55. It is also pertinent to remember that Hans Sebald's sister, Ottilie, was married to Lutheran critic Sebastian Franck; see cat. nr. 84.

6. See Hampe, *Nürnberger Ratsverlässe*, nrs. 1621, 1629, 1631–1634; cat. nr. 95.

7. Peltzer, ed., *Sandrarts Academie*, p. 77.

8. He collaborated on this book and a second prayer book for Duke Johann Albrecht von Mecklenburg with Nuremberg illuminator Nikolaus Glockendon. See *Nuremberg: Meister um Dürer*, nrs. 69–70; esp. A. Biermann, "Die Miniaturenhandschriften des Kardinals Albrecht von Brandenburg (1514–1545)," *Aachener Kunstblätter* 46 (1975): 15–310, esp. pp. 232–239, figs. 305–322.

9. See Pauli, *Hans Sebald Beham*, or Hollstein, III, for listings of the books.

10. On the *Siege of Vienna*, see Geisberg, nrs. 283–288. It was published in 1529 in Nuremberg by Niclas Meldemann.

11. The term *kleinmeister* is applied to both Beham brothers and to Pencz. The term was already in use by 1890.

176

74. MAN OF SORROWS

1520; monogram
Engraving
13 × 8.6 cm
B. 26; Pauli, *Hans Sebald Beham*, nr. 28; Hollstein, III: p. 26
Lent by the New York Public Library, Prints Division, Astor, Lenox and Tilden Foundations

The *Man of Sorrows* is among Beham's earliest prints.[1] In spite of certain weaknesses in the formation of the chest and shoulder, the style of the figure reveals that Beham is already a highly skilled printmaker. He was successful in creating a wide range of chiaroscuro contrasts. The figure of Christ with his brilliant halo is isolated against a dark background. These features suggest that Beham was emulating Dürer's engravings, notably the *Man of Sorrows* and the Virgin and Child prints of 1519 and 1520.[2]

The iconography of Beham's print is unusual. Customarily, the Man of Sorrows is represented either displaying his wounds, as in Schäufelein's engraving (cat. nr. 48) and Traut's woodcut (cat. nr. 59), or surrounded by the Passion instruments, as in Dürer's *Mass of St. Gregory* (cat. nr. 13). Beham's Christ is alone at the foot of the cross. His blood drips into the eucharistic chalice. The emphasis on the chalice and the omission of the host may be an explicit reference to the contemporary chalice controversy.[3] In Roman Catholic communion services, only the priest drank from the chalice, while the congregation received just the host. In his "Sermon on the New Testament" of 1520, Luther demanded that the laity receive both the wine and the host. This would become a central Lutheran tenet and was frequently represented in Protestant art, as, for instance, in Zündt's *The Apostle Ship* etching of 1570 (cat. nr. 185).[4]

1. In 1519–1520, Beham made three other engravings of the head of Christ that are stylistically related to the *Man of Sorrows*. In the *Man of Sorrows*, Christ stares not at the chalice but at some unseen object outside the composition. This gesture tends, I think, to weaken the religious impact of the print. In a lecture titled "Sow's Ears and Silk Purses: Judging Quality in Art and Its Significance for the Historian of the Reformation" delivered on 3 October 1981 in Detroit, Charles Talbot noted that the glances and figure positions of the Virgin and Child in Beham's prints often diffuse the drama and personal interaction of the pair. He speculated that Beham's own lack of religious conviction may have impaired the designs of these prints. Dürer's prints of the same subject exhibit the tender love of mother and child.
2. Meder, nrs. 3, 39–41.
3. Panofsky, *Dürer*, p. 222; Talbot, ed., *Dürer*, nr. 206.
4. For other examples, see Christensen, *Art and the Reformation in Germany*, pp. 137, 141, 146–154.

75. TWO LOVERS SEATED BEFORE A FENCE

ca. 1522; monogram
Woodcut
12.5 × 8.5 cm
B. 161; Pauli, *Hans Sebald Beham*, nr. 1229; Hollstein, III: p. 244
Lent by the Fine Arts Museums of San Francisco, Achenbach Foundation for Graphic Arts, Gift of Julius Landauer, 1961

This woodcut, one of Beham's earliest, first appeared in 1522. The second edition, without a date, likely followed soon afterward. In spite of the apparent simplicity of the composition, Beham's technical talents are already evident. The couple is seated on the grass before a wooden fence.[1] His figures are set in shadow and only gradually emerge into the sunlight.[2] Thus Beham experimented with a wide range of tonal values from the sun-drenched knee and thigh of the woman to the rich blacks around the man's wrist. In this woodcut, Beham seemed to respond to the chiaroscuro contrasts of Dürer's graphic work.

In 1526 Beham etched a reverse copy of this print.[3] The etching technique permitted more subtle shading and greater details. Beham's fascination with etching was short-lived, however, since most of his prints in this technique date between 1520 and 1526.[4]

1. Beham used a similar design of two lovers before a fence on several occasions; see B. 202 (engraving), Geisberg, nr. 250 (woodcut).

2. Compare cat. nr. 74. After his departure from Nuremberg, Beham rarely used the woodcut technique for his chiaroscuro experiments. The major innovations are found in his engravings.

3. B. 209; Pauli, *Hans Sebald Beham*, nr. 1229a; Hollstein, III: p. 122.

4. For instance, B. 61, 66, 139, 147, 195, 203, 205, 206.

76. THE ENTOMBMENT

ca. 1522; later inscription at bottom: albert
Dürer
Drawing: pen and black ink
23.1 cm diameter
Lent by the Wadsworth Atheneum, Hartford,
Henry and Walter Keney Fund

The Entombment belongs to a series of drawings
of the life of Christ that Beham created in about
1522. The drawings are all circular, measuring
about 23 cm in diameter, and most have the
penned inscription "albert Dürer" added at the
very bottom. The spelling of Dürer's name and
the calligraphy are identical in every case. This
association with Dürer is understandable, if incorrect, since Beham used several of the compositions in Dürer's *Small Woodcut Passion* for his
models. *The Entombment* closely follows Dürer's
print of this subject.[1]

Friedländer was the first critic to relate the
drawings of *Christ before Pilate* and the *Descent
from the Cross*, both in Berlin (Kupferstichkabinett), and to suggest that these formed part of a
larger series.[2] Since then, other art historians
have identified the *Massacre of the Innocents*
(Berlin, Kupferstichkabinett), the *Crucifixion*
(Frankfurt, Städelsches Kunstinstitut), and
sketches in London (British Museum) and Oxford (Ashmolean Museum) as belonging to this
series.[3] To this group, *The Entombment* can now
be added.

The drawings were intended as designs for
stained-glass roundels. To the *Massacre of the
Innocents*, Beham added a color wash and lettered color notations for the glazer. Schmitz
published an *Ecce Homo* roundel, now in an
American collection, that was made by the
Hirschvogel family workshop in Nuremberg
after one of Beham's drawings.[4] Other windows
and drawings in this series may well exist.

1. For Dürer's *The Entombment*, see Meder 153.
2. M. J. Friedländer, "Zwei Zeichnungen Hans
Sebald Behams," *Amtliche Berichte aus dem Preussischen
Kunstsammlungen* 30 (1908–1909): cols. 300–302, figs.
183–184.
3. *Massacre of the Innocents* (ex - Oppenheimer Col-
lection in London): K. T. Parker, *Drawings of the Early
German Schools* (New York, 1926), nr. 29; *Nuremberg:
Meister um Dürer*, nr. 85 (see nrs. 86–87 for the other
two Berlin drawings); *Dürer et son Temps*, exh. cat.
(Brussels: Palais des Beaux-Arts, 1964), nr. 78. *Crucifix-
ion*: E. Schilling, *Städelsches Kunstinstitut Frankfurt am
Main. Katalog der deutschen Zeichnungen: Alte Meister*
(Munich, 1973), nr. 40. On the Oxford drawings, see
K. T. Parker, *Catalogue of the Collection of Drawings in the
Ashmolean Museum* (Oxford, 1938), I: nrs. 274 (*The Mul-
tiplication of the Loaves and Fishes*), 275 (*The Temptation of
Christ*), 276 (*Christ in Limbo*). I wish to thank Mr.
Martin Royalton-Kisch, assistant keeper, Department
of Prints and Drawings at the British Museum, for
supplying me with information about *The Mocking of
Christ* and *St. Peter Denying Christ* drawings in the museum's collection. He also brought to my attention that
a version of *St. Peter Denying Christ* was in the
Oppenheimer sale (1956, lot 358).
4. Schmitz, *Die Glasgemälde*, I: p. 160, fig. 267. This
roundel was formerly in the Felix collection. I do not
know the present location of this window.

77. EIGHT PLAYING CARDS FROM A SET OF FORTY-EIGHT

ca. 1523; monogram
Woodcut: each mounted on a backing
9.6 × 6.5 cm each
B. 159–160; Pauli, *Hans Sebald Beham*, nrs.
1290–1337; Geisberg, nrs. 323–330; Hollstein,
III: pp. 268–269
Lent by the John M. Wing Foundation of The
Newberry Library, Chicago

By the sixteenth century printed decks of cards were quite common.[1] Amman, Flötner, Schäufelein, Schön (two sets), and Solis, among other Nuremberg artists, designed decks of either forty-eight (without aces) or fifty-two cards.[2] Decks by Hanns Facunde, listed in 1397 as Nuremberg's first cardmaker, and other early craftsmen were hand painted and therefore relatively expensive.[3] During the fifteenth century, most of the thirty-eight recorded cardmakers in the city printed their decks, often in crude woodcut editions.[4] A 1518 city ordinance banning cardmakers from working in Nuremberg seems to have had little impact since such artists as Beham and Flötner continued to design cards.[5]

Most German decks differed from their modern counterparts both in suit and in number.[6] The traditional suits (clubs, diamonds, hearts, and spades) were already used in Italy and France in the sixteenth century, but German cardmakers continued until the mid-seventeenth century to label their suits with bells, goblets, books, hearts, crowns, fishes, thistles, bagpipes, hunting horns, and a variety of animals and plants. Beham's deck consists of acorns, leaves, pomegranates, and roses.[7] The number of cards also varied, although the standard set consisted of forty-eight cards. A mid-fifteenth-century set by the Master of the Playing Cards, active along the Rhine, contained sixty-five cards in five suits. By the mid-sixteenth century, thirteen card suits, which included an ace, were very common.

Beham's set was printed in Nuremberg as indicated by the city's coat of arms on the two of acorns. Only eight well-worn cards survive from this particular deck. A complete set is in Dresden (Kupferstichkabinett).[8]

1. On this subject, see *Katalog der im Germanischen Museum befindlichen Kartenspiele und Spielkarten* (Nuremberg: Germanisches Nationalmuseum, 1886); C. P. Hargrave, *A History of Playing Cards* (New York, 1930); K. Pilz, intro., *Tarok-Skat-17 + 4: Spielkarten in*

Nürnberg, exh. cat. (Nuremberg: Stadtbibliothek, 1970); *The Art of the Playing Card*, exh. cat. (New Haven: Yale University Library, 1973).
2. Geisberg, nrs. 868 (Flötner), 1112–1117 (Schäufelein), 1308–1311 (Schön); Hollstein, II: p. 50 (Amman); Pilz, *Tarok-Skat-17 + 4*, cat. nrs. 15, 17, 19, 114–118. Nr. 114 is Beham's set, which Pilz dated ca. 1523.
3. Pilz, *Tarok-Skat-17 + 4*, p. 2. Hensel von Wissenburg, recorded in 1391 in Frankfurt, is the first known German cardmaker.
4. Ibid., p. 10.
5. Ibid., pp. 4, 10 (a listing of sixteenth-century cardmakers).
6. Ibid., p. 3.
7. Exhibited are the two, knave, and queen of roses; the two and king of pomegranates; and the two, knave, and king of acorns.
8. Illustrated in Geisberg, nrs. 323–330.

78. MARTIN LUTHER(?) AND HANS SACHS(?), DAS BABSTUM MIT SEYNEN GLIEDERN GEMALET VND BESCHRYBEN GEBESSERT VND GEMEHRT (Nuremberg: Hans Wandereisen(?), 1526)

73 woodblocks; hand colored
7.8–8 × 5–6 cm (each woodcut)
Pauli, *Hans Sebald Beham*, nrs. 1124–1196;
Geisberg, nrs. 226–233; Hollstein, III: pp. 236–237
Lent by the New York Public Library, Spencer Collection, Astor, Lenox and Tilden Foundations

---

The Papacy and Its Organization is an antipapal satire on the Roman Catholic church and its profusion of different religious orders.[1] The pamphlet consists of a prose preface and postscript attributed to Luther, Beham's seventy-four woodcuts, and short poems ascribed to Hans Sachs underneath each woodcut. The poems criticize the Catholic church and its hierarchy for permitting the proliferation of countless religious groups, each distinguished by its costumes and minor doctrinal distinctions, rather than clearly preaching God's word. The church was said to obscure God's truth rather than reveal it.

Sixty-four separate monastic orders, from the Antonites to the Hospitalers are identified, often with the date of their founding. The Dominicans (Predigers), the Franciscans (Barfussers, or barefooted ones), the Augustinians, and the Brothers of Our Lady are represented on pages C i verso and C ii recto, illustrated here. Sachs(?) mentioned that Martin Luther came from the Augustinians. In spite of the polemic intent of this pamphlet, the cataloguing of the different orders and their respective costumes provides an important record of the diversity of the church during the Reformation.

---

1. This pamphlet is one of the few that Beham illustrated while still living in Nuremberg. It was published in at least five separate editions, including being printed on eight sheets of paper, each measuring about 27.5 × 38.5 cm; see Geisberg, nrs. 226–233, Hollstein, III: p. 236. Also see *Nuremberg: Meister um Dürer*, nr. 138. There are seventy-four woodcuts since the woodblock of the pope was printed twice.

Der Prediger orden vñ
derm Babst Honorio.3.im.j220

Hernach folgent vier betler ózden
Welche nůr kůntten seelen mózden
Ir tugent zeygten sie zů Bern
Das gerůcht in ewig wirt wern
Keysser Heinrich endte seyn leben
Durch dise die jm hand vergeben
Weyß, daruber schwartz/ist jr kleydt
Vnd zů betlen dringt sie jr eydt

Der barfusser orden vñ
derm Babst Honorio.3.im.j222

Graw gekleydet mit blossen füssen
Wolten dise jr sünde büssen
Auch gürtent vmb eyn seyl mit knöpff
Darzů seind jn geschorn die köpff
Fasten vnd betten sie auch seer
Doch was jr küche nysser lehr
Machten eyn münch mit fünff wundt
Damit sie alle welte schunden

Der Augustiner orden

Augustiner gantz schwartz gekleyd
Ir orden helt nicht vil vnderscheyd
Alß man tausent fünff hundert jar
Darzů neuntzehen zelt für war
Aldo auß jr seckt erstandt
Martin Luther in Saxer landt
Gotts wort ehr vns wider lert
Des Babsts reych hat ehr gar verhert

Vnser frawen brůd.ord.
vnderm Babst Hono.3.im.j278.

Der Babst Marie brůder nendt
Ich weyß/sie hat jr nye erkendt
Am Berck Helie wart jn geben
Nach Helie weyß zů leben
Ir rock ist schwartz/der mantel weyß
Nůr auff bettlen stat all jr fleyß
Ir frůmer scheyn hat vns gepleut
Ich hoff es hab mit jn ein end.

C ij

79. DESIGN FOR A MEDAL OF KING FERDINAND OF HUNGARY AND BOHEMIA

ca. 1530–1531; monogram
Engraving
3.8 cm diameter (outer borderline); 5.8 × 4.3 cm (plate)
B. 85; Pauli, *Hans Sebald Beham*, nr. 222; Hollstein, III: p. 132
Lent by the National Gallery of Art, Washington, Rosenwald Collection, 1943

Ferdinand I (1503–1564) was the younger son of Philip the Fair, brother of Emperor Charles V, and grandson of Emperor Maximilian I. Following the death of his brother-in-law Ludwig II in 1526, Ferdinand was crowned king of Hungary and Bohemia. In 1531 he was elected king of the Romans, heir to the imperial crown, which he obtained on 24 March 1558.

Like Hans Krafft the Elder's *Portrait of Emperor Charles V* (cat. nr. 138), Beham's print stresses Ferdinand's role as king by means of his dress, which includes his royal crown, scepter of office, and sword of justice, and his elaborate coat of arms, which is represented on the pendant engraving showing the reverse of the medal.[1] Beham's emphasis on Ferdinand's princely role suggests that the print was made to commemorate either the 1526 coronation or, more likely, the 1531 election.[2] Although portraits of Ferdinand were generally available in Germany, Beham may have made a portrait sketch of Ferdinand on 10 June 1530 when Ferdinand and Charles V triumphantly entered Munich. Beham was in Munich, as evidenced by his large woodcut of the entry.[3]

While I am unaware of any contemporary medals made after Beham's engraving, these may have existed.[4] More likely, Beham's design was intended to be used by other printmakers, goldsmiths, and furniture makers much in the way these masters used his portraits of ancient Roman emperors.[5]

1. Pauli, *Hans Sebald Beham*, nr. 223; Hollstein, III: p. 132; not exhibited here.
2. The coat of arms contains the heraldic shields of Austria-Castile, Bohemia, and Hungary. Ferdinand could not have used the arms of Bohemia and Hungary until 1526 at the earliest. Therefore, the dating of these two related engravings to about 1519, as suggested in *Nuremberg: Meister um Dürer*, nrs. 98–99, is incorrect.
3. B. 169; Geisberg, nrs. 292–296; Hollstein, III: p. 228. Barthel Beham's more elaborate portrait engraving of Ferdinand dates to 1531 and was made to celebrate his new title; see B. 61; Pauli, *Hans Sebald Beham*, nr. 91; and Hollstein, II: p. 229.
4. Beham made a triple portrait medal design that is much simpler than the engraving of Ferdinand. See B. 221; Pauli, *Hans Sebald Beham*, nr. 224; and Hollstein, III: p. 133. Beham created drawings for medals. See the comments for Matthes Gebel's *Portrait of Dorothea von der Pfalz* (cat. nr. 151).
5. For instance, a Nuremberg sculptor, active during the second quarter of the sixteenth century, used a medal of Ferdinand I, though not Beham's example, as the source for a wooden model for a girdle or belt to be made with precious metals. The medal of Ferdinand is set in the center and flanked by ornamental grotesque patterns. See Kohlhaussen, *Nürnberger Goldschmiedekunst*, nr. 441 (Nuremberg, Germanisches Nationalmuseum, inv. Pl. 535).

81. THE WOMEN'S BATHHOUSE

1530–1535; monogram
Woodcut
29.3 cm diameter (outer borderline)
B. 167; Pauli, *Hans Sebald Beham*, nr. 1223;
Geisberg, nr. 267; Hollstein, III: p. 241
The University of Texas at Austin, Archer M.
Huntington Art Gallery

Bathhouses were congenial gathering places that men and women visited as much for social as for hygienic reasons.[1] The nine women, four children, and a male attendant are engaged both in conversation and in the act of washing. The women in the foreground are scraping their legs or rinsing their hair in buckets, while the women behind are seated in or beside a shallow pool.

Beham's interior setting, with its carefully devised perspective, and the considerable range of figure positions may have been inspired by Dürer's 1496 drawing *Women's Bath*.[2] Unlike Dürer, Beham was not particularly interested in representing textures or subtle tonal variations. Beham's woodcut has been dated about 1530 and about 1540.[3] I favor a dating of 1530–1535 since this print seems to predate slightly the closely related *Fountain of Youth* woodcut (cat. nr. 85) of the mid-1530s. Many identical figure types are common to these two prints.

The elaborate frame around the *Women's Bathhouse* suggests that the artist designed the woodcut not only as a model for stained glass but also as an independent decoration, perhaps for a wall or a box.[4] Jost Amman later created woodcuts with similarly elaborate frames that were intended to ornament boxes.[5]

---

1. See Dürer's *The Bathhouse* (cat. nr. 5).
2. Bremen (Kunsthalle); see Winkler, *Zeichnungen Dürers*, I: nr. 152. Beham is credited with making the woodcut after Dürer's drawing that appeared with a text by Hans Sachs around 1545. See Pauli, *Hans Sebald Beham*, nr. 1223a; *Die Welt des Hans Sachs*, nr. 205.
3. It is dated ca. 1530 in *Berlin: Der Mensch um 1500*, fig. 97, and ten years later by Geisberg (nr. 267).
4. A stained-glass roundel after Beham's woodcut was made by an unknown Nuremberg glazer active during the early 1530s. The roundel was in Berlin (Kunstgewerbemuseum, inv. KGM nr. 295); see Schmitz, *Die Glasgemälde*, I: p. 165, fig. 279.
5. Strauss, *The German Single-Leaf Woodcut*, *1550–1600*, I: nrs. 31, 32, 35.

80. BIBLISCH HISTORIEN FIGÜRLICH FÜRGEBILDET DURCH DEN WOLBERÜMPTEN SEBALD BEHEM VON NÜREMBERG ⱨⱬ (Frankfurt: Christian Egenolff, 30 June 1533)

8 title pages and 80 woodcuts
5 × 7 cm (average woodcut)
B. 1–73; Pauli, *Hans Sebald Beham*, nrs. 271–358;
Hollstein, III: p. 166
Lent by the Library of Congress, Washington,
Lessing J. Rosenwald Collection

This is a rare copy of the first edition of Beham's historiated Bible. According to Dodgson, who did not know of this example, copies of this edition exist only at Coburg, Göttingen, and London (British Museum).[1] The *Biblisch Historien* proved to be one of the most successful collaborations between Beham and Frankfurt publisher Egenolph. A total of seven editions were printed between 1533 and 1539.[2] Many of Beham's woodcuts subsequently appeared in other books issued by Egenolph, who apparently did not pay Beham whenever the woodcuts were reused.

The initial title page with its six scenes from Exodus is the most elaborate of the woodcuts.

Beham depicted the crossing of the Red Sea, the gathering of manna, Moses receiving the law, the breaking of the tablets, Moses and the brazen serpent, and Aaron and the Golden Calf. The majority of the other woodcuts in this book also illustrate events from the Old Testament. The book has no text other than a brief description of each scene and the appropriate book and chapter references.

Several of Beham's woodcuts were used by a Nuremberg workshop around 1550 as designs for a stained-glass series. A few of these glass roundels were formerly in Berlin (Kunstgewerbemuseum).[3]

---

1. Dodgson, I: p. 440. Also see L. Rosenthal, "Hans Sebald Behams Alttestamentarische Holzschnitte und deren Verwendung zur Bücher-Illustration (1529–1612)," *Repertorium für Kunstwissenschaft* 5 (1882): 379–405, esp. 384 (nr. 11). The woodcuts are reproduced in *The Illustrated Bartsch*, 15: pp. 135–161.
2. Hollstein, III: p. 166, also lists editions of 1557 and n.d. On the 1534 edition, see H. Dornick-Eger, *Albrecht Dürer und die Graphik der Reformationzeit* (Vienna, 1969), nr. 50.
3. Schmitz, *Die Glasgemälde*, I: p. 165, figs. 280, 282a, 282b. Included among this series are David watching Bathsheba at her bath and Jonah and the whale. I am unsure whether any of these roundels survived the last world war.

82. THE FEAST OF HERODIAS

ca. 1530–1535
Woodcut: two blocks
38.8 × 52.8 cm
Pauli, *Hans Sebald Beham*, nr. 832; Geisberg, nrs.
179–180; Hollstein, III: p. 188
The University of Texas at Austin, The Humanities Research Center, Iconography Collection

The feast of Herodias, the subject of the print, occupies only the upper left-hand quarter of the composition.[1] Without the inclusion of Salome with the head of John the Baptist on the platter, the scene could be a sixteenth-century German banquet with accompanying outdoor festivities. The biblical subject simply provided Beham with an excuse to represent a festive occasion. The revelers, all dressed in contemporary not biblical attire, are shown dancing, eating and drinking, bathing, and courting. The mood and the figures are quite similar to those of Beham's *Fountain of Youth* (cat. nr. 85), which dates a few years later.

Amid the lightheartedness of the feast, Beham has included warnings about the wiles of women and about man's mortality. Salome was frequently included along with Delilah, Phyllis, the daughter of Augustus(?), and others in series of the power of women over men.[2] Women were believed to be capable of dominat-ing even the most powerful rulers or the wisest men by means of their feminine charms. At the banquet of Herod and his wife Herodias, Herod was so captivated by the skillful dancing of his step-daughter Salome that he swore he would grant whatever she might ask. At Herodias's instigation, Salome requested the head of the prophet John the Baptist, who was at that moment a prisoner in Herod's jail because he had criticized the marriage of Herod and his former sister-in-law Herodias. Salome and Herodias thus manipulated Herod to secure the death of John the Baptist. In the rest of the composition, men are succumbing to the sensual attractions of women.

In the middle of the print, just beneath Salome, Death approaches one of the well-dressed couples. He holds an hour glass and a scythe, his traditional attributes. He is a reminder that death can come at any time and usually when he is least expected. Sensuality and life are both fleeting, as Beham warns in his woodcut.

1. This is the second edition of this print. It lacks the colophon of publisher Albrecht Glockendon that is found on the first edition. The Humanities Research Center possesses a second, hand-colored copy of the second edition of this woodcut; however, it is too fragile and damaged to be exhibited. On the feast of Herodias, see *The Golden Legend of Jacobus de Voragine*, tr. G. Ryan and H. Ripperger (1941; reprint New York,

1969), pp. 502–510; Réau, *Iconographie de l'Art Chrétien*, II.1: pp. 452–459. The feast day of the beheading of St. John is 29 August.

2. See Pencz's *Samson and Delilah* (cat. nr. 104A), *Salome Presenting the Head of John the Baptist* (cat. nr. 104B), and *Virgil in a Basket* (cat. nr. 105A) for other images and a discussion of the power of women.

3. Beham's woodcut inspired a painting, now in Bayreuth, that is dated 1540; see K.-A. and U. Knappe, "Das Bayreuther Gemälde 'Fest des Herods' und sein Vorbild," *Archiv für Geschichte Oberfranken* 47 (1967): 289–301. In 1612 Adrian Grebber of Haarlem made a copy of Beham's print.

83. THE VIRGIN AND CHILD WITH ST. ANNE

1534 (see below); monogram of Albrecht Dürer added later
Drawing: pen and black ink
19.6 × 16.2 cm
Lent by the Museum of Fine Arts, Boston, Charles Hitchcock Tyler Fund

This drawing bears the date 1514.[1] Since Beham was only fourteen years old in 1514, either the attribution to this artist or the date is suspect. In an old engraved facsimile, the date reads 1534.[2] That the date has been tampered with is born out by a recent examination of the drawing with a microscope and with an ultraviolet light.[3] 1534 would seem to be the correct date.

Although the drawing is not signed with Beham's monogram, the attribution is, I believe, correct. The Christ Child with his puffed cheeks, drawn with circular strokes, is a characteristic infant type that can be seen in Beham's prints and drawings.[4] The highly abbreviated face of the Virgin can be compared with the earlier *Entombment* drawing (cat. nr. 76), where several of the faces are defined with simple outlines on one side and crude shading strokes on the other side. Beham probably made this drawing as a design for a woodcut that was never executed.

1. I wish to thank Sue W. Reed of the Department of Prints, Drawings & Photographs at the Museum of Fine Arts for the dating information contained in this paragraph. The date was altered sometime in this century prior to the museum's purchase of the drawing from P. & D. Colnaghi & Co. Ltd. of London in 1962. See *Exhibition of Old Master Drawings* (London: P. & D. Colnaghi & Co. Ltd, 19 June to 21 July 1962), nr. 2, pl. I. The drawing was formerly in the Karl Eduard von Liphart Collection in Leipzig.
2. The facsimile (Babcock 88, Anonymous) is in the collection of the Museum of Fine Arts.
3. Reed and her colleagues conducted this examination.
4. Compare the children in his series *Old Testament Patriarchs* (B. 74–83; Geisberg, nrs. 168–177) published in Nuremberg in 1530.

84. LARGE CHURCH FESTIVAL

1535
Woodcut (four blocks)
36.2 × 114.2 cm
B. 168; Pauli, *Hans Sebald Beham*, nr. 1245;
Geisberg, nrs. 251–254; Hollstein, III: p. 255
Lent by the Art Institute of Chicago. Potter
Palmer Collection. 1967.491

Beham's *Large Church Festival* of 1535 presents a panorama of events that occurred at religious festivals, the celebrations of the anniversaries of a church's consecration that, by the late Middle Ages, had become the peasants' most important holiday.[1] This print represents numerous events that took place over several days: a wedding before a church door (top left), a dentist extracting a tooth and money from a patient (left center), the celebration before an inn by lovers and a preacher alike (center bottom), and dancing, game-playing, and fighting (right). Despite the enjoyment of peasants, burghers (right bottom), and clergy (center), the inclusion of the symbolic bear (left bottom) and copulating chickens (center) points to the sins of anger and unchastity that they represent, which are acted out on the game field and around the inn. At the center bottom, a peasant vomits. The cause of his excessive behavior is no doubt wine, which was produced from the kind of plant growing in front of the inn. As lust, anger, and drunkenness were considered at this time to number among the effects of wine, the placement of this key idea at the center bottom is certainly appropriate.[2]

Because of the licentious behavior of the celebrants at church festivals, the Nuremberg city council issued an ordinance on 24 May 1525 that reduced the number of holidays by half to about twenty-five.[3] The remaining holidays celebrated events from the life of the Virgin and Christ and the name days of the twelve apostles. The ordinance was printed and distributed to the city's preachers and posted about the countryside.[4] On 30 August 1526, the council sought to ban all church festivals on the grounds that they resulted in sinful behavior that led to the dishonor of God's holy word.[5] A further mandate of 1530 suggests that the practice continued in spite of the council's efforts.[6]

This print has been variously interpreted. Zschelletzschky suggested that Beham was a friend of the peasants and shows them in a favorable light.[7] Other critics, however, believe that Beham expressed the contemporary scorn of the peasant by the city dweller;[8] that is, the peasant was a plump, country bumpkin with bad manners. Moxey explained the *Large Church Festival* as a repressive Lutheran satire of church festivals.[9] Luther and his colleagues criticized the festivals and the behavior of the participants. Although Luther's attitudes were shared to a degree by the Nuremberg city council, his thoughts differed from Hans Sebald Beham's. Is the minister seated before the inn a portrait of Luther? This man resembles Hans Brosamer's portrait of Luther that was printed in Nuremberg by Wolfgang Resch in 1530.[10] There are two possible ways to explain his presence. First, it adds fuel to the argument against these festivals

to portray a critic of them in their midst. Second, and even more intriguing, is the possibility that Luther's presence may have alluded to contemporary criticism of his followers by members of the left wing of the Reformation. The failure to achieve a renewal or cleansing of popular customs was hurled at Luther by Sebastian Franck, who later left the Reformed movement for this reason. Franck stated in his *On the Horrible Vice of Drunkenness* of 1528 that being drunk is the Bible for many Lutherans, while stressing that asceticism is called papist and hypocritical.[11]

It is perhaps more than of passing interest to note that Franck was Hans Sebald's brother-in-law. Luther gave Franck's wife, Ottilie, credit for inspiring Franck, for placing the spirit in him, thereby suggesting that her politics were similar to those of her agnostic, left-wing brother.[12]

Beham's *Large Church Festival* thus represents a cabaret-like view of the church festival in Nuremberg—enjoyable, sinful, still actual, and possibly critical of the Reformed movement.[13]

1. This catalogue entry was written by Alison G. Stewart, NEA intern in the Department of Prints, Drawings, and Photographs at the Philadelphia Museum of Art. The content of this entry is taken from her dissertation in progress, which is entitled "The First 'Peasant Festivals': Eleven Woodcuts Produced in Nuremberg by Barthel Beham, Sebald Beham, and Erhard Schön (ca. 1524 to 1535)" (Columbia University, New York). This print is the culmination of seven woodcut versions of the theme made in Nuremberg, over twenty-five years before Pieter Bruegel the Elder took up the subject in his paintings and prints. These Nuremberg examples will be examined in Stewart, "The First 'Peasant Festivals,'" chs. 4, 5. The date for the *Large Church Festival* is 1535, not 1539. The five slipped during the printing. The exhibited version, which was once owned by Johann Friedrich, Elector of Saxony, lacks the date and the colophon of the publisher, Albrecht Glockendon.

2. Stewart, "The First 'Peasant Festivals,'" ch. 5.

3. G. Seebass, "Ratschläge zur Aufhebung von Feiertagen 1525," in *Andreas Osiander d. Ä. Gesamtausgabe*, ed. G. Müller and G. Seebass (Gütersloh, 1977), II: pp. 127–129.

4. G. Pfeiffer, *Quellen zur Nürnberger Reformationsgeschichte* (Nuremberg, 1968), p. 93, nr. 696.

5. Stewart, "The First 'Peasant Festivals,'" ch. 5.

6. Ibid.

7. Zschelletzschky, *Die 'Drei gottlosen Maler' von Nürnberg*, p. 333.

8. *Das Bild vom Bauern. Vorstellungen und Wirklichkeit vom 16. Jahrhundert bis zur Gegenwart*, exh. cat. (Berlin: Museum für Deutsche Volkskunde, 1978), p. 18.

9. K. P. F. Moxey, "Sebald Beham's Church Anniversary Holidays: Festive Peasants as Instruments of Repressive Humor," *Simiolus* 12 (1981–1982): 107–130.

10. Geisberg, nr. 423.

11. H. Weigelt, *Sebastian Franck und die lutherische Reformation* (Gütersloh, 1972), pp. 15–16.

12. H. Weigelt, "Sebastian Franck," in *Gestalten der Kirchengeschichte*, Reformationszeit, vol. 2 (Stuttgart, 1981), p. 120.

13. I would like to thank Dr. Johannes Willers of the Germanisches Nationalmuseum, who described Beham's church festival to me as a *kabarettistisch*.

85. FOUNTAIN OF YOUTH

ca. 1536; monogram
Woodcut (4 blocks)
37 × 108.3 cm
B. 165; Pauli, *Hans Sebald Beham*, nr. 1120;
Geisberg, nrs. 263–266; Hollstein, III: p. 234
Lent by the National Gallery of Art, Washington, Rosenwald Collection, 1943

Beham published this print in two editions. The first, exhibited here, lacks the inscription "ALBRECHT GLOCKENDON ILLUMINIST ZW NURMBERGK" found on the second edition.[1] This print demonstrates Beham's continued ties with Nuremberg artists and printers long after his departure from the city.

By foot and by stretcher, the elderly approach the fountain seeking rejuvenation.[2] Four figures celebrate their transformations by dancing merrily around a fire fueled with the crutches of the elderly. Once youth is restored, thoughts turned immediately to sensual pleasure as the couples engage in conversation, music making, and amorous pursuits. The fountain of youth is linked with the elaborate Renaissance-style bathhouse at the right. Beham joins the two halves of the composition by the jet of elixir aimed at the bottom of the woman in the gallery.

Although the mood of Beham's gathering is joyous, the artist did add two figures to warn the viewer about seeking impossible panaceas. On the ends of the balcony are a man dressed in a fool's cap and holding a fool's stick and, opposite, a fully dressed, elderly woman playing a hurdy-gurdy, an instrument commonly associated with fools, beggars, and peasants. The dream of the fountain of youth is simply a dream, and one would be foolish to think otherwise.[3]

The decorative features in the *Fountain of Youth* are frequently found in other prints by the artist.

The lintel frieze with the medallions of rulers can be compared with Beham's *Ornament with Two Genii* (cat. nr. 94) and his portraits of classical emperors.[4] Other details derive from Italian prints. For instance, in the second woodcut with the fountain and the artist's monogram, the figure with leaves in her hair on the front edge of the fountain is borrowed directly from Marcantonio Raimondi's *The Judgment of Paris* engraving after Raphael.[5] The man immediately behind her in the water and the blindfolded man further to the left are also loosely patterned after two other figures in Raimondi's engraving.

in Nuremberg and other German towns. For instance, a similar frieze design by Flötner was the source for the carved wooden lintel formerly seen in the courtyard of the house at Tucherstrasse 15; see Schwemmer, *Bürgerhaus*, pl. 85c.

5. B. XIV, 245, and Shoemaker and Broun, *The Engravings of Marcantonio Raimondi*, exh. cat., nr. 43.

1. Hollstein, III: p. 234. Glockendon also published Beham's *Feast of Herodias* (cat. nr. 82) and *Large Church Festival* (cat. nr. 84), Pencz's *Venus* (cat. nr. 103), and Schön's *Twelve Clean and Twelve Unclean Birds* (cat. nr. 70).

2. Beham's woodcut and Lucas Cranach the Elder's 1546 painting (Berlin, Staatliche Museen) are the best known representations of the fountain of youth theme during this period. On Cranach's picture, see W. Schade, *Cranach: A Family of Master Painters*, tr. H. Sebba (New York, 1980), pl. 182. On the theme, see Anna Rapp, *Der Jungbrunnen in Literatur und bildender Kunst des Mittelalters* (Zurich, 1976).

3. In Erhard Schön's *Fountain of Youth* woodcut of ca. 1535, the fountain is crowned with the figure of a fool who spouts water from a penis shaped like a cock's head. The essential message of Schön's and Beham's prints is the same. See *Die Welt des Hans Sachs*, nr. 153; Röttinger, *Schön*, nr. 195.

4. B. 129–131 woodcut portraits of emperors. Also see his engravings of ornaments and architectural forms, B. 243–253. Such friezes did appear on houses

86. MELENCOLIA (MELANCHOLY)

1539; monogram
Engraving
7.9 × 5.2 cm
B. 144; Pauli, *Hans Sebald Beham*, nr. 145; Hollstein, III: p. 85
Lent by the Detroit Institute of Arts, Gift of Charles E. Feinberg in Memory of Sarah Lambert Brown Nirenberg

Beham's engraving is largely a simplification of Dürer's *Melencolia I* of 1514 (cat. nr. 19).[1] Beham retained the saw, globe, chisel, compass, hourglass, and book represented by Dürer; however, he stripped away most of the symbols used in Dürer's complicated allegory. Beham's figure of melancholy appears asleep, while Dürer's figure is lost in thought, deeply brooding over her inabilities.

During the years 1539–1541, Beham created several independent prints representing allegorical figures.[2] In each case, the figure is set in the extreme foreground and surrounded by the appropriate symbols. This formula may have been inspired by plaquettes, such as those by Flötner (cat. nrs. 128–131).

1. On the iconography of melancholy, see the comments about Dürer's print. Also see Klibansky, Panofsky, and Saxl, *Saturn and Melancholy*, pp. 329, 377. For the six different editions of this print, see Hollstein, III: p. 85.
2. Cf. B. 137 (*Charity*), 138 (*Patience*), 140 (*Fortune*), 141 (*Misfortune*).

87. RETURN OF THE PRODIGAL SON

1540; monogram
Drawing: pen and black ink with gray wash
5.9 × 9.8 cm
Lent by the Metropolitan Museum of Art, New
York, Rogers Fund, 1919

88. PARABLE OF THE PRODIGAL SON

1540; monogram
Engraving: series of four
5.0–5.8 × 9.2–9.8 cm (borderline)
B. 31–34; Pauli, *Hans Sebald Beham*, nrs. 33–36;
Hollstein, III: p. 30
Lent by the St. Louis Art Museum

The four engravings illustrate the principal events of the parable of the prodigal son (Luke 15:11–32): the son's departure from his family, his squandering of his inheritance on wine and women, his abject poverty that forced him to tend swine, and his return to and reconciliation with his father.[1]

The *Return of the Prodigal Son*, one of Beham's rare surviving drawings for a print, provides valuable information about the artist's working method. In this drawing, Beham rapidly outlined his figures and the other compositional forms. Whereas in his earlier drawings (cat. nrs. 76 and 83) he used hatching patterns to define shading and chiaroscuro contrasts, here he applied a gray wash.[2] These washed areas were later reinterpreted as lines in the copper engraving plate. For instance, the face of the foreground figure holding a robe is in shadow with only a slight patch of light by the ear. In the drawing, the wash covers all but this small spot. In the engraving, the diagonal hatching strokes are less closely spaced in this area. Interestingly, Beham seemed to add most of the secondary details directly on the plate, not in the drawing.

Nuremberg mechanic and sculptor Leonhard Danner (1507–1587) made four plaquettes after Beham's prints.[3] These plaquettes were used as individual decorations and, in another instance, together as the side panels for a table clock in Berlin (Kunstgewerbemuseum).

---

1. Around 1535 Beham made a large (65.7 × 95.2 cm) woodcut, printed with eight blocks, showing these four episodes; see B. 128; Pauli, *Hans Sebald Beham*, nr. 831; Geisberg, nrs. 219–220; Hollstein, III: p 187.
2. Did Beham learn this new drawing style from a Netherlandish artist? This sketch and the *Designs for Medallions* (cat. nrs. 89–90) of 1540 are very similar to some of the drawings of Pieter Coecke van Aelst of Antwerp. See Coecke's *Triumph of Mordecai* (Paris, Louvre) of the early 1540s in G. Marlier, *La Renaissance flamande: Pierre Coeck d'Alost* (Brussels, 1966), pp. 86–87.
3. Pechstein, *Bronzen und Plaketten*, nrs. 187, 188 (clock; 1550s).

89. CONSTANTIA TRIUMPHANS

1540; monogram
Inscription: CONSTANTIA TRIUMPHANS
(and around the edge) HOFNUNG GEDULDT
BESTENDIGKEIT ERLANGT DIE KRON DER
SEELIGKHEIT
Drawing: pen and black ink with wash
4.3 cm diameter
Lent by the Nelson-Atkins Museum of Art,
Kansas City, Missouri (Nelson Fund)

90. STATVA PACIS

1540; monogram
Inscription: PERVIGILIVM DEI // LI RE-
GIO // V[erbum] D[omini] M[anet] I[n] AE[ter-
num] MDXXXX (and around the edge) ACH
HERR DEIN VOLCK UND WORT BEHUT
REIN WIE EIN AUG BEY WAHREM
FRIED // CVSTODI ME VT PVPIL LAM OCVLI
PSAL: 17
Drawing: pen and black ink with wash
4.1 cm diameter
Lent by the Nelson-Atkins Museum of Art,
Kansas City, Missouri (Nelson Fund)

DESIGNS FOR TWO SEALS: CONSTANTIA TRIUMPHANS AND STATVA PACIS

Beham's two drawings are designs for two seals or medals or the obverse and reverse of one seal.[1] The first drawing represents hope and patience pulling the chariot of constancy. According to the inscription, these allegorical figures are receiving the crown of salvation. The second sketch shows the personification of peace holding a chalice and a column, attributes usually associated with faith and constancy (or fortitude).[2] Behind is a tranquil landscape with a small town dominated by a church. Perhaps the allusion is to the need for religious peace.

The patron of these two drawings may have been Johann Friedrich, elector of Saxony. The inscription on the base of the *Statva Pacis* drawing reads "V.D.M.I.AE," or "Verbum Domini Manet in Aeternum" (the word of God will last forever). This phrase is first found on a portrait medal of Elector Friedrich the Wise that is dated 1522 and attributed to Hans Krafft the Elder of Nuremberg.[3] After Friedrich's death in 1525, this motto, with its Lutheran emphasis on the word of God, was adopted by his successor, Johann Friedrich. It can be seen inscribed on Pencz's *Portrait of Johann Friedrich* of 1543 (cat. nr. 110).[4] While additional evidence is needed to prove conclusively that Johann Friedrich commissioned these drawings, it is not irrelevant to recall that he did collect the prints of Hans Sebald Beham, including the *Large Church Festival* (cat. nr. 84).

In these two drawings and the *Return of the Prodigal Son* (cat. nr. 87), Beham's style differs somewhat from the earlier sketches of the *Entombment* (cat. nr. 76) and the *Virgin and Child with St. Anne* (cat. nr. 83). The figures are now much more Italianate and the classical draperies cling to the bodies. These same trends can be found in Beham's prints of the late 1530s and 1540s as the artist increasingly absorbed the forms and motifs of his younger brother, Barthel.[5]

---

1. I am inclined to see these drawings as medal designs since elaborate religious and allegorical medals were made in Nuremberg and other German cities at this time. See Pechstein, *Bronzen und Plaketten*, nrs. 160–162, 166–167. On Nuremberg seals, most of which predate the sixteenth century, see Kohlhaussen, *Nürnberger Goldschmiedekunst*, pp. 11–78.
2. Cf. Beham's engravings *Faith and Fortitude*, which belong to his 1539 series of the *Seven Virtues*; see Bartsch 133 and 135. I am unsure which emblem book, if any, Beham used when preparing his designs.
3. Washington (National Gallery; Samuel H. Kress Collection). See Hill and Pollard, nr. 618.
4. Lucas Cranach the Younger's 1547 woodcut portrait of Johann Friedrich as the Lutheran champion has the letters "V.D.M.I.E." inscribed on the elector's sword of authority. In this year Johann Friedrich led the Protestant forces against those of Charles V at the battle of Mühlberg. See Jahn, *Lucas Cranach d. Ä., 1472–1553*, p. 643.
5. See Hans Sebald's *Labors of Hercules* (cat. nr. 92), Barthel's *Battle for the Banner* (cat. nr. 97), and *Virgin and Child by the Window* (cat. nr. 98). For brief comments on Hans Sebald's copying the engravings of Barthel, see *Death and the Three Nude Women* (cat. nr. 91).

91. DEATH AND THREE NUDE WOMEN

early 1540s; monogram
Engraving
7.7 × 5.4 cm
B. 151; Pauli, *Hans Sebald Beham*, nr. 152; Hollstein, III: p. 92
The University of Texas at Austin, Archer M. Huntington Art Gallery

The theme of death was common in the art of Beham and his contemporaries.[1] Beham's prints illustrate Death visiting young women and amorous couples; in this instance, Death approaches three women of varying ages.[2] He focuses on the youngest, his quarry. The arrival of Death is usually unexpected, a point also conveyed by the skull at the bottom of the print, which the viewer notices only after examining the rest of the composition.

The creator of this composition was not Hans Sebald but his brother Barthel.[3] Particularly after Barthel's death in 1540, Hans Sebald reworked and reissued several of his brother's prints under his own monogram.[4] Barthel's engraving is not dated but was probably made during the late 1520s. Even more than in Hans Sebald's *Two Lovers Seated before a Fence* (cat. nr. 75), Barthel's figures emerge from the darkness, as light, not line, is the principal means of defining form.

---

1. For instance, see Beham's *Feast of Herodias* (cat. nr. 82) and B. 146–147, 149–152. On the subject of death in the art of this period, see C. Olds, R. G. Williams, and W. R. Levin, *Images of Love and Death in Late Medieval and Renaissance Art*; see the comments on Hans Schwarz's wooden relief of *Death and the Maiden* (Berlin, Staatliche Museen) in *Berlin: Der Mensch um 1500*, nr. 25.

2. The three women do not seem to represent the three graces or the three ages of women. For examples by Baldung Grien of these themes, see Marrow and Shestack, ed., *Hans Baldung Grien*, figs. 32–34.

3. B. 42; Pauli, *Hans Sebald Beham*, nr. 40; and Hollstein, II: p. 199.

4. For instance, among Hans Sebald's prints after his brother are B. 70, 75, 146, 147, 198, 207, 208, 215.

92. THE LABORS OF HERCULES

1542–1548; monogram
Engraving: series of twelve
4.8–5.2 × 7–7.8 cm (borderline)
B. 96–107; Pauli, *Hans Sebald Beham*, nrs.
98–109; Hollstein, III: pp. 67–69
Lent by the New York Public Library, Prints Division, Astor, Lenox and Tilden Foundations

Beham is known as a *kleinmeister*, or small master, largely because of the minute scale of many of his prints. The small sizes are especially evident in his engraved series, such as the *Labors of Hercules*, the *Seven Virtues*, or the *Seven Planets*, which would neatly fit on a sheet of paper.[1]

The labors of Hercules or, more accurately, the story of Hercules consists of twelve prints designed over a period of seven years.[2] The arrangement is as follows:

1. Hercules fighting against the Centaurs (1542)
2. Hercules killing the Nemean Lion (1548)
3. Hercules slaying the Hydra (1545)
4. Hercules carrying the columns of Gaza (1545) (illustrated)
5. Hercules killing Cacus (1545)
6. Hercules killing Anthaeus (1545)
7. Hercules capturing Cerberus (1545)
8. Hercules fighting the Trojans (1545)
9. Hercules killing Nessus (1542)
10. Hercules abducting Iole (1544)
11. Lichas bringing the garment of Nessus to Hercules (n.d.)
12. Death of Hercules (1548).

In designing this series, Beham borrowed liberally from the prints of his brother Barthel and Georg Pencz. Many of the battling figures, especially in *Hercules Fighting against the Centaurs*, derive from or were inspired by Barthel's *Battle for the Banner* (cat. nr. 97) and its two companion battle engravings.[3] The setting used in the scene of Hercules carrying the columns of Gaza is modeled after that of Pencz's *Virgil in a Basket* (cat. nr. 105A).

1. B. 129–136 (*Seven Virtues*), 96–107 (*Seven Planets*).
2. For representations of Hercules in German art, see O. Lenz, "Über den Ikonographischen Zusammenhang und die Literarische Grundlage einiger Herkuleszyklen des 16. Jahrhunderts und zur Deutung des Dürerstiches B. 73," *MJBK* N.F. 1 (1924): 80–103; E. Panofsky, *Hercules am Scheidewege und andere antike Bildstoffe in der neueren Kunst* (Leipzig, 1930).
3. Barthel Beham's prints are B. 16–18.

93. ADAM AND EVE

1543; monogram
Engraving
8.1 × 5.6 cm (borderline)
B. 6; Pauli, *Hans Sebald Beham*, nr. 7; Hollstein, III: p. 5
Lent by the Detroit Institute of Arts, City of Detroit Purchase

As in the case of the engraving *Death and Three Nude Women* (cat. nr. 91), Hans Sebald directly copied a print by his brother Barthel. Barthel's engraving of *Adam and Eve* dates between 1526 and 1529.[1] Hans Sebald added little beyond his monogram and the 1543 date.

Barthel's representation of Adam and Eve beside the tree of knowledge is very different from the more conventional depictions of this theme by Springinklee (cat. nr. 53) or Krug (cat. nr. 114). Barthel focused not on the temptation of

Adam but on the consequences of Adam and Eve's transgression. As the first pair ate the forbidden fruit, they gained knowledge, including sin, and mortality. Barthel transformed the tree into a skeleton symbolizing death.[2] The fall of man led to the expulsion from the Garden of Eden; Adam already holds the flaming sword of the Archangel Michael that was used to drive Eve and himself from paradise. Once outside Eden, Adam and Eve would have to toil and eventually to die. Thus Barthel interpreted the fall of man as the original *memento mori*.

1. B. 1; Pauli, *Hans Sebald Beham*, nr. 1; Hollstein, II: p. 173. For a general discussion of these two prints, see Zschelletzschky, *Die 'Drei gottlosen Maler' von Nürnberg*, pp. 190–193.
2. Hans Baldung Grien also developed the association of knowledge and death in his painting *Eve, the Serpent, and Death* (Ottawa, National Gallery of Canada) of 1510–1512. See R. A. Koch, *Hans Baldung Grien: Eve, the Serpent, and Death* (Ottawa, 1974), pp. 5–6, 24–29.

94. ORNAMENT WITH TWO GENII RIDING ON TWO CHIMERAS

1544; monogram
Engraving
3.4 × 10 cm
B. 236; Pauli, *Hans Sebald Beham*, nr. 241; Hollstein, III: p. 143
Lent by the Fine Arts Museums of San Francisco, Achenbach Foundation for Graphic Arts

This engraving is typical of the many small decorative prints that Beham produced for use by other artists.[1] Like Flötner, Solis, and Amman, Beham created designs for medals (cat. nr. 79), columns and capitals, goblets and cups, and a variety of ornamental products. His compositions were copied by goldsmiths, plaquette makers, tinsmiths, ceramists, furniture makers, wood designers, and other craftsmen. The narrow, horizontal format of this particular print was most appropriate for furniture decorations and architectural friezes.[2]

Engravings and, more often, woodcuts were also glued directly on furniture and on walls.[3] During the early 1520s, Beham devised large-scale ornamental patterns, such as tendrils with pomegranates, for use as wallpaper.[4] Multiple impressions of a single woodcut, when placed side by side, formed a continuous, repeating design that decorated an entire room. Beham's *Great Garland* consisted of eight separate woodblocks that could be arranged in various combinations, without repetition, to create a frieze measuring 560 by 28 cm.[5]

1. B. 223–253; Geisberg, nrs. 332–345, 349.
2. See Beham's *Fountain of Youth* (cat. nr. 85). A lead plaquette with a triumphal procession, modeled after two of Beham's engravings, is in Berlin (Kunstgewerbemuseum). See Pechstein, *Bronzen und Plaketten*, nr. 189.
3. Appuhn and von Heusinger, *Riesenholzschnitte und Papiertapeten der Renaissance*, esp. pp. 11–25, 87–103; see cat. nr. 81.
4. Ibid., pp. 18–20, figs. 10–11.
5. Ibid., pp. 20–22, fig. 12; Geisberg, nrs. 338–345.

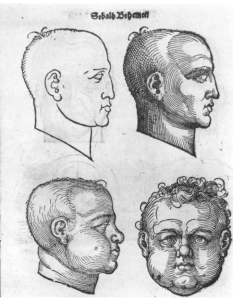

95. DAS KUNST UND LERE BÜCHLIN SEBALDEN BEHEMS. MALEN VND REISSEN ZU LERNEN NACH RECHTER PROPORTION MASS VND AUSSTEYLUNG DES CIRCKELS. ANGEHNDEN MALERN VND KUNSTBAREN WERCKLEUTEN DIENLICH (Frankfurt: Christian Egenolff, 1552)

B. 140–158; Pauli, *Hans Sebald Beham*, nrs. 1270–1289; Hollstein, III: p. 267
Lent by the New York Public Library, Spencer Collection, Astor, Lenox and Tilden Foundations

Beham's *Art and Instruction Manual for Learning Painting and Drawing, According to Proper Proportion, Measures, and Division by the Compass, Useful for Young Painters and Artisans* contains a very brief text, didactic diagrams, and illustrative woodcuts.[1] On page A i, the table of contents lists the four principal chapters: the use of the compass and ruler, the correct method of drawing human faces using predrawn squares, how to do the same without a grid, and the proper techniques for representing horses.

The thirteen-page section on horses is the most thoroughly planned part of the treatise. It originally appeared separately under the title *Dises buchlein zeyget an und lernt ein mass oder proporcion der Ross*, published in Nuremberg by Hieronymus Andreae in 1528.[2] Most of Beham's ideas were borrowed from Dürer's theoretical writings, including the as yet unpublished *Art of Measurement* (cat. nr. 31), which first appeared in October 1528. The Nuremberg city council accused Beham of using Dürer's writings and ordered Beham and Andreae not to publish any further copies of the treatise and not to sell those copies already printed.[3]

Although the series of civic actions prevented Beham from printing a large number of copies of the treatise on horses, the artist subsequently included much of the treatise in his *Art and Instruc-*

tion Manual. This volume first appeared in 1546. The exhibited copy is the second edition. Egenolff printed a third edition in 1557, and his heirs published further versions in 1565, 1566, 1582, 1584, 1594, and 1605. The arrangement of the woodcuts varies slightly between the 1552 and 1565 editions.[4]

---

1. A partial translation of the 1565 edition of this treatise is published in *The Illustrated Bartsch*, 15: pp. 219–272.
2. *Nuremberg: Meister um Dürer*, nr. 140.
3. "Iheronimus [Andreae], formschneidern, und Sebald Behem, malern, soll man verpieten, nichts der proporcion halben ausgeen zu lassen, pis das exemplar, vom Dürer gemacht, ausganngen unnd gefertigt ist, bey straff eins erbern rats, die man gegen iren leib und gütern furnemen würd." Hampe, *Nürnberger Ratsverlässe* I: nr. 1621 (22 July 1528); also see nrs. 1629 (26 August), 1631 (31 August), 1632 (1 September), 1633 (1 September), 1634 (2 September).
4. The editions are listed in Hollstein, III: p. 267.

Barthel Beham, younger brother of Hans Sebald, was a painter and a printmaker.[1] He was born in Nuremberg in 1502, a date verified by Ludwig Neufahrer's 1531 portrait medal of Barthel at age 29.[2] Little is known about his training. Although there is no firm evidence to prove that Dürer was his teacher, Dürer's art and technical skills greatly influenced Barthel's work throughout the 1520s. Barthel may also have studied briefly with his brother.

Along with Hans Sebald and Georg Pencz, Barthel was expelled from Nuremberg on 26 January 1525 because of his atheistic views.[3] At the urging of Melchior Pfinzing, provost of St. Sebaldus, Barthel was permitted to return to Nuremberg by 26 November. In 1527 Barthel permanently left the city. It is perhaps ironic that Barthel moved to Munich to become the court painter for Ludwig X and, later, Wilhelm IV, dukes of Bavaria, who were among the staunchest Catholic princes in Germany. For Wilhelm IV, Barthel painted several religious pictures, notably the *Miracle of the Cross* of 1530 (Munich, Alte Pinakothek).[4] Barthel soon became one of Germany's most important portrait painters. Baldass credited Barthel with introducing the hip-length portrait, seen here in the *Portrait of a Nobleman* (cat. nr. 102), into German painting.[5]

While at the Bavarian court, Barthel developed a strong interest in Italian art and classical motifs. According to Neudörfer, Wilhelm IV sent Barthel to Italy at court expense.[6] The trip south was probably made in 1536. Sandrart added that Barthel lived in Rome and Bologna, where he reportedly worked with Marcantonio Raimondi.[7] Sandrart claimed that several of Barthel's prints were published under Raimondi's name. Barthel remained in Italy until his death in 1540.

---

1. G. Pauli, "Beham, Barthel," in Thieme-Becker (Leipzig, 1909), 3: pp. 191–193; Pauli, *Barthel Beham*; H. Röttinger, *Die Holzschnitte Barthel Behams*; *Nuremberg: Meister um Dürer*, pp. 64–72, nrs. 30–68; Zschelletzschky, *Die 'Drei gottlosen Maler' von Nürnberg*. A thorough critical monograph on Beham is needed.
2. P. Grotemeyer, *'Da ich het die gestalt': Deutsche Bildnismedaillen des 16. Jahrhunderts*, fig. 60; also in Zschelletzschky, *Die 'Drei gottlosen Maler' von Nürnberg*, fig. 4.
3. See Section 3 above and Zschelletzschky, *Die 'Drei gottlosen Maler' von Nürnberg*, pp. 31–55, 65 (return to Nuremberg).
4. *Alte Pinakothek München Katalog II: Altdeutsche Malerei* (Munich, 1963), pp. 206–207.
5. Von Baldass, "Zur Bildniskunst der Dürerschule, II. Die Bildniskunst des Jörg Pencz und Bartel Beham," p. 258.
6. Neudörfer, *Nachrichten von Künstlern*, p. 138.
7. Peltzer, ed., *Sandrarts Academie*, p. 77.

96. PORTRAIT OF LEONHARD VON ECK

1527; monogram
Engraving: first of two states
10.8 and 8 cm
B. 64; Pauli, *Barthel Beham*, nr. 94; Hollstein, II:
p. 232
Lent by the Nelson-Atkins Museum of Art,
Kansas City, Missouri (Gift of Mr. Robert B.
Fizzell)

Shortly after his arrival at the Bavarian court in
Munich, Barthel Beham made three portraits of
Leonhard von Eck (or Egkh; 1480–1550), the
brilliant chancellor and humanist.[1] A single
drawing, now lost, served as the basis for Barthel's painting of von Eck, now in New York
(Metropolitan Museum of Art), and two very
different states of the same engraving.[2] Dürer's
influence upon Beham is clearly seen in the engraving. Beham employed the same strong outlining of the features, strong chiaroscuro contrasts to enhance the facial modeling, emphasis
on the textures and details of the clothing, and
the hatched background that can be found in
Dürer's *Portrait of Friedrich the Wise* (cat. nr. 29).
An important distinction between their works
is, however, already evident in Beham's engraving. His five printed and many painted portraits
are characterized by a coolness or reserve.[3]
Beham rarely incorporated an understanding of
the sitter's personality, a trait that is an integral
part of Dürer's better portraits of the 1520s.

The exhibited print is the first state of the engraving. In the same year, Beham radically reworked the copper plate. He dressed von Eck in
a fur coat and placed a hat over his cap. The coat
obscures part of his monogram, while the hat
covered the words "VON EGKH" and "AET" in
the inscription. These words were rewritten
underneath "LEONHART" and "XXXXVII."
However, in spite of scraping the plate to remove the center of the original inscription, the
letters "VO" and "T" are still legible.

1. Von Eck studied at Ingolstadt and in Siena before
returning to Germany to become the teacher and,
from 1512, advisor to Wilhelm IV. He was appointed
chancellor in 1519. He was a staunch supporter of Catholicism and the independence of Bavaria from both
church and imperial influences. He is credited with establishing the foundation for Bavaria's emergence as
the pre-eminent Roman Catholic power in Germany
later in the sixteenth century. See *Neue Deutsche Biographie* (Berlin, 1959), 4: pp. 277–279.

2. H. Wehle and M. Salinger, *Metropolitan Museum of
Art, a Catalogue of Early Flemish, Dutch, and German
Painting* (New York, 1947), pp. 191–193. The painting
is identical to the exhibited print except that it is a half-
length, not bust, portrait and the orientation of the
portrait has been reversed in the print. The prints are
inscribed "LEONHART VON EGKH AET XXXXVII"
(Leonhard von Eck at age 47). See below for comments
on the second state of this print.

3. Leonhard von Eck is the first of his portrait engravings. In 1531 he made portraits of Charles V (cat.
nr. 100) and Ferdinand I. He also depicted Ludwig X
of Bavaria (ca. 1532) and Erasmus Baldermann (1535),
who was an imperial advisor in Nuremberg. See Hollstein, II: pp. 228–232.

97. BATTLE FOR THE BANNER

ca. 1528–1530
Engraving
6.5 × 28.9 cm
B. 18; Pauli, *Barthel Beham*, nr. 26; Hollstein, II: p. 192
Lent by the Bowdoin College Museum of Art, Brunswick, Maine

Following his departure from Nuremberg, Beham became increasingly interested in Italian and classical art. Around 1528 he engraved the *Battle for the Banner*, the *Battle of Eighteen Nude Men*, and *Titus Gracchus*, each of which resembles a Roman frieze or sarcophagus filled with violently twisted nude men engaged in mortal combat.[1] Beham was concerned with the individual gestures, the presentation of the developed anatomies, and the dramatic groupings of his combatants. The actual subject, if there was one, and the allegiances of the warriors in the *Battle for the Banner* are unknown.

Beham's three engravings belong to the tradition of classical battle scenes that became popular in the decades after Antonio Pollaiuolo's famous *Battle of the Nudes* engraving (ca. 1470).[2] Beham's specific sources were prints after Michelangelo's *Battle of Cascina* cartoon (1504–1505).[3] His tightly muscled figures, the exaggerated gestures, and the flame-like hair are very similar to Marcantonio Raimondi's *The Climbers* of 1510, which depicts three of Michelangelo's nude men.[4] Beham's engraving is, however, an original response to the Italian models rather than a simple pastiche.

Beham's battle prints were used as designs for armor decoration. The *Battle for the Banner* and his *Rape of Helen* can be found engraved on breastplates made by Valentin Siebenbürger in the 1530s.[5]

1. B. 16 and 17.
2. Levenson, Oberhuber, and Sheehan, *Early Italian Engravings*, nr. 13.
3. C. de Tolnay, *The Youth of Michelangelo* (Princeton, 1943), pp. 209–219.
4. Shoemaker and Broun, *The Engravings of Marcantonio Raimondi*, nr. 19.
5. W. Boeheim, "Nürnberger Waffenschmiede und ihre Werke in den Kaiserlichen und in anderen Sammlungen," *JKSAK* 16 (1895): 364–399, esp. 376–377, fig. 8, pl. XLIV (armor of Konrad von Bemelberg of ca. 1533 with the *Rape of Helen* [B. 89] engraved onto the armor by Albrecht Glockendon).

98. VIRGIN AND CHILD BY THE WINDOW

ca. 1529
Engraving
10.6 × 8.5 cm (plate)
B. 8; Pauli, *Barthel Beham*, nr. 9; Hollstein, II: p. 180
Lent by the New York Public Library, Prints Division, Astor, Lenox and Tilden Foundations

This engraving is a good example of how Barthel blended his Nuremberg training with his interest in Italian art. The basic setting of a woman seated beside a large window derives from Marcantonio Raimondi's *Pensive Woman* (after Raphael or Parmigianino).[1] Raimondi's woman is replaced by the Virgin, now an Italian matron, and the Christ Child. In Raimondi's print, the interest in lighting effects was secondary. For Beham, the light was his real subject.[2] The warm sunlight suffuses the chamber. It models the furniture, the walls, and the figures. The subtle

tonal contrasts may not be as varied or as rich as in Dürer's *St. Jerome in His Study* (cat. nr. 18), yet Beham learned his virtuoso technique from studying and imitating Dürer's prints. Of all Dürer's pupils and followers, Barthel Beham best understood Dürer's style.

There are two drawings after this print by a follower of Beham in Berlin (Kupferstichkabinett).[3]

1. *The Illustrated Bartsch*, 27: nr. 460. The Virgin is generally patterned after women in other Raimondi prints.
2. Similar interest in lighting effects and contrasts can be seen in many of Barthel's prints, including the *Virgin and Child with a Vase* (B. 6; Pauli, *Barthel Beham*, nr. 7; Hollstein, II: p. 178).
3. Bock, *Staatliche Museen zu Berlin*, I: p. 12, nrs. 336, 4768.

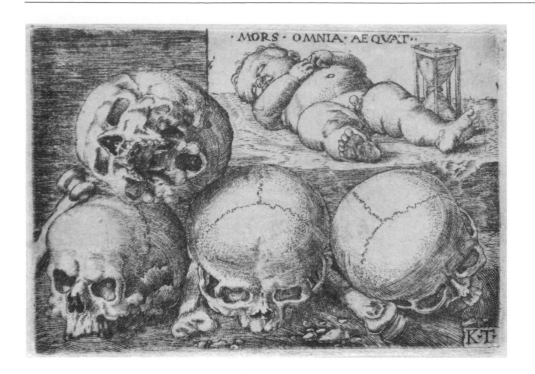

99. SLEEPING CHILD WITH FOUR SKULLS

ca. 1530 (late sixteenth century); monogram K.T.
Engraving
5.4 × 7.6 cm
B. 28; Pauli, *Barthel Beham*, nr. 36; Hollstein, II: p. 197
Lent by the Pennsylvania Academy of the Fine Arts, Philadelphia, John S. Philips Collection

"MORS OMNIA AEQVAT" (death equalizes everything) reads the inscription above the sleeping child. As the infant dozes, time, here symbolized by the hourglass, passes and the child comes inexorably closer to death. The four skulls are posed at what appears to be the door of a charnel house. The anonymity of the skulls reinforces the central message that death equalizes the rich and poor and the young and old alike. Beham's print lacks any of the connotations of sloth or hedonism or melancholy that Janson has identified in Italian and other Northern European versions of this theme.[1]

Death is a common subject in Barthel's prints, as is evident in his *Bookplate of Hieronymus Baumgartner* (cat. nr. 101) and *Death and Three Nude Women* (copy by Hans Sebald Beham, cat. nr. 91). Beham first experimented with the theme of the child and a skull in 1525, when he made an engraving of a putto reclining upon a skull.[2] He also devised other prints just of the skull, a sleeping child with three skulls, and the Virgin and Child with a skull and an hourglass.[3] All refer to the passing of and the brevity of time.

Barthel's print enjoyed tremendous popularity. Pauli has identified at least fifteen copies after the *Sleeping Child with Four Skulls*.[4] The exhibited print is a reversed copy of Barthel's engraving; the inscription has been properly ori-

ented. It is by monogramist K.T., whom Nagler has determined was a German engraver active at the end of the sixteenth century.[5] No other works by this master are known.

1. H. W. Janson, "The Putto with the Death's Head," *Art Bulletin* 19 (1937): 423–449, esp. 437–440; G. de Tervarent, *Attributs et Symboles dans l'Art Profane, 1450–1600* (Geneva, 1959), cols. 373–375; Zschelletzschky, *Die 'Drei gottlosen Maler' von Nürnberg*, pp. 183–187.
2. B. 31; Pauli, *Barthel Beham*, nr. 37.
3. Pauli, *Barthel Beham*, nr. 34 (skull); B. 27 and Pauli, *Barthel Beham*, nr. 35 (*Child with Three Skulls*); B. 5 and Pauli, nr. 6 (*Virgin and Child with a Skull*).
4. Pauli, *Barthel Beham*, nr. 36.
5. G. K. Nagler, *Die Monogrammisten* (1858–1920; reprint: Nieuwkoop, 1966), 4: nr. 845.

HIERONYMVS·BAVMGARTNERSSQ·

101. BOOKPLATE OF HIERONYMUS BAUMGARTNER

1530s
Engraving
8.6 × 6.9 cm (plate)
B. 57; Pauli, *Barthel Beham*, nr. 89; Hollstein, II: p. 227
Lent by the National Gallery of Art, Washington, Rosenwald Collection, 1948

Although printed portraits and coats of arms were occasionally used to mark the ownership of a book, many humanists and wealthy merchants had special bookplates made. For instance, Dürer designed bookplates for Pirckheimer and Hieronymus Ebner of Nuremberg.[1] Beham's bookplate for Hieronymus Baumgartner (1498–1565), a Nuremberg patrician and senator, conforms to a basic type.[2] In the center is Baumgartner's coat of arms. The surrounding inscription is written in Latin, Hebrew, and Greek, the three languages of the scholar.[3] These three languages were used in Pirckheimer's bookplate as well. Baumgartner's motto refers to the brevity of life and the passing of time. This *memento mori* image is reinforced by the addition of an hourglass, a clock, a skull, and a shield struck with stars, an allusion perhaps to the vanity of temporal honors.

Beham's bookplate is meticulously designed and executed. The elaborate coat of arms and secondary symbols are carefully drawn and shaded. This contrasts with the cruder woodcut bookplates by Dürer.

The copper plate for this print is probably still extant. In 1896 it was in the collection of Ilse Warnecke in Germany.[4]

1. Meder, nrs. 280, 282. Solis's bookplate of Jacob Muffel is in cat. nr. 47.
2. For a biography of Baumgartner (Paumgartner), see the comments for Joachim Deschler's portrait medal of the patrician (cat. nr. 152).
3. The Latin inscription reads: "Stat sua qui[s]q[ue] dies, breve & irreparabile tempus," or, roughly translated, "Each of his days is fixed, his time is short and irretrievable."
4. E. Doepler the Younger, "Baumgartners Ex-Libris von Barthel Beham," *Zeitschrift für Bücherzeichen, Bibliothekenkunde und Gelehrtengeschichte* 6 (1896): 101–102. The specific city is not given.

PROGENIES·DIVVM·QVINTVS·SIC·CAROLVS·ILLE
IMPERII·CAESAR·LVMINA·ET·ORA·TVLIT
AET · SVAE · XXXI
ANN · M·D· XXXI

100. PORTRAIT OF EMPEROR CHARLES V

1531; monogram
Engraving: fourth of four states
20.8 × 13.8 cm (plate)
B. 60; Pauli, *Barthel Beham*, nr. 90; Hollstein, II: p. 228
Lent by the Nelson-Atkins Museum of Art, Kansas City, Missouri

On 10 June 1530, Emperor Charles V (1500–1558) and his brother, Ferdinand I (1503–1564), visited Munich.[1] On this occasion Barthel made portrait sketches, now lost, that served as the designs for his 1531 engraved portraits of the two nobles. Although the portrait of Ferdinand is slightly smaller in size, the two prints were conceived and probably sold as a pair to commemorate the election of Ferdinand in 1531 as the king of the Romans, the heir to the imperial throne.[2] Both are bust-length portraits with

hatched backgrounds and elaborate stone tablets inscribed with their names, titles, ages, and the date 1531. When the prints are set side by side, the brothers are arranged to face each other. Both men wear hats, the simplified form of the collar of the Order of the Golden Fleece, and rich robes.

In comparison with the *Portrait of Leonhard von Eck* (cat. nr. 96), Beham's modifications to the *Charles V* plate were minor and primarily restricted to reinforcing the hatchings of the clothes or the background. Only in the fourth state of the print was the artist's monogram added.

1. Their entry is recorded in a woodcut by Hans Sebald Beham; see Geisberg, nrs. 292–296.
2. This print measures 20.5 × 13.1 cm; see B. 61, Pauli, *Barthel Beham*, nr. 91, Hollstein, II: p. 229; Zschelletzschky, *Die 'Drei gottlosen Maler' von Nürnberg*, pp. 94–95. Both prints were copied by Agostino Veneziano (Musi); see *The Illustrated Bartsch*, 27: nrs. 499–500. On Ferdinand, see cat. nr. 79.

102. PORTRAIT OF A NOBLEMAN

1535–1540
Painting: oil on canvas (transferred from panel)
62.7 × 48.3 cm
Lent by the National Gallery of Canada (Galerie Nationale du Canada), Ottawa

Barthel Beham's success at the Bavarian court in Munich was due largely to his talents as a portraitist.[1] His best portraits, including those of Ludwig X (1530), Wilhelm IV (1533), and Ottheinrich (1535) in Munich (Alte Pinakothek), share a meticulous attention to details and materials. Beham captured the dignity, if not always the humanity, of his sitters. Beham's style largely derived from his assimilation of Dürer's late portraits, such as those of Jakob Muffel and Hieronymus Holzschuher of 1526.[2]

After his arrival in Munich in 1527, Beham blended his Nuremberg training with the innovations of contemporary Italian painting. The *Portrait of a Nobleman*, executed either in Munich or during the last years of his life in Bologna or Rome, is a good example of Beham's fusion of styles.[3] The identity of the sitter is unknown other than he appears to be German and he is Catholic since he wears a pendant crucifix adorned with pearls. Beham painted the gentleman in a hip-length view, a feature that was found only in Italian art until Beham introduced it into Germany in 1527 in his *Portrait of Leonhard von Eck* (New York, Metropolitan Museum of Art).[4] He used this format frequently in his subsequent portraits. It has the advantage of enhancing the monumentality and sense of motion through the actions of the arms.

1. A. L. Mayer, "Barthel Beham als Bildnismaler," *Pantheon* 11 (1933): 1–4; von Baldass, "Zur Bildniskunst der Dürerschule, II. Die Bildniskunst des Jörg Pencz und Bartel Beham," pp. 258–259; esp. Löcher, "Studien zur oberdeutschen Bildnismalerei des 16. Jahrhunderts," pp. 50–58, and on his influence upon Hans Schöpfer the Elder and Hans Mielich, see pp. 58–76.
2. Both paintings are in Berlin (Staatliche Museen). See Anzelewsky, *Dürer*, nrs. 178–179. For a comparison of Dürer's *Hieronymus Holzschuher* and Beham's *Ottheinrich*, see O. Benesch, *La Peinture Allemande—De Dürer à Holbein* (Geneva, 1966), color plates on pp. 138–139.
3. The painting has been attributed to Hans Holbein the Younger and Georg Pencz, among others, in the past. See C. L. Kuhn, *A Catalogue of German Paintings of the Middle Ages and Renaissance in American Collections* (Cambridge, Mass., 1936), nr. 219; Gmelin, "Georg Pencz als Maler," nr. 92.
4. Wehle and Salinger, *A Catalogue of Early Flemish, Dutch, and German Paintings*, pp. 191–193. On Beham's introduction of the hip-length portrait, see Baldass, "Zur Bildniskunst der Dürerschule, II. Die Bildniskunst des Jörg Pencz und Bartel Beham," p. 258. This format was used by Titian, Pontormo, and others during the 1520s.

Also see Hans Sebald Beham's copies after Barthel Beham's *Death and Three Nude Women* (cat. nr. 91) and *Adam and Eve* (cat. nr. 93).

Georg Pencz

Georg Pencz was Nuremberg's leading painter and printmaker during the second quarter of the sixteenth century.[1] He was born around 1500, probably in Breslau. Although Pencz did not become a Nuremberg citizen until 8 August 1523, he may have been a member of Dürer's workshop prior to 1521. Because of his association with Dürer, Pencz participated in the redecoration of the great hall of the Nuremberg Rathaus between 1521 and late 1522.[2] In January 1525 Pencz, along with the Beham brothers, was expelled from Nuremberg because of his lack of orthodox religious convictions.[3] After settling briefly at Windsheim, he returned to Nuremberg.

Very little is known about his artistic activities during the 1520s. Friedländer and other scholars have claimed that Pencz was the Master I. B., presumably I[J]örg Bentz, a printmaker influenced by Dürer and working in Nuremberg during this decade.[4] Since Pencz's own signed prints date only from the 1530s and Master I. B.'s late prints date to 1529, it is tempting to identify Master I. B. as the youthful Pencz. Unfortunately, because serious stylistic differences exist between the two corpora of works the association is highly questionable.[5] The lack of early paintings by Pencz offers no solution to this problem.

Pencz's subsequent career is better documented. He is recorded back in Nuremberg in January 1530. Paintings and prints (cat. nr. 103) of his are known dating from 1531, and on 31 May 1532, Pencz was appointed the official Nuremberg city painter with an annual salary of 10 gulden.[6] It was certainly in his capacity as city painter that Pencz made replicas of Dürer's *Emperors Charlemagne and Sigismund*, then in the Rathaus, for Johann Friedrich (see cat. nr. 110), and of Cranach's *Portrait of Luther* (1533).[7] In 1534 Pencz collaborated with Peter Flötner in the decoration of the garden room of the Hirschvogelhaus.[8] Inspired by Giulio Romano, whose paintings Pencz had studied during a trip to Mantua in about 1529, he made the *Fall of Phaeton*, an illusionistic ceiling painting (fig. 33).

Pencz returned to Italy sometime between 19 April 1539, when his civic salary was raised to 24 gulden per year, and 6 November 1540.[9] Besides visiting Mantua, Venice, and Ferrara, Pencz stayed in Rome, where he made careful drawings and prints after Michelangelo, Raphael, Polidoro da Caravaggio, and Romano. Romano's influence is evident in Pencz's *Siege of Carthage* (cat. nr. 107) and the *Triumphs of Petrarch* (cat. nr. 108). Pencz's *The Deluge* drawing in Washington (National Gallery) is a study after Michelangelo's famous scene on the ceiling of the Sistine Chapel (fig. 57).[10]

Pencz was back in Nuremberg by 6 November 1540 at the latest and became immediately involved in the preparations for the long-awaited visit of Emperor Charles V on 16 February 1541. Pencz, perhaps with the help of Flötner, designed the great triumphal arch honoring the emperor (fig. 32).[11] Among the city's gifts to Charles was Pencz's painting of the castle in Ghent in which the prince had been born in 1500.[12] Other civic projects from this period include a portrait of Cardinal Nicolas Granvella, who stopped in Nuremberg in February 1543,

and, in the same year, a relief plan of Nuremberg that Pencz made with sculptor Sebald Beck (Peck).[13]

By the mid-1540s Pencz had achieved considerable fame as a portraitist (see cat. nrs. 110 and 111).[14] This talent led to his appointment as the court painter to Albrecht, duke of Prussia, on 5 September 1550. Pencz died in Leipzig on 17 October 1550 while en route to his new post at Königsberg (Kaliningrad).[15]

1. The literature on Pencz is extensive. For the following, I have relied primarily upon Neudörfer, *Nachrichten von Künstlern*, p. 137; Peltzer, ed., *Sandrarts Academie*, pp. 78, 318, 320; A. Kurzwelly, *Forschungen zu Georg Pencz*; H. Röttinger, *Die Holzschnitte des Georg Pencz*; *Nuremberg: Meister um Dürer*, pp. 151–164, nrs. 253–287; Gmelin, "Georg Pencz als Maler," pp. 49–126, esp. 49–52, 115–122; Zschelletzschky, *Die 'Drei gottlosen Maler' von Nürnberg*; D. Landau, *Catalogo completo dell' opera grafica di Georg Pencz*.

2. See Section 6 A.

3. See Section 3 C.

4. M. J. Friedländer, "Georg Pentz, Jörg Bentz, der Meister IB," *Repertorium für Kunstwissenschaft* 20 (1897): 130–132.

5. Landau, *Pencz*, pp. 1off., discusses the problems with this identification.

6. Gmelin, "Georg Pencz als Maler," pp. 50, 73 (nr. 1), Pencz's *Judith* (Munich, Alte Pinakothek). Gmelin (pp. 50–61) discusses Pencz's early style and several paintings that may date to the 1520s.

7. Ibid., pp. 88 (nrs. 27–28), 99–100 (nr. 48, *Luther* in the North Carolina Museum of Art in Raleigh).

8. See Section 6 A for a discussion of this and other decorative cycles by Pencz. Pencz and Flötner worked together on other projects, notably the *Silver Altar* made in 1535–1536 for King Sigismund's chapel in Cracow Cathedral; see Gmelin, "Georg Pencz als Maler," pp. 76–79 (nr. 6); Kohlhaussen, *Nürnberger Goldschmiedekunst*, nr. 458; the comments in Section 6 E.

9. Landau, *Pencz*, pp. 42, 44; also see the comments for the catalogue entries cited below.

10. Geissler, *Zeichnung in Deutschland*, I: pp. 38–39, nr. A35. In 1546 Pencz made the *Romulus and Remus* drawing now in Kansas City (Nelson-Atkins Museum of Art), which may reflect some model he had seen when in Rome. This drawing was once in the Nuremberg collection of Paulus Praun; see Kurzwelly, *Pencz*, p. 92, nr. 21. For a brief discussion of this sketch, see T. D. Kaufmann, *Drawings from the Holy Roman Empire, 1540–1680: A Selection from North American Collections*, nr. 6.

11. See Section 6 A.

12. Gmelin, "Georg Pencz als Maler," p. 51.

13. Ibid.; Schnelbögl, *Dokumentie zur Nurnberger Kartographie*, p. 12.

14. For a good discussion of Pencz's portraits, see Gmelin, "Georg Pencz als Maler," pp. 69–72, 89–103 (nrs. 30–52); also see Section 6 A.

15. Gmelin, "Georg Pencz als Maler," pp. 51–53; Landau, *Pencz*, p. 74. Pencz's widow, Margarete, accused him of pawning certain works of silver that he was supposed to take to Königsberg. The Nuremberg city council settled the case "in view of his many sons, his great poverty, and the fact that he was a fine artist." The council censured Margarete for her behavior before and after Pencz's death. Margarete was the daughter of Michael Graf. I have found no evidence to support the often repeated claim that Pencz married Suzanna, Dürer's maid during his 1520–1521 Netherlandish trip.

57. Georg Pencz, *The Deluge* (after Michelangelo), drawing, 1539 or 1540, Washington, National Gallery of Art.

103. VENUS (from the SEVEN PLANETS)

1531
Woodcut
30.2 × 20.7 cm
Geisberg, nr. 990; Röttinger, *Pencz*, nr. 8
Lent by the Metropolitan Museum of Art, New York, The Elisha Whittelsey Collection, The Elisha Whittelsey Fund, 1957

Throughout the Renaissance, scholars and artists alike were fascinated by the influence of the seven planets upon the activities of mankind.[1] Each planet was thought to have direct effect upon humanity consistent with the character of the pagan deity for which it was named. Jupiter, king of the gods, held sway over kings, emperors, popes, and other leaders. Mars, the god of war, held dominion over soldiers; Saturn, over laborers; and Mercury, over men of science and art. Venus, as seen in the woodcut from Pencz's *Seven Planets* series, encouraged lovers and musicians.[2] The inscription at the top reads:

Venus children like to be gay
They prefer wooing to anything else on earth.
In a mere 365 days
I complete my entire circuit.[3]

Other factors influencing one's temperament and the degree of planetary dominance were the relationship of one's birth date to the planet's ascendance or descendance and the planet's position in the heavens relative to the constellations of stars.

Here, Venus is seated in her chariot above the world. She holds a blindfolded Cupid whose bow and arrow are poised. The wheels of the chariot are decorated with the zodiacal signs of Taurus and Libra. A pair of birds, probably doves, pulls the chariot. Below is a great garden of love, reminiscent of, though earlier than, Hans Sebald Beham's *Fountain of Youth* (cat. nr. 85) and *Feast of Herodias* (cat. nr. 82). Amorous couples are shown making music, strolling arm in arm, cavorting in the water, and drinking at a table.

Pencz's general source for *Venus* and the other planets was a set of Florentine engravings made about 1460.[4] For instance, the symbolic features of Venus's chariot are based upon the Italian print, but the actual design is Pencz's. None of Pencz's figures are directly copied from the engraving.

A complete impression of Pencz's *Venus* contains a long inscription at the bottom of the print. The text, which is similar to that on the Florentine engraving, reads

Venus is kind, cold, humid, feminine, and fortunate.
An oracle for [a symbol of] all women and
Effeminate men who occupy themselves with
Feminine things such as singers, lutenists, pipers,
Organ players, painters, suitors, adulterers, gluttons,
Drunkards and all sorts of unchaste people.
Also for [of] those who deal with pure and pleasant
Smelling things such as apothecaries and the like,
And those who deal with precious stones, jewelry,
Gems and ornaments appropriate to women and practice a pure trade.
Her art is medicine and music and all instruments that serve joy and pleasure.
Her sicknesses come from cold, damp, immoderate eating,
Drinking, unchaste activities and the like, usually
Affecting the secret parts and the genitals of both
Sexes, male and female, etc. She has Friday and Monday night.
Her colors on clothes are green, brown, liver-colored,
And some say white as well; on horses, bay and chestnut.
Her houses [mansions] in the zodiac are Taurus and Libra.
In the ascendant she is Pisces; in the descendant, Virgo.
At times of Venus it is propitious to travel across country,
Play chess, marry and take medicine.
It is not propitious to travel in ships.[5]

Pencz's *Seven Planets* enjoyed considerable popularity and were reproduced in various other media. For instance, Peter Flötner based his Mars and Venus plaquettes largely on Pencz's woodcuts.[6] When Emperor Charles V visited Nuremberg in 1541, the city council presented him with a silver goblet with raised figures of the seven planets and their effects.[7] This goblet, valued at 460 gulden and filled with another 2,000 gulden, is certainly after Pencz's series, especially since Pencz designed the other artistic decorations for this imperial visit (fig. 32).[8]

---

1. On this general subject, see J. Seznec, *Survival of the Pagan Gods*, ch. 2, esp. pp. 69–77. The planets were often associated with the liberal arts (cf. cat. nr. 109). In 1533 Martin Schaffner of Ulm painted a table with the planets, the liberal arts, the virtues, the colors, and the metals to illustrate their interconnections. According to Schaffner's scheme, which was relatively standard, the Sun governed Grammar; the Moon, Rhetoric; Mars, Arithmetic; Mercury, Logic; Jupiter, Geometry; Venus, Music; and Saturn, Astronomy. The table is in Kassel (Hessisches Museum); see D. Hay, ed., *The Age of the Renaissance* (New York, 1965), p. 208.
2. Geisberg, nrs. 990–996, for the entire series; the Sun (nr. 993) is inscribed with the name of publisher Albrecht Glockendon and the date 1 August 1531. Also see A. Hoyt, "Woodcuts of the Planets," *Bulletin of the Museum of Fine Arts* (Boston) 52 (1954): pp. 2–10, with an erroneous attribution to Barthel Beham; *Nuremberg: Meister um Dürer*, nr. 286; *Reformation in Nürnberg*, nr. 43; Zschelletzschky, *Die 'Drei gottlosen Maler' von Nürnberg*, pp. 134–168, esp. 157ff. This series was first attributed to Pencz by Röttinger; previously it had been ascribed to either Hans Sebald or Barthel Beham.
3. Translation by Hubert Heinem (University of Texas at Austin).
4. A. Hind, *Early Italian Engraving* (1938; reprint: Nendeln, 1970), I: pp. 77–83 (A. III 1–9). This series has been attributed to Baccio Baldini; see Levenson, Oberhuber, and Sheehan, *Early Italian Engravings*, pp. 15–16, figs. 2–8. Also see Zschelletzschky, *Die 'Drei gottlosen Maler' von Nürnberg*, fig. 110 (Venus).
5. Translation by Hubert Heinem (University of Texas at Austin).
6. Lange, *Flötner*, p. 124, nrs. 18–19, pl. VII. Only the chariots are copied after Pencz since the landscapes are quite different and without figures. Also copied in prints by Virgil Solis; see B. 163ff.
7. Christensen, "The Nuernberg City Council," p. 135.
8. See Section 6 for a discussion of Pencz's involvement with this event.

Venus kind sind frölich geren
Bulschafft liebt yhn fur als aufferen.

Inn .3 6 5. tagen gering
Ich meinen gantzen lauff verbring

Venus.

104A. SAMSON AND DELILAH

ca. 1531–1532; monogram
Engraving
4.8 × 7.7 cm
B. 28; Landau, *Pencz*, nr. 30
Lent by the Detroit Institute of Arts, Bequest of
Hal H. Smith

104B. SALOME PRESENTING THE HEAD OF JOHN THE BAPTIST

ca. 1531–1532; monogram
Engraving
4.7 × 7.6 cm
B. 29; Landau, *Pencz*, nr. 57
Lent by the Detroit Institute of Arts, Bequest of
Hal H. Smith

These two prints belong to a series of nine Old
Testament scenes illustrating the power of
women over men.[1] Ever since the fall of Adam
and Eve, women have been labeled as temptresses who, by virtue of their beauty or their
cunning, could make fools of even the wisest or
most powerful of men. Delilah used her wiles to
learn the secret of Samson's strength, his hair,
which she is shown trimming with a pair of
shears. Salome's dancing so impressed Herod
that he granted her a wish and was then com-
pelled, at her bidding, to order the execution of
John the Baptist. Women were not always seen
as evil temptresses, however. Bathsheba or Susanna were innocent victims of men's lust. Judith, on the other hand, was a heroine and
savior of the Israelites when she used her
charms to overcome Holofernes.

Pencz's prints were intended to warn man to
be the master of his own senses. In 1520–1521,
Pencz and others, using Dürer's designs,
painted the south wall of the great hall of the
Nuremberg Rathaus with scenes of the power of
women.[2] Just as Wolgemut's *Last Judgment* and
Pencz's *Calumny of Apelles* in this chamber admonished the lawyers and counsellors to be
truthful, the power-of-women roundels warned
the patricians, who used the hall for their
dances, to beware of feminine wiles. The popularity of these themes can be explained by the
voyeurism of the stories, for they illustrate licentious tales of incest, adultery, deceit, and feminine cunning.

1. The series consists of *Lot and his Daughters* (B. 20),
David and Bathsheba (B. 21), *Solomon Worshipping Idols*
(B. 22), *Judgment of Solomon* (B. 23), *Judith and Holofernes Dining* (B. 24), *Judith and her Servant with the Head
of Holofernes* (B. 25), *Susanna and the Elders* (B. 26 with a
second version as B. 27), and the two prints included
here. The story of the decapitation of John the Baptist
is often included with tales from the Old Testament.
Also see Pencz's *Virgil in a Basket* and *Virgil's Revenge*
(cat. nrs. 105A–B). On the subject of the power of
women, see J. Hutchinson, "The Housebook Master
and the Folly of the Wise Man," *Art Bulletin* 48 (1966):
97–107; M. Kahr, "Delilah," *Art Bulletin* 54 (1972):
282–299.
2. See Section 6 and Mende, *Rathaus*, I: pp. 245–
296, esp. nr. 273 (Dürer's drawing for the south wall
with medallions of David and Bathsheba, Samson and
Delilah, and Aristotle and Phyllis). The general position of these paintings can be seen in cat. nr. 213. The
designs of Pencz's prints are unrelated to the Rathaus
cycle.

105A. VIRGIL IN A BASKET

ca. 1541; monogram
Engraving
5.7 × 8.1 cm
B. 87; Landau, *Pencz*, nr. 94
Lent by the Art Institute of Chicago, Gift of Mr.
and Mrs. Potter Palmer, 1919.2313

105B. VIRGIL'S REVENGE

ca. 1541; monogram
Engraving
5.8 × 8.2 cm
B. 88; Landau, *Pencz*, nr. 95
Lent by the Art Institute of Chicago, Gift of Mr.
and Mrs. Potter Palmer, 1919.2314

Pencz's two engravings illustrate the "Lay of Virgil," a popular fable that probably originated in France in the first half of the fourteenth century.[1] According to the story, Virgil (70–19 B.C.), the famous Roman poet, had fallen deeply in love with the daughter of Emperor Augustus. Believing that she loved him in return, Virgil accepted her invitation to visit her one night in her tower room. On the appointed evening, the emperor's daughter lowered a basket to the poet; however, when she had hoisted Virgil halfway up to her window she stopped. She chided him and left him to be discovered by the citizens of Rome the next morning. Stung by the ridicule, Virgil exacted a just revenge. Throughout the Middle Ages he was thought to be a sorcerer, and so, according to the story, Virgil cast a spell over Rome that left the city without light for several days. Only by touching their torches to the private parts of the emperor's daughter could the citizens of Rome relight their lamps.

The story once again demonstrates the power of women over men.[2] Often the story appears in conjunction with the tales of Samson and Delilah, David and Bathsheba, Aristotle and Phyllis, or Judith and Holofernes.

The architectural setting of *Virgil in a Basket* with the foreground steps and round temple-like structure behind is modeled loosely upon Marcantonio Raimondi's *St. Paul Preaching in Athens* (after Raphael).[3] Pencz's print, in turn, was the source for Hans Sebald Beham's *Hercules Carrying the Columns of Gaza* (cat. nr. 92).

1. For a good discussion of the theme, see Olds, Williams, and Levin, *Images of Love and Death*, nr. 53A–B.
2. Also see Pencz's *Samson and Delilah* (cat. nr. 104A) and *Salome Presenting the Head of John the Baptist* (cat. nr. 104B) on the subject of the power of women.
3. *The Illustrated Bartsch*, 26: nr. 50; Shoemaker and Broun, *The Engravings of Marcantonio Raimondi*, nr. 47. This print was made between 1517 and 1520.

Ein yeder trag sein Joch dise zeit/ Und vberwinde sein vbel mit gedult.

Eins morgens gieng ich durch ein Wald/ Ob sie möchten den Jeger fellen. Jch wölt euch drucket wie ich wolt/
Es het geschneit vnd war grimm Kalt/ Jn dem hört ich ein Horen schellen. Das jr mich alzeit fliehen solt
Neben der strassen hört ich wispern Vnd auch jauchtze der Hunde hauffe/ Nach aller Hasen natur vnd art.
Etwas hind einem gestreuß laut zispern/ Anfiengen die Hasen zu lauffen Jetz so jr haltet widerpart
Jch gugt hin durch/sah das da sassen Hinab gen thal dem Jeger zů/ Vnd jr mein Meister worden seit/
Etwas in die zwey hundert Hasen/ Jch stůnd ein weil/ vnd in eim nů Erkenn ich erst mein groß torheit.

106. RABBITS CATCHING THE HUNTERS

1534–1535 (1550)
Woodcut: hand colored
25.4 × 39.3 cm (woodcut); 52.3 × 39.5 cm (sheet)
Röttinger, *Pencz*, nr. 40; Geisberg, nr. 1014; Landau, *Pencz*, nr. 153
Lent by the Museum of Fine Arts, Boston, Horatio Greenough Curtis Fund

This remarkable broadsheet is benignly titled *Everyone Should Bear His Yoke at This Time and Overcome His Misfortune with Patience.*[1] The accompanying woodcut, however, presents a disturbing and disorienting scene, for it is a gory reversal of the natural order of things. Hares, normally gentle timid forest creatures, have turned murderous, going busily and matter-of-factly about the task of butchering and preparing to eat two hunters and their hounds.

The woodcut was first made about 1534–1535. The text, which was added by Hans Sachs on 25 April 1550, relates how the poet was walking through the forest one cold morning when he encountered this bizarre scene. The hares had captured their traditional tormentors. After an interrogation and trial, the hunters and dogs were condemned to death.

The image and poem are classic examples of the world upside down, where the normal hierarchical relationships in nature or society are purposefully inverted.[2] In this case, the usual associations of man versus animal and animal versus animal have been reversed so that the hunters become the hunted. Although images of the world upside down existed in antiquity, their popularity expanded with the development of the print in the fifteenth and, especially, sixteenth centuries.

These images were frequently metaphors for human social relations. The hares symbolized the citizens oppressed by the laws and customs of the day. The text of this print tells how the hares came together to avenge themselves. The final lines read in translation:

It is true, as Seneca says,
That whatever man practices great
Tyranny, levies high taxes and
Exploits his people,
Thinking to oppress his subjects
So that they fear and respect his person,
Must himself fear many of them.
And if he should overdo it
His actions will perhaps be rewarded
With violence . . .[3]

While the specific reasons for this revolt are unstated, it may refer to the increased taxes and suppression of rights of the peasants following the 1525 rebellion.[4]

1. Röttinger, *Die Bilderbogen des Hans Sachs*, nr. 3296; Nuremberg: *Die Welt des Hans Sachs*, nr. 166; Zschelletzschky, *Die 'Drei gottlosen Maler' von Nürnberg*, pp. 354–358.
2. On this topic, see D. Kunzle, "Bruegel's Proverbs, Painting, and the World Upside Down," *Art Bulletin* 59 (1977): 197–202, and "The World Upside Down: Iconography of a European Broadsheet Type," in *Reversible World*, ed. B. Babcock (Ithaca, 1978), pp. 39–94; Scribner, *For the Sake of Simple Folk*, pp. 148–189. Several examples can be found in the paintings of Hieronymus Bosch and Pieter Bruegel the Elder.
3. The translation is by Professor Hubert Heinem (University of Texas at Austin).
4. See Zschelletzschky, *Die 'Drei gottlosen Maler' von Nürnberg*, p. 356, for the social context of the peasants.

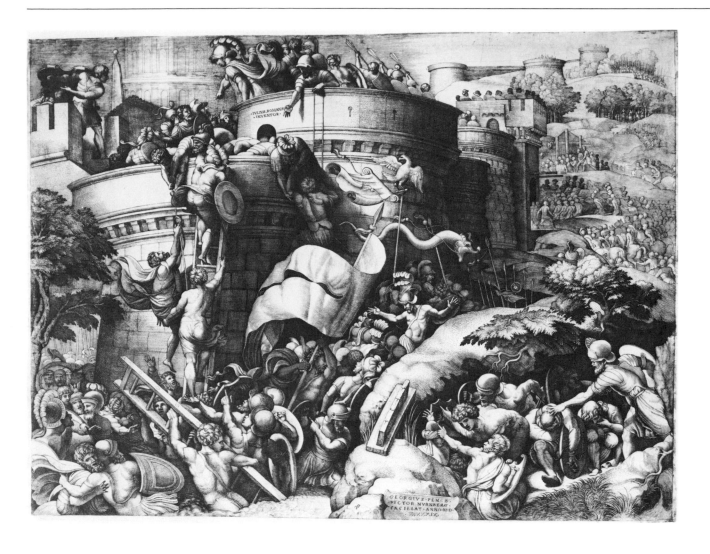

107. THE SIEGE OF CARTHAGE

1539; monogram and inscribed: GEORGIVS
PENCZ PICTOR NVRNBERG FACIEBAT
ANNO M.D. XXXIX (and) IVLIS ROMANS
INVENTOR
Engraving: second of six states
41.8 × 60.3 cm
B. 86; Landau, *Pencz*, nr. 93
Lent by the New York Public Library, Prints Division, Astor, Lenox and Tilden Foundations

Sometime between 19 April 1539 and November
1540, Pencz returned to Italy. He stopped in
Mantua and Rome, where he made drawings of
Michelangelo's *The Deluge* (fig. 57) and one of the
prophets from the Sistine Chapel, as well as
Raphael's frescoes in the Stanza della Segnatura.[1] Our knowledge of his visit to Mantua is
based largely upon *The Siege of Carthage* engraving of 1539 since it is a copy of a composition by
Giulio Romano. Between 1531 and 1533, Romano and his assistant Gianfrancesco Penni designed the twenty-two–piece *History of Scipio*
tapestries for Francis I, king of France.[2] Romano's patron Federico Gonzaga, duke of
Mantua, served as the king's agent and was responsible for the selection of the designers. The
small tapestry cartoons were sent via Fontainebleau to weaver Marc Crétif in Brussels.
The tapestries were completed by 12 August

1535, the date of the final payment. These sumptuous weavings remained in the French royal
collection until 1797, when they were intentionally burned to recover the precious gold and
silver woven into the fabric.

While Pencz was in Mantua, he had access to
several of the preparatory drawings for the *Siege
of Carthage*, the fourth event in the cycle. The
scene depicted is the attack of Carthago Nova by
the Roman troops of Scipio Africanus (236–ca.
184 B.C.) in 210 B.C., one of the climactic events
of the Second Punic War (218–201 B.C.). Two
drawings attributed by some critics to Romano
and others to Penni are in Paris (Louvre).[3] Although both illustrate the same event, one
drawing is much more spontaneous, more
vibrant than the drier, somewhat more detailed
second sketch. Pencz's engraving was probably
made from this second drawing since it matches
it detail for detail.

The *Siege of Carthage* was published in Italy
and the plate seems to have remained in Rome
until the sixth, and last, edition was printed by
Carlo Losi in 1773.[4] The first edition includes
Pencz's inscription. The attribution to Romano
was added in the second edition, exhibited here.
Antonio Salamanca (active 1530 to ca. 1562) published a third edition in Rome.

1. *The Deluge* (Washington, National Gallery of Art)
is in poor condition. See Geissler, ed., *Zeichnung in*

Deutschland, I: nr. A 35. Geissler mentions that an unpublished Apostle drawing by Pencz is in a private collection in Hannover. Also see K. T. Parker, "Georg
Pencz(?)—Copy of the Octagon of the Ceiling of the
Stanza della Segnatura—Oxford, Ashmolean Museum," *Old Master Drawings* 14 (1939–1940): 19–20. On
the influence of Michelangelo and Giulio Romano on
Pencz's art, see Section 6. Selective borrowings of figures by Michelangelo, Raphael, and Romano can be
found in many of Pencz's prints, as, for instance, in
the *Triumph of Death* (cat. nr. 108).

2. The following is based upon Hartt, *Giulio Romano*, I: pp. 227–231, II: figs. 474–483; esp. *Jules Romain: L'Histoire de Scipion, tapisseries et dessins*, exh. cat.
(Paris, Grand Palais, 1978), pp. 5–15, 31–38.

3. *Jules Romain: L'Histoire de Scipion*, nrs. II 1, II 2,
with a discussion of the attribution problems. Both
drawings are approximately the same size as Pencz's
print.

4. Ibid., nr. II 3. The print was praised by Sandrart;
see Peltzer, ed., *Sandrarts Academie*, p. 78. For the different editions, see Landau, *Pencz*, nr. 93.

108. THE TRIUMPHS OF PETRARCH

1539–1540; monogram
Engraving: series of six
13.9/15.1 × 20.5/20.9 cm (each print)
B. 117–122; Landau, *Pencz*, nrs. 116–121
Lent by the Philadelphia Museum of Art: William S. Pilling Collection

NASCENTES·MORIMVR·FINISQZ·AB·ORIGINE·PENDET·
LONGIVS·AVT·PROPIVS·MORS·SVA·QVENOZ·MANET·

Between the late 1330s and his death in 1374, Florentine poet Francesco Petrarch composed six *trionfi*, loosely autobiographical poems about the different stages of life.[1] The *Triumph of Love* describes his youthful affection for Laura, which subsequently was held in check by the triumph of Chastity. After Laura's death in the plague of 1348, Petrarch penned the *Triumph of Death*. Each triumph is overcome by a greater force. Death yields to fame, fame to time, and time to eternity.

Petrarch's *Triumphs* inspired numerous artistic series from the late fourteenth century on. Rarely, however, do any of the Italian cycles match the innovation and power of expression that characterize Pencz's six engravings.[2] For instance, the *Triumph of Death*, illustrated here, is an apocalyptic vision.[3] Riding on a chariot pulled by two wild oxen, Death cuts down mankind, sparing neither king nor pope. The desperate throng futilely attempts to flee, the violently twisting figures heightening the commotion. Several of the struggling or dead men, including the pair by the wheel of the chariot, are borrowed from Giulio Romano's *Battle of the Milvian Bridge* (ca. 1524) in the Sala di Constantino in the Vatican, which Pencz visited in 1539 or early 1540.[4] In two other Petrarch series published in Venice in 1490 and in Milan in 1494, Death is a rather benign figure who is not physically involved in the destruction of mankind.[5] Similarly, the Italian woodcuts show simple scenes of angels carrying souls to heaven and the devils transporting the damned to hell. Pencz has transformed these scenes into a vast panoramic landscape. At the right, Charon ferries the damned across the River Styx toward a great hell mouth, behind which is a city in flames. Opposite, the saved wait on the shore of the river for angels to transport them to paradise, which is depicted as a long procession toward the distant sun. In the center is the enthroned Christ and a large fountain of life. Pencz's vision recalls Denis the Carthusian's *Dialogue on the Particular Judgment of God*, a popular account that inspired paintings by Netherlandish artists Dirk Bouts and Hieronymus Bosch.[6]

In each of the engravings, Pencz has expanded the traditional iconographies and settings. In the *Triumph of Fame*, the procession passes by such recognizable Roman monuments as the fragmentary colossal statue of Emperor Constantine, now in the Palazzo dei Conservatori in Rome, the Pyramid of Cestius, the Temple of Vesta, the Colosseum, and other structures from the Forum Romanorum and the Forum of Trajan. Pencz's ability to transcend his models and expand the well-worn themes makes the *Triumphs of Petrarch* one of Pencz's finest graphic cycles.

1. E. H. Wilkins, *The Triumphs of Petrarch* (Chicago, 1962).

2. For an excellent discussion of Pencz's series and some of the Italian precedents, see Olds, Williams, and Levin, *Images of Love and Death*, nrs. 54 (Pencz), 27 (1494 Milan edition); Hind, *Early Italian Engraving*, I: pp. 32–37, A.1 nrs. 18–23, with a list of other Italian examples. Pencz incorrectly numbered the *Triumph of Death* as the fifth rather than third print in the sequence.
3. The inscription reads in translation:

Being born, we die, and the end hangs from the beginning;
Farther or nearer, his death awaits every man.

This and translations for the other five engravings are given in Olds, Williams, and Levin, *Images of Love and Death*, nr. 54.
4. Landau, *Pencz*, p. 44. See Hartt, *Giulio Romano*, I: pp. 42–51, II: fig. 58.
5. The Milanese edition, which is copied after the Venetian edition, is discussed and illustrated in Olds, Williams, and Levin, *Images of Love and Death*, nr. 27. A copy of the Venetian edition was owned by Michael Wolgemut in 1493; see Panofsky, *Dürer*, p. 31.
6. See A. Châtelet, "Sur un Jugement dernier de Dieric Bouts," *Nederlandsch Kunsthistorisch Jaarboek* 16 (1965): 17–42.

109. THE SEVEN LIBERAL ARTS

ca. 1541; monogram
Engraving: series of seven
7.4 × 5.2 cm (each)
B. 110–116; Landau, *Pencz*, nrs. 109–115
Lent by the St. Louis Art Museum

The seven liberal arts formed the traditional curriculum of medieval and Renaissance learning. The arts are divided into two groups: the trivium (grammar, logic or dialectic, and rhetoric) and the quadrivium (arithmetic, astronomy, geometry, and music). The latter provides the means for understanding the world and the former provides the ability to communicate this knowledge. Images of the seven liberal arts were commonplace on medieval churches and in manuscripts. The iconographies of the arts were typically based upon the descriptions of Martianus Capella, an African grammarian of the fifth century, and Alanus de Insulis, a monk at Cîteaux in the twelfth century, though various minor embellishments and modifications occurred during the Renaissance.[1]

Pencz's series deviates little from the standard representations of the liberal arts.[2] For instance, Astrologia (astrology or astronomy), illustrated here, was described by Alanus de Insulis as the last of the arts, with her head lifted toward the heavens, her body dressed in a tunic sparkling with diamonds, and her hand carrying a globe.[3] Capella added that she had wings and carried an instrument for observing the stars.[4] Pencz's maiden wears a thin tunic, though without the covering of diamonds. She points at the stars and rests her right arm on a globe. The wings now belong to her accompanying putto who uses a sextant to sight the stars. A compass for measuring and plotting rests against the right-hand wall. Finally, Pencz numbered this print with a 7 to indicate that it was the final figure in the series.

While Pencz's series is undated, the highly Italianate figures would suggest that he devised the engravings shortly after returning from his second trip to Italy in 1539–1540. Corroborating this dating is a set of seven drawings after Pencz's series by a follower that is inscribed with Pencz's monogram and the year 1541.[5]

One set of Pencz's *Seven Liberal Arts* found its way to India in the 1590s. Emperor Jahangir, who ruled from 1605 to 1627, was strongly interested in European art and requested the Jesuit priests at his court to supply him with paintings and prints, including numerous graphic works by Pencz, Dürer, and the Behams. Some of these prints were then copied in the imperial manuscripts by Jahangir's artists. For instance, *Geometry*, complete with Pencz's monogram, appears on one of the pages of the *Album of Jahangir*, now in Washington (Freer Gallery of Art).[6] Famous Mughal painter Manohar copied Pencz's *Arithmetic* in another of the emperor's albums, today in Leningrad (Institute of Peoples of Asia).[7]

1. E. Mâle, *The Gothic Image—Religious Art in France of the Thirteenth Century*, tr. D. Nussey (1913; reprint: New York, 1958), pp. 75–90. On the association of the liberal arts with the planets, see cat. nr. 103, note 1. On the liberal arts in German art, see K.-A. Wirth, "Die Kolorierten Federzeichnungen im Cod. 2975 der Österreichischen Nationalbibliothek—ein Beitrag zur Ikonographie der Artes Liberales im 15. Jahrhundert," *AGNM* (1979): 67–110.

2. Compare the contemporary prints of the liberal arts by Hans Sebald Beham, which are only slightly different albeit artistically inferior, to Pencz's; see *The Illustrated Bartsch*, 15: nrs. 121–127.

3. Mâle, *The Gothic Image*, p. 81.

4. Ibid., p. 79.

5. Erlangen (Universitätsbibliothek); see Bock, *Zeichnungen*, nrs. 299–305.

6. Freer 56.12B. The drawing is in ink and gold on paper and dates to the 1590s before Jahangir attained the throne. See M. C. Beach, *The Imperial Image: Paintings from the Mughal Court*, exh. cat. (Washington: Freer Gallery of Art, 1981), pp. 162–163, nr. 16c. Also see A. K. Das, *Mughal Painting during Jahangir's Time* (Calcutta, 1978), pp. 229–249, on the general subject of European prints in India, and p. 238 note 93 for *Geometry*.

7. Das, *Mughal Painting*, p. 238 note 93.

110. PORTRAIT OF JOHANN FRIEDRICH

1543; monogram
Engraving
33 × 21.4 cm
B. 126; Landau, *Pencz*, nr. 124
Lent by the St. Louis Art Museum; Gift of Mrs. Moyer S. Fleischer in Memory of Dr. Moyer S. Fleischer, 192:1968

Johann Friedrich (1503–1554) succeeded his father, Johann the Steadfast as the elector of Saxony in 1532.[1] He held this title until the battle of Mühlberg in April 1547, when the Protestant forces under his direction were routed by those of Emperor Charles V. Charles stripped him of his title and, temporarily, his lands because of his ardent support for the Lutheran cause.

This is Pencz's only engraved portrait. The elaborateness of the costume, the inscription, and the frame with Johann Friedrich's coats of arms (which has been cut from this particular impression) suggest that the print was commissioned by the prince.[2] Pencz based his portrait upon one of Lucas Cranach the Elder's many representations of Johann Friedrich rather than upon a life sketch. Cranach's woodcut portrait of Johann Friedrich of about 1533 contains almost identical renderings of the face and the beard, as well as the fur-trimmed robe, the shirt style though not its decoration, and the pendant gem.[3] The sleeves, beret, and feather can be found in other portraits by Cranach and his son Lucas the Younger. This was not the first time that Pencz copied Cranach's art—his portrait of Luther (Raleigh, North Carolina Museum of Art) is a replica of a Cranach painting.[4]

Pencz's preparatory drawing on parchment, dated 1543, was listed in the inventory of the collection of Paulus Praun of Nuremberg in the late sixteenth–early seventeenth centuries.[5] A second drawing by a follower(?) is in Dresden (Kupferstichkabinett).[6]

Although Pencz's portrait is based upon one by Cranach, the overall design of the print is modeled after Dürer's *Portrait of Friedrich the Wise* (cat. nr. 29). Like Dürer, Pencz placed a half-length figure seated behind a stone parapet or tablet. The shadow of the prince is cast against the back wall with its horizontal hatchings.

The print is inscribed:

My hope is in God
Johann Friedrich by the benefit [grace] of God, Duke of Saxony, Archmarshal and Elector of the Holy Roman Empire, Landgrave of Thuringia [and] the March of Misnia [Meissen], and Burggrave of Magdeburg etc.
The word of God will last forever. 15 $\frac{P}{G}$ 43[7]

SPES MEA IN DEO EST
IOHANNES FRIDERICVS DEI BENEFICIO SAXONIÆ DVX.
SACRI ROMANI IMPERII ARCHIMARSCHALCHVS ET
ELECTOR LANDGRAVIVS THVRINGIÆ, MARCHIO MISNIÆ,
ET BVRGGRAVIVS MAGDEBVRGI ETO: 15 P 43
VERBVM DOMINI MANET IN ÆTERNVM, &

1. On his life, see *Allgemeine Deutsche Biographie* (Leipzig, 1881), 14: pp. 326–330; *Neue Deutsche Biographie* (Berlin, 1974), 10: pp. 524–525.
2. The print with its frame and fourteen coats of arms measures 40.5 × 31 cm. For a reproduction, see *The Illustrated Bartsch*, nr. 126; Landau, *Pencz*, nr. 124.
3. Jahn, *1472–1553 Lucas Cranach d. Ä.*, p. 409, also see 643, 690.
4. Gmelin, "Georg Pencz als Maler," nr. 48 (dated 1533).
5. De Murr, *Description du Cabinet de Monsieur Paul de Praun à Nuremberg*, p. 12, nr. 100; also cited by A. Kurzwelly, Pencz, p. 92.
6. Kurzwelly, *Pencz*, p. 92 (without the coats of arms).

7. The motto "SPES MEA IN DEO EST" (My hope is in God) appears on Matthes Gebel's portrait medal of Johann Friedrich of about 1532 (cat. nr. 150). For a discussion of the concluding motto, "VERBVM DOMINI MANET IN AETERNVM" (The word of God will last forever), see cat. nrs. 89–90.

111. PORTRAIT OF A GIRL

ca. 1547; inscribed "AETATIS SVE. 20"
Painting: oil on canvas
60.96 × 49.53 cm
Lent by the Minneapolis Institute of Arts, Bequest of Miss Tessie Jones in Memory of Herschel V. Jones

The precise identity of this twenty-year-old girl is unknown. Gmelin has identified her, based upon the coat of arms at the right, as a member of the patrician Kuetraffer family of Regensburg.[1] The portrait is a fine example of Pencz's mature painting style. In contrast with his powerful, three-quarters–length male portraits of the mid-1540s, the *Portrait of a Girl* is more subdued.[2] The subject is strongly silhouetted against the background, her face bathed in cool light, which Pencz exploited to heighten the clarity of the features. He stopped, however, just short of the enamel-like flesh found in contemporary portraits of Agnolo Bronzino or, a decade earlier, Barthel Beham.[3] As in his *Portrait of Johann Friedrich* (cat. nr. 110), Pencz lavishly attended to the details of the costume and the hands. The dress appears somewhat flatter than the more three-dimensionally developed head.

The background is rather confused. Is the parapet behind the girl's left arm an extension of the shelf at the rear? The glass vase and the coat of arms define two parallel planes joined by the intersecting corner of the room. An identical spatial setting can be seen in Pencz's 1547 *Portrait of Lienhart*[?] *Hirschvogel*.[4] While these specific paintings are not pendants, both may have once been joined with companion portraits that completed the architecture of the back wall.

1. Gmelin, "Georg Pencz als Maler," nr. 30, fig. 61. For additional bibliography, see A. Clark et al., *European Paintings from the Minneapolis Institute of Arts* (New York, 1971), nr. 184.

2. Compare his portraits of *Sebald Schirmer* (Nuremberg, Germanisches Nationalmuseum) or *Jörg Herz* (Karlsruhe, Staatliche Kunsthalle); Gmelin, "Georg Pencz als Maler," nrs. 47, 42, figs. 54, 55. As Gmelin has observed (nr. 30 and see fig. 62), Pencz's *Portrait of a Girl* is quite similar to a drawing that Pencz made after a now lost portrait of a girl by Christoph Amberger. The drawing is dated 1548 and was formerly in the Koenig Collection in Haarlem.

3. See the comments in Section 6.

4. Schloss Puchhof, Thyssen Collection; see Gmelin, "Georg Pencz als Maler," nr. 43, fig. 60.

Ludwig Krug was a highly versatile printmaker, sculptor, and goldsmith.[1] He was born between 1488 and 1490 in Nuremberg, where he later trained with his father, Hans Krug, the goldsmith. His earliest dated work is the 1514 *Adam and Eve* stone relief in Berlin (Staatliche Museen), the first of many representations of this theme.[2] Between 1515 and about 1520, Ludwig made two woodcuts and sixteen engravings; he then seems to have abandoned printmaking. His prints are all signed with his monogram and his pitcher (*krug*). During these years he was also a die cutter and, perhaps, a painter, though no examples of his painting are known.

Krug's achievements as a goldsmith are highly praised. Hayward ranked Krug second only to Dürer as an interpreter of Renaissance ideas in German goldsmith work.[3] The crucial work for defining his skill as a goldsmith is the monogrammed ciborium, formerly in the collection of Cardinal Albrecht von Brandenburg and preserved only in an illustration in the *Hallesche Heiltumsschatz* (ca. 1526).[4] Based on this drawing of the ciborium, Kohlhaussen and others have attributed a small corpus of lavish goldsmith pieces to Krug.[5] Among these is the *Raudnitz Cup*, now lost, which was decorated with scenes from the life of Hercules that were carved in shell cameos.[6] Neudörfer praised Krug for this sort of shell carvings.[7] Still other items, including the famous *Apple Cup* (cat. nr. 116), must be ascribed to the large Krug workshop rather than to either Ludwig or his father, Hans.

Ludwig died in 1532 in Nuremberg.

1. There is no complete monograph on Krug. See E. Schilling, "Zeichnungen von Ludwig Krug," *AGNM* (1932–1933): 109–118; E. Bock, "The Engravings of Ludwig Krug of Nuremberg," *Print Collector's Quarterly* 20 (1933): 87–115; Kohlhaussen, *Nürnberger Goldschmiedekunst*, pp. 357–371. Bock states that Krug was a master in 1513, while others give the date as 1522.

2. See the comments for cat. nrs. 114–115.

3. Hayward, *Virtuoso Goldsmiths*, pp. 98–99.

4. Kohlhaussen, *Nürnberger Goldschmiedekunst*, nr. 397.

5. Ibid., nrs. 397–398, 403, 405, 414, 417–418, 423 (a wooden model of a naked man).

6. Present location unknown; formerly in Raudnitz (near Prague). Ibid., nr. 398.

7. Neudörfer, *Nachrichten von Künstlern*, pp. 124–125. Neudörfer also mentioned that Ludwig cast or embossed the works by Hans Frey, Dürer's father-in-law, and the wooden portraits of Hans Schwarz.

112. THE ADORATION OF THE MAGI

1515 or 1516; signed "Ludw. Krug" in ink on the verso
Drawing: pen and brown ink on tan paper
25 × 17.5 cm
Lent by the Crocker Art Museum, Sacramento, Crocker Collection

113. THE ADORATION OF THE MAGI

1516; monogram
Engraving
16.3 × 12.1 cm
B. 2
Lent by the Cleveland Museum of Art, Leonard C. Hanna, Jr., Collection

In 1515 or 1516, Krug started working on an Adoration of the Magi composition that he intended to engrave. He created at least two drawings of this theme, the example exhibited and the final preparatory sketch now in Nuremberg (Germanisches Nationalmuseum).[1] The latter is blackened with graphite on the verso so that when the drawing was placed directly on the copper plate the image could be transferred by simply tracing the design. While the Nuremberg drawing contains the same basic figure and architectural arrangements as in the engraving, most of the subtle facial and shading details, as well as the Hercules frieze on the back wall, were incorporated directly onto the copper plate.[2]

The Sacramento drawing is contemporary to the engraving, although, because of its much

greater size, it cannot have been made specifically for the print. The composition of the drawing is much simpler, with only the three kings, Mary, and the Christ Child. The palace is replaced by a humble stable. Yet these works share many common features. The side-turned Moor at the right of the drawing wears exactly the same attire as his engraved counterpart. The boots are folded at the knee and have strapped-on spurs. The robe is bunched over the inside shoulder, creating sharp, angular folds with their deliberate play of chiaroscuro contrasts. The robe is tied with bows at the back and, borrowing a motif from Martin Schongauer, is pushed aside by the diagonally hanging sword.[3] The Moor's turban has the same intertwined arrangement. The lobed dish in his hand in the drawing is held by the third king, at the rear of

the engraving. Similar analogies can be found for the other figures, especially in the designs of their draperies. Even the architecture, while different in style, is based upon a shallow chamber with its back wall parallel to the picture plane combined with two columns or piers placed diagonally behind the Virgin and Child.[4]

Although it is impossible to determine whether the print or the drawing was made first, both works must have been made at about the same time. Together with the Nuremberg sketch, they provide important insights into Krug's working practices.

---

1. On the engraving, see Bock, "The Engravings of Ludwig Krug," p. 111, nr. 2. On the Nuremberg drawing, see Schilling, "Zeichnung von Ludwig Krug," pp. 109, 114–115, fig. 71; Zink, *Die Handzeichnungen*, nr. 77. The Sacramento drawing is not mentioned in any

of these studies; see J. A. Mahey, *Master Drawings from Sacramento* (Sacramento, 1971), nr. 3 (without any text).

2. The copper plate for *The Adoration of the Magi* and its pendant, *The Nativity* (B. 1 and Bock, nr. 1), are today in Bamberg (Staatliche Bibliothek). In the sixteenth century, these two plates and copies of the engravings were in the possession of Paulus Praun of Nuremberg; see de Murr, *Description du Cabinet de Monsieur Paul de Praun à Nuremberg*, p. 197; also cited by Bock, "The Engravings of Ludwig Krug," p. 111, nrs. 1, 2.

3. See Schongauer's *The Adoration of the Kings* (B. 6); Shestack, *The Complete Engravings of Martin Schongauer*, fig. 8.

4. Krug's initial indecision about the architectural design of the back wall is evident upon close inspection. Directly over the standing king in the center a small double lancet window was added and then covered over by the brick pattern.

114. ADAM AND EVE

ca. 1515
Woodcut: third of three states
17.7 × 12.5 cm
Dodgson, I: p. 524; Geisberg, nr. 890
Lent by the Metropolitan Museum of Art, New
York, Harris Brisbane Dick Fund, 1947

Between 1514 and 1524, Krug treated the theme of Adam and Eve by the tree of knowledge at least four times in sculpture and in the exhibited woodcut.[1] That Krug was inspired by Dürer's engraving of the subject (cat. nr. 11) is particularly evident here. Like Dürer, Krug has placed Adam and Eve against a dense forest with jagged rocks. Of the four principal animals in Dürer's engraving, only the elk has been retained. Krug has adopted the body of Dürer's Eve from the shoulders down; however, the arm and hand with the apple cupped in the palm have been changed from the left to the right side. The head and left arm of Krug's Eve are also different. The seated Adam, with his wonderful subdued, or resigned, expression, is Krug's own invention.

Krug was a better engraver than woodcut artist. His use of hatching in the woodcut is much less sophisticated than in his *Adoration of the Magi* engraving (cat. nr. 113). The chest of Adam is oddly flat as the grid of lines is insufficiently differentiated to convey either the rounding of the body or the patterns of light across the limbs. The two figures scarcely stand out from the background. By contrast, an artist like Hans Springinklee more fully comprehended both Dürer's composition and his style, as is evident, for example, in his *Adam and Eve* (cat. nr. 53) of about 1512.

The *cartellino* in the foreground is blank.[2] In the first state of this print it contained both Krug's initials and his pitcher (*krug*); the only extant example is now in Dresden (Kupferstichkabinett).[3] A second state, probably made later in the sixteenth century, lacks the pitcher, and the hatching on Eve's legs has been simplified. According to Dodgson and Bock, the British Museum in London possesses the only copy of the second state. Much more common is the third state, exhibited here, in which the artist's initials have been removed. Most third-state impressions date to later centuries, especially the nineteenth, when the original woodblock (Berlin, Derschau Collection) was reused.

1. On the sculptural examples, see cat. nr. 115. On the woodcut, also see C. Dodgson, "Zwei Holzschnitte von Ludwig Krug," *Repertorium für Kunstwissenschaft* 20 (1897): 303; Bock, "The Engravings of Ludwig Krug," p. 115, woodcut nr. 1. This woodcut was paired with *The Expulsion from Eden* (Geisberg, nr. 891; Bock, woodcut nr. 2).

2. On the different states, see Dodgson, I: p. 524; Bock, "The Engravings of Ludwig Krug," p. 115, woodcut nr. 1. Dodgson was unaware of the third state.

3. The first state is illustrated in Geisberg, nr. 890.

115. ADAM AND EVE

1515 [1518]; monogram
Plaquette: bronze (solid cast), natural brown
and red opaque patina with remnants of dark
brown lacquer
12.2 × 10.8 cm
Weber, *Renaissanceplaketten*, p. 55, nr. 28
Lent by the Cleveland Museum of Art, John
Severance Fund, 48.359

This plaquette, the only signed and dated work
in bronze by Krug,[1] exists in two examples. The
first, cast with only the date of 1515 on the front
side, is in Brno (Kunstgewerbemuseum). Although the Cleveland example is also inscribed
1515, it bears a second cast date of 1518 on the
reverse.

As observed in the previous entry, Krug repeatedly returned to the subject of Adam and
Eve between 1514 and 1524 since it offered him
the opportunity to experiment with nude figures. In 1514 Krug carved a *solnhofen* (limestone) stone relief (Berlin, Staatliche Museen), in
which the standing figures of Adam and Eve
face each other as the apple is offered to Adam.[2]
Eve is, once again, borrowed from Dürer's 1504
engraving (cat. nr. 11), but Adam, except for his
profile, is Krug's own invention. The Cleveland
plaquette exhibits a more adventurous composition. Eve is shown reclining on a small rocky

ledge. She appears to be in conversation with
the serpent, who is wrapped around one
branch. Adam's body is sharply twisted as he
bends around the tree to watch Eve and the serpent. The arrangement of Adam and Eve forms
a circular motion that unifies the composition.
In this case, Krug owes little to Dürer beyond
the interest in muscular physiques. In about
1524 Krug carved the red marble *Adam and Eve*
relief now in Munich (Bayerisches Nationalmuseum).[3] Eve still harks back to Dürer's engraving; otherwise, the contorted figure of
Adam and the elaborate tree with the large
dangling serpent are much more animated than
their predecessors.[4]

1. Also see W. D. Wixom, *Renaissance Bronzes from
Ohio Collections*, nr. 165 (with further bibliography).
2. Kohlhaussen, *Nürnberger Goldschmiedekunst*, fig.
526; I. Weber, *Deutsche, niederländische und französische
Renaissanceplaketten*, nr. M27; esp. *Berlin: Der Mensch
um 1500*, nr. 28.
3. T. Müller, *Die Bildwerke in Holz, Ton und Stein,
Bayerisches Nationalmuseum·München*, p. 196; *Berlin: Der
Mensch um 1500*, fig. 121. The Munich relief measures
35 × 27.2 cm, while the Berlin carving is only 14 × 9
cm.
4. Kohlhaussen, *Nürnberger Goldschmiedekunst*, nr.
401, credits the Krug workshop with the creation of a
now lost pomegranate cup with Adam and Eve, together with the serpent, on its foot. The cup was formerly in the Schloss Raudnitz near Prague.

116. APPLE CUP (APFELPOKAL)

ca. 1510–1515; inscribed with an "N" (Nuremberg civic goldsmiths' mark)
Goldsmith work: gilt silver
Height 21.5 cm
Lent by the Germanisches Nationalmuseum, Nuremberg, HG. 8399

Before entering Michael Wolgemut's workshop in 1486, Dürer had begun his training as a goldsmith under his father's tutelage. In spite of his career change, Dürer's fascination with goldsmith work never disappeared. Throughout his life he incorporated elaborately shaped cups and dishes into his prints and paintings, for example, in *The Babylonian Whore* (cat. nr. 6B). Dürer produced numerous goldsmith designs; one drawing of six cups, now in Dresden (Sächsische Landesbibliothek), is inscribed "Tomorrow I shall draw more of these," which conveys his delight in devising new, ever more intricate forms.[1]

The *Apple Cup* is certainly the most famous goldsmith work directly associated with Dürer.[2] The shape is that of a smooth, polished apple resting on a foot in the form of a branch with leaves. Although the apple appears to be growing still, its stem has been severed and the fruit has been turned right side up. Included among the six goldsmith cups penned by Dürer on the Dresden drawing mentioned above is one for an apple cup. The shape is simpler, especially with its short base, and a handle has been formed in the shape of the serpent in the Garden of Eden. Even closer to the Nuremberg cup is the example held by the Moorish king in Dürer's *Adoration of the Magi* painting of 1504 in Florence (Uffizi); here the serpent has been turned into a finial on the lid of the cup.[3] The Nuremberg cup may have been inspired by either of these works or, more likely, by another drawing that has not survived.

The artist of the *Apple Cup* is unknown. Von Falke attributed the cup to Ludwig Krug, while Kohlhaussen tentatively ascribed it to Hans Krug the Elder.[4] Schiedlausky correctly observed that, while the cup certainly belongs to an artist working in the Krug workshop, it is at present impossible to be any more precise, given the similarities of style and the constant collaboration within this large atelier.[5]

1. Kohlhaussen, *Nürnberger Goldschmiedekunst*, fig. 456; Strauss, ed., *The Human Figure by Albrecht Dürer*, nr. 162 (with translation used here). On the subject of Dürer's designs for goldsmith works, see the comments of G. Schiedlausky in *Nuremberg: Dürer (1971)*, pp. 364–378, nrs. 660–698.
2. The city goldsmith's mark on the foot is R³ 3687; M. Rosenberg, *Der Goldschmiede Merkzeichen*, III: p. 13. It is a reversed capital N.
3. Anzelewsky, *Dürer*, nr. 82. Kohlhaussen, *Nürnberger Goldschmiedekunst*, nr. 390, also mentions other apple cups. He relates the example formerly in Cardinal Albrecht von Brandenburg's collection at Halle to a design by Dürer; see nr. 391. In the 1531 inventory of the possessions of one of Willibald Pirckheimer's granddaughters, a gilt silver apple cup is listed. Yet another is mentioned in the correspondence of Wenzel Jamnitzer in 1545.
4. O. von Falke, "Silberarbeiten von Ludwig Krug," *Pantheon* 6 (1933): 189; Kohlhaussen, *Nürnberger Goldschmiedekunst*, nr. 390.
5. Schiedlausky in *Nuremberg: Dürer (1971)*, nr. 671. On the production of this workshop, see Kohlhaussen, *Nürnberger Goldschmiedekunst*, nrs. 387a–425.

The Vischers, a Nuremberg family of sculptors and bronze casters, ran Germany's foremost foundry from the mid-fifteenth century until the 1530s.[1] The foundry and workshop were established by Hermann the Elder (died 1488), who acquired Nuremberg citizenship in 1453 and is best known for his bronze tomb slabs and the baptismal font, dated 1457, in Wittenberg. He was succeeded by his son Peter the Elder (ca. 1460–1529), the most illustrious member of the family, whose interest in classical sculpture and coins is reflected in his *Branch Breaker* of 1490 and in the later workshop interpretations of Italian art.[2] Between 1488 and 1519, Peter the Elder designed, cast, and placed the *Tomb of St. Sebaldus* (figs. 21 and 22), and in 1513 he created the over-life-size bronze statues of King Arthur and Theodoric, king of the Ostrogoths (died 526), after the designs of Albrecht Dürer, for the tomb of Emperor Maximilian I, now in the Hofkirche at Innsbruck.[3]

While preparing the *Tomb of St. Sebaldus*, Peter the Elder was greatly assisted by his sons, Hermann (1486–1517), Peter the Younger (1487–1528), and, to a much lesser degree, Hans (ca. 1489–1550). In the past few decades critics have come to the conclusion that, while the initial design for the tomb was by Peter the Elder, from 1507 on his role was primarily that of the caster of the figures conceived and sculpted by Hermann and Peter the Younger. Both Hermann and Peter the Younger traveled to Italy on one or, more likely, two occasions, trips that greatly changed both the form and figure styles of the tomb statues and, significantly, introduced north Italian sculptural ideas into German art.[4] For instance, these two created the first known or, at least, the oldest surviving German portrait medals, both self-portraits.[5] Pilz and others credit Peter the Younger with the transmission of the lost wax casting technique, which he learned while presumably in the workshop of Andrea Riccio in Padua in about 1512.[6] From this time on, the Vischer workshop produced hollow cast statues, such as the *Candlestick in the Form of a Man* (cat. nr. 118), for local collectors, who, as did their Italian counterparts, decorated their studies with small independent bronzes of allegorical, mythological, or, occasionally, genre subjects.

With Hermann's death in 1517 and his father's activities restricted primarily to casting, Peter the Younger assumed control of the family workshop. Already in 1513, Peter had fashioned the *Epitaph of Dr. Anton Kress* (fig. 29) in St. Lorenz, which is probably the earliest Renaissance-style funerary monument in Germany. Peter the Younger later was commissioned to make the epitaphs for Cardinal Albrecht von Brandenburg (1525), now in the Stiftskirche in Aschaffenburg, and Elector Friedrich the Wise (1527) in the Schlosskirche in Wittenberg.[7] In a highly unusual move, the Nuremberg city council issued a decree in 1527 accepting this funerary monument for Friedrich the Wise as Peter the Younger's official masterpiece.[8]

Hans took over the workshop following the deaths of Peter the Younger in 1528 and his father in the following year. From this point on, the fame of the workshop quickly declined. Hans may have cast Peter Flötner's *Apollo Foun-* *tain* (fig. 35) and he did complete the monumental metal grille for the great hall of the Rathaus, a work begun and largely executed by his brothers.[9] His son Jörg maintained the shop until his death in 1592.

1. On the family, see the comments in Section 6 D; Neudörfer, *Nachrichten von Künstlern*, pp. 21, 31–33; H. Stafski, "Die Vischer-Werkstatt und ihre Probleme," *ZfK* 21 (1958): 1–26, and *Der Jüngere Peter Vischer*; Pilz, *Das Sebaldusgrabmal*, esp. pp. 41, 58–60. Although these and other more specialized studies provide a good introduction to the family and, especially, the career of Peter the Younger, a thorough critical monograph is needed.
2. Von der Osten, "Über Peter Vischers Törichten Bauern und den Beginn der 'Renaissance' in Nürnberg," pp. 71–83.
3. On the tomb of St. Sebaldus, see note 1 and cat. nr. 117. On the tomb of Maximilian I, see Egg, *Die Hofkirche in Innsbruck*, p. 32, figs. 50–53.
4. Their first trips may have occurred as early as 1507. Peter the Younger went back to northern Italy in 1512 for at least a year. Hermann was in Mantua, Siena, and Rome. His architectural drawings after Roman and contemporary Italian buildings are unrivalled in Germany; see Section 6 C. On their trips, see generally Pilz, *Das Sebaldusgrabmal*, pp. 53, 58–59.
5. See the brief introduction to portrait medals before cat. nr. 137.
6. Pilz, *Das Sebaldusgrabmal*, p. 59. On modeling in wax and the lost wax technique, see A. Radcliffe, *European Bronze Statuettes*, pp. 14–17; Weihrauch, *Europäische Bronzestatuetten*, pp. 11–32; E. P. Bowron, *Renaissance Bronzes in the Walters Art Gallery*, pp. 18–21, which provides excellent summaries, as well as discussions about the origins of and contemporary taste for bronze statues.
7. Stafski, *Der Jüngere Peter Vischer*, pp. 40–44, figs. 80–81.
8. Hampe, *Nürnberger Ratsverlässe*, I: nr. 1563 (22 May 1527). For various reasons Peter the Younger had avoided joining the bronze workers' guild by working as an assistant or journeyman for Peter the Elder.
9. On the *Apollo Fountain*, see Flötner's biography. On the grille, see Section 6 D and cat. nr. 213.

117. PORTRAIT OF PETER VISCHER THE ELDER

Nineteenth-century replica
Bronze statue
38.1 cm (height)
Lent by the Metropolitan Museum of Art, New
York, The Jules S. Bache Collection, 1949

This statue is a replica of the bronze figure of Peter the Elder on the east side of the *Tomb of St. Sebaldus* (figs. 21 and 22) in Nuremberg.[1] Peter Vischer the Younger designed the original statue in honor of his father, the principal artist of the tomb and Germany's most famous bronze caster. Peter the Elder began working on the tomb as early as 1488, the date of his first preparatory drawing; yet, because of funding problems and design changes, the tomb was not erected until between 1507 and 1519.[2] An inscription on the base of the eastern face of the tomb, which reads "EIN ANFANG DVRCH MICH PETER VISCHER 1508" (A beginning by me Peter Vischer 1508), provides an approximate date for the statue. It was certainly completed by 1512, when the second phase of the tomb was finished.

Peter the Elder is shown dressed in his leather apron and holding a hammer and chisel. Like Adam Kraft's self-portrait on the *Sacrament House* of 1493 in St. Lorenz (figs. 19 and 20), this is an image of the pious, hard-working artist devoting his skills to the erection of a Christian monument.[3] The many self-portraits of Albrecht Dürer in religious paintings have the same intent.[4] That this is indeed a portrait of Peter the Elder is confirmed by Neudörfer in 1547 and many later writers.[5]

During the eighteenth and nineteenth centuries, Peter the Elder was widely recognized as Germany's greatest sculptor and was occasionally represented as Sculptura to Dürer as Pictura.[6] Copies of the statue were made before 1836 by Jacob Daniel Burgschmiet and his pupil Georg Howalt. Another replica, by Johann Christoph Phörtsch of 1844 and now in the Fembohaus (Stadtgeschichtliche Museen), was created for the meeting hall of the guild of bronze workers in Nuremberg. Peter the Elder was considered a perfect patron or model for their organization.

1. It was exhibited in *Master Bronzes*, exh. cat. (Buffalo: Buffalo Fine Arts Academy, 1937), nr. 146.
2. On the history of the tomb, see Stafski, *Der Jüngere Peter Vischer*, pp. 9–36, figs. 1 (the 1488 drawing)–74; Pilz, *Das Sebaldusgrabmal*, esp. pp. 54, 61, on the figure of Peter the Elder. Also see the comments in Section 3 A.
3. See Section 3 A.
4. Anzelewsky, *Dürer*, nrs. 93, 105, 115, 118.
5. Neudörfer, *Nachrichten von Künstlern*, p. 21.
6. For what follows, see Anzelewsky, Mende, and Eeckhout, *Albert Dürer aux Pays-Bas*, nr. 35.
7. Ibid., fig. p. 10. Inv. Z. 1121.

118. CANDLESTICK IN THE FORM OF A MAN

1518–1528
Bronze statue with surface fire-gilt
34.5 cm (height: statue only); the base is
unrelated
Lent by the Walters Art Gallery, Baltimore

This candlestick of a slender yet athletic nude male supporting two candle holders in his outstretched arms is one of the very few first-rate Nuremberg bronzes in the United States.[1] It probably once adorned the desk of a scholar or a humanistically educated patrician. The figure with its symmetrical posture and lack of contrapposto is based on contemporary German, not classical or north Italian, models. As Weihrauch has correctly observed, the statue immediately recalls the oeuvre of Peter Vischer the Younger, whose nudes tend to be rather elongated, with thin, muscular legs and a taut torso emphasizing the anatomical structure of the chest.[2] Like the apostles on the *Tomb of St. Sebaldus* (fig. 21), the candle bearer possesses a relaxed demeanor and characteristic upturned tilt to the head that imparts a sense of detachment or even hauteur. He is closest in spirit to the figures of Sts. Peter, James the Minor, and Simon, which Pilz attributed to Peter the Younger, or Judas Thaddeus, by Peter or the workshop.[3] The beard and moustache types reflect current tastes and again may be found on the tomb figures or on the nude Hercules in Peter's *The Dream of Hercules* drawing in Berlin.[4] This statue was done by Peter the Younger sometime after the completion of the *Tomb of St. Sebaldus* in 1518–1519.

1. Weihrauch, *Europäische Bronzestatuetten*, pp. 277, 281, fig. 329; Bowron, *Renaissance Bronzes*, p. 16 (illustration only).
2. Weihrauch, *Europäische Bronzestatuetten*, p. 277. Weihrauch does not explain his reasons for the attribution to Peter the Younger; he simply says (p. 281) that the artist may have been influenced by Dürer's proportional studies (cf. cat. nr. 34). For Peter the Younger's male nudes, see Stafski, *Der Jüngere Peter Vischer*, figs. 4–11 (*Tomb of St. Sebaldus*—probably by the workshop), 76–77 (the two Orpheus plaquettes; cf. fig. 34), 88 (*Orpheus and Eurydice* drawing, dated 1514, in the Grange Collection in London), 90 (*The Dream of Hercules* drawing in the Kupferstichkabinett in Berlin).
3. Stafski, *Der Jüngere Peter Vischer*, figs. 54–56, 60. On the specific attributions of these figures to Peter the Younger, see Pilz, *Das Sebaldusgrabmal*, pp. 71–72.
4. See note 2.

119. HERCULES AND THE LION

First quarter of the sixteenth century
Bronze statue
24.1 × 16.5 cm
Lent by the Museum of Fine Arts, Boston, Harriet Otis Craft Fund

As the first of his twelve labors, Hercules was required to kill a monstrous lion that lived in the valley of Nemea. After failing to vanquish the lion with his arrows and his club, Hercules strangled it. In the Boston statue, Hercules grabs the lion's mane and prepares to strike the beast with his left hand. The lion is rather misproportioned and oddly tame looking as it lacks the physicality of its counterpart in Dürer's *Samson and the Lion* woodcut of about 1497–1498.[1] Dürer was much more successful in imparting a sense of a violent, life-or-death struggle. Only Hercules's exaggerated contrapposto enlivens this statue group.

Although *Hercules and the Lion* has been attributed to Peter the Younger and dated about 1500, the two figures have little in common with either the various male nudes or the several lions on the St. Sebaldus tomb; furthermore, in 1500, Peter the Younger was only thirteen.[2] The master of this statue group was only loosely influenced by the Vischer workshop and his localization to Nuremberg, while plausible, cannot be proven.

1. Meder 107.
2. This information is provided in the curatorial files of the Museum of Fine Arts and is likely based upon the dealer's report. See Stafski, *Der Jüngere Peter Vischer*, figs. 4–11 (male nudes), 12–13, 20–22 (lions); cf. the Boston statue with cat. nr. 118.

120. SEATED BOY HOLDING A BIRD

1520s or 1530s
Bronze statuette: brown with traces of gilding
6.5 cm (height)
Lent by the National Gallery of Art, Washington, Samuel H. Kress Collection

In his description of the *Tomb of St. Sebaldus* (fig. 21), Eobanus Hessus praised the Vischers for their skill in fashioning so many figures. He writes, "What shall I say of so many animals, of so many cast lions' bodies? Of the thousand figures of nude infants?"[1] While Hessus inflated the number of statues, the tomb is covered with dozens of putti (or cherubs) cast in almost every imaginable pose. Peter the Younger was responsible for the execution of most of these nude figures.

It is therefore not surprising that many of the independent statuettes of nude children that were made in southern Germany during the first half of the sixteenth century are attributed to Peter the Younger or his workshop. In the case of the Washington statuette, the boy is reminiscent of several of the tomb figures; however, he is thinner and has straighter hair than his counterparts on the tomb.[2] He is much closer to the figure in the *Boy with a Bird* and the *Boy with a Dog* (Braunschweig, Herzog Anton Ulrich–Museum) that Bange ascribed to Vischer.[3] As Pope-Hennessy observed, the pose of the Washington statuette is an inversion of the legs of the *Boy with a Dog*, while the upper torso, notably the twisting of the arms, and the tilted head are also very similar.[4] In this case, the artist of the *Seated Boy Holding a Bird* does seem to have been a Nuremberg master either in Peter the Younger's workshop or strongly influenced by his style.

1. Stechow, *Northern Renaissance Art*, p. 126. On Hessus, see cat. nr. 33. For illustrations of these putti, see Stafski, *Der Jüngere Peter Vischer*, figs. 5, 6, 10, 16, 20–23, 40–41.
2. J. Pope-Hennessy, *Renaissance Bronzes from the Samuel H. Kress Collection*, nr. 552, fig. 576. The hole at the navel is plugged with lead.
3. Bange, *Die Deutschen Bronzestatuetten des 16. Jahrhunderts*, nrs. 48–49.
4. Pope-Hennessy, *Renaissance Bronzes*, nr. 552. He also relates it to another workshop piece in Munich; see H. R. Weihrauch, *Die Bildwerke in Bronze und in anderen Metallen*, Bayerisches Nationalmuseum, München, nr. 23.

Jörg Vischer

Jörg (ca. 1520–1592) was a sculptor and bronze caster. After the death of Peter Vischer the Elder in 1529, the family workshop passed to his third son, Hans (ca. 1489–1550), the father of Jörg. The importance of the workshop continued to decline until Hans left Nuremberg in 1549. Under the guidance of Jörg, attractive bronzes continued to be cast; however, the foundry never regained its former vigor.

Jörg's small oeuvre has been assembled around a bronze inkstand in Berlin (Staatliche Museen) that is inscribed with the initials G.F. and the date 1547.[1] Because of their stylistic associations with the nude woman on the Berlin inkstand, Bange has attributed the statues *Allegory of Fertility* in Providence (Rhode Island School of Design) and *Venus* (Eve?) in Paris (Louvre), among other works, to Jörg.[2]

Little else is known about Jörg's life or his career.

1. "Vischer, Jörg" in Thieme-Becker (1940), 34: p. 413; Bange, *Die Deutschen Bronzestatuetten des 16. Jahrhunderts*, pp. 26, 32, 121, nr. 70; Berlin: *Der Mensch um 1500*, nr. 26.
2. Bange, *Die Deutschen Bronzestatuetten des 16. Jahrhunderts*, nrs. 71–73b.

121. EVE

Mid-sixteenth century
Bronze statuette with some gilding on the surface
19.1 cm (height of figure only)
Lent by the Walters Art Gallery, Baltimore

Weihrauch was the first to attribute this small statuette of Eve to Jörg Vischer or, more likely, his workshop.[1] Eve's graceful lines, her hair style, and, especially, the forms of her eyes, nose (which is partially damaged), and mouth recall the features of the *Allegory of Fertility* statue in Providence that is attributed to Jörg.[2] Eve is not, however, as elongated or as finely finished as the figure of Fertility. Eve's pose is based ultimately on classical statues of the *Venus pudica*, or chaste Venus, that were frequently copied by Andrea Riccio and other north Italian bronze sculptors of the early sixteenth century.[3]

1. Weihrauch, *Europäische Bronzestatuetten*, pp. 281ff., fig. 330.
2. Bange, *Die Deutschen Bronzestatuetten des 16. Jahrhunderts*, nr. 71.
3. W. S. Sheard, *Antiquity in the Renaissance*, nrs. 37, 37a.

Flötner was one of the most innovative sculptors and printmakers of the German Renaissance.[1] In 1547, a year after Flötner's death, Johann Neudörfer wrote in his biography of the artist that it was unfortunate Flötner had never received a great commission worthy of his talents.[2] His fame, then as now, rested primarily upon his smaller sculptures, his decorative programs for patrician houses, his models for goldsmiths, and, above all, his dozens of prints and plaquettes. His creative ideas and his interpretations of classical architectural motifs were disseminated throughout central Europe. Flötner's role was certainly not as great as Dürer's had been, yet his designs significantly influenced artists working in other media.

He was born between 1486 and 1495, probably in Thurgau (Switzerland). Little firm evidence exists to document his early career.[3] Flötner may have been trained in Augsburg, for occasionally he is linked with the Fugger Chapel in St. Anna in that city. In 1520 or 1521 Flötner may have traveled to Italy. He was active briefly in Ansbach before arriving in Nuremberg in 1522. On 8 August 1523 he took the oath of citizenship in Nuremberg, where he would remain until his death. Mende has suggested that Flötner's earliest carvings in Nuremberg were the capitals and consoles of the renovated Rathaus.[4]

From the mid-1520s on, Flötner began producing designs for organs; elaborate epitaphs, such as the *Transfiguration of Christ* drawing of the 1530s at Erlangen (Universitätsbibliothek; fig. 58); and fountains, both wall and freestanding types.[5] He carved the wooden models for the fountain in the marketplace at Mainz, which Cardinal Albrecht von Brandenburg had ordered in 1526, and another in the palace at Trient.[6] Much more important is his *Apollo Fountain* of 1532, cast in bronze by either Hans Vischer or Pankraz Labenwolf, which was originally set in the shooting yard of the Herrenschiesshaus, the gentlemen's archery clubhouse in Nuremberg (fig. 35).[7]

During the 1530s and 1540s, Flötner designed furniture and the interior decorations of several patrician houses, including the Tucherhaus (1533–1544).[8] Flötner may have contributed to the architectural plans of the garden room of the Hirschvogelhaus that was erected in 1534.[9] For this room he carved the stone chimneypiece, the wall paneling, and the doorways (fig. 17); Pencz painted the ceiling (fig. 33).

Neudörfer claimed that most of Flötner's carved work was purchased by goldsmith Jacob Hoffmann.[10] While no works by Hoffmann have survived, let alone goldsmith pieces based on Flötner's designs, Flötner's associations with Master M. E. and, especially, with Melchior Baier can be studied.[11] Flötner and Baier collaborated upon several major goldsmith projects, including the *Silver Altar* (1531–1538) and the Reliquary of St. Sigismund (1533), both in Cracow (Cathedral); the *Pfinzing Dish* (1534–1538) and *Holzschuher Covered Cup* (before 1540), both in Nuremberg (Germanisches Nationalmuseum; figs. 38 and 39); and the *Agate Dish* (1536) in Munich (Residenz).[12] Flötner's soapstone model for the foot of a dish, now in Cambridge (Massachusetts; Busch-Reisinger Museum), was intended to be cast in silver.[13]

Goldsmiths and artists working in virtually all other media eagerly collected Flötner's woodcuts of architectural forms and plaquettes.[14] Flötner carved wooden (see cat. nr. 129) and stone models of biblical, mythological, and allegorical themes. These were cast in lead, bronze, silver, or, occasionally, tin. Since the models were pressed into fine sand and molten metals were poured into the resulting depressions in the sand, multiple copies of plaquettes were made. *Christ and the Samaritan Woman* (cat. nr. 126), exhibited here in lead and bronze, was repeatedly recast during the sixteenth and seventeenth centuries. Goldsmiths as great as Wenzel Jamnitzer employed Flötner's plaquettes in their production (see cat. nr. 198). Plaquettes were also sought out by collectors. When the famous Amerbach family collection in Basel was inventoried in 1586, five drawers filled with Flötner's plaquettes were listed.[15] A representative sampling of the variety of the artist's plaquettes is included in the exhibition.

Flötner died on 23 October 1546 in his house on Spitzenberg. He was buried in the Johannisfriedhof.

1. Although the Flötner bibliography is extensive, a new critical monograph is needed. The basic studies are Lange, *Flötner*; E. F. Bange, *Peter Flötner*, and "Die Handzeichnungen Peter Flötners," *JPKS* 57 (1936): 169–192; *Peter Flötner und die Renaissance in Deutschland*; the studies cited in the notes below.

2. Neudörfer, *Nachrichten von Künstlern*, p. 115. See Hill and Pollard, nr. 610, for a medal attributed to Hoffmann.

3. Lange, *Flötner*, pp. 3–19, provides a basic biographical discussion. It should be noted that there is no documentary, only stylistic, evidence for Flötner's trip to Italy. A second Italian trip around 1530 has also been proposed.

4. Mende, *Rathaus*, I: pp. 78ff.

5. See the artist's drawings at Berlin and Erlangen; see Bock, *Staatliche Museen zu Berlin*, I: p. 42, nrs. 390–391 (organs), 1263 (a wall fountain in the form of a mountain waterfall); Bock, *Zeichnungen*, nrs. 370 (an attributed drawing of the organ of the Fugger Chapel in Augsburg), 357 (the *Transfiguration of Christ* epitaph). On Flötner's designs for altars and altarframes, see J. Rasmussen, *Die Nürnberger Altarbaukunst der Dürerzeit*, pp. 92–96.

6. Lange, *Flötner*, pp. 81–82; E. W. Braun, "Ein Nürnberger Bronzebrunnen von 1532/33 im Schlosse zu Trient," *MJBK* 3 Folge, 2 (1951): 195–203; Weihrauch, *Europäische Bronzestatuetten*, pp. 287–293, esp. 289.

7. See Section 6 D; Weihrauch, *Europäische Bronzestatuetten*, pp. 288–289, 318.

8. On Flötner's furniture and interior designs, see O. von Falke, "Peter Flötner und die süddeutsche Tischlerei," *JPKS* 7 (1916): 121ff.; H. Kreisel, *Die Kunst des deutschen Möbels* (Munich, 1968), I: pp. 63–74. On the Tucherhaus, see Lange, *Flötner*, pp. 74ff.; Schwemmer, *Bürgerhaus*, pls. 57a, 95, 120b.

9. Lange, *Flötner*, pp. 64–73; Glück, *Die Kunst der Renaissance*, p. 492; Schwemmer, *Bürgerhaus*, pls. 23a, 105c; see Section 6 A and C.

10. Neudörfer, *Nachrichten von Künstlern*, p. 115.

11. See Kohlhaussen, *Nürnberger Goldschmiedekunst*, nr. 475 (the *Lucretia Cup*, dated 1535, in Copenhagen [National Museum]).

12. Ibid., pp. 437–448, cat. nrs. 458, 464–465, 467, 469.

13. J. D. Farmer, *The Virtuoso Craftsman: Northern European Design in the Sixteenth Century*, nr. 9. Flötner's drawing for this piece is in Braunschweig (Herzog Anton Ulrich–Museum); see Geissler, *Zeichnung in Deutschland*, I: nr. A19.

14. On his woodcuts and book illustrations, see cat. nrs. 123–124, 136; Lange, *Flötner*, pp. 20–49; H. Röttinger, *Peter Flettners Holzschnitte*; Bange, *Flötner*; Hollstein, VIII. For a posthumous edition of some of his prints, see cat. nr. 124. On his plaquettes, see Lange,

Flötner, pp. 118–157, 141 to 151 consists of a listing of objects in other media patterned after Flötner's plaquettes; I. Weber, "Bemerkungen zum Plakettenwerk von Peter Flötner," *Pantheon* 28 (1970): 521–525, esp. *Renaissanceplaketten*, pp. 56–85. Flötner's role as the designer of medals has been challenged. In 1538 he did design the commemorative medal for the campaign to rebuild the fortifications of the Burg; it was cast by Hans Maslitzer. See Kohlhaussen, *Nürnberger Goldschmiedekunst*, nr. 457.

15. P. Ganz, "Die Entstehung des Amerbach'schen Kunstkabinets und die Amerbach'schen Inventare," *Berichte, Öffentliche Sammlungen, Basel* 59 (1907): 45–46.

58. Peter Flötner, *Design for an Epitaph*, drawing, 1530s, Erlangen, Universitätsbibliothek, B 357.

122. DAVID AND BATHSHEBA

ca. 1530; inscription "R 20" is not original
Drawing: black chalk
19.9 × 16.8 cm
Lent by the National Gallery of Canada (Galerie nationale du Canada), Ottawa

"And it came to pass in an eveningtide, that David arose from off his bed, and walked upon the roof of the king's house; and from the roof he saw a woman washing herself; and the woman was very beautiful to look upon" (II Samuel 11:2). David, the Old Testament king of Israel, is first seen in the window at the upper left. He stares down at Bathsheba and her two handmaidens. The abbreviated figures of the women lack sufficient definition to distinguish which is Bathsheba. David next appears on the roof at the center of the composition. Again it is not clear whether he is continuing to stare at Bathsheba bathing or whether the single figure standing to the right on the roof is Bathsheba, whom he has summoned into the palace.

The majority of Flötner's drawings are very precise pen-and-ink designs for goldsmith work or sculpture (see fig. 58).[1] Only in a few drawings, such as the exhibited piece or his *Presentation in the Temple* in Erlangen (Universitätsbibliothek), did Flötner use chalk, with its characteristic soft, fuzzy lines.[2] The light, nervous strokes of the trees, sky, and figures contrast with the tighter construction of the Renaissance-style palace, the lines of which converge to a single point midway up the tree on the right. Although Schilling, the first critic to attribute this drawing to Flötner, linked it with a series of Old Testament drawings (Erlangen, Universitätsbibliothek) that Flötner made around 1523, *David and Bathsheba* is actually much closer in style and date to the more mature prints and plaquettes of the 1530s.[3] The Erlangen Old Testament drawings are very crude pen sketches on a much smaller scale; these works do not begin to approach the deep spatial design and atmospheric features that are evident in the Ottawa drawing or, in a more developed and slightly later form, in his plaquettes (cf. cat. nrs. 125–128).

1. See, for example, the elaborate drawing for a standing covered cup in Paris (Bibliothèque Nationale); F. Lugt and J. Vallery-Radot, *Bibliothèque Nationale, Cabinet des Estampes, Inventaire Général des Dessins des Écoles du Nord* (Paris, 1936), nr. 29 (with the artist's monogram).
2. On the Ottawa drawing, see E. Schilling, "Peter Flötner," *Old Master Drawings* 14 (1939–1940): 62–63; A. E. Popham and K. M. Fenwick, *European Drawings in the Collection of the National Gallery of Canada*, pp. 129–130, nr. 187. On the Erlangen drawing, see Bock, *Zeichnungen*, nr. 356. Schilling first noted the similarities between these two drawings.
3. Schilling, "Flötner," pp. 62–63; Bock, *Zeichnungen*, nrs. 324–355. And see his woodcuts the *Nine Vices*; the *Power of Women*, which includes a somewhat similar image of David and Bathsheba; and the *Allegory of Avarice and Charity*. See Geisberg, nrs. 817, 818, 821.

123. THE PROCESSION OF THE CLERGY

ca. 1530–1535
Woodcut
11.6 × 56.4 cm
Geisberg, nrs. 825–826; Röttinger, *Flötner*, nr. 28; Hollstein, VIII: nr. 5
Lent by the New York Public Library, Prints Division, Astor, Lenox and Tilden Foundations

The exhibited impression of this woodcut lacks the title and the verses underneath. The full title reads, in translation, *The Pious pilgrimage and procession of gluttonous friars and sisters from one church dedication festival to another to get indulgences.*[1] Although the print is unsigned, as were most anti-Catholic woodcuts, the attribution to Flötner was first made in 1547 by Johann Neudörfer, who singled out this print in his biography of the artist.[2] It is one of three stinging satires of the Roman Catholic church and its hierarchy by Flötner; he also made the *Triumphal Arch for Johann Eck* and the *New Passion of Christ*, in which Christ's tormentors are represented as the pope and other ecclesiastics.[3]

Flötner here parodied the many religious processions that had become part of the Roman Catholic ritual. Eucharist or reliquary processions in which the Host or a shrine would be carried through the streets or from town to town were quite common during the late fifteenth and early sixteenth centuries.[4] In this case, the artist condemns the indulgences obtained by ecclesiastics at church dedication ceremonies.

The participants move from left to right.[5] At the head of the procession are a pig, a fat monk with an incense burner, and a curate sprinkling holy water that he has taken from a kettle held by a woman in secular dress. This woman is probably a priest's concubine. They are followed by two vomiting friars and two canons with beer steins. Two children, dressed as monks, hold sticks with lanterns, the flames of which are burning piles of excrement. In the center is an obese abbot carried on a litter by two fools. The nuns behind the abbot carry sausages on a spit; two hay forks with codpieces, a reference to the sexual license of the clergy; a backgammon board, which is being used in place of a hymnal; a roast goose; a wine decanter and glass; and, finally, an illegitimate child in swaddling clothes. The participants attend to their physical, not spiritual, needs. The texts beneath the print criticize the quest for indulgences, the corpulence of the abbot, and the clergy's example of religious turpitude.

Mock religious processions were occasionally held in Germany.[6] In 1503 in Augsburg, a goat was placed on a cushion, decorated with ribbons, and then baptized by a mock priest. Carnival revelers in Naumberg in 1525 conducted a comic procession of the church hierarchy through the streets. Similar parodies occurred at Münster (1532), Hildesheim (1543), and in other German towns.

1. C. Dodgson, "Rare Woodcuts in the Ashmolean Museum—IV," *Burlington Magazine* 66 (1935): 93, pl. II a and b. Dodgson noted that various copies after Flötner's print exist, including the later example published by Geisberg (nrs. 825–826). The exhibited print is by Flötner and is considerably finer in the execution of the figures and of details than the later versions.
2. Neudörfer, *Nachrichten von Künstlern*, p. 115.
3. Geisberg, nrs. 814, 823–824.
4. On contemporary processions in Nuremberg before 1525, see K. Schlemmer, *Gottesdienst und Frömmigkeit in der Reichsstadt Nürnberg am Vorabend der Reformation*, pp. 261ff.
5. The following description and comments are based largely upon Scribner, *For the Sake of Simple Folk*, pp. 96–98.
6. Ibid., pp. 68, 97.

124. THREE HORIZONTAL ORNAMENTS

mid-1530s
Woodcut
16.2 × 28.6 cm
Geisberg, nr. 865; Röttinger, *Flötner*, nr. 68;
Hollstein, VIII: nrs. 80–82
Lent by the Metropolitan Museum of Art, New
York, Harris Brisbane Dick Fund, 1927
(27.54.79)

Flötner's designs for architectural forms, cups, pitchers, beds, game boards, and general decorative motifs inspired artists throughout central Europe.[1] The popularity of Flötner's prints can be gauged by the frequent appearance of his ideas in other media and by the fact that Zurich *formschneider* Rudolff Wijffenbach assumed there was still a market for Flötner's art when in 1549, three years after the artist's death, he published *Das Kunstbuch des Peter Flotner*, a compendium of forty decorative designs by the Nuremberg master.[2]

Three Horizontal Ornaments is one of three woodcuts of friezes that Flötner produced in the 1530s or early 1540s.[3] Unicorns, sirens, putti, masks, and other forms are intertwined with foliage. The compositions are perfectly symmetrical and planned so that several impressions can be placed end to end to form a continuous repeating pattern. The ornaments are very similar to those on the carved wooden frieze and stone chimneypiece formerly in the garden room of the Hirschvogelhaus (fig. 17). Another of Flötner's woodcuts of friezes was the source for the carved wooden gallery in the courtyard of the house at Tucherstrasse 15 in Nuremberg.[4]

1. Geisberg, nrs. 833–867.
2. His influence upon other arts was a principal point made in *Peter Flötner und die Renaissance in Deutschland; Aufgang der Neuzeit*, esp. sections D and H. On the art book published by Wijffenbach, see *Das Kvnstbuch des Peter Flötner Zeichners Bildhavers vnd Formschneiders von Nvernberg Gestorben im Jahre Fünfzehn Hvndert Sechs vnd Vierzig. . . . Nach den Originalen im Besitz der Königlich Prevssischen Kvnstsammlungen nev heravsgegeben*, ed. F. L. and R. D. (Berlin: Kunstgewerbemuseum, 1881).
3. Also see Geisberg, nrs. 866–867. None of these woodcuts are dated. Geisberg suggested a dating of about 1544–1545 for all three examples. The exhibited print is unusual since it is a negative or white-line woodcut. Normally, the figures and the principal forms are printed in black—that is, these features are on the surface of the original block and the background is cut away from the block and reads white. In this case the background is the surface of the woodblock and the figures have been cut away. This technique first appears in Flötner's work in the woodcut *Six Putti and a Nude* (Geisberg, nr. 863), which is signed and dated 1533. Since the style of *Three Horizontal Ornaments* is almost identical to the 1533 woodcut, there is no reason to preclude a contemporary dating.
4. Schwemmer, *Bürgerhaus*, pl. 85c. This house is dated by Schwemmer to the 1530s; it was destroyed in 1945.

125. BAPTISM OF CHRIST

ca. 1530–1535 (a later cast with seventeenth-century inscriptions)
Plaquette: bronze gilt
5.3 × 10.2 cm
Weber, *Renaissanceplaketten*, nr. 34.1
Lent by the Metropolitan Museum of Art, New York, Rogers Fund, 1909

126. CHRIST AND THE SAMARITAN WOMAN

A. ca. 1530–1535
Plaquette: lead
5.5 × 11.1 cm
Weber, *Renaissanceplaketten*, nr. 34.2
Lent by the Bowdoin College Museum of Art, Brunswick, Maine, The Molinari Collection

B. ca. 1530–1535 (a later cast with seventeenth-century inscriptions)
Plaquette: bronze gilt
5.3 × 10.2 cm
Weber, *Renaissanceplaketten*, nr. 34.2
Lent by the Metropolitan Museum of Art, New York, Rogers Fund, 1909

127. CHRIST ON THE ROAD TO EMMAUS

ca. 1530–1535 (a later cast with seventeenth-century inscriptions)
Plaquette: bronze gilt
5.3 × 10.2 cm
Weber, *Renaissanceplaketten*, nr. 34.3
Lent by the Metropolitan Museum of Art, New York, Rogers Fund, 1909

These three scenes are characteristic of Flötner's early plaquette style.[1] Flötner has placed his small figures in the foreground of each composition and then surrounded them with verdant, panoramic landscapes. The spatial depth of the landscapes and the myriad of details, including the careful rendering of different types of trees and grasses, are unique among German or Italian plaquettes of this period. Precedents for Flötner's landscapes are to be found instead in the prints of the Danube School artists, notably Albrecht Altdorfer.[2] In 1547 Johann Neudörfer wrote in his biography of Flötner that the artist once carved a cow horn with 113 different human faces.[3] One can hardly accuse Neudörfer of hyperbole given the complexity of the landscape forms included in these small, low-relief plaquettes.

1. On these plaquettes, also see Lange, *Flötner*, nrs. 8–10; J. De Coo, *Museum Mayer van den Bergh. Catalogus 2—Beeldhouwkunst, Plaketten, Antiek*, nrs. 2376–2378; A. S. Norris and I. Weber, *Medals and Plaquettes from the Molinari Collection at Bowdoin College*, nr. 370. Two examples of *Christ and the Samaritan Woman* are exhibited to demonstrate that both lead and bronze were used for plaquettes and how the individual impressions vary slightly in the strength of the details. The general chronology of Flötner's plaquettes was established by E. F. Bange and modified by Weber. See Bange, "Zur Datierung von Peter Flötners Plakettenwerk," *Archiv für Medaillen- und Plaketten-Kunde* 3 (1921–1922): 45–52, esp. 46, for these landscape plaquettes.

2. Talbot and Shestack, eds., *The Danube School*, pp. 31–60, on Altdorfer. None of Flötner's landscape plaquettes have been shown to derive from specific prints by Altdorfer or any other artists. Nevertheless, the general approach to landscape is similar. Flötner's landscapes anticipate those by Hans Lautensack (cat. nrs. 165 and 169).

3. Neudörfer, *Nachrichten von Künstlern*, p. 115.

129. FEMALE FIGURE

ca. 1535–1540
Boxwood model for a plaquette
7 × 3.65 cm
Lent by the Nelson-Atkins Museum of Art, Kansas City, Missouri (Nelson Fund)

128. ATE AND THE LITAE

ca. 1535–1540
Plaquette: lead (three holes in the top)
15.8 cm diameter
Morgenroth, nr. 361; Weber, *Renaissanceplaketten*, nr. 42
Lent by the University Art Museum, University of California, Santa Barbara, Morgenroth Collection

Ate and the Litae is Flötner's largest and most beautiful plaquette.[1] Flötner has further refined the design of the landscape with its deep space and its subtly graduated relief. The larger format permitted Flötner to incorporate more naturalistic details than in the three previous examples (cat. nrs. 125–127). The scrollwork cartouche is blank, except for the faintly scratched name Henricus de Honthorst, which was added at a later date.

The story of *Ate and the Litae* is based upon the account in Homer's *Iliad* (9, 502ff., and 19, 91ff.). Flötner's specific source was Andrea Alciati's *Emblematum Libellus*, either the 1531 Augsburg edition or, more likely, the larger 1534 Paris edition.[2] Ate was the clawfooted daughter of Jupiter who caused strife and misfortune wherever she went. At the top of the composition is Jupiter, with his thunderbolts, banishing Ate from Mount Olympus. As Ate flies over the world the castle at the left is consumed by fire and the traveler in the forest at the right is attacked. The three older women in the foreground are the Litae, also Jupiter's daughters, who pursue their half-sister by foot to repair some of the damage that she has caused.

---

1. Lange, *Flötner*, nr. 38; De Coo, *Museum Mayer van den Bergh*, nr. 2379.
2. Lange, *Flötner*, nr. 38, first identified Flötner's dependence upon Alciati for the subject alone. In the 1542 Paris edition, the emblem of Ate and the Litae is number XCII; see Andreas Alciatus, *Emblematum Libellus* (reprint: Darmstadt: Wissenschaftliche Buchgesellschaft, 1967), pp. 204–205. For a discussion of the different issues of Alciati, see M. Praz, *Studies in Seventeenth-Century Imagery*, pp. 248–252; H. Homann, *Studien zur Emblematik des 16. Jahrhunderts*, pp. 25–40.

The identity of the woman is uncertain. The female type with the head turned upward and to the side to express grief or intense emotion, with the hair blowing in the wind, and the seminude body conceived in contrapposto is found in German and Italian representations of Lucretia and Cleopatra, or, less frequently, Dido.[1] In her right hand, now broken off, the woman would have presumably held a knife, if she were Lucretia, or an asp, if she were Cleopatra.

The plaquette design with a full-size figure with raised left foot and a simple landscape behind is very similar to the compositions of *Vanity* (cat. nr. 130), *Choler* (cat. nr. 131), or *Sol* (cat. nr. 133). The relief carving in this boxwood model is unusually deep and would have been difficult to cast, which may explain why there are no known plaquettes after this model. Flötner may have conceived the female figure as a high-relief goldsmith model or as an independent carving.

---

1. I wish to thank Roger Ward of the Nelson-Atkins Museum of Art for the suggestion that Flötner based his figure upon Agostino Veneziano's engraving after Baccio Bandinelli's *Cleopatra*; see *The Illustrated Bartsch*, 26: nr. 193. By the 1530s the general figure type had become relatively common in the prints of Marcantonio Raimondi (ibid., 26: nr. 192B), Barthel Beham (ibid., 15: nr. 12), Hans Sebald Beham (ibid., 15: nrs. 77–79), and Georg Pencz (ibid., 16: nr. 85), among other artists. The woman is not Daphne, as formerly listed by the museum.

130. VANITY (VANITAS)

ca. 1537–1543
Plaquette: bronze (with hole)
8.25 × 4.75 cm
Weber, *Renaissanceplaketten*, nr. 56.1
Lent by the Spencer Museum of Art, University of Kansas, Lawrence

131. CHOLER

ca. 1537–1543
Plaquette: bronze (with four holes)
7 × 5.1 cm
Weber, *Renaissanceplaketten*, nr. 56.6
Lent by the Spencer Museum of Art, University of Kansas, Lawrence

These two plaquettes belong to a series of the seven deadly sins.[1] Each female personification is shown with wings and with the appropriate attributes. Vanity gazes at a large mirror. Her seminaked body is ornamented with two pendant necklaces. The horse behind her was traditionally associated with the prideful side of vanity since a wild horse refuses to be ridden. Choler is clad in ancient armor. Because of her anger, she pierces her breast with a sword. In her left hand she holds a flaming torch, symbol of the heat and dryness associated with the choleric temperament. She wears a lion's head for a hat and has a lion cub at her feet. The lion, like the cat in Dürer's *Adam and Eve* (cat. nr. 11), signifies the cruelty of choler.

Both of these plaquettes were frequently copied.[2] For instance, the workshop of Wenzel Jamnitzer made a cast after *Vanity* and used it, along with two other Flötner plaquettes, to decorate the sides of the mortar (cat. nr. 198) now in Cleveland.

1. Lange, *Flötner*, nrs. 95, 98, 95–101, for the entire series. The iconography of the vices was well established by the sixteenth century. See M. W. Bloomfield, *The Seven Deadly Sins* (Lansing, Mich., 1952). Pencz's engraved series of the vices or sins contains the same symbolic attributes; see *The Illustrated Bartsch*, 16: nrs. 98–104, esp. 98 (*Vanity* or *Pride*), 103 (*Choler*).
2. For example, Virgil Solis made prints after these plaquettes. See Bartsch IX: nrs. 179 (*Choler*), 213 (*Vanity*).

132. CHARITY (CARITAS)

ca. 1540
Plaquette: bronze
9 × 6.7 cm
Weber, *Renaissanceplaketten*, nr. 55.3
Lent by the Walters Art Gallery, Baltimore

Charity is from a series of seven cardinal virtues.[1] A standing woman with two children is set against a landscape reminiscent of the artist's earlier plaquettes. The iconography of Charity as a woman nursing or playing with one or more children was well established by the sixteenth century.[2] Flötner produced two other plaquettes of this theme that vary only in the positions of the figures.[3]

1. Lange, *Flötner*, nrs. 81, 81–87 (series); and De Coo, *Museum Mayer van den Bergh*, nr. 2418.
2. R. Freyhen, "The Evolution of the Caritas Figure in the Thirteenth and Fourteenth Centuries," *Journal of the Warburg and Courtauld Institutes* 11 (1948): 68–86. This article contains comments on several Renaissance examples as well. Also see Hans Sebald Beham's engraving of *Charity*; *The Illustrated Bartsch*, 15: nrs. 131, 129–136 (series of the virtues).
3. The formats of the other two *Charity* plaquettes are different. One is trapezoidal and the other circular; see Lange, *Flötner*, nrs. 89, 59. The stone model for the circular *Charity* is in the Kunsthistorisches Museum in Vienna. A second, later soapstone model is in the Victoria & Albert Museum in London. This second model may have been made in 1556, when Johannes Neudörfer of Nuremberg commissioned a christening coin (a *patenpfenning*) for a godson; see Pechstein, *Bronzen und Plaketten*, nr. 163. Wenzel Jamnitzer copied the circular *Charity* for his *Kaiserpokal* in Berlin (Kunstgewerbemuseum; fig. 50, but not visible in this particular view).

133. SOL

ca. 1540
Plaquette: bronze
7 × 4.75 cm
Weber, *Renaissanceplaketten*, nr. 57.4
Lent by the Spencer Museum of Art, University of Kansas, Lawrence

Sol, the sun god, is from a series of seven planetary deities.[1] He is presented as a crowned and bearded king holding a scepter. His shield, emblazoned with the sun insignia, rests against a crouching lion, his symbol.

Sol and several other plaquettes in this set were inspired by the 1528 engravings of the planets by Master I. B., who is traditionally identified as Georg Pencz.[2] In each case, Flötner altered the composition slightly but retained the essential features. For instance, Flötner's *Sol* and the print of the same subject show a single figure standing against a landscape. The tree on the left side extends from the bottom to the top margins. The designs of the shields and the positionings of the lions with their winding tails are almost identical.

1. Lange, *Flötner*, nrs. 14, 11–17 (series); De Coo, *Museum Mayer van den Bergh*, nr. 2404.
2. *The Illustrated Bartsch*, 16: nrs. 11–17, esp. 14 (*Sol*). Also see Hans Sebald Beham's 1539 engraved series; *The Illustrated Bartsch*, 15: nrs. 113–120, esp. 117 (*Sol*).

134. SENSE OF TOUCH: VENUS AND AMOR

ca. 1543–1546
Plaquette: lead (hole in the top)
6.9 × 9.3 cm
Morgenroth, nr. 370
Lent by the University Art Museum, University of California, Santa Barbara, Morgenroth Collection

This scene of Venus and Amor (or Cupid) clearly illustrates the sense of touch.[1] Amor, having reached into a tree to get some honey, is now being pursued by a swarm of angry bees. By the distressed look on his face, Amor has obviously already been stung. He rushes toward Venus for protection. This theme is ultimately based upon Theocritus's *Idylls* (XIX). During the Renaissance it was frequently painted by the Cranach workshop to illustrate the pain often associated with love.[2] Whether Flötner borrowed the theme from Cranach or from Andrea Alciati's *Emblematum Libellus* is uncertain.[3] The landscape and buildings surrounding Venus and Amor are reminiscent of, if not as detailed as, the artist's earlier plaquettes.

1. Lange, *Flötner*, nr. 111, cf. nrs. 109–110; De Coo, *Museum Mayer van den Bergh*, nr. 2427. Wenzel Jamnitzer copied this plaquette for the decoration on his mortar of the 1550s in Berlin (Kunstgewerbemuseum); Pechstein, *Bronzen und Plaketten*, nr. 8.

2. Koepplin and Falk, eds., *Lukas Cranach*, II: nr. 569, provides a brief iconographic discussion. The earliest example of this theme in Germany was in Dürer's drawing of 1514 (Vienna, Kunsthistorisches Museum); Winkler, *Zeichnungen Dürers*, III: nr. 665.

3. *Emblematum Libellus* (Paris, 1542 ed.), nr. XC. For Flötner's use of Alciati's emblem book, see *Ate and the Litae* (cat. nr. 128).

135. KING IN A FRAME OF SCROLL ORNAMENT

Second half of the sixteenth century
Plaquette: bronze
Parabolical (12.2 × 8 cm)
Morgenroth, nr. 379; Weber, *Renaissanceplaketten*, after nr. 46.13
Lent by the University Art Museum, University of California, Santa Barbara, Morgenroth Collection

The standing figure of a king is a replica of one of the rulers in Flötner's plaquette series the *Ancient Kings of Germany*.[1] His precise identity is unknown. The Nuremberg artist of this plaquette added an elaborate scroll frame around the king. The style of the scrollwork with the secondary figures is reminiscent of the decorative prints of Virgil Solis, such as the frame on the title page of his *Biblische Figuren* of 1562 (cat. nr. 178). The scroll pattern at the top of the plaquette also can be compared with the more complicated design on Hans Bolsterer's wooden cartouche (cat. nr. 204).

1. Lange, *Flötner*, nr. 57. The series consists of twelve kings with this figure as either a thirteenth ruler or an alternate design. See Lange, nrs. 45–56, for the others. This series was frequently copied. Jonas Silber used the original twelve kings as models for the interior of the lid of the *Weltallschale of Emperor Rudolf II* (dated 1589; fig. 52, but not visible); see Pechstein, *Goldschmiedewerke der Renaissance*, nr. 101. Flötner also made woodcuts of the kings for Burchard Waldis's *Vrsprung vnd Herkumen der zwolff ersten alten Konig vnd Fürsten devtscher Nation* (Nuremberg: Hans Guldenmund, 1543); see Röttinger, *Flettners Holzschnitte*, pp. 3–10.

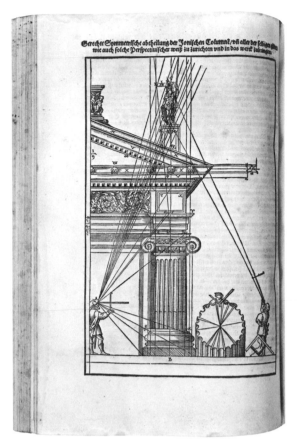

136. VITRUVIUS POLLO, VITRUUIUS TEUTSCH . . . DURCH GUALTHERU H. RIUIUM (Nuremberg: Johann Petrius, 1548)

193 woodcuts (190 woodblocks)
Lange, *Flötner*, pp. 29–35
Lent by the Library of Congress, Washington, Lessing J. Rosenwald Collection

Between 27 and 23 B.C., Vitruvius, Roman architect and engineer, wrote *De Architectura* (commonly known as the *Ten Books on Architecture*), which was destined to be one of the most influential artistic treatises during both his era and the Renaissance.[1] It provided the theoretical basis for the treatises of Alberti, Sebastiano Serlio, and other Renaissance authors. Although Vitruvius's text was widely known through manuscript copies, it was initially published by J. Sulpicius da Veroli in Rome in about 1486. This treatise was frequently reprinted in new editions during the sixteenth century. Walter Rivius issued the first northern European edition at Strassburg in 1543. Rivius was also responsible for publishing the first German translation of Vitruvius's treatise, the *Vitruvius teutsch*, which is exhibited here.[2]

Excepting Serlio's *General Rules of Architecture* of 1542, the *Vitruvius teutsch* was the first significant architectural treatise published in German.[3] Much of the technical information was still relevant to sixteenth-century architects and artists. The treatise, which is divided into ten books, offers discussions about the education of the architect (Book I); materials and technical matters (Book II); the construction of temples and the three classical orders (Books III–IV); the construction of public buildings, such as forums, basilicas, theaters, baths, and harbors (Book V); domestic buildings (Book VI); decorative materials and their applications (Book VII); the finding of water and the building of wells, aqueducts, and so forth (Book VIII); studying of the stars and the measurement of time (Book IX); and the construction of hoisting, pumping, and siege machines (Book X).

The attribution of the 190 new woodcuts in the Nuremberg edition is problematic.[4] Peter Flötner's monogram appears on page CXCVIII verso, a demonstration of how to use the sun to start a fire; the remaining woodcuts are unsigned. Röttinger has questioned Flötner's participation because the artist died in 1546, two years before the treatise was published.[5] Nevertheless, the inclusion of his monogram on this page and the close correspondence between the text illustrations and Flötner's graphic and sculptural oeuvre lead one to conclude that he was the principal artist of the project and that his designs were essentially followed by Virgil Solis and, less clearly, Georg Pencz, who completed the treatise.[6]

Reproduced here are pages XI and CXXVII verso. In the first, a child stands upon a block and is surrounded by all the books and tools necessary for the education of an architect. Vitruvius writes "The architect should be equipped with knowledge of many branches of study and varied kinds of learning, for it is by his judgment that all work done by the other arts is put to test. This knowledge is the child of practice and theory."[7] On page CXXVII verso, three architects study the base, capital, and entablature of an Ionic temple.[8] The figure of the child and the architectural forms of the Ionic temple recall Flötner's Hirschvogelhaus chimneypiece (fig. 17) or the artist's many woodcuts of columns and capitals.[9]

---

1. *Vitruvius: The Ten Books on Architecture*, tr. M. H. Morgan (New York: 1914; reprint: Dover Publications, 1960). On Vitruvius and his influence, see J. von Schlosser, *La Letteratura artistica*, pp. 251–258; R. Martin, "Vitruvius," *Encyclopedia of World Art* (New York, 1967), 14: cols. 805–811. Among the most important editions of Vitruvius's text are those of Fra Giovanni Giocondo (Venice, 1511, 1513, 1522, and 1525) and Cesare Cesariano (Como, 1521).

2. H. Röttinger, *Die Holzschnitte zur Architektur und zum Vitruvius Teutsch des Walther Rivius*, esp. pp. 24–35; Schlosser, *La Letteratura artistica*, pp. 277, 280. For a recent reprint of the original edition, see E. Forssman (foreword), *Zehen Bücher von der Architectur und künstlicher Bauen Marcus Vitrivius Pollio; Erstmals verteutscht durch Gualther Hermenius Rivius* (Hildesheim: G. Olms, 1973).

3. Pieter Coecke van Aelst produced a German edition of Serlio's treatise at Antwerp in 1542. See Schlosser, *La Letteratura artistica*, pp. 418–419; G. Marlier, *La Renaissance flamande: Pierre Coeck d'Alost* (Brussels, 1966), pp. 379–383.

4. Röttinger, *Vitrivius Teutsch*, pp. 41ff. Many of the woodcuts are elaborations upon or reinterpretations of the illustrations in the 1521 Como edition of Vitruvius, Francesco Colonna's *Hypnerotomachia Poliphili* (Venice: Aldus Manutius, 1499), and Serlio's treatise.

5. Röttinger, *Vitrivius Teutsch*, pp. 41–43.

6. Ibid., pp. 43–48, for Solis and Pencz. On Flötner, see the next paragraph.

7. *Vitruvius: The Ten Books on Architecture*, p. 5 (Book I, chapter 1).

8. Ibid., pp. 9off. (Book III, chapter V).

9. For instance, see Geisberg, nrs. 835, 841, 845–855.

Portrait Medals

As an art form, the portrait medal dates back to Roman antiquity.[1] North Italian painter Pisanello (ca. 1395–1455) is generally credited with reviving the portrait medal when in 1438 he cast the likeness of John VIII Palaeologus, Emperor of Constantinople (1425–1448).[2] From the courts of Mantua and Ferrara, the taste for these antique-style metallic portraits quickly spread among nobles and humanists. Although Italian medals are mentioned in Germany as early as 1459, it was not until 1507 and 1509, when Nuremberg sculptors Hermann and Peter Vischer the Younger made their own portraits, that medals began to be produced in Germany.[3] Nuremberg quickly became the German center for their manufacture. The earliest medalists, such as Hans Schwarz (cat. nrs. 139–143) and Matthes Gebel (cat. nrs. 144–151), were trained sculptors, whereas Joachim Deschler (cat. nrs. 152–154) and Valentin Maler (cat. nrs. 155–157), among others, were trained as goldsmiths and metalworkers. As a result, the later medals are often of higher quality casting, yet these lack, in some instances, the finer modeling and understanding of the facial structure of the earlier medals.

It has been estimated that approximately four thousand different portrait medals were created in Germany in the sixteenth century.[4] The majority were by German and Italian artists. One positive result, beyond the inherent aesthetic value of these medals, is the broad surviving pictorial legacy of Germany's nobles, patricians, scholars, and artists.

A typical medal, such as Gebel's *Portrait of Johann Friedrich* (cat. nr. 150), presents the portrait, as well as the name, the age, the motto, and the coat of arms of the individual, although not all these features are included on every medal. Occasionally, an allegorical scene will be depicted on the reverse. The medal is ringed with a raised edge, often in a pearl or laurel pattern.

A medal served much the same purpose as a painted portrait: it immortalized the individual. Medals made popular gifts, and humanists and merchants alike collected and exchanged them well as for a variety of other reasons. Schwarz's *Portraits of the Five Pfinzing Brothers* (cat. nr. 141) was ordered to celebrate their fraternal ties. Medals made popular gifts, and Humanists and merchants alike collected and exchanged them with their friends.[5] In preparation for Emperor Charles V's planned visit to Nuremberg in 1521, the city council commissioned Albrecht Dürer to design and Hans Krafft the Elder to execute a sumptuous silver medal decorated with the prince's portrait, his mottos and emblems, and his coats of arms (cat. nr. 138). Medals, like plaquettes, were usually stored in drawers in a collector's cabinet. Others were pierced with a hole at the top or attached to a ring and then affixed to clothing or worn around the neck.[6] From the 1530s such artists as Melchior Baier and Peter Flötner incorporated portrait medals into lavish goldsmith works, as for instance the *Pfinzing Dish* (fig. 38).

The production process began with a drawing of the individual to be portrayed. In the case of the *Portrait of Willibald Pirckheimer* (cat. nr. 137),

the unknown Nuremberg artist worked from existing portraits of the humanist by Albrecht Dürer. Since these preparatory drawings were considered to be of relatively little importance in their own right, very few survive today. The extant corpus of drawings by Hans Schwarz is unique.

Next, a relief model was carved. Schwarz and many early masters favored a wooden model, usually of boxwood or pearwood or, less often, oak or limewood (lindenwood). Matthes Gebel (cat. nrs. 146 and 147), Valentin Maler (cat. nr. 155), and other later medalists preferred to use stone, such as the light-colored *solnhofen* or the darker *kehlheim*, both types of limestone. By the 1560s, the Italian practice of employing a wax model on slate became increasingly popular.

There were two principal means for producing a medal: casting and striking. In the first, a bed of very fine, firmly packed sand was prepared. The wooden, stone, or wax model was pressed into the surface of the sand and, when removed, it left a positive impression. Multiple impressions of the same model could be created simultaneously. Next, the molten metal was poured into the depressed sand. Lead, bronze, and silver were the favored metals; however, tin or gold was occasionally used. If the medal was to have cast reliefs on both sides, each half could be cast separately and the two later joined together, as in the case of Deschler's *Portrait of Hieronymus Paumgartner* (cat. nr. 152), or some form of hinged frame that permitted a simultaneous double casting was used.

The second technique, striking, was used most often for lettering and the low-relief coats of arms on the reverse of the medal. The desired inscription or image had been cut into the die, which was then used to punch or stamp the warm metal. Frequently, a metal press, similar to a coin press, was used. In Gebel's earliest medal (cat. nr. 144), he had yet to master fully the integration of the cast bust and the struck text. Both were created separately and the two pieces were fitted together, albeit rather awkwardly. Occasionally, the coat of arms or motto on the reverse was engraved (e.g., cat. nr. 156).

Once the medal was cast or cut, any surface imperfections, such as might be caused by an air bubble or grains of sand that had shifted, were trimmed away and the blemish smoothed over. Finally, the medalist would typically either varnish or gild the medals before presenting them to their owners.

---

1. The basic sources for the following are Habich, I.1, pp. XIIIff.; Suhle, *Die Deutsche Renaissance-Medaille*, esp. pp. 7–12; Grotemeyer, *'Da ich het die gestalt,'* esp. pp. 5–13; *Berlin: Der Mensch um 1500*, pp. 85–90.
2. Hill and Pollard, nr. 1.
3. Grotemeyer, *'Da ich het die gestalt,'* p. 5, figs. 7–8. It is not accidental that these two sons of Peter Vischer the Elder created what may be the earliest German medals. The elder Vischer owned a collection of coins and medals that is believed to have included both Roman and early medieval examples. See von der Osten, "Über Peter Vischers Törichten Bauern und den Beginn der 'Renaissance' in Nürnberg," pp. 80–81.
4. Grotemeyer, *'Da ich het die gestalt,'* pp. 13–14. Habich catalogued 3,700 examples. Some medals were issued in unique impressions, while others survive in larger quantities. Hans Krafft the Elder's *Portrait of Emperor Charles V* (cat. nr. 138) was produced in an edition of at least one hundred medals.

5. Ibid., pp. 5–6. For Paulus Praun's extensive holding of antique and contemporary medals, see Murr, *Description du Cabinet de Monsieur Paul de Praun à Nuremberg*, pp. 389–483.
6. See the portraits by Lucas Cranach the Elder and his son Lucas illustrated in Grotemeyer, *'Da ich het die gestalt,'* pl. IV; *Berlin: Der Mensch um 1500*, fig. 54. Also see Hans Lautensack's *Portrait of Hieronymus Schurstab* (cat. nr. 166).

137. PORTRAIT OF WILLIBALD PIRCKHEIMER

1517
Obverse: bust to right; inscription:
BILIBALDVS PIRCKHEYMER
Reverse: coat of arms; inscription: MDXVII
INICIV SAPIAE TIMOR DOMINI
Medal: silver
7.4 cm diameter
Habich 17; Morgenroth 152; *Nuremberg: Dürer*
(1971), nr. 695
Lent by the University of California, Santa Barbara, University Art Museum, Morgenroth Collection

The artist of this medal has yet to be identified. The attribution to Peter Vischer the Younger, based upon general similarities of the style of the lettering, is unconvincing.[1] For the design of the medal, the unknown artist used drawings by Dürer and his workshop that were probably already in Pirckheimer's possession. The profile portrait of Pirckheimer on the medal recalls Dürer's two silverpoint and charcoal sketches of the humanist that were made in 1503.[2] The reverse of the medal with Pirckheimer's coat of arms, a stylized birch tree, surrounded by a laurel wreath derives from a Dürer workshop drawing of 1514–1517.[3]

1. *Nuremberg: Dürer (1971)*, nr. 695. On Pirckheimer, see cat. nr. 30.
2. Winkler, *Zeichnungen Dürers*, II: nrs. 268, 270, both in Berlin (Kupferstichkabinett); *Nuremberg: Dürer (1971)*, nr. 529. A version of this medal, now in Augsburg, is signed with Dürer's monogram. This reflects the recognition that Dürer's drawings of Pirckheimer were the source for the medal.
3. Zink, *Die Handzeichnungen*, nr. 73. Toward the end of the sixteenth century, oval plaquettes of lead or carved mother-of-pearl after this medal were made in southern Germany. See Beck and Decker, *Dürers Verwandlung in der Skulptur zwischen Renaissance und Barock*, nr. 67, fig. 29.

Krafft was a goldsmith and maker of coins and medals in Nuremberg.[1] By 1509 he was producing seal and coin stamps for the city. Between 1510 and 1513 he minted coins and medals for Elector Friedrich the Wise. Krafft is best known for casting the *Portrait of Emperor Charles V* (cat. nr. 138), the most famous portrait medal of the sixteenth century. He is documented making stamps for the city in 1527. Krafft died in 1542 or 1543.

1. See the bibliography for cat. nr. 138. Also see Hampe, *Nürnberger Ratsverlässe*, I: nrs. 932, 934, 1024, 1586, 1588.

138. PORTRAIT OF EMPEROR CHARLES V

1521
Obverse: bust to right; inscription: CAROLVS V RO IMPER; around the edge are Charles V's devices, pillars of Hercules and the flint and firestone of the Order of the Golden Fleece; his motto, PLV[s] VLTR[a]; and fourteen coats of arms
Reverse: imperial double-headed eagle charged on the breast with the shield of Austria-Burgundy, the date 1521, the letter N for Nuremberg, and thirteen coats of arms
Medal: silver
7.15 cm diameter
Habich 18; Kohlhaussen, *Nürnberger Goldschmiedekunst*, nr. 453; *Nuremberg: Dürer (1971)*, nr. 267
Lent by the Germanisches Nationalmuseum, Nuremberg, Med. 8008

In June 1520 the Nuremberg city council commissioned Albrecht Dürer to design an elaborate commemorative medal with the portrait of Charles V to be presented to the emperor during the Reichstag that was to be held in Nuremberg the following year.[1] Dürer's drawing for the medal has not survived. The artist's model for the portrait of Charles V was a medal of the emperor by Hans Schwarz. Charles V is crowned and dressed in armor with a Golden Fleece collar around his neck. Dürer patterned the double-headed imperial eagle after a single-headed eagle on a medal of Friedrich the Wise designed by Lucas Cranach the Elder and cast by Hans Krug the Elder of Nuremberg around 1510.[2] The heraldic program was devised by Willibald Pirckheimer and Lazarus Spengler, who consulted with Johannes Stabius.

Dürer's design was then given to goldsmith Hans Krafft the Elder, who cast the bust of Charles V. The surrounding coats of arms on the front and back, as well as the double-headed eagle, are made from three separate stamps. Krafft produced an edition of one hundred medals, many of which were marked with the impression number. This is a rare occasion where the actual quantity of the edition is known.

Although an outbreak of the plague forced the Reichstag to be moved from Nuremberg to Worms, on 17 February 1521 the city council instructed its envoys Kaspar Nützel, Leonhard Groland, and Christoph Kress to deliver at least eleven copies of the medal to Charles V. Contemporary descriptions of the medal attest to its beauty and artistic merit, features befitting an important gift to the emperor.[3]

1. Besides the sources cited at the beginning of this entry, also see Grotemeyer, *'Da ich het die gestalt,'* pp. 42–43, which quotes three documents related to this medal. These documents are published in full in *JKSAK* 10 (1889): Rep. 5829, 5831–5832.
2. This medal has also been attributed to Hans Krafft the Elder. See Kohlhaussen, *Nürnberger Goldschmiedekunst*, nr. 448; *Nuremberg: Dürer (1971)*, nr. 268. Dürer's use of designs by Schwarz and Cranach may in part be due to his desire to complete the project quickly since he departed for the Netherlands on 20 July 1520.
3. See Grotemeyer, *'Da ich het die gestalt,'* pp. 42–43; Kohlhaussen, *Nürnberger Goldschmiedekunst*, p. 436.

Schwarz, a sculptor, was Germany's first major medalist.[1] He was born in 1492 in Augsburg, where he began studying with sculptor Stephan Schwarz in 1506. Hans Holbein the Elder twice sketched Schwarz as a youth.[2] These drawings and Schwarz's adoption of Holbein's drawing technique suggest that Schwarz may have briefly been in Holbein's workshop.[3] Although Schwarz was not an independent artist until 1517, he carved an elaborate wooden *Lamentation* relief in 1516 and signed it with his monogram.[4] His first portrait medal, of Konrad Peutinger, a humanist, is dated 1517.[5] In the following year he made medals of artist Hans Burgkmair and at least fifteen of the imperial courtiers and princes who attended the Reichstag in Augsburg.[6]

In 1519 Schwarz moved to Nuremberg, apparently at the invitation of Melchior Pfinzing, provost of St. Sebaldus (cat. nr. 140). According to Neudörfer, Schwarz resided in Pfinzing's house.[7] In this year Schwarz made several medals for members of the Pfinzing family (cat. nr. 141). During his two years in Nuremberg, Schwarz produced numerous drawings for medals (cat. nr. 139); many medals, including a self-portrait and a portrait of Dürer (cat. nr. 143); and an occasional wooden carving, such as *Death and the Maiden*, an oak relief in Berlin (Staatliche Museen).[8]

From 1521 Schwarz traveled across Europe from court to court seeking commissions for his portrait medals. In 1521 he journeyed to Speyer and to the Reichstag at Worms. He then went to Heidelberg. During the mid-1520s Schwarz returned to Nuremberg. He is credited with carving the *Allegory of Justice* statues for the council chamber of the Nuremberg Rathaus during this period.[9] Subsequently, Schwarz was in Poland (1527); Denmark; Paris (1532), where he designed the portrait medal of Jean Clouet, the court painter of King Francis I; the Netherlands; and Westphalia (mid-1530s).[10] He probably died shortly after 1535, the date on his last medal.[11]

Habich attributed 175 medals and wooden models for medals to Schwarz. Undoubtedly, many more medals were made. At least 136 portrait drawings for medals by Schwarz also survive.[12]

1. Much of the biographical information is in Habich I.1, pp. 23–49, nrs. 111–285; Suhle, *Renaissance-Medaille*, pp. 13–28.

2. Bock, *Staatliche Museen zu Berlin*, I: p. 51, nrs. 2553–2554; II: pl. 71.

3. See cat. nr. 139.

4. Berlin (Staatliche Museen); Suhle, *Renaissance-Medaille*, fig. 7.

5. Habich 111.

6. Habich 127 (Burgkmair).

7. Neudörfer, *Nachrichten von Künstlern*, pp. 124–125.

8. *Berlin: Der Mensch um 1500*, nr. 25, pp. 142–147 (relief), fig. 82 (self-portrait). The self-portrait is Habich 171.

9. Pfeiffer and Schwemmer, *Bilddokumenten*, fig. 52; Mende, *Rathaus*, I: fig. 67, and it will be discussed in Mende, *Rathaus*, II: nrs. 606–607. These statues are on display in the Fembohaus in Nuremberg. The statues have also been incorrectly attributed to Hans Leinberger.

10. Suhle, *Renaissance-Medaille*, fig. 11 (Clouet).

11. The medal depicts Johann von Leyden.

12. See cat. nr. 139; M. Bernhardt, "Die Porträtzeichnungen des Hans Schwarz," *MJBK* 11 (1934): 65–95.

139. PORTRAIT OF A MAN IN PROFILE

ca. 1518–1521
Inscription (19th century): Maister Arnold
Drawing: black chalk on paper, cut along the outlines and pasted on a second sheet of paper
22.6 × 18.3 cm
Lent by the Metropolitan Museum of Art, New York, Robert Lehman Collection, 1975

The sitter portrayed in this drawing is unknown.[1] The inscription was added probably in the nineteenth century and, as in the case of many of Schwarz's drawings with later inscriptions, is inaccurate. This drawing is one of 136 known portrait sketches by Schwarz.[2] The majority of the others are in Bamberg (Staatsbibliothek), Berlin (Kupferstichkabinett), and Weimar (Kunstmuseum).[3] Ninety-two of the others are designs for known medals by Schwarz that date, with a few exceptions, between 1518 and 1521.[4]

Gebel, Deschler, Maler, and the other major Nuremberg medalists presumably also made portrait drawings; however, only the sketches by Schwarz survive. Schwarz's drawing technique consists of strongly outlining the contour of the face, emphasizing the principal facial characteristics, and quickly adding a modicum of shading. His style parallels that of Hans Holbein the Younger, who dashed off innumerable sketches for painted portraits.[5] Schwarz probably learned portraiture from Hans Holbein the Elder in Augsburg. The elder Holbein made at least two portrait drawings of Schwarz as a youth, which proves that the two artists were in contact.[6]

Once the drawing was completed, Schwarz prepared the wooden model. In his 1520 self-portrait, Schwarz depicted himself holding a compass and a wood carving knife.[7] Although Schwarz did cast his own medals, he also employed sculptors, such as Ludwig Krug, for this task.[8]

1. Bernhardt, "Die Porträtzeichnungen des Hans Schwarz," nr. 126; G. Szabo, XV–XVI Century Northern Drawings from the Robert Lehman Collection, Metropolitan Museum of Art (New York, 1978), nr. 32.
2. The arrangement of this drawing with the figure wearing a hat tilted slightly to his right, long hair covering the ear, cleanly shaved face, and a heavy robe is a type found in many of Schwarz's sketches. See Bernhardt, "Die Porträtzeichnungen des Hans Schwarz," nrs. 33, 43–45, 48, 55–56, 60, 70, etc.
3. Ibid., nrs. 68–69, 90–95 (a table of the drawings). According to Bernhardt (pp. 67–68), the provenance of these drawings can be traced back to the eighteenth century, when they were owned by the Pfinzing family. As noted in the biography of Schwarz, the artist lived in the house of Melchior Pfinzing in 1519 and 1520 and he made medals of several family members (cat. nrs. 140–142). Melchior or one of his brothers may have obtained the drawings from the artist who might otherwise have thrown them away.
4. Ibid., p. 74. No medal can be associated with the Lehman Collection drawing. The dates are listed in Bernhardt's table of drawings (pp. 90–95). Only a few drawings are dated 1523 or 1528.
5. K. T. Parker, The Drawings of Hans Holbein in the Collection of His Majesty the King at Windsor Castle (London, 1945).
6. Bock, Staatliche Museen zu Berlin, I: p. 51, nrs. 2553–2554; II: pl. 71.
7. Habich 171.
8. Neudörfer, Nachrichten von Künstlern, pp. 124–125, mentioned that Krug cast some of Schwarz's medals.

140. PORTRAIT OF MELCHIOR PFINZING

1519
Obverse: bust to left; inscription: MCCCCXIX AET XXXVII
Reverse: inscription: XIX DEO VINDICTA ET IPSE RETRIBVET AN MD
Medal: bronze
4.4 cm diameter
Habich 134; Hill and Pollard 585
Lent by the National Gallery of Art, Washington, Samuel H. Kress Collection

Melchior Pfinzing (1481–1535) was the provost of St. Sebaldus from 1512 and of St. Alban in Mainz from 1517. He served as the principal editor of Maximilian's Theuerdank (cat. nr. 47). According to Neudörfer, Pfinzing was responsible for bringing Schwarz to Nuremberg where they resided together in the Pfarrhof.[1] Neudörfer also mentioned that he was present when Pfinzing commissioned Schwarz to create the wooden model for this medal. Ludwig Krug was to cast the medal. Although the account probably refers to the exhibited medal, Schwarz made a total of four separate but similar medals of Pfinzing between 1518 and 1521.[2] Schwarz's drawing for this 1519 medal is today in Berlin (Kupferstichkabinett).[3] Interestingly, it is a half-length, not a bust, portrait, which suggests that Schwarz initially planned a slightly different design for his medal. This depiction of Pfinzing in his clerical robe and hat is also unusually detailed and carefully sketched.

Pfinzing left Nuremberg in 1521 because of the growing civic support for the Lutheran cause.[4] He settled in Mainz, where he remained until his death.

1. Neudörfer, Nachrichten von Künstlern, pp. 124–125. The Pfarrhof, or parish house, is located just west of St. Sebaldus. See the map in fig. 2, location nr. 29. Pfinzing had Kulmbach and others make stained-glass windows for the Pfarrhof. Dürer penned a wheel-of-fortune drawing in one of Pfinzing's books; see Winkler, Zeichnungen Dürers, III: nr. 704.
2. Habich 133–136.
3. Bernhardt, "Die Porträtzeichnungen des Hans Schwarz," nr. 50, pl. VI,3. Also see nr. 22, pl. I,7, a more abbreviated bust drawing for Schwarz's 1518 medal (Habich 133); this drawing is in Bamberg (Staatsbibliothek).
4. Pfinzing did maintain his Nuremberg ties. Around 1528 Gebel made a portrait medal of Pfinzing that is unrelated to any of Schwarz's works. See Habich 970; Morgenroth 160.

141. PORTRAITS OF THE FIVE PFINZING BROTHERS

1519

Obverse: five busts to left; inscription: CON-CORDIAE FRATERNAE

Reverse: inscription: EFFIGIES SIGISMVNDI MELCHIORIS PREPOSITI ECCLESIE SANCTI ALBANI MOGVNTINENSIS VDALRICI ABBATIS SANCTI PAVLI VALLIS LAVINII SEYFRIDI ET MARTINI PFINCZING FRATRVM ANN M CCCCC XIX

Medal: lead

4.75 cm diameter

Habich 177; Morgenroth 155

Lent by the University of California, Santa Barbara, University Art Museum, Morgenroth Collection

---

Schwarz's medal celebrates the fraternal ties of Melchior Pfinzing and his four brothers.[1] The five busts overlap and are arranged by age. From right to left and front to back are Sigmund, Melchior, Ulrich, Seyfried, and Martin, the sons of Seyfried Pfinzing (died 1514) and his second wife, Barbara Grundherrin (died 1517). Sigmund (1479–1554) was a member of the Nuremberg city council from 1513 to 1515 and later a magistrate at Marloffstein; he died in Leipzig. Ulrich (1484–1530) was an advisor to Maximilian, abbot of St. Paul in Kärnten, and, like Melchior, provost of St. Alban in Mainz. Seyfried (1485–1545) was a preacher at Weigelshof. Martin I von Henfenfeld (1490–1552) was a member of the city council in 1523.[2] In 1532 and 1542 he directed Nuremberg's troops in the wars against the Turks. He was married twice and had nineteen children.

In preparing this medal, Schwarz reused the drawings and medals he had made in 1519 of both Melchior and Martin.[3] This is immediately evident when, for instance, the medal of Melchior (cat. nr. 140) is compared with his depiction on the fraternal medal. Drawings of the other three brothers do not survive. Schwarz next carved a wooden model, probably the example now in Stuttgart (Staatsgalerie).[4] It is impossible to determine how many copies of the fraternal medal were cast. The exhibited example contains a ring so the medal could be worn around the neck and it may have been intended for one of the brothers or another family member.[5]

In 1534 Sigmund, Seyfried, and Martin ordered another fraternal work, the *Pfinzing Dish* (Nuremberg, Germanisches Nationalmuseum) made by Peter Flötner and Melchior Baier (fig. 38).[6] This dish is decorated with three portrait medals by Gebel and is an artistically important example of the use of medals to personalize a goldsmith's work.

---

1. Habich 177 for the biographical information. Also see Pechstein, *Bronzen und Plaketten*, nr. 151.
2. While Dürer was in Aachen in October 1520, he made a drawing of Martin Pfinzing in his travel sketchbook. Winkler, *Zeichnungen Dürers*, IV: nr. 761 (Berlin, Kupferstichkabinett). The inscription on this drawing has been trimmed. Martin was thirty not twenty years old.
3. For Melchior, see the previous entry. Schwarz's drawing of Martin is in Berlin (Kupferstichkabinett); Bernhardt, "Die Porträtzeichnungen des Hans Schwarz," nr. 60, pl. XX,6. The medal is Habich 185. Both are illustrated in *Berlin: Der Mensch um 1500*, figs. 56–57.
4. Habich I.1, pl. XXXIX,4.
5. Since several silver and bronze copies of this medal are known, this lead example was probably for a family member and not one of the brothers. Other copies of this medal are in Berlin, Munich, Nuremberg, and other collections. Pechstein, *Bronzen und Plaketten*, nr. 151.
6. See the comments in Section 6 and Kohlhaussen, *Nürnberger Goldschmiedekunst*, nr. 465.

142. PORTRAIT OF SEBALD IV PFINZING

1519

Obverse: bust to left; inscription: SEBALDVS PFINCZING AETA XXXI

Reverse: coat of arms; inscription: MDXVIIII

Medal: bronze gilt

4.7 cm diameter

Habich 149; Morgenroth 154

Lent by the University of California, Santa Barbara, University Art Museum, Morgenroth Collection

---

Sebald IV Pfinzing von Lichtenhof (1487–1543) was part of a different branch of the Pfinzing family than that of Melchior and his four brothers.[1] Sebald's father, Sebald III, owned the house in which Dürer was raised. When Dürer acquired the property rights from Sebald III on 8 May 1507, Sebald IV was one of the witnesses. In 1510 Sebald IV married Katharina, daughter of Leinhard von Ploben. From 1511 on Sebald was a member of the city council. In 1522 he was the elder burgermeister and in 1536 the senior government officer.

The drawing for this medal is in Berlin (Kupferstichkabinett).[2] Once a drawing was made, Schwarz rarely altered the facial design. In this instance, the drawing and the medal are virtually identical.

---

1. Habich 149 says that Sebald died in 1543. Pfeiffer, ed., *Nürnberg*, p. 601 (index), gives the death date as 1537.
2. Bernhardt, "Die Porträtzeichnungen des Hans Schwarz," nr. 34, pl. XIV,1.

143. PORTRAIT OF ALBRECHT DÜRER

1520
Obverse: bust to left; inscription: ALBERTVS
DVRER PICTORIS GERMANICVS
Medal: bronze
5.8 cm diameter
Habich 201
Lent by the Germanisches Nationalmuseum,
Nuremberg, Med. 9401

While in Antwerp in September 1520, Dürer wrote in his travel diary: "I have sent Hans Schwarz 2 fl[orins] in gold for my picture, in a letter by the Antwerp Fuggers to Augsburg."[1] The picture to which Dürer referred is the box-wood model for a portrait medal now in Braunschweig (Herzog Anton Ulrich–Museum).[2] This wooden model was made in 1519 and was used the following year to produce a series of portrait medals, including the example exhibited here.[3]

To what degree Dürer participated in the designing of the medal is uncertain. In 1519 Dürer drew a plan for the obverse and reverse of a proposed medal of himself,[4] but the drawing contains only inscriptions and his coat of arms. If he created a self-portrait for this project, it has not survived. Since Schwarz was an accomplished portraitist and usually made his own drawings (see cat. nr. 139), it is reasonable to assume that he was responsible for the likeness. Schwarz may have studied Dürer's 1500 *Self-Portrait* (Munich, Alte Pinakothek), since the styles of the fur-trimmed robe and long, wavy hair are quite similar.[5] Dürer had yet to adopt the shorter haircut that can be seen in the 1527 medal by Gebel and in Schön's woodcut portrait (cat. nr. 66).

By 1519–1520, portrait medals of German artists were no longer unusual. Schwarz created medals of Hans Burgkmair (1518) and himself (1520).[6] Hermann II Vischer produced a self-portrait with an antique-style figure on the reverse in 1507.[7] A self-portrait of his brother, Peter the Younger, dates to 1509.[8] Later Gebel designed a portrait of Hans Sebald Beham, and Ludwig Neufahrer made a medal of Barthel Beham (1531).[9] These medals reflect the improving social status of artists in Nuremberg and other German towns. For example, Dürer was a celebrity within his own lifetime as well as after his death. Schwarz's medal was frequently copied by Hans Petzoldt (1628) and others, demonstrating that there was a demand for portraits of the artist.[10]

1. Conway, *Writings of Dürer*, p. 104; Rupprich, *Dürer schriftlicher Nachlass*, I: p. 157 (lines 81–84).

2. H. J. Erlanger, "The Medallic Portraits of Albrecht Dürer," *Museum Notes* (American Numismatic Society) 10 (1962): 145–172, esp. 154–155; *Nuremberg: Dürer (1971)*, nr. 76; *Selbstbildnisse und Künstlerportraits von Lucas van Leyden bis Anton Raphael Mengs*, exh. cat. (Braunschweig: Herzog Anton Ulrich–Museum, 1980), pp. 88–90, nr. 22. On the reverse of the wooden model is the inscription IMAGO ALBERTI DVRER ALEMANI QVAM SVIS MET IPSE EFFINXIT MANIBVS ANNO AETATIS SVAE XLVIII SALVTIS VERO MDXIX. The model measures 5.8 cm in diameter.

3. Schwarz also made a smaller version, measuring 2.75 cm in diameter; see Habich 202.

4. London (British Museum). Winkler, *Zeichnungen Dürers*, III: nr. 720. The inscriptions on the drawing do not correspond to that on the medal.

5. Anzelewsky, *Dürer*, nr. 66.

6. Habich 127 (Burgkmair), 171 (self-portrait).

7. Grotemeyer, *'Da ich het die gestalt,'* figs. 7, 8.

8. Ibid., fig. 6.

9. Ibid., fig. 60 (Barthel Beham); Suhle, *Renaissance-Medaille*, pl. 23, fig. 1 (Hans Sebald Beham).

10. Petzoldt's medal was made to celebrate the centennial of Dürer's death. See *Nuremberg: Dürer (1971)*, nr. 78; Beck and Decker, eds., *Dürers Verwandlung in der Skulptur zwischen Renaissance und Barock*, nrs. 59–61.

Gebel was a sculptor and prolific medalist.[1] He was born around 1500 somewhere outside Nuremberg, perhaps at Wiener-Neustadt, and acquired Nuremberg citizenship on 14 August 1523. Excepting brief trips to Speyer in 1529 and Augsburg in 1530, Gebel remained in Nuremberg until his death on 22 April 1574. Few of his sculptures have been identified. He carved the attractive wooden busts of Friedrich II, Elector of Palatine, and Philipp von Pfalz that are now in Munich (Bayerisches Nationalmuseum).[2] Habich attributed 330 portrait medals to Gebel, most of which date between 1526 (cat. nr. 144) and 1543.[3] Only after 1542 did Gebel begin to sign his medals. After 1550 Gebel produced few new medals, but rather he and his workshop reissued older works. Gebel was married twice and had a large family.

1. Habich I.2, pp. 140–177, nrs. 957–1286; Suhle, *Renaissance-Medaille*, pp. 52–62, for the following biographic information.
2. Inv. K919–920. Jahn, *Deutsche Renaissance*, pl. 141a. These portrait busts were made about 1530. He also produced portrait medals of both princes. See the related comments in cat. nrs. 149 and 151.
3. Habich I.2, p. 140. Suhle, *Renaissance-Medaille*, p. 52, estimates that Gebel made as many as 350 medals prior to 1554.

144. PORTRAIT OF CHRISTOPH KRESS VON KRESSENSTEIN

1526
Obverse: bust to right; inscription: CRISTOF KRES XXXXII IAR ALT
Reverse: coat of arms; inscription: CISTOFF KRES VOM KRESENSTAIN M D XXVI
Medal: silver with traces of light gilding
3.9 cm diameter
Habich 957; Morgenroth 158; Hill and Pollard 596b
Lent by the University of California, Santa Barbara, University Art Museum, Morgenroth Collection

Christoph Kress (1484–1535), son of Anton Kress and Katharina Löffelholz, spent his youth studying in Milan (1497), Antwerp (1500–1502), and London (1502–1503) before returning to Nuremberg in 1504.[1] In 1513 he married Helen Tucher and became a member of the city council. Kress was actively involved in the city government, especially in his capacity as military advisor.[2] From 1532 he was the city's principal military officer (*kriegshauptmann*). He also headed Nuremberg's delegations to the Reichstag at Speyer in 1526 and Augsburg in 1530. In 1532 Charles V rewarded Kress with the title "von Kressenstein." His marble tomb with an effigy of him as a military officer in armor is in the church of Nürnberg-Kraftshof.[3]

According to Habich, this is Gebel's earliest medal.[4] Gebel's style is already firmly established in this medal and will vary little over the course of the artist's long career. The bust is strongly outlined, often in moderately high relief. Gebel typically emphasizes surface patterns and contrasts the different material textures.

The reverse of this medal poses a dating problem. On it are inscribed Kress's title von Kressenstein and the date 1526, six years before he received this title. Suhle suggested that Kress had Gebel create a new reverse to go with the older medal.[5] If this is true, there should be casts of this medal either without a reverse or with the original reverse if, indeed, these ever existed.

1. *Allgemeine Deutsche Biographie* (Leipzig, 1906), 51: pp. 376–388.
2. In a letter dated about 30 July 1515, Dürer requested Kress's assistance in obtaining his annual stipend of 100 gulden from Emperor Maximilian I. At the time, Kress was on city business in Vienna. See Rupprich, *Dürer schriftlicher Nachlass*, I: pp. 77–78.
3. Pfeiffer and Schwemmer, *Bilddokumenten*, fig. 168.
4. Habich 957. Habich 958 is the same medal with a smaller inscription; the medal measures 2.2 cm in diameter. A lead impression of Habich 957 is in Washington (National Gallery of Art); see Hill and Pollard 596b. Hans Krafft the Younger(?) made another portrait medal of Kress in 1533; see Habich 1296 and Morgenroth 169.
5. Suhle, *Renaissance-Medaille*, p. 56, pl. 20, 1 and 2.

145. PORTRAIT OF ALBRECHT SCHEURL

1527

Obverse: bust to right; inscription: ALBRECHT SCHEVERL GE IM MCCCC LXXXII IAR AM XXVII NOVEMB
Reverse: coat of arms; inscription: OHERR GOT DVR CHRISTVM ERBARM DIGII VNSER M D XXVII
Medal: lead with blackish varnish
4.0 cm diameter
Habich 961; Morgenroth 159
Lent by the University of California, Santa Barbara, University Art Museum, Morgenroth Collection

Albrecht Scheurl (1482–1531) was a Nuremberg patrician who is best remembered for having been murdered by robber knights.[1] On 3 February 1523 he married Anna Zingel. Albrecht Dürer was the godfather of their son Albrecht, who was baptized on 3 February 1525.

Gebel's portrait exhibits a strong, clear profile view of the sitter. He wears the same high-collared shirt as Christoph Kress (cat. nr. 144). The style of braided cap shown was popular during the first third of the century. Gebel also used it in his portrait medal of Dr. Christoph Scheurl (1533) of Nuremberg.[2]

---

1. Rupprich, *Dürer schriftlicher Nachlass*, I: p. 297, G. Hirschmann, "Albrecht Dürer Abstammung und Familienkreis," in Hirschmann and Schnelbögl, *Albrecht Dürers Umwelt*, p. 47.
2. Suhle, *Renaissance-Medaille*, pl. 22, fig. 5; also see pls. 3, fig. 1 (Schwarz's *Portrait of Jakob Fugger* [1518]), 4, fig. 3 (Schwarz's *Portrait of Hans Burgkmair* [1518]).

MODELS FOR TWO MEDALS
146. MODEL FOR THE REVERSE OF THE PORTRAIT OF MARTIN III GEUDER

1528

Reverse only: coat of arms; inscription: SOLA VIRTVS MDXXVIII
Kehlheim stone
3.8 cm diameter
Lent by the Cleveland Museum of Art, Purchase, John L. Severance Fund

147. MODEL FOR THE OBVERSE OF THE PORTRAIT OF A SON OF MARTIN III GEUDER

1535–1540

Obverse only: bust to right; inscription: REMEDIVM INIVKIAE CONTEMPTVS
Kehlheim stone
3.65 cm diameter
Lent by the Cleveland Museum of Art, Purchase, John L. Severance Fund

Although these two stones at first seem to be the models for the same portrait medal, they are instead the obverse and reverse for two separate medals. The reverse (cat. nr. 146) is identical in design and size with the reverse of the 1528 medal of Martin III Geuder von Heroldsberg und Stain (1455–1532).[1] Geuder was a member of the Nuremberg city council from 1483 on, the elder *bürgermeister* in 1499, the *alter herr*, or senior counsellor, from 1509, and the first treasurer, the highest civic officer, in 1532.[2] He married Willibald Pirckheimer's sister Juliana, who bore three sons, Johann (born 1496), Sebald (born 1498), and Georg (1500–1552).[3] The obverse of Gebel's 1528 medal is completely different in its design and the physiognomy of its figure from the Cleveland obverse model.

The obverse model represents one of Martin III's three sons. Johann and Georg were both members of the city council. Emperor Charles V knighted Georg for his military accomplishments in 1530. The obverse model is identical in design to a medal that Gebel produced between 1535 and 1540.[4] The reverse of this medal depicts four maidens and the inscription TRIBVLATIO TOLERANTIA INVIDIA SPES.

---

1. Habich 973. Habich 974 is a smaller (3.0 cm) version of 973. The reverse design also was used on Gebel's 1532 medal of Geuder; see Habich 1083. Gebel's stone model for the obverse of the 1532 medal is in Berlin (Staatliche Museen); see Suhle, *Renaissance-Medaille*, p. 57, pl. 20, fig. 6.
2. The biographical information is from Habich 973.
3. For information on the sons, see Johann Heinrich Zedler, *Grosses Vollständiges Universal-Lexikon* (1735; reprint: Graz, 1961), 10: cols. 1353–1354; Kurras and Machilek, *Caritas Pirckheimer*, nr. 31.
4. The obverse and reverse of this medal are illustrated in Suhle, *Renaissance-Medaille*, pl. 20, figs. 4, 5.

148. PORTRAIT OF HIERONYMUS HOLZSCHUHER

1529
Obverse: bust to right; inscription: HIERO-
NYMVS HOITZSCHVER SENIOR AETATIS
SVAE LX
Reverse: shield of arms with crest and man-
tling; inscription: MVNIFICENTIA AMICOS
PATIENTIA INIMICOS VINCE M DXXIX
Medal: silver
4.0 cm diameter
Habich 993; Hill and Pollard 597a
Lent by the National Gallery of Art, Washing-
ton, Samuel H. Kress Collection

Hieronymus Holzschuher (1469–1529) was a
Nuremberg patrician and a friend of Albrecht
Dürer, who painted his portrait in 1526.[1] In 1498
Holzschuher married Dorothea, daughter of Dr.
Hieronymus Münzer, famed Nuremberg physi-
cian and humanist.[2] In the following year he be-
came a member of the city council. He served as
the elder *bürgermeister* in 1509 and again in 1520.[3]
Holzschuher was also a member of the Sodalitas
Staupitziana.[4]

Although the dress and the profile view that
Gebel used in his medal differ from Dürer's
painting of Holzschuher, Gebel may have consulted this picture. The lines and the construction of the face as represented in the medal seem
to derive in part from Dürer's portrait.

1. Berlin (Staatliche Museen); Anzelewsky, *Dürer*,
nrs. 179–180.
2. The biographical information is taken from
Habich 993 and Anzelewsky, *Dürer*, p. 271.
3. On this group, see the comments above in Section 3 C.
4. On Gebel's medal, also see Suhle, *Renaissance-
Medaille*, p. 58. Gebel's portrait medal of Albrecht
Dürer, used by Schön for the woodcut portrait (cat. nr.
66), displays the same general portrait type as the
Holzschuher medal.

149. PORTRAIT OF OTTHEINRICH, COUNT PALATINE

1531
Obverse: bust to right; inscription: OTTO
HENRICVS DEI GRACIA CO PA RHE INFERI
SUPE ZZ BAIO DVX ZC
Reverse: allegorical figure of Spes (Hope) in a
ship; inscription: SPES MEA DEVS FOR-
TVNAM EXPECTANS ETATIS SVE XXVIIII
MDXXXI
Medal: silver
4.3 cm diameter
Habich 1054
Lent by the University of Wisconsin, Madison,
Elvehjem Museum of Art, Vernon Hall
Collection

Ottheinrich (1502–1559) was the elder son of
Rupprecht, Count Palatine.[1] Upon his father's
death in 1505, Ottheinrich and his brother
Philipp (1503–1548) co-ruled and, from 1522
to 1541, administered the county of Pfalz-
Neuburg. Between 1527 and 1538 Ottheinrich
erected the new wing of the castle at Neuburg.[2]
In 1529 he married Susanna, daughter of Duke
Albrecht IV of Bavaria. When Ottheinrich became a Lutheran in 1542, he had Nuremberg
preacher Andreas Osiander write the official an-
nouncement. In 1551 he took sole control of
Pfalz-Neuburg. Five years later, after the death
of Friedrich II, Ottheinrich became the Elector of
Palatine. Ottheinrich was an active patron of the
arts, having founded the Palatina Library, now
in Rome; reorganized the university at Heidelberg; and enlarged Heidelberg castle between
1556 and 1559.[3]

Gebel made eleven portrait medals of Ottheinrich between 1528 and 1535.[4] In the exhibited example he is dressed in a robe with a chain
around his neck and wearing a hat.[5] His hair is
cut short to reveal his right ear. Other medals
depict the prince dressed in armor, bareheaded,
and with longer hair.[6] In 1532 Gebel portrayed
Ottheinrich in a frontal rather than profile pose.[7]
The motif of Spes holding the sails of a ship
being tossed by the sea appears on two other
medals of Ottheinrich and his brother Philipp,
both dated 1531, by Gebel.[8]

1. *Allgemeine Deutsche Biographie* (Leipzig, 1887), 24:
pp. 713–719.
2. Hitchcock, *German Renaissance Architecture*, pp.
64–67, 73–77, pls. 74–76, 90–91.
3. Ibid., pp. 132–140, 143–146, 149–152, pls. 139,
177–179.
4. Habich 980, 982–984, 1044, 1045, 1049, 1050,
1054, 1056, 1072.
5. Also see V. Hall, *Catalogue of the Vernon Hall Collection of European Medals: Elvehjem Museum of Art, University of Wisconsin* (Madison, 1978), nr. 186.
6. Habich 983. See also *Berlin: Der Mensch um 1500*,
nr. 12.
7. Suhle, *Renaissance-Medaille*, pl. 22, fig. 1.
8. Habich 1050 (Ottheinrich), 1055 (Philipp).

150. PORTRAIT OF JOHANN FRIEDRICH, ELECTOR OF SAXONY

ca. 1532
Obverse: bust to right; inscription: IO FR I IO I
RO IMPELECT PRIMOG D SAX
Reverse: blazon of arms; inscription: SPES MEA
IN DEO EST
Medal: silver
4.6 cm diameter
Habich 1080; Morgenroth 163; Hill and Pollard
599c
Lent by the University of California, Santa Bar-
bara, University Art Museum, Morgenroth
Collection

Johann Friedrich the Magnanimous (1503–1554),
son of Johann the Steadfast, became elector of
Saxony in 1532.[1] To commemorate the occasion,
Gebel created four separate portrait medals of
the prince of varying size and design.[2] In the exhibited example, Johann Friedrich is in his everyday court attire, while in another medal the
prince wields a large sword, symbolizing his
new office.[3]

1. On Johann Friedrich's life and artistic patronage,
see the comments for Pencz's *Portrait of Johann Friedrich*
(cat. nr. 110). In 1532 Johann Friedrich had not yet
grown as corpulent as he appears in Pencz's print and
other late portraits.
2. Habich 1077–1080. 1077 and 1079 are smaller,
dated versions of 1080.
3. Habich 1078.

151. PORTRAIT OF DOROTHEA VON DER PFALZ

1537
Obverse: bust to left; inscription: DOROTHEA
VON GOTTES GNADEN PFALCZ GREFFIN
No reverse
Medal: lead with gray varnish
3.85 cm diameter
Habich 1146; Morgenroth 165
Lent by the University of California, Santa Bar-
bara, University Art Museum, Morgenroth
Collection

Dorothea von der Pfalz (1520–1580) was the
daughter of King Christian II of Denmark and
Isabella of Austria, who was the sister of Emperor Charles V.[1] Dorothea was raised in Flanders following the expulsion of her father from
Denmark in 1523. In 1535 she married Friedrich
II, Elector of Palatine (1482–1556).[2]

This particular impression of the medal lacks
the reverse with the coat of arms and the inscription found on other versions.[3] A 1536 drawing of the coat of arms and inscription design for
this medal, attributed to Hans Sebald Beham, is
in Berlin (Kupferstichkabinett).[4]

1. *Dansk Biografisk Leksikon* (Copenhagen, 1935), 6:
pp. 59–60, for the following.
2. Gebel also made medals of her husband in 1531,
1535, and 1545.
3. See Habich 1146. The inscription normally found
on the reverse reads BEI RHEIN HERCZOGIN IN
BAIERN DER DENMARKISCHEN // KHONIGREICH
PRINCESSIN VND ERBIN M D XXXVII.
4. Bock, *Staatliche Museen zu Berlin*, I: p. 13, nr. 341;
II: pl. 16.

Deschler (ca. 1500–1571/72) was a medalist and a sculptor.[1] He was married in Nuremberg in 1532 but did not acquire citizenship until 1537.[2] Excluding a two-year trip to Italy and frequent journeys to Vienna, Deschler lived in Nuremberg until the late 1550s. Habich attributed 113 medals, dating between 1540 and 1569, to Deschler.[3] Deschler also carved the alabaster portrait bust of Ottheinrich, Count Palatine, now in Paris (Louvre), an onyx portrait of Emperor Charles V, and a boxwood portrait of Dürer.[4] In 1543 and 1553 Deschler is documented working for Archduke, later Emperor, Maximilian II. During the late 1550s he moved permanently to Maximilian's court in Vienna. In 1566 he was appointed imperial sculptor, a post he held until his death in either 1571 or 1572.[5]

1. Habich I.2: pp. 221–236.
2. Ibid., p. 221.
3. Ibid., nrs. 1555–1667. Among the best of these is the medal of Hieronymus Paumgartner (cat. nr. 152).
4. The bust of Ottheinrich is 16 cm high and dates to the mid-sixteenth century; *Berlin: Der Mensch um 1500*, fig. 21. This bust has also been attributed to Dietrich Schro of Mainz; see Kauffmann, *Die Kunst des 16. Jahrhunderts*, nr. 173. The portrait of Charles V is in Vienna (Kunsthistorisches Museum); see F. Eichler and E. Kris, *Die Kameen im Kunsthistorisches Museum, Wien* (Vienna, 1927), nr. 406. The portrait of Dürer is listed in the 1659 inventory of Archduke Leopold-Wilhelm in Vienna; cited by Habich, p. 221.
5. His monthly salary in 1569 was 9 gulden 4 Kreuzen; Habich, p. 221.

152. PORTRAIT OF HIERONYMUS BAUMGARTNER (PAUMGARTNER)

1553; signed on underside of bust on obverse
Obverse: frontal bust; inscription: HIERO-NYMVS PAVMGARTNER ANNO AETATIS 56; on underside of bust: 1553 (and the initials) ID
Reverse: coat of arms with helmet and mantling; inscription: IN VMBRA ALARVM TVARVM SPERABO DONEC TRANSEAT INIQVITAS
Medal: bronze
6.8 cm diameter
Habich 1611
Lent by the Museum of Fine Arts, Boston, Theodora Wilbour Fund Nr. 1

Baumgartner (1498–1565) was a humanist and Nuremberg statesman.[1] Between 1513 and 1518 he studied at Ingolstadt before entering the university at Wittenberg. Through his association with Luther and Melanchthon, he became a Lutheran and a strong supporter of the Protestant cause after his return to Nuremberg.[2] As a member of the city council, Baumgartner was frequently sent on diplomatic missions. He was among Nuremberg's envoys to the Reichstags at Speyer in 1529 and Augsburg in 1530. On his return trip from a Reichstag held at Speyer in 1544, he was kidnapped by Albrecht von Rosenberg, a rebellious knight, and held for fourteen months until a steep ransom was paid. This event was the subject of a sensationalistic print by Matthias Zündt.[3] Baumgartner was the guardian of St. Sebaldus (1536) and St. Lorenz (1537). He also held a variety of civic offices.

This is among the finest of Deschler's medals.[4] The bust is carved in very high relief. Special attention has been given to the modeling of the face, particularly the musculature of the cheeks and the patterns of the beard. The coat of arms with the helmet and mantling is more symmetrical in design than in Barthel Beham's engraved book plate (cat. nr. 101).

1. The biographical information is from Habich 1611 and *Neue Deutsche Biographie* (Berlin, 1953), 1: pp. 664–665. His name is also spelled Paumgartner.
2. Baumgartner was one of the co-founders of the Obere Schule, which became the Egidien, or Melanchthon, Gymnasium in 1526.
3. Andresen, I: nr. 37; illustrated in G. Hirth, *Kulturgeschichtliches Bilderbuch aus drei Jahrhunderten: Picture Book of the Graphic Arts, 1500–1800* (Munich, 1882–1890; reprint: New York, 1972), II: nr. 1015.
4. Deschler made three other smaller medals for Baumgartner; see Habich 1612–1614.

153. PORTRAIT OF JOHANN NEUDÖRFER

1554
Obverse: bust to right; inscription: IOHANN
NEVDORFFER ARITHM AET SVE LVII
Reverse: coat of arms; inscription: INDVS-
TRIAM ADIVVAT DEVS
Medal: bronze with light patina
2.4 cm diameter
Habich 1617; Morgenroth 170
Lent by the University of California, Santa Bar-
bara, University Art Museum, Morgenroth
Collection

Neudörfer (1497–1563) was a famous mathematician, calligrapher, and biographer of artists.[1]
This tiny medal conveys little of the intellect that
Neufchâtel captured so successfully in his 1561
painting of Neudörfer (fig. 40). Nevertheless,
the basic image is the same. Deschler, like Neufchâtel, emphasized Neudörfer's large nose and
down-turned mouth. Deschler's face in the
medal is rather fleshier than that in the painted
version. The dress type is essentially the same in
both works.

1. For a discussion of Neudörfer's life, see cat. nr.
164. A variant of this medal exists in which "57" is
used in place of "LVII."

154. PORTRAIT OF MARGARETHE BALBUS, NÉE GANZHORN

1565
Obverse: bust to left; inscription: MARGARETA
DOCTOR WILHELM GANCZHORNS ELEIB-
LICHE DOCHT
Reverse: below, two coats of arms; above, in-
scription: ANNO 65 DOCTOR IOA BALBVS
VICE CAN ELICHE HAVS FRAV IRES ALTERS
XXV
Medal: silver
3.9 cm diameter, with ring at top
Habich 1680; Hill and Pollard 609
Lent by the National Gallery of Art, Washing-
ton, Samuel H. Kress Collection

Margarethe Balbus was the daughter of Wilhelm
Ganzhorn, a lawyer and advisor for the prince-
bishop of Würzburg. Her husband, Johann Balbus, was also a lawyer in Würzburg.[1]

Deschler has set the portrait against a foliate-
pattern background. Although the face is seen
in profile, Margarethe's body is twisted into a
three-quarters position. The reverse depicts the
coats of arms of her father and her husband.

1. Deschler's portrait medal of the husband is dated
17 July 1565; Habich 1679. Habich was unsure whether
these two medals were by Deschler or, less likely, by a
follower working in Würzburg.

Maler was a prolific medalist.[1] He was born at Iglau (Mähren) but his birth date and early history are unknown. He was probably in Nuremberg by about 1567 and he is first listed in the city records in 1569. On 2 November 1569, Maler married Maria, daughter of Wenzel Jamnitzer. Although local goldsmiths objected to Maler's request for citizenship, the city council granted it to him because of his talents. In 1579 he purchased a house, the "Chanler'sche Haus unter der Vesten." He acquired another in 1597. Maler frequently traveled outside Nuremberg, including trips to Prague (1571), Munich (1572), Dresden (1574), and Stuttgart (1582). He worked periodically for the Saxon court, as well as for Emperors Maximilian II and Rudolf II at Prague.

Maler had five sons and two daughters. He remained active until at least 1593. He died shortly before 1 September 1603, when he was listed in the death book of St. Sebaldus. He was buried at the Johannisfriedhof.

1. The following biography is based entirely upon Habich, II.1, pp. 352–381, esp. 352–353. To my knowledge, no major new research has been done on Maler since Habich.

155. MODEL FOR A PORTRAIT OF ANDREAS IMHOFF

1569
Obverse: frontal bust; inscription: 1569 AN-DREAS IM HOFF DER ELTER AET. LXXVII
Stone: blackened
9.7 × 5.3 cm
Lent by the Nelson-Atkins Museum of Art, Kansas City, Missouri (Nelson Fund)

156. PORTRAIT OF ANDREAS IMHOFF

1569
Obverse: frontal bust; inscription: ANDREAS IM HOFF DER ELTER GE BORN IN S AN-DREAE NACHT ANNO MCCCCXCI (and flanking the bust) MDL XIX
Reverse: engraved coat of arms
Medal: silver gilt
5.85 cm diameter
Habich 2425
Lent by the Germanisches Nationalmuseum, Nuremberg, Med. K. 442

Andreas Imhoff (1491–1579) was a member of one of Nuremberg's oldest and wealthiest patrician families.[1] He was among the family's most illustrious members because of his long service as a member of the city council (from 1523 on) and as first treasurer (from 1544).

In 1569, the year Maler is first documented in Nuremberg, the artist created at least five portraits of Andreas Imhoff, commissioned to commemorate Imhoff's seventy-eighth birthday. All derive from the same source. Imhoff is represented with a long beard, bulbous nose, and deeply wrinkled brow and is wearing a cap that is deeply creased.

The precise order in which the five portraits were made is unclear. The finest example, now in Nuremberg (Germanisches Nationalmuseum), is made of wax on slate that has been painted with body colors.[2] There are two stone models for medals, one in Berlin and the other in Kansas City.[3] The oval format of the latter is highly unusual, and its fine smooth surface and the beveled edges of the stone suggest that it was admired as a sculptural portrait rather than actually used to cast medals. The circular stone model in Berlin was the probable source for both the exhibited medal and a second, slightly smaller (5.5 cm diameter) version.[4] The second medal was signed (VM) and dated (1569) on the underside of the bust. The exhibited medal is ornamented with pearl beading and a ring to permit it to be hung around the neck.

1. On the family, see von Imhoff, "Die Imhoff-Handelsherren und Kunstliebhaber," pp. 1–42, esp. fig. 20 (a contemporary painted portrait of Andreas Imhoff); L. Veit, "Die Imhoff. Handelsherren und Mäzene des ausgehenden Mittelalters und der beginnenden Neuzeit," in *Das Schatzhaus der Deutschen Geschichte*, ed. R. Pörtner, pp. 503–531, esp. 508, 523.
2. Veit, "Die Imhoff," fig. 22 (in color).
3. On the Berlin model, see Habich 2426. It was then in the Kaiser Friedrich Museum. The Kansas City model is, I believe, unpublished.
4. The smaller medal is Habich 2424. It is inscribed "ANDREAS IM HOFF DER ELTER AET. LXXVII."

157. PORTRAIT OF PAUL SCHEURL

1583; monogram on underside of bust
Obverse: bust to right; inscription: PAVLVS SCHEVRL AETAT XXVII
Reverse: coat of arms; inscription: PACIEN-TIAM SPES NVTRIT
Medal: silver with traces of gilding on the reverse
3.6 cm diameter
Habich 2533; Morgenroth 175
Lent by the University of California, Santa Barbara, University Art Museum, Morgenroth Collection

Paul Scheurl von Deffersdorf (1555–1618) was the son of Albrecht VI Scheurl.[1] Little is known about his life other than that he married Anna Kastner in 1579 and was mentioned in the 1598 records of the city council.

Portrait medals provide valuable information about changes in fashions during the sixteenth century. Paul Scheurl wears his hair short. His jacket has prominent buttons along the front and a high neck, above which can be seen his ruffled lace collar. Almost identical hair and costume styles can be observed in Hans Hoffmann's 1591 *Portrait of Paulus Pfinzing* (cat. nr. 208).

1. The biographical information is given in Habich 2533.

Labenwolf was the principal bronze caster active in Nuremberg during the middle third of the sixteenth century.[1] He was born in 1492 in Nuremberg, where he trained in the Vischer family workshop. By 1519 Labenwolf was a master, and four years later he had his own workshop. In 1537 the city council permitted Labenwolf to erect his own foundry. He collaborated with Peter Flötner, among others, in the creation of the *Silver Altar*, ordered in 1531 by King Sigismund I of Poland for the Cathedral in Cracow, and a fountain in the palace at Trient, commissioned by Cardinal Bernhard von Cles in 1532 or 1533.[2] Either Labenwolf or Hans Vischer cast Flötner's *Apollo Fountain* in 1532 (fig. 35). In 1535 Labenwolf made a fountain for the bath chamber of Ottheinrich's palace at Neuburg; since 1917 this fountain has been located on the Marstallplatz behind the Residenz in Munich.[3] Labenwolf is best known for his *Goose-Bearer* (ca. 1550) and *Putto* (ca. 1555) fountains in Nuremberg (fig. 36).[4] Hans Peisser's two wooden models for these fountains are also still in Nuremberg. Labenwolf also cast several epitaphs and funerary monuments, including the monumental bronze marker for the count of Zimmern in Messkirch, which is signed "Bangratz Labenwolf zu Nurnberg auf der Schmelczhütten gos mich."[5]

With the waning of the Vischer family's foundry in the 1530s, Labenwolf's workshop quickly became the city's pre-eminent metalworking establishment. Pankraz was succeeded by his son Georg (died 1585) and his grandson Benedikt Wurzelbauer (see cat. nr. 209).[6]

1. On Labenwolf, see D. Stern, "Labenwolf, Pankraz," in Thieme-Becker, XX: p. 165; Weihrauch, *Europäische Bronzestatuetten*, pp. 318–319.

2. On the *Silver Altar* (completed in 1538), see Kohlhaussen, *Nürnberger Goldschmiedekunst*, nr. 458. On the Trient fountain, see E. W. Braun, "Ein Nürnberger Bronzebrunnen von 1532/33 im Schlosse zu Trient," *MJBK* 3 Folge, 2 (1951): 195–203.

3. G. Habich, "Ein Brunnen von Pankraz Labenwolf in München," *MJBK* 10 (1916–1918): 217–222.

4. See Section 6 D and note 80.

5. Weihrauch, *Europäisch Bronzestatuetten*, p. 319.

6. D. Stern, "Labenwolf, Georg" in Thieme-Becker, XX: pp. 165–166.

158. THE WRATH OF NEPTUNE (QUOS EGO)

Third quarter of the sixteenth century
Bronze statue: hollow cast with a dark brown lacquer patina
38.5 × 11.7 × 16.4 cm (diameter)
Lent by the Walters Art Gallery, Baltimore

The powerful nude figure of Neptune, god of the seas, stands on a rather diminutive chariot pulled through the turbulent waves by two winged seahorses (or hippocampi).[1] Originally, Neptune held a trident in his right hand. The statue is believed to represent the wrath of Neptune, an event described by Virgil in the *Aeneid* (I: 125–140). As Aeneas and his followers were fleeing Troy and heading for Carthage by boat, Juno instructed Aeolus, the northern wind god, to unleash the winds upon the fleet. Neptune, angered by Aeolus's actions, shouts "Quos ego—sed motos praestat componere fluctus" (Who am I—but it is better to calm the turbulent waves). Neptune's intercession permitted Aeneas's ships to reach the African shore. The subject was widely known because of Marcantonio Raimondi's engraving (after Raphael), which may be the source for the many later bronze depictions of Neptune.[2]

The Baltimore statue was first attributed to the Labenwolf workshop by Weihrauch in 1967.[3] It was directly inspired by the bronze Neptunes of Tiziano Minio (ca. 1511/12–1552), who was active in Venice and Padua. Two of Minio's Neptune statues are in Braunschweig and Cleveland.[4] The artist of the Baltimore statue carefully reproduced Minio's base design with the straining horses. Minio's figure of Neptune, with his wind-swept beard and hair, is altered slightly by the Nuremberg artist. While Minio's Neptune is turned to our left and stares upward, the Nuremberg example reverses the pose, brings the trident-carrying arm closer to the body, and has the figure staring downward. What really distinguishes the Nuremberg statue is the stocky, less classically proportioned body.

In this and other works, the Labenwolf workshop continued the manufacture of small bronzes, an art form first popularized in Nuremberg by the Vischer workshop (cat. nrs. 118–121) and, later, by Peter Flötner.[5]

1. P. Verdier, "Newly Acquired Bronzes," *Bulletin of the Walters Art Gallery* 12 (1960): 1–2, nr. 4 (attributed to Jacopo Sansovino); Weihrauch, *Europäische Bronzestatuetten*, p. 330, fig. 401; Bowron, *Renaissance Bronzes*, pp. 55–56 (the quotation cited below is taken from here).

2. *The Illustrated Bartsch*, 27: nr. 352-1.

3. Weihrauch, *Europäische Bronzestatuetten*, p. 330. Weihrauch (pp. 329–330) traces the development of this figure into the late sixteenth and early seventeenth centuries. Cf. cat. nr. 209.

4. Ibid., fig. 400 (Braunschweig); Wixom, *Renaissance Bronzes from Ohio Collections*, nr. 114.

5. Flötner made, among other pieces, the bronze standing horse in Stuttgart (Schlossmuseum); see Bange, *Die Deutschen Bronzestatuetten des 16. Jahrhunderts*, fig. 90.

159. AMOR (CUPID)

ca. 1550
Walnut wood
24.5 cm (height)
Lent by the Germanisches Nationalmuseum,
Nuremberg, PL. 2553

The artist of this wooden statue is unknown.[1] Although it was once attributed to Peter Flötner, it is closer in style to Hans Peisser's wooden statue for Labenwolf's *Putto Fountain* of about 1555 (fig. 36).[2] The twisting pose with the raised left leg and the arms positioned to shoot a bow is somewhat more adventurous than the lance-bearing putto of Labenwolf's fountain.

The image of Amor, or Cupid, with his bow appears frequently in Nuremberg art. A blindfolded cupid standing on one leg is found in Dürer's 1503 drawing of *Venus on a Dolphin* in Vienna (Albertina).[3] He reappears in a 1530 drawing by Schön in Berlin (Kupferstichkabinett) and in Pencz's *Venus* woodcut (cat. nr. 103).[4] A Nuremberg artist is credited with casting the bronze Cupid statue in Berlin (Staatliche Museen), which Bange dates to about 1545 to 1550.[5]

The *Amor* carving was intended as the preparatory model for a bronze statue, most likely for a fountain.[6] Once it was transferred to a foundry, such as Labenwolf's, wax and clay molds repeating the shape of the figure would have been prepared. A bronze statue would then have been cast using the lost wax technique. Given the small scale of the wooden figure, the resulting bronze statue would certainly have been displayed in the courtyard or garden of a patrician house rather than in a public place.

1. W. Josephi, *Die Werke plastischer Kunst*, pp. 303–304, nr. 499; *Peter Flötner und die Renaissance in Deutschland*, nr. 46 (with the attribution to Flötner).
2. Peisser's wooden putto is displayed next to the Amor statue in the Germanisches Nationalmuseum. On Peisser's putto and Goose-Bearer models, see Pechstein, "Der Bildschnitzer Hans Peisser," pp. 84–106, esp. 84–92, figs. 1–2, 7–8.
3. Winkler, *Zeichnungen Dürers*, II: nr. 330.
4. Bock, *Staatliche Museen zu Berlin*, II: pl. 109, nr. 2086.
5. Bange, *Die Deutschen Bronzestatuetten des 16. Jahrhunderts*, nr. 83. Bange also cited the Dürer and Schön drawings mentioned above. This Berlin statue is considerably less accomplished in design than the exhibited work. They are both about the same size. Also see cat. nr. 187.
6. Compare the cupid fountain in Johann Wechtlin's *Pyramus and Thisbe* woodcut of about 1515; Geisberg, nr. 1495.

Siebenbürger was among the most celebrated of Nuremberg's armorers.[1] His birth date is unknown, but in 1531 he became a master armorer, having trained with Wilhelm von Worms the Elder, his future father-in-law.[2] From 1533 until 1562, Siebenbürger's name is frequently listed in the city council records, which mention his brief stay in prison in 1533 for some unspecified offense. Siebenbürger repeatedly petitioned the council to permit him to employ additional help or to extend the working hours in order to keep up with his workload. The artist and his wife, Anna, lived in the house known as Pilate's House by the Tiergärtnertor. Wilhelm von Worms resided with them until his death in 1538. According to Neudörfer, Wilhelm shared all his knowledge and clients with his son-in-law.[3]

Siebenbürger's works are identified by his monogram and mark, a jousting helmet in right profile with a lily as a crest.[4] Although the monogram is usually V S, several pieces with the monogram F S are also attributed to Siebenbürger. His clients included the city of Nuremberg, Charles V and his court, Duke Albrecht of Prussia, and customers from Poland. Siebenbürger's best known set of arms is the 1553 suit for Konrad von Bemelberg (1494–1567), now in Vienna (Kunsthistorisches Museum).[5] He died in 1564.

1. On Siebenbürger, see Boeheim, "Waffenschmiede," pp. 364–399, esp. 370–388, from which most of the following information is taken; Uhlemann, "Siebenbürger, Valentin" in Thieme-Becker (1936), 30: p. 592; A. Frhr. von Reitzenstein, "Die Nürnberger Plattner," *Beiträge zur wirtschaftsgeschichte Nürnbergs* (Nuremberg, 1967), 2: pp. 700–725, specifically 720–722. I wish to thank Stuart W. Pyhrr for providing me with information about Nuremberg armorers.
2. On Wilhelm the Elder, see Boeheim, "Waffenschmiede," pp. 368ff.; Reitzenstein, "Nürnberger Plattner," pp. 715–719.
3. Neudörfer, *Nachrichten von Künstlern*, p. 64.
4. Boeheim, "Waffenschmiede," p. 370, fig. 3.
5. Ibid., pp. 375–377, pls. XLIII, XLV (a painting showing Bemelberg wearing his armor). This suit was made by Siebenbürger and his brother-in-law, Wilhelm the Younger. The etched decoration is attributed to Albrecht Glockendon; see the comments for cat. nr. 160. On this suit, also see B. Thomas, "Nürnberger Platterkunst in Wien," *AGNM* (1963): 89–99, esp. fig. 4.

160. BREASTPLATE

ca. 1530; marks: (1) Nuremberg guild, (2) F.S.
Armor steel with etched decorations
45.7 × 34.5 cm
Lent by the Metropolitan Museum of Art, New
York, Gift of Mrs. John Stoneacre Ellis and Au-
gustus Van Horne Ellis, 1896

During the late fifteenth and the sixteenth centuries, Nuremberg had a thriving armor indus-
try, second only to Augsburg's in importance.
The principal masters were, in chronological
order, Hans Grünewald, Wilhelm von Worms
the Elder and Wilhelm the Younger, Siebenbürger, Georg Hartlieb, and Kunz Lochner (cat.
nr. 161).[1]

The breastplate exhibited here, a representative early work by Siebenbürger, is all that remains of a complete suit; the lance rest is modern. Siebenbürger's mark is punched into the
metal just beneath the collar. The breastplate is
ornamented with bands of etched foliate decorations. The frieze beneath the roped collar depicts a Roman emperor flanked by lions, putti,
and birds. Its general design recalls the ornamental prints by Hans Sebald Beham (cat. nr. 94)
and Peter Flötner (cat. nr. 124). Such prints were
frequently copied by armorers or, more commonly, the printmakers they hired to embellish
their work. The suit of armor of Konrad von
Bemelberg by Siebenbürger and Wilhelm von
Worms the Younger contains a large etched image of Bemelberg kneeling before the crucified
Christ and, beneath the collar, a copy of Barthel
Beham's *Rape of Helen* (B. 13); both of these decorations were applied by printmaker Albrecht
Glockendon.[2]

The style of the breastplate can be compared
with other pieces by Siebenbürger now in Rennes

and Solothurn.[3] The Solothurn breastplate is
also marked with the monogram F S, which according to Pyhrr is found on a few of Siebenbürger's earliest works before he adopted the
V S monogram.[4]

1. See Boeheim, "Waffenschmiede," pp. 364–399;
Reitzenstein, "Nürnberger Plattner," pp. 700–725,
with a fairly complete history of the armor of this period. One of the masters of the Mendelsche Hausbuch
and Jost Amman represented local armorers at work; see
Treue et al., *Des Hausbuch der Mendelschen Zwölfbrüderstiftung*, II: p. 222 (folio 147v) brother Conz Falck,
who died in 1533; B. A. Rifkin, ed., *The Book of Trades
(Ständebuch) Jost Amman and Hans Sachs*, nr. 79; see cat.
nr. 190.
2. See Siebenbürger biography, note 5.
3. A. von Reitzenstein, "Ein Harnisch Valentin Sie-
benbürgers in französischem Museumbesitz," *Waffen-
und Kostümkunde, Zeitschrift der Gesellschaft für historische Waffen- und Kostümkunde* (1973), pp. 99–108. On
the Solothurn breastplate, see R. Wegeli, *Katalog der
Waffen- Sammlung im Zeughause zu Solothurn* (Solothurn, 1905), pp. 3–4, nr. 9, pl. 1.
4. Stuart W. Pyhrr mentioned this issue in our conversations. The monogrammist F S has also been identified as Friedrich Schmid of Nuremberg; see N. Vital,
Das Alte Zeughaus Solothurn (Solothurn, 1980), pp.
120–121 (Friedrich Schmid?). The letters *F* and *V* were
commonly interchanged in sixteenth-century German.
See the combined *F* and *V* listing in Hampe,
Nürnberger Ratsverlässe, III: pp. 19–25 (index).

Lochner (1510–1567) trained with his father, Kunz the Elder of Nuremberg.[1] Comparatively little is known about his life beyond his almost annual requests to the city council to be permitted to employ additional journeymen and apprentices above the limit set by the local ordinances.[2] Lochner's clients included Ferdinand I in 1543; Archduke Maximilian II, who, from 1544 on, provided Lochner with an annual salary; Albrecht V of Bavaria (1550–1579); and King Sigismund August of Poland.[3] According to Neudörfer, Lochner's armor was prized for its skillful shape and its finish, which simulated silver.[4] His works, such as the parade armor of Albrecht V of about 1550 (fig. 59), are identified by his mark, a lion rampant within a shield.[5]

---

1. Boeheim, "Waffenschmiede," pp. 388–399; "Lochner, Kunz" in Thieme-Becker (1929), 23: p. 306; B. Thomas, "Kaiser Ferdinands I. Harnisch von Kunz Lochner," *JKSW* 50 (1953): 131–136.
2. Hampe, *Nürnberger Ratsverlässe*, I: nrs. 3034, 3094, 3138, 3191, 3307.
3. Ibid., nrs. 2817, 2819, 2856; also Thomas, "Kaiser Ferdinands I. Harnisch." In 1559 Lochner went to Poland to collect money from King Sigismund August. Four years earlier he made the suit of armor and horse armor for Nikolaus IV, Prince of Radziwill of Poland, that is now divided between New York, Paris, and Vienna; see Thomas, "Nürnberger Platterkunst in Wien," fig. 6.
4. Neudörfer, *Nachrichten von Künstlern*, p. 64.
5. Boeheim, "Waffenschmiede," p. 390, fig. 23. The suit of armor illustrated here is in New York (Metropolitan Museum of Art) and is believed to have been made for Albrecht V or, less likely, Emperor Charles V.

59. Kunz Lochner, *Parade Armor of Albrecht V, Duke of Bavaria*, 1549, New York, Metropolitan Museum of Art (Rogers Fund and Pratt Gift, 1933).

161. CLOSE HELMET FOR TILT

ca. 1550; marks: (1) Nuremberg guild, (2) artist's symbol
Armor steel with etched decorations
34.3 × 20.6 cm
Lent by the Metropolitan Museum of Art, New York, Gift of Mrs. Theodore Offerman, 1939, in memory of her husband

This helmet was intended to be used primarily during jousting tournaments, such as that illustrated in Jost Amman's woodcut *Tournament of Maximilian II* of 1565 (cat. nr. 189).[1] The three holes on the bowl of the helmet were to permit the attachment of a panache, a feather plume, and its holder, of the sort worn by the jousters in Amman's print. The helmet has an attractive long, streamlined shape and pointed beaver, which is ornamented with rosettes and the marks of the city and the artist. It is decorated with etched bands of foliage and, on either side of the roped crest of the bowl, the figures of Tritons, who seem to be trumpeting the fame of the wearer.

The shape and the style of the helmet are particularly close to Lochner's suit of armor for Maximilian II of about 1545, now in Vienna.[2] The ribbons of foliate decorations can also be compared to Lochner's suit of parade armor that he made probably for Duke Albrecht V of Bavaria in about 1550 (fig. 59). Since this suit was worn during ceremonial events rather than during

jousts, the front of the helmet is open to permit Albrecht V to see and be seen. The breastplate is etched with the figures of the apocalyptic Virgin and Christ Child.

---

1. The helmet was published by S. V. Grancsay, "A Helmet by Kunz Lochner," *Bulletin of the Metropolitan Museum of Art* 34 (1939): 114–116.
2. Boeheim, "Waffenschmiede," fig. 24; Thomas, "Nürnberger Platterkunst in Wien," fig. 5.

Although Neudörfer (1497–1563) was technically not an artist, he is included here for his work as a calligrapher.[1] He was renowned as a strict teacher of arithmetic, geometry, and related disciplines. Neudörfer was also Germany's first biographer of artists. His *Nachrichten von Künstlern und Werkleuten* (*Account of Artists and Workmen*) was published in Nuremberg in 1547, three years before Giorgio Vasari completed his first edition of the lives of Italian artists.[2] Neudörfer's account provides invaluable information about most of the artists of the first half of the sixteenth century who are included in the present exhibition. His text was continued by Andreas Gulden (died 1683) in the seventeenth century.

Neudörfer lived at Gasse unter den Veste 16, the modern Burgstrasse, directly across the street from the house where Albrecht Dürer resided until 1509, which may explain their occasional collaboration during the 1510s and 1520s. According to Kapr, Dürer had Neudörfer design the script used for his *Map of the Eastern Hemisphere* of 1515, the *Portrait of Ulrich Varnbüler* of 1522 (cat. nr. 25), the *Four Apostles* (fig. 26), and possibly the *Triumphal Arch of Emperor Maximilian I* of 1515 (cat. nr. 20) and the *Treatise on Fortification* of 1527.[3]

Numerous portraits of Neudörfer exist, beginning with the medals by Hans Schwarz (1523), Matthes Gebel (1531), Joachim Deschler (1554; cat. nr. 153), and Jacob Bink (undated).[4] The so-called Master of the Neudörfer Portraits painted Johann and his wife, Magdalena, in 1527.[5] The

best known example is Nicolas Neufchâtel's *Portrait of Johann Neudörfer and His Son* of 1561 (fig. 40), which was commissioned by the Nuremberg city council and was displayed in the Rathaus. A second version, now in Lille (Musée des Beaux-Arts), was made the same year for Neudörfer himself.[6]

When Neudörfer died in 1563, he was buried in the Johannisfriedhof.

1. A Kapr, intro., *Johann Neudörffer d. Ä. der grosse Schreibmeister der deutschen Renaissance*, esp. pp. 7–38, on his life.
2. See Neudörfer, *Nachrichten von Künstlern*, for the complete bibliographic reference.
3. Kapr, *Neudörffer*, p. 17. On the map and the treatise, see Meder, nr. 261, p. 287. Neudörfer was involved in other artistic projects; see cat. nr. 195.
4. Kapr, *Neudörffer*, p. 17.
5. *Nuremberg: Meister um Dürer*, nrs. 246–247, pls. 48–49. These paintings are in the Staatliche Gemäldegalerie in Kassel.
6. Anzelewsky, Mende, and Eeckhout, *Albert Dürer aux Pays-Bas*, nr. 31. These authors mention that the preparatory drawing for these pictures is in Berlin (Kupferstichkabinett, inv. 5352). On the placement of the city's copy of the painting, see Mummenhoff, *Rathaus*, p. 290.

162. JOHANN NEUDÖRFER, EINE GUTE ORDNUNG VND KURTZE VNTERRRICHT DER FURNEMSTEN GRUNDE . . . (Nuremberg, 1538)

Lent by the John M. Wing Foundation of The Newberry Library, Chicago

Besides his many other talents, Neudörfer was a master calligrapher, whose *Fundament*, published in 1519 in Nuremberg by Hieronymus Andreae, was the first writing manual printed in Germany.[1] In it Neudörfer offered his reader a grounding in the fundamentals of shaping letters. He may have been encouraged in this project by Dürer, who included a section on the just shaping of letters in his *Art of Measurement* (cat. nr. 31), much of which was already completed by 1519 but not published until 1525.

In 1538 Neudörfer completed his finest treatise, *Eine gute Ordnung . . .* (A good Classification and a short Instruction about the most important basics [of writing]), a catalogue of the different styles of script, the proper way to hold

a pen, and the correct manner to form each letter. The diversity of writing styles is underscored in the title page, where the lengthy book title is in flourishing Gothic script while the phrase "Nvlla dies sine linea" (never a day without a line [of writing]) is in Roman script.

The success of this book inspired Neudörfer to write two other manuals in 1544 and 1549.[2] It also prompted his son Johann the Younger and a host of other scribes to add to this growing category of instructional literature.[3]

1. Kapr, *Neudörffer*, pp. 9–10, on this book and the prior history of writing manuals, and 26–32 for Neudörfer's contributions to the development of type designs.
2. *Anweysung vnd eygentlicher bericht . . .* (Nuremberg, 1544) and *Ein Gesprechbüchlein . . .* (Nuremberg, 1549).
3. Johann the Younger's text was composed by 1558 but never printed. For lists of the authors and titles of other sixteenth-century German writing manuals, see *Aufgang der Neuzeit*, pp. 183–184, nrs. T 168–176; Pechstein et al., *Paul Wolfgang Merkel und die Merkelsche Familienstiftung*, nrs. D 71–73, for later examples 74–78.

N VL LA D I E S S I N E L I N E A

Hans Lautensack

Although Hans (Hanns) Lautensack was renowned for his landscape and portrait etchings, he was also a talented medalist and, reportedly, painter.[1] Hans was born in Bamberg in about 1520, the son of Paul Lautensack (1478–1558), Bamberg painter, organist, and mystic.[2] The family moved from Bamberg to Nuremberg in 1527, and the father acquired citizenship here in the following year.

Hans was one of the few Nuremberg artists who specialized in making landscapes, a fact that is all the more surprising given the strong interest in landscape in southern German art of the first half of the sixteenth century. Hans likely trained with his father, about whose work little is known. Hans's earliest dated compositions, two landscape etchings of 1544, reveal the influence of Danube school artists Albrecht Altdorfer and, especially, Wolf Huber of Passau.[3] There also exist general affinities with Nuremberg's two other landscapists, Augustin Hirschvogel, who left the city in 1536 but continued to publish his prints, and the Master of 1544.[4] While most of Lautensack's landscapes are evocative, imaginary vistas, his finest prints are his two 1552 views of Nuremberg (cat. nrs. 163 and 164), detailed catalogues of the city's monuments and the surrounding countryside.

Lautensack's career can be divided into his Nuremberg and Vienna periods. In late 1554 Lautensack moved to Vienna to become a court artist to King Ferdinand I.[5] He was charged specifically with the task of copying the royal collection of classical coins and medals.[6] When six Roman stelae were unearthed in Vienna in 1559, Lautensack prepared prints of them that were published in the booklet *Exempla Aliquot S. Vetustatis Rom. in Saxis Quibusdam . . .* (Vienna: Raphael Hofhalter, 1560).[7] Besides continuing to produce an occasional landscape, including the *Turkish Siege of Vienna* (1558), and several etched portraits, Lautensack designed portrait medals of Ferdinand I and several prominent Viennese citizens.[8]

Lautensack lived in Vienna until his death, which occurred sometime between 1564, the date on his last work, a medal of Agnes Marb, and 6 January 1566, when his wife, Barbara, was referred to as a widow in a court document.[9]

1. The best study is A. Schmitt, *Hanns Lautensack*. Schmitt credits Lautensack with making seventy-nine etchings and two woodcuts. A third woodcut (cat. nr. 170) has been discovered in the interim. Lautensack is referred to as a painter; however, no pictures by him are known. Schmitt provides a good discussion of his art, including a complete catalogue, and his biographical documentation. Lautensack's monogram is traditionally read as H.S.L., which was interpreted to mean Hans (or Hanns) Sebald Lautensack. Schmitt has, however, demonstrated (pp. 1–2) that the monogram should be understood as H.L.S. with the last two letters taken from his surname Lautensack. Hans Springinklee and Heinrich Aldegrever, among others, used double initials to signify their last names. On the artist, also see the brief comments in Oberhuber, ed., *Zwischen Renaissance und Barock*, pp. 135–139; Geissler, ed., *Zeichnung in Deutschland*, I: nr. A 28.
2. See Schmitt, *Lautensack*, nr. 1, for his 1552 portrait of his father, Paul. Hans had three brothers, including Heinrich, a talented goldsmith who was active in Frankfurt and Nuremberg. Heinrich composed an important perspective and proportional treatise, *Des Cirkels und Richtscheyts, auch der Perspectiva und Proportion der Menschen und Rosse, . . .* (Frankfurt: S. Feyerabend, 1564), a copy of which is in Washington (Library of Congress).
3. Schmitt, *Lautensack*, pp. 18–19, nrs. 45–46. See the comments for cat. nr. 165.
4. On these artists, see cat. nr. 165; Talbot and Shestack, eds., *Prints and Drawings of the Danube School*, pp. 88–93 (Hirschvogel), 97–99 (the Master of 1544).
5. Schmitt, *Lautensack*, p. 50, doc. nr. XXXVI (16 August 1554).
6. Ibid., p. 51, doc. XLV (20 August 1556).
7. Ibid., nrs. 36–41.
8. Ibid., nr. 32 (*Turkish Siege of Vienna*). See also cat. nr. 169. On the late etched portraits, see Schmitt, pp. 11–14, nrs. 11–26; on his stone models for medals, see pp. 14–18, nrs. 87–92.
9. Ibid., p. 52, doc. LV, nr. 91.

163. VIEW OF NUREMBERG FROM THE EAST

1552; monogram
Etching (on three plates)
29.7 × 152.8 cm (total); left and right plates:
29.7 × 49.2 cm; center plate: 29.5 × 54.4 cm
B. 59; Schmitt, *Lautensack*, nr. 50; Hollstein, XXI:
nr. 4
Lent by the National Gallery of Art, Washington, Rosenwald Collection

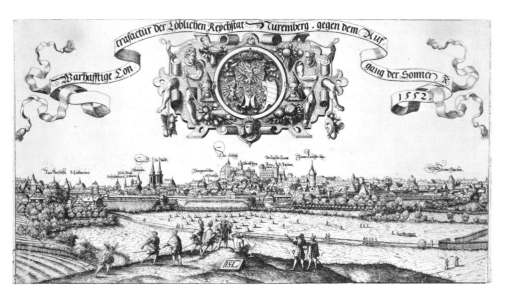

164. VIEW OF NUREMBERG FROM THE WEST

1552; monogram
Etching (on three plates)
29.4 × 150.1 cm (total); left plate: 29.4 × 48.4
cm; center plate: 29.4 × 53 cm; right plate:
29.4 × 48.7 cm
B. 58; Schmitt, *Lautensack*, nr. 51; Hollstein, XXI:
nr. 5
Lent by the National Gallery of Art, Washington, Rosenwald Collection

Ever since the Master of the *Krell Altar* incorporated a western view of Nuremberg in the background of his painting in St. Lorenz of about 1483, local artists have repeatedly copied the city's distinctive skyline or select vistas in its neighborhoods.[1] Michael Wolgemut's woodcut in the *Nuremberg Chronicle* (cat. nr. 3) is the best known, though not the most accurate, version. Albrecht Dürer's watercolors *Nuremberg from the West* (Bremen, Kunsthalle), the Johannisfriedhof (Bremen, Kunsthalle), and two of the local mills are among his finest early works.[2] Neudörfer's biography of Veit Stoss praised a relief map by Stoss, presumably of Nuremberg.[3] This relief plan may have looked like the detailed example made in 1540 by Hans Beheim that is now in Munich (Bayerisches Nationalmuseum).[4] Three years later Georg Pencz and sculptor Sebald Peck (Beck?) made an elaborate relief plan for the Nuremberg city council.[5]

Lautensack's views of Nuremberg from the east and the west are an outgrowth of this tradition of cartographic depictions of the city. While an artist like Wolgemut tampered with the specific features of the skyline, especially in the number of towers that ring the city walls, Lautensack's etchings were extremely precise. The eastern view (cat. nr. 163) extends from the suburbs south of the Frauentor to the Laufertor and the village of Wöhrd to the northeast. The western view (cat. nr. 164) encompasses the vista from St. Johannis and the Johannisfriedhof to the

northwest to the Spittlertor to the southwest. Each notable building and monument is carefully labeled for the viewer's benefit.[6] As if to convince the viewer that he made the designs from life, as opposed to compiling scenes from older representations, Lautensack has incorporated himself in the center of both series. He is seated sketching the panoramas, while groups of curious onlookers watch him work.

Both sets are ornamented with elaborate scrolled frames and laudatory inscriptions.[7] The text for the western view (cat. nr. 164) reads, beginning with the central title:

A Truthful Picture of the Praiseworthy Imperial
Town
Nuremberg Toward the West.[8]

The Latin inscription on the left panel reads:

This is a view of the city seen from varying
directions.
Where Phoebus draws near to the western
waters of Atlantis
Here where Pegasus passing through the
pleasant walls
Washes the meadows of Alerius—meadows
which are near to the sun.
Where far away from the top of Mount Artos,
the aquilis citadel, powerful on the north,
looks into the city.

The Middle High German inscription on the right panel reads:

This is the city portrayed towards the west
Where the river flows forth
Where we can see the royal castle
That overlooks the town
Which God in his mercy will keep in peace.

The inscriptions on the eastern view (cat. nr. 163) are in the same spirit; however, the last two lines of the Latin text provide a clue to Lautensack's reason for creating the prints.

Here we have drawn the towers and walls of
this city,
To paint its riches was too great a task.

These two series are encomia to Nuremberg's prosperity. It was a well-fortified city filled with beautiful churches and houses, and Lautensack appealed to local civic pride. Not surprisingly, the city council rewarded Lautensack with a gift of 50 gulden for his efforts, a considerable improvement over the miserly 20 gulden it presented to Conrad Celtis for his *Norimberga* a half-century earlier.[9]

1. Pfeiffer and Schwemmer, *Bilddokumenten*, fig. 136.
2. Winkler, *Zeichnungen Dürers*, I: nrs. 61–62, 113, 116. The two drawings in Bremen were destroyed in World War II.
3. Neudörfer, *Nachrichten von Künstlern*, p. 84; Schnelbögl, *Dokumentie zur nürnberger Kartographie*, p. 11.
4. Oberstleutnant Mayer-München, "Relief Nürnbergs vom Jahre 1540 im Nationalmuseum zu München," *MVGN* 20 (1913): 261–274; Schnelbögl, *Dokumentie zur nürnberger Kartographie*, p. 75.
5. Schnelbögl, *Dokumentie zur nürnberger Kartographie*, p. 12.
6. The reader should compare these etchings with figs. 1 and 2, as well as the description of the city in Section 1. A year after Lautensack completed the etchings, Jörg Nöttelein (died 1567) began work on the first, or at least oldest extant, ground plan of Nuremberg. See F. Schnelbögl, "Zur Geschichte der älteren nürnberger Kartographie, Teil II. Jörg Nöttelein," *MVGN* 50 (1960): 286–298, *Dokumentie zur nürnberger Kartographie*, pp. 97–98. This plan is in the Stadtarchiv in Nuremberg; Pläne nr. 515.
7. Schmitt, *Lautensack*, pp. 87–88, fig. 24, has shown that Lautensack borrowed the designs for his cartouches from prints by contemporary Netherlandish artist Cornelis Bos. See S. Suhéle, *Cornelis Bos: A Study of the Origins of the Netherland Grotesque* (Stockholm, 1965), pp. 185–187, figs. 177, 179, 183, 187; these were published sometime between 1540 and 1550.
8. This print with the translation given here were published in Talbot and Shestack, eds., *Prints and Drawings of the Danube School*, nr. 104.
9. See Schmitt, *Lautensack*, p. 50, docs. XXXIV–XXXV (21 March 1552). On Celtis, see Section 4.

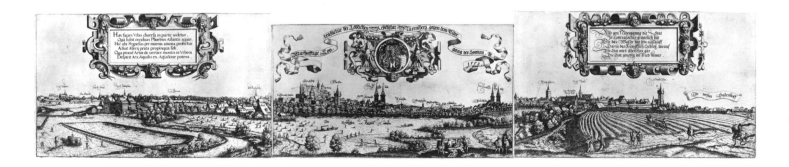

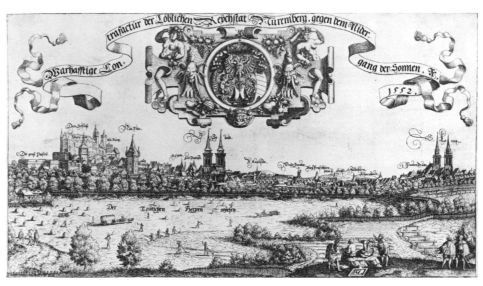

165. LANDSCAPE WITH A TOWN ON A RIVER

1553; monogram (altered to look like that of
Hans Sebald Beham)
Etching: second of two states
11.8 × 16.7 cm
B. 41; Schmitt, *Lautensack*, nr. 54; Hollstein, XXI:
nr. 31
Lent by the New York Public Library, Prints Di-
vision, Astor, Lenox and Tilden Foundations

In 1553 Lautensack created at least twelve landscape etchings that clearly establish him as one
of the pre-eminent landscape artists in Germany.[1] As in the example exhibited here, most
of these prints follow a conventional scheme. In
the foreground Lautensack placed a strip of land
that moves diagonally into the composition. A
few tall pines and moss-covered trees are added
to establish the scale. Behind is a broad vista
with rolling hills, punctuated with small castles
and church steeples. Lautensack used winding paths or rivers to link the foreground with
the middle ground. Each print is given one or
two distinguishing features, as, for instance, the
sturdy wooden bridge and the small town seen
here.

Lautensack was strongly influenced by the
prints and drawings of the two leading practitioners of the Danube school landscape style,
Albrecht Altdorfer (ca. 1480–1538) and Wolf Huber (by 1490–1553).[2] From these masters, Lautensack developed an interest in broad, expressive landscapes, and he borrowed such specific
motifs as the gnarled, stunted tree (left), the tall
trees covered only with whisps of moss (right),
and the simplified architectural forms. More important, Lautensack emulated their different
uses of line. The fields and hills in the exhibited
print are formed with a myriad of minute wavy
contour lines that convey an impression of physical structure while also animating the surface of

the countryside through their irregular placement. These lines impart a sense of motion that
reads as wind pushing through the trees and
fields. While Lautensack could not match the
depth of understanding of nature and its moods
that is evident in the better works of Altdorfer
and Huber, he was, nevertheless, capable of for-
mulating very pleasing, highly detailed panoramic vistas. Most of his views, as here, are
imaginary rather than records of actual geo-
graphic sites.

1. Cf. Schmitt, *Lautensack*, nrs. 52–63.
2. Ibid., pp. 31–34. See Stange, *Malerei der Donauschule*, figs. 15, 28, 29, 131, 135 (Altdorfer), 195,
198–204 (Huber); Talbot and Shestack, *Prints and
Drawings of the Danube School*, nrs. 56–57, 59–60 (Altdorfer), 77–78, 81, 83 (Huber); esp. F. Winzinger, *Wolf
Huber: Das Gesamtwerk*, I: p. 47 (a brief discussion of
Huber's influence on Lautensack), and see the catalogue of Huber's drawings. Lautensack may also have
been generally influenced by the landscape etchings of
Nuremberg ex-patriot Augustin Hirschvogel; see the
above studies and the bibliography listed in Section 6,
note 2. Also see Schmitt, *Lautensack*, nrs. 77, 82–85,
for Lautensack's landscape drawings, which, however,
are rarely as elaborate as his printed scenes.

166. PORTRAIT OF HIERONYMUS SCHÜRSTAB

1554; monogram
Etching: second of two states
19.8 × 29.6 cm
B. 7; Schmitt, *Lautensack*, nr. 8; Hollstein, XXI: nr. 68
Lent by the University of Michigan Museum of Art, Ann Arbor (acc. nr. 1958/1.97)

Before leaving Nuremberg for Vienna in 1554, Lautensack produced several etched portraits of prominent Nuremberg citizens, including Schürstab (1512–1573) and Georg Roggenbach (cat. nr. 167). In most of these prints, the sitter is presented half-length, standing or seated by a window in a room.[1] The portraits consist of four components: the sitter, the coat of arms on the adjacent wall, a laudatory inscription, and a landscape visible through the background window. While the vertical format of the Roggenbach print (cat. nr. 167) is more consistent with contemporary painted portraits, the horizontal arrangement in the Schürstab etching is unusual.[2]

Schürstab was a prominent member of the Nuremberg city council. From 1545 he served as the *bürgermeister* and from 1558 as the *alter bürgermeister* (elder or senior mayor). The Latin inscription in the cartellino reads: "I had seen my times for forty-two years when my face was such as you see; And I was mourning the disasters of my country and the sad wars of the nobles; but give Thou better times, O God; and govern our land, our House, our kings that they may spend their time in holy and tranquil peace, that Your kingdom may spread far and wide through the world, and the true seeds of Your word may grow. IN THE YEAR OF CHRIST 1554."[3] He wears a brocaded robe, a portrait medal on a chain, and a cap.

The inscription above the landscape viewed through the window identifies the site as St.

Leonhard, a church and infirmary located to the southwest of Nuremberg, just outside the city walls. Hermann Schürstab, one of Hieronymus's ancestors, established the infirmary in 1317. Hieronymus served as one of the guardians, or overseers, of St. Leonhard; however, he was not appointed until 1559, five years after Lautensack had completed the print. The print exists in two states. The first, or original, state lacks the inscription "S. Leonhardskirch" that is seen in the second state exhibited here. Zink has suggested that the church behind Schürstab is St. Peter's, not St. Leonhard.[4] Schürstab had been a guardian of the church and infirmary of St. Peter's, which is located to the north of Nuremberg, since 1549. Presumably, when his interest shifted to St. Leonhard's in 1559, Schürstab hired an artist to add the inscription to the copper plate in his possession, and the second edition was prepared.

1. See Schmitt, *Lautensack*, nrs. 1, 4–7, 10, besides the two examples exhibited here, for this portrait type.
2. Lautensack used the horizontal format only one other time—his double portrait of Hieronymus and Johannes Lauterbachius in 1558; see ibid., nr. 21.
3. I wish to thank David Armstrong of the University of Texas at Austin for preparing this translation.
4. F. Zink, "Der Benennbare Fensterausblick im Porträt," *AGNM* (1963): 100–109, esp. 102. For brief comments on these two institutions, see Pfeiffer, ed., *Nürnberg*, pp. 43, 68, 498.

167. PORTRAIT OF GEORG ROGGENBACH

1554; monogram
Etching: second of two states
34 × 24.1 cm
B. 9; Schmitt, *Lautensack*, nr. 9; Hollstein, XXI: nr. 65
Lent by the Philadelphia Museum of Art, Charles M. Lea Collection

Dr. Georg Roggenbach (1517–1581) was a Nuremberg lawyer who served as a counsel to the city and to the bishop-elector of Mainz. The setting for his portrait is similar to that used in the likeness of Schürstab (cat. nr. 166). He is seated in a chamber, surrounded by his books and an hour glass. His family coat of arms is set against the left-hand wall. In the first state of this print, the shape of the helmet is slightly different than in the second state exhibited here; otherwise, the two versions are identical.[1] The landscape serves simply as a backdrop and has no specific association with Roggenbach. The inscriptions on the parapet beneath Roggenbach read, "In the thirty-eighth year of his life" and, below, in poorly composed Greek, "You see the image of a good man, whose intelligence no one could paint; the art of graphics [that is, the print] pictures only bodies."[2]

Although Lautensack would continue to design similar interior portraits after he left Nuremberg in 1554, his better likenesses either show the sitter silhouetted against a full landscape and surrounded by an elaborate architectural frame, such as in *Archduke Charles* (1554) and *King Ferdinand I* (1556), or restrict the portrait to a profile bust view that is, again, set within an elaborate scrolled frame, as in his *Archduke Maximilian* (1555).[3]

1. The original copper plate is in Bamberg (Staatsbibliothek).
2. I wish to thank David Armstrong of the University of Texas at Austin for preparing this translation. He notes that Roggenbach tried to apply Latin scansion to Greek composition.
3. Schmitt, *Lautensack*, nrs. 11 (Charles), 17 (Maximilian), 19 (Ferdinand).

168. PORTRAIT OF JOHANNES AVENTINUS

1554; monogram
Woodcut
26.4 × 17.3 cm (with inscriptions)
B. 1 (woodcut); Schmitt, *Lautensack*, nr. 13; Hollstein, XXI: nr. 48
The University of Texas at Austin, The Humanities Research Center, Iconography Collection

Johannes Aventinus, or Johann Turmair (1477–1534), was a prominent Bavarian scholar and historian.[1] He had been a pupil of Conrad Celtis at Ingolstadt and Vienna before becoming the tutor to the two sons of Wilhelm IV, duke of Bavaria, from 1509 to 1517. He was a close friend of Chancellor Leonhard von Eck (see cat. nr. 96), who brought Aventinus back to Ingolstadt in 1533 to teach his own son Oswalt. Aventinus's principal work was the *Annales Boiorum* (Bavarian Chronicle), published posthumously in 1554 by Alexander and Samuel Weissenhorn of Ingolstadt.

Lautensack's portrait of Aventinus is based on a carved likeness on the scholar's gravestone in St. Emmeram in Regensburg. Aventinus, dressed in an academic cap and gown, is represented at work on his *Annales Boiorum*. I am uncertain whether the lower inscription, written as a eulogy, was also on the Regensburg tomb. It reads: "In the name of God greatest and highest. Johannes Aventinus, a man endowed with singular erudition and piety, an ornament to his country, and a wonder to foreigners; a great student of Bavaria and Germany, a most sagacious investigator of earlier times, a favorer of true religion and of everything that is noble. To whom [this picture] is [dedicated] that posterity may remember him. He died 9 January 1534."[2]

The upper inscription was most likely added by the artist or the publisher. It reads: "Aventinus the Bavarian was such as this in face and appearance, and was to be seen in this sort of dress. He was a great writer of history, and set forth the works of the ancients; he will live as long as the world turns."

Lautensack's portrait appeared both as an independent print and as an illustration in the *Annales Boiorum* of 1554.[3] Since the exhibited example lacks the printed text on the verso, it must have been intended as a print for sale.

---

1. The biographical information is taken from Schmitt, *Lautensack*, nr. 13. On his career, see G. Strauss, *Historian in an Age of Crisis: The Life and Work of Johannes Aventinus, 1477–1534* (Cambridge, Mass., 1963).
2. I wish to thank David Armstrong of the University of Texas at Austin for preparing this and the following Latin translations.
3. Schmitt, *Lautensack*, nr. 13, lists copies after Lautensack by Jost Amman, Tobias Stimmer, and Theodor de Bry. I am unsure whether Lautensack was commissioned to make this portrait by the Weissenhorns of Ingolstadt or, conceivably, by Oswalt von Eck. In 1553 Lautensack prepared portrait prints of Oswalt and his parents, Leonhard and Felicitas; see Schmitt, nrs. 4–6. It is possible that Oswalt initiated the three family portraits and that of his tutor Aventinus. Lautensack's *Leonhard von Eck* is a copy after Barthel Beham's earlier engraving (cat. nr. 96).

Boius Auentinus faciem sic gessit, & ora,
Atq habitu tali conspiciendus erat.
Magnus in historijs scriptor, ueterum monumenta
Explicuit:uiuet dum uagus orbis erit.

D O M
IOAN. AVENTINVS VIR SINGVLARI ERVDI.
FIDE AC PIETATE PRÆDITVS: PATRIÆ SVÆ
ORNAMENTO, EXTERIS ADMIRATIONI FVIT:
BOIORVM, ET GERMANIÆ STVDIOSISSIMVS:
RERVM ANTIQVARVM INDAGATOR SAGACISSIMVS:
VERÆ RELIGIONIS OMNISQ. HONESTI AMATOR.
CVI H M AD POSTERIT. MEMORIAM P EST
☩ V IDVS IAN. ANNO M. D. XXXIIII.

169. LANDSCAPE WITH WORKERS IN A VINEYARD

1559; monogram
Etching
19.4 × 29.5 cm
B. 53; Schmitt, *Lautensack*, nr. 75; Hollstein, XXI: nr. 10
Lent by the Philadelphia Museum of Art, Gift of Lessing J. Rosenwald

This etching is Lautensack's last dated landscape. The nucleus of this print was formulated when the village and castle in the center of the composition were placed in the background of the artist's double portrait of Hieronymus and Johannes Lauterbachius of Vienna.[1] According to Schmitt, Lautensack's landscapes underwent a stylistic change during 1558 and 1559 when the artist became increasingly influenced by Netherlandish masters, such as Cornelis Massys or some of the other Antwerp artists whose prints were published by Hieronymus Cock.[2] What he learned from the Antwerp school was not an interest in fantastic landscapes, since this taste was already well entrenched in his art, or the demonstrable borrowing of figures from Cornelis Bos, features pointed out by Schmitt, but instead a better understanding of the representation of space. If this print is compared with *Landscape with a Town on a River* (cat. nr. 165), the changes are obvious. Lautensack now made the foreground the center of attention. His figures tend the vineyard and walk through the countryside. The expansive horizontally composed foreground extends more convincingly into the middle distance, whereas in many of the early prints this spatial transition is masked by a conveniently located stand of trees or an intervening river.

1. Schmitt, *Lautensack*, nr. 21.
2. Schmitt, *Lautensack*, pp. 28–31. See Franz, *Niederländische Landschaftsmalerei im Zeitalter des Manierismus*; Winner, ed., *Pieter Bruegel d. Ä. als Zeichner*, esp. nrs. 172–177 (C. Massys); T. A. Riggs, *Hieronymus Cock (1510–1570): Printmaker and Publisher* (New York, 1977).

170. THE FLOOD

after 1554; monogram
Woodcut
6 × 28.2 cm
Hollstein, XXI: nr. 1
Lent by the Davison Art Center, Wesleyan University, Middletown (1940.D1-146)

Although this woodcut was periodically referred to in the scholarly literature, no copies were known until the exhibited print entered the Davison Art Center. It was first published by Schwarz in 1964, and it is believed to be a unique impression.[1]

The subject is the great flood, as recounted in Genesis 6–8. Noah's ark is seen floating in the midst of the rising waters. Parts of the city behind have already been consumed, while the remnants of humanity, left and right, struggle to reach higher ground. Schwarz demonstrated that Lautensack's ark is copied from Bernard Salomon's woodcut of this subject that was published in Claude Paradin's *Quadrins historiques de la Bible* (Lyon: Jean de Tournes, 1553 and 1554).[2] Lautensack's woodcut therefore must date to late 1554 or afterward. The general arrangement of the composition with groups of figures on either side and the ark in the center, as well as a few specific motifs, notably the cloak draped about the tree on the right side, ultimately derive from Michelangelo's fresco on the ceiling of the Sistine Chapel. Lautensack knew this painting only through graphic copies; unlike Georg Pencz, whose drawing after Michelangelo's scene (fig. 57) is now in Washington (National Gallery), Lautensack never traveled to Rome.

Lautensack's woodcut is much less detailed, less expressive than his etched landscapes. The figures are summarily outlined and provided with only minimal shading lines.

1. H. Schwarz, "A Unique Woodcut by Hanns Lautensack," *Pantheon* 22 (1964): 143–150. Schwarz provides a list of early references to this woodcut. He also speculates (p. 148) that *The Flood* either may have been intended to be used on a large broadsheet (cf. cat. nr. 58) or was the only print to be finished from a large story of Noah cycle.
2. Ibid., p. 146, figs. 4, 5. Jost Amman copied the boat in his woodcut of the Flood that was published in *Neuwe Biblische Figuren* (Frankfurt: Sigmund Feyerabend, 1564, 1566); see Schwarz, fig. 3.

Glaser was active as a printer, *formschneider*, and *briefmaler* between about 1540 and 1571.[1] Although mentioned in the Nuremberg records as early as 1540, he only became a citizen on 4 April 1546. Glaser frequently listed his address on his prints; from 1553 he lived just off the square in front of St. Lorenz.

Strauss attributed forty-two woodcuts to Glaser. Many of these are direct copies after the prints of Dürer, Erhard Schön, and Niklas Stoer of Nuremberg.[2] On 1 November 1558, the Nuremberg city council warned him against printing unauthorized texts. Thirteen years later the council refused Glaser permission to publish a broadsheet about Cyprus.

Information about Glaser's career is sketchy. The majority of his woodcuts treat sensational themes, such as battles and miraculous apparitions, including the *Bearded Grape Found in a Vineyard near Prague* and various celestial disturbances over Nuremberg.[3]

---

1. On Glaser, see Strauss, *The German Single-Leaf Woodcut, 1550–1600*, I: pp. 333–372, esp. 333; *Nuremberg: Vorbild Dürer*, p. 16, nr. 174. It is uncertain whether Hans Glaser was related to Hans Wolf Glaser, another Nuremberg printer and *briefmaler*, who was active in Nuremberg between 1562 and 1567. See Strauss, pp. 373–380.
2. Glaser made a copy of Schön's *Portrait of Albrecht Dürer*; see cat. nr. 66. For a discussion of his replica of Dürer's *St. Jerome in a Cave* (Meder 229), see *Nuremberg: Vorbild Dürer*, nr. 174.
3. Strauss, *The German Single-Leaf Woodcut, 1550–1600*, I: nrs. 30, 32–35.

171. HOLY FAMILY WITH ST. ANNE

1550s(?); monogram of Albrecht Dürer
Chiaroscuro woodcut
30.3 × 22 cm
Lent by the Museum of Fine Arts, Boston,
Harvey D. Parker Collection

Hans Springinklee or another master associated with Dürer's workshop devised this composition in 1519.[1] St. Anne is shown seated holding the Christ Child while the kneeling Virgin, St. Joseph, and Joachim look on adoringly.

The *Holy Family with St. Anne* is a typical example of an early print that was periodically reissued and copied well into the middle of the century.[2] One copy, attributed to Niklas Stoer (active 1532–1562), was published by Hans Glaser. Since his address is given as just off the square by St. Lorenz, a location added to his prints starting in 1553, this provides a rough dating perimeter. According to Strauss, there exist four states of the Stoer copy. The last state, exhibited here, is a chiaroscuro woodcut in which a reddish-brown-inked tone block was added to the original line block. This impression is fairly strong, though the registration in the halos is slightly askew.[3] The stone block at the lower left is now imprinted with Dürer's monogram. Since this fourth state lacks Glaser's name, it is unclear whether Glaser or another, perhaps later, printer was responsible for its production.

---

1. Geisberg, nr. 770 (Dürer school, perhaps Springinklee).
2. For what follows, see Strauss, *Chiaroscuro*, nr. 51, *The German Single-Leaf Woodcut, 1550–1600*, I: p. 370, nr. 40.
3. The Museum of Fine Arts, Boston, possesses a second, darker, but less carefully registered fourth-state impression (Allen 427).

Solis was the most prolific graphic artist in mid-sixteenth-century Germany.[1] Over two thousand prints and book illustrations have been attributed to him and his large workshop. He was born in 1514, a date deduced from the inscription accompanying Balthasar Jenichen's 1562 portrait print of Solis.[2] His birth place is unknown; however, it was probably not Nuremberg, as is frequently cited, because his father(?), Hans Sollis, a painter, only acquired Nuremberg citizenship in 1525.[3] Virgil Solis probably became a master in 1539 shortly before his marriage on 29 April to Dorothea Dalmenin, his first wife, who bore him twelve children.

From 1540, the date of his first print, until his death in 1562, Solis was active as a graphic artist and, presumably, as a painter. He was noted for his designs for goldsmiths (see cat. nrs. 172 and 176) and for his frequent copies after other masters (see cat. nrs. 175 and 177). Following the death of Hans Sebald Beham in 1550, Solis became the principal book illustrator for Sigmund Feyerabend and other Frankfurt publishers. The *Biblische Figuren des Alter und Neuwen Testaments* (cat. nr. 178) contains 218 of his finest woodcuts. During the last ten or twelve years of Solis's life, his oeuvre became increasingly mechanical as he relied more and more on the participation of his many shop assistants.[4] As a result, the quality of his work is very uneven.

Solis is documented buying and quickly selling a house on Neuen Gasse in 1554.[5] A year later he purchased a house behind the Tetzelhof from goldsmith Hieronymus Peter. In 1556 his wife, Dorothea, died. He was remarried the following year to Margareta Lehwin, who bore him four more children. Solis died on 1 August 1562, perhaps a victim of the plague that killed 2,583 citizens of Nuremberg that year. In 1564 his widow, Margareta, married Balthasar Jenichen, Solis's principal assistant, who presumably inherited his workshop.

1. The following biographical information is taken primarily from O'Dell-Franke, *Solis*, esp. pp. 8–9, 14–18. Additional literature on Solis can be found in this study.
2. Ibid., pp. 14–15 (text), frontispiece (illustration); Andresen, II: nr. 42.
3. O'Dell-Franke, pp. 1, 14. It is uncertain whether Hans Sollis was the father or even a relative of Virgil. O'Dell-Franke notes that the name Virgil was highly unusual in Nuremberg and may suggest a birthplace near Salzburg.
4. Ibid., pp. 17–26, on the workshop. Many designs by the pupils and journeymen bear Solis's monogram; as a result, many drawings attributed to Solis are actually the work of others or, in other cases, were copied after the many prints by Solis and his workshop. See Geissler, ed., *Zeichnung in Deutschland*, I: A 39–A 41. I have been unable to obtain a copy of I. Franke, "Die Handzeichnungen Virgil Solis," dissertation (Göttingen, 1968), the only thorough study of Solis's drawings.
5. O'Dell-Franke, *Solis*, pp. 8, 9, for the following.

172. STUDY FOR AN ELABORATE DRINKING CUP

mid-sixteenth century(?)
Drawing: pencil and wash
29.2 × 19 cm
Lent by the Wadsworth Atheneum, Hartford, Bequest of Warren H. Lowenhaupt

Solis was a prolific creator of designs for cups, pitchers, and other goldsmith objects.[1] Solis's concern for the practical application of his designs is especially evident in one print series of the mid-1550s in which several tall covered cups are labeled with the words *Leuchter* (candlestick), *Salcz f.* (salt), *Geschir* (dish), *Schmek* (wine taster), and *Urlein* (little clocks) to indicate that the individual parts of his designs could also be used to make any one of these other objects.[2] Most of Solis's drawings and prints for goldsmith works display the decorative motifs then current in the workshop of Wenzel Jamnitzer (cf. cat. nrs. 183, 184, and 197).[3]

The *Study for an Elaborate Drinking Cup* has been attributed to Solis by the Wadsworth Atheneum. The attribution is very problematic because any similarities between the drawing and Solis's known graphic oeuvre are remote at best. The individual decorative features, such as the hanging garland, putto heads and, below, terms that alternate with embossed lobes, tendrils, and cartouches, all may be found in contemporary Nuremberg goldsmith work and related prints; however, collective application to a single cup is unique. In most of Solis's prints (see cat. nr. 178), the cartouches are in the form of thick, rather rigid, high-relief strapwork and not the irregularly curved pattern used in the Hartford drawing. Whether the drawing is by Solis, an artist in his workshop, or another artist, perhaps in the Netherlands, is uncertain.

1. Hayward, *Virtuoso Goldsmiths*, pp. 206–207; O'Dell-Franke, *Solis*, nrs. i 1–124, pls. 102–122.
2. This example is given in J. S. Byrne, *Renaissance Ornament Prints and Drawings*, nr. 133.
3. Hayward, *Virtuoso Goldsmiths*, pls. 118–122.

173. PORTRAIT OF EDWARD VI, KING OF ENGLAND, ON HORSEBACK

ca. 1550; monogram
Woodcut: colored; published by Stefan Hamer of Nuremberg
30 × 39.9 cm (bottom margin partially trimmed)
The University of Texas at Austin, The Humanities Research Center, Iconography Collection (formerly in the Duke of Gotha collection)

174. PORTRAIT OF ALBRECHT, MARGRAVE OF BRANDENBURG, ON HORSEBACK

ca. 1550 or later
Woodcut: colored; published by Hans Weigel of Nuremberg
24.8 × 34.2 cm
The University of Texas at Austin, The Humanities Research Center, Iconography Collection (formerly in the Duke of Gotha collection)

In about 1550 Virgil Solis created a series of equestrian portraits of some prominent German and foreign rulers. The exact extent of this cycle is difficult to determine since many of the woodcuts survive in only one or two impressions and little scholarly attention has been given to this subject.[1] These woodcuts were published in Nuremberg by Stefan Hamer.[2]

The design is essentially the same in all cases. At the top is an inscription "by the grace of God" plus the name and title of the individual. Below, the king or prince, mounted on his horse, is surrounded by an escort of four or five soldiers on foot. In every example that I have examined, the scene is treated as a procession moving from left to right. The arrangement seen here in the portrait of Edward VI is repeated identically in related portraits of Henri I, King of France, and Christian, King of Sweden and Norway; the only differences are the head and, occasionally, the colors applied, using a stencil, to each print.[3] Frequently, the portraits are purely imaginary. Edward VI was born in 1537, became king in 1547 following the death of Henry VIII, and died in 1553. Therefore, when this print was produced he was a lad of about thirteen rather than the mature adult represented. The king's coat of arms is placed in the upper right corner. Solis's monogram is inserted between the legs of the second or first soldier depending on whether a five- or four-member escort was used. Finally, at the bottom is the publisher's signature "Steffan Hamer Brieffmaler zu Nürnberg auff der Schmeltzbütten" (Stefan Hamer illuminator of Nuremberg [located] near the foundry). Hamer was responsible for the printing and coloring of the woodcuts.

The attribution and dating of the portrait of Margrave Albrecht Alcibiades of Brandenburg-Kulmbach (1536–1557) are more problematic. This woodcut lacks Solis's monogram, its design does not conform to that outlined above, and the publisher was Hans Weigel, not Hamer.[4] Although the composition of the portrait of Albrecht Alcibiades is not as vigorous as that of Edward VI, it may be seen that the undersized horse and the slightly awkward, unbalanced placement of the figures, the costumes, and the facial types are very similar to Solis's. The por-

Von Gottes genaden Eudardus König von Engelland.

Steffan Hamer Brieffmaler zu Nürnberg auff der Schmeltzbütten.

Von Gottes gnaden Albrecht Marggraff zu Brandenburg/zu Stetin/Pomern/der Cassuben vnnd Wenden Hertzog/Burggraff zu Nürnberg/vnnd Fürst zu Rügen/rc.

Gedruckt zu Nürnberg durch Hanns Weygel Formschneyder.

trait of Albrecht Alcibiades should be attributed either to Solis or, more likely, to a member of his workshop. It belongs to a second series of celebrity portraits published by Weigel, who frequently collaborated with Hamer. Interestingly, the likeness of Albrecht Alcibiades bears little resemblance to the portrait of him in the original equestrian series published by Hamer. Presumably, this second cycle was issued sometime before Albrecht's death in 1557.

1. H. Röttinger, "Neue Mitteilungen über Virgil Solis," *Zeitschrift für Bücherfreunde* N.F. 16 (1924): 77ff., esp. 82; Geisberg, nrs. 1328-1, 2, 3; Strauss, *The German Single Leaf Woodcut, 1550–1600*, I: pp. 404–405, nrs. 15–18. On the subject of woodcut portraits of nobles, including equestrian images, see *Vorstenportretten uit de eerste Helft van de 16de Eeuw: Houtsneden als Propaganda*, esp. pp. 15–27 (for German prints), nrs. 24–29 (Solis).

2. Hamer was active in Nuremberg between 1531 and 1562. He frequently was in trouble with the civil authorities for publishing woodcuts of miraculous apparitions. In one instance, in July 1550, he was jailed for three days and when his woodblocks of an apparition were returned to him by the city, they had been slashed to prevent further printings. On Hamer, see Strauss, *The German Single-Leaf Woodcut, 1550–1600*, I: pp. 391–405, with biographical information on 391.

3. Ibid., p. 404, nrs. 15–16. Each print in this series is composed from two separate woodblocks. In the portrait of Edward VI, a second square block for his head and shoulders and the tip of the soldier's ax has been added to the core block used for the remainder of the scene.

4. Ibid., III: pp. 1107–1138, with biographical information on 1107. Weigel was active in Nuremberg from about 1549 until 1577. Weigel was imprisoned along with Hamer (see note 2) for publishing a depiction of a miraculous apparition without first obtaining civic permission.

176. HEART DECORATION

1550–1555; monogram
Engraving
6.7 cm diameter
B. 464; O'Dell-Franke, *Solis*, nr. i 82
Lent by the New York Public Library, Prints Division, Astor, Lenox and Tilden Foundations

This tiny engraving was intended as a design for the interior of a cup or dish. The centers of dishes were often ornamented with animals, mythological scenes, or coats of arms.[1] This print is one of at least six, probably unrelated, circular prints with animals, including a lion and a goat, or ancient heroes, including Hector, in the center.[2]

The image used here is a love emblem. In the middle are two harts and a doe. Presumably, the closer male is protecting his mate from the amorous overtures of the second. The idea of love is repeated in the marginal scenes of the single and double crowned hearts. The design is filled out with two ornamental patterns.

---

1. O'Dell-Franke, *Solis*, pp. 68, 172. These ornaments could be either flat or in relief. See Pechstein, *Goldschmiedewerke der Renaissance*, nrs. 19–25, 53, 165, for examples.
2. O'Dell-Franke, *Solis*, nrs. i 80–85.

175. THE BATH
(after Heinrich Aldegrever)

ca. 1540(?); monograms of Solis and Aldegrever
Engraving
33.6 × 28.5 cm plate
B. 265; O'Dell-Franke, *Solis*, nr. f 71
Lent by the Fine Arts Museums of San Francisco, Achenbach Foundation for Graphic Arts
(1963.30.1494)

Solis frequently copied the drawings and prints of other masters.[1] *The Bath* is believed to be based upon a drawing, now lost, by Heinrich Aldegrever (1502–1556/61), a talented northern German printmaker.[2] The attribution of the design to Aldegrever is supported both by the inclusion of his monogram on the plaque in the center of the print and by the figure style, which can be compared with that in his engravings *Susanna* (B. 30) or *Bathsheba* (B. 37).[3] How Solis came into possession of Aldegrever's drawing is uncertain. Zschelletzschky and other older critics suggested that Aldegrever, who frequently reproduced Dürer's prints, was briefly in Dürer's workshop in Nuremberg; however, this has been discounted in more recent literature.[4]

The subject is ostensibly a mixed bathhouse, although it has more of the mood of Beham's *Fountain of Youth* (cat. nr. 85), with the amorous interplay, than of Dürer's *The Bathhouse* (cat. nr. 5). It has also been referred to as the bath of the Anabaptists. Some members of this religious sect believed in polygamy and, in a very few cases, nakedness based on the examples of the Old Testament patriarchs and prophets.[5] Their notoriety was all the greater in the aftermath of their seizure of Münster (which is near Soest, where Aldegrever lived) and their subsequent slaughter by the combined Protestant and Catholic forces in 1535 (see cat. nr. 69).

---

1. See cat. nr. 177 and *Nuremberg: Vorbild Dürer*, nrs. 80, 138, 144, 148, 151–152, 180, for examples of Solis's repeating the work of other masters.
2. H. Zschelletzschky, *Das Graphische Werk Heinrich Aldegrevers* (Strassburg, 1933), p. 259, nr. 158; cited by O'Dell-Franke, *Solis*, p. 53.
3. *The Illustrated Bartsch*, 16: nrs. 30, 37.
4. *Nuremberg: Vorbild Dürer*, p. 13, nr. 172. Aldegrever even patterned the style of his monogram after Dürer's.
5. R. H. Bainton, *The Reformation of the Sixteenth Century*, pp. 95–109, esp. 106.

177. VIRGIL SOLIS, . . . BUCHLIN VON DEN ALTEN GEBEUEN . . . (Nuremberg[?], 1550 or later)

Thirteen engraved plates plus title page
14.7/15 × 9.5/9.9 cm (each)
B. 352–363; O'Dell-Franke, *Solis*, nrs. f. 138–150
Lent by the John M. Wing Foundation of The Newberry Library, Chicago

In 1550 French artist and architect Jacques Androuet Du Cerceau (ca. 1520–ca. 1585) issued a booklet of prints after the drawings of Léonard Thiry. These represented rather fanciful views of Roman ruins.[1] This booklet, like the contemporary prints of Roman buildings published in Antwerp by Hieronymus Cock, was aimed at an ever increasing public interested in images and information about the ancient world.[2]

Shortly after the appearance of Du Cerceau's booklet, Virgil Solis published his own edition.[3] The orientation of the original plates was reversed in the copies and Solis's monogram was added to each plate, otherwise the images are identical. In his prologue, Solis acknowledged that he was reproducing the work of Du Cerceau and Thiry ("Leonhard Theodorico"), a comparatively rare instance of artistic honesty during this period.

In the third plate, illustrated here, three artists are shown busily sketching the Roman wall decorations and a male statue that is incongruously placed over a broken vault.[3] In spite of very loose analogies with the Basilica of Constantine and the Column of Trajan, the entire scene is imaginary.[4]

---

1. *Fragmenta Structurae Veteris* (Orleans, 1550). See Oberhuber, *Zwischen Renaissance und Barock*, nr. 298, pl. 43. Thiry was active at Fontainebleau between 1536 and 1542 before moving to Antwerp, where he died in 1550.
2. Ibid., nrs. 11–15; L. De Pauw-De Veen, *Jérôme Cock: Éditeur d'estampes et graveur, 1507?–1570*, exh. cat. (Brussels: Bibliothèque Royale Albert Ier, 1970), pp. 69–77; T. A. Riggs, *Hieronymus Cock (1510–1570):*

178. BIBLISCHE FIGUREN DES ALTER UND NEUWEN TESTAMENTS . . . DURCH VIRGILIUM SOLIS (Frankfurt: David Zephelium, Johann Raschen, and Sigmund Feyerabend, 1562)

Original vellum binding
20 × 26 cm (book)
B., IX: pp. 316–317 (1565 edition)
Lent by the University of Illinois at Urbana-Champaign, Rare Book Collection

Before his death in 1562, Solis and his atelier completed work on 218 woodcuts and 2 title pages for this illustrated Bible published by his frequent patron and collaborator Sigmund Feyerabend of Frankfurt.[1] As in Hans Sebald Beham's *Biblische Historien* (Frankfurt: Christian Egenolff, 1533; cat. nr. 80), the format consists of illustrations with accompanying texts rather than the complete biblical account. The 1562 Bible was the second edition on which Solis worked. In 1560 Feyerabend published a Bible with 147 illustrations by Solis, as well as Hans Sebald Beham, Anton Woensam, and others.[2] Perhaps the success of this venture prompted Feyerabend to order the more extensive 1562 cycle.[3] Ten subsequent editions were printed by

Feyerabend's establishment between 1565 and 1606.[4]

The title page for the New Testament is illustrated here. The cartouche recalls those of Cornelis Bos that were copied by Lautensack (cat. nrs. 163 and 164) and other Nuremberg artists; however, Solis's design is oddly two dimensional by comparison.[5] The eagle (of St. John?) is flanked by the phoenix and pelican, traditional symbols of Christ. Below are two sphinxes.

---

1. This copy of the 1562 Bible is imperfect. It lacks the title page and twenty-six leaves of volume I (Old Testament) and twenty of volume II (New Testament). Both volumes are bound together. On the Bible, see E. von Ubisch, *Virgil Solis und seine biblischen Illustrationen für den Holzschnitt*, pp. 43–83, esp. 57–68, for the 1562 edition; von Ubisch provides a complete listing of the woodcuts and any artist or *formschneider* monograms. Also see P. Schmidt, *Die Illustrationen der Lutherbibel* (Basel, 1962), pp. 236ff.
2. Von Ubisch, *Virgil Solis*, pp. 43ff.
3. Ibid., pp. 68–69.
4. Ibid., pp. 78–83.
5. Schéle, *Cornelis Bos*, pls. 49–55.

Also see cat. nrs.
47 Pfinzing, *Theuerdank* (bookplate by Solis)
136 *Vitruvius teutsch*
194 Rumpolt, *Ein new Kochbuch . . .*

Printmaker and Publisher (New York, 1977), pp. 165–169.
3. O'Dell-Franke, *Solis*, pp. 46–47, 133–134, nrs. f. 138–150.
4. Ibid., nr. f. 145. Compare Oberhuber, *Zwischen Renaissance und Barock*, nr. 298, which is Du Cerceau's etching that Solis copied. Solis's own attempts at devising antique-style scenes are rather weak. See his *Landscape with Ruins* drawing of 1560 in Berlin (Kupferstichkabinett); see Geissler, ed., *Zeichnung in Deutschland*, I: nr. A 41.

Hornick was among the most talented designers of goldsmith works and jewelry.[1] He is believed to have been born in the 1520s in the Low Countries, perhaps in Antwerp, where he was probably trained. Hornick settled in Augsburg sometime prior to his marriage to Afra Haug, daughter of a prominent patrician family, on 27 July 1555.[2] This would suggest that he was already quite well established in Augsburg. He moved to Nuremberg in 1559, and the city council granted him citizenship without the customary charge, "inasmuch as he is an outstanding artist in the goldsmiths' craft."[3] Hornick joined the Nuremberg goldsmith guild in 1563. He resided in Nuremberg until 1566, when he surrendered his citizenship and, presumably, returned to Augsburg, where he is documented between 1568 and 1570. In 1578 he sought employment in Nuremberg as a military engineer. Emperor Rudolf II appointed him goldsmith in the imperial workshop in Prague in 1582; he died there in October of the following year.[4]

Hornick's Nuremberg period seems to have been his most productive.[5] He published five sets of pattern books that provided the stylistic basis for the many drawings that Hayward and others have attributed to him in recent years (cat. nrs. 179–182).[6] Although his basic forms often derive from Wenzel Jamnitzer and other contemporary goldsmiths, Hornick created imaginative new design combinations. Because few actual goldsmith works can be linked with any of Hornick's prints and drawings, his exact influence is difficult to assess.[7]

1. On the artist, see "Hornick, Erasmus" in Thieme-Becker (1924), 17: p. 521. J. F. Hayward, "The Mannerist Goldsmiths, 3: Antwerp IV: Italian Influence in the Designs of Erasmus Hornick," *Connoisseur* 158 (1965): 144–149; "The Goldsmiths' Designs of the Bayerische Staatsbibliothek Reattributed to Erasmus Hornick" and "The Drawings and Engraved Ornaments of Erasmus Hornick," *Burlington Magazine* 110 (1968): 201–207, 383–389; *Virtuoso Goldsmiths*, pp. 243–251. Also see Y. Hackenbroch, "Erasmus Hornick as a Jeweller," *Connoisseur* 166 (1967): 54–63.

2. Hayward, "The Goldsmiths' Designs of the Bayerische Staatsbibliothek," p. 205.

3. "Erassmussen Hornay von Anndtorff [Antwerp] alls einen treffenlichen künstler ufm goldtschmidt-hanndtwerckh zu bürger annemen unnd ime das bürgerrecht schennkhen" (23 November 1559); see Hampe, *Nürnberger Ratsverlässe*, nr. 3788; Hayward, *Virtuoso Goldsmiths*, p. 244.

4. Hayward, *Virtuoso Goldsmiths*, pp. 246–247.

5. For a summary of Hornick's activities in Nuremberg, see K. Pechstein, "Bemerkungen zu Erasmus Hornick in Nürnberg," *AGNM* (1979): 116–120.

6. The first three sets are signed by Hornick, published in Nuremberg, and dated. These consist of (1) twenty designs for jewelry and bottles (1562); (2) twenty designs for pendants (1565); and (3) eighteen designs for vases, ewers, and other goldsmith works. Two additional sets of medallion designs that lack either dates or places of publication are believed to belong to this period. See Hayward, *Virtuoso Goldsmiths*, p. 244; the various articles cited in notes 1 and 5. All these prints exist in very limited quantities. Most are in Berlin (Kunstbibliothek), Coburg (Veste), London (British Museum), and Vienna (Albertina).

7. Hornick and Wenzel Jamnitzer are credited with designing and executing the stands for two globes by Johann Praetorius of 1566 now in Nuremberg (Germanisches Nationalmuseum); see Schnelbögl, *Dokumentie zur Nürnberger Kartographie*, pp. 80–81. I am unsure about the reasons for this attribution.

179. DESIGN FOR A COVERED TUREEN WITH TWO HANDLES

Before 1559(?)
Drawing: pen and ink with gray and yellow wash
41.6 × 21.9 cm
Lent by the National Gallery of Canada (La Galerie nationale du Canada), Ottawa, inv. nr. 6193

180. TWO DESIGNS FOR GOBLETS

Before 1559(?)
Drawing: pen and ink with gray and yellow wash
41.9 × 20.8 cm
Lent by the National Gallery of Canada (La Galerie nationale du Canada), Ottawa, inv. nr. 6194

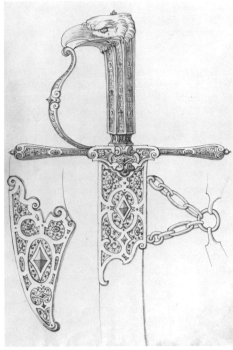

181. DESIGN FOR A PLATTER WITH THE BATTLE OF THE SEA-GODS

ca. 1560 or earlier
Drawing: pen and ink with gray and yellow wash
41.6 × 29.8 cm
Lent by the Metropolitan Museum of Art, New York, Rogers Fund, by exchange 1958 (58.525.9)

182. DESIGN FOR THE HILT AND SCABBARD OF A SWORD

ca. 1560
Drawing: pen and ink with gray and yellow wash
41.3 × 28.8 cm
Lent by the Metropolitan Museum of Art, New York, Bequest of Harry G. Sperling, 1975 (1975.131.71)

These four goldsmith designs are attributed to Erasmus Hornick, perhaps with contributions by his assistants. The sketches were once in an album of at least one hundred drawings formerly in the possession of the princes of Liechtenstein at Vaduz.[1] This was one of three sets of drawings by Hornick and his workshop that passed into the collection of Emperor Rudolf II in Prague following Hornick's death in 1583. The largest of these albums, containing 275 drawings, is now in London (Victoria & Albert Museum). Another group of thirteen drawings is in Vienna (Österreichisches Museum für Angewandte Kunst).

According to Hayward, these three sets originally belonged to a single large group of designs that Hornick intended to publish in a series of pattern books similar to those that were printed in Nuremberg in the 1560s. The Victoria & Albert Museum album contains at least four drawings for title pages. One of these drawings is dated 1560 and illustrates a lion skin spread out and suspended by nails and ribbons, a motif used in the printed title page of one of his 1565 printed pattern books.[2] Such pattern books were in great demand by goldsmiths, woodcarvers, and other craftsmen who depended on artists, such as Hornick, Flindt, Zan, and Zündt, to invent designs for their use. Hornick may also have sold his drawings directly to local goldsmiths. Some sketches, including these four, remained in his possession for his own creative use and, probably, as designs to show to a prospective patron.

The *Design for a Covered Tureen with Two Handles* (cat. nr. 179) is for a container to hold sweetmeats, as the pen inscription "per Confetti" indicates.[3] It is believed to date prior to Hornick's Nuremberg period largely because of the particular lobe and scroll patterns. Hayward attributed this drawing to a follower rather than to Hornick; however, Popham, while recognizing that it is closest to several of the drawings by Italian masters in the Victoria & Albert album, sees Hornick's hand in the two exhibited Ottawa drawings and in a third sketch of a salver.[4]

The *Two Designs for Goblets* (cat. nr. 180) also seems to date to before 1560.[5] The Moresque decorations, the strapwork, the lion masks, and the putti are motifs frequently found on other Hornick drawings.

The *Design for a Platter with the Battle of the Sea-Gods* (cat. nr. 181) is particularly impressive. Amid the central strapwork decorations are four masks with streams of water issuing from their mouths. The revolving scene depicts battling Nereids. This sketch is almost identical in theme and style to a Hornick drawing of a plate in the Victoria & Albert Museum album.[6] Contemporary plates and dishes were frequently embellished with scenes of aquatic battles.[7]

Goldsmiths of the sixteenth century produced such men's adornments as splendid sword hilts, scabbards, and belt mounts that were prized by the nobility. As in the *Design for the Hilt and Scabbard of a Sword* (cat. nr. 182) and other Hornick sword drawings of about 1560, these objects were to be wrought in fine metals and set with precious stones.[8] Because of their costly materials, the swords were frequently melted down, and few prime pieces survive today.[9] In this instance, the hilt and scabbard are covered with strapwork, filled in with Moresque forms and precious stones. The pommel and grip are in the form of an eagle's head and neck.

1. After the album was purchased by Colnaghi of London, it was broken up and dispersed to several private and public collections, including the National Gallery of Canada, the Metropolitan Museum of Art, the National Gallery of Victoria in Melbourne, and the Paul Wallraf Collection in London. For a general discussion of this album, the others cited below, and at least three additional albums attributed to Hornick or his workshop, see Hayward, "The Goldsmiths' Designs of the Bayerische Staatsbibliothek," pp. 201–207, esp. 205, "The Drawings and Engraved Ornaments," pp. 383–389, esp. 384, 387–388.
2. Hayward, *Virtuoso Goldsmiths*, pls. 138–139.
3. Popham and Fenwick, *European Drawings*, nr. 189; Hayward, *Virtuoso Goldsmiths*, p. 248. The Victoria & Albert album has drawings by Hornick and several Italian artists working in his style.
4. On the salver, see Popham and Fenwick, *European Drawings*, nr. 188; Farmer, *Virtuoso Craftsman*, nr. 17; Kaufmann, *Drawings from the Holy Roman Empire*, nr. 25.
5. Popham and Fenwick, *European Drawings*, nr. 190.
6. Hayward, *Virtuoso Goldsmiths*, pl. 201, cf. 200.
7. Ibid., pl. 498, Christoph Lencker's gilt basin (Vienna, Kunsthistorisches Museum) of the early seventeenth century provides a very general idea of this type of platter with relief decorations. The subject is Europa and the bull.
8. Ibid., pls. 224 (New York), 225 (London); Hayward, "The Drawings and Engraved Ornaments," p. 282, fig. 18.
9. J. Schöbel, *Fire Arms and Armor: Treasures in the Dresden Collection* (New York, 1975).

Matthias Zündt

Zündt was a printmaker, sculptor, and goldsmith.[1] His early history is unknown. His birth date has been placed as early as about 1498, but he is first documented only in 1551 as a journeyman and son-in-law of Wenzel Jamnitzer in Nuremberg. In that year he published the *Novum Opus Craterographicum . . . oder Ein new Kunstbuch*, a highly influential pattern book with designs for elaborate goldsmith cups, dishes, and pitchers (cat. nrs. 183 and 184).

With Wenzel Jamnitzer's help, Zündt became a Nuremberg citizen in 1556, two years after the city council denied his initial request. Although he only became a master goldsmith in 1560, he was sufficiently talented for Jamnitzer to send him to Prague in 1559 to work on a lavish Adam and Eve table fountain commissioned by Archduke Ferdinand.[2] Zündt specialized in modeling and casting tiny insects, animals, and grasses in silver. Due to the lack of silver, this table fountain was still unfinished in 1561, when the project was apparently abandoned.

Zündt's activities as a goldsmith were quite limited. He is referred to as a carver or hard stone cutter in the local documents.[3] He seems to have worked primarily as a designer and sculptor of goldsmith models, such as the copper dagger sheath in Berlin (Kunstgewerbemuseum) that is attributed to him.[4]

Zündt was also an accomplished printmaker.[5] Besides the plates in the *Craterographicum*, he published twelve brooch designs in an untitled booklet of 1553, and many individual designs for goldsmith works.[6] Zündt produced the plates for Hans Lencker's *Perspectiva Literaria* (Nuremberg, 1567).[7] He created portraits; religious images, including *The Apostle Ship* (cat. nr. 185); maps of Cyprus, Malta (1565), Hungary (1566), and other countries; images of contemporary battles; and many coats of arms.[8]

Zündt died in 1572 or as late as 1581.[9]

1. There exists no adequate study of Zündt's career. See "Zündt, Matthias" in Thieme-Becker (1947), 36: pp. 584–585; Farmer, *Virtuoso Craftsman*, p. 104; Hayward, *Virtuoso Goldsmiths*, pp. 206–207.

2. Hayward, *Virtuoso Goldsmiths*, pp. 46–47.

3. Hampe, *Nürnberger Ratsverlässe*, I: nrs. 3496 ("staynschneyder"; 3 August 1554), 3613 ("goldtschmid"; 23 May 1556, when he acquired his citizenship).

4. Pechstein, *Bronzen und Plaketten*, nr. 212. Various jewelry models have been attributed (incorrectly?) to Zündt; see Y. Hackenbroch, "Jewellery at the Court of Albrecht V at Munich," *Connoisseur* 165 (1967): 74–82, esp. p. 75; Farmer, *Virtuoso Craftsman*, nr. 54.

5. Andresen, I: pp. 1–46.

6. Ibid., nrs. 59–70 (1553 booklet), 57–58, 71–78.

7. Ibid., nr. 56. A copy is in the Metropolitan Museum of Art in New York.

8. Ibid., nrs. 1–14 (portraits), 15–20 (religious images), 26–30 (maps), 32–36 (battles), 38–55 (coats of arms). The Nuremberg city council purchased his maps of Malta and Hungary; see Hampe, *Nürnberger Ratsverlässe*, I: nrs. 4078, 4128.

9. The anonymous author of the article in Thieme-Becker (see note 1) gives Zündt's death date as 25 February 1572. Pechstein, *Bronzen und Plaketten*, nr. 212, lists it as 1581(?).

183. DESIGN FOR AN ORNATE EWER WITH A FIGURE OF NEPTUNE

1551
Engraving
25 × 16.2 cm
Lent by the Cooper-Hewitt Museum, The Smithsonian Institution's National Museum of Design, New York (1946-37-1)

184. DESIGN FOR A DOUBLE DISH

1551
Engraving
12.4 × 17.5 cm (trimmed)
Lent by the New York Public Library, Prints Division, Astor, Lenox and Tilden Foundations

These engravings are two of the highly mannered designs for goldsmith works contained in the *Novum Opus Craterographicum . . . oder Ein new Kunstbuch (A Work of New Vessel Shapes . . . or a New Art Book)*, published in Nuremberg in 1551.[1] Although the name of the artist is lacking, the plates have long been attributed to Zündt based on comparison with his other prints and because of the artist's obvious debt to his father-in-law, Wenzel Jamnitzer.[2] Just as Jamnitzer's *Merkel Table Decoration* (figs. 47 and 48) introduced a new, even more bizarre style to the art of the goldsmith, Zündt's engravings mark the concomitant rise of a new direction for prints and drawings of goldsmith works. According to Farmer, "This book marks the formal beginnings of a rejection of the rational Renaissance taste in favor of a crowded, sometimes seemingly formless decorative style frequently utilized on vessels which assumed new asymmetrical and organic forms."[3]

Zündt's ewer would have been difficult, if not impossible, to use unless the figure of Neptune and his dolphin-drawn chariot were part of a detachable lid. The surface of the ewer is hidden beneath a wealth of grotesque forms, masks, insects, and foliate patterns. The aquatic function of this ewer is playfully reinforced by the choice of Neptune on the spout, an ass(?) with water issuing from its mouth, the scene of tritons on the underside of the vessel, and even the fish-scale pattern below.

Similar use of the cast shells and the strapwork is evident in the *Design for a Double Dish*. Other motifs, such as the pendant garlands of fruit and foliage and the winged angels, are frequently found in other plates in this series. Many of the plates are also characterized by intense cross-hatching to form shadows on the right side and, to a much lesser degree, on the left side of the goldsmith pieces; this provides depth and a sense of structure to the objects.

1. On these and other plates, see Hayward, *Virtuoso Goldsmiths*, pp. 206–207, pls. 134 (the ewer)–136; Byrne, *Renaissance Ornament Prints and Drawings*, nrs. 136–137. Also see J. Hayward, "Four Carved Wood Models for a Clock-Case," *AGNM* (1975): 65–71, for a discussion of carved pearwood models after Zündt's plates. On a drawing of a ewer by a follower of Zündt, see Farmer, *Virtuoso Craftsman*, nr. 53; C. M. Rosenberg, "A Drawing by Mathias Zündt, an Engraving by Hans Sebald Beham, and a Seventeenth Century German Tankard," *University of Michigan Museum of Art, Bulletin* 5 (1970–1971): 18–25.
2. Wenzel Jamnitzer may well have provided the designs or at least many of the ideas for Zündt's plates; see K. Pechstein, "Zeichnungen von Wenzel Jamnitzer," *AGNM* (1970): 81–95, esp. 82.
3. Farmer, *Virtuoso Craftsman*, p. 104.

185. THE APOSTLE SHIP

1570; signed
Etching: retouched with pen
26.3 × 36.1 cm
Andresen, I: p. 15, nr. 19
Lent by the Germanisches Nationalmuseum, Nuremberg, HB 34

The Apostle Ship is one of the few important religious prints made in Nuremberg during the second half of the sixteenth century.[1] Represented is the ship of the Christian church, with Christ and the Protestant sacraments (baptism, communion, and confession) symbolically depicted on the deck, under the constant attack of its enemies. Christ is shown as the mast of the ship. "Watch ye, stand fast in the faith, quit you like men, be strong" (1 Corinthians 16:13) reads the inscription directly above Christ. A trinitarian image is formed with the Holy Spirit and God the Father above. Christ stands on an altar, and his blood flows into the baptismal font and toward those partaking in the double (wine and host) communion. Nearby stand the four archangels holding the instruments of the Passion.

The Apostle Ship is not stridently anti-Catholic in its imagery. It expresses the Protestant view that the reformers Luther and Melanchthon were not radical separatists but guardians of the Church's fundamental teachings. They are

shown, together with the Church fathers(?) and the emperors since Constantine, as oarsmen of the Christian ship; they maintain the continuity of the Church. The ship's navigators are the four Evangelists, John the Baptist, and St. James the Major, while the helmsmen include Sts. Peter and Paul and several of the Apostles.

The Church's enemies are shown in the water beside the ship. They denote the anti-Christian forces that are constantly trying to damage the Church and its authority. The eight swimmers are Nero, Caiphas, Pilate, Sergius, Nestorius, Pelagius, Arius, and Mahomet. Their eight mounted colleagues are Antiochus, Attila, Genserich, Herod, the Turk, the Tartar, the Whore of Babylon (cf. cat. nr. 6), and Jezebel.

In the upper corners are representations of God protecting Shadrach, Meshach, and Abednego from the flames of the fiery furnace of King Nebuchadnezzar (Daniel 3), and the conversion of St. Paul (Acts 9). Both tales emphasize the importance of one's belief in God in the face of persecution, an apt analogy to the Lutheran struggle against the institution of the Roman Catholic church.

The image of the Christian church is based on a passage in Matthew 9:23–27. It reads: "And when he was entered into a ship, his disciples followed him. And, behold, there arose a great tempest in the sea, insomuch that the ship was covered with the waves; but he was asleep. And

his disciples came to him, and awoke him, saying, Lord, save us: we perish. And he saith unto them, Why are ye fearful, O ye of little faith? Then he arose, and rebuked the winds and the sea; and there was a great calm. But the men marvelled, saying, What manner of man is this, that even the winds and the sea obey him!" The etching is thus a call for faith and strength of conviction in the face of contemporary assaults and seeming setbacks to the Protestant cause.

A year or two after Zündt completed this print, Hans Weigel the Elder of Nuremberg published a huge broadsheet, measuring 69 × 104 cm, entitled *The Christian Ship*.[2] Weigel's woodcut contains only minor modifications.

---

1. This print is published with brief descriptions in *Reformation in Nürnberg*, nr. 148; Scribner, *For the Sake of Simple Folk*, p. 115. See the general comments in Section 3 C.
2. Strauss, *The German Single-Leaf Woodcut, 1550–1600*, III: pp. 1124–1125, nr. 34.

Bernhard Zan

Zan was a goldsmith and engraver active in Nuremberg during the 1580s.[1] As a journeyman in 1580, he published a set of twelve prints of cups decorated in low strapwork interspersed with masks, fruits, and flowers.[2] In the following year he produced at least forty punch engravings of goldsmith designs. These were published by goldsmith Stephan Herman of nearby Ansbach in 1584 in a pattern book entitled *Allerley Gebuntznierte Fisirungen . . . (All Kinds of Dotted Designs . . .).*[3] Nothing else about Zan's career is known.

1. Andresen, III: pp. 256–262; Heye, "Zan, Bernhard" in Thieme-Becker (1947), 36: p. 399; Oberhuber, *Zwischen Renaissance und Barock,* nr. 205; Farmer, *Virtuoso Craftsman,* p. 139; Hayward, *Virtuoso Goldsmiths,* pp. 43, 238.
2. Andresen, III: pp. 256–257, nrs. 1–12. The title is *12 STICK. ZVM VERZAICHEN STECHEN VERFERTIGT BERNHART ZAN GOLDSCHMID GESEL. INN NIERNBERG 1580.* On Zan's activities as a punch engraver, see A. Winkler, "Die Gefäss- und Punzenstecher der deutschen Hochrenaissance," *JPKS* 13 (1892): 93–107, esp. 97.
3. Andresen, III: pp. 258ff., nrs. 13–52; Winkler, "Die Gefäss- und Punzenstecher," p. 97.

186. DESIGN FOR A COVERED CUP

1581; monogram
Punch engraving: hand colored in blue and gold
21.2 × 11.1 cm
Andresen, III: p. 259, nr. 20
Lent by the Museum of Fine Arts, Boston, Horatio Greenough Curtis Fund (M-35092)

This print is an early example of two stylistic innovations: low-relief strapwork and punch engraving.[1] According to Winkler and Hayward, low-relief, or flat, strapwork was first introduced by Nuremberg painter Georg Wechter in a series of thirty goldsmith designs published in 1579.[2] By the next year Bernhard Zan was issuing his own flat strapwork patterns. These contrast with the immensely popular high strapwork style that had been created in the 1530s at Fontainebleau and then quickly was spread throughout the continent by Cornelis Bos of Antwerp and others. The cartouches in Lautensack's two views of Nuremberg (cat. nrs. 163 and 164) and Hans Bolsterer's *Cartouche with a Female Mask* (cat. nr. 204) are representative examples of the high strapwork style.

Zan's engravings immediately influenced Nuremberg goldsmiths. Melchior Königsmüller's *Covered Cup* (cat. nr. 206) is a three-dimensional translation of Zan's ideas. The low-relief strapwork is barely raised above the surface of the cup. It is combined with clusters of fruit, tiny floral buttons, and female masks that are almost identical to those in Zan's engraving. The shape of Königsmüller's cup derives from yet another of Zan's prints.

Zan's *Design for a Covered Cup* was made with a goldsmith's handpunch rather than a burin.[3] A close examination of this print reveals that the lines are actually a series of closely spaced dots. Zan punched or, with a punch and a hammer, tapped these dots directly into the surface of the metal plate. When the plate was printed, these stippled dots gave the initial appearance of a continuous line. This method of making prints was an adaptation of the punch engraving technique long used by goldsmiths either as a preparatory step in the decoration of the metal or as an ornamental process. Before embossing the metal, the goldsmith would designate the areas to be decorated with fine lines of dots driven into the metal by a punch. If a record of the design was desired, a rubbing or even an inked impression could be made on paper. This technique enjoyed considerable popularity in Nuremberg during the last two decades of the century. Most of its practitioners, notably Zan, Jonas Silber, and Paul Flindt the Younger, were trained goldsmiths who also were printmakers.[4] They simply applied the tools of their trade to printmaking.

1. This print was reissued in 1584 in the pattern book *Allerley Gebuntznierte Fisirungen . . . ,* published by goldsmith Stephan Herman at Ansbach.
2. Winkler, "Die Gefäss- und Punzenstecher," p. 97; Hayward, *Virtuoso Goldsmiths,* p. 237; Byrne, *Renaissance Ornament Prints and Drawings,* nr. 25, reproduces the title page of Wechter's pattern book.
3. On punch engraving, see Winkler, "Die Gefäss- und Punzenstecher," pp. 93–107, for the best discussion. Also see A. Hind, *A History of Engraving & Etching,* 3d ed. (1923; reprint: New York, 1963), pp. 10–11; Farmer, *Virtuoso Craftsman,* nr. 71 (Zan's print); Hayward, *Virtuoso Goldsmiths,* pp. 237–238.
4. Winkler, "Die Gefäss- und Punzenstecher," pp. 97–107. Winkler's Master JS is now identified as Jonas Silber. On Silber, see Section 7 E and fig. 52.

Flindt was active as a printmaker and a gold-smith.[1] He was born in 1567, the son of Nuremberg goldsmith Paul Flindt the Elder (died 1571/72) and worked in Nuremberg until his death sometime after 1631. The majority of his prints represent cups, plates, candlesticks, pitchers, and other goldsmith objects. He published two pattern books in Vienna in 1592 and 1593 and a third in Nuremberg in 1594 (cat. nr. 187).[2] Like Zan (cat. nr. 186), he frequently made dot or punch engravings. Two drawings attributed to Flindt are now in Berlin (Kupferstichkabinett).[3] Rosenberg ascribed an oval platter decorated with a trumpeter and a tambourine player to Flindt.[4]

1. T. Hampe, "Flindt, Paul" in Thieme-Becker (1916), 12: p. 101; Farmer, *Virtuoso Craftsman*, pp. 141–142; Hayward, *Virtuoso Goldsmiths*, pp. 238–239, pls. 162, 178, 180, 182.
2. On these three pattern books, together with others from 1603 and 1618, see Winkler, "Die Gefäss- und Punzenstecher," pp. 102–107.
3. Bock, *Staatliche Museen zu Berlin*, I: pp. 41–42, nrs. 2119 (*The Judgment of Paris*), 2661 (*Dolphin's Head with a Scene from the Story of the Prodigal Son*); also see nrs. 2662–2663. On the *Judgment of Paris*, also see Geissler, ed., *Zeichnung in Deutschland*, nr. E 20.
4. In 1885 this work was in the Patriarchs' Treasury in Moscow. See Rosenberg, *Der Goldschmiede Merkzeichen*, III: pp. 169–170, nr. 4110A, which cites a reference to Flindt's activities as a goldsmith. Various plaquettes have also been attributed to Flindt; however, most of these are after his prints. See Weber, *Renaissanceplaketten*, p. 204.

187. DESIGN FOR A COVERED CUP WITH A CUPID FINIAL

1594; monogram
Punch engraving
30.3 × 13.3 cm
Lent by the Metropolitan Museum of Art, New York, Harris Brisbane Dick Fund, 1937 (37.40.5(32))

188. DESIGN FOR A DECORATED GOBLET WITH JUPITER AND CALLISTO

early 1590s; monogram
Punch engraving
26.1 × 14.6 cm
Lent by the Cleveland Museum of Art, Gift of Mrs. Warren H. Corning, Sr.

Flindt was strongly influenced by the prints of Zan and Jonas Silber, notably in the use of the punch engraving technique and the flat strapwork decoration. Flindt's style was more complex, more pictorial than Zan's. His application of the strapwork, masks, foliate forms, and figural scenes in the *Design for a Covered Cup with a Cupid Finial* reveals his taste for intricate, yet carefully controlled, decoration. This was one of several columbine cup designs that Flindt made with the Nuremberg apprentice goldsmiths in mind.[1] These young goldsmiths were required to produce columbine cups as their master, or test, pieces; they were not, however, required to create their own designs, and so they frequently used Flindt's ideas.[2]

Flindt's *Design for a Decorated Goblet with Jupiter and Callisto* can be compared with the shape and decoration of contemporary Nuremberg goldsmith cups, including those by Hans Kellner (cat. nr. 205) and Melchior Mager (cat. nr. 207). Especially similar in type are the strapwork-framed scene at the top of the cup, the base and urn-shaped stem, and the specific decorative forms.

1. This print was published in Flindt's 1594 pattern book, which is entitled *Dieses buch mit 40 Stücken eingetheilet Fecit Paulus Flindt Nurmbergensis Ao 1594*; see Winkler, "Die Gefäss- und Punzenstecher," p. 103, for a summary of its contents. This print is also illustrated in Byrne, *Renaissance Ornament Prints and Drawings*, nr. 128. For another of his columbine cup designs, see Hayward, *Virtuoso Goldsmiths*, pl. 178.
2. Compare the late-sixteenth-century columbine cup (London, Victoria & Albert) attributed to the workshop of Christoph Jamnitzer; see Hayward, *Virtuoso Goldsmiths*, pl. 515.

Jost Amman was a painter, printmaker, and designer of stained-glass windows, jewelry, and goldsmith works.[1] He was born on 13 June 1539 in Zurich, where he was later educated at the Collegium Carolinum.[2] His father, Johann Jacob Amman, was the choir director and professor of rhetoric and classical languages at this school. Amman received his artistic training in Zurich and Basel; he may have worked in Basel as early as 1557.[3] While in Schaffhausen two years later, Amman was influenced by and possibly collaborated with glass painter Hieronymus Lang and printmaker Tobias Stimmer (1539–1584). Stimmer and Amman were destined to become the period's two finest graphic artists.

Amman settled in Nuremberg sometime before 3 March 1561, the date on his painting of the *Gesellenstechen*, a patrician tournament that took place in the Hauptmarkt.[4] There is no documentary evidence to support the claim that Amman came to Nuremberg to study with Virgil Solis and, following the death of Solis in 1562, that he took over the workshop.[5] Solis's atelier certainly passed to his long-time pupil Balthasar Jenichen, who married his widow, Margareta, in 1564.[6] Amman's proposed association with Solis results from the fact that after Solis's death Amman became the principal supplier of book illustrations for Frankfurt publisher Sigmund Feyerabend.[7] Beginning with his 133 woodcuts for the *Neuwe Biblische Figuren des Alten und Neuwen Testaments* of 1564, Amman provided the illustrations for at least fifty books printed by or for Feyerabend.

During the 1560s, Amman worked closely with other Nuremberg artists, notably Wenzel Jamnitzer. Amman and Jamnitzer collaborated on several projects, the most significant of which was the *Perspectiva Corporum Regularium* of 1568 (cat. nr. 197). Amman continued to work as a painter. When he painted the *Portrait of a Thirty-Year-Old Man*, now in Basel (Kunstmuseum), in 1565, he signed the picture "IAGVZR 1565," or Jost Amman Glasmaler von Zurich (glass painter of Zurich) 1565.[8]

As this inscription suggests, Amman continued to think of his stay in Nuremberg as a temporary one. Not until 1574 did he marry Barbara Wilke, the widow of a local goldsmith, and settle into a house on the Obere Schmiedgasse.[9] On 14 June 1577, the city council of Nuremberg granted Amman citizenship in recognition of his skillfulness.[10] The document lists Amman as a painter and designer of art objects.

From the mid-1570s until Amman's death in March 1591, he was primarily active as a graphic artist and as a designer for local jewelers and goldsmiths. In 1578 Feyerabend published Amman's *Kunst und Lehrbüchlein*, a manual of art and painting with 108 woodcuts.[11] An expanded edition with 156 woodcuts appeared in 1580. Artistic commissions required Amman to travel to Frankfurt, Venice, and Zurich in 1574; to Augsburg in 1578; and to Frankfurt and Heidelberg in 1583.

In spite of his prolific output, which Amman's pupil Jörg Keller claimed was enough to fill a haywagon with four years' worth of drawings, Amman never achieved financial success.[12] In 1590 he is mentioned earning money by teaching drawing to an unnamed English earl at nearby Altdorf, the site of the recently created university of Nuremberg. On his death in 1591, his estate was valued at only 338 florins.

1. A good monograph on the artist still needs to be written. The best study on Amman is K. Pilz, "Jost Amman, 1539–1591," *MVGN* 37 (1940): 201–252, from which most of the biographical information given here is drawn. Also see Andresen, I: pp. 99–147; C. Becker, *Jobst Amman, Zeichner und Formschneider, Kupferätzer und Stecher*; Thieme-Becker, I: pp. 410–413; Hollstein, II: pp. 8–57; Oberhuber, *Zwischen Renaissance und Barock*, pp. 141–146; Strauss, *The German Single-Leaf Woodcut, 1550–1600*, I: pp. 25–80, esp. 25; O'Dell-Franke, *Solis*, esp. pp. 22–23; Geissler, ed., *Zeichnung in Deutschland*, I: pp. 194–198. Other specialized studies are given below.

2. Pilz, "Amman," pp. 203–204, on his early history.

3. P. L. Ganz, *Die Basler Glasmaler der Spätrenaissance und Barockzeit*, pp. 40ff. Pilz, "Amman," p. 204, says that in 1560 Amman was in the Basel workshop of glass painter Ludwig Ringler (1535–1605).

4. Pilz, "Amman," pp. 205–206. This picture is now in the Bayerisches Nationalmuseum in Munich; see Pfeiffer and Schwemmer, *Bilddokumenten*, fig. 61, with a brief commentary. It does not show a duel of apprentices as is sometimes claimed.

5. This suggestion was made in Pilz, "Amman," p. 205, among others. It is noteworthy that Amman's earliest drawing of a soldier (The Hague, Collection of Dr. Hans Schneider in 1940), dated 1556, is a copy after a Solis print (B. 249). O'Dell-Franke, *Solis*, p. 22, was the first to challenge Amman's association with Solis.

6. O'Dell-Franke, *Solis*, pp. 23–25.

7. On Amman's work for Feyerabend, see Pilz, "Amman," pp. 207ff. A listing of Amman's prints for Feyerabend and other book publishers is given in Hollstein, II: pp. 37–56.

8. See Pilz, "Amman," pp. 224–225, for this and other paintings by Amman.

9. His first wife, Barbara, died in early 1586. Amman remarried in December of this year.

10. Hampe, *Nürnberger Ratsverlässe*, II: nr. 282.

11. Andresen, I: nr. 237; Becker, *Amman*, nr. 27; Hollstein, II: p. 51. The fourth edition, with supplemental woodcuts, published in 1599, has been reprinted as Jost Amman, *293 Renaissance Woodcuts for Artists and Illustrators*, intro. A. Werner (New York: Dover Publications, 1968). The influence of Amman's drawings and prints on all media has been studied by many critics. In particular, see Y. Hackenbroch, "Renaissance Pendants after Designs of Jost Amman," *Connoisseur* 160 (1965): 58–65.

12. Peltzer, ed., *Sandrarts Academie*, p. 106; also cited in Strauss, *The German Single-Leaf Woodcut, 1550–1600*, I: p. 25.

Diß ift ein Figur vnd eigentliche anzeygung eins gantzen Thurniers / wie der vor
zeyten durch die Ritterschafft vnd vom Adel gehalten. Wie vnd was darinn / mit Seyl abhauwen durch die Grießwertel/
Empfahung/ Cleinoter abhauwung mit den Schwerdten/Straffung deß Schlagens/Schranckenfetzens vnd
außziehens/rc.gehandelt worden.

189. TOURNAMENT OF MAXIMILIAN II

1565; monogram
Woodcut: second of five states
20.3 × 35.4 cm
Andresen, I: nr. 69; Hollstein, II: p. 28
Lent by the Cleveland Museum of Art, Purchase, Dudley P. Allen Fund

Amman's woodcut first appeared in 1565 and was frequently reused in the following years.[1] The page number (E iiii) at the bottom right indicates its placement in Georg Rüxner's *Thurnierbuch* (or Tournament Book) that was published by Sigmund Feyerabend in Frankfurt in 1566. Either Feyerabend or Amman pulled numerous, independent impressions of this woodcut, including the exhibited copy, while preparing this book.[2]

Jousting had long been a favorite pastime of the nobility and the Nuremberg patricians. Amman's first painting made in Nuremberg depicts a patrician joust held in the Hauptmarkt in 1561.[3] Both Amman's painting and woodcut recall Lucas Cranach the Elder's famous woodcut of a Saxon jousting tournament held in 1506.[4] All

three examples illustrate the German jousting style, in which chaos seems to reign as several combatants tilt simultaneously. This contrasts with the more common French-style joust, in which only two participants compete at any one time and they are separated by a long wooden list.[5]

According to the inscription accompanying the first state of this print, the tournament was held in honor of Maximilian II in Vienna. A problem arises about which one of Maximilian's Viennese contests is represented since he held major jousts there in 1558, 1560, and 1563; none was held in 1565.[6] Fortunately, the solution also is provided by this inscription. Maximilian is referred to as the king of Bohemia and the future Roman emperor (or, more correctly, the king of the Romans), titles that he received in 1562. Following Ferdinand I's death in 1564, Maximilian became the new emperor. Therefore, if the inscription is correct, the tournament could only have been held in the years 1562 to 1563. To celebrate his new status, sumptuous jousts were held in Prague in September 1562 and in Vienna in the following March.[7] Amman's view of the old Burg, or castle, in Vienna is purely imaginary, as is immediately apparent when it is com-

pared with Hans Lautensack's etching of the 1560 Viennese joust.[8] Lautensack faithfully copied the surrounding buildings.

1. On the different editions, see Andresen, I: nr. 69.
2. Becker, *Amman*, nr. 8.
3. On the 1561 painting, see Amman biography, note 4. Jousting remained popular in Nuremberg. A notable joust that took place there on 8 October 1616 was immortalized three years later in Heinrich and Hans Kuhn's stucco ceiling decorations for the upper gallery of the new wing of the Rathaus; unfortunately, this cycle was destroyed in World War II. See Mummenhoff, *Rathaus*, pp. 152, 155.
4. Jahn, *Lucas Cranach*, p. 380; Geisberg, nr. 620. Compare the similar compositional and figural arrangements.
5. See note 8 below.
6. T. D. Kaufmann, *Variations on the Imperial Theme in the Age of Maximilian II and Rudolf II*, pp. 22–28. I wish to thank Thomas Kaufmann for sharing his knowledge of these events.
7. Ibid., pp. 26–27.
8. Schmitt, *Lautensack*, nr. 35. This French-style tournament was held to celebrate the visit of Duke Albrecht V of Bavaria.

190. HANS SACHS, EYGENTLICHE BESCHREIBUNG ALLER STÄNDE AUFF ERDEN, . . . (Frankfurt: printed in the shop of Georg Raben for Sigmund Feyerabend, 1574)

115 woodcuts
7.8 × 6 cm (approximate size of each woodcut)
Andresen, I: nr. 231; B., IX: p. 381, 8; Becker, *Amman*, nr. 13; Hollstein, II: p. 47
Lent by the Philadelphia Museum of Art, The SmithKline Corporation Collection
A. (Not shown) Complete second German edition (first edition appeared in 1568)
B. *Der Formschneider* (The Woodblock Cutter), separate woodcut
C. *Der Brieffmaler* (The Illuminator), separate woodcut

The Exact Description of All Ranks on Earth, as the title translates, is better known as the *Book of Trades*.[1] Jost Amman and poet Hans Sachs provide a catalogue of the different occupations of the day, from pope and ecclesiastic to emperor and noble to artist and laborer to three categories of fool. Each is described in an eight-line poem by Sachs and a woodcut by Amman. The text beneath *Der Formschneider* reads:

I am a skilled *formschneider*
Given a design drawn with feather [pen] upon the woodblock, this I engrave with my tool. When a print is struck, the image appears on the paper as sharply and as artistically drawn as on the design.[2]

Only in a few instances, such as the monks or the pilgrims, did Sachs use his satirical wit to comment upon the groups' usefulness. Otherwise, the book is free of moralizing. That the book is intended for a broad audience is evident in its composition since it begins with the pope and members of the Roman Catholic church, much despised by the Lutherans in Nuremberg. This may reflect the religious accommodations that resulted from the 1555 Treaty of Augsburg, which established peace and imperial recognition of the current religious divisions within Germany.

Amman provided accurate illustrations of the individual craftsmen at work. His woodcuts, however, add little new to our understanding of technical procedures. The *Book of Trades* may have been inspired by the *Haushuch* (Housebook) of the Mendel Zwölfbrüderhaus, the charitable house for elderly craftsmen founded in 1388 by Konrad Mendel the Elder.[3] The *Hausbuch*, now in the Stadtbibliothek in Nuremberg, consists of three volumes of watercolor sketches of the deceased brothers of the house, each represented at work in his respective trade, which included weaving, painting, gardening, metalworking, and other forms of manual labor. Volume one consists of 330 sketches made between 1425 and 1545. Although the numerous painters who executed the images sought to represent the various crafts, they did not intend to provide the sweeping survey found in the *Book of Trades*. Amman certainly knew this work and may have referred to it while devising his own scenes.

The *Book of Trades* begins with a portrait of Wenzel Jamnitzer, to whom the work is dedicated.[4] Jamnitzer, Amman's frequent collabora-

Der Formschneider.

Ich bin ein Formenschneider gut/
Als was man mir fürreissen thut/
Mit der Federn auff ein Formbrät/
Das schneid ich denn mit meim Gerät/
Wenn mans denn druckt so findt sich scharff
Die Bildnuß/wie sie der entwarff/
Die steht denn druckt auff dem Papier/
Künstlich denn außzustreichen schier.
F   Der

tor, may have embodied the virtuous, successful craftsman that Amman and Sachs sought to inspire. The portrait is followed by Feyerabend's long foreword, completed on 24 December 1567, and the 114 occupational woodcuts. Sachs concluded with the advice to the reader to be industrious in whatever job he selects.

The book enjoyed immediate popularity.[5] A Latin edition was published by Feyerabend also in 1568. To this he added eighteen woodcuts used in other books illustrated by Amman. Second German and Latin editions appeared in 1574. Many of the woodcuts reappear in related texts in the following century.

---

1. A good general introduction is provided in Rifkin, ed., *Book of Trades*.
2. The translation is by Sigrid Knudsen and Annegreth Nill.
3. On the *Hausbuch* and related craft illustrations, see Treue et al., *Des Hausbuch der Mendelschen Zwölfbrüderstiftung*, esp. I: pp. 71–92, 93–97; H. Zirnbauer, "Nachträge zur Geschichte und Datierung des Mendelbuches I," and W. Schultheiss, "Das Hausbuch des Mendelschen Zwölfbrüderhauses zu Nürnberg von 1388/1425 bis 1549. Nürnberger Beiträge zur Geschichte der deutschen Technik," *MVGN* 54 (1966): 91–93, 94–108.
4. The age of Jamnitzer is given as fifty-nine. This print was also issued separately. See Andresen, I: nr.

13; Hollstein, II: p. 23. It is illustrated in Rifkin, ed., *Book of Trades*, p. 3.
5. On the different editions and later uses of many of the woodcuts, see Becker, *Amman*, pp. 64–65; Rifkin, ed., *Book of Trades*, p. xliii.

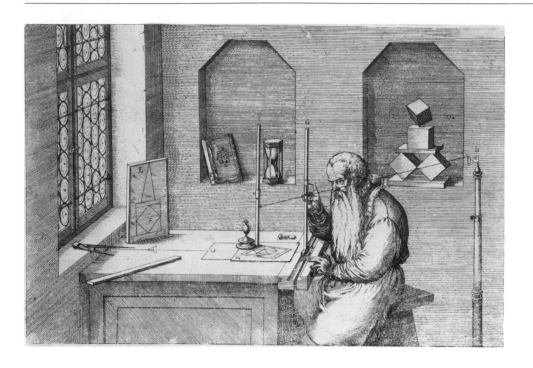

191. WENZEL JAMNITZER IN HIS STUDIO

ca. 1572–1575
Etching
17.6 × 25.8 cm
Andresen, I: nr. 6; Becker, *Amman*, nr. 122;
Hollstein, II: p. 11
Lent by the Metropolitan Museum of Art, New
York, The Elisha Whittelsey Collection, The
Elisha Whittelsey Fund, 1956 (56.510.2)

When Nicolas Neufchâtel painted a portrait of
Jamnitzer in about 1565, he depicted the famous
artist as a learned goldsmith (fig. 40).[1] About a
decade later, Amman chose to show his friend
and colleague not as a goldsmith but as a mathematician.[2] Jamnitzer is shown seated in his study
adjusting a siting instrument as he prepares to
draw a stereographic form of the sort that Amman etched for his *Perspectiva Corporum Regularium* of 1568 (cat. nr. 197). Amman's composition
may have been inspired by Dürer's *Art of Measurement* (cat. nr. 31), which contains two or four,
depending on the edition, scenes of artists using drawing devices to assist their perspective
renderings.

In this woodcut Jamnitzer is somewhat older
looking than in either the Neufchâtel painting or
Amman's other portrait of the artist that appeared in Sachs's *Book of Trades* of 1568 (cat. nr.
190). This would suggest a slightly later dating
for Amman's etched portrait. In all three cases,
Jamnitzer is shown with a long flowing beard
and wearing a heavy robe with a high collar.

1. On this painting, see Section 7 A.
2. Hollstein, II: p. 11, says that this print is the
counterpart to the *Landscape with the Surveyor* (Andresen, I: nr. 216; Hollstein, p. 20), which measures
17.4 × 25.7 cm. The identity of the surveyor has not
been determined.

192. THE DISPLAY OF FIREWORKS ON THE CASTLE OF NUREMBERG

Signed and dated at the lower right: 1570/Jos Amman F
Etching and engraving
23.7 × 34.7 cm
Andr. 70; B. 14; Becker, *Amman*, nr. 109; Hollstein, II: p. 15
Lent by the Fine Arts Museums of San Francisco, Achenbach Foundation for Graphic Arts, 1964.142.45

On 7 June 1570, Maximilian II, as emperor (1564–1576), made his inaugural entry into Nuremberg. The city welcomed him with elaborate pageants and festivities, including a great fireworks display at the Burg. From his vantage point in the grassy field just north of the Burg, Amman offers us a clear view of the rockets exploding in the sky above the castle.[1] He successfully captures the excitement of the crowd and the commotion of the barking dogs, bolting horses, and gesturing spectators. At the right are two temporary structures of Islamic design shown being consumed by flames. These were included by the city as a flattering reference to Maximilian II's vow to push the Turks out of his kingdom of Hungary.[2]

Amman provides an accurate view of the Burg. From left to right are the Kaiserstallung, the tall Sinwell Tower, the Heathens' Tower, and the imperial apartments (cf. fig. 11). The massive ramparts are those built by Italian fortification engineer Antonio Fazuni between 1538 and 1545. Amman's depiction of the Burg from the north

nicely complements the southern vista used in Dürer's *Virgin and Child Seated by the Wall* of 1514 (cat. nr. 15) and the panorama in Lautensack's *View of Nuremberg from the West* of 1552 (cat. nr. 164).

The *Display of Fireworks on the Castle of Nuremberg* is one of Amman's rare prints representing a contemporary event. In order to benefit economically from the local interest in Maximilian II's entry, Amman designed and produced his print within a couple weeks of the entry. This is proven by the fact that on or before 26 June, Amman presented a copy of the print to the Nuremberg city council.[3] He also created a tempera-on-paper painting of the fireworks display, which later is listed in the inventory of the collection of Paulus Praun (1548–1616).[4] Since this painting is lost, its stylistic and chronological relationships to the print cannot be determined. Conceivably, this painting was a rapid study, rather than a highly finished picture, done during the fireworks display.

Besides the fireworks, Maximilian II was honored with an elaborate triumphal arch arranged across Burgstrasse between the Rathaus and the Burg.[5] This was the arch that Georg Pencz had originally designed and constructed for Emperor Charles V's entry into Nuremberg on 16 February 1541 (fig. 32). Pencz's arch was re-used repeatedly during the second half of the sixteenth century.[6] Each time the individual ruler's coats of arms and emblems were changed. Otherwise, only minor repainting and restorations were required. On this occasion, the city council presented Maximilian II with various gifts, including Wenzel Jamnitzer's beautiful *Kaiserpokal* (fig. 50).[7]

1. The entry occurred on 7 June and the fireworks display took place on the following night. This print was occasionally published with the following text: "Eigentliche und ware Abconterfactur der zweyer Schlösser vnd anderm Feuerwerk, so zu Närmberg auff der Vesten geworffen vnd verbrent find worden, Zu Ehren dem Grossmechtigsten—Kaiser Maximiliano dem andern—im Jar 1570 den 8. Junii. Als nach Christi gepurt zelt war—sein Genad, Amen. Zugericht und in Druck verfertigt zu Nürmberg durch Jos Amman." The text is given in Becker, *Amman*, nr. 109.
2. For anti-Turkish pageantry at Maximilian II's court, see Kaufmann, *Variations on the Imperial Theme*, p. 28.
3. Hampe, *Nürnberger Ratsverlässe*, I: nr. 4277.
4. Murr, *Description du Cabinet de Monsieur Paul de Praun à Nuremberg*, paintings, nr. 238.
5. Amman made an etching of the triumphal arch; see Andresen, I: nr. 71; Becker, *Amman*, nr. 110; Hollstein, II: p. 16 (with illustration).
6. On Pencz's arch, see the comments in Section 6 A. The arch was to be used again for the proposed entry of Emperor Rudolf II into Nuremberg in 1580, which was subsequently canceled. See Kaufmann, *Variations on the Imperial Theme*, figs. 5–6.
7. On Jamnitzer's *Kaiserpokal*, see the comments in Section 7 E.

193. PORTRAIT OF HANS SACHS AT AGE EIGHTY-ONE

Signed and dated: IA 1576
Etching and engraving
31.2 × 21 cm
Andr. 11; B. 19; Becker, *Amman*, nr. 116; Hollstein, II: p. 12
Lent by the New York Public Library, Prints Division, Astor, Lenox and Tilden Foundations

Amman's print celebrates the eighty-first birthday of Nuremberg's most popular poet, playwright, and Meistersinger, Hans Sachs (1494–1576). Sachs is credited with writing upward of two thousand poems and four thousand songs during his long career.[1] His witty, satirical verses provided the commentary to several of the pamphlets and prints in this exhibition.[2] Sachs worked closely on occasion with Schön, Schäufelein, Pencz, and Flötner. In 1568 Sachs teamed with Amman to produce the *Book of Trades* (cat. nr. 190).

Amman's portrait is based upon a painting by local artist Andreas Herneisen (1538–1610), dated 1576 and now in the Fembohaus in Nuremberg.[3] So great was Sachs's fame during this period that Herneisen painted another picture showing himself in Sachs's library in the act of portraying the poet.[4] Amman's print, executed a few months prior to Sachs's death, served as the model for several later portraits, including the 1617 engraving by Lucas Kilian of Augsburg.[5] Other portraits of Sachs predate those of Herneisen and Amman.[6]

The inscription on Amman's print was certainly penned by Sachs. It reads:

Zwai monat ein vnd achzg Jahr alt,
War ich Hans Sachs in der gestalt.
Von Endres Herrneysen abgemalt

Ein kind war ich auff dwelt gevorn,
Zum Kind bin ich auch wider worn,
Den all mein Krefft hab ich verlorn,

Gott Bescher mir nun ein Seligs ennd,
Vnd nem mein feel in seine Hennd,
Geb mir auch ein Fröhlich Vrstennd.

For two months and eighty-one years,
I, Hans Sachs, have been known by this presence.
Andreas Herneisen painted me so.

As I was born as a child,
So have I become a child again,
Having lost all my strength.

May God grant me a blessed end,
And take my soul in his hand,
And also give me a joyous spirit.[7]

Amman published a second edition of this portrait with a slightly different text in 1576.[8] Two years later he created a woodcut portrait of Sachs, who is now shown turned toward the opposite direction.[9]

1. On Sachs's career, see A. von Keller and E. Goetze, eds., *Hans Sachs Werke*, 26 vols. (Stuttgart, 1870–1908); Röttinger, *Die Bilderbogen des Hans Sachs*; *Nuremberg: Die Welt des Hans Sachs*; Willers, ed., *Hans Sachs und die Meistersinger*.
2. For instance, see cat. nrs. 50, 65, 70, 166.
3. The painting belongs to the Germanisches Nationalmuseum (on loan to the Fembohaus); see Schwemmer and Kriegbaum, *Nürnberg*, p. 138.
4. Willers, ed., *Hans Sachs und die Meistersinger*, nr. 123 (Wolfenbüttel, Herzog-August-Bibliothek).
5. Ibid., nrs. 124 (Amman), 126 (Killian). Nr. 125 is Valentin Maler's portrait medal of Sachs, which is based upon Amman's print.
6. Ibid., nr. 121 (Michael Ostendorfer [Geisberg, nr. 977]), for instance.
7. The translation is by Sigrid Knudsen.
8. Andressen, I: nr. 12; Becker, *Amman*, nr. 116; Hollstein, II: p. 12.
9. *Nuremberg: Die Welt des Hans Sachs*, nr. 336.

Ein new Kochbuch/
Das ist Ein
gründtliche beschreibung
wie man recht vnd wol/ nicht allein von vierfüssigen/ heymischen
vnd wilden Thieren/ sondern auch von mancherley Vögel vnd Federwildpret/ darzu von allem grünen vnd dürren Fischwerck/ allerley Speiß/ als gesotten/ gebraten/ gebacken/ Pre-
solen/ Carbonaden/ mancherley Pasteten vnd Füllwerck/ Gallrat/ etc. auff Teutsche/ Vngerische/ Hispanische/ Ita-
lianische vnnd Frantzösische weiß/ kochen vnd zubereiten solle: Auch wie allerley Gemüß/
Obß/ Salsen/ Senff/ Confect vnd Latwergen/ zuzurichten seye.

Auch ist darinnen zu vernemmen/ wie man herrliche grosse Panckten/ sampt
gemeinen Gastereyen/ ordentlich anrichten vnd bestellen soll.

Allen Menschen/ hohes vnd nidriges Standts/ Weibs vnd Manns Personen/ zu nutz
jetzundt zum ersten in Druck gegeben/ dergleichen vor nie ist außgegangen/

Durch
M. Marxen Rumpolt/ Churf. Meintzischen Mundtkoch.

Mit Röm. Keyserlicher Maiestat special Priuilegio.

I S   8 L.

Sampt einem gründtlichen Bericht/ wie man alle Wein vor allen zufällen
bewaren/ die breshafften widerbringen/ Kräuter vnd andere Wein/ Bier/
Essig/ vnd alle andere Getränck/ machen vnd bereiten soll/ daß sie natür-
lich/ vnd allen Menschen vnschädlich/ zu trin-
cken seindt.

Gedruckt zu Franckfort am Mayn/ In verlegung M.
Marx Rumpolts/ Churf. Meintz. Mundtkochs/
vnd Sigmundt Feyerabendts.

194. MARX RUMPOLT, EIN NEW KOCHBUCH. DAS IST, EIN GRÜNDTLICHE BESCHREIBUNG . . . (Frankfurt: Sigmund Feyerabend, 1581)

Andresen, I: nr. 255; Becker, *Amman*, nr. 32; Hollstein, II: p. 56
Lent by the New York Public Library, Spencer Collection, Astor, Lenox and Tilden Foundations

Rumpolt's *A New Cookbook—That Is, a Fundamental Description . . .* , dedicated to Anna (1532–1585), duchess of Saxony, is one of the most important early German cookbooks.[1] It contains almost two thousand recipes, numerous practical household tips, and directions concerning the storage, selection, and serving of wine. The volume is filled with advice about "how to organize a party for princes and lords," "how to shop," "how to deal with servants," "how to plan the various courses," and even a section on music to accompany the meal. Rumpolt even explained how to prepare pastries out of which live animals will appear. Rumpolt tried to impress his readers by including culinary specialties of other countries. He listed recipes for over 150 different edible animals, including eighty-three for ox and forty-three for boar. Each chapter is fittingly introduced with a woodcut of the appropriate animal, bird, or fish. The entire volume extends to two hundred double pages with about 150 woodcuts.

Rumpolt was the chef for Anna of Saxony and, earlier, Daniel Brendel, the archbishop of Mainz from 1555 to 1582. His stated purpose, like that of Dürer's in his theoretical treatises (cat. nrs. 31 and 34), was to educate future generations. Rumpolt sought to share his vast culinary knowledge with young master chefs. Up until this time, recipes and food preparation had been carefully guarded secrets.[2]

Amman contributed at least eight woodcuts, including the title page illustrated here. Others are attributed to Virgil Solis; however, the majority are unsigned and of inferior quality.[3]

1. This entry was prepared by Sigrid Knudsen. The primary source is *Ein new Kochbuch . . .* (Leipzig: Edition Leipzig, 1976 facsimile edition with an afterword by M. Lemmer). Five editions were published between 1581 and 1604.

2. The first German cookbook is the anonymous *Kuchemaistrey*, published in Nuremberg in 1485 by Peter Wagner and subsequently reprinted in thirteen editions in the next fifteen years. Ibid., afterword p. 4.

3. Becker, *Amman*, p. 110.

195. ALLEGORY OF COMMERCE

1585; Amman's name is listed in the second
state
Woodcut: fourth of five states
87.5 × 60.3 cm
Andresen, I: nr. 81; Becker, *Amman*, nr. 56;
Hollstein, II: p. 32
Lent by the University of Minnesota, James
Ford Bell Library, Minneapolis

The *Allegory of Commerce* is among the largest
and most complex of all sixteenth-century woodcuts.[1] It exists in at least five states, the first of
which was printed by Johann Schultes and published by Wilhelm Peter Zimmermann, both of
Augsburg, in 1585.[2] In the accompanying title,
Johann Neudörfer (see cat. nr. 162) is credited
with the thematic idea and Kaspar Brunner, his
pupil, with the final execution. Jost Amman is
listed as the artist in the second edition, also of
1585. The later editions vary mainly in their
titles; the 1622 edition also has texts along the
expanded side margins.[3]

The print illustrates the various facets of contemporary mercantile life, including its rewards
and risks. At the top center is Mercury, the patron of commerce, who holds a scale balancing
the book of debtors and creditors. The encircling
scroll lauds his quickness and versatility, qualities necessary for the successful merchant. On
either side of Mercury, beginning at the lower
left, are the crests of various European cities arranged in monthly order according to the dates
of their trade fairs.

Below Mercury stands Fortune, precariously
balanced on a journal or account book. The
column is marked Circumstantia, or circum-
stance, and on the basin beneath are the various
branches of commerce, such as the wool, metal,
and spice trades. On the ground behind the
fountain are shown the possibilities for loss and
gain in trade, including death, war, shipwreck,
mining, and land commerce. Beyond is a view of
the skyline of Antwerp, which, until the political
upheavals of the 1560s and 1570s, had been the
commercial and financial capital of Europe.

The everyday activities of a large trading company are depicted in the lower section of the
print. In the center, the head of the company is
seated beneath the "Book of Secrets," the firm's
master journal, which only he can consult.
Bookkeepers, clerks, cashiers, and couriers are
shown working. Goods are packed, dispatched,
and received; money is counted at large tables.
Allegorical references are made to the moral
strengths and intellectual qualities—including
integrity, silence, obligation, and knowledge of
languages—required for successful business
dealings.

In the lower foreground stands Luck, an ever
present reminder to mankind of the fickleness of
fate. The inscription beneath her reads:

Sphere on which the riches of the world rest
All things, soon shattered,
Meet here with death their end.
Therefore, note the wind-blown smoke,
Be pious, fearing God, and do penance.[4]

This figure of Luck seems to provide the key to
understanding at least part of the print's message. By 1585 Antwerp had lost its primacy—

Eigentliche Abbildung deß ganzen Gewerbs der löblichen Kaufmannschafft/ samt etlich der nahmhaffte und fürnehmsten Handelstädt
Signatur und Wappen/ darinnen zum Theil fürnehmlich die Märckt und Messen begriffen seyn/ so deß Jahrs über in jedem Monath einfallen/ auch hin und wider in
Europa zu unterschidlichen Zeiten erhalten/ und von fürnehmen und geringen Gewerbs- und Handelsleuthen/ auß allerley Nationen besucht und gebaucht werden; wie durch vielerlei mancherley Gschäfft und Waaren hie unten
und zum Eingang bey dem elZerzartus angezeigt ist. Samt der jetzigen schönen vralten kunst des Buchhaltens/ darinnen alle Kaufmanns-Gewerb schönen/ und richtig vnterhalten werden; Neben andern welgemeinten Erinnerungen/
welche dem Handelstreibenden notwendig zu wissen und zu bedachten sind.

that is, its luck had changed for the worse. Even
the most powerful cities are subject to the same
misfortunes that can befall the unwary
merchant.

Beyond this moralistic message, the particu-
lars of which could not have occurred to Neudörfer, who died in 1563, the purpose and the
origin of this print are unknown.

1. This entry was prepared by Sigrid Knudsen.
Other than that listed above, there is little literature on
this print. It is mentioned briefly in writings on commerce in Nuremberg. See L. Veit, *Handel und Wandel
mit aller Welt*, p. 14; generally, W. von Stromer, "Das
Wirtschaft vom 14.–16. Jahrhundert," *Beiträge zur*

wirtschaftsgeschichte Nürnbergs (Nuremberg, 1967), 2:
pp. 751–799.
2. The states are discussed in Andresen, I: nr. 81;
Becker, *Amman*, nr. 56. The fourth state, exhibited
here, probably dates to the early seventeenth century.
Andresen mentioned that the blocks were in the library of Prince Wallerstein at Maihingen.
3. Some of the inscription texts within the cartouches vary from edition to edition. The 1622 edition
with the side texts is illustrated, and incorrectly dated,
in *Reformation in Nürnberg*, nr. 10.
4. This translation is given in E. Simon, *The Reformation* (New York, 1966), p. 69, which reproduces the
lower portion of the print and provides English
inscriptions.

196. THE DAUGHTER OF JEPHTHAH

1575–1585; monogram; later penned inscriptions at the bottom
Drawing: pen and black ink with gray wash
30.7 × 19.6 cm (upper right corner is missing)
Lent by the Germanisches Nationalmuseum, Nuremberg, HZ. 64

And Jephthah vowed a vow unto the Lord, and said, if Thou shalt without fail deliver the children of Ammon into mine hands, Then it shall be, that whatsoever cometh forth of the doors of my house to meet me, when I return in peace from the children of Ammon, shall surely be the Lord's, and I will offer it up for a burnt offering. . . . And Jephthah came to Mizpeh unto his house, and, behold, his daughter came out to meet him with timbrels and with dances: and she was his only child; beside her he had neither son nor daughter. And it came to pass, when he saw her, that he rent his clothes, and said, Alas, my daughter! Thou has brought me very low, and thou art one of them that trouble me: for I have opened my mouth unto the Lord, and I cannot go back. (Judges 11:30–35)

Amman illustrated the moment of Jephthah's arrival back at his house after his victory over the Ammonites. His daughter and her servants greet him with music. Jephthah, distraught, tears at his cape and looks to heaven. In the background, the vow is fulfilled as he sacrifices his daughter. In other versions of the story, Jephthah's daughter was permitted to live but was condemned to a life of celibacy.

The story of Jephthah and his daughter is contrasted with another intemperate vow in the upper corners. Because of Herod's promise to grant Salome's wish, John the Baptist was beheaded. The decapitation occurs at the upper left, while opposite is, presumably, the figure of Salome. The drawing is torn in the right corner, and the upper half of the woman has been penned in on an affixed piece of paper. It is impossible to determine whether Salome held a charger with John the Baptist's head or whether she was shown dancing.

The *Daughter of Jephthah* is a preparatory drawing for a stained-glass window. In many of Amman's glass designs he completed only half of the ornamental frame, which the glazer would reproduce when preparing the window. Other examples of this working practice include the *Coat of Arms of Count von Zimmern* (Schaffhausen, Dr. H. H. von Ziegler Collection) of 1573, *Curius Dantatus and Cincinnatus* (Zurich, Schweizerisches Landesmuseum) of 1575, and *St. Paul Preaching* (London, British Museum) of about 1585.[1]

Although the *Daughter of Jephthah* is undated, it may be assigned to the years between 1575 and 1585. Because Amman's style varied little during this period, it is difficult to be more precise. The figures of Jephthah, his daughter, and her servants are stock male and female types that reappear in almost identical fashion in the *Curius Dantatus and Cincinnatus* and *St. Paul Preaching* drawings. Amman favored clinging drapery that revealed the body and, in the case of the women, billowed in the wind. Even as late as his 1590 printed series on antique armor, the same male costumes are used.[2]

1. Pilz, "Amman," pp. 218–224, does not mention the Nuremberg drawing, but see 213–215, figs. 3–4 for the Schaffhausen and London drawings. On the Zurich drawing, see Geissler, *Zeichnung in Deutschland*, I: nr. E 10. For Amman's early work as a stained-glass designer, see Ganz, *Basler Glasmaler*, pp. 40ff.
2. Andresen, I: nrs. 73–80; Becker, *Amman*, nr. 89; Hollstein, II: p. 17 (with illustration).

Also see cat. nr.

197 Wenzel Jamnitzer, *Perspectiva Corporum Regularium*, with prints by Amman.

Jamnitzer, Germany's finest goldsmith in the sixteenth century, was born in 1508 in Vienna, where he may have been trained, and is first mentioned in Nuremberg on 23 May 1534, when he obtained his citizenship.[1] He married Anna Braunreuch on 22 June of that year in St. Sebaldus. In 1544 he was appointed the city's official coin-and-seal-die cutter. He became a member of the greater city council in 1556 and of the smaller council, a position usually reserved only for patricians, in 1573. Throughout his career Wenzel was repeatedly involved in civic affairs. He died on 19 December 1585.

Wenzel and his brother Albrecht (died 1555) established a large workshop, located on the modern Albrecht-Dürer-Strasse 17, where he trained his sons Wenzel the Younger, Hans (cat. nrs. 200–203), and Abraham, as well as many pupils, including Jonas Silber (see fig. 52), Nikolaus Schmidt (died 1609), and his two sons-in-law, Matthias Zündt (cat. nrs. 183 and 184) and Hans Straub (active 1568–1610).[2] Beginning with his first great piece, the *Merkel Table Decoration* (figs. 47–49), which was sold to the city council in 1549, Jamnitzer transformed both the style and the techniques of German goldsmith work. He introduced methods of casting grasses, insects, and small animals directly from nature (see cat. nr. 198). Later he would invent new tools, such as the roller stamp, a mechanism for repeating decorative patterns. Other important examples of his goldsmith work include the *Emperor's Cup* (fig. 50), several collector's chests (fig. 51), the highly mannered ewer in Munich, and the monumental table fountain for Maximilian II.[3] Jamnitzer's designs were widely circulated through his own prints (cat. nr. 197) and those of his followers (see cat. nr. 183).

Jamnitzer is represented both as a goldsmith and as a mathematician in his portraits by Nicolas Neufchâtel (fig. 41) and Jost Amman (cat. nr. 191). His interest in geometry and perspective led to the publication of his small treatise the *Perspectiva Corporum Regularium* (cat. nr. 197) in 1568.

1. The following biography is brief due to the lengthy discussion of Jamnitzer and his art in Section 7 E. The biographical information is taken primarily from G. Kuhr, "Stammfolge der Familie Jamnitzer in Nürnberg," *MVGN* 61 (1974): 122–126, esp. 123–124. In spite of the numerous articles and booklets on individual works by Jamnitzer, a new thorough critical monograph is needed. Klaus Pechstein informs me that he is preparing a major exhibition on Jamnitzer to be held at the Germanisches Nationalmuseum in 1985 to celebrate the four-hundredth anniversary of the artist's death.

2. On his house, see E. Mulzer, "Das Jamnitzerhaus in Nürnberg und der Goldschmied Wenzel Jamnitzer," *MVGN* 61 (1974): 48–89; it was extensively damaged on 3 October 1944. On his sons and pupils, see Hayward, *Virtuoso Goldsmiths*, pp. 212–218.

3. For a discussion of and literature on these works and Wenzel's technical innovations, see Section 7 E and notes 72–89; the excellent summary of Wenzel's career in Hayward, *Virtuoso Goldsmiths*, pp. 208–215. Also see the comments for cat. nrs. 196–199.

197. WENZEL JAMNITZER, PERSPECTIVA CORPORUM REGULARIUM (Nuremberg[?], 1568)

50 etchings by Jost Amman after Jamnitzer
37.3 × 26.8 cm (book); 26.5 × 20 cm (title page)
Andresen, I: nr. 217; Becker, *Amman*, nr. 82;
Hollstein, II: p. 217
Lent by the New York Public Library, Prints Division, Astor, Lenox and Tilden Foundations

Jamnitzer's *Perspectiva Corporum Regularium* (*Perspective of Ruled Shapes*) is a treatise on the correct perspectival construction of stereometric forms.[1] The book consists of a dedication to Emperor Maximilian II, a brief foreword (the only text) explaining the project and identifying Jost Amman as the printmaker, the title page (illustrated here), six chapter title pages, and forty-three plates (G. VI illustrated here). The first five of the six chapters are related to the four elements—fire, air, earth, and water—and the

60. Wenzel Jamnitzer, *Mirror Frame*, ca. 1568, New York, Metropolitan Museum of Art (Gift of J. Pierpont Morgan, 1917).

heavens that encompass them all.[2] These chapters are devoted to tetrahedrons, octahedrons, hexahedrons, icosahedrons, and dodecahedrons, with the final one on the formation of letters, spheres, cones, and rings. The plate on page G. VI representing two variations on spheres is typical. Unlike Dürer, who provided step-by-step didactic explanations to accompany his discussion of three-dimensional forms in his *Art of Measurement* (cat. nr. 31), Jamnitzer simply offered his reader completed examples of the different geometric shapes. The book functions more as a pattern book than a theoretical discourse or pedagogical aid.

The opening title page is the most elaborate of the plates. Surrounding the text are the figures of Arithmetic, Geometry, Perspective, Architecture, and, in the guise of two putti, Inclination and Diligence. Presumably, the successful artist must be grounded in these mathematical disciplines and should possess these personality traits. The elaborate high strapwork frame on which these figures rest seems to derive from the ornamental prints of Cornelis Bos.[3] Jamnitzer later used his design for this title page as the model for a silver gilt mirror frame (fig. 60) now in the Metropolitan Museum of Art in New York.[4] This frame is an autograph work since it bears the goldsmith marks of both Nuremberg and Jamnitzer; however, whether it was originally intended as a mirror frame or for some other purpose is uncertain. The print and the frame vary only slightly. The print lacks the decorated strapwork patterning and the frame lacks the background foliage.

Two sets of drawings attributed to Jamnitzer have been associated with the plates for this treatise. According to Franke, the thirty-six hand-colored drawings in Wolfenbüttel (Herzog-August Bibliothek) are Jamnitzer's preparatory designs, while those in Berlin (Kupferstichkabinett) are copies after the Wolfenbüttel drawings by either Jost Amman or a member of his workshop.[5] The quality of the Wolfenbüttel drawings is much better than that of those in Berlin.

1. Amman's *Portrait of Wenzel Jamnitzer* (cat. nr. 191) shows Jamnitzer at his desk preparing related drawings. There exist two facsimiles of this book; see A. Flocon, *Jamnitzer: Orfèvre de la rigeur sensible. Étude sur la Perspectiva Corporum Regularium* (Paris, 1964); Wenzel Jamnitzer, *Perspectiva Corporum Regularium. Nachdruck der ausgabe Nürnberg 1568 mit fünfzig Kupferstichen von Jost Amman*, Instrumentaria Artium 3 (Graz, 1973). Also see Farmer, *Virtuoso Craftsman*, nr. 49; M. M. Prechtl, *Jamnitzer, Lencker, Stoer. Drei Nürnberger Konstruktivisten des 16. Jahrhundert*. One interesting note about this treatise is the imperial copyright, listed at the bottom of the title page, which forbids anyone else from reproducing the book and its contents for fifteen years. Artists, such as Jamnitzer, sought increasingly to halt the unauthorized copying of their ideas.

2. For an explanation of the relationship between the elements and the different forms, see Prechtl, *Jamnitzer, Lencker, Stoer*, introduction (unpaginated), which summarizes Flocon's research.

3. Schéle, *Cornelis Bos*, figs. 123–124, 128, 177, 180, 187, 191, 193, 198, for loosely related designs.

4. Farmer, *Virtuoso Craftsman*, nr. 50; Hayward, *Virtuoso Goldsmiths*, comments to pl. 437.

5. I. Franke, "Wenzel Jamnitzer's Zeichnungen zur Perspectiva," *MJBK* 23 (1972): 165–186. On Jamnitzer's drawings, see also Pechstein, "Jamnitzer-Studien," pp. 237–283, esp. 241–263, 278–282, and "Zeichnungen von Wenzel Jamnitzer," pp. 81–95; Geissler, ed., *Zeichnung in Deutschland*, I: nrs. E 1–4.

198. MORTAR

ca. 1550–1560
Bronze: dark brown to yellowish brown patina
11.8 (height) × 14.6 cm (diameter across the
rim)
Lent by the Cleveland Museum of Art, Purchase from the J. H. Wade Fund 51.444

The Jamnitzer workshop was famed for its silver and bronze casts from natural objects, such as grasses, insects, small lizards, and other tiny animals.[1] These were sold separately or applied to such lavish goldsmith pieces as the *Merkel Table Decoration* (figs. 47 and 48), where Mother Earth is surrounded by different types of grasses and grains, as well as minute turtles. In 1565 Archduke Ferdinand of Tirol ordered two dozen small cast animals and a supply of cast grasses, perhaps to supplement those already in his possession from the abandoned *Adam and Eve in Paradise* table fountain that he had commissioned from Jamnitzer in about 1556 but which remained incomplete a decade later.[2] Exquisite examples of Jamnitzer's nature casts, in bronze and silver, are on display in Berlin (Kunstgewerbemuseum) and Nuremberg (Germanisches Nationalmuseum).[3] The silver vase with grasses in the niche at the rear of Neufchâtel's *Portrait of Wenzel Jamnitzer* (fig. 41) alludes to Jamnitzer's technical virtuosity.

Jamnitzer and his workshop used cast grasses and animals to ornament a series of at least four mortars that are today in Berlin, Cleveland, and London (2).[4] The Cleveland mortar lacks the near pristine condition of its Berlin counterpart since many of the grasses and figures have been flattened and the tails of several of the lizards are broken. Nevertheless, the mortar's design and the application of the grasses to the side and the lizards to the underside of the lip are almost identical to the Berlin mortar. Furthermore, inserted into the sides of both mortars are casts

after plaquettes by Peter Flötner. The thematic selection is odd in each instance since the Cleveland mortar pairs Faith and Hope, two of the three cardinal virtues, with Vanity (cf. cat. nr. 130), a vice, while the Berlin mortar is decorated with Faith and Hope plus the *Allegory of Touch* (cf. cat. nr. 134) and a *Memento Mori*.

It is impossible to determine the degree of Jamnitzer's personal involvement in the completion of any of these mortars. Most likely, once a prototype was made by the master, the successive variants were workshop products. One of Jamnitzer's assistants, his son-in-law Matthias Zündt, is documented in conjunction with the *Adam and Eve in Paradise* table fountain project as being unusually skilled in casting after natural forms.[5] Zündt's etching *Design for an Ornate Ewer* (cat. nr. 183) reveals his own interest in integrating cast natural forms into goldsmith works. It is quite possible that Zündt was one of the shop assistants who worked on this group of mortars.

1. Casting after natural forms can be found on earlier works by Andrea Riccio (died 1532) and other goldsmiths in Padua; however, none exploited the technique's potential as did Jamnitzer. On the subject see Kris, "Der Stil 'Rustique,'" pp. 137–208; Pechstein, "Silberglocken," pp. 36–43.
2. Hayward, *Virtuoso Goldsmiths*, pp. 46–47.
3. Pechstein, *Bronzen und Plaketten*, nrs. 134–138.
4. Ibid., nr. 8; Wixom, *Renaissance Bronzes from Ohio Collections*, nr. 183, with references to the mortars in the Victoria & Albert Museum and the Wallace Collection in London.
5. See note 2 above and Zündt's biography.

199. CANDLESTICK IN THE FORM OF A GROTESQUE MAN

Third quarter of the sixteenth century
Brass
29.2 cm (height)
Lent by the Metropolitan Museum of Art, New York, Gift of George Blumenthal, 1941

If Peter Vischer the Younger's *Candlestick in the Form of a Man* (cat. nr. 118) embodies the order and harmony inherent in early Renaissance art in Nuremberg, the *Candlestick in the Form of a Grotesque Man* reflects the fascination of Jamnitzer and his contemporaries with bizarre, distorted forms. The shaft of this later candlestick is shaped like a bearded man wearing a turban and cloak. His lower body has been transformed into two twisting tree trunks with exposed roots.

The design of the candlestick is based on one of Agostino Veneziano's 1536 prints of terms after Roman models.[1] Veneziano's print was subsequently copied by Cornelis Bos and, in Nuremberg, Virgil Solis in Rivius's *Vitruvius teutsch* (cat. nr. 136).[2] The artist of the candlestick has exaggerated the figure's contrapposto and repositioned the head slightly while also transforming the single knotted tree into a pair of spiraling, twisting trunks. Otherwise, he has followed the print rather closely.

The association of this candlestick with the circle of Jamnitzer is problematic. Of contemporary German goldsmiths, Jamnitzer most frequently used terms, of a more conventional style, on his collector's chests (cf. fig. 51) and, in combination with other contorted figures, to form the shafts of his scales in Berlin and Cleveland.[3] At best, the candlestick was fashioned by a Nuremberg(?) artist inspired by the term published in the *Vitruvius teutsch* and influenced by Jamnitzer, Zündt (cf. cat. nr. 183), and other members of this workshop.

1. I wish to thank James Draper for informing me that his colleague Janet S. Byrne had identified Veneziano's print as the source for the candlestick. See *The Illustrated Bartsch*, 26: nr. 304.
2. See Schéle, *Cornelis Bos*, nr. 81; Röttinger, *Vitruvius teutsch*, pl. V (fol. 15 verso).
3. Pechstein, *Bronzen und Plaketten*, nr. 7; Wixom, *Renaissance Bronzes from Ohio Collections*, nr. 184.

Hans (1538–1603), Wenzel's second and most talented son, was a goldsmith, sculptor, and, on at least one occasion in 1600, when he created a portrait of his father for the city council, a painter.[1] Hans trained with his father and spent his period as a journeyman working for the duke of Ferrara in 1558. He was back in Nuremberg by 30 November 1561, when his masterpiece was accepted.[2] During the next couple of decades Hans was periodically in trouble with the local authorities, for instance in 1569, when, shortly after he received the position of official seal-die cutter for the city, the appointment was revoked because he had swindled Christoph Lindenberger, another goldsmith, out of two drinking cups. In 1582 the city council admonished Hans for making enameled medals, since this was the domain of other craftsmen. Two years later, Wenzel wrote in his will that he was now pleased with his son, who had presumably settled down. From 1596 until his death on 23 April 1603, Hans was a member of the greater city council.

Through his marriage to Susanna Wagner, Hans had six children, including Christoph (see cat. nrs. 210–212), the last great member of the Jamnitzer family.

Hans's most beautiful goldsmith piece is the silver-gilt casket, decorated with mother-of-pearl and hardstone, made for one of the dukes of Württemberg and now in Stuttgart (Württembergisches Landesmuseum).[3] Numerous *tazzas* (dishes) and plaquettes, including several signed with the monogram H. G., are attributed to Hans. Although most critics accept the identification of Hans with Master H. G., it is by no means certain.[4]

1. The following biographical information is drawn primarily from Kuhr, "Stammfolge der Familie Jamnitzer," p. 125; Hayward, *Virtuoso Goldsmiths*, esp. pp. 215–216. The painting by Hans hung in the Regimentsstuben and Hans was paid 50 gulden; see Mummenhoff, *Rathaus*, p. 72, note 222. The first critical study of Jamnitzer's oeuvre was E. Kris and O. von Falke, "Beiträge zu den Werken Christoph und Hans Jamnitzer," *JPKS* 47 (1926): 186–207.
2. This date is given by Kuhr, "Stammfolge der Familie Jamnitzer," p. 125, whereas Hayward, *Virtuoso Goldsmiths*, p. 215, says that he obtained his master's status in 1563.
3. Hayward, *Virtuoso Goldsmiths*, pl. 447.
4. Ibid., p. 216, summarizes the controversy while also observing that Hans's name was frequently spelled Hans Gamnitzer in the local records; for instance, see Hampe, *Nürnberger Ratsverlässe*, II: nr. 1412. The topic was initiated in I. Weber, "Fragen zum Oeuvre des Meister H. G.," *MJBK* 22 (1971): 133–145; however, in her book *Renaissanceplaketten*, pp. 159ff., she seems to revert toward the traditional identification of this master as Hans Jamnitzer.

200. REBECCA AND ELIEZER

Before 1565
Plaquette: bronze, hollow cast with brown natural patina
9.7–9.8 cm diameter
Weber, *Renaissanceplaketten*, nr. 280
Lent by Oberlin College, Allen Memorial Art Museum, Oberlin, Mrs. F. F. Prentiss Fund
61.27

This plaquette illustrates the story of Rebecca and Eliezer as recounted in Genesis 24:15–20.[1] Abraham, seeking a wife for his son Isaac, sent his servant Eliezer to Mesopotamia and instructed him that God would reveal the chosen bride by having her fetch water for Eliezer and his camels. Jamnitzer has selected the moment when Rebecca raises her pitcher to Eliezer, who stares at her in amazement. They stand by the fountain outside the city of Nahor. While Jamnitzer lacked Peter Flötner's talent for creating naturalistic landscapes, his scene is enlivened by the energetic motion of the trees and the waves.[2]

Until recently this plaquette was believed to postdate 1571 because the same scene appears in Jost Amman's woodcut in the *Sacra Biblia*, published by Sigmund Feyerabend in Frankfurt in that year.[3] Pechstein has demonstrated that Amman borrowed the composition from Jamnitzer rather than vice versa, and Weber dates it before 1565, which would make this one of the artist's earliest pieces.[4]

These plaquettes had essentially the same function as those by Flötner; however, many of Jamnitzer's better plaquettes were used to ornament silver *tazzas* (dishes) and goldsmith works.[5] *Rebecca and Eliezer* was copied by Lüneberg goldsmith Heinrich Folman on the inside of the lid of his sumptuous *Seven Electors Cup* of about 1570 now in Berlin (Kunstgewerbemuseum).[6]

1. The plaquette was published in Wixom, *Renaissance Bronzes from Ohio Collections*, nr. 187.
2. Compare it with Flötner's *Christ and the Samaritan Woman* (cat. nr. 126) or *Ate and the Litae* (cat. nr. 128).
3. Andresen, I: nr. 182; Becker, *Amman*, nr. 3; Hollstein, II: p. 37, on the Bible.
4. K. Pechstein, "Neuentdeckte Arbeiten von Hans Jamnitzer," *Berliner Museen, Berichte* N.F. 20 (1970): 61–66, esp. 62–63; Weber, *Renaissanceplaketten*, nr. 280.
5. Hayward, *Virtuoso Goldsmiths*, p. 215, pl. 658.
6. Pechstein, "Neuentdeckte Arbeiten von Hans Jamnitzer," p. 63, and *Goldschmiedewerke der Renaissance*, nr. 15.

201. DAVID ANOINTED BY SAMUEL

After 1575
Plaquette: silverplated bronze
17 cm diameter
Morgenroth, nr. 382; Weber, *Renaissanceplaketten*, nr. 281
Lent by the University of California, Santa Barbara, University Art Museum, Sigmund Morgenroth Collection

At the Lord's bidding, Samuel went to Bethlehem to anoint one of the sons of Jesse as the future king of Israel, an event recounted in 1 Samuel 16:12–13. Having examined and rejected Jesse's sons, Samuel learned that the youngest, David, was in the field tending the sheep. At the rear David is seen playing his harp and being fetched by a servant. In the foreground Samuel anoints David with oil as Jesse and, opposite, two of his sons look on. The burning offering on the altar was a ploy that Samuel used to enter Bethlehem without incurring the suspicion of King Saul, whom David would eventually replace.

Jamnitzer's background treatment, notably the style of architecture in the distant towns, recalls that in the previous entry. The figures are larger and occupy more of the composition than in his earlier work. The source for the plaquette seems to be an engraving after Maerten van Heemskerck by an artist working for Hieronymus Cock in Antwerp in the mid-1550s.[1]

1. This was suggested by the authors of Morgenroth, nr. 382. I have not seen a copy of this print; however, if it is like the Heemskerck drawing of this subject, then Jamnitzer adopted only general costume motifs. See F. Lugt, *Inventaire général des dessins des écoles du Nord. Musée du Louvre. Maîtres des anciens Pays-Bas nés avant 1550* (Paris, 1968), p. 65, nr. 229, pl. 103. Jamnitzer's figures of Samuel and, to a lesser degree, David recall the poses of the father and son in Heemskerck's *Return of the Prodigal Son* of 1559; see R. Grosshans, *Maerten van Heemskerck—Die Gemälde* (Berlin, 1980), nr. 87, fig. 120. Prints after Heemskerck circulated widely throughout the continent. At least one Heemskerck painting, *St. Luke Painting the Virgin and Child*, was listed in the 1711 inventory of the Nuremberg Rathaus; see Mummenhoff, *Rathaus*, p. 292.

202. THE JUDGMENT OF SOLOMON

After 1575
Plaquette: pewter
16.5 cm diameter
Weber, *Renaissanceplaketten*, nr. 282
Lent by the Museum of Fine Arts, Houston,
Museum purchase

The story of the Judgment of Solomon (I Kings
3:16–28) was among the most popular tales of
the Old Testament. In Jamnitzer's plaquette, Solomon, enthroned, orders his soldier to divide
the living child between the two harlots who
claimed to be its mother. While the woman
kneeling on the ground pleads for the child's life,
the other points at the child with her left hand
and makes a chopping gesture with the right to
signify her desire to deny the true mother her
child. In this way the false mother is exposed
and justice is performed.

Jamnitzer probably conceived of this plaquette
as part of a larger Old Testament cycle that included *David Anointed by Samuel* (cat. nr. 201).
Both plaquettes are characterized by a similar
handling of the classicizing drapery that clings
to the bodies, the use of bold gestures and twisting poses, and nearly identical landscape motifs.
They are approximately the same size and have
the same pattern of decorative trim.

1. J. L. Schrader, "Recent Acquisitions: Three
Nürnberg Renaissance Plaquettes," *Bulletin of the Museum of Fine Arts, Houston* 3 (1972–1973): 57–60.

203. VULCAN FORGING CUPID'S WING

1570–1580
Plaquette: bronze
17 cm diameter
Lent by the Museum of Fine Arts, Boston,
Frederick Brown Fund

This plaquette is based upon Maerten van Heemskerck's grisaille painting *Vulcan Forging Cupid's Wing* of 1536, now in Prague (National-galerie), which was reproduced in a 1546 print by Cornelis Bos.[1] Vulcan and his assistants beat the wing into the proper shape as Venus and Cupid look on. In both the painting and the print the scene is set indoors, whereas Jamnitzer has chosen an outdoor setting.

Wixom questioned the traditional attribution of this plaquette to Jamnitzer, assigning it instead to a Netherlandish artist working sometime after the print was published in 1546.[2] Although Wixom gave no reasons for his change in attribution, it is easy to see that the heavily muscled figures contrast strongly with those in the three plaquettes described above. It is important to recognize that Jamnitzer liberally borrowed from Heemskerck and many other artists, and in each instance he bent his own style to conform to that of his model. His personal traits are more evident in how he placed the borrowed figures within his own composition, how he used specific types of plants to fill out the foreground, and how he provided a deep landscape background for almost all his plaquettes. In this case, the landscape is dotted with obelisks and columned buildings as well as a mill with a water wheel on the right. These motifs and a fuller, somewhat more organic tree type are seen in Jamnitzer's signed and dated plaquettes of fishing scenes that Hayward has published.[3] In the years since completing the *Rebecca and Eliezer* plaquette, Jamnitzer had gained a better understanding of architectural forms, both classical and contemporary, and of landscape construction by examining the earlier plaquettes of Flötner.

1. Grosshans, *Maerten van Heemskerck—Die Gemälde*, pp. 119–124, figs. 22–23, 176, 178; Schéle, *Cornelis Bos*, fig. 51. On the iconography, which derives from Virgil's *Aeneid* VIII: 416–453, see M. A. Jacobsen, "Vulcan Forging Cupid's Wing," *Art Bulletin* 54 (1972): 418–429.
2. Wixom, *Renaissance Bronzes from Ohio Collections*, nr. 220 (a lead impression in the Allen Memorial Art Museum at Oberlin College).
3. Hayward, *Virtuoso Goldsmiths*, pls. 438 (dated 1572), 440 (dated 1570). The foliate pattern of the border of the former is identical to the Boston plaquette.

Bolsterer was a sculptor and medalist active in Nuremberg from about 1540 until his death in 1573.[1] Habich noted that Bolsterer used five different monograms. His early history is unknown before he began making medals of Nuremberg citizens in 1540. Bolsterer resided briefly in Frankfurt around 1547, when he created the double medal of *Johann Fichard and His Wife Elisabeth* and others, but he had returned to Nuremberg by 1551, when he received his citizenship.[2] During the early 1550s he designed a medal of Wenzel Jamnitzer (1552) and several of Emperor Charles V.[3] In 1554–1555 he participated with Hans Kels in the competition for the commission to carve the high altar in the Hofkirche in Innsbruck.[4] Bolsterer also sculpted the grave monument of Bishop Weigand von Redwitz (died 1546) of Bamberg and the epitaph of Wolf Müntzer von Babenberg in Nuremberg.[5] Although he gave up his Nuremberg citizenship in 1562, Bolsterer is recorded in Nuremberg in 1566 and he died there on 26 December 1573.

1. Habich, I.2: pp. 250–254, nrs. 1771–1804; "Bolsterer, Hans," in Thieme-Becker (1910), 4: p. 254, for the following biography.
2. Habich, I.2: nr. 1779; Hill and Pollard, nr. 607.
3. Habich, I.2: nrs. 1785–1788 (Charles V), 1793 (Jamnitzer).
4. Habich, I.2: p. 250, refers to this as a competition, while Egg, *Die Hofkirche in Innsbruck*, p. 73, gives the date as 1553 and mentions that Bolsterer's price for carving the altar was too expensive.
5. Habich, I.2: p. 250, fig. 225 (Müntzer's epitaph in the Germanisches Nationalmuseum), and the bishop's is in Michaelskirche in Bamberg. Also see H. Rascher, "Die Kleiderstiftung des Wolfgang Münzer von 1577," *MVGN* 57 (1970): 1–123.

204. CARTOUCHE WITH A FEMALE MASK

1560–1570
Relief model: pear wood(?)
8.7 × 11.5 cm
Lent by the Germanisches Nationalmuseum, Nuremberg, PL 553

In the 1659 inventory of the art collection of Archduke Leopold Wilhelm of Austria was the entry "Ein flach ablang Stückhel in Pirnholcz, von Laubwerckh geschnitten, auf schwartz Holcz geleimbt. Vom Bolsterer" (A flat, oblong piece in pearwood, carved with foliage, glued on black wood. By Bolsterer).[1] This item was a wooden relief model, much like the exhibited example, that was flat on the back and richly carved with foliage and perhaps, as here, high strapwork.[2] Such wooden models were used by goldsmiths for the production of cast metal decorations.[3] From the wooden relief a negative model was made in plaster and glue. Wax was pressed into the recesses of this negative model to form a new positive model. This wax model was then encased in plaster or clay; holes for the wax to flow out and air to get in were bored; and molten metal was poured in, displacing the wax and assuming the original shape of the wax model. When the metal had cooled, the plaster or clay mould was broken away, the casting removed, and the metal surface chased and polished. The initial wooden model was only necessary when multiple copies, rather than a single one, were required, since an unlimited number of negative models could be created from a single wooden model whereas the wax model was lost during the casting. The cartouche shown here would have been used to make decorative borders, chest ornaments, and related embellishments.

Very few wooden relief goldsmith models sur-

vive since with repeated use they were damaged and discarded.[4] The Nuremberg cartouche is slightly later in date than the three boxwood cartouches, now in Berlin (Kunstgewerbemuseum), that were carved in Nuremberg during the 1550s.[5] All four pieces reflect the influence of Wenzel Jamnitzer's designs, especially the introduction of high strapwork, floral flourishes, and classical masks.

The attribution of the Nuremberg cartouche to Bolsterer is tentative since the piece is not signed. That he was active as a model maker is proven by the 1659 inventory entry.[6]

1. The inventory was published by A. Berger in *JKSAK* 1 (1883): clxxiii, nr. 272; also cited by Habich, I.2: p. 250. The initial draft for this entry was prepared by Sigrid Knudsen.
2. This relief was first published in Josephi, *Die Werke plastischer Kunst*, nr. 518; later in *Germanisches Nationalmuseum*, nr. 381.
3. See Hayward, *Virtuoso Goldsmiths*, pp. 59–60.
4. Ibid., pls. 733, 735; esp. Pechstein, *Goldschmiedewerke der Renaissance*, nrs. 149–165.
5. Pechstein, *Goldschmiedewerke der Renaissance*, nrs. 160–162.
6. This attribution is now given by the Germanisches Nationalmuseum.

Hans Kellner

Hans Kellner (or Keller) was one of Nuremberg's major goldsmiths during the last two decades of the sixteenth century and the opening decade of the seventeenth. He was born in Nuremberg on 9 March 1561, perhaps a relative of goldsmith Lorenz Kellner (died 1560), and he trained under Wenzel Jamnitzer before becoming a master goldsmith in 1582.[1] Kellner sold his work to both princely patrons and the city of Nuremberg.[2] Rosenberg lists fifteen pieces bearing his mark, a scepter, including the *St. George and the Dragon Tablepiece* and a lavish nautilus cup, both in Dresden (Grünes Gewölbe).[3] Using the designs of Jost Amman, Kellner prepared the silver-gilt decorative mounts for the *Geschlechtsbuch*, or record book, of the Tucher family; the mounts are today in Berlin (Kunstgewerbemuseum) while the book is in Nuremberg (Germanisches Nationalmuseum).[4] He died on 4 October 1609.

1. C. Steinbrucker, "Kellner, Hans," in Thieme-Becker (1927), 20: p. 123; Hayward, *Virtuoso Goldsmiths*, p. 220; esp. K. Pechstein, who gives new information about his birth and training, in *Germanisches Nationalmuseum, Erwerbungen, Geschenke und Leihgaben im Jahre 1976*, p. 140. His birth date was previously given as about 1555.
2. Mummenhoff, *Rathaus*, pp. 265–266, nrs. 4, 9; also cited by Pechstein (see note 1).
3. Rosenberg, *Der Goldschmiede Merkzeichen*, III: nrs. 4031–4032.
4. Pechstein, *Bronzen und Plaketten*, nrs. 217–220; Weber, *Renaissanceplaketten*, pp. 174–175.

205. CUP (HALF OF A DOUBLE CUP)

ca. 1590; marks: (1) Nuremberg, (2) Kellner
Gilt silver
24.3 cm (height)
Lent by the Germanisches Nationalmuseum, Nuremberg, HG 11786

The drinking cup was an object of considerable social importance during the sixteenth century in Germany as is attested by the number of extant examples and by the amazing variety of shapes and types.[1] Cups assumed the forms of apples (cat. nr. 116) and pears (cat. nr. 206) or were embellished with sumptuous designs, as for instance Baier and Flötner's *Holzschuher Cup* (fig. 39), Jamnitzer's *Emperor's Cup* (fig. 50), and Petzoldt's *Ostrich Egg Cup* and *Diana Cup* (figs. 53 and 54).[2] One major category was the double cup, in which both halves of identical design could be fitted together lip to lip.

Only this half remains of Kellner's double cup.[3] It is a fine example of the transformations that were occurring in goldsmith designs during the 1580s and the 1590s. The shape is fairly conventional and can be compared with Wenzel Jamnitzer's signed drawing for half of a double cup.[4] Certain features, such as the band of rollwork in the form of triglyphs and metopes, are characteristic qualities of the Jamnitzer workshop; however, Kellner has also adopted the flat strapwork, rather than the now-outmoded high strapwork, that first appeared in Nuremberg around 1580 and is seen in Bernhard Zan's punching engraving of 1581 (cat. nr. 186).[5] He has blended the embossed strapwork, with its garlands of fruit and masks, in alternation with three relief figures of women.

1. For a discussion of the importance and styles of drinking cups, see Pechstein, "The 'Welcome' Cup," pp. 180–187, and "Von Trinkgeräten und Trinksitten: Von der Kindstaufe zum Kaufvertrag—Pokale als Protokolle des Ereignisses," in *Das Schatzhaus der deutschen Geschichte*, ed. R. Pörtner, pp. 385–411.
2. Kellner created the huge *Pineapple Cup with a Figure of Bacchus*, now in Baltimore (Walters Art Gallery); see A. Gabhart, *Treasures & Rarities—Renaissance, Mannerist, and Baroque*, pp. 24–25. This cup is almost 74 cm tall.
3. It is published by K. Pechstein in *Germanisches Nationalmuseum, Erwerbungen, Geschenke und Leihgaben im Jahre 1976*, pp. 140, 142 (illustration), and "Von Trinkgeräten," p. 398, fig. 5 (in color).
4. Hayward, *Virtuoso Goldsmiths*, pl. 125. The drawing is in the Germanisches Nationalmuseum.
5. On the rollwork, see Wenzel Jamnitzer's lead model and two of his chests illustrated in ibid., pls. 427–429.

This artist is one of the many talented Nuremberg goldsmiths about whom little is known today.[1] He was born in Nuremberg into a large goldsmith family. He became a master goldsmith in 1567 and died in 1611. His only extant work is the covered cup (cat. nr. 206) in the Germanisches Nationalmuseum in Nuremberg.

1. Rosenberg, *Der Goldschmiede Merkzeichen*, III: nr. 3964 (which lists no known works); *Barock in Nürnberg*, p. 140, nr. E 1.

206. COVERED CUP

1580s or early 1590s; marks: (1) Nuremberg, (2) Königsmüller
Silver gilt
33.2 cm (height)
Lent by the Germanisches Nationalmuseum, Nuremberg, HG 10913

This cup, the only known piece bearing Königsmüller's mark, is shaped like a pear and set on a knotted stem in the form of a tree trunk, upon which a tiny bearded man is climbing.[1] The owner's coat of arms is held by the sea-lion finial figure.[2] Königsmüller's use of a naturalistic shape for the cup and the tree trunk stem recall the *Apple Cup* (cat. nr. 116) by the Krug workshop or the *Holzschuher Cup* (fig. 39) by Baier and Flötner. The artist and many of his colleagues in late sixteenth-century Nuremberg consciously revived cup designs and decorative motifs that were common at the outset of the century. It was part of a general movement that Falke has labeled neo-Gothic; in painting, Königsmüller's contemporaries, notably Hans Hoffmann, produced pictures in the style of Albrecht Dürer.[3]

The shape and decorative scheme for Königsmüller's cup derive from the punch engravings of Bernhard Zan. The form of Zan's *Design for a Pear Cup* is identical to Königsmüller's with the minor exceptions of a different finial, a longer stem, and a woodsman rather than a putto on the goldsmith cup.[4] Zan's punch engravings were an important factor in the dissemination of the new flat strapwork style that was adopted by Königsmüller and other Nuremberg goldsmiths. The exhibited cup can be compared with Zan's engraving cited above or his *Design for a Covered Cup* (cat. nr. 186). Each example displays the same strapwork application combined with masks and fruit clusters. Königsmüller's cup underscores the significance of drawn and printed designs for contemporary goldsmiths, who, more often than not, were competent craftsmen rather than inventive artists. They relied on the creative talents of Zan, Zündt, Flindt, Hornick, and others for their inspiration.

1. For the artist's mark, see Rosenberg, *Der Goldschmiede Merkzeichen*, III: nr. 3964. The cup has been published with little commentary in *Barock in Nürnberg*, p. 140, nr. E 1; Pechstein, "Von Trinkgeräten," p. 398, fig. 5 (in color).
2. I have not had the opportunity to try to determine the identity of the patron.
3. Von Falke, "Die Neugotik im deutschen Kunstgewerbe der Spätrenaissance," pp. 75–92; see the comments in Section 7. On Hoffmann, see his biography and cat. nr. 208.
4. Hayward, *Virtuoso Goldsmiths*, pl. 179, cf. pl. 521 (Heinrich Jonas's *Pear Cup* in Leningrad [The Hermitage Museum], which was made in Nuremberg during the 1580s or 1590s and is very similar in conception to both Zan's print and Königsmüller's cup).

Melchior Mager

Mager was a journeyman goldsmith in Nuremberg as early as 12 July 1583, when he was mentioned in the city council records questioning certain points of a new goldsmith code for apprentices and journeymen.[1] He became a master goldsmith in 1586 and acquired his Nuremberg citizenship in the following year. How long he remained in Nuremberg is uncertain since he died in 1618 while living in Frankfurt.

---

1. Rosenberg, *Der Goldschmiede Merkzeichen*, III: nr. 4036, was uncertain whether Mager became a master in 1582 or 1586. For documentary references to Mager, see Habich, *Nürnberger Ratsverlässe*, II: nrs. 684, 754 (2 December 1584), 2484.

207. COVERED CUP

1590s; marks: (1) Nuremberg, (2) Mager
Silver gilt
20.5 cm (height)
Lent by the Germanisches Nationalmuseum, Nuremberg, HG 3889

During the 1590s and the first decades of the seventeenth century, artists rejected the use of rigid strapwork that dominated the goldsmith design, as seen for example in Zan's *Design for a Covered Cup* (cat. nr. 186) and Königsmüller's *Covered Cup* (cat. nr. 206), in favor of a more subtle integration of strapwork, foliage, and pictorial scenes.[1] This trend is evident in Flindt's *Design for a Decorated Goblet with Jupiter and Callisto* (cat. nr. 188) and, more clearly, in Mager's *Covered Cup*.[2] The cartouches on the side of the cup are broader; masks are replaced by depictions of men wearing contemporary dress (see cat. nr. 208). Beneath the lip are three hunting scenes set within scrollwork frames. Flindt and Mager, however, continued to use putto masks and fruit clusters as secondary decorative motifs.[3]

---

1. This is Mager's only known work. On his mark, see Rosenberg, *Der Goldschmiede Merkzeichen*, III: nr. 3964. The soldier finial is quite similar to that on Hans Petzoldt's *Ostrich Egg Cup* of 1594 (fig. 53).
2. This tendency continued as late as 1626, the date on Hans Petzoldt's *Covered Cup* in a private collection in Switzerland; see Hayward, *Virtuoso Goldsmiths*, pl. 484.
3. The influence of Flindt on Mager appears to have been considerable in terms of the form and the decoration of this cup.

Hoffmann was one of Nuremberg's most important painters during the last third of the sixteenth century.[1] He was born in about 1530. His place of origin is uncertain since he is mentioned in a city council record dated 19 August 1557 as "Hannsen Hofman, dem Niderlennder," or the Netherlander, yet he is never mentioned acquiring Nuremberg citizenship.[2] Either the citizenship records are incomplete, which is unlikely given the general thoroughness of the civic accounts, or Hoffmann may have been born in Nuremberg and traveled to Antwerp or another Netherlandish city to receive his training. Hoffmann may have worked with Nicolas Neufchâtel, who strongly influenced his portrait style.[3] A Hans Hoffmann and his wife, Eva, baptized their son in St. Sebaldus on 8 December 1572; unfortunately, it cannot be determined whether this refers to the artist.[4]

After 1573, the date on his *Portrait of Barbara Möhringer*, Hoffmann's career is better documented.[5] He is mentioned as a Nuremberg citizen in a letter of 30 June 1576.[6] During the 1570s and early 1580s, Hoffmann achieved success as a portraitist and as a copyist of other artists. Famed Nuremberg collector Paulus Praun owned at least fifty-two paintings by Hoffmann, including copies after Titian (2), Parmigianino, Paris Bordone, and Dürer, as well as portraits of Hans Sachs, Dürer, and sculptor Johann Gregor van der Schardt.[7] Hoffmann was best known, then and now, for his ability to copy Dürer's art and to create new works in his style. His *Dead Blue Jay* (Cleveland Museum of Art) of 1583 is the best example of his reproductive talents in the United States.[8]

Hoffmann left Nuremberg in 1584 to work for Duke Wilhelm V of Bavaria (1579–1597) in Munich and from 1585 on he was a court painter for Emperor Rudolf II in Prague.[9] He received an annual salary of 100 thalers up until his death sometime between 14 October 1591 and 12 June 1592.[10]

---

1. The biographical information is taken primarily from Pilz, "Hoffmann," pp. 236–272. Also see R. A. Peltzer, "Hoffmann, Hans," in Thieme-Becker (1924), 17: pp. 257–258; *Barock in Nürnberg*, p. 38, nrs. A 1–5; Geissler, ed., *Zeichnung in Deutschland*, I: pp. 192–193, nrs. E 6–7.
2. Hampe, *Nürnberger Ratsverlässe*, I: nr. 3679; also cited in Pilz, "Hoffmann," p. 236.
3. Pilz, "Hoffmann," p. 242.
4. Ibid., p. 238. I suspect that this must be the artist since the son's name is given as Matthes, who must certainly be the same Mathias Hoffman who received payment from Emperor Rudolf II in 1592 following the death of Hans. See Pilz, p. 241.
5. Ibid., pp. 242, 248, nr. 1, fig. 1. The painting is in Munich.
6. Ibid., p. 237. The letter is recorded in the city council records; see Hampe, *Nürnberger Ratsverlässe*, II: nr. 238.
7. Murr, *Description du Cabinet de Monsieur Paul de Praun à Nuremberg*, pp. 3ff. (paintings), nrs. 28, 32, 36, 38–39, 56, 58–66, 76–78, 102–103, 128–148, 157, 162, 169–171, 174, 198, 203, 221, 236–237.
8. Kaufmann, *Drawings from the Holy Roman Empire*, nr. 26, provides a good discussion of this work and of Hoffmann's talent for copying Dürer's work. Also see the comments in Section 7 A.
9. Pilz, "Hoffmann," pp. 239–241.
10. Ibid., p. 241.

208. PORTRAIT OF PAULUS PFINZING

1591; monogram
Drawing: black and white chalk on gray paper; repaired at the lower right
36.9 × 25.5 cm
Lent by the Germanisches Nationalmuseum, Nuremberg, HZ. 4958

Paullus Pfintzing der Ernuest,
Ist Conterfet ufs aller Best,
Als er wahr Im 37. Jar
fec 1591, Es verfertigt wahr.

Paulus Pfinzing the Elder
Is portrayed at his very best,
As he was at age 37
made in 1591, it is made true.

This inscription at the top of the drawing identifies the sitter as Paulus Pfinzing von Henfenfeld the Elder (1554–1599) at age thirty-seven in 1591.[1] Pfinzing was one of Nuremberg's most famous geometricians and cartographers.[2] His plan of Nuremberg, one of the watercolor drawings from the *Pfinzing-Atlas* of about 1596, is illustrated in figure 1 at the beginning of the catalogue.

This portrait must have been the last or one of the last made by Hoffmann since the artist died either in 1591 or in the following year. Hoffmann was working in Prague at this time, so Pfinzing presumably requested the portrait while he was in Prague on business, though it is conceivable that Hoffmann had returned briefly to Nuremberg. Pfinzing stares intently at the viewer. His short hair and beard, high buttoned coat, and ruffled collar reflect the changes in fashion in the years since Neufchâtel depicted Wenzel Jamnitzer (fig. 41) in the mid-1560s. Similar hair and costume styles are evident in Lorenz Strauch's *Portrait of Christoph Jamnitzer* of 1597 (fig. 42) and in Valentin Maler's portrait medal of Paul Scheurl of 1583 (cat. nr. 157). No other late portraits by Hoffmann survive with which the Pfinzing drawing could be compared. The Netherlandish influence on the portraiture of the Prague school and Germany in general can be seen.

Although Hoffmann's drawing could have been intended as a preparatory study for a painted portrait, it was more likely considered as a finished piece because of the detail and the painterly white highlights. Hoffmann's drawings were widely collected. This portrait of Paulus Pfinzing, after his death, entered the collection of Paulus Praun where it was but one of at least twenty-one drawings by Hoffmann.

---

1. Pilz, "Hoffmann," pp. 264–265, nr. 32; *Barock in Nürnberg*, p. 38, nr. A 5; Geissler, ed., *Zeichnung in Deutschland*, I: nr. E 7.
2. On Pfinzing's career, see E. Gagel, *Pfinzing, der Kartograph der Reichsstadt Nürnberg (1554–1599)* (Nuremberg, 1957); Schnelbögl, *Dokumentie zur Nürnberger Kartographie*, pp. 15–18, 100–104. His two principal writings were *Methodus geometrica* (1598) and *Extrakt der Geometrie und Perspektive* (1599; 2d ed.: Augsburg, 1616), both of which build on Dürer's treatise (cat. nr. 31), Rivius's *Vitruvius teutsch* (cat. nr. 136), and Jamnitzer's *Perspectiva Corporum Regularium* (cat. nr. 197).
3. On the Prague school, see the forthcoming book by T. D. Kaufmann, *L'École de Prague, La Peinture à la Cour de Rodolphe II* (Paris, 1983).
4. Murr, *Description du Cabinet de Monsieur Paul de Praun à Nuremberg*, p. 59, on Hoffmann's drawings. For the complete provenance of this drawing, see Pilz, "Hoffmann," p. 265.

Sculptor and bronze caster Benedikt Wurzelbauer, born in Nuremberg on 25 September
1548, was the grandson of Pankraz Labenwolf
(see cat. nr. 158) and the nephew of Georg Labenwolf, with whom he studied.[1] In 1583 he
married Margaretha Kronberger and began
work on the *Fountain of the Virtues* (fig. 46), his
most famous creation, which was designed by
Johannes Schünnemann and completed in 1589.[2]
Wurzelbauer is credited with making small table
or courtyard fountains (cat. nr. 209), as well
as such large fountains as the one he cast for
Bishop Ernst von Mengersdorf of Bamberg at
Geyerswörth between 1590 and 1592 or the
Venus Fountain that was erected in Prague in
1599–1600. Several funerary monuments and
small bronze statuettes are also attributed to
Wurzelbauer.[3] In 1599 he was named to the
greater city council.[4] The Wurzelbauer foundry
remained Nuremberg's most important casting
center through the careers of Benedikt, who
died on 2 October 1620, and his son and heir
Johann (1595–1656).[5]

---

1. The following biographical information is from
F. Schulz, "Wurzelbauer, Benedikt," in Thieme-Becker
(1947), 36: pp. 313–314.
2. See the comments in Section 7 D; Bange, *Die
Deutschen Bronzestatuetten des 16. Jahrhunderts*, pp.
108–109, 150, figs. 189–201; Herkommer,
"Heilsgeschichtliches Programm," pp. 212–216.
3. Bange, *Die Deutschen Bronzestatuetten des 16. Jahrhunderts*, nr. 188; Weihrauch, *Europäische Bronzestatuetten*, pp. 256–257, 259, 318, 327; *Europäische Kleinplastik
aus dem Herzog Anton Ulrich-Museum Braunschweig*, exh.
cat. (Braunschweig, 1976), nr. 38.
4. Hampe, *Nürnberger Ratsverlässe*, II: nr. 1580.
5. On Johann Wurzelbauer, see Thieme-Becker
(1947), 36: pp. 314–315.

209. FOUNTAIN WITH NEPTUNE AND TWO DOLPHINS

ca. 1600
Bronze
37.3 cm (height with socle); the base is a later
addition
Lent by the Germanisches Nationalmuseum,
Nuremberg, PL. 2875

Statues of Neptune, god of the sea, frequently
adorned Renaissance fountains as varied as Bartolommeo Ammanati's colossal ensemble, dating
from 1560 to 1575, that dominates the Piazza
della Signoria in Florence to such small examples
as the exhibited bronze.[1] The surface corrosion
on this figure of Neptune and his accompanying
dolphins, both with water spouts protruding
from their mouths, is evidence that this sculptural group was once positioned in an uncovered
courtyard or, less likely given the small scale and
single viewpoint of the statues, a garden.[2]

Grasping his trident (now broken) in his right
hand, Neptune has a bold, open stance as he
stares out across the waves. His pose offers
a nice contrast with the bulkier, more compact
Neptune (cat. nr. 158) by the workshop of Pankraz Labenwolf, Wurzelbauer's grandfather.[3]
The Nuremberg Neptune, while powerful, is
more naturally proportioned and lacks the excessive attention to the musculature that characterizes the Labenwolf statue.

The Nuremberg Neptune is tentatively attributed to Wurzelbauer based on its relationship to other known Neptune bronzes by or associated with the Wurzelbauer workshop.[4] The
figure is virtually identical to the bronze Neptune statue in Schloss Tratzberg in Tyrol that
Weihrauch ascribes to Wurzelbauer and relates,
in turn, to other Neptune statues in the Kunsthistorisches Museum in Vienna, the Huntington
Library in San Marino, and a third piece on the
art market. The *Fountain with Neptune and Two
Dolphins* has been in Nuremberg at least since
the eighteenth century, when it was in the important collection of Paul Wolfgang Merkel
(1756–1820).[5]

---

1. On the exhibited bronze, see Josephi, *Die Werke
plastischer Kunst*, nr. 170 (without an attribution);
Aufgang der Neuzeit, nr. H 40; Anzelewsky, Mende,
and Eeckhout, *Albert Dürer aux Pays-Bas*, nr. 36 (anonymous Nuremberg artist, ca. 1570); Pechstein et al.,
Paul Wolfgang Merkel und die Merkelsche Familienstiftung,
nr. K 25 (Wurzelbauer workshop?, ca. 1600). On the
Neptune fountain by Ammanati and the related example in Bologna by Giovanni Bologna, see John Pope-
Hennessy, *Italian High Renaissance and Baroque Sculpture*, 3 vols. (London and New York, 1963 [repr. 1 vol.,
1970]), I: figs. 94, 98. In the 1660s sculptor Georg
Schweigger cast a large bronze Neptune fountain for
the city of Nuremberg; however, this work was not
erected until its purchase in 1797 by Czar Paul I of
Russia and its transportation to Leningrad. A copy is
visible today in the Stadtpark in Nuremberg. See the
reference in Section 7, note 70.
2. This is mentioned in Anzelewsky, Mende, and
Eeckhout, *Albert Dürer aux Pays-Bas*, nr. 36.
3. The artist of the Nuremberg Neptune bronze
may have been familiar with Giovanni Bologna's Neptune bronzes, many of which were in the possession
of Nuremberg collector Paulus Praun. For instance,
Bologna's Neptune in the Nationalmuseum in Stockholm is represented with his right leg raised to rest on
a dolphin while his weight is placed fully on the stiff
left leg on the base. His left arm, rather than the right,
is extended out and the right arm falls down at his
side. In his right hand is a staff that is either missing
from or was never included in the Nuremberg statue.
The overall pose of the Nuremberg statue seems to be
a variation on Giovanni Bologna's piece or one of its
many variants; the Nuremberg artist has, however,
not adopted the muscular body or the facial type. See
the reference to Giovanni Bologna in note 1 and Avery
and Radcliffe, *Giambologna, 1529–1608*, nr. 32.
4. On the following, see Weihrauch, *Europäische
Bronzestatuetten*, pp. 327, 329–330, figs. 396, 399,
402, 403.
5. See Josephi, *Die Werke plastischer Kunst*, nr. 170;
Pechstein, *Merkel*, nr. K 25.

Christoph (1563–1618) was the leading German goldsmith of the early seventeenth century, as well as the last member of the great Jamnitzer dynasty, which included his grandfather, Wenzel, and his father, Hans, with whom he probably trained.[1] Over thirty goldsmith works, at least twenty-nine drawings, and the famous pattern book, the *Neuw Grottessken Buch* of 1610 (cat. nr. 212), by Christoph survive.[2] He seems to have traveled in Italy before becoming a master goldsmith in Nuremberg in 1592 since many of his finial statues and embossed figures derive from Giovanni Bologna, Michelangelo, and Jacopo Sansovino (1486–1570).[3] The small Bacchus that Christoph is carving in his 1597 portrait (fig. 42) by Lorenz Strauch has been interpreted as a variant of Michelangelo's statue in the Bargello in Florence.[4]

Jamnitzer's original, highly refined goldsmith works, including the Elephant (fig. 55) in Berlin, the elaborate ewer in Dresden, and the 1616 *Shell Dish with Milo of Crotona* in Nuremberg, were made for princely patrons.[5] Although he was never a court goldsmith to Emperor Rudolf II, he traveled to Prague to deliver commissioned pieces on several occasions. In 1603 Rudolf II paid Jamnitzer the considerable sum of 4,024 florins, presumably for the silver ewer and basin, now in Vienna (Kunsthistorisches Museum), that was used only for such ceremonies as the imperial coronations.[6] The basin showing the gods on Mount Olympus is boldly signed "Christoforo Jamnitzer fezit," while the triumphs of Petrarch are embossed on the ewer. The triumph-of-death relief (see cat. nr. 108) includes the portraits of Petrarch, Dürer, Michelangelo, and, presumably, Wenzel Jamnitzer and Hans von Aachen.

In 1607 Christoph was named a member of the greater city council and six years later he was a sworn counselor (*geschworener*), a high civic distinction. Christoph designed one of the few monumental sculpture projects in Nuremberg—the stone statues carved by Joachim Toppmann and Leonhard Kern in 1616 and 1617 for the three portals of the new west façade of the Rathaus (see fig. 8).[7] These sculptures prove that Christoph had the talent to fashion monumental programs as well as the intricate goldsmith designs that he is better known for.

1. On his life and career, see M. Frankenburger, "Jamnitzer, Christoph," in Thieme-Becker (1925), 18: pp. 366–368; Kris and von Falke, "Beiträge zu den Werken Christoph und Hans Jamnitzer," pp. 186–207; *Barock in Nürnberg*, p. 38; Hayward, *Virtuoso Goldsmiths*, pp. 220–223; K. Pechstein, "Zum Werk von Christoph Jamnitzer," AGNM (1977): 95–104, and "Christoph Jamnitzer (+ 1618)," *Fränkische Lebensbilder* 10 (1982): 179–192. I wish to thank Dr. Pechstein for sending me a copy of his 1982 article. Also see the comments in Section 7 D and E.

2. On his goldsmith works, see Rosenberg, *Der Goldschmiede Merkzeichen*, III: nr. 3839; the references below. On his drawings, see H. W. Williams, "Supplementary Note Regarding Four Drawings Attributed to Christoph Jamnitzer," *Art Bulletin* 19 (1937): 112; Pechstein, "Jamnitzer-Studien," and "Eine unbekannte Entwurfsskizze für eine Goldschmiedeplastik von Christoph Jamnitzer," *ZfK* 31 (1968): 314–321; Geissler, ed., *Zeichnung in Deutschland*, I: nrs. E 13–15; G. Irmscher, "Motiventlehnungen in neuentdeckten und bekannten Handzeichnungen Christoph Jamnitzers," AGNM (1981): 84–106, which provides a catalogue of the drawings.

3. See H. Weihrauch, "Italienische Bronzen als Vorbilder deutscher Goldschmiedekunst," in *Studien zur Geschichte der europäischen Plastik—Festschrift Theodor Müller*, ed. K. Martin, pp. 263–280, esp. 270; Hayward, *Virtuoso Goldsmiths*, pp. 221–222; Pechstein, "Zum Werk von Christoph Jamnitzer," esp. pp. 95ff.

4. Pechstein, "Christoph Jamnitzer (+ 1618)," p. 182.

5. Pechstein, *Goldschmiedewerke der Renaissance*, nr. 102 (the Elephant); Hayward, *Virtuoso Goldsmiths*, pls. 516 (Dresden ewer), 517 (the Elephant); Pechstein, "Eine unbekannte Entwurfsskizze," p. 321, fig. 7 (shell dish).

6. Hayward, *Virtuoso Goldsmiths*, pp. 221–222, pls. 511–514.

7. Mummenhoff, *Rathaus*, pp. 134ff.; Pechstein, "Zum Werk von Christoph Jamnitzer," pp. 99–102.

210. STUDY OF TWENTY PUTTI

1600–1610
Drawing: pen and brown ink with light blue wash, pasted onto a second sheet of paper
24 × 21 cm
Lent by the Germanisches Nationalmuseum, Nuremberg, HZ. 3899

Twenty putti are represented frolicking among the clouds.[1] As some are shown blowing a trumpet, dancing, drinking wine, or carrying a punch bowl, others are depicted passing gas, holding an apple, playing with swords, or simply posing. They would be appropriate at a bacchanal or some other mythological festival. Each is sketched with a quick, free outline that captures the putto's inherent pudginess and animated pose.

This is one of three sketches of putti that Jamnitzer created during the first decade of the seventeenth century.[2] The purpose of the drawings is uncertain, although putti do occasionally figure on the artist's goldsmith works, as, for example, on the ewer of Rudolf II in Vienna.[3] Conceivably, Jamnitzer planned a large table fountain or related piece covered with cavorting putti. He also included putti, intermixed with fictitious monsters, in the etchings in his *Neuw Grottessken Buch* of 1610 (cat. nr. 212); however, only one of the putti in the exhibited drawing is incorporated into that book, on page 6. This appealing drawing, together with his many other, more pictorial sketches, demonstrates that Jamnitzer was a talented draftsman and highly versatile artist. Unlike most goldsmiths, he created the majority of his own designs.[4]

1. The drawing is published in *Barock in Nürnberg*, nr. A 7 (no text); H. G. Franz, intro., *Christoph Jamnitzer, Neuw Grottessken Buch. Nachdruck der ausgabe Nürnberg 1610*, p. 27, fig. 3; Irmscher, "Handzeichnungen Christoph Jamnitzers," p. 106.
2. Franz, *Jamnitzer*, pp. 26–27, figs. 1–3, cf. 4; Irmscher, "Handzeichnungen Christoph Jamnitzers," pp. 105–106. Of the other two drawings, one is in the Nationalgalerie in Budapest and the second is in the Germanisches Nationalmuseum in Nuremberg.
3. Hayward, *Virtuoso Goldsmiths*, pl. 513.
4. See the articles on his drawings cited in the biography, note 2. One of the most impressive is his design for a cup or dish stem with a figure of Bacchus (Erlangen, Universitätsbibliothek); see Geissler, ed., *Zeichnung in Deutschland*, I: nr. E 13.

211. RELIEF WITH THE FIGURE OF JUPITER

ca. 1610(?)
Silver gilt with a red stone affixed to Jupiter's chest
8.7 × 7.5 cm
Lent by the Germanisches Nationalmuseum, Nuremberg, HG 7789

In this small cast relief, Jupiter, king of the gods, stares menacingly down at someone or something outside the composition that has incurred his wrath.[1] His strong, muscular body has a wide, open stance as he prepares to hurl the bolt of lightning in his right hand. Jamnitzer is considerably more successful than Georg Pencz had been in his *Fall of Phaeton* (fig. 33) in expressing Jupiter's violent anger. Jupiter is clad in classical armor much like that seen in the basin of Rudolf II or in Jost Amman's *The Daughter of Jephthah* drawing (cat. nr. 196); it is ornamented with gems, including an actual red-colored stone set into the middle of his chest. Jupiter is placed against a rather simple landscape with a river, small town, and distant mountains—features that preclude its identification as Mount Olympus. Beneath him is his symbol, the eagle.

The purpose of this relief is uncertain. While it could be an independent decoration, it is much more likely that it belonged on the side or top of a chest or reading desk of the sort frequently made by Wenzel Jamnitzer, Hans Straub, or Nikolaus Schmidt of Nuremberg.[2] For example, Wenzel Jamnitzer's collector's chest (fig. 51) in Chicago has twelve cast reliefs of classical gods, several of whom are shown seated before simple landscapes.[3] Given that the chests produced by the Jamnitzer and related workshops were the finest created in Germany during the later sixteenth century, it is probable that Christoph Jamnitzer also received commissions for similar chests.[4]

1. This relief is unpublished. The attribution to Jamnitzer, given by the Germanisches Nationalmuseum, is certainly correct when the figure of Jupiter is compared with Jamnitzer's other works, notably the ewer and basin of Rudolf II, the Dresden ewer, the warriors of the elephant (fig. 55), and, especially, Milo of Crotona on the shell dish in Nuremberg. See the biography of Christoph Jamnitzer, notes 5 and 6, for references to illustrations.
2. See Pechstein, *Goldschmiedewerke der Renaissance*, nrs. 88–89; Hayward, *Virtuoso Goldsmiths*, pls. 427–428, cf. 448–451. Given the relatively large size of the relief, it is unlikely that it could have been worn on a chain; however, see Hayward, pl. 154, for one of Erasmus Hornick's designs for a large pendant with the figures of Mars and Venus.
3. On this chest, see the comments in Section 7 E.
4. One writing desk has been attributed to Christoph Jamnitzer; see M. Rosenberg, *Jamnitzer, Alle erhaltenen Goldschmiedearbeiten. Verlorene Werke. Handzeichnungen*, pl. 61.

212. GROTESQUE DESIGN FROM CHRISTOPH JAMNITZER, NEUW GROTTESSKEN BUCH (Nuremberg, 1610)

Etching
14.3 × 17.8 cm (trimmed)
Andresen, IV: nr. 34
Lent by the New York Public Library, Prints Division, Astor, Lenox and Tilden Foundations

This bizarre image of a hybrid creature being attacked by a female beast with wings, who excretes candlewick trimmers, is characteristic of the plates in Christoph Jamnitzer's *Book of New Grotesques*, one of the most wonderfully imaginative pattern books ever published.[1] Jamnitzer has created a world inhabited by monstrous figures, part animal and part ornament, whose features seem to melt and to metamorphose into something even more fanciful. The book consists of three title pages, a two-page foreword, and sixty etched plates, without any text. The inspiration for his book, as he relates in the foreword, was the tales of Christopher Columbus's and Hernando Cortez's voyages to the New World and the accounts of marvelous new creatures never before seen in Europe. Jamnitzer decided to make his own menagerie of animals. Although several of the plates did inspire a group of lead plaquettes, the book was intended more for the amusement of the reader than the instruction of the goldsmith or the furniture deco-rator in search of designs.[2] Indeed, the creature illustrated here would be extremely difficult to translate into a plastic ornament.

While some of his figures recall the phantasmagoric inventions of Hieronymus Bosch, they are in fact outgrowths of the Renaissance decorative tradition of grotesques.[3] Inspired by the wall paintings found in Roman imperial houses that were excavated in Rome and Tivoli at the end of the fifteenth century, Italian and later northern European artists adopted the decorative motifs. From the *grottesche* by Raphael and his assistants in the Vatican loggia to Primaticcio's rooms at Fontainebleau, grotesques, notably terms, satyrs, and other classically dressed figures, placed within floral or architectural settings, entered into the main stream of European pictorial forms by the 1540s. With time and considerable imagination, Cornelis Bos, Cornelis Floris, and others radically transformed the original models.[4] The strapwork patterns of Bos that were copied by Wenzel Jamnitzer and other Nuremberg artists barely recall their original sources, and new decorative motifs were continually being generated, as seen for instance in the prints of Zan (cat. nr. 186) or Flindt (cat. nrs. 187 and 188).

Christoph Jamnitzer's etchings parody the rigid strapwork and stock masks and floral flourishes that dominated goldsmith designs in Nuremberg throughout the second half of the six-teenth century. The strap- and scrollwork of his predecessors here blossom into monstrous tendrils whose volutes are actually withered breasts and fanciful wings. The whole design is supremely logical, albeit a perverted and highly Manneristic application of Renaissance balance and symmetry. The playful mocking of contemporary tastes is also clearly evident in Jamnitzer's placement of his fanciful creatures upon a very traditional dolphin pedestal as he contrasts the new with the old.

1. The principal source for the following is Franz, intro., *Christoph Jamnitzer*. Also see P. A. Wick, "A New Book of Grotesques by Christoph Jamnitzer," *Bulletin of the Museum of Fine Arts, Boston* 60 (1962): 83–104. I have not seen the recent published dissertation, G. Juchheim, *Das Neuw Grottessken Buch Nürnberg 1610 von Christoph Jamnitzer* (Munich, 1976). The entire volume is Andresen, IV: pp. 244–264, nrs. 1–62. Only one of Jamnitzer's drawings, now in Würzburg (Universitätsbibliothek), is specifically related to this book; however, other sketches of putti, including cat. nr. 210, also provided a few of the preparatory designs; see Franz, *Christoph Jamnitzer*, pp. 26–28, figs. 1–4.
2. Pechstein, *Bronzen und Plaketten*, nr. 221; Weber, *Renaissanceplaketten*, nr. 753.
3. For the following, see Franz, *Christoph Jamnitzer*, pp. 10–13; also the comments in Farmer, *Virtuoso Craftsman*, nrs. 97–98.
4. Schéle, *Cornelis Bos*, chs. II, III, provides an excellent discussion of grotesque decoration and the roles of Bos and Floris in disseminating the style by means of their prints.

Paul Juvenel the Elder

Juvenel, one of Nuremberg's most talented seventeenth-century painters, was baptized on 22 December 1579, and he trained with his father, Nicolas (before 1540–1597), a Netherlandish painter who had settled in Nuremberg.[1] In 1607 Paul Juvenel and Frederick van Valckenborch, another Netherlandish ex-patriot residing in Nuremberg, were commissioned by Archduke Maximilian I of Bavaria (1597–1651) to copy the middle panel of Dürer's *Heller Altar* in the Dominikanerkirche in Frankfurt; the copy, like the original painting, is lost.[2] In the same year Martin Peller had Juvenel paint the *Fall of Phaeton* cycle (fig. 43) on the ceiling of the so-called Schöne Zimmer (or beautiful chamber) in his lavish new townhouse (figs. 13 and 14).

Sometime prior to 1613, when he was working on the restoration of the great hall of the Rathaus in Nuremberg, Juvenel traveled to Italy, where he visited Mantua and Rome.[3] While in Rome he was greatly influenced by the landscapes of Adam Elsheimer, who had died in 1610, and Paulus Brill as seen already in a painting dated 1611.[4]

During the 1610s Juvenel established his reputation as a painter of illusionistic ceilings and house façades, including those of the Meierhaus at Hauptmarkt 26 and the Viatishaus (fig. 44), which was executed between 1615 and 1620.[5] The city council paid him 400 gulden in 1622 for painting scenes of Roman history on the ceiling of the Schönen Saal of the Rathaus.[6] Another ceiling painting dating to 1623 was once in the house at Albrecht Dürer Platz 10.[7]

Juvenel left Nuremberg in 1638, perhaps because of the wars that sapped Nuremberg's economic strength, and settled in Vienna briefly before he moved on to Pressburg in Hungary, where he died in 1643.[8]

1. See R. A. Peltzer, "Juvenel, Paul," in Thieme-Becker (1926), 19: pp. 365–367; *Barock in Nürnberg*, p. 47, nrs. A 51–57; Geissler, ed., *Zeichnung in Deutschland*, I: E 24–26, for the following biographical information.
2. Peltzer, ed., *Sandrarts Academie*, p. 136. On the *Heller Altar*, see Anzelewsky, *Dürer*, nr. 115K.
3. His drawing of the walls of Mantua is in Berlin; see Bock, *Staatliche Museen zu Berlin*, I: p. 196, nr. 8632; II: pl. 164.
4. This influence is evident in Juvenel's *Presentation in the Temple* of 1611 in Danzig (Stadtmuseum); see W. Drost, "Ein frühes Architekturbild des Paul Juvenel," *Pantheon* 9 (1932): 122–123.
5. See the comments in Section 7 A; *Barock in Nürnberg*, nrs. A 53–54.
6. Mummenhoff, *Rathaus*, pp. 144–145, 292.
7. Two other drawings for ceiling decorations are in Berlin; see Bock, *Staatliche Museen zu Berlin*, I: pp. 195–196, nrs. 8629 (dated 1626), 8630.
8. His last known dated work is his *Presentation in the Temple* drawing of 1642 now in Munich (Staatliche Graphische Sammlung); see Geissler, ed., *Zeichnung in Deutschland*, I: nr. E 26.

213. VIEW OF THE INTERIOR OF THE GREAT HALL OF THE NUREMBERG RATHAUS

ca. 1614
22 × 16 cm
Painting: oil on copper
Lent by the Germanisches Nationalmuseum, Nuremberg, GM 1051

On 8 April 1613 the city council ruled that since the paintings adorning the great hall of the Rathaus had become difficult to read it would commission artists Paul Juvenel the Elder, Georg Gärtner, Jobst Harrich, and Gabriel Weyer to restore the various pictorial cycles.[1] In the first campaign of 1613 and 1614, Juvenel, Gärtner, and Harrich renewed the 1521 wall paintings and the ceiling decorations. A second campaign, dating mainly from 1619, included the destruc-

tion of the old west wall, which was necessary because of the new western façade (fig. 8) that Jakob Wolff the Younger was then erecting, and new painting series by Weyer for the western and eastern walls.

When the first campaign was initiated in 1613, the city architect was Wolf Jakob Stromer von Reichenbach, who frequently commissioned paintings and drawings as records of the buildings erected or restored under his supervision. The small copper painting exhibited here bears Stromer's coat of arms flanked by the allegorical figures of Civil Architecture and Glory (Fame), which suggests that the painting, like others, was ordered by Stromer to document the restoration campaign of 1613 to 1614.[2] The painting certainly was completed by 1614, the year of Stromer's death. The picture is attributed to Paul Juvenel the Elder because of the stylistic similarities with other paintings by the artist; Juvenel was also one of the four artists executing the restoration.[3] A Juvenel portrait of Stromer exists, thus proving at the very least the business relationship between the two men.

This painting is extremely important since it is the oldest view of the interior of the great hall and the only surviving record of the room's appearance before the second restoration campaign that destroyed, among other things, the huge *Last Judgment* mural on the west wall that is attributed to Michael Wolgemut.[4] Juvenel's depiction of the hall is from east to west. On the right side, or the north wall, are the *Great Triumphal Chariot*, based upon Dürer's print (cat. nr. 26), the civic musicians, who are painted behind an actual balcony where local musicians performed during the patrician dances and other important occasions, and, barely visible, the *Calumny of Apelles*, which is patterned after Dürer's drawing now in Vienna (Albertina).[5] On the left side, or the south wall, are images of the power of women over men, including the figures of David and Bathsheba, Samson and Delilah, and Phyllis and Aristotle, and several virtues that derive from a Dürer drawing in New York (Pierpont Morgan Library) and other now-lost sketches.[6] In front of the west wall with its *Last Judgment* stands the monumental bronze grille completed by Hans Vischer in 1540 and flanked by the stone frames carved by Sebald Beck.[7] The east wall, not visible in the painting, included the imperial throne and stained-glass windows with the city's coats of arms, which were designed by Hans von Kulmbach and created by Veit Hirschvogel the Elder in 1521.

The great hall and its decorations were among the crowning artistic glories of Nuremberg. The chamber was constructed between 1332 and 1340 and measures forty meters in length and fourteen meters in height, which made it the largest civic room in northern Europe in the fourteenth century. The paintings, with the exception of the *Last Judgment* attributed to Wolgemut, were executed in 1521–1522 by Georg Pencz, Hans von Kulmbach(?), and Hans Springinklee, among others, after the designs of Albrecht Dürer, who received 100 guldens as payment from the city council in early 1522. This pictorial cycle reflected the room's multiple functions. Besides being the site of the occasional patrician dance, it served as the meeting room for imperial as-semblies, which prompted the inclusion of the triumph of Maximilian I. The western portion of the hall, behind the grille, was the civic tribunal; the *Calumny of Apelles* illustrated the perversion of justice while the *Last Judgment* warned those who would either lie or give false testimony of the ultimate punishment they would face on Judgment Day. The paintings provided marvelous background decorations that mirrored the multiple uses of the great hall. Unfortunately, very little survived the bombardment of Nuremberg in 1945.

---

1. Mummenhoff, *Rathaus*, p. 116. On the paintings in this room and their restoration, see Mummenhoff, pp. 92–158; Christensen, "The Nuernberg City Council," pp. 82–89; esp. Mende, *Rathaus*, I: pp. 38–88, 192–409, and see the forthcoming volume two of his study. The paintings are discussed in Section 6 A.

2. On the painting, see Anzelewsky, Mende, and Eeckhout, *Albert Dürer aux Pays-Bas*, nr. 6; *Reformation in Nürnberg*, nr. 77; esp. Mende, *Rathaus*, I: nr. 110, color pl. II. Also see L. Sporhan-Krempel (with assistance of Wolfgang von Stromer), "Wolf Jacob Stromer, 1561–1614, Ratsbaumeister zu Nürnberg," *MVGN* 51 (1962): 273–310.

3. See Mende, *Rathaus*, I: p. 180, for the attribution and for the following sentence. Also see Sporhan-Krempel, "Wolf Jacob Stromer," fig. 1.

4. Ibid., II: nr. 604, will discuss the Last Judgment and its attribution. Compare Juvenel's view with that in Lorenz Hess's painting of 1626; Mende, I: nr. 112.

5. Winkler, *Zeichnungen Dürers*, IV: nr. 922.

6. Ibid., nr. 921.

7. On the grille, see Section 6 A, note 67.

MELCHIOR BAIER (master 1525; died 1577)

Baier was one of Nuremberg's finest goldsmiths. His greatest period of activity occurred during the 1530s and 1540s, when he collaborated with Peter Flötner to produce, among other works, the *Silver Altar* of King Sigismund I of Poland, the *Pfinzing Dish* (fig. 38), the agate dish in Munich, and the *Holzschuher Covered Cup* (fig. 39). See Section 6 E.

HANS BEHEIM (BEHAIM) THE ELDER (ca. 1455–1538)

For almost forty years, Beheim was Nuremberg's leading architect. From 1503 he served as the master mason of the city; however, he was permitted to design as well as to erect buildings. Beheim constructed the Waage, or weighing house, the three civic granaries, the additions to the Heilig-Geist-Spital and the Rathaus, the chapel of the Zwölfbrüderhaus (fig. 15), the Holzschuherkapelle in the Johannisfriedhof, the Rochuskapelle (design only), and many important houses. See Section 6 C.

HANS BEUTMÜLLER (master 1588; died 1622)

After receiving his training in Venice(?), Beutmüller moved to Nuremberg and became a leading goldsmith. Among the twenty-five or so pieces attributed to him is the covered cup in the Toledo Museum of Art.

HANS DÜRER (1490–1534/35 or 1538)

Hans trained in the workshop of his brother Albrecht Dürer and is known to have assisted with the painting of Albrecht's *Heller Altar*, formerly in Frankfurt. By 1527 Hans had moved to Cracow, where two years later he became the court painter of King Sigismund I of Poland.

JACOB ELSNER (died 1517)

One of the city's principal manuscript illuminators who worked for Anton Kress and Friedrich the Wise, among others. Several portraits, including two in the Germanisches Nationalmuseum in Nuremberg, are by his hand.

HANS FREY (1450–1523)

Frey was a bronzesmith who specialized in creating table fountains, such as the example with a mountain scene and Morris dancers illustrated in a drawing (fig. 30) attributed to him, now in the Universitätsbibliothek at Erlangen. Frey and his wife, Anna Rummel, had two daughters, including Agnes, the wife of Albrecht Dürer.

ALBRECHT GLOCKENDON THE ELDER (died 1545)

Albrecht and his son Albrecht the Younger were important manuscript illuminators whose major works include the *Prayer Book of Duke Wilhelm IV of Bavaria* in Vienna and the *Glockendon Missal* in Nuremberg. Albrecht the Elder was also a *formschneider* and print publisher (see cat. nrs. 70, 82, 84, 85, and 103).

GEORG GLOCKENDON THE ELDER (died 1514)

Georg the Elder was a manuscript illuminator and *briefmaler* who was active from 1484, the year in which he acquired his Nuremberg citizenship. He painted Martin Behaim's *Erdapfel* (Earth Apple) of 1492, the oldest terrestrial globe, now in Nuremberg. He also printed cat. nr. 1. His son Georg the Younger was a manuscript illuminator from about 1530 until 1555.

NIKOLAUS GLOCKENDON (died 1534)

Nikolaus, son of Nikolaus the Elder, was a manuscript illuminator and *briefmaler*. He is first mentioned in 1515. Nikolaus was certainly the finest German book illuminator; his style was strongly influenced by the Bening family of Bruges. He painted several manuscripts for Albrecht von Brandenburg, including a missal and a book of hours of the Virgin in Aschaffenburg and a prayer book in Kassel.

AUGUSTIN HIRSCHVOGEL (HIRSVOGEL; 1503–1553)

The son of Veit Hirschvogel the Elder, Augustin made stained-glass windows; however, his greatest accomplishments were as an etcher and a cartographer. He left Nuremberg in 1536 and settled in Ljubljana (Laibach) in modern Yugoslavia, where he was active designing maps, including the map of the Turkish border that the

Nuremberg city council commissioned in 1539. By 1543 he moved to Vienna, his home until his death ten years later. During this period he produced three hundred etchings, including thirty-five landscapes.

VEIT HIRSCHVOGEL (HIRSVOGEL) THE ELDER (1461–1525)

Veit the Elder was the head of Nuremberg's most important stained-glass workshop. He collaborated closely with Albrecht Dürer, Hans Baldung Grien, Hans von Kulmbach, and other contemporary Nuremberg artists who supplied him with stained-glass designs (cat. nr. 35). Veit the Elder and his workshop made windows for St. Lorenz; the Chapel of St. Anne at St. Lorenz; the *Bamberg, Margrave's,* and *Emperor's Windows* in St. Sebaldus; the Sebalder Pfarrhof; the Tucherhaus; and the Imhoffkapelle in the Rochusfriedhof. He frequently worked with his son Veit the Younger (1485–1553), who is credited with producing the windows in the Chapel of the Zwölfbrüderhaus (cat. nr. 35 and fig. 15).

ADAM KRAFT (ca. 1455/60–1509)

Kraft was the leading stone sculptor in Nuremberg during the 1490s and first decade of the sixteenth century. Most of his work was for local civic buildings, such as the Waage and the Rathaus, churches, and private residences rather than for patrons outside Nuremberg. His principal sculptures include the *Schreyer-Landauer Epitaph* (1490–1492) on the exterior of St. Sebaldus, the *Sacrament House* (1493; figs. 19 and 20) in St. Lorenz, and the *Stations of the Cross* (fig. 18) that lined the road from Pilate's House to the Johannisfriedhof. See Section 3 A.

HANS KRUG THE ELDER (master 1484; died 1519)

Krug was a goldsmith and, from 1494 until 1509, the city mint master. He was also the stamp cutter for Friedrich the Wise from 1508 until 1510. Goldsmiths Hans the Younger (died 1528) and Ludwig (see cat. nrs. 112–116) were his sons.

ELIAS (died 1591) AND HANS LENCKER (master 1550; died 1585)

These two brothers were highly skilled goldsmiths who specialized in the use of translucent enameling. Their principal works include the reading desk of about 1560 in Vienna and the writing casket of about 1585 in Munich. Several cups, including the *Holzschuher Double Cup* of about 1575 in Hamburg, bear Elias's mark.

NICOLAS NEUFCHÂTEL (ca. 1527–after 1573)

Neufchâtel was born and worked in Mons (Hainaut) during the 1540s and 1550s, after completing his apprenticeship in 1539 with Pieter Coecke van Aelst in Antwerp. By 1561 Neufchâtel had settled in Nuremberg, where he quickly became the leading painter. About forty paintings are attributed to him, including the *Portrait of Johann Neudörfer and His Son* (1561; fig. 40) and the *Portrait of Wenzel Jamnitzer* (ca. 1565; fig. 41). What happened to Neufchâtel after 1573, the date of his last known portrait, is uncertain. See Section 7 A.

HANS PEISSER (ca. 1505–ca. 1575)

Peisser, a prominent stone and wood sculptor, acquired his Nuremberg citizenship in 1526, about the time he had completed the ornate frame of the *Welser Altar,* formerly the high altar of the Frauenkirche (see fig. 6). He carved the wooden models, several of which survive, for Pankraz Labenwolf's *Goosebearer Fountain* and *Putto Fountain* (fig. 36) in Nuremberg, as well as the *Planet Gods Fountain* in Linz and others in Friesach (Kärntnen) and Prague. Peisser renounced his Nuremberg citizenship in 1559 and was active in Prague by 1562. See Section 6 D.

HANS PETZOLDT (1551–1633)

After the death of Wenzel Jamnitzer in 1585, Petzoldt became the city's leading goldsmith. He was a master in 1578 and acquired his Nuremberg citizenship the following year. Although he worked for Emperor Rudolf II in Prague in 1605, as well as for other princely patrons, most of his commissions were from the Nuremberg city council, for which he made at least eighty cups plus other goldsmith objects, most of which were presented as gifts to notable visitors to Nuremberg. Among his finest pieces are the *Ostrich Egg Cup* (1594; fig. 53) in Minneapolis and the *Diana Cup* (ca. 1610; fig. 54) in Berlin.

JÖRG RUEL (master 1598; died 1625)

Ruel was another of the city's talented goldsmiths active at the opening of the seventeenth century. The *Agate Dish* (early seventeenth century) in Minneapolis is perhaps his best work.

JOHANN GREGOR VAN DER SCHARDT (JAN DE ZAR; ca. 1530–after 1581)

Schardt was born and trained in Nijmegen (Gelderland). During the 1560s he studied and worked in Rome, Florence, and, by 1569, Venice. While in the employment of Emperor Maximilian II, Schardt arrived in Nuremberg in either late 1569 or 1570, the date of his terra-cotta *Portrait Bust of Willibald Imhoff* (fig. 45). During the 1570s he produced numerous wax and terra-cotta sculptured portraits of Nuremberg patricians. Schardt also carved wooden statues to be cast by Benedikt Wurzelbauer and other local bronze founders. He either died or left Nuremberg sometime shortly after 1581. See Section 7 D.

NIKOLAUS SCHMIDT (master 1582; died 1609)

Schmidt trained with Wenzel Jamnitzer, with whom he collaborated on a casket now in Dresden. He specialized in elaborate forms, such as the nautilus-shell cup owned by Queen Elizabeth II, the unusual ewer and basin in Dresden, and another ewer in Vienna.

JONAS SILBER (master 1572)

Silber was one of Wenzel Jamnitzer's most talented pupils. He was the court goldsmith in Heidelberg from 1578 to 1580 and in 1587 a coin cutter in Danzig. Silber returned to Nuremberg sometime prior to 1589, the date on his finest piece, the *Weltallschale*, or *World Dish*, of Emperor Rudolf II (fig. 52). He was also active as a plaquette maker and a punch engraver. See Section 7 E.

VEIT STOSS (1447[?]–1533)

Although renowned as one of Germany's greatest sculptors of the late Middle Ages and the early Renaissance, Stoss was also a painter, cartographer, and engraver. He was born at Horb am Neckar and was active in Nuremberg until 1477, when he renounced his citizenship and moved to Cracow, where he remained until 1496. In this year he returned to Nuremberg, where he lived until his death. Stoss's career was marked by great successes, most notably his *Angelic Salutation* (fig. 23) in St. Lorenz and the *Mary Altar*, made for the Karmeliterkloster in Nuremberg and now in Bamberg Cathedral. He also suffered reversals, including the draping of his *Angelic Salutation* because it was considered idolatrous, and, in 1503, Stoss was convicted of fraud, branded as punishment, and pardoned by Emperor Maximilian I only three years later. Notwithstanding his conflicts with the city council, Stoss carved an elaborate chandelier (fig. 31) after Dürer's drawing for the Rathaus in 1522. See Section 3 A.

HANS STRAUB (master 1568; died 1610)

Straub was a follower and son-in-law of Wenzel Jamnitzer. He obtained his Nuremberg citizenship in 1569. Straub's goldsmith works, including his sumptuous chest of about 1580, now in Berlin, continue the stylistic motifs of Jamnitzer. Straub served as a member of the larger city council from 1583 on, he was a sworn member from 1586, and a friend of the council (*ratsfreund*) from 1596.

LORENZ STRAUCH (1554–ca. 1630/32)

Strauch excelled as a portraitist and painter of architectural views. He was active as early as 1573, though his first dated work is 1581. Among Strauch's better portraits is *Christoph Jamnitzer* (fig. 42) of 1597. His views of the Hauptmarkt (1599; fig. 5) and the west façade of the Rathaus (1621; fig. 8) were engraved by Johann Troschel, among others. See Section 7 A.

FREDERICK VAN VALCKENBORCH (ca. 1570–1623)

A member of the talented Valckenborch family of landscape painters, Frederick lived in Antwerp, Frankfurt, and, between 1590 and 1592 with his brother Gillis, in Rome and Venice. Although he acquired his Frankfurt citizenship in 1597, Frederick had settled in Nuremberg by 1602 and became a citizen there in 1607. Valckenborch and

Paul Juvenel the Elder spent most of 1607 in Frankfurt copying Dürer's *Heller Altar* for Archduke Maximilian I of Bavaria. In 1610 he became a member of the greater city council and two years later he was responsible for planning the triumphal pageant in Nuremberg for Emperor Matthias's visit.

HERMANN AND PETER VISCHER THE ELDER

See Sections 3 A and 6 D and the biography of Peter Vischer the Younger and the Vischer workshop.

GABRIEL WEYER (1576–1632)

Painter Weyer was active from 1597. After returning from his two-year journeyman's trip to the Netherlands in 1604, he became a master painter in Nuremberg. Weyer participated in the restoration of the great hall of the Rathaus (see cat. nr. 213) in 1613 and the subsequent repainting of the eastern and western walls of this chamber later in the decade. In 1615 he was named as the official city painter.

JAKOB WOLFF THE ELDER (ca. 1546–1612)

Wolff was the leading Nuremberg architect of the late sixteenth and early seventeenth centuries. He was probably the architect of the Fembohaus (1591–1600; fig. 10). Between 1602 and 1607 he erected the Pellerhaus (figs. 13 and 14). See Section 7 C.

JAKOB WOLFF THE YOUNGER (1574–1620)

As the *stadtwerkmeister*, or city architect, Jakob the Younger supplied many of the architectural drawings that are now in the *Baumeisterbuch* of Wolf Jakob Stromer in Schloss Grünsberg. He built the early Baroque west wing of the Nuremberg Rathaus (fig. 8), a project that began in 1616 and was completed only in 1622, two years after his death.

Bibliography

The following is a very select bibliography with few articles on individual paintings, drawings, prints, sculptures, and other objects. The reader should check the biographies and entries for the individual artists.

Abraham, E. *Nürnberger Malerei der zweiten Hälfte des 15. Jahrhunderts.* Strassburg, 1912.

Ahlborn, J. *Die Familie Landauer, vom Maler zum Montanherrn.* Nuremberg, 1969.

Albrecht Dürer: Master Printmaker. Ed. E. Sayre et al. Exh. cat. Boston: Museum of Fine Arts, 1971.

Albrecht Dürer, 1471–1971. Exh. cat. Nuremberg: Germanisches Nationalmuseum, 1971.

Andersson, C. "Religiöse Bilder Cranachs im Dienste der Reformation." In *Humanismus und Reformation als kulturelle Kräfte in der deutschen Geschichte,* ed. L. Spitz, pp. 43–79. Berlin, 1981.

Andresen, A. A. *Der Deutsche Peintre-Graveur.* 5 vols. Leipzig, 1864–1878.

Anzelewsky, F. *Albrecht Dürer: Das malerische Werk.* Berlin, 1971.

——. *Dürer: His Art and Life.* Tr. H. Grieve. New York, 1981.

——, M. Mende, and P. Eeckhout. *Albert Dürer aux Pays-Bas: Son voyage (1520–1521), son influence.* Exh. cat. Brussels: Palais des Beaux-Arts, 1977.

Appelbaum, S., ed. *The Triumph of Maximilian I: 137 Woodcuts by Hans Burgkmair and Others.* New York, 1964.

Appuhn, H., and C. von Heusinger. *Riesenholzschnitte und Papiertapeten der Renaissance.* Unterschneidheim, 1976.

Aufgang der Neuzeit: Deutsche Kunst und Kultur von Dürers Tod bis zum Dreissigjährigen Kriege, 1530–1650. Nuremberg: Germanisches Nationalmuseum, 1952.

Augsburg: Welt im Umbruch: see *Welt im Umbruch.*

Avery, C., and A. Radcliffe. *Giambologna, 1529–1608: Sculptor to the Medici.* Exh. cat. London: Victoria & Albert Museum, 1978.

Bachmann, E. *Imperial Castle Nuremberg: Official Guide.* 5th English ed. Munich, 1978.

Bainton, R. H. "Dürer and Luther as the Man of Sorrows." *Art Bulletin* 29 (1947): 269–272.

——. *The Reformation of the Sixteenth Century.* Boston, 1956.

Baldass, L. von. "Zur Bildniskunst der Dürerschule. I. Zur Bildniskunst des Wolf Traut und H. L. Schäufelein." *Pantheon* 26 (1940): 225–229; "Zur Bildniskunst der Dürerschule. II. Die Bildniskunst des Jörg Pencz und Bartel Beham." Ibid., pp. 253–259.

Baltrusaitis, J. *Anamorphic Art.* Tr. W. J. Strachan. New York, 1976.

Bange, E. F. "Zur Datierung von Peter Flötners Plakettenwerk." *Archiv für Medaillen- und Plaketten-Kunde* 3 (1921–1922): 45–52.

——. *Die Deutschen Bronzestatuetten des 16. Jahrhunderts.* Berlin, 1949.

——. "Die Handzeichnungen Peter Flötners." *JPKS* 57 (1936): 169–192.

——. *Die Kleinplastik der deutschen Renaissance in Holz und Stein.* Leipzig, 1928.

——. *Peter Flötner.* Leipzig, 1926.

Barock in Nürnberg, 1600–1750. Exh. cat. Nuremberg: Germanisches Nationalmuseum, 1962.

Bartsch, A. *The Illustrated Bartsch.* Gen. ed. W. L. Strauss. 1ff. vols. New York, 1978–.

——. *Le Peintre-Graveur.* 21 vols. Vienna, 1803–1870.

Bauer, H., G. Hirschmann, and G. Stolz, eds. *500 Jahre Hallenchor St. Lorenz zu Nürnberg, 1477–1977.* Nuremberg, 1977.

Baxandall, M. *The Limewood Sculptors of Renaissance Germany.* New Haven, 1980.

Beck, H., and B. Decker, eds. *Dürer's Verwandlung in der Skulptur zwischen Renaissance und Barock.* Exh. cat. Frankfurt: Liebieghaus Museum alter Plastik, 1981.

Becker, C. *Jobst Amman, Zeichner und Formschneider, Kupferätzer und Stecher.* Leipzig, 1854; reprinted: Nieuwkoop, 1961.

Beenken, H. "Zeichnungen aus der Nürnberger Frühzeit Hans Baldungs." *Jahrbuch für Kunstwissenschaft* 5 (1928): 169–175.

Bellm, R. *Der Schatzbehalter—Ein Andachts- und Erbauungsbuch aus dem Jahre 1491.* 2 vols. Wiesbaden, 1962.

——. *Wolgemuts Skizzenbuch—im Berliner Kupferstichkabinett.* Strassburg, 1959.

Benzing, J. "Humanismus in Nürnberg, 1500–1540. Eine Liste der Druckschriften." In *Albrecht Dürers Umwelt,* ed. Hirschmann and Schnelbögl, pp. 255–299.

Berlin: Der Mensch um 1500: see *Der Mensch um 1500.*

Bernhardt, M. "Die Porträtzeichnungen des Hans Schwarz." *MJBK* 11 (1934): 65–95.

Betz, G. "Der Nürnberger Maler Michael Wolgemut und seine Werkstatt." Dissertation, Freiburg-i. B., 1955.

Bialostocki, J. *The Art of the Renaissance in Eastern Europe.* Ithaca, N.Y., 1976.

Bibel und Gesangbuch in Zeitalter der Reformation, 1517–1967. Exh. cat. Nuremberg: Germanisches Nationalmuseum, 1967.

Bock, E. "The Engravings of Ludwig Krug of Nuremberg." *Print Collector's Quarterly* 20 (1933): 87–115.

——. *Staatliche Museen zu Berlin, Die Zeichnungen alter Meister im Kupferstichkabinett: Die deutschen Meister.* 2 vols. Berlin, 1929.

——. *Die Zeichnungen in der Universitätsbibliothek Erlangen.* 2 vols. Frankfurt, 1929.

Boeheim, W. "Nürnberger Waffenschmiede und ihre Werke in den Kaiserlichen und in anderen Sammlungen." *JKSAK* 16 (1895): 364–399.

Böllinger, K. *Das Toplerhaus in Nürnberg.* Berlin, 1916.

Borchardt, F. L. *German Antiquity in Renaissance Myth.* Baltimore, 1971.

Boston: Dürer: see *Albrecht Dürer: Master Printmaker.*

Bowron, E. P. *Renaissance Bronzes in the Walters Art Gallery.* Baltimore, 1978.

Brady, T. A., Jr. "The Social Place of a German Renaissance Artist: Hans Baldung Grien (1484/85–1545) at Strasbourg." *Central European History* 8 (1975): 295–315.

Bräutigam, G. "Nürnberg als Kaiserstadt." In *Kaiser Karl IV.—Staatsmann und Mäzen*, ed. F. Seibt, pp. 339–343. Munich, 1978.

Bruck, R. *Friedrich der Weise als Förderer der Kunst.* Strassburg, 1903.

Buchner, E. "Der junge Schäufelein als Maler und Zeichner." In *Festschrift für Max J. Friedländer zum 60. Geburtstage*, pp. 46–76. Leipzig, 1927.

Buck, A. "Enea Silvio Piccolomini und Nürnberg." In *Albrecht Dürers Umwelt*, ed. Hirschmann and Schnelbögl, pp. 20–28.

Busch, R. von. *Studien zu deutschen Antikensammlungen des 16. Jahrhunderts.* Tübingen, 1973.

Bussmann, G. *Manierismus im Spätwerk Hans Baldung Grien: Die Gemälde der zweiten Strassburger Zeit.* Heidelberg, 1966.

Byrne, J. S. *Renaissance Ornament Prints and Drawings.* New York: Metropolitan Museum of Art, 1981.

Caesar, E. "Sebald Schreyer, ein Lebensbild aus dem vorreformatorischen Nürnberg." *MVGN* 56 (1969): 1–213.

Charles-Quint et son Temps. Exh. cat. Ghent: Musée des Beaux-Arts, 1955.

Chmelarz, E. "Die Ehrenpforte des Kaisers Maximilian I." *JKSAK* 4 (1886): 289–319.

Christensen, C. C. *Art and the Reformation in Germany.* Athens, Ohio, 1979

———. "Iconoclasm and Preservation of Ecclesiastical Art in Reformation Nürnberg." *Archiv für Reformationsgeschichte* 61 (1970): 205–221.

———. "The Nuernberg City Council as a Patron of the Fine Arts, 1500–1550." Dissertation, Ohio State University, 1965.

Conway, W. M., ed. and tr. *The Writings of Albrecht Dürer.* New York, 1958.

De Coo, J. *Museum Mayer van den Bergh. Catalogus 2—Beeldhouwkunst, Plaketten, Antiek.* Antwerp, 1969.

Demonts, L. *Musée du Louvre—Inventaires général des Dessins des Écoles du Nord—Écoles Allemande et Suisse.* 2 vols. Paris, 1938.

Derschau, H. A. von. *Holzschnitte alter Meister gedruckt von den Originalstöcken der Sammlung Derschau im Besitz des Staatliche Kupferstichkabinetts zu Berlin.* Intro. M. J. Friedländer. Leipzig, 1922.

Dettenthaler, J. "Hans Springinklee als Maler." *MVGN* 63 (1976): 145–182.

Dodgson, E. *Catalogue of Early German and Flemish Woodcuts Preserved in the Department of Prints and Drawings in the British Museum.* 2 vols. London, 1903, 1911.

———. "Rare Woodcuts in the Ashmolean Museum—IV." *Burlington Magazine* 66 (1935): 89–93.

Doppelmayr, J. G. *Historische Nachricht von den Nürnbergischen Mathematicis und Künstlern.* Nuremberg, 1730.

Dotzauer, D. von. "Das Zeughaus der Reichsstadt Nürnberg." *MVGN* 16 (1904): 151–178.

Douglass, E. J. D. *Justification in Late Medieval Preaching: A Study of John Geiler of Kaisersberg.* Leiden, 1966.

Eckert, W. P., and C. von Imhoff. *Willibald Pirckheimer. Dürers Freund im Spiegel seines Lebens, seiner Werke und seiner Umwelt.* Cologne, 1971.

Egg, E. *Die Hofkirche in Innsbruck.* Innsbruck, 1974.

Erlanger, H. J. "The Medallic Portraits of Albrecht Dürer." *Museum Notes* (American Numismatic Society) 10 (1962): 145–172.

Falke, O. von. "Die Neugotik im deutschen Kunstgewerbe der Spätrenaissance." *JPKS* 40 (1919): 75–92.

Farmer, J. D. *The Virtuoso Craftsman: Northern European Design in the Sixteenth Century.* Exh. cat. Worcester: Worcester Art Museum, 1969.

Field, R. *Fifteenth Century Woodcuts and Metalcuts from the National Gallery of Art.* Washington, 1965.

Fillitz, H. *Die Insignien und Kleinodien des Heiligen Römischen Reiches.* Vienna, 1954.

Franz, H. G., intro. *Christoph Jamnitzer, Neuw Grottessken Buch. Nachdruck der Ausgabe Nürnberg 1610.* Graz, 1966.

———. *Niederländische Landschaftsmalerei im Zeitalter des Manierismus.* 2 vols. Graz, 1969.

Frenzel, G. "Entwurf und Ausführung in der Nürnberger Glasmalerei der Dürerzeit." *ZfKW* 15 (1961): 31–59.

Frenzel, U. "Michael Wolgemuts Tätigkeit für die Nürnberger Glasmalerei. Dargestellt an der Bildnisscheibe des Dr. Lorenz Tucher von 1485." *AGNM* (1970): 27–46.

Gabhart, A. *Treasures & Rarities—Renaissance, Mannerist, and Baroque.* Baltimore: Walters Art Gallery, 1971.

Ganz, P. *Die Basler Glasmaler der Spätrenaissance und Barockzeit.* Basel, 1960.

———. "Die Entstehung des Amerbach'schen Kunstkabinets und die Amerbach'schen Inventare." *Berichte, Öffentliche Sammlungen, Basel* 59 (1907): 1–68.

———. *The Paintings of Hans Holbein.* London, 1950.

Geisberg, M. *The German Single-Leaf Woodcut: 1500–1550.* Rev. and ed. W. L. Strauss. 4 vols. New York, 1974.

Geissler, H., ed. *Zeichnung in Deutschland: Deutsche Zeichner, 1540–1640.* Exh. cat. 2 vols. Stuttgart: Staatsgalerie, 1979.

Geldner, F. *Die Deutschen Inkunabeldrucker.* 2 vols. Stuttgart, 1968, 1970.

Germanisches Nationalmuseum Nürnberg: Führer durch die Sammlungen. 2d ed. Munich, 1980.

Glück, G. *Die Kunst der Renaissance in Deutschland, den Niederlanden, Frankreich, etc.* 2d ed. Berlin, 1928.

Gmelin, H. G. "Georg Pencz als Maler." *MJBK* 17 (1966): 49–126.

Goldberg, G. "Zur Ausprägung der Dürer-Renaissance in München." *MJBK* 31 (1980): 129–175.

Goldmann, K. *Geschichte der Stadtbibliothek Nürnberg.* Nuremberg, 1957.

Greenfield, K. R. "Sumptuary Law in Nürnberg: A Study in Paternal Government." *Johns Hopkins University—Studies in Historical and Political Science* 36 (1918): 7–139.

Grimm, H. J. *Lazarus Spengler, a Lay Leader of the Reformation.* Columbus, 1978.

Grote, L. *Die Romantische Entdeckung Nürnbergs.* Munich, 1967.

———. *Die Tucher: Bildnis einer Patrizierfamilie.* Munich, 1961.

———. "Die 'Vorder-Stube' des Sebald Schreyer—Ein Beitrag zur Rezeption der Renaissance in Nürnberg." *AGNM* (1954–1959): 43–67.

Grotemeyer, P. *'Da ich het die gestalt': Deutsche Bildnismedaillen des 16. Jahrhunderts.* Munich, 1957.

Habich, G. *Die Deutschen Schaumünzen des XVI. Jahrhunderts.* 5 vols. Munich, 1929–1935.

Hackenbroch, Y. *Renaissance Jewellery.* Munich, 1979.

Haebler, H. C. von. *Das Bild in der evangelischen Kirche.* Berlin, 1957.

Haller von Hallerstein, H., and E. Eichhorn. *Das Pilgrimspital zum Heiligen Kreuz vor Nürnberg. Geschichte und Kunstdenkmäler.* Nuremberg, 1969.

Halm, P. M., and R. Berliner. *Das Hallesche Heiltum: Man. Aschaffenb. 14.* Berlin, 1931.

Hampe, T. "Kunstfreunde im alten Nürnberg und ihre Sammlungen." *MVGN* 16 (1904): 57–124.

———. *Nürnberger Ratsverlässe über Kunst und Künstler im Zeitalter der Spätgotik und Renaissance (1449), 1474–1618 (1633).* 2 vols. Vienna, 1904.

Händler, G. *Fürstliche Mäzene und Sammler in Deutschland von 1500–1620.* Strassburg, 1933.

Harbison, C. *Symbols in Transformation: Iconographic Themes at the Time of the Reformation.* Exh. cat. Princeton: Art Museum, 1969.

Hartmann, G. *Reichserzkanzler, Kurfürst und Kardinal Albrecht II. von Brandenburg, der Führer deutscher Renaissancekunst.* Nuremberg, 1937.

Hartt, F. *Giulio Romano.* 2 vols. New Haven, 1958.

Hase, O. *Die Koberger.* Leipzig, 1885.

Häussler, H. *Brunnen, Denkmale und Freiplastiken in Nürnberg.* Nuremberg, 1977.

Hayward, J. F. *Virtuoso Goldsmiths.* London, 1976.

Held, J., ed. *Dürer through Other Eyes: His Graphic Work Mirrored in Copies and Forgeries of Three Centuries.* Exh. cat. Williamstown, Mass.: Clark Art Institute, 1975.

Hempel, E. *Baroque Art and Architecture in Central Europe.* Baltimore, 1965.

Herkommer, H. "Heilsgeschichtliches Programm und Tugendlehre—Ein Beitrag zur Kultur- und Geistesgeschichte der Stadt Nürnberg am Beispiel des Schönen Brunnens und des Tugendbrunnens." *MVGN* 63 (1976): 192–216.

Hildebrand, J., and C. Theuerkauff. *Die Brandenburgisch-Preussische Kunstkammer: Eine Auswahl aus den alten Beständen.* Exh. cat. Berlin: Staatliche Museen, 1981.

Hill, G. F., and G. Pollard. *Renaissance Medals from the Samuel H. Kress Collection at the National Gallery of Art.* London, 1967.

Hirschmann, G., and F. Schnelbögl, eds. *Albrecht Dürers Umwelt—Festschrift zum 500. Geburtstag Albrecht Dürers am 21. Mai 1971.* Nuremberg, 1971.

Hitchcock, H.-R. *German Renaissance Architecture.* Princeton, 1981.

Höhn, H. *Nürnberger Renaissanceplastik.* Nuremberg, 1924.

Hoffmann, K. "Typologie Exemplarik und reformatorische Bildsatire." In *Kontinuität und Umbruch,* ed. J. Nolte, pp. 189–210. Stuttgart, 1978.

Hofmann, J. E. "Dürers Verhältnis zur Mathematik." In *Albrecht Dürers Umwelt,* ed. Hirschmann and Schnelbögl, pp. 132–151.

Hollstein, F. W. H., ed. *German Engravings, Etchings, and Woodcuts, ca. 1400–1700.* 1ff. vols. Amsterdam, 1954–.

Holsberg, N. "Willibald Pirckheimer als Wegbereiter der griechischen Studien in Deutschland." *MVGN* 67 (1980): 60–78.

Homann, H. *Studien zur Emblematik des 16. Jahrhunderts.* Utrecht, 1971.

I. Höss. "Das religiösgeistige Leben in Nürnberg am Ende des 15. und am Ausgang des 16. Jahrhunderts." In *Miscellanea Historiae Ecclesiasticae,* pp. 17–36. Bibliothèque de la Revue d'Histoire Ecclésiastique, fasc. 38. Louvain, 1961.

———. "Das religiöse Leben vor der Reformation." In *Nürnberg,* ed. Pfeiffer, pp. 137–146.

Husband, T., and G. Gilmore-House. *The Wild Man: Medieval Myth and Symbolism.* Exh. cat. New York: Metropolitan Museum of Art, 1980.

Huth, H. *Künstler und Werkstatt der Spätgotik.* Augsburg, 1923; reprinted Darmstadt, 1967.

Hütt, W. *Deutsche Malerei und Graphik der frühbürgerlichen Revolution.* Leipzig, 1973.

Imhoff, C. Frhr. von. "Die Imhoff- Handelsherren und Kunstliebhaber." *MVGN* 62 (1975): 1–42.

Irmscher, G. "Motiventlehnungen in neuentdeckten und bekannten Handzeichnungen Christoph Jamnitzers." *AGNM* (1981): 84–106.

Jaffé, M. "Rubens as Collector of Drawings." *Master Drawings* 2 (1964): 383–397; 3 (1965): 21–35.

Jahn, J. *Deutsche Renaissance.* Leipzig, 1969.

———. *Lucas Cranach d. Ä., 1472–1553. Das gesamte graphische Werk.* Munich, 1972.

Janeck, A. *Zeichen am Himmel: Flugblätter des 16. Jahrhunderts.* Exh. cat. Nuremberg: Germanisches Nationalmuseum, 1982.

Janssen, J. *History of the German People at the Close of the Middle Ages.* Tr. M. Mitchell and A. Christie. 16 vols. London, 1905–1925.

Josephi, W. *Die Werke plastischer Kunst.* Nuremberg: Germanisches Nationalmuseum, 1910.

Kaiser Maximilian I. (1459–1519) und die Reichsstadt Nürnberg. Exh. cat. Nuremberg: Germanisches Nationalmuseum, 1959.

Kapr, A., intro. *Johann Neudörffer d. Ä., der grosse Schreibmeister der deutschen Renaissance.* Leipzig, 1956.

Kauffmann, G. *Die Kunst des 16. Jahrhunderts.* Berlin, 1970.

Kauffmann, H. "Dürer in der Kunst und im Kunsturteil um 1600." *AGNM* (1940–1953): 18–60.

Kaufmann, T. D. *Drawings from the Holy Roman Empire, 1540–1680: A Selection from North American Collections.* Exh. cat. Princeton: Art Museum, 1982.

———. *Variations on the Imperial Theme in the Age of Maximilian II and Rudolf II.* New York, 1978.

Kircher, A. *Deutsche Kaiser in Nürnberg: Eine Studie zur Geschichte des öffentlichen Lebens der Reichsstadt Nürnberg von 1500–1612.* Nuremberg, 1955.

Klauner, F. "Gedenken zu Dürers Allerheiligenbildern." *JKSW* 75 (1979): 57–92.

Knappe, K.-A. *Albrecht Dürer und das Bamberger Fenster in St. Sebald in Nürnberg.* Nuremberg, 1961.

———. "Das Löffelholz-Fenster in St. Lorenz in Nürnberg und Hans Baldung." *ZfKW* 12 (1958): 163–178.

Koch, C., et al. *Hans Baldung Grien.* Exh. cat. Karlsruhe: Staatliche Kunsthalle, 1959.

Koepplin, D., and T. Falk. *Lukas Cranach.* Exh. cat. 2 vols. Basel: Kunstmuseum, 1974, 1976.

Kohlhaussen, H. *Nürnberger Goldschmiedekunst des Mittelalters und der Dürerzeit, 1240 bis 1540.* Berlin, 1968.

Kris, E. "Georg Pencz als Deckenmaler." *Mitteilungen der Gesellschaft für vervielfältigende Kunst* 46 (1923): 45–53.

———. "Der Stil 'Rustique,' die Verwandlung des Naturabgusses bei Wenzel Jamnitzer und Bernard Palissy." *JKSW* 1 (1926): 137–208.

———, and O. von Falke. "Beiträge zu den Werken Christoph und Hans Jamnitzer." *JPKS* 47 (1926): 186–207.

Kurras, L., and F. Machilek. *Caritas Pirckheimer, 1467–1532.* Exh. cat. Nuremberg: Kaiserburg; Munich, 1982.

Kurzwelly, A. *Forschungen zu Georg Pencz.* Leipzig, 1895.

Kuspit, D. "Dürer and the Lutheran Image." *Art in America* 63 (1975): 56–61.

Landau, D. *Catalogo completo dell' opera grafica di Georg Pencz.* Milan, 1978.

Lange, K. *Peter Flötner, ein Bahnbrecher der deutschen Renaissance auf Grund neuer Entdeckungen.* Berlin, 1897.

Legner, A., et al., eds. *Die Parler und der schöne Stil, 1350–1400.* Exh. cat. 5 vols. Cologne: Kunsthalle, 1978–1980.

Lehrs, M. *Late Gothic Engravings of Germany & the Netherlands.* New York, 1969.

Levenson, J., K. Oberhuber, and J. Sheehan. *Early Italian Engravings from the National Gallery of Art.* Washington, 1973.

Lieb, N. *Die Fugger und die Kunst.* 2 vols. Munich, 1952, 1958.

Löcher, K. "Dürers Kaiserbilder—Nürnberg als Hüterin der Reichsinsignien." In *Das Schatzhaus der deutschen Geschichte,* ed. R. Pörtner, pp. 305–330. Düsseldorf, 1982.

———. "Studien zur oberdeutschen Bildnismalerei des 16. Jahrhunderts." *Jahrbuch der Staatlichen Kunstsammlungen in Baden-Württemberg* 4 (1967): 31–84.

Lutze, E. "Hans Behaim der Ältere." *ZDVK* 5 (1938): 181–203.

———. *Veit Stoss.* 3d ed. Munich, 1968.

Machilek, F. "Klosterhumanismus in Nürnberg um 1500." *MVGN* 64 (1977): 10–45.

Mahn, H. H. *Lorenz und Georg Strauch.* Reutlingen, 1927.

Marrow, J., and A. Shestack, eds. *Hans Baldung Grien—Prints & Drawings.* Exh. cat. New Haven: Yale University Art Gallery, 1981.

Maximilian I. 1459–1959. Exh. cat. Vienna: Österreichische Nationalbibliothek, 1959.

Meder, J. *Dürer-Katalog.* Vienna, 1932.

Meister um Albrecht Dürer. Ed. P. Strieder. Exh. cat. Nuremberg: Germanisches Nationalmuseum, 1961.

Melanchthon und Nürnberg. Exh. cat. Nuremberg: Stadtbibliothek, 1960.

Mende, M. *Das Alte Nürnberger Rathaus.* Exh. cat. Vol. 1. Nuremberg: Stadtgeschichtliche Museen, 1979. [Vol. 2 forthcoming.]

———. *Dürer-Bibliographie.* Wiesbaden, 1971.

Der Mensch um 1500: Werke aus Kirchen und Kunstkammern. Ed. H. Gagel. Exh. cat. Berlin: Staatliche Museen, 1977.

Middeldorf, U., and O. Goetz. *Medals and Plaquettes from the Sigmund Morgenroth Collection.* Chicago: Art Institute of Chicago, 1944.

Mielke, H. *Manierismus in Holland um 1600.* Exh. cat. Berlin: Kupferstichkabinett, 1979.

Moeller, B. "Piety in Germany around 1500." In *The Reformation in Medieval Perspective,* ed. S. Ozment, pp. 50–75. Chicago, 1971.

Mongan, A., and P. J. Sachs. *Drawings in the Fogg Museum of Art.* Cambridge, Mass., 1946.

Müller, A. "Zensurpolitik der Reichsstadt Nürnberg. Von der Einführung der Buchdruckkunst bis zum Ende der Reichsstadtzeit." *MVGN* 49 (1959): 66–169.

Müller, T. *Die Bildwerke in Holz, Ton und Stein, Bayerisches Nationalmuseum München.* Munich, 1959.

———. *Sculpture in the Netherlands, Germany, France, and Spain, 1400 to 1500.* Baltimore, 1966.

Mulzer, E. *Der Wiederaufbau der Altstadt von Nürnberg, 1945 bis 1970.* Erlangen, 1972.

Mummenhoff, E. *Das Rathaus in Nürnberg.* Nuremberg, 1891.

———. "Studien zur Geschichte und Topographie des Nürnberger Marktplatzes und seiner Umgebung." In *Aufsätze und Vorträge zur Nürnberger Ortsgeschichte,* pp. 194–279. Nuremberg, 1931.

Murr, C. T. de. *Description du Cabinet de Monsieur Paul de Praun à Nuremberg.* Nuremberg, 1797.

———. *Journal zur Kunstgeschichte.* Nuremberg, 1776.

Neudörfer, Johann. *Des Johann Neudörfer Nachrichten von Künstlern und Werkleuten daselbst aus dem Jahre 1547.* Ed. G. W. K. Lochner. Vienna, 1875.

Norris, A. S., and I. Weber. *Medals and Plaquettes from the Molinari Collection at Bowdoin College.* Brunswick, Maine, 1976.

Nuremberg: Dürer (1971): see *Albrecht Dürer, 1471–1971.*

Nuremberg: Meister um Dürer: see *Meister um Albrecht Dürer.*

Nuremberg: Vorbild Dürer: see *Vorbild Dürer.*

Nuremberg: Die Welt des Hans Sachs: see *Die Welt des Hans Sachs.*

Oberhuber, K., ed. *Die Kunst der Graphik IV: Zwischen Renaissance und Barock—Das Zeitalter von Bruegel und Bellange.* Exh. cat. Vienna: Graphische Sammlung Albertina, 1967.

O'Dell-Franke, I. *Kupferstiche und Radierungen aus der Werkstatt des Virgil Solis.* Wiesbaden, 1977.

Oettinger, K. "Zu Dürers Beginn." *ZDVK* 8 (1954): 153–168.

———, and K.-A. Knappe. *Hans Baldung Grien und Albrecht Dürer in Nürnberg.* Nuremberg, 1963.

Oldenbourg, M. C. *Die Buchholzschnitte des Hans Schäufelein.* 2 vols. Baden-Baden, 1964.

———. *Hortulus Animae (1494)–1523: Bibliographie und Illustration.* Hamburg, 1973.

Olds, C., E. Verheyen, and W. Tresidder. *Dürer's Cities: Nuremberg and Venice.* Exh. cat. Ann Arbor: University of Michigan Museum of Art, 1971.

Olds, C., R. G. Williams, and W. R. Levin. *Images of Love and Death in Late Medieval and Renaissance Art.* Exh. cat. Ann Arbor: University of Michigan Museum of Art, 1975.

Osten, G. von der. "Über Peter Vischers Törichten Bauern und den Beginn der 'Renaissance' in Nürnberg." *AGNM* (1963): 71–83.

———, and H. Vey. *Painting and Sculpture in Germany and the Netherlands, 1500 to 1600.* Baltimore, 1969.

Panofsky, E. "Albrecht Dürer and Classical Antiquity." In *Meaning in the Visual Arts,* pp. 236–294. Garden City, N.Y., 1955.

———. *The Life and Art of Albrecht Dürer.* 4th ed. Princeton, 1955.

Pauli, G. *Barthel Beham, ein kritisches Verzeichnis seiner Kupferstiche.* Strassburg, 1911.

———. *Hans Sebald Beham, ein kritisches Verzeichniss seiner Kupferstiche, Radierungen, und Holzschnitte.* Strassburg, 1901.

Pechstein, K. "Allerlei Visierungen und Abriss Wegen der Fleischbrücken 1595." *AGNM* (1975): 72–89.

———. "Der Bildschnitzer Hans Peisser." *AGNM* (1973): 84–106.

———. *Bronzen und Plaketten vom ausgehenden 15. Jahrhundert bis zur Mitte des 17. Jahrhunderts—Kataloge des Kunstgewerbemuseums Berlin III.* Berlin, 1968.

———. "Christoph Jamnitzer (+ 1618)." *Fränkische Lebensbilder* 10 (1982): 179–192.

———. *Goldschmiedewerke der Renaissance—Kataloge des Kunstgewerbemuseums Berlin V.* Berlin, 1971.

———. "Jamnitzer-Studien." *Jahrbuch der Berliner Museen* 8 (1966): 237–283.

———. "Der Merkelsche Tafelaufsatz von Wenzel Jamnitzer." *MVGN* 61 (1974): 90–121.

———. "Neuentdeckte Arbeiten von Hans Jamnitzer." *Berliner Museen, Berichte* N.F. 20 (1970): 61–66.

———. "Von Trinkgeräten und Trinksitten: Von der Kindstaufe zum Kaufvertrag—Pokale als Protokolle des Ereignisses." In *Das Schatzhaus der deutschen Geschichte,* ed. R. Pörtner, pp. 385–411. Düsseldorf, 1982.

———. "The 'Welcome' Cup—Renaissance Drinking Vessels by Nuremberg Goldsmiths." *Connoisseur* 199 (November 1978): 180–187.

———. "Wenzel Jamnitzers Silberglocken mit Naturabgüssen." *AGNM* (1967): 36–43.

———. "Zeichnungen von Wenzel Jamnitzer." *AGNM* (1970): 81–95.

———. "Zu den Altarskulpturen und Kunstkammerstücken von Hans Peisser." *AGNM* (1974): 38–74.

———. "Zum Werk von Christoph Jamnitzer." *AGNM* (1977): 95–104.

———, et al. *Paul Wolfgang Merkel und die Merkelsche Familienstiftung.* Exh. cat. Nuremberg: Germanisches Nationalmuseum, 1979.

Peltzer, R. A., ed. *Joachim von Sandrarts Academie der Bau-, Bild- und Mahlerey-Künste von 1675—Leben der berühmten Maler, Bildhauer und Baumeister.* Munich, 1925.

———. "Johann Gregor van der Schardt (Jan de Zar) aus Nymwegen, ein Bildhauer der Spättrenaissance." *MJBK* 10 (1916–1918): 198–216.

———. "Nicholas Neufchâtel und seine Nürnberger Bildnisse." *MJBK* N.F. 3 (1926): 187–231.

Peter Flötner und die Renaissance in Deutschland. Exh. cat. Nuremberg: Germanisches Nationalmuseum, 1946.

Peters, J. S. "Early Drawings by Augustin Hirschvogel, 1503–1553." *Master Drawings* 17 (1979): 359–392.

———. "Frühe Glasgemälde von Augustin Hirschvogel." *AGNM* (1980): 79–92.

Pfeiffer, E. "Der 'Augustiner-Hochaltar' und vier weitere Altäre des ausgehenden 15. Jahrhunderts." *MVGN* 52 (1963–1964): 305–398.

———. "Dürers Masseinheiten und Werkzahlen in der Unterweisung der Messung." *MVGN* 64 (1977): 111–164.

Pfeiffer, G., ed. *Nürnberg, Geschichte einer europäischen Stadt.* Munich, 1971.

———, and W. Schwemmer. *Geschichte Nürnbergs in Bilddokumenten.* 3d ed. Munich, 1977.

Pilz, K. "Hans Hoffmann—Ein Nürnberger Dürer-Nachahmer aus der 2. Hälfte des 16. Jahrhunderts." *MVGN* 51 (1962): 236–272.

———. "Jost Amman, 1539–1591." *MVGN* 37 (1940): 201–252.

———. "Nürnberg und die Niederlande." *MVGN* 43 (1952): 1–153.

———. *Das Sebaldusgrabmal im Ostchor der St.-Sebaldus-Kirche in Nürnberg—Ein Messinggus aus der Giesshüte der Vischer.* Nuremberg, 1970.

Pope-Hennessy, J. *The Portrait in the Renaissance.* Washington, 1966.

———. *Renaissance Bronzes from the Samuel H. Kress Collection.* London, 1965.

Popham, A. E., and K. M. Fenwick. *European Drawings in the Collection of the National Gallery of Canada.* Ottawa, 1965.

Pörtner, R. "Der 'Erdapfel,' der Wie ein Augapfel gehütet wird." In *Das Schatzhaus der deutschen Geschichte,* ed. R. Pörtner, pp. 277–304. Düsseldorf, 1982.

Praz, M. *Studies in Seventeenth-Century Imagery.* 2d ed. Rome, 1964.

Prechtl, M. M. *Jamnitzer, Lencker, Stoer. Drei Nürnberger Konstruktivisten des 16. Jahrhundert.* Exh. cat. Nuremberg: Stadtgeschichtliche Museen, 1969.

Pröll, F. X. *Willibald Pirckheimer, 1470–1970—eine Dokumentation in der Stadtbibliothek Nürnberg.* Exh. cat. Nuremberg: Stadtbibliothek, 1970.

Radcliffe, A. *European Bronze Statuettes.* London, 1966.

Rasmussen, J. *Die Nürnberger Altarbaukunst der Dürerzeit.* Hamburg, 1974.

Rauch, C. *Die Trauts.* Strassburg, 1907.

Réau, L. *Iconographie de l'Art Chrétien.* 6 vols. Paris, 1955–1959.

Reformation in Nürnberg: Umbruch und Bewahrung. Exh. cat. Nuremberg: Germanisches Nationalmuseum, 1979.

Reitzenstein, A. Frhr. von. "Die Nürnberger Plattner." In *Beiträge zur Wirtschaftsgeschichte Nürnbergs,* 2 vols., II: pp. 700–725. Nuremberg, 1967.

Rifkin, B. A., ed. *The Book of Trades (Ständebuch) Jost Amman and Hans Sachs.* New York: Dover Publications, 1973.

Ringbom, S. *Icon to Narrative: The Rise of the Dramatic Close-up in Fifteenth-Century Devotional Painting.* Abo, 1965.

Roach, W. "William Smith: *A Description of the Cittie of Noremberg* (Beschreibung der Reichsstadt Nürnberg) 1594." Foreword by K. Goldmann. *MVGN* 48 (1958): 194–245.

Robinson, W. W. "'This Passion for Prints': Collecting and Connoisseurship in Northern Europe during the Seventeenth Century." In *Printmaking in the Age of Rembrandt,* by C. S. Ackley, pp. xxvii–xlviii. Boston, 1981.

Rosenberg, M. *Der Goldschmiede Merkzeichen.* 4 vols. Frankfurt a. M., 1925.

———. *Jamnitzer, Alle erhaltenen Goldschmiedearbeiten. Verlorene Werke. Handzeichnungen.* Frankfurt a. M., 1920.

Rosenthal-Metzger, J. "Das Augustinerkloster in Nürnberg." *MVGN* 30 (1931): 1–106.

Röttinger, H. *Die Bilderbogen des Hans Sachs.* Strassburg, 1927.

———. *Erhard Schön und Niklas Stör, der Pseudo-Schön.* Strassburg, 1925.

———. *Die Holzschnitte Barthel Behams.* Strassburg, 1921.

———. *Die Holzschnitte des Georg Pencz.* Leipzig, 1914.

———. *Die Holzschnitte zur Architektur und zum Vitruvius Teutsch des Walther Rivius.* Strassburg, 1914.

———. *Peter Flettners Holzschnitte.* Strassburg, 1916.

Rucker, E. *Die Schedelsche Weltchronik—Das grösste Buchunternehmen der Dürer-Zeit.* Munich, 1973.

Rupprich, H., ed. *Dürer: schriftlicher Nachlass.* 3 vols. Berlin, 1956–1969.

———. "Dürer und Pirckheimer, Geschichte einer Freundschaft." In *Albrecht Dürers Umwelt,* ed. Hirschmann and Schnelbögl, pp. 78–100.

———. *Die Frühzeit des Humanismus und der Renaissance in Deutschland.* Leipzig, 1938.

Schaffer, R. *Das Pellerhaus in Nürnberg.* Nuremberg, 1931.

———. "Die Siegel und Wappen der Reichsstadt Nürnberg." *Zeitschrift für bayerische Landesgeschichte* 10 (1937): 157–203.

Schaper, C. "Studien zur Geschichte der Baumeisterfamilie Behaim." *MVGN* 48 (1958): 125–182.

Schéle, S. *Cornelis Bos: A Study of the Origins of the Netherland Grotesque.* Stockholm, 1965.

Schestag, F. "Kaiser Maximilian I. Triumph." *JKSAK* 1 (1883): 154–181.

Schiller, G. *Iconography of Christian Art.* Tr. J. Seligman. 2 vols. Greenwich, Conn., 1966, 1972.

Schilling, E. *Nürnberger Handzeichnungen des XV. und XVI. Jahrhunderts.* Freiburg, 1929.

———. "Zeichnungen von Ludwig Krug." *AGNM* (1932–1933): 109–118.

Schlemmer, K. *Gottesdienst und Frömmigkeit in der Reichsstadt Nürnberg am Vorabend der Reformation.* Würzburg, 1980.

Schlosser, J. von. "Aus der Bildnerwerkstatt der Renaissance." *JKSAK* 31 (1913–1914): 67–136.

———. *La Letteratura artistica.* 3d Italian ed. Florence, 1977.

Schmidt, U. P. *Stephan Fridolin. Ein Franziskanerprediger des ausgehenden Mittelalters.* Munich, 1911.

Schmitt, A. *Hanns Lautensack.* Nuremberg, 1957.

Schmitz, H. *Die Glasgemälde des königlichen Kunstgewerbemuseums in Berlin.* 2 vols. Berlin, 1913.

Schnelbögl, F. *Dokumente zur Nürnberger Kartographie—mit Katalog.* Nuremberg, 1966.

———. "Life and Work of the Nuremberg Cartographer Erhard Etzlaub (+ 1532)." *Imago Mundi—a Review of Early Cartography* 20 (1966): 11–26.

———. "Das Nürnberg Albrecht Dürers." In *Albrecht Dürers Umwelt,* ed. Hirschmann and Schnelbögl, pp. 56–77.

Schnelbögl, J. "Die Reichskleinodien in Nürnberg. 1424–1523." *MVGN* 51 (1962): 78–159.

Schönberger, A. "Die 'Weltallschale' Kaiser Rudolfs II." In *Studien zur Geschichte der europäischen Plastik: Festschrift für Theodor Müller,* pp. 253–262. Munich, 1965.

Schramm, A. *Die Bilderschmuck der Frühdrucke.* Vols. 17 and 18. Leipzig, 1934, 1935.

Schultheiss, W. "Albrecht Dürers Beziehungen zum Recht." In *Albrecht Dürers Umwelt,* ed. Hirschmann and Schnelbögl, pp. 220–254.

———. "Das Hausbuch des Mendelschen Zwölfbrüderhauses zu Nürnberg von 1388/1425 bis 1549. Nürnberger Beiträge zur Geschichte der deutschen Technik." *MVGN* 54 (1966): 94–108.

———. "Der Nürnberger Architekt Hans Behaim d. Ä., seine Herkunft und Bautätigkeit bis 1491." *MVGN* 47 (1956): 426–443.

Schulz, F. T. "Die Nürnberger Fassadenmalerei—Das XVI. Jahrhundert." *Mitteilungen aus dem Germanischen Nationalmuseum Nürnberg* (1911): 106–140.

Schwarz, K. *Augustin Hirschvogel: Ein deutscher Meister der Renaissance.* 2 vols. Berlin, 1917.

Schwemmer, W. *Adam Kraft.* Nuremberg, 1958.

———. "Aus der Geschichte der Kunstsammlungen der Stadt Nürnberg." *MVGN* 40 (1949): 97–206.

———. *Das Bürgerhaus in Nürnberg.* Tübingen, 1972.

———. "Das Mäzenatentum der Nürnberger Patrizierfamilie Tucher vom 14.–18. Jahrhundert." *MVGN* 51 (1962): 18–59.

———, and H. Clauss. *Das Albrecht-Dürer-Haus in Nürnberg.* Nuremberg, 1959.

———, and W. Kriegbaum. *Nürnberg, historische Entwicklung einer deutschen Stadt in Bildern.* Nuremberg, 1960.

———, and M. Lagois. *Die Sebalduskirche zu Nürnberg.* Nuremberg, 1979.

Scribner, R. W. *For the Sake of Simple Folk: Popular Propaganda for the German Reformation.* Cambridge, 1981.

Seebass, G. "Dürers Stellung in der reformatorischen Bewegung." In *Albrecht Dürers Umwelt,* ed. Hirschmann and Schnelbögl, pp. 101–131.

Selig, H. *Die Kunst der Augsburger Goldschmiede, 1529–1868.* 3 vols. Munich, 1980.

Seznec, J. *The Survival of the Pagan Gods: The Mythological Tradition and Its Place in Renais-*

sance Humanism and Art. Tr. B. F. Sessions. Princeton, 1972.

Sheard, W. S. *Antiquity in the Renaissance.* Exh. cat. Northampton: Smith College Museum of Art, 1979.

Shestack, A. *The Complete Engravings of Martin Schöngauer.* New York, 1969.

——. "An Introduction to Hans Baldung Grien." In *Hans Baldung Grien,* ed. Marrow and Shestack, pp. 3–18.

——. *Master E. S.—Five Hundredth Anniversary Exhibition.* Exh. cat. Philadelphia: Philadelphia Museum of Art, 1967.

Shoemaker, I. H., and E. Broun. *The Engravings of Marcantonio Raimondi.* Exh. cat. Lawrence, Kansas: Spencer Museum of Art, 1981.

Spitz, L. *Conrad Celtis: The German Arch-Humanist.* Cambridge, Mass., 1957.

——. "The Course of German Humanism." In *Itinerarium Italicum,* ed. H. Oberman and T. Brady, Jr., pp. 371–436. Leiden, 1975.

——. *The Religious Renaissance of the German Humanists.* Cambridge, Mass., 1963.

The Splendors of Dresden: Five Centuries of Art Collecting. Exh. cat. New York: Metropolitan Museum of Art, 1978.

Springer, A. "Inventare der Imhoff'schen Kunstkammer zu Nürnberg." *Mitteilungen der kaiserl. königl. Central Commission* (Wien) 5 (1860): 352–357.

Sprusansky, S., ed. *Der Heilige Sebald, seine Kirche und seine Stadt.* Exh. cat. Nuremberg: Stadtmuseum, 1979.

Stadler, F. *Hans von Kulmbach.* Vienna, 1936.

——. *Michael Wolgemut und der nürnberger Holzschnitt im letzten Drittel des fünfzehnten Jahrhunderts.* Strassburg, 1913.

Stafski, H. *Der Jüngere Peter Vischer.* Nuremberg, 1962.

——. "Die Vischer-Werkstatt und ihre Probleme." *ZfK* 21 (1958): 1–26.

Stange, A. *Malerei der Donauschule.* 2d ed. Munich, 1971.

Stechow, W. *Northern Renaissance Art, 1400–1600—Sources and Documents.* Englewood Cliffs, N.J., 1966.

Steingräber, E. "Süddeutsche Goldemailplastik der Frührenaissance." In *Studien zur Geschichte für europäischen Plastik—Festschrift für Theodor Müller,* ed. K. Martin, pp. 223–233. Munich, 1965.

Stewart, A. G. "Early Woodcut Workshops." *Art Journal* 39 (1980): 189–194.

——. *Unequal Lovers.* New York, 1977.

Stirm, M. *Die Bilderfrage in der Reformation.* Gütersloh, 1977.

Strauss, G. *Nuremberg in the Sixteenth Century: City Politics and Life between Middle Ages and Modern Times.* Bloomington, 1976.

Strauss, W. L. *Albrecht Dürer: Woodcuts and Woodblocks.* New York, 1980.

——. *Chiaroscuro: The Clair-Obscur Woodcuts by the German and Netherlandish Masters of the XVIth and XVIIth Centuries.* London, 1973.

——. *The Complete Drawings of Albrecht Dürer.* 6 vols. New York, 1974.

——. *The German Single-Leaf Woodcut, 1550–1600.* 3 vols. New York, 1975.

——. *The Human Figure by Albrecht Dürer: The Complete Dresden Sketchbook.* New York, 1972.

——, ed. *The Painter's Manual.* New York, 1977

Strieder, P. *Albrecht Dürer: Paintings, Prints, Drawings.* Tr. N. M. Gordon and W. L. Strauss. New York, 1982.

——. "Antike Vorbilder für Dürers Kupferstich 'Das Meerwunder.'" *AGNM* (1971–1972): 42–47.

——. "Copies et interprétations du cuivre d'Albrecht Dürer *Adam et Eve.*" *Revue de l'Art* 21 (1973): 44–47.

——. "Noch einmal zu Albrecht Dürers Kaiserbildern." *AGNM* (1979): 111–115.

——. "Zur Entstehungsgeschichte von Dürers Ehrenpforte für Kaiser Maximilian." *AGNM* (1954–1959): 128–142.

——. "Zur Nürnberger Bildniskunst des 16. Jahrhunderts." *MJBK* 7 (1956): 120–137.

Suhle, A. *Die Deutsche Renaissance-Medaille.* Leipzig, 1950.

Sumberg, S. L. *The Nuremberg Schembart Carnival.* New York, 1941.

Talbot, C. W., ed. *Dürer in America: His Graphic Work.* Notes by G. F. Ravenel and J. A. Levenson. Exh. cat. Washington: National Gallery of Art, 1971.

——, and A. Shestack, eds. *Prints and Drawings of the Danube School.* Exh. cat. New Haven: Yale University Art Gallery, 1969.

Thieme, U., and F. Becker, eds. *Allgemeines Lexikon der bildenden Künstler von der Antike bis zur Gegenwart.* 37 vols. Leipzig, 1907–1950.

Thomas, B. "Nürnberger Platterkunst in Wien." *AGNM* (1963): 89–99.

Treue, W., et al. *Das Hausbuch der Mendelschen Zwölfbrüderstiftung zu Nürnberg. Deutsche Handwerkerbilder des 15. und 16. Jahrhunderts.* 2 vols. Munich, 1966.

Ubisch, E. von. *Virgil Solis und seine biblischen Illustrationen für den Holzschnitt.* Leipzig, 1889.

Veit, L. *Handel und Wandel mit aller Welt.* Munich, 1960.

——. "Die Imhoff. Handelsherren und Mäzene des ausgehenden Mittelalters und der beginnenden Neuzeit." In *Das Schatzhaus der deutschen Geschichte,* ed. R. Pörtner, pp. 503–531. Düsseldorf, 1982.

Viebig, J., et al. *Die Lorenzkirche in Nürnberg.* Königstein im Taunus, 1971.

Vienna: Maximilian I. 1459–1959: see *Maximilian I. 1459–1959.*

Vollmer, H. "Die Illustratoren des 'Beschlossen gart des rosenkranz mariae.' Ein Beitrag zur Kenntnis des Holzschnittes der Dürerschule." *Repertorium für Kunstwissenschaft* 31 (1908): 18–36, 144–158.

Vorbild Dürer: Kupferstiche und Holzschnitte Albrecht Dürers im Spiegel der europäischen Druckgraphik des 16. Jahrhunderts. Exh. cat. Nuremberg: Germanisches Nationalmuseum; Munich, 1978.

Vorstenportretten uit de eerste Helft van de 16de Eeuw: Houtsneden als Propaganda. Exh. cat. Amsterdam: Rijksprentenkabinett, 1972.

Voss, W. "Eine Himmelskarte vom Jahre 1503 mit den Wahrzeichen des Wiener Poetenkollegiums als Vorlage Albrecht Dürers." *JPKS* 64 (1943): 89–150.

Weber, I. *Deutsche, niederländische und französische Renaissanceplaketten.* Munich, 1975.

Weihrauch, H. R. *Die Bildwerke in Bronze und in anderen Metallen, Bayerisches Nationalmuseum, München.* Munich, 1956.

———. *Europäische Bronzestatuetten.* Braunschweig, 1967.

———. "Italienische Bronzen als Vorbilder deutscher Goldschmiedekunst." In *Studien zur Geschichte der europäischen Plastik—Festschrift für Theodor Müller*, ed. K. Martin, pp. 263–280. Munich, 1965.

Weinberger, M. *Nürnberger Malerei an der Wende zur Renaissance und die Anfänge der Dürerschule.* Strassburg, 1921.

Weiss, E. "Albrecht Dürer's geographische, astronomische und astrologische Tafeln." *JKSAK* 7 (1888): 207–220.

Die Welt des Hans Sachs. Ed. R. Freitag-Stadler et al. Exh. cat. Nuremberg: Stadtgeschichtliche Museen, 1976.

Welt im Umbruch: Augsburg zwischen Renaissance und Barock. Exh. cat. 2 vols. Augsburg: Stadt Augsburg, 1980.

Wenke, W. "Das Bildnis bei Michael Wolgemut." *AGNM* (1932–1933): 61–73.

Wiederanders, G. *Albrecht Dürers theologische Anschauungen.* Berlin, 1976.

Willers, J. K. W., ed. *Hans Sachs und die Meistersinger in ihrer Zeit.* Exh. cat. Bayreuth: Neuen Rathaus; Nuremberg: Germanisches Nationalmuseum, 1981.

Wilson, A. "The Early Drawings for the Nürnberg Chronicle." *Master Drawings* 13 (1975): 115–130.

———. *The Making of the Nuremberg Chronicle.* Amsterdam, 1976.

Winkler, A. "Die Gefäss- und Punzenstecher der deutschen Hochrenaissance." *JPKS* 13 (1892): 93–107.

Winkler, F. *Hans von Kulmbach.* Kulmbach, 1959.

———. *Die Zeichnungen Albrecht Dürers.* 4 vols. Berlin, 1936–1939.

———. *Die Zeichnungen Hans Süss von Kulmbachs und Hans Leonhard Schäufeleins.* Berlin, 1942.

Winner, M., ed. *Pieter Bruegel d. Ä. als Zeichner: Herkunft und Nachfolge.* Exh. cat. Berlin: Kupferstichkabinett, 1975.

Winzinger, F. *Wolf Huber: Das Gesamtwerk.* 2 vols. Munich, 1979.

Wixom, W. D. *Renaissance Bronzes from Ohio Collections.* Exh. cat. Cleveland: Cleveland Museum of Art, 1975.

Zimmermann, E. H. "Zur Nürnberger Malerei der II. Hälfte des XV. Jahrhunderts." *AGNM* (1932–1933): 43–60.

Zink, F. "Der Benennbare Fensterausblick im Porträt." *AGNM* (1963): 100–109.

———. *Die Deutschen Handzeichnungen I: Die Handzeichnungen bis zur Mitte des 16. Jahrhunderts (Kataloge des Germanischen Nationalmuseums Nürnberg).* Nuremberg, 1968.

Zschelletzschky, H. *Die 'Drei gottlosen Maler' von Nürnberg: Sebald Beham, Barthel Beham und Georg Pencz.* Leipzig, 1975.

Index

Note: Roman page numbers indicate principal references.

Clouet, Jean, *236*
Cochlaeus, Johannes, *23, 24*
Cock, Hieronymus, *262, 267, 289*
Coecke van Aelst, Pieter, *69, 191, 233, 304*
Coligny, Gaspar de, *75*
Colmar, *46, 96*
Colonna, Francesco, *233*
Columbus, Christopher, *39, 300*
Cordus, Euricius, *128*
Correggio (Antonio Allegri), *58*
Cortez, Hernando, *300*
Cracow, *53, 60, 63, 130, 135, 305*
Cranach, Lucas the Elder, *35, 36, 53, 58, 74,*
    110, 124, 148, 159, 166, 189, 203, 212, 234,
    235, 276
Cranach, Lucas the Younger, *35, 192, 212, 234*
Cranach school/workshop, *35 (fig. 28), 36, 232*
Crétif, Marc, *209*

Danhauser, Peter, *40*
Danner, Leonhard, *191*
Danube School, *228, 254, 258*
Denck, Hans, *20, 31*
Denis the Carthusian, *210*
Deschler, Joachim, *78, 201, 234, 237, 244–245*
    (cat. nrs. 152–154), 253
Dietmair, Hans, *6, 13, 76*
Dietrichstein, Sigismund von, *145*
Doppelmayr, Johann Gabriel, *152*
Dorothea von der Pfalz, *243 (cat. nr. 151)*
Drechsel, Wolfgang, *168, 169*
Dresden, *63*
Du Cerceau, Jacques Androuet, *267*
Dürer, Albrecht, passim; especially *3, 4, 12, 14*
    (fig. 15), 25–26, 29 (fig. 25)–31, 32 (fig. 26),
    33, 40–42, 45–50, 53–55, 58–59, 71–72, 92,
    95, 96–129 (cat. nrs. 4–34), 130–131, 134,
    136, 139–141, 152–154, 160, 168–169 (cat.
    nrs. 66–67) 176, 179, 190, 196, 203, 216, 218
    (cat. nr. 116), 235 (cat. nrs. 137–138), 239 (cat.
    nr. 143), 256, 263, 296, 302
Dürer, Albrecht the Elder, *12, 54, 64, 96*
Dürer, Hans, *46, 63, 136, 303*

Ebner, Hieronymus, *29, 30, 160, 201*
Eck, Johann, *35, 226*
Eck (Egkh), Leonard von, *197 (cat. nr. 96), 201,*
    202, 261
Edward VI (king of England), *264 (cat. nr. 173)*
Egenolff, Christian, *176, 183, 196*
Elsheimer, Adam, *72, 74, 301*
Elsner, Jacob, *303*
Erasmus, *35, 45, 62, 109, 110*
Erfurt, *58*
Ernst von Mengersdorf (bishop of Bam-
    berg), *297*
Esprinchard, Jacques, *72*
Etzlaub, Erhard, *3, 75, 90–91 (cat. nr. 1)*

Facunde, Hanns, *180*
Falck, Conz, *251*
Fazuni, Antonio, *12, 107, 279*
Ferdinand I (archduke of Austria, king of
    Bohemia and Hungary, emperor), *113, 120,*
    145, 154, 156, 170, 182 (cat. nr. 79), 197, 201,
    252, 260
Ferdinand II (archduke of Tirol), *58, 270, 286*
Ferdinand of Aragon, *150*
Feyerabend, Sigmund, *74, 75, 254, 262, 264,*
    267, 275, 276, 277, 281, 288
Ficino, Marsilio, *111*

Flindt, Paul the Elder, *274*
Flindt (Vlindt), Paul the Younger, *74, 269, 273,*
    274 (cat. nrs. 187–188), 294, 295, 300
Florence, *79, 297*
Floris, Cornelius, *61, 76–77, 300*
Flötner, Peter, *3, 4, 13–14 (fig. 17), 35, 53, 57,*
    59, 60–65 (figs. 35, 38, 39), 77, 81, 82, 162,
    180, 189, 190, 203, 204, 219, 224 (fig. 58)–233
    (cat. nrs. 122–136), 234, 238, 248, 249, 251,
    286 (cat. nr. 198), 288, 291, 293, 294
Folman, Heinrich, *288*
Francis I (king of France), *170, 209*
Franck, Sebastian, *187*
Francken, Frans II, *58*
Frankfurt, *3, 69, 72, 74, 176*
Franz von Waldeck, *171*
Freiburg, *136*
Frey, Agnes, *47, 96, 101, 129*
Frey, Hans, *49 (fig. 30), 64, 83, 96, 214, 303*
Fridolin, Stephan, *24, 93*
Friedrich III (emperor), *5, 12, 40, 92, 112, 154*
Friedrich the Wise (elector), *3, 27, 35, 41, 49,*
    53, 58, 62, 96, 124 (cat. nr. 29), 130, 139, 159,
    192, 197, 212, 219, 235, 303, 304
Friedrich II von Pfalz (elector), *62, 240, 242, 243*
Fuggers, *3, 49, 62, 239*

Gabriel (Munich painter), *92*
Ganzhorn, Wilhelm, *245*
Gärtner, Georg the Younger, *72, 73, 301*
Gebel, Matthes, *62, 78, 145, 168, 176, 212, 234,*
    236, 238, 239, 240–243 (cat. nrs. 144–151),
    253
Geiler von Kaiserberg, Johann, *23, 33*
Gerhaert, Nikolaus, *61*
Gerhard, Hubert, *77, 79*
Gerung, Matthias, *99*
Geuder, Georg, *241*
Geuder, Johann, *241*
Geuder, Martin III, *29, 241 (cat. nr. 146)*
Geyerswörth, *297*
Ghent, *203*
Giocondo, Fra Giovanni, *233*
Glaser, Hans, *59, 263 (cat. nr. 171)*
Glaser, Hans Wolff, *168–169, 263*
Glockendon, Albrecht, *59, 91, 164, 172, 176,*
    184, 187–189, 198, 204, 250, 251, 303
Glockendon, Georg (Jörg) the Elder, *59, 90, 91,*
    303
Glockendon, Georg the Younger, *303*
Glockendon, Nikolaus, *46, 303*
Goltzius, Hendrik, *75*
Gonzaga, Federico, *209*
Graf, Hans, *56*
Graf, Michael, *56, 90, 203*
Graff, Johann Andreas, *7 (fig. 3), 8 (fig. 4), 10*
    (figs. 6, 7), 23
Granvella, Nicolas, *203*
Grebber, Adrian, *184*
Greenwich, *77*
Greff, Hieronymus, *99*
Greiffenberger, Hans, *34*
Grimani, Ottavio, *78*
Grimm, Jakob, *8*
Groland, Leonhard, *235*
Gross, Konrad, *8*
Grünewald (Matthaus Gotthard Neithart), *58,*
    144
Grünewald, Hans, *251*
Guicciardini, Luigi, *78*
Gulden, Andreas, *71, 253*

Photographic Credits

The photographs for the objects included in the exhibition were all supplied by the lending institutions. The photographs for the text figures were supplied by the following:

Amsterdam, Rijksmuseum-Stichting: *47, 48*
Author: *11, 19–22, 29, 46*
Berlin, Kunstgewerbemuseum: *50, 52, 54, 55*
Berlin, Staatliche Museen: *45*
Chicago, The Martin D'Arcy Gallery, Loyola University of Chicago: *51*
Erlangen, Universitätsbibliothek: *30, 58*
Geneva, Musée d'Art et d'Histoire: *41*
Minneapolis, The Minneapolis Institute of Arts: *53*
Munich, Alte Pinakothek: *26, 40*
New York, The Metropolitan Museum of Art: *59, 60*
Nuremberg, Bayerisches Staatsarchiv: *1, 24, 32*
Nuremberg, Germanisches Nationalmuseum: *2–8, 15, 25, 27–28, 31, 33, 37–39, 42, 49*
Nuremberg, Hochbauamt-Bildstelle: *10, 12–14, 16–18, 23, 35–36, 43, 44*
Vienna, Graphische Sammlung Albertina (Lichtbildwerkstätte "Alpenland"): *9*
Washington, National Gallery of Art: *34, 57*

Archer M. Huntington Art Gallery

Full- and Part-time Personnel

Eric S. McCready, *Director*

Eric Anderson, *Technical Staff Assistant*
Carolyn Appleton, *Senior Secretary*
Carole Black, *Administrative Assistant*
Miriam Blum, *Research Assistant*
Ellie Francis, *Administrative Secretary*
Joseph Fronek, *Conservator*
Christy Grill, *Education Secretary*
Patricia Hendricks, *Assistant Curator*
Clyde Holleman, *Carpenter*
George Holmes, *Photographer*
Sue Ellen Jeffers, *Registrar*
Robert Jones, *Technical Staff Assistant*
Judith Keller, *Curator of Prints and Drawings*
Forrest McGill, *Assistant Director*
Susan Mayer, *Educational Coordinator*
Cindy Neuschwander, *Assistant Registrar*
Andrea S. Norris, *Chief Curator*
Jessie Taylor Otto, *Assistant Curator*
Fran Prudhomme, *Coordinator, Art Enrichment Program*
Thomas Puryear, *Technical Staff Coordinator*
Becky Duval Reese, *Educational Curator*
Tim Reilly, *Technical Staff Assistant*
John Sager, *Technical Staff Assistant*
Susan Sternberg, *Museum Intern*
Donna Vliet, *Art Teacher, Art Enrichment Program*
Tanya Walker, *Administrative Secretary*

PACE UNIVERSITY LIBRARIES
BIRNBAUM STACKS
N6886.N9 S64 1983
Nuremberg, a Renaissance city, 1500–1618

3 5061 00535 4536